Modern Sociological Issues

Modern Sociological Issues

2/e

BARRY J. WISHART and LOUIS C. REICHMAN

Macmillan Publishing Co., Inc.
New York

Collier Macmillan Publishers
London

Macmillan Publishing Co., Inc.
866 Third Avenue, New York, New York 10022

Collier Macmillan Canada, Ltd.

Library of Congress Cataloging in Publication Data

Wishart, Barry J   comp.
  Modern sociological issues.

  Includes bibliographical references.
  1. Sociology—Addresses, essays, lectures.
2. Social psychology—Addresses, essays, lectures.
3. United States—Social conditions—Addresses,
essays, lectures.   I. Reichman, Louis C., joint author.
II. Title.
HM51.W57 1979   301   78-7359
ISBN 0-02-428760-1

Printing: 1 2 3 4 5 6 7 8   Year: 9 0 1 2 3 4 5

Preface to the Second Edition

A second edition is always gratifying to authors and publishing companies. This is true for both practical and idealistic reasons. With the second edition of *Modern Sociological Issues* we feel justified in another gratification. The success of the first edition has demonstrated the truth of a fundamental educational premise: meaningful education in a complex subject can also be interesting. The adjustments that we have made to fulfill this premise in terms of 1979 relevance contrasted to 1974 emphasize such newly emerging sociological issues as stereotyping of the aged, the misapplication of science to support political ideology, and the amorphous nature of the Women's Liberation movement, to mention a few. It is hoped that such changes will assist the reader to understand American society in the 1980's.

B. J. W.
L. C. R.

Preface

Teachers and students of introductory sociology are plagued by a seemingly irreconcilable gap: The casual orientation of most introductory sociology students in contrast to sophisticated but often unimaginative and incomprehensible theories and concepts that seem to constitute the discipline of sociology. If introductory sociology students were asked what they expected to gain from the class (other than good grades and meeting the prescribed requirements!) a large majority would give some version of the following answer: "We want to learn why we behave as we do, and what can be done to help us live life so we can be happier." On the other hand, ask almost any introductory sociology teacher what he expects his students to learn and his response will stress the necessity of objective and critical analysis which emphasizes the scientific method and inductive logic as means of arriving at "value free" and tentative conclusions about man and his behavior. Many—perhaps most—introductory sociology teachers would add to this basic teaching responsibility the necessity of exploring alternative assumptions and values pertaining to the scientific conclusions.

This student-teacher gap stems from a variety of factors. One of the most important factors is the discrepancy between experience levels of students and teachers. Unfortunately, many teachers are backed into a position which attempts an uncomfortable resolution of the gap between student readiness and teacher responsibility. Some introductory sociology teachers feel obligated to de-emphasize sociology as a legitimate scientific discipline. Such an attitude can have the effect of relegating sociology to a study of man and his interrelationships without any serious differentiation of evidence and methodology. Others, in their commendable regard for the discipline of sociology, have unintentionally made it become for introductory students so abstract, esoteric, and incomprehensible that it seems alien to the world of casual sensible experience. These approaches have the effect of exacerbating the problem, widening the gap, and carrying the seeds of an educational standoff. If sociology is as vital to the intelligent understanding of man's behavior in society today as we believe it to be, the gap between the needs of introductory sociology students and the understanding of the discipline of sociology must be bridged. We feel this can be accomplished by a book of readings which satisfies both student and teacher while facilitating the bridging.

This book of readings has been selected, organized, and abridged in such a way that it is readable, provocative, and close to the student's realm of experience. The articles aid the teacher by providing *practical* examples of sociological concepts as they are found in the world of the student. For example, to illustrate changing family structure, the student is offered a *specific* instance of "Marriage as a Wretched Institution" which describes how the American family has completed the transition "from institution to companionship." Similarly, for a relevant example of the process of social mobility, the student is referred to "The Dying Art of Social Climbing." This article describes techniques of social climbing such as manipulation of associations and the cultivation of class-typed behavior. Such examples gradually and gently expose and make meaningful the world of sociological concepts on a level that is understandable for the introductory sociology student. Perhaps most important these lively articles generate the sense of excitement basic to all learning and understanding. Finally, these articles aid the development of the skill of generalizing from the specific examples provided by the readings to sociological concepts and theories. Not only is this skill at the heart of all learning, it is also a practical necessity for the development of a sociological perspective.

The widespread use of books of readings in introductory sociology courses suggests that most teachers of these courses recognize the importance of this skill of moving from the specific to the general. Our review of the available readers led us to the conclusion that the gap between student readiness and the formal discipline of sociology was unresolved because of the following shortcomings: (1) The books were too narrow and specialized for a comprehensive introductory course. For example, several introductory sociology readers contained many good articles, but covered only the following subjects: "social interaction," "social activities," "institutions," and "social problems." Most introductory courses in sociology cover between 18 and 25 subjects which include: "science," "the family," "social stratification," "social power," "demography," etc. Surely all of these subjects require specific examples. (2) The articles are so "heavy" that they require extensive interpretation by the teacher. Almost all traditional introductory sociology readers suffer from this malady. (3) The articles are so removed from the experiences and concerns of introductory sociology students that they are seen as irrelevant and insignificant. Therefore, while sociology readers generally are premised on the need to aid introductory sociology students in bridging the student-teacher discipline gap, these books fail to recognize that most students in the introductory sociology course are not majors in sociology and hold no innate interest in a sociological perspective. *Modern Sociological Issues* is an effort to resolve this problem.

The outline of this book is designed to approximate the outline of the major texts used in introductory sociology courses. Introductions are provided for each chapter to review the major sociological concepts on which the chapter focuses. Separate article introductions further focus the student's attention on the basic sociological point(s). These introductions are offered as guideposts which direct the student in terms of what to look for and how to interpret what he will see from a solid sociological perspective. This continued sociological focusing process with the lively and relevant articles will facilitate the relationship between the discipline of sociology and the experiences of everyday life. Discussion questions follow each article to give further help to the student in summarizing and generalizing from the specific relevant example to the pertinent sociological concept.

The kind of reconciliation we are attempting here is a perennial educational concern. Alfred North Whitehead, writing in the 1920s, stressed the responsibility of higher education to unite "the young and the old in the imaginative consideration of learning" which so transformed mere knowledge that "A fact is no longer a bare fact: it is invested with all its possibilities. It is no longer a burden on the memory: it is energizing as the poet of our dreams, and as the architect of our purposes. . . . Fools act on imagination without knowledge; pedants act on knowledge without imagination." Our hope in assembling this book is that it may play a significant role in welding together knowledge, imagination, and experience for students and teachers of introductory sociology.

B. J. W.
L. C. R.

Contents

1 / Sociology as a Science

Sociology is the scientific study of human behavior in groups. It not only describes the range of human behavior from a fleeting contact between strangers to a permanent complex relationship developed over a lifetime, it also offers explanations to questions such as, What causes inequalities between rich and poor? Why does war and social conflict persist? What causes the rising crime rates? And why are some religious sects experiencing unprecedented growth while others are declining? These fundamental questions on the nature of social life have been the source of considerable debate and speculation by the philosophers and poets since the beginning of time. Many of their observations were highly perceptive, but because their conclusions were based largely on intuition and commonsense reasoning, they lacked the qualities of accuracy and reliability that social scientists demand today. In order to provide accurate and reliable conclusions about human behavior in groups, social scientists employ the *scientific method*, which

is a special technique—a test—for knowing that something is true or correct.

The scientific method can be defined as a set of assumptions, characteristics, and procedures that yields a systematic body of knowledge about the universe. Because the universe is so large and complex, the quest for knowledge has been divided into general areas such as the physical sciences, the biological sciences, and the social sciences. Sociology is one of the social sciences and, as such, it shares the same assumptions, characteristics, and procedures as the other sciences.

One *assumption* of sociology as a science is that the universe is patterned and orderly. The most basic assumption of sociology is that human behavior follows patterns similar to those of other natural phenomena in the universe, whether it is the patterned relationship of earth, sun, and moon or the metamorphosis of the catapillar into a beautiful butterfly. Sociology has similarly discovered and described patterns in numerous social activities such as dating, deviancy, political participation, and birth rates. These patterns allow sociologists to closely predict much of our behavior.

One *characteristic* of the scientific method is ethical neutrality, which insists that the scientist—whether a physicist or sociologist—must not place moral issues or ideology ahead of the search for knowledge about how humans act in groups. However, recent concerns with social reform and social action have caused many sociologists to argue for more direct involvement in solving society's problems. Other social scientists, moreover, argue that ethical neutrality is in fact an impossible ideal and that no matter how competent the scientist, his values will somehow influence the "scientific" conclusions.

The most basic procedures of the scientific method are observation and replication. Replication involves the repeating of an experiment or observation using the same methods to see if there are the same results. For example, if a scientific study of middle-class residents in Los Angeles concluded that suburban life-styles caused a high divorce rate, replication would require that the same study be made of middle-class residents in the suburbs of Chicago, Houston, and other similar suburban areas. If these studies confirm the results of the original study, sociologists may conclude that they have accurately observed a pattern of behavior.

Some *forms* of scientific observations used by sociologists are planned experiments, case studies, and statistical comparative studies. These techniques provide the sociologist with a kind of observation that differs from the common way of looking at things because scientific observation has special requirements. Scientific observation is accurate, precise, systematic, recorded, trained, and objective. These procedures are designed to reduce the possibility of deception and fraud, and to ensure that research will provide knowledge rather than mere opinion.

It would be misleading, however, to conclude that as a scientific endeavor sociology involves the simple application of the scientific method. Actually there is no such thing as *the* scientific method, that is, there is not one and only one way to study human behavior. As such, applying the scientific method in sociology is much like playing baseball. Baseball players never talk about *the method* of playing baseball. Instead, baseball players talk about the various techniques of hitting, running bases, stealing bases, and winning games. The procedures and techniques employed depend of course on the circumstances of a particular game. Sociology similarly employs a variety of techniques and procedures in obtaining knowledge about human behavior. For example, the first article of the book, by Herbert J. Gans, describes how one sociologist used the participant-observer procedure in seeking to accurately describe the emergence and development of suburban life-styles. Given this diversity, employing the scientific method to study human behavior is fraught with difficulties and pitfalls. It is no wonder, therefore, that one eminent scientist remarked that "the scientist has no other method than doing his damndest." Examples of sociological applications of the scientific method and the difficulties and pitfalls are provided in this chapter.

HERBERT J. GANS

The Levittowners

All sciences use planned experiments. Sociology is no exception. However, the individuals being studied in a sociological study know they are being studied. Therefore, they often react to the study itself. Because of this problem, sociology depends heavily on techniques other than the planned experiments. Examples of some of these techniques are statistical comparative studies, questionnaire interviews, and participant-observation studies such as the one this article reviews. Participant-observation studies assume that some things can be understood only by experiencing them. The sociologist becomes a member of the group he is studying. He discreetly records his observations, assesses their implications, and eventually formulates generalizations that help to describe the group structure and function under study. Herbert J. Gans, a well-known sociologist, describes his efforts to use this method in his study of *The Levittowners.*

The Setting, Theory, and Method of the Study

This study had its beginnings sixteen years ago when I concluded some research in the new town of Park Forest, Illinois, near Chicago. Having come to Park Forest when it was fourteen months old and already a community, I decided that someday I would study a new town from its very beginnings. Soon after I left Park Forest, it and other postwar suburban developments suddenly became a topic of widespread popular interest. Journalists and critics began to write articles suggesting that life in these new suburbs was radically different from that in the older cities and towns and that these differences could be ascribed both to basic changes in American values and to the effects of suburban life. In the first and most perceptive of these reports, Whyte's articles on Park Forest, the author described drastic increases in visiting and club activity, shifts in political party affiliation and church-going habits, and a more equalitarian mode of consumer behavior and status competition (keeping down with the Jones) which he explained as a decline in individualism and the rise of a new Social Ethic—most evident in and partly created by the new suburbs.

Later reports by less searching and responsible writers followed, and so did a flood of popular fiction, eventually creating what Bennett Berger has called the myth of suburbia. Its main theme took off where Whyte stopped: the suburbs were breeding a new set of Americans, as mass produced as the houses they lived in, driven into a never ending round of group activity ruled by the strictest conformity. Suburbanites were incapable of real friendships; they were bored and lonely, alienated, atomized, and depersonalized. As the myth grew, it added yet more disturbing elements: the emergence of a matriarchal family of domineering wives, absent husbands, and spoiled children, and with it, rising marital friction, adultery, divorce, drunkenness, and mental illness. In unison, the authors chanted that individualism was dying, suburbanites were miserable, and the fault lay with the homogeneous suburban landscape and its population. John Keats, perhaps the most hysterical of the mythmakers, began his book as follows: *"For literally nothing down . . . you too can find a box of your own in one of the fresh-air slums we're building around the edges of American cities . . . inhabited by people whose* age, income, number of children, problems, habits, conversation, dress, possessions and perhaps even blood type are also precisely like yours. . . . They are developments conceived in error, nurtured by greed, corroding everything they touch. They . . . actually drive mad myriads of housewives shut up in them."

.   .   .

I watched the growth of this mythology with misgivings, for my observations in various new suburbs persuaded me neither that there was much change in people when they moved to the suburbs nor that the change which took place could be traced to the new environment. And if suburban life was as undesirable and unhealthy as the critics charged, the suburbanites themselves were blissfully unaware of it; they were happy in their new homes and communities, much happier than they had been in the city. Some of the observations about suburbia were quite accurate, and the critics represented a wide range of political and cultural viewpoints, so that it is perhaps unfair to lump them all together—although I do so as a shorthand in the chapters that follow. Nevertheless, it seemed to me that a basic inaccuracy was being perpetrated by those who give American society its picture of itself, and when I learned that city planners also swallowed the suburban myth and were altering their professional recommendations accordingly, I felt it was time to do a study of the new suburbs. Lacking the grants to do a large comparative study of several communities that was—and still is—needed, and leaning toward participant-observation by my training, I decided the best way to do the research was to live in one such community. That community turned out to be Levittown, New Jersey.

The Setting

On a sunny Saturday in June 1958, Levittown was officially opened to potential purchasers, and that day my wife and I were among hundreds of others who looked over the houses. Since I wanted to be among the very first residents, we selected the model we liked best, a four-bedroom "Cape Cod," and made the required down payment of $100. A few weeks later, the first group of about 100 purchasers was asked to come to Levittown to pick a lot, and we chose one in the middle of a short block—to make sure that we would literally be in the middle of things. During the second week of October, we were among the first 25 families who moved into the new community—none of them, I was pleased to discover, coming to study it.

The Theory of the Study

The study I wanted to do focused around three major but interrelated questions: the origin of a new community, the quality of suburban life, and the effect of suburbia on the behavior of its residents. Later, I added a fourth question on the quality of politics and decision-making.

My first task was to determine the processes which transform a group of strangers into a community, to see if I could identify the essential prerequisites for "community." But I also wanted to test the critics' charge that the Levittowns were inflicted on purchasers with little choice of other housing by a profit-minded builder unwilling to provide them with a superior home and community. Consequently, I intended to study how the community was planned: to what extent the plans were shaped by Levitt's goals and to what extent by the goals of the expected purchasers. For this purpose, I needed also to study the purchasers—why they were moving to Levittown and what aspirations they had for life in the new community. Once they had moved in, I wanted to observe the community formation process from the same perspective: how much specific groups were shaped by their founders, how much by their members, and how much by the group's function for the larger community. I hoped to know after several years to what extent the emerging community reflected the priorities of builder, founders, and other community leaders and to what extent the goals for which people said they had moved to Levittown.

These questions were grounded in a set of theoretical issues of relevance to both social science and public policy. Sociologists have long been asking what and who bring about innovation and social change, and what role elite leaders and experts, on the one hand, and the rank-and-file citizenry, on the other, play in this process. As a policy matter, the same question has been raised by the concept of mass society, which implies that many features of American society—whether television programs, Levittowns, or Pentagon policies—are imposed by an intentional or unintentional conspiracy of business and governmental leaders acting on passive or resigned Americans who actually want something entirely different.

This issue is of more than academic interest to makers of community policy, be they politicians or city planners. The city planner is an expert with a conception of the ideal community and good life, which he seeks to translate into reality through his professional activities. If a small number of leaders shape the community, he need only proselytize them effectively to establish his conception. If the residents themselves determine the community, however, he is faced with a more difficult task: persuading them of the desirability of his plans or somehow changing their behavior to accord with them. The further and normative issue is even more perplexing: whose values *should* shape the new community, the residents' or the planner's?

The second question of the study sought to test the validity of the suburban critique, whether suburban ways of life were as undesirable as had been claimed. Are people status-seekers, do they engage in a hyperactive social life which they do not really enjoy, do they conform unwillingly to the demands of their neighbors, is the community a dull microcosm of mass society? Are the women bored and lonely matriarchs, and does suburban life produce the malaise and mental illness which the critics predicted? And if not, what dissatisfactions and problems *do* develop.

The third question followed logically from the second: were undesirable changes (and desirable ones too) an effect of the move from city to suburb or of causes unrelated to either the move or suburbia? My previous observations led me to suspect that the changes were less a result of suburban residence than of aspirations for individual and family life which encouraged people to move to the suburbs in the first place. Consequently, I wanted to discover whether the changes people reported after coming to Levittown were *intended,* planned by them before the move, or *unintended,* encouraged or forced on them afterwards by the community. If unintended changes outweighed intended ones, the community probably had significant effects on its residents. And if so, what *sources* and *agents* within the community created them—the physical environment of suburbia, the distance from urban facilities, the social structure and the people who made it, and/or the builder or organizational founder?

· · ·

I should note that when I began my research, I had not formulated the questions as clearly or compactly as they are here written, and I had no intention of limiting myself only to them. One of the major pleasures of participant-observation is to come upon unexpected new topics of study, and these are reflected in the occasional tangential analyses that occur throughout the book.

The Methods of the Study

The main source of data was to be participant-observation. By living in the community for the first two years, I planned to observe the development of neighbor relations and social life and to be on hand when organizations and institutions were being set up. In addition to observing at public meetings, I would also be able to interview founders and members, and once having gotten to know them, follow their groups as they went through their birth pains. Meanwhile I would do much the same with churches, governmental public bodies, and political parties; I would talk to doctors, lawyers, local reporters, and the Levitt executives, as well. Eventually I would get to know all the important people and a sizeable sample of other residents, and interview them from time to time as the community building process unfolded. The nature of everyday life I would discover principally on my own street, where I could observe my neighbors and myself in our roles as homeowners and block residents. These plans came to fruition, and I spent most of my days making the rounds of the community to find out what was happening, much like a reporter. For a year after organizations first sprang up, I went to at least one meeting every week night.

I tried not to act like a formal researcher and rarely took notes during the thousands of informal conversational interviews. Instead I memorized the answers, made quick notes as soon as I could, and later wrote the whole interview in my field diary. (Although a famous novelist has recently garnered considerable publicity for memorizing his interviews, this has long been standard practice for many sociologists.) Social occasions were a fruitful source of data about community attitudes, but I was always careful not to ask too many questions or questions inappropriate to the neighborly role. I recall feeling frustrated about this at one social gathering, only to hear a neighbor ask exactly the questions I felt I could not ask. This made me wonder about the similarity between sociology and gossip, but then she was the block's nosy neighbor. Actually, in life on the block I often acted spontaneously as a neighbor, and only after I got home would I become the researcher again, writing down my and my neighbors' conversations and activities.

The main problem in being a participant-observer is not to get people to give information, but to live with the role day after day. As a researcher, I could not afford to alienate any present or potential sources, or become identified with any single group or clique in the community. Consequently, I had to be neutral, not offering opinions on controversial local issues or on national politics if they were too different from prevailing opinions—as they often were. Even in social situations, I could never be quite myself, and I had to be careful not to take a dominant role. The life of the party makes a poor participant-observer, but being shy anyway, I did not have to pretend. I also had to restrain the normal temptation to avoid people I did not like, for had I given in, my sample would have been biased and my conclusions inaccurate. The participant-observer must talk to a fairly representative cross section of the population. I had to be sure not to act like a professor, for fear of losing access to people who feel threatened by academic degrees or by their own lack of education. This was not too difficult, for I am not entirely comfortable in a professional role anyway. And having enough interest in small talk about sports, sex, automobiles, weather, and other staples of male conversation, I had no difficulty in participating in the regular evening and Saturday morning bull sessions on the front lawn. Relaxed conversation with women was more difficult, except in a group of couples, and observing women's meetings was out of the question. Perhaps they would have let me in, but we would all have been uncomfortable. However, women enjoyed being interviewed—they liked having their housework interrupted—and I could always go to see anyone I wished to find out what happened at their meetings.

A participant-observer is much like a politician, for he must always watch his words and his behavior, think about the next question to ask, and plan strategy for studying a prospective event. There was anxiety too, about figuring out what to study and what not to study, and particularly about the possibility of missing something important that could not be retrieved in the rapid flow of events. I also felt guilty sometimes about not telling people why I was asking questions and about the deceptions that inevitably accompany the research role, but I felt secure in the knowledge that none of the information so gathered would ever be used against anyone.

Yet even the strain of playing a role that inhibits one's personality is more than matched by the excitement of doing research, watching society from close up, seeing the textbook social processes in operation, and constantly getting ideas about social theory from what people say and do. There was enjoyment in meeting many hundreds of people, and above all, in being in the middle of and in on things. Often, I felt I was watching dozens of continuing serials, some pitting heroes against villains, others with temporary cliff-hanger endings, but all of them stimulating my curiosity as to how they would come out. And before one serial was over, several others were sure to have begun. This is why I could never answer properly when city people asked me whether I *really* enjoyed living in Levittown. I did enjoy it, but as a researcher, I was not a normal resident. Had I been one, I would have enjoyed the many opportunities for community activity which came my way (partly because of my training in city planning)—all of which I had to turn down as a researcher—but sometimes I found the community personally unsatisfying because of the shortage of people and facilities to meet my own intellectual and cultural needs. Even so, I would not judge Levittown, or any community, negatively simply because it could not fully satisfy my personal needs.

Studying the quality of life implies evaluation, and this means personal value judgments. I was guided by at least three. First and foremost, my evaluation reflects the standards of the residents themselves, for I begin with the judgment that, more often than not, they are the best authority of the quality of their own life. In a pluralistic society, there is no single standard for the good life, and in a democratic one, people have the right to set their own. For example, if Levittowners report that they find their community satisfying, as they do, their opinion ought to be respected. Although the suburban critics insist that these satisfactions are spurious and self-deceptive, they offer no valid evidence, so that their charge only indicates their differing standards for the good life. Of course, if the Levittowners' statements include latent suggestions of dissatisfation, something is clearly wrong.

Implicit in this value judgment is a second which goes beyond the dictates of pluralism and democracy. Specifically, I believe that there are an infinite number of ways of living well and of coping with problems, all of them valid unless they hurt the people practicing them or others. Our society generates too much social criticism consisting essentially of complaints that people are not behaving as the critics would like or themselves behave. Without proof that certain behavior is pathological for individual or society, such criticism can be rejected for what it is, an objection to diversity and pluralism.

But it would be foolhardy to base an evaluation solely on what people say, for if sociology has discovered anything, it is that often people do not know all they are doing or what is happening to them. The observer always sees more than anyone else, if only because that is his job, but if he evaluates what he alone sees, he must still do so by the standards of the people whom he is observing. Of course, here and there I make personal judgments which do not practice what I have just preached and which reject one or another of the Levittowners' standards. At the conscious level, I have limited myself to those judgments which I consider of higher importance than the Levittowners' standards—including the practice of democracy—but unconscious judgments surely creep in too. One cannot live intimately with a community for several years without making them, and I only regret not being aware of those that might bias the study unduly.

Discussion Questions

1. Develop a review statement of these three aspects of Gans' study: Setting, Theory, Method.
2. How "biased" would you guess the final detailed findings of Gans' study were? Discuss.
3. From Gans' point of view, what were the major mistakes of previous studies of the suburbs? Do you tend to agree with him? Why or why not?
4. Reread the last two paragraphs. From what Gans says and from what you believe, what should be the role of "personal judgments" in scientific sociological studies?

CHRISTOPHER JENCKS, HENRY M. LEVIN

Inequality . . . as an Illustration of the Social Science Objectivity Gap

After the sociologist has collected his data, he must subject it to analysis and interpretation if it is to serve as a contribution to the fund of social science knowledge. However, it has been argued that this interpretive process introduces the all-too-human element of bias, which violates the standards of ethical neutrality. Also, the very nature of sociology's subject matter is too complex, varied, and unpredictable for the kind of precise study that is possible in the natural sciences. These factors prevent the achievement of total objectivity in social science studies.

Although bias, complexity, variation, and unpredictability are formidable challenges, sociologists agree that the scientific method is the best available method to separate truth from mere opinion. This is because all the interpretations of the social scientists are available for public scrutiny and criticism. Therefore, says the social scientist, those interpretations influenced by wishful thinking, vested interests, and outright fraud will be detected and exposed in the long run.

What follows is a brief excerpt from Christopher Jencks' interpretations of the volatile and controversial relationships between family, education, and economic variables in determining economic success. These findings are critiqued by another social scientist, Henry M. Levin. This interplay of findings, research techniques used, interpretations offered, and subsequent criticism offers an excellent example of the role played by public scrutiny and criticism in the scientific method.

JENCKS on Inequality

Our work suggests, then, that many popular explanations of economic inequality are largely wrong. We cannot blame economic inequality primarily on genetic differences in men's capacity for abstract reasoning, since there is nearly as much economic inequality among men with equal test scores as among men in general. We cannot blame economic inequality primarily on the fact that parents pass along their disadvantages to their children, since there is nearly as much inequality among men whose parents had the same economic status as among men in general. We cannot blame economic inequality on differences between schools, since differences between schools seem to have very little effect on any measurable attribute of those who attend them.

Economic success seems to depend on varieties of luck and on-the-job competence that are only moderately related to family background, schooling, or scores on standardized tests. The definition of competence varies greatly from one job to another, but it seems in most cases to depend more on personality than on technical skills. This makes it hard to imagine a strategy for equalizing competence. A strategy for equalizing luck is even harder to conceive.

The fact that we cannot equalize luck or competence does *not* mean that economic inequality is inevitable. Still less does it imply that we cannot eliminate what has traditionally been defined as poverty. It only implies that we must tackle these problems in a different way. Instead of trying to reduce people's capacity to gain a competitive advantage on one another, we would have to change the rules of the game so as to reduce the rewards of competitive success and the costs of failure. Instead of trying to make everyone equally lucky or equally good at his job, we would have to devise "insurance" systems which neutralize the effects of luck, and income-sharing systems which break the link between vocational success and living standards.

This could be done in a variety of ways. Employers could be constrained to reduce wage disparities between their best- and worst-paid workers. The state could make taxes more progressive, and could provide income supplements to those who cannot earn an adequate living from wages alone. The state could also provide free public services for those who cannot afford to buy adequate services in the private sector. Pursued with vigor, such a strategy would make "poverty" (i.e. having a living standard less than half the national average) virtually impossible. It would also make economic "success," in the sense of having, say, a living standard more than twice the national average, far less common than it now is. The net effect would be to make those with the most competence and luck subsidize those with the least competence and luck to a far greater extent than they do today.

This strategy was rejected during the 1960s for the simple reason that it

Reprinted from Christopher Jencks et al., *Inequality: A Reassessment of the Effect of Family and Schooling in America* (New York: Basic Books, Inc., 1972), pp. 8–9.

commanded relatively little popular support. The required legislation could not have passed Congress. Nor could it pass today. But that does not mean it was the wrong strategy. It simply means that until we change the political and moral premises on which most Americans now operate, poverty and inequality of opportunity will persist at pretty much their present level.

LEVIN on Schooling and Inequality

About a century ago the books of Horatio Alger, Jr., began to enthrall the nation. Typically they revolved around a fifteen-year-old boy who made his fortune by somehow being in the right place at the right time. When the child of a rich man was drowning, there was one of Alger's boys to save him; when a wealthy man lost his wallet, one of Alger's honest but impoverished heroes would find it. This familiar plot repeated itself in over 120 books that sold some twenty million copies.

Now the Horatio Alger myth has been resurrected, not by a latter-day novelist, but by a group of social scientists at the Harvard University Center for Educational Policy Research. Their conclusion is not rendered in the sentimental and repetitive prose of the Alger parables. Rather it is stated in the precise-sounding terminology of the social sciences. Thus, Christopher Jencks and his colleagues conclude in *Inequality* that computerized analyses employing immense sources of data have shown that "neither family background, cognitive skill, educational attainment, nor occupational status explains much of the variation in men's incomes."

Instead we are told that economic success depends primarily on competencies and chance factors that are almost unrelated to one's class of origin, genes, or schooling. As the authors noted in a recent summary of their work, . . . their results suggest that "school reform is never likely to have any significant effect on the degree of inequality among adults."

· · ·

At the outset Jencks notes two concepts of equality: equality of opportunity and equality of results. He suggests that most people are willing to accept a world with unequal incomes and status if they believe that these differences are based on such merits as ability, training, industriousness, and so on. Most people regard equality of opportunity to compete for life's unequal rewards as a social objective, and schools represent a major instrument to attain that goal. Accordingly, Jencks weighs the relative importance of inequalities in school resources, genetic endowments, and family backgrounds —and, surprisingly, finds that they are not strongly related to economic outcomes. They do not account for a person's income in his adult life.

Reprinted from Henry M. Levin, "Schooling and Inequality: The Social Science Objectivity Gap," *Saturday Review* (November 11, 1972), 49–51. Copyright 1972 by Saturday Review Co. First appeared in *Saturday Review,* November 11, 1972. Used with permission.

The authors proceed to draw two major conclusions from their analyses. First, since inequalities in schooling, test scores, and family background do not appear to be strongly related to differences in income, "equality of opportunity" in an economic sense already exists. While we should attempt to make schools more pleasant places for young people, we should not view them as important social instruments for obtaining equality of results. Second, as long as the available economic and occupational roles provided by society are so unequal, large inequalities in economic outcomes will persist. Therefore, Jencks and his colleagues argue that, if we wish to reduce large inequalities in income between rich and poor—the top fifth of the population receives seven times what the bottom fifth receives—we should redistribute income directly by increasing the taxes of the rich and raising the minimum incomes provided for the poor.

The second conclusion seems eminently reasonable from a technical point of view. If we wish to improve the distribution of income, we should adopt policy measures that affect income directly. Yet, if the nature of our society is such that the present, large inequalities in income have existed for almost fifty years, it is difficult to believe that there is a powerful enough political coalition to effect a major redistribution. (Witness the recent decision by Congress to postpone welfare reform for several years.)

We might consider whether the competition for the present unequal rewards is a fair one, as Jencks and his coauthors imply. This is the single most crucial finding of the book, since it represents the basis for the author's derogation of social policies aimed at improving equality of opportunity. Stated explicitly, the lack of relationship between family background, schooling, and test scores with income leads to the conclusion that policies to alter schools and family background will have little impact on eliminating economic inequalities.

Certainly, Jencks's assertion that the advantages with which one starts life have little to do with one's economic success seems to defy empirical verification for both the very poor and the very rich, although it may reflect accurately substantial mobility in the middle class. Surveys of the poverty population suggest that the "permanently poor" (in contrast with the transient poor, such as students, or the elderly who are living on pensions and social security payments) were themselves born into impoverished households and have low educational attainments. The very rich also seem to be able to sustain their position from generation to generation. Only the tumultuous economic upheaval associated with the Great Depression provided any appreciable movement from riches to rags, and only the calamity of World War II seemed to provide any appreciable movement from rags to riches over the last half-century. To assert that the forces of luck and other random factors give the children of the poor about the same chance in life as the children of the rich is in substantial conflict with this evidence.

In addition, many previous studies by economists on the subject have found that both schools and family background appear to have substantial effects on earnings. How is it possible, then, that Jencks's conclusions are in such sharp contrast to those of other researchers? The answer seems to lie in differences in interpretation and in the treatment of the data. For example, some differences that Jencks interprets as small ones would not seem trivial to other observers. Even according to the findings presented in the book, an extra year of elementary or secondary schooling appears to boost future income by about 4 per cent, an extra year of college by about 7 per cent, and a year of graduate school by about 4 per cent. According to these data a comparison of high school graduates and college graduates, who were otherwise identical, would show the college graduates earning about 30 per cent more than their less-educated peers. Jencks apparently believes that such differences are small, but two men separated by such income disparities might not agree. Thus, part of the conflict appears to revolve around the rather subjective issue of what magnitudes are important.

Clearly, the more serious discrepancies between Jencks and other researchers appear to be due to differences in the statistical treatment of data. The book's principal finding on the inefficacy of schools is that test scores, family background, and related factors account for only 12–15 per cent of differences in income. In contrast, other studies have found that from one-third to one-half of the variance in income can be explained by these and similar influences; according to their results, we should seriously consider the policy implications of improving the distribution of schooling.

It is not difficult to find the sources of the differences between these studies and that of Jencks. In fact, the *Inequality* study omitted data that would have improved considerably the amount of variance in income inequality. The most notable of these omissions include data on age and place of residence.

Ordinarily, when economists attempt to explain the determinants of income or earnings, they are concerned with *real* difference, not just artificial differences that are due to variations in price levels. Much of the differences in income among the various regions of the United States is really attributable to differences in the cost of living. The U.S. Bureau of Labor Statistics found that in 1970 the annual costs of a four-person urban family at an intermediate standard of living varied from about $9,200 in Austin, Texas, to over $12,000 in the New York area and almost $13,000 in Honolulu. There are also large differences within metropolitan areas and regions. Thus, much of what appear to be differences in income among a national population are really due to differences in price levels and do not represent differences in *real* incomes. In order to adjust for these effects, other studies have done their analyses within regions or have adjusted the data for the place of residence. Jencks's failure to do this resulted in a substantial overstatement of the "unexplained" variance in income relative to that of other studies.

A second omission that biases Jencks's results is the failure to include the age of the income recipient. Persons with the same educational and family background show large differences in their income over the life cycle. In the early stages of a career incomes rise briskly as individuals advance through on-the-job training, experience, and occupational upgrading. Peak earnings and advancement are reached at about forty-five to fifty years of age, and at this point many workers and self-employed professionals begin to withdraw from the labor market through early retirement or a reduction of hours worked. Thus, earned incomes decline considerably over the latter segment of the life cycle. Since Jencks's income data are based upon white, nonfarm men, twenty-five to sixty-four years of age, they include large components of income differences that are due to this normal life-cycle phenomenon. His failure to adjust the estimates for the age of the worker will serve to increase the amount of "unexplained" variations in income. Researchers usually treat this adjustment as a matter of standard procedure.

Finally, the fact that Jencks's data include income from property, social security, pensions, and other sources also tends to weaken the relationship between schooling, family background, and income. The statistical treatment in *Inequality* uses virtually the same variables to explain the income of the fully productive worker as it does the one who is retired and receives only a pension or social security payments. It uses the same attributes to explain the 15–20 per cent of income that is derived from nonproperty sources such as rents, dividends, and interest, even though such income is not derived from employment. Thus, the statistical formulation itself does not lend itself to explaining components of income that have little to do with individual labor-market productivity. Jencks does not take these important adjustments into account.

Further, the Jencks approach to explaining differences in income does not take noncognitive personality traits into account—even though recent research has found that schools and family appear to have a greater impact on the development of attitudes and values such as independence and conformity than on test scores. Such attributes appear to play an important role in determining social and economic outcomes. Jencks agrees that noncognitive traits ". . . play a larger role than cognitive skills in determining economic success or failure." Yet he omits such effects because of his stated inability to assess and measure them.

The result of all these omissions is to understate seriously the ways in which incomes vary systematically with differences in schooling and family background. If Jencks had corrected the data for such idiosyncrasies and if he had included data on place of residence, age, and noncognitive attributes, his formulation would probably have explained from three to four times as much of the inequality in income as did the more naïve formulation he actually used.

In a sense this example illustrates the fragility of social-science research in complex areas where theories are mere speculations and the techniques of analysis are subject to wide differences in application, usage, and interpretation. Jencks concluded that, because such a small portion of the variance in income was explained statistically by the family-background, schooling, and test-score variables, differences in income must be due primarily to differences in luck and competences that are not related to an individual's educational and family experiences. Yet the obvious alternative explanation is that the omission of important variables, as well as problems in the quality of the data, were the culprits and that differences in family and schooling do indeed affect economic success of adults.

Though Jencks gives the impression that his results are derived strictly from his statistical model and social-science methodology, in fact, the application of that model and its methodology are based upon numerous judgments and opinions. The omission of important variables because of "ignorance of their effects," the casual ordering of the variables, assumptions of linear relationships and normal distributions, the scavenging and use of data collected for other purposes and the questionable treatment of their measurement errors, as well as the ambiguity of many of the results, means that the actual findings and interpretations are at least as much a product of the value perspectives and opinions of the researcher as they are of this methodology and data. Unfortunately, the values and biases of the researcher are built into his procedures and interpretations at every stage.

Using similar data and techniques of analysis, Jencks's colleagues at Harvard, Herbert Gintis and Samuel Bowles, have found powerful support for the theory that social class and income inequality are indeed transmitted from generation to generation by rather powerful noncognitive effects of both family background and schools. They have constructed their model on the assumption that the vast inequality in society is a reflection of the class structure that corresponds to men's relations to the means of production under a system of monopoly-capitalism. In this Marxian model, schools and other institutions work to reproduce the social division of labor and the class structure. Placed in this context, the data and methods used by Jencks would engender very different interpretations. For example, in the Bowles-Gintis context the fact that society spends about twice as much on the schooling of the rich child as on the poor one hardly seems an innocuous accident.

In contrast, Jencks feigns neutrality in the important value issues of how society functions. Schools, family, and the distribution of income appear to operate in a conceptual vacuum, and Jencks seems to shy away from any socio-political-economic theory that might relate them. This places the reader in a position of having to evaluate conclusions based upon statistical evidence that in turn could be derived and interpreted in many different ways. Unless we know the overall value perspectives of the author, it is very difficult to ascertain why he intrepreted the data in the particular way he did in the face of many possible alternative explanations.

Discussion Questions

1. From the brief excerpt of Jencks' interpretations, how would you summarize his major conclusions about this question: What are the most important causes of economic success?

2. Levin disagrees with Jencks' conclusions in answer to question 1. Review at least three or four of Levin's major disagreements. How do you think Jencks would answer these disagreements?

3. Give two or three examples of Jencks' "personal judgments" entering into his interpretations of his data (assuming

Levin's statement of these is correct).
4. What is Levin's criticism concerning Jencks' omission of data? Can any scientific study of such complex vari-

ables as the ones the Jencks study concentrates on resolve this problem? Discuss.

JACKSON TOBY

Undermining the Student's Faith in the Validity of Personal Experience

It has been argued that one of the benefits of twentieth-century progress is that we no longer depend on myths and legends to explain nature and guide us through life. After all, we have verified knowledge revealed to us by the scientific method. It is an irony of our times, however, that while we extol the virtues of science we still seem to retain our tendency to rely on our personal observations and experience and commonsense reasoning. The results of carrying this tendency into sociological studies are discussed by Jackson Toby in this article.

After listening to me talk for a half-hour on research in the field of child socialization, a freshman raised his hand to comment, "In all of my eighteen years, I never came across any of those things you were talking about." The class laughed, but I found that other students are also unwilling to believe anything that they cannot confirm by their own experience. It does no good to point out that they get to meet in a lifetime only an insignificant proportion of the human race and that, moreover, a white Protestant New Yorker has little chance of knowing Southern Negroes, European priests, or even American farmers. Personal experience is so convincing that they discourse with assurance on topics about which I dare to make only the most tentative observations. At first I was non-plussed. Then I got an idea. If I could shake their confidence in the validity of personal experience, perhaps they would prefer the cautious, pedestrian conclusions of social science.

My program of subversion includes the following illustration of the limitations of "experience": I ask the class whether anyone has noticed, in traveling by bus or streetcar, that there are more public conveyances going by in the *wrong* direction. A few students agree that this is so. "You mean that, no matter which way you wish to go, more buses come by going in the opposite direction?" The class begins to mumble that you see the same number in both directions, that it only *seems* there are more buses coming the other way. The handful of students who spoke up first feel trapped and hasten to disavow their original position.

Reprinted from Jackson Toby, "Undermining the Student's Faith in the Validity of Personal Experience," *American Sociological Review*, Vol. 20, No. 6 (December 1955), 717–718, by permission of The American Sociological Association and the author.

"No, it is not an illusion," I assure them, "you actually have observed more buses going in the wrong direction!" No matter which direction you want to go in? How can that be? Disbelief is writ large on their faces. "Suppose you want to travel *east*. A bus comes heading *west*. Do you take it?" Of course not, they snort. "You wait five minutes more, and another bus comes heading *west*. Do you take it?" No. "How many buses do you see heading west that day?" It depends on how long it takes for *my* bus to come. "As many as five?" Possibly. "How many do you see heading east?" They begin to catch on. Only *one* because, as soon as a bus comes going in my direction, I take it!

"Over the years you can accumulate quite a bit of experience testifying that public transportation companies are engaged in a conspiracy to frustrate your travel plans. Of course, it is neither the bus company nor a malevolent deity. You observe the comings and goings of buses while waiting for one, and this biases your conclusions. When buses go by in the wrong direction, you may fume, curse the bus company, or spend your time counting them. But no matter how many there are, you do not board any of them. Let one bus come on your side of the street, and you get on. This is your mistake. If you want to prove to yourself that paranoid conclusions are unjustified, you have to restrain the impulse to get someplace. Station yourself at the bus stop at 6 A.M. and stay there until sunset, counting the buses as they go by in *both* directions. This is the only scientific way to mobilize the testimony of experience on this problem."

So far, none of my students has been scientist enough to accept my challenge.

Discussion Questions

1. Why, do you think, is "personal experience so convincing" to many people?
2. What is wrong with relying on personal experience for authoritative conclusions about human behavior?
3. Do you believe that Toby's "illustration of the limitations of experience" proves his point? Discuss.

2 / Culture

Drawing by D. Reilly; in Look, 3-24-70

"Shouldn't we be putting a little something aside for our irrelevant years?"

Why are young adults in America given so much freedom in their choice of marital partners and occupations? Why do the traditional Maoris of New Zealand *hongi* (rub noses) when greeting a friend instead of shaking hands? Why did the Japanese willingly participate in Banzai charges that seem so senseless to Americans? Why do most mothers on Niue Island give their third or fourth child away at birth? These differences are explained by the concept of *culture.* The most classic definition of culture was framed by Edward Tyler in the nineteenth century: "Culture is a complex whole which includes knowledge, belief, art, morals, law, custom, and other capabilities acquired by man as a member of society." It is culture that determines whether we think a person is beautiful or ugly, a government is legitimate or illegitimate, a type of entertainment is desirable or undesirable, and a type of food is edible or not. Culture, therefore, is much more than an inclination toward opera music, browsing through art galleries, and the possession of social graces. It includes the entire way of life of a particular society. It even includes swearing, "obscene" jokes, and other relatively trivial things. Culture, in effect, determines the way an individual will view the world.

While social scientists differ in their interpretation of the meaning and content of culture, sociologists generally approach it as learned behavior. The use of "four-letter words" and the reciting of jokes—sexual, ethnic, or otherwise—are skills learned within a group.

Similarly, other aspects of culture were learned as man developed techniques to adapt to the environment around him.

In complex societies such as the United States, any one individual will learn only a small proportion of the society's culture. The influence of industrialization has not only set in motion a seemingly endless series of cultural changes, but it has also created such vast amounts of knowledge and added so many traits that it is impossible to learn all of the culture. Also, in a society as complex as ours we find many religious and ethnic groups whose norms and behavior differ from that of the dominant culture. To explain these variations from the dominant culture the concepts of *subculture* and *counterculture* are introduced.

The concept of *subculture* refers to behavior patterns related to the general culture and yet distinguishable from it. Subcultures can be distinguished from the dominant culture and other subcultures by such characteristics as language, dress, diet, religion, political beliefs, or occupation. The boxing profession is a good example of an occupational subculture. Boxers share a common background of extensive training, a common goal of winning the fight, a specialized jargon, and a number of specialized material traits such as mouth guards, boxing gloves, and punching bags. Subcultures are important because individuals live and func-tion within them. *Counterculture,* on the other hand, is not merely different from the dominant culture; it opposes it. The "hippie," for example, looks with disdain on the vulgar materialistic ambitions of the dominant culture.

The significance of culture, however, stems from the fact that it furnishes a method of regulating behavior. As a system of norms, culture defines the situation for the individual and tells him how he is supposed to behave. This is especially applicable to the repetitive activities of an organized group. Emily Post, for example, clarifies the norms (etiquette) regarding the use of forks, knives, and napkins at a lavish banquet table. Violation of these norms does not usually result in severe repercussions. Consider, however, the chaos and bedlam on the roads and highways if we were deprived of guidelines for behavior. Upon learning the highway code (norms for the group called "highway drivers") you will *define the situation* of a red light as requiring you to stop, and a green light will be defined as allowing you to proceed. The norms regarding highway driving not only regulate your own behavior, they also provide you with an expectation that other members of the group will similarly conform to the guidelines. Such expectations are the springboard to organized behavior.

The examples provided in the following articles show both the subtle and the more obvious influences of culture.

THOMAS KOCHMAN

"Rapping" in the Black Ghetto

Every complex society includes groups of people whose behavior patterns differ from the dominant culture. Sociologists define such a group as a *subculture*. Subcultures refer to the values and behavior patterns that are characteristic of a particular profession, such as that of a boxer or a physician; a church, such as Catholic or Mormon; or even an ethnic community. Each of these subcultures has unique ways of dealing with issues that are important to it, such as power, money, prestige, diet, clothes, or companionship. Boxers, for example, wear shorts at work. A Catholic priest has much more elaborate clothing, and Mormons advocate abstinence from alcohol and

Reprinted from Thomas Kochman, "Rapping in the Black Ghetto," *Society,* Vol. 6, No. 4. Copyright © 1969 by Transaction Inc. Reprinted with permission.

tobacco. In the following article, Thomas Kochman describes the distinctive aspects of an ethnic ghetto, which involve skills of "rapping," "shucking," "jiving," "sounding," and "gripping." Notice how the distinctive verbal patterns establish personality, stir up excitement, and exhibit respect for power and manipulation.

"Rapping," "shucking," "jiving," "running it down," "gripping," "copping a plea," "signifying," and "sounding" are all part of the black ghetto idiom and describe different kinds of talking. Each has its own distinguishing features of form, style, and function; each is influenced by, and influences, the speaker, setting, and audience; and each sheds light on the black perspective and the black condition—on those orienting values and attitudes that will cause a speaker to speak or perform in his own way within the social context of the black community.

I was first introduced to black idiom in New York City, and, as a professional linguist interested in dialects, I began to compile a lexicon of such expressions. My real involvement, however, came in Chicago, while preparing a course on black idiom at the Center for Inner City studies, the southside branch of Northeastern Illinois State College.

Here I began to explore the full cultural significance of this kind of verbal behavior. My students and informants within black Chicago, through their knowledge of these terms, and their ability to recognize and categorize the techniques, and to give examples, gave me much reliable data. When I turned for other or better examples to the literature—such as the writings of Malcolm X, Robert Conot, and Iceberg Slim—my students and informants were able to recognize and confirm their authenticity.

While often used to mean ordinary conversation, rapping is distinctively a fluent and a lively way of talking, always characterized by a high degree of personal style. To one's own group, rapping may be descriptive of an interesting narration, a colorful rundown of some past event. An example of this kind of rap is the answer from a Chicago gang member to a youth worker who asked how this group became organized:

Now I'm goin to tell you how the jive really started. I'm going to tell you how the club got this big. 'Bout 1956 there used to be a time when the Jackson Park show was open and the Stony show was open. Sixty-six street, Jeff, Gene, all of 'em, little bitty dudes, little bitty . . . Gene wasn't with 'em then. Gene was cribbin (living) over here. Jeff, all of 'em, real little bitty dudes, you dig? All of us were little.

Sixty-six (the gang on sixty-sixth street), they wouldn't allow us in the Jackson Park show. That was when the parky (?) was headin it. Everybody say, If we want to go to the show, we go! One day, who was it? Carl Robinson. He went up to the show . . . and Jeff fired on him. He came back and all this was swelled up 'bout yay big, you know. He come back over to the hood (neighborhood). He told (name unclear) and them dudes went up there. That was when mostly all the main sixty-six boys was over here like Bett Riley. All of 'em was over here. People that quit gang-bangin (fighting, especially as a group), Marvell Gates, people like that.

They went on up there, John, Roy and Skeeter went in there. And they start humbuggin (fighting) in there. That's how it all started. Sixty-six found out they couldn't beat us, at *that* time. They couldn't *whup* seven-o. Am I right Leroy? You was cribbin over here then. Am I right? We were dynamite! Used to be a time, you ain't have a passport, Man, you couldn't walk through here. And if didn't nobody know you it was worse than that. . . .

Rapping to a woman is a colorful way of "asking for some pussy." "One needs to throw a lively rap when he is 'putting the make' on a broad." (John Horton, "Time and Cool People," *trans*action, April, 1967.)

According to one informant the woman is usually someone he has just seen or met, looks good, and might be willing to have sexual intercourse with him. My informant says the term would not be descriptive of talk between a couple "who have had a relationship over any length of time." Rapping then, is used at the beginning of a relationship to create a favorable impression and be persuasive at the same time. The man who has the reputation for excelling at this is the pimp, or mack man. Both terms describe a person of considerable status in the street hierarchy, who, by his lively and persuasive rapping ("macking" is also used in this context) has acquired a stable of girls to hustle for him and give him money. For most street men and many teenagers he is the model whom they try to emulate. Thus, within the community you have a pimp walk, pimp style boots and clothes, and perhaps most of all "pimp talk," is a colorful literary example of a telephone rap. One of my informants regards it as extreme, but agrees that it illustrates the language, style and technique of rapping. "Blood" is rapping to an ex-whore named Christine in an effort to trap her into his stable:

Now try to control yourself baby. I'm the tall stud with the dreamy bedroom eyes across the hall in four-twenty. I'm the guy with the pretty towel wrapped around his sexy hips. I got the same hips on now that you X-rayed. Remember that hump of sugar your peepers feasted on?

She said, "Maybe, but you shouldn't call me. I don't want an incident. What do you want? A lady doesn't accept phone calls from strangers."

I said, "A million dollars and a trip to the moon with a bored, trapped, beautiful bitch, you dig? I'm no stranger. I've been popping the elastic on your panties ever since you saw me in the hall. . . ."

Rapping between men and women often is competitive and leads to a lively repartee with the women becoming as adept as the men. An example follows:

A man coming from the bathroom forgot to zip his pants. An unescorted party of women kept watching him and laughing among themselves. The man's friends "hip" (inform) him to what's going on. He approaches one woman— "Hey baby, did you see that big black Cadillac with the full tires? ready to roll in action just for you." She answers—"No, mother-fucker, but I saw a little gray Volkswagen with two flat tires." Everybody laughs. His rap was "capped" (excelled, topped).

When "whupping the game" on a "trick" or "lame" (trying to get goods or services from someone who looks like he can be swindled), rapping is often descriptive of the highly stylized verbal part of the maneuver. In well established "con games" the rap is carefully prepared and used with great skill in directing the course of the transaction. An excellent illustration came from an adept hustler who was playing the "murphy" game on a white trick. The "murphy" game is designed to get the *trick* to give his money to the hustler, who in this instance poses as a "steerer" (one who directs or steers customers to a brothel), to keep the whore from stealing it. The hustler then skips with the money.

> Look Buddy, I know a fabulous house not more than two blocks away. Brother you ain't never seen more beautiful, freakier broads than are in that house. One of them, the prettiest one, can do more with a swipe than a monkey can with a banana. She's like a rubber doll; she can take a hundred positions."
> At this point the sucker is wild to get to this place of pure joy. He entreats the con player to take him there, not just direct him to it.
> The "murphy" player will prat him (pretend rejection) to enhance his desire. He will say, "Man, don't be offended, but Aunt Kate, that runs the house don't have nothing but highclass White men coming to her place. . . . You know, doctors, lawyers, big-shot politicians. You look like a clean-cut White man, but you ain't in that league are you? (Iceberg Slim, *Pimp: The Story of My Life.*)

After a few more exchanges of the "murphy" dialogue, "the mark is separated from his scratch."

An analysis of rapping indicates a number of things.

For instance, it is revealing that one raps *to* rather than *with* a person supporting the impression that rapping is to be regarded more as a performance than verbal exchange. As with other performances, rapping projects the personality, physical appearance and style of the performer. In each of the examples given, the intrusive "I" of the speaker was instrumental in contributing to the total impression of the rap.

The combination of personality and style is usually best when "asking for some pussy." It is less when "whupping the game" on someone or "running something down."

In "asking for some pussy" for example, where personality and style might be projected through nonverbal means: stance, clothing, walking, looking, one can speak of a "silent rap." The woman is won here without the use of words, or rather, with words being implied that would generally accompany the nonverbal components.

As a lively way of "running it down" the verbal element consists of personality and style plus information. To someone *reading* my example of the gang member's narration, the impression might be that the information would be more influential in directing the listener's response. The youth worker might be expected to say "So that's how the gang got so big," instead of "Man, that gang member is *bad* (strong, brave)" in which instance he would be responding to the personality and style of the rapper. However, if the reader would *listen* to the gang member on tape or could have been present when the gang member spoke he more likely would have reacted more to personality and style as my informants did.

Remember that in attendance with the youth worker were members of the gang who *already knew* how the gang got started (e.g., "Am I right Leroy? You was cribbin' over here then") and for whom the information itself would have little interest. Their attention was held by the *way* the information was presented.

The verbal element in "whupping the game" on someone, in the preceding example, was an integral part of an overall deception in which information and personality-style were skillfully manipulated for the purpose of controlling the "trick's" response. But again, greater weight must be given to personality-style. In the "murphy game" for example, it was this element which got the trick to trust the hustler and leave his money with him for "safekeeping."

The function of rapping in each of these forms is *expressive*. By this I mean that the speaker raps to project his personality onto the scene or to evoke a generally favorable response. When rapping is used to "ask for some pussy" or to "whup the game" on someone its function is *directive*. By this I mean that rapping becomes an instrument to manipulate and control people to get them to give up or to do something. The difference between rapping to a "fox" (pretty girl) for the purpose of "getting inside her pants" and rapping to a "lame" to get something from him is operational rather than functional. The latter rap contains a concealed motivation where the former does not.

"Shucking," "shucking it," "shucking and jiving," "S-ing" and "J-ing" or just "jiving," are terms that refer to language behavior practiced by the black when confronting "the Man" (the white man, the establishment, or *any* authority figure), and to another form of language behavior practiced by blacks with each other on the peer group level.

In the South, and later in the North, the black man learned that American society had assigned to him a restrictive role and status. Among whites his behavior had to conform to this imposed station and he was constantly reminded to "keep his place." He learned that it was not acceptable in the presence of white people to show feelings of indignation, frustration, discontent, pride, ambition, or desire; that real feelings had to be concealed behind a mask of innocence, ignorance, childishness, obedience, humility and deference. The terms used by the black to describe the role he played before white folks in the South was "tomming," or "jeffing." Failure to accommodate the white Southerner in this respect was almost certain to invite psychological and often physical brutality. A description related by a black psychiatrist, Alvin F. Poussaint, is typical and revealing:

Once last year as I was leaving my office in Jackson, Miss., with my Negro secretary, a White policeman yelled, "Hey, boy! Come here!" Somewhat bothered, I retorted: "I'm no boy!" He then rushed at me, inflamed, and stood towering over me, snorting "What d'ja say, boy?" Quickly he frisked me and demanded, "What's your name boy?" Frightened, I replied, "Dr. Poussaint. I'm a physician." He angrily chuckled and hissed, "What's your first name, boy?" When I hesitated he assumed a threatening stance and clenched his fists. As my heart palpitated, I muttered in profound humiliation, "Alvin."

He continued his psychological brutality, bellowing, "Alvin, the next time I call you, you come right away, you hear? You hear?" I hesitated. "You hear me, boy?" My voice trembling with helplessness, but *following my instincts of self-preservation*, I murmured, "Yes, sir." *Now fully satisfied that I had performed and acquiesced to my "boy" status*, he dismissed me with, "Now, boy, go on and get out of here or next time we'll take you for a little ride down to the station house!" (Alvin F. Poussaint, "A Negro Psychiatrist Explains the Negro Psyche," *The New York Times Magazine*, August 20, 1967 [emphasis mine].)

In the northern cities the black encountered authority figures equivalent to Southern "crackers": policemen, judges, probation officers, truant officers, teachers and "Mr. Charlies" (bosses), and soon learned that the way to get by and avoid difficulty was to shuck. Thus, he learned to accommodate "the Man," to use the total orchestration of speech, intonation, gesture and facial expression for the purpose of producing whatever appearance would be acceptable. It was a technique and ability that was developed from fear, a respect for power, and a will to survive. This type of accommodation is exemplified by the Uncle Tom with his "Yes sir, Mr. Charlie," or "Anything you say, Mr. Charlie."

Through accommodation, many blacks became adept at concealing and controlling their emotions and at assuming a variety of postures. They became competent actors. Many developed a keen perception of what affected, motivated, appeased or satisfied the authority figures with whom they came into contact. Shucking became an effective way for many blacks to stay out of trouble, and for others a useful artifice for avoiding arrest or getting out of trouble when apprehended. Shucking it with a judge, for example, would be to feign repentance in the hope of receiving a lighter or suspended sentence. Robert Conot reports an example of shucking in his book, *Rivers of Blood, Years of Darkness*: Joe was found guilty of possession of narcotics. But he did an excellent job of shucking it with the probation officer.

The probation officer interceded for Joe with the judge: "His own attitude toward the present offense appears to be serious and responsible and it is believed that the defendant is an excellent subject for probation."

Some field illustration of shucking to get out of trouble came from some seventh-grade children from an inner-city school in Chicago. The children were asked to talk their way out of a troublesome situation.

You are cursing at this old man and your mother comes walking down the stairs. She hears you.

To "talk your way out of this":

"I'd tell her that I was studying a scene in school for a play."

What if you were in a store stealing something and the manager caught you?

"I would start stuttering. Then I would say, 'Oh, Oh, I forgot. Here the money is.' "

A literary example of shucking comes from Iceberg Slim's autobiography. Iceberg, a pimp, shucks before "two red-faced Swede rollers (detectives)" who catch him in a motel room with his whore. My italics identify which elements of the passage constitute the shuck.

> I put my shaking hands into the pajama pockets . . . *I hoped I was keeping the fear out of my face. I gave them a wide toothy smile.* They came in and stood in the middle of the room. Their eyes were racing about the room. Stacy was open mouthed in the bed.
>
> I said, *"Yes, gentlemen, what can I do for you?"*
>
> Lanky said, "We wanta see your I.D."
>
> I went to the closet and got the phony John Cato Fredrickson I.D. I put it in his palm. I felt cold sweat running down my back. They looked at it, then looked at each other.
>
> Lanky said, "You are in violation of the law. You signed the motel register improperly. Why didn't you sign your full name? What are you trying to hide? What are you doing here in town? It says here you're a dancer. We don't have a club in town that books entertainers."
>
> I said, *"Officers, my professional name is Johnny Cato. I've got nothing to hide. My full name had always been too long for the marquees. I've fallen into the habit of using the shorter version.*
>
> *"My legs went out last year. I don't dance anymore: My wife and I decided to go into business. We are making a tour of this part of the country. We think that in your town we've found the ideal site for a Southern fried chicken shack. My wife has a secret recipe that should make us rich up here."* (Iceberg Slim, *Pimp: The Story of My Life.*)

Another example of shucking was related to me by a colleague. A black gang member was coming down the stairway from the club room with seven guns on him and encountered some policemen and detectives coming up the same stairs. If they stopped and frisked him he and others would have been arrested. A paraphrase of his shuck follows: "Man, I gotta get away from up there. There's gonna be some trouble and I don't want no part of it." This shuck worked on the minds of the policemen. It anticipated their questions as to why he was leaving the club room, and why he would be in a hurry. He also gave *them* a reason for wanting to get up to the room fast.

It ought to be mentioned at this point that there was not uniform agreement among my informants in characterizing the above examples as shucking. One informant used shucking only in the sense in which it is used among peers, e.g., bull-shitting, and characterized the above examples as jiving or whupping game. Others however, identified the above examples as shucking, and reserved jiving and whupping game for more offensive maneuvers. In fact, one of the apparent features of shucking is that the posture of the black when acting with members of the establishment be a *defensive* one.

Frederick Douglass, in telling of how he taught himself to read, would challenge a white boy with whom he was playing, by saying that he could write as well as he. Whereupon he would write down all the letters he knew. The white boy would then write down more letters than Douglass did. In this way, Douglass eventually learned all the letters of the alphabet. Some of my informants regarded the example as whupping game. Others regarded it as shucking. The former were perhaps focusing on the maneuver rather than the language used. The latter may have felt that any maneuvers designed to learn to read were justifiably defensive. One of my informants said Douglass was "shucking *in order to* whup the game." This latter response seems to be the most revealing. Just as one can rap to whup the game on someone, so one can shuck or jive for the same purpose; that is, assume a guise or posture or perform some action in a certain way that is designed to work on someone's mind to get him to give up something.

"Whupping game" to con whitey

The following examples from Malcolm X illustrate the shucking and jiving in this context though jive is the term used. Today, whupping game might also be the term used to describe the operation. Whites who came at night got a better reception; the several Harlem nightclubs they patronized were geared to entertain and jive (flatter, cajole) the night white crowd to get their money. (Malcolm X, *The Autobiography of Malcolm X.*)

The maneuvers involved here are clearly designed to obtain some benefit or advantage.

> Freddie got on the stand and went to work on his own shoes. Brush, liquid polish, brush, paste wax, shine rag, lacquer sole dressing . . . step by step, Freddie showed me what to do.
>
> "But you got to get a whole lot faster. You can't waste time!" Freddie showed me how fast on my own shoes. Then because business was tapering off, he had time to give me a demonstration of how to make the shine rag pop like a firecracker. "Dig the action?" he asked. He did it in slow motion. I got down and tried it on his shoes. I had the principle of it. "Just got to do it, faster," Freddie said. *"It's a jive noise, that's all. Cats tip better, they figure you're knocking yourself out!"* (Malcolm X, *The Autobiography of Malcolm X.*)

An eight-year-old boy whupped the game on me one day this way:

My colleague and I were sitting in a room listening to a tape. The door to the room was open and outside was a soda machine. Two boys came up in the elevator, stopped at the soda machine, and then came into the room.

"Do you have a dime for two nickels?" Presumably the soda machine would not accept nickels. I took out the change in my pocket, found a dime and gave it to the boy for two nickels.

After accepting the dime, he looked at the change in my hand and asked, "Can I have two cents? I need carfare to get home." I gave him the two cents.

At first I assumed the verbal component of the maneuver was the rather weak, transparently false reason for wanting the two cents. Actually, as was pointed out to me later, the maneuver began with the first question which was designed to get me to show my money. He could then ask me for something that he knew I had, making my refusal more difficult. He apparently felt that the reason need not be more than plausible because the amount he wanted was small. Were the amount larger, he would no doubt have elaborated on the verbal element of the game. The form of the verbal element could be in the direction of rapping or shucking and jiving. If he were to rap the eight-year-old might say, "Man, you know a cat needs to have a little bread to keep the girls in line." Were he to shuck and jive he might make the reason for needing the money more compelling, look hungry, etc.

The function of shucking and jiving as it refers to blacks and "the Man" is designed to work on the mind and emotions of the authority figure for the purpose of getting him to feel a certain way or give up something that will be to the other's advantage. Iceberg showed a "toothy smile" which said to the detective, "I'm glad to see you" and "Would I be glad to see you if I had something to hide?" When the maneuvers seem to be *defensive* most of my informants regarded the language behavior as shucking. When the maneuvers were *offensive* my informants tended to regard the behavior as "whupping the game."

Also significant is that the first form of shucking described, which developed out of accommodation, is becoming less frequently used today by many blacks, because of a new-found self-assertiveness and pride, challenging the system. The willingness on the part of many blacks to accept the psychological and physical brutality and general social consequences of not "keeping one's place" is indicative of the changing self-concept of the black man. Ironically, the shocked reaction of some whites to the present militancy of the black is partly due to the fact that the black was so successful at "putting Whitey on" via shucking in the past. This new attitude can be seen from a conversation I recently had with a shoe-shine attendant at O'Hare Airport in Chicago.

I was having my shoes shined and the black attendant was using a polishing machine instead of the rag that was generally used in the past. I asked whether the machine made his work any easier. He did not answer me until about ten seconds had passed and then responded in a loud voice that he "never had a job that was easy," that he would give me "one hundred dollars for any *easy* job" I could offer him, that the machine made his job "faster" but not "easier." I was startled at the response because it was so unexpected and I realized that here was a new "breed of cat" who was not going to shuck for a big tip or ingratiate himself with "Whitey" anymore. A few years ago his response probably would have been different.

The contrast between this "shoe-shine" scene and the one illustrated earlier from Malcolm X's autobiography, when "shucking Whitey" was the common practice, is striking.

Shucking, jiving, shucking and jiving, or S-ing and J-ing, when referring to language behavior practiced by blacks, is descriptive of the talk and gestures that are appropriate to "putting someone on" by creating a false impression. The terms seem to cover a range from simply telling a lie, to bullshitting, to subtly playing with someone's mind. An important difference between this form of shucking and that described earlier is that the same talk and gestures that are deceptive to "the Man" are often transparent to those members of one's own group who are able practitioners at shucking themselves. As Robert Conot has pointed out, "The Negro who often fools the White officer by 'shucking it' is much less likely to be successful with another Negro. . . ." Also, S-ing and J-ing within the group often has play overtones in which the person being "put on" is aware of the attempts being made and goes along with it for enjoyment or in apprecation of the style.

"Running it down" is the term used by speakers in the ghetto when it is their intention to give information, either by explanation, narrative, or giving advice. In the following literary example, Sweet Mac is "running this Edith broad down" to his friends:

> Edith is the "saved" broad who can't marry out of her religion . . . or do anything else out of her religion for that matter, especially what I wanted her to do. A bogue religion, man! So dig, for the last couple weeks I been quoting the Good Book and all that staff to her; telling her I am now saved myself, you dig. (Woodie King, Jr., "The Game," *Liberator*, August, 1965.)

The following citation from Claude Brown uses the term with the additional sense of giving advice:

> If I saw him (Claude's brother) hanging out with cats I knew were weak, who might be using drugs sooner or later, I'd run it down to him.

It seems clear that running it down has simply an informative function, that of telling somebody something that he doesn't already know.

"Gripping" is of fairly recent vintage, used by black high school students in Chicago to refer to the talk and facial expression that accompanies a *partial* loss of face or self-possession, or showing of fear. Its appearance along-side "copping a plea," which refers to a total loss of face, in which one begs one's adversary for mercy, is a significant new perception. In linking it with the street code which acclaims the ability to "look tough and inviolate, fearless, secure, 'cool,' " it suggests that even the slightest weakening of this posture will be held up to ridicule and contempt. There are always contemptuous overtones attached to the use of the term when applied to the others' behavior. One is tempted to link it with the violence and toughness required to survive on the street. The intensity of both seems to be increasing. As one of my informants noted, "Today, you're *lucky* if you end up in the hospital" —that is, are not killed.

Reaction to fear and superior power

Both gripping and copping a plea refer to behavior produced from fear and a respect for superior power. An example of gripping comes from the record *"Street and Gangland Rhythms"* (Band 4 Dumb Boy). Lennie meets Calvin and asks him what happened to his lip. Calvin says that a boy named Pierre hit him for copying off him in school. Lennie, pretending to be Calvin's brother, goes to confront Pierre. Their dialogue follows:

> Lennie: "Hey you! What you hit my little brother for?"
> Pierre: "Did he tell you what happen man?"
> Lennie: "Yeah, he told me what happened."
> Pierre: "But you . . . but you . . . but you should tell your people to teach him to go to the school, man." (Pause) "I, I know, I know I didn't have a right to hit him."

Pierre, anticipating a fight with Lennie if he continued to justify his hitting of Calvin, tried to avoid it by "gripping" with the last line.

Copping a plea originally meant "to plead guilty to a lesser charge to save the state the cost of a trial" (with the hope of receiving a lesser or suspended sentence), but is now generally used to mean "to beg," "plead for mercy," as in the example "Please cop, don't hit me. I give." (*Street and Gangland Rhythms,* Band 1 "Gang Fight.") This change of meaning can be seen from its use by Piri Thomas in *Down These Mean Streets.*

> The night before my hearing, I decided to make a prayer. It had to be on my knees, 'cause if I was gonna cop a plea to God, I couldn't play it cheap.

The function of gripping and copping a plea is obviously to induce pity or to acknowledge the presence of superior strength. In so doing, one evinces noticeable feelings of fear and insecurity which also result in a loss of status among one's peers.

Signifying is the term used to describe the language behavior that, as Abrahams has defined it, attempts to "imply, goad, beg, boast by indirect verbal or gestural means." (Roger D. Abrahams, *Deep Down in the Jungle.*) In Chicago it is also used as a synonym to describe language behavior more generally known as "sounding" elsewhere.

Some excellent examples of signifying as well as of other forms of language behavior come from the well known "toast" (narrative form) "The Signifying Monkey and the Lion" which was collected by Abrahams from Negro street corner bards in Philadelphia. In the above toast the monkey is trying to get the lion involved in a fight with the elephant:

Now the lion came through the jungle one peaceful day,
When the signifying monkey stopped him, and that is what he started to say:
He said, "Mr. Lion," he said, "A bad-assed mother-fucker down your way,"
He said, "Yeah! The way he talks about your folks is a certain shame.
I even heard him curse when he mentioned your grandmother's name."
The lion's tail shot back like a forty-four
When he went down that jungle in all uproar.

Thus the monkey has goaded the lion into a fight with the elephant by "signifying," that is, indicating that the elephant has been "sounding on" (insulting) the lion. When the lion comes back, thoroughly beaten up, the monkey again "signifies" by making fun of the lion:

. . . lion came back through the jungle more dead than alive,
When the monkey started some more of that signifying jive.
He said, "Damn, Mr. Lion, you went through here yesterday, the jungle rung.
Now you come back today, damn near hung."

The monkey, of course, is delivering this taunt from a safe distance away on the limb of a tree when his foot slips and he falls to the ground, at which point,

Like a bolt of lightning, a stripe of white heat,
The lion was on the monkey with all four feet.

In desperation the monkey quickly resorts to "copping a plea":

The monkey looked up with a tear in his eyes,
He said, "Please, Mr. Lion, I apologize."

His "plea" however, fails to move the lion to show any mercy so the monkey tries another verbal ruse, "shucking":

He said, "You lemme get my head out of the sand,
Ass out the grass, I'll fight you like a natural man."

In this he is more successful as,

The lion jumped back and squared for a fight.
The mother-fucking monkey jumped clear out of sight.

A safe distance away again, the monkey returns to "signifying":

> He said, "Yeah, you had me down, you had me at last,
> But you left me free, now you can still kiss my ass."

This example illustrates the methods of provocation, goading and taunting artfully practiced by a signifier.

Interestingly, when the *function* of signifying is *directive* the *tactic* employed is *indirection,* i.e., the signifier reports or repeats what someone else has said about the listener; the "report" is couched in plausible language designed to compel belief and arouse feelings of anger and hostility. There is also the implication that if the listener fails to do anything about it—what has to be "done" is usually quite clear—his status will be seriously compromised. Thus the lion is compelled to vindicate the honor of his family by fighting or else leave the impression that he is afraid, and that he is not "king" of the jungle. When used for the purpose of directing action, "signifying" is like "shucking" in also being deceptive and subtle in approach and depending for success on the naiveté or gullibility of the person being "put on."

When the function of signifying is to arouse feelings of embarrassment, shame, frustration or futility, to diminish someone's status, the tactic employed is direct in the form of a taunt, as in the example where the monkey is making fun of the lion.

"Sounding" to relieve tensions

Sounding is the term which is today most widely known for the game of verbal insult known in the past as "Playing the Dozens," "The Dirty Dozens" or just "The Dozens." Other current names for the game have regional distribution: Signifying or "Sigging" (Chicago), Joning (Washington, D.C.), Screaming (Harrisburg), etc. In Chicago, the term "sounding" would be descriptive of the initial remarks which are designed to sound out the other person to see whether he will play the game. The verbal insult is also subdivided, the term "signifying" applying to insults which are hurled directly at the person and "the dozens" applying to insults hurled at your opponent's family, especially the mother.

Sounding is often catalyzed by signifying remarks referred to earlier such as "Are you going to let him say that about your mama" to spur an exchange between members of the group. It is begun on a relatively low key and built up by verbal exchanges. The game goes like this:

> One insults a member of another's family; others in the group make disapproving sounds to spur on the coming exchange. The one who has been insulted feels at this point that he must reply with a slur on the protagonist's family which is clever enough to defend his honor (and therefore that of his family). This, of

course, leads to other (once again, more due to pressure from the crowd than actual insult) to make further jabs. This can proceed until everyone is bored with the whole affair, until one hits the other (fairly rare), or until some other subject comes up that interrupts the proceedings (the usual state of affairs). (Roger D. Abrahams, "Playing the Dozens," *Journal of American Folklore*, July–September, 1962.)

Mack McCormick describes the dozens as a verbal contest:

. . . in which the players strive to bury one another with vituperation. In the play, the opponent's mother is especially slandered. . . . Then, in turn fathers are identified as queer and syphilitic Sisters are whores, brothers are defective, cousins are "funny" and the opponent is himself diseased. (Mack McCormick, "The Dirty Dozens," book jacket in the record album *The Unexpurgated Folksongs of Men,* Arhoolie Records.)

An example of the "game" collected by one of my students goes:

Frank looked up and saw Leroy enter the Outpost.
Leroy walked past the room where Quinton, "Nap," "Pretty Black," "Cunny," Richard, Haywood, "Bull" and Reese sat playing cards. As Leroy neared the T.V. room, Frank shouted to him.
Frank: "Hey Leroy, your mama—calling you man."
Leroy turned and walked toward the room where the sound came from. He stood in the door and looked at Frank.
Leroy: "Look mother-fuckers, I don't play that shit."
Frank (signifying): "Man, I told you cats 'bout that mama jive" (as if he were concerned about how Leroy felt).
Leroy: "That's all right Frank; you don't have to tell these funky mother-fuckers nothing; I'll fuck me up somebody yet."
Frank's face lit up as if he were ready to burst his side laughing. "Cunny" became pissed at Leroy.
"Cunny": "Leroy, you stupid bastard, you let Frank make a fool of you. He said that 'bout your mama."
"Pretty Black": "Aw, fat ass head 'Cunny' shut up."
"Cunny": "Ain't that some shit. This Black slick head motor flicker got nerve 'nough to call somebody 'fat-head.' Boy, you so black, you sweat Perma-lube Oil."

This eased the tension of the group as they burst into loud laughter.

"Pretty Black": "What 'chu laughing 'bout 'Nap,' with your funky mouth smelling like dog shit."
Even Leroy laughed at this.
"Nap": "Your mama mother-fucker."
"Pretty Black": "Your funky mama too."
"Nap" (strongly): "It takes twelve barrels of water to make a steamboat run; it takes an elephant's dick to make your Grandmammy come; she been

elephant fucked, camel fucked and hit side the head with **your Grandpappy's nuts.**"

Reese: "Godorr-damn; go on and rap mother-fucker."

Reese began slapping each boy in his hand, giving his positive approval of "Nap's" comment. "Pretty Black" in an effort not to be outdone, but directing his verbal play elsewhere stated:

"Pretty Black": "Reese, what you laughing 'bout? You so square, you **shit** bricked shit."

Frank: "Whooooowee!"

Reese (sounded back): "Square huh, what about your nappy ass hair before it was stewed; that shit was so bad till, when you went to bed at night, it would leave your head and go on the corner and meddle."

The boys slapped each other in the hand and cracked up.

"Pretty Black": "On the streets meddling, bet Dinky didn't offer me no pussy and I turned it down."

Frank: "Reese scared of pussy."

"Pretty Black": "Hell, yeah; the greasy mother rather fuck old ugly, funky cock Sue Willie than get a piece of ass from a decent broad."

Frank: "Godorr-damn! Not Sue Willie."

"Pretty Black": "Yeah, ol meat-beating Reese rather screw that cross-eyed clapsy bitch, who when she cry, tears rip down her ass."

Haywood: "Don't be so mean, Black."

Reese: "Aw shut up, you half-White bastard."

Frank: "Wait, man, Haywood ain't gonna hear much more of that half-White shit; he's a brother too."

Reese: "Brother, my Black ass; that White ass landlord gotta be this mother-fucker's paw."

"Cunny": "Man, you better stop foolin with Haywood; he's turning red."

Haywood: "Fuck yall" (as he withdrew from the "sig" game).

Frank: "Yeah, fuck yall; let's go to the stick hall."

The group left enroute to the billiard hall. (James Maryland, "Signifying at the Outpost," unpublished term paper for the course *Idiom of the Negro Ghettos,* January 1967.)

The above example of sounding is an excellent illustration of the "game" as played by 15–17-year-old Negro boys, some of whom have already acquired the verbal skill which for them is often the basis for having a high "rep." Ability with words is apparently as highly valued as physical strength. In the sense that the status of one of the participants in the game is diminished if he has to resort to fighting to answer a verbal attack, verbal ability may be even more highly regarded than physical ability.

The relatively high value placed on verbal ability must be clear to most black boys at early age. Most boys begin their activity in sounding by compiling a repertoire of "one liners." When the game is played the one who has the greatest number off such remarks wins. Here are some examples of "one liners" collected from fifth- and sixth-grade black boys in Chicago:

Yo mama is so bowlegged, she looks like the bite out of a donut.
Yo mama sent her picture to the lonely hearts club, and they sent it back and said, "We ain't that lonely!"
Your family is so poor the rats and roaches eat lunch out.
Your house is so small the roaches walk single file.
I walked in your house and your family was running around the table. I said, "Why you doin that?" Your mama say, "First one drops, we eat."

Real proficiency in the game comes to only a small percentage of those who play it. These players have the special skill in being able to turn around what their opponents have said and attack them with it. Thus, when someone indifferently said "fuck you" to Concho, his retort was immediate and devastating: "Man, you haven't even kissed me yet."

The "best talkers" from this group often become the successful street-corner, barber shop, and pool hall story tellers who deliver the long, rhymed, witty, narrative stories called "toasts." They are, as Roger D. Abrahams has described, the traditional "men of words" and have become on occasion entertainers such as Dick Gregory and Redd Foxx, who are virtuosos at repartee, and preachers, whose verbal power has been traditionally esteemed.

The function of the "dozens" or "sounding" is to borrow status from an opponent through an exercise of verbal power. The opponent feels compelled to regain his status by "sounding" back on the speaker or other group member whom he regards as more vulnerable.

The presence of a group seems to be especially important in controlling the game. First of all, one does not "play" with just anyone since the subject matter is concerned with things that in reality one is quite sensitive about. It is precisely *because* "Pretty Black" has a "black slick head" that makes him vulnerable to "Cunny's" barb, especially now when the Afro-American "natural" hair style is in vogue. Without the control of the group "sounding" will frequently lead to a fight. This was illustrated by a tragic epilogue concerning Haywood, when Haywood was being "sounded" on in the presence of two girls by his best fried (other members of the group were absent), he refused to tolerate it. He went home, got a rifle, came back and shot and killed his friend. In the classroom from about the fourth grade on fights among black boys invariably are caused by someone "sounding" on the other person's mother.

Significantly, the subject matter of sounding is changing with the changing self-concept of the black with regard to those physical characteristics that are characteristically "Negro," and which in the past were vulnerable points in the black psyche: blackness and "nappy" hair. It ought to be said that for many blacks, blackness was always highly esteemed and it might be more accurate to regard the present sentiment of the black community toward skin color as reflecting a shifted attitude for only a *portion* of the black community. This suggests that "sounding" on someone's light skin color is not new. Nevertheless, one can regard the previously favorable attitude toward light skin color and "good hair" as the prevailing one. "Other things being equal, the more closely a women approached her white counterpart, the more attractive she was considered to be, by both men and women alike. 'Good hair' (hair that is long and soft) and light skin were the chief criteria." (Elliot Liebow, *Tally's Corner.*)

"The dozens" has been linked to the overall psycho-social growth of the black male. McCormick has stated that a "single round of a dozen or so exchanges frees more pent-up aggressions than will a dose of sodium pentothal." The fact that one permits a kind of abuse within the rules of the game and within the confines of the group which would otherwise not be tolerated, is filled with psychological import. It seems also important, however, to view its function from the perspective of the nonparticipating members of the group. Its function for them may be to incite and prod individual members of the group to combat for the purpose of energizing the elements, of simply relieving the boredom of just "hanging around" and the malaise of living in a static and restrictive environment.

A summary analysis of the different forms of language behavior which have been discussed above permit the following generalizations:

The prestige norms which influence black speech behavior are those which have been successful in manipulating and controlling people and situations. The function of all of the forms of language behavior discussed above, with the exception of "running it down," was to project personality, assert oneself, or arouse emotion, frequently with the additional purpose of getting the person to give up or do something which will be of some benefit to the speaker. Only running it down has as its primary function to communicate information and often here too, the personality and style of the speaker in the form of rapping is projected along with the information.

The purpose for which language is used suggests that the speaker views the social situations into which he moves as consisting of a series of transactions which require that he be continually ready to take advantage of a person or situation or defend himself against being victimized. He has absorbed what Horton has called "street rationality." As one of Horton's respondents put it: "The good hustler . . . conditions his mind and must never put his guard too far down, to relax, or he'll be taken."

I have carefully avoided limiting the group within the black community of whom the language behavior and perspective of their environment is characteristic. While I have no doubt that it is true of those who are generally called "street people" I am uncertain of the extent to which it is true of a much larger portion of the black community, especially the male segment. My informants consisted of street people, high school students, and blacks, who by their occupation as community and youth workers, possess what has been described as a "sharp sense of the streets." Yet it is difficult to find a black male in the community who has *not* witnessed or participated in "the dozens" or heard of signifying, or rapping, or shucking and jiving at some time during his growing up. It would be equally difficult to imagine a high school student in a Chicago inner-city school not being touched by what is generally regarded as "street culture."

In conclusion, by blending style and verbal power, through rapping, sounding and running it down, the black in the ghetto establishes his personality; through shucking, gripping and copping a plea, he shows his respect for power; through jiving and signifying he stirs up excitement. With all of the above, he hopes to manipulate and control people and situations to give himself a winning edge.

Discussion Questions

1. Review one example of each of the following:
   rapping
   shucking
   jiving
   sounding
   gripping
2. What difference do you see—if any—between ghetto achievement based on these skills and more highly valued achievements of the dominant culture.

WILLIAM ARENS

The Great American Football Ritual

Our culture includes such a complex array of subcultures, countercultures, cultural complexes, institutions, values, beliefs, and rules that it seems to defy both a systematic description by sociologists and a clear understanding by students. But our culture can be understood, and the place to begin is with familiar cultural patterns that we participate in on a regular basis. Football, for example, is described below by William Arens in much the same way a social scientist would describe the exotic rituals of a newly discovered tribe, or the mobility structure of a large multinational corporation. Football, like all other cultural patterns in our society, requires rules, specialized skills, a division of labor, and group coordination, and it places great emphasis on the value of winning. Just as William Arens provides new insights into the familiar cultural pattern of football, sociologists can provide systematic description and understanding of other aspects of our culture.

Lear. O, you sir, you! Come you hither, sir. Who am I, sir?
Oswald. My lady's father.
Lear. "My lady's father"? My lord's knave, you whoresome dog, you slave, you cur!

From William Arens, "The Great American Football Ritual." Reprinted with permission, from *Natural History* Magazine, October, 1975. Copyright © The American Museum of Natural History, 1975.

Oswald.   I am none of these, my lord; I beseech your pardon.
Lear.   Do you bandy looks with me, you rascal? [*Striking him*]
Oswald.   I'll not be strucken, my lord.
Kent.   Nor tripped neither, you base football player.

King Lear. Act I, Scene 4

The attitude toward the football player has obviously changed since Shakespeare's time. Today the once "base football player" occupies the hearts minds, and television screens of millions. He is emulated and sought after, and the stratagems he uses in the game are often followed at the highest levels of government and business.

As an anthropologist I would contend that football, although only a game, tells us much about who and what we Americans are as a people.

This belief owes its impetus to the hundreds of football games I have watched on television. Feelings of guilt led me to muse in an academic fashion about the game and turned me to books written by players, as well as to the rare anthropological accounts of sport in other societies. This research has led me to believe that if an anthropologist from another planet visited here, he would be struck by the American fixation on this game and would report on it with the glee and romantic intoxication anthropologists normally reserve for the exotic rituals of a newly discovered tribe. This assertion is based on the theory that certain significant symbols are the key to understanding a culture; football is such a symbol.

This argument requires a short detour in time to examine the evolution of the game from its European origins. Mythology states that it was first played by a group of English soldiers who celebrated their victory over a Viking settlement by using the skulls of the dead enemy in a kicking match. Sometime later, an inflated animal bladder was substituted for the skull, and the sport became known as "Dane's head."

During the early Middle Ages, the game often took the form of a disorganized, all-day competition between neighboring towns. A ball was placed midway between two villages and the object was to kick it along the countryside to the opposing village green for a score. In the twelfth century the pastime became so popular with the English peasantry that Henry II banned it because it interfered with the practice of archery. The sport was not reinstated until the seventeenth century, by which time the longbow had become an obsolete weapon.

According to sociologists David Reisman and Reuel Denny, who have charted the game's evolution, kicking a ball remained a dominant part of the game until 1823 when, as popular legend has it, one William Ellis, of Rugby School, "with a fine disregard for the rules of football, as played in his time, first took the ball in his arms and ran with it. . . ." This innovation became institutionalized at the school and shortly thereafter was adopted by others, hence the name Rugby.

In America, the honor of playing the first game of what was to emerge as football should go to Harvard and McGill, which in 1874 played a game that essentially followed Rugby regulations. In the remaining decades of the nineteenth century, the sport began to take on a more American form as a definite line of scrimmage and the center snap replaced the swaying "scrum" and "heel out" of English Rugby. This meant that possession of the ball was now given to one team at a time. The introduction of the forward pass in the early years of this century, however, signaled the most radical break with the past. These revisions on Rugby not only resulted in greater structure and order, but they also provided more variety and flexibility since running, kicking, and forward passing were incorporated as offensive maneuvers.

Football has now emerged as an item of our cultural inventory that we share with no other country except Canada, where it is of minor interest. We share our language, kinship system, religions, political and economic institutions, and a variety of other traits with many nations, but our premier spectator sport remains ours alone. This is important when we consider that other societies have taken up baseball, which is derived from cricket, and basketball, a domestic product. Like English beer, the American brand of football is unexportable, even to the colonies.

Football, in contrast to our language and many of our values, was not forced upon us. We chose to accept it. Our society, like any other complex one, is divided by race, ethnicity, income, political affiliation, and regionalism. Yet 79 percent of all the households in the country tuned in the first Super Bowl on television, implying that the event cut through many of these divisive factors. The game does not represent Middle America, as is so often claimed, but rather the whole of America. A love of football is one of the few interests we share with few outside our borders, but with almost everyone within them.

The salient features of the game reflect some striking similarities to the society that created and nourished it. More than any other sport, football combines the qualities of group coordination through a complex division of labor with highly developed specialization. Every professional and major college team today includes a player whose only function is place-kicking, while another player is used only for punting. Individuals on some teams have the sole responsibility of centering, or holding the ball for the point after a touchdown. Football is also a game where success now demands extensive reliance on sophisticated electronic technology—from telephones to computers—to relay instructions while the match is in progress. In short, football, as opposed to its ancestor, Rugby, epitomizes the spirit and form of contemporary American society.

Violence is one of our society's most obvious traits, and its expression in football, where bodily contact and territorial incursion are essential, clearly accounts for part of the game's appeal. It is hardly surprising, therefore, that books by participants are replete with symbolic references to war. Jerry Kramer, a Green Bay Packer during the 1960s and coauthor of *Instant Replay,* divides the book into the following sections: Preliminary Skirmishes, Basic Training, Mock Warfare, Armed Combat, War's End. And Frank

Leahy, a former coach at Notre Dame wrote in his memoirs that "the Stars and Stripes have never taken second place on any battlefield. With this in mind, we ask you to think back and ask yourself where our young men developed the qualities that go to make up a good fighting man. . . . These traits are something that cannot be found in textbooks nor can they be learned in the lecture room. It is on the athletic fields that our boys acquire these winning ways that are as much a part of the American life as are freedom of speech and of the press."

Mike Holovak, a former coach with the New England Patriots, waxed even more lyrical in reminiscing on his World War II military service. He refers to those years as the time he was on "the first team" in the "South Pacific playground" where the tracers arced out "like a long touchdown pass" and the artillery fired "orange blobs—just like a football."

To single out violence as the sole or even primary reason for the game's popularity is a tempting oversimplification. Boxing, for example, allows for an even greater display of legitimate blood spilling. Yet boxing's popularity has waned over the last few decades, an indication, perhaps, that reliance on naked individual force has less appeal for us than aggression acted out in a more tactical and sophisticated context. Football's violence is expressed within the framework of teamwork, specialization, mechanization, and variation, and this combination accounts for its appeal. But we cannot explain football's popularity on the basis of violence alone because we are not unique in this respect. There have been many other violent nations, but they did not enshrine football as a national symbol.

Although baseball—the national pastime—has not suffered the same fate as boxing, interest in this game has also ebbed. Like boxing, baseball is not in step with the times. Its action does not entail the degree of complexity, co-ordination, and specialization that now captures our fancy. The recent intro-duction of players who only bat or run bases, and who never field, are moves to inject specialization and heighten the game's appeal to modern America. Baseball, however, belongs to a past era when life was a bit less complicated.

While football, representing the typical American outlook, overshadows class, race, and economic differences in our society, it emphasizes the division between the sexes. The game is a male preserve that manifests and symbolizes both the physical and cultural values of masculinity. Entrance into the arena of football competition depends upon muscle power and speed, which only a very few males and probably no females possess. Women can and do excel in a variety of other sports, but football totally excludes them from participation.

In an informal game between females in a Long Island community, the husbands responded by appearing on the sidelines in women's clothes and wigs. The message was clear. If the women were going to act like men, then the men were going to transform themselves into women. These "rituals of rebellion" involving an inversion of sex roles have often been recorded by anthropologists. It is not surprising that this symbolic rebellion in our culture involved a bastion of male supremacy.

If this argument seems farfetched, consider the extent to which football gear accents the male physique. The donning of the required items results in an enlarged head and shoulders and a narrowed waist, with the lower torso poured into skintight pants accented only by a metal codpiece. The result is not an expression but an exaggeration of maleness. Dressed in this manner, players can engage in hand holding, hugging, and bottom patting that would be disapproved of in any other context, but which is accepted on the gridiron without a second thought. Admittedly, there are good reasons for wearing the gear, but that does not mean that we should dismiss the symbolic significance of the visual impression. The game could just as easily be played without the major items such as the helmet, shoulder pads, and cleats. They are as much offensive as defensive in function. Indeed, in comparison, Rugby players seem to manage quite well in the flimsiest of uniforms.

Just as the players' uniforms symbolize exaggerated masculinity, their activities symbolize an aloofness from the profane business of everyday life. This is a common aspect of ritual behavior in any part of the world. Especially relevant for the participants in rituals is the avoidance of what anthropologists refer to as "pollution"—an impure ritual state—as the result of contact with contaminating acts or situations.

In many rituals performed entirely for and by males, sexual contact with females is avoided because it is considered an expression of man's animal, or profane, nature. In some societies, prior to an important activity such as hunting or warfare, community members are admonished to refrain from sexual behavior for fear of disastrous consequences. In the world of sport, and in football in particular, abstinence before a game is therefore not too surprising. In this context I am reminded of anthropologist E. Adamson Hoebel's statement, "The Cheyenne feeling about male sexuality is that it is something to be husbanded and kept in reserve as a source of strength for the great crises of war."

This attitude is common in football training camps. At these virtually monastic facilities, all the players, including married men, are sequestered during practice days. Since there is no practice on Sunday, players are allowed to visit their wives on Saturday nights. In consideration of Monday practice, however, players must return to the all-male atmosphere on Sunday evening. The result is that sex and football, the profane and the sacred, are segregated in time and space.

During the season a variation of the procedure prevails. Since the games are played on Sundays, the players and staff spend Saturday nights together. In each instance there is a clear-cut attempt to avoid the symbolic danger of contact with females prior to the event. This segregation was impressed on me when I traveled with my university's team by chartered bus to a game to be played at the opponent's field. Since there were a few unoccupied seats, two of the players asked the coach if their girl friends could ride along. He said in all seriousness that they would not be permitted on the bus with us, but that they could join us on the way home.

A writer who spent the season with the Rice University football squad mentioned a similar instance. When the bus pulled up in front of the dormitory on the opponent's campus where the team would spend the night, a number of the girls from the college entered the vehicle and began to flirt with the players. The Rice coach, who was in an accompanying car, stormed onto the bus and ordered the girls off immediately. He then told the players that they should have known better since the incident was a dirty trick instigated by the foe.

As another example, Jerry Kramer describes the night before the first Super Bowl, when the Green Bay Packers were allowed to bring their wives along as a reward for championship play. "My wife's been here for the past few days, and so has Chandler's. Tonight we're putting the girls in one room, and Danny and I are sharing one. It's better for the girls to be away from us tonight. We're always grumpy and grouchy before a game."

There are, of course, some perfectly reasonable arguments for segregating the players before a game. The coaches argue that the team members get an undistracted night's sleep and will thus be better able to concentrate on the upcoming event.

The inhibition of sexual activity prior to an athletic event, however, has no apparent scientific rationale. The latest research argues that sex is actually beneficial since it induces a more restful night's sleep. A British physician who advised and interviewed his country's Olympic competitors mentioned that one informant admitted setting the world record in a middle distance track event an hour after sexual intercourse. Another athlete said that an hour and a half after the same activity, he ran the mile in less than four minutes. One must look beyond rationality for an explanation of the negative attitude toward sex on the part of the elders who control professional football. If we grant that the sport involves a significant ritual element, then the idea does make some sense. From this standpoint, scientific reasoning is not relevant.

Accounts of rituals in other cultures also indicate a prevalent belief in symbolic contamination through contact with illness or physical imperfection. Examples of this sort of avoidance also crop up in football. Players avoid and ridicule those who become sick to their stomachs in the summer heat of training camp.

In a similar vein participants are admonished to stay away from an injured player so that the trainer can attend to him. The players, however, do not appear to need the advice since after a momentary glance they studiously avoid a downed colleague. Injured, inactive players on the team I was associated with as faculty sponsor were not allowed to mingle with the active participants during the game. The loquacious professional Jerry Kramer also writes that when he was hurt and disabled, he felt like an "outsider," "isolated" and "separated" from the rest of the group. Others have written that they were ignored during these times by their teammates and coaches.

Eating is another profane act; as a further indication of our animal nature, it renders an individual unfit to participate in rituals. In contrast to sexuality and physical imperfection, however, nourishment cannot be avoided for any length of time. Instead, under controlled conditions, the act of eating is incorporated into the ritual, and the food becomes charged with a sacred character. Not just any type of food is acceptable. What is more appropriate in our society than males eating beef prior to the great event? Imagine the scorn that would be heaped on a team if it were known that its members prepared themselves for the competition by eating chicken.

The problem with eating any meat on the day of the competition is that meat is not converted into potential energy until hours after the game has ended. Although the players must appear for this meal because it is part of the ritual, few actually eat what is presented to them. Instead, in contradiction to the ritual leaders, the participants prefer a high-energy snack, such as a pill, that has more immediate value. Nevertheless, as in the other instances, those who control the players' behavior adhere to a less functional course by forcing their charges to confront a symbolic substance. If this situation were presented to an anthropologist in the heart of the Amazon, I wonder how long it would take to suggest ritual cannibalism on the part of the natives.

A ritual has a variety of levels, components, and consequences. The slaughter of a white bull during a *rite de passage* for males among cattle-keeping people in Africa has an obvious nutritional benefit for those who consume it. At the same time, this does not obviate the ritual significance of the act. If I am making too much of the symbolic element of American football, then perhaps we ought to reconsider the ease with which we accept this type of analysis for other, supposedly simpler cultures. Accounts of team log-racing among the Shavante Indians of Brazil as an attempt to restore harmony to a social order beset by political divisions and the analysis of cockfighting in Bali as an expression of national character have caused little stir. Unless we consider ourselves something special, our own society is equally suitable grist for the anthropological mill. It is reasonable to suppose that if other people symbolically express their basic cultural themes in rituals, then we are likely to do the same.

Discussion Questions

1. How does football reflect U.S. society?
2. The author approaches football in the United States as a subcultural ritual. Do you agree with this kind of analysis? Discuss.

JOHN STEINBECK

And the World Was Built in an Evening

Culture develops as man meets the challenges posed by his environment. The following article describes how a group of migrants developed rules and regulations to cope with a new environment. By obedience to the rules of this subculture, order rather than chaos prevailed. As such, culture served as a survival kit during a period of economic hardship and social turmoil.

The cars of the migrant people crawled out of the side roads onto the great cross-country highway, and they took the migrant way to the West. In the daylight they scuttled like bugs to the westward; and as the dark caught them, they clustered like bugs near to shelter and to water. And because they were lonely and perplexed, because they had all come from a place of sadness and worry and defeat, and because they were all going to a new mysterious place, they huddled together; they talked together; they shared their lives, their food, and the things they hoped for in the new country. Thus it might be that one family camped near a spring, and another camped for the spring and for company, and a third because two families had pioneered the place and found it good. And when the sun went down, perhaps twenty families and twenty cars were there.

In the evening a strange thing happened: the twenty families became one family, the children were the children of all. The loss of home became one loss, and the golden time in the West was one dream. And it might be that a sick child threw despair into the hearts of twenty families, of a hundred people; that a birth there in a tent kept a hundred people quiet and awestruck through the night and filled a hundred people with the birth-joy in the morning. A family which the night before had been lost and fearful might search its goods to find a present for a new baby. In the evening, sitting about the fires, the twenty were one. They grew to be units of the camps, units of the evenings and the nights. A guitar unwrapped from a blanket and tuned—and the songs, which were all of the people, were sung in the nights. Men sang the words, and women hummed the tunes.

Every night a world created, complete with furniture—friends made and enemies established; a world complete with braggarts and with cowards, with quiet men, with humble men, with kindly men. Every night relationships that make a world, established; and every morning the world torn down like a circus.

At first the families were timid in the building and tumbling worlds, but gradually the technique of building worlds became their technique. Then leaders emerged, then laws were made, then codes came into being. And as the worlds moved westward they were more complex and better furnished, for their builders were more experienced in building them.

The families learned what rights must be observed—the right of privacy in the tent; the right to keep the past black hidden in the heart; the right to talk and to listen; the right to refuse help or to accept, to offer help or to decline it; the right of son to court and daughter to be courted; the right of the hungry to be fed; the rights of the pregnant and the sick to transcend all other rights.

And the families learned, although no one told them, what rights are monstrous and must be destroyed: the right to intrude upon privacy, the right to be noisy while the camp slept, the right of seduction or rape, the right of adultery and theft and murder. These rights were crushed, because the little worlds could not exist for even a night with such rights alive.

And as the worlds moved westward, rules became laws, although no one told the families. It is unlawful to foul near the camp; it is unlawful in any way to foul the drinking water; it is unlawful to eat good rich food near one who is hungry, unless he is asked to share.

And with the laws, the punishments—and there were only two—a quick and murderous fight or ostracism; and ostracism was the worst. For if one broke the laws his name and face went with him, and he had no place in any world, no matter where created.

In the worlds, social conduct became fixed and rigid, so that a man must say "Good morning," when asked for it, so that a man might have a willing girl if he stayed with her, if he fathered her children and protected them. But a man might not have one girl one night and another the next, for this would endanger the worlds.

The families moved westward, and the technique of building the worlds improved so that the people could be safe in their worlds; and the form was so fixed that a family acting in the rules knew it was safe in the rules.

There grew up government in the worlds, with leaders, with elders. A man who was wise found that his wisdom was needed in every camp; a man who was a fool could not change his folly with his world. And a kind of insurance developed in these nights. A man with food fed a hungry man, and thus insured himself against hunger. And when a baby died a pile of silver coins grew at the door flap, for a baby must be well buried, since it has had nothing else of life. An old man may be left in a potter's field, but not a baby.

A certain physical pattern is needed for the building of a world—water, a river bank, a stream, a spring, or even a faucet unguarded. And there is needed enough flat land to pitch the tents, a little brush or wood to build the fires. If there is a garbage dump not too far off, all the better; for there can be found equipment—stove tops, a curved fender to shelter the fire, and cans to cook in and to eat from.

And the worlds were built in the evening. The people, moving in from the highways, made them with their tents and their hearts and their brains.

In the morning the tents came down, the canvas was folded, the tent poles tied along the running board, the beds put in place on the cars, the pots in their places. And as the families moved westward, the technique of building up a home in the evening and tearing it down with the morning light became fixed; so that the folded tent was packed in one place, the cooking pots counted in their box. And as the cars moved westward, each member of the family grew into his proper place, grew into his duties; so that each member, old and young, had his place in the car; so that in the weary, hot evenings, when the cars pulled into the camping places, each member had his duty and went to it without instruction: children to gather wood, to carry water; men to pitch the tents and bring down the beds; women to cook the supper and to watch while the family fed. And this was done without command. The families, which had been units of which the boundaries were a house at night, a farm by day, changed their boundaries. In the long hot light, they were silent in the cars moving slowly westward; but at night they integrated with any group they found.

Thus they changed their social life—changed as in the whole universe only man can change. They were not farm men any more, but migrant men. And the thought, the planning, the long staring silence that had gone out of the fields, went now to the roads, to the distance, to the West.

Discussion Questions

1. List at least five rules of this migrant culture. How are they similar to rules of the dominant culture?
2. How were these rules enforced?
3. In what ways did these rules (norms) establish order?
4. Do the rules of a culture (dominant or migrant) contradict man's individual freedom? Discuss.

MARYA MANNES

Dear Mummy

When we think of the conflict between the *real* and *ideal* culture we sometimes conjure up examples about someone else, somewhere else, at some other time. For example, there is a widely quoted story about the residents of a town in Kansas who drank in private while supporting the "temperance"

Reprinted from Marya Mannes, *But Will It Sell?* ("Dear Mummy," pp. 97–103) by Marya Mannes. Copyright © 1964, 1963, 1962, 1961, 1959, 1958, 1955 by Marya Mannes. Reprinted by permission of J. B. Lippincott Company.

morality. No matter how superior we might feel to this kind of contradiction, almost all of us—the "educated" as well as the "uneducated"—participate in this conflict between the real and the ideal. Marya Mannes, in the following series of fictional letters, clearly depicts this conflict.

Mrs. Howard Andrews
Our Place
Crestview, Ohio

Dear Addie,

Your father and I are very disturbed about something we just heard from the Maitlands (they came aboard yesterday for drinks). Ginny said that just before they left for Flat Key, Ann Rossiter called her from Oakdale and said that the Westover girl had given a birthday party that turned into something of a riot. She was very vague about the details, but it seems things got very rough and the house was a shambles. We are very worried because we remembered that Doug had been seeing something of the Westover girl, and we naturally hope he wasn't involved.

Please let us know what, if anything, happened.

Love,
Mummy

Mr. and Mrs. Curtis Munson
Fool's Paradise
Flat Key, Bahamas

Dearest Mummy,

It's just like Ginny Maitland to go gabbing away like that upsetting people for no reason. We are all trying to keep the affair in the family, so to speak, and Howie even saw to it that Ed Bates didn't print anything about it in the Oakdale Sentinel.

Franny Westover *did* give a birthday party for about a hundred kids, and I guess it went on a little late and the boys wanted some fun and threw a few things around. Doug doesn't seem to remember what exactly happened, he said they "twisted" and then someone thought it would be funny if they had a "book-wetting," so they took all the books in the house and threw them in the swimming pool, and then someone else (I think it was a girl) thought it would be fun to have everyone take off their ordinary clothes and dress in window curtains. Dick Westover was very unpleasant over the phone yesterday (we never liked him anyway) and accused Doug of being one of the boys who cut up the living room rug with pruning shears, but it was a hideous mustard broadloom (the house is in the *worst* taste) and I don't much blame them.

The point is, Daddy, it was a simple case of high spirits and no real harm done. Just to smooth things over, I gave Doug a check for $300 to cover some glassware and the rug business (he swears he didn't burn any curtains).

So please don't worry about it, Doug is a fine boy, really, and those were the nicest kids anyone would want to know, all from the best homes and Yale and Princeton and all that.

Love and Kisses,
Addie

Mrs. Howard Andrews
Our Place
Crestview, Ohio

Dear Addie,

Your father had one of his indigestion attacks after getting your letter, and has asked me to write you.

I need hardly say we were appalled. How is it possible for boys of decent families to destroy the property of other people who are giving them a party? And why weren't there any grownups at the party to stop them? In my days, the parents and older people were always around.

Your Distressed Mother,
Mother

P.S. If I'd been you and Howie I'd have made Doug pay for the damage out of his own pocket and taken away his college tuition for a semester. How else will these spoiled young ruffians ever learn?

Dad

Mrs. Curtis Munson
Fool's Paradise
Andros, Bahamas

Dear Mummy,

Your letter shows how out of touch you two have been with things today. No self-respecting parent would *dream* of being in the house when the kids are having a party, it inhibits them so. Howie and I just engage the band and the caterer and have our fun somewhere else. Just to be on the safe side, we *did* hire a policeman for Carol's last party to see that the "crashers" didn't get too out of hand. In case you didn't know, it's the custom for a lot of kids to drive to a party they haven't been asked to, and in a way I think it's very democratic even if they do make a sort of mess of the place. But we always get a house-cleaning crew in the next day to sweep up the broken glass, refinish the furniture, and plant new bushes. It's just part of the expense of entertaining these days.

Also I don't see how you can say Doug is spoiled. He deserved a new Thunderbird for getting into Yale (Howie never thought he'd make it), and as for his speedboat this summer, you couldn't really expect him to take his dates across the lake in an outboard.

Doug is *not* a "ruffian." Why only the other day, Mr. Ballard (he's Vice

President of Western Swivel) told Howie that Doug was a natural leader with a real feeling for money.

Love,
Addie

Mrs. Howard Andrews
Our Place
Crestview, Ohio

Dear Addie,

"Natural leaders with a real feeling for money" have been known to land in jail. Doug may too some day if you and Howie don't set him straight before it's too late.

Speaking of which, have you ever bothered to tell the kid about Right and Wrong and Responsibility? Where's his father been all this time? How can you possibly expect kids who drink hard liquor from fourteen on and crash parties and need policemen to keep them in order to turn into decent citizens?

High spirits my hat! Those boys need a flogging or a psychiatric examination. Not that I believe in that stuff, it's mostly mumbo-jumbo, but something must be wrong inside if a boy has to destroy something to feel good.

Love,
Dad

Mrs. Curtis Munson
Fool's Paradise
Eleuthera, Bahamas

Dear Mummy,

I can't write to Dad in his present condition, he just doesn't understand the realities of today.

For one thing, Doug went to Sunday School from the ages of 8 to 10, and then at prep school they had the Lord's Prayer every morning before they banned it. So he's had as good a Christian upbringing as anyone.

For another, Dad seems to forget that when Doug was fifteen he won the D.A.R. prize for the best essay on Why Our Way of Life is the Best Way. So don't talk to me about ethics.

And what does Dad mean asking where Howie's been? Howie's in town every day as he well knows, working so that we can all have a decent standard of living, and it isn't his fault that he doesn't see his son from one end of the week to the other. It's the mother's responsibility anyway, and God knows I've given Doug everything since he was a tiny baby.

What Dad refuses to realize is that it's terribly hard growing up, with the bomb and insecurity and China, and boys like Doug don't know what's going to happen to them so they have to have some outlet somewhere.

Love,
Addie

Telegram to Mrs. Howard Andrews
RE OUTLET HOW ABOUT HONEST WORK OR THE PEACE CORPS?

Dad

Mr. Curtis Munson
Fool's Paradise
St. James, Barbados

Dear Curtis,

Addie has just showed me your letter and telegram, and as she is rather emotional about all this, I thought I'd write to you directly.

My personal view is that the Communists were behind all these so-called riots you read about. I don't doubt that some Harvard red got into that Westover party and planted the whole thing so that it would reflect badly on our society.

Anyway, you have no cause to worry about Doug. He's a fine red-blooded kid with a great sense of humor and a lot of git-up-and go.

What it all comes down to is, what would you rather have: a free society or a socialist state?

Cordially,
Howie

Miss Frances Westover
Oakdale, Ohio

Dear Fran,

I'm sorry you thought I sounded mad when you phoned me the news yesterday, but you can understand why it was something of a shock, especially as I don't remember a thing that happened that night, any more than you did. Somebody shot the lights out and I couldn't see who the hell I was with.

Honest, I'm really glad it was you and we might as well have a family now as later anyway.

I'll break the news to my old bag next weekend. It'll take her mind off this price-fixing and Dad's company you've probably read about.

Anyway, relax, I'll be calling you.

Your everloving Doug

Mr. and Mrs. Curtis Munson
Fool's Paradise
Tobago, Trinidad

Dear Dad and Mom,

I know you'll be as happy as I am to know that Doug is engaged to Francis Westover and they hope to be married very soon. She's a darling girl (they're Mainland Steel), and they seem in a romantic daze about each other. So you see, the little Doug who worried you so is now about to be a responsible married man and, of course, some day, the father of a family.

I am hoping that after he finishes college (Howie naturally will see them through that), they'll settle somewhere near us so that the children can grow up in a fine healthy community with people who think alike and have the same values.

Doug will write you himself, I know. In spite of his sometimes casual manner, he is really very fond of you both, even if the generations don't always mix. Young people are more realistic, don't you think?

Lovingly,
Addie

Discussion Questions

1. Give at least four examples of the norms of both the *ideal* and the *real* culture as described by the letters.
2. In spite of the direct conflict described in these letters between the *ideal* and real culture, a showdown is avoided. How? Discuss.
3. Is your guess that "little Doug" will become a "responsible married man . . ."? Why?

3 / Personality and Socialization

Drawing by Craig Boyd

"Good Lord! Is it REALLY ME?"

Because of the wide variations of personality within our culture, and because personality is so complex and dynamic, sociologists have yet to arrive at an agreed-upon specific definition of personality. In general terms, *personality* can be defined as including all of an individual's behavioral and emotional traits—his attitudes, values, beliefs, habits, goals, fears, and so on. It includes all of a person's learned preparations to behave, such as the habits and skills necessary to survive and master his environment, his style of interacting with other persons, as well as the things he believes with regard to faith.

Social scientists have approached personality from different points of view. *Biological determinism* argues that personality is the result of inborn drives and instincts. Although the simplicity of instinct theory is a tempting explanation of human behavior, it has not stood the test of scientific research. Sociologists do recognize man as a biological or-

ganism, but consider it the source of potentialities that other factors such as group experience may channel and develop. *Cultural determinism* argues that culture determines personality. Although culture provides all members of a society with a uniform set of common experiences, sociologists consider cultural determinism as altogether too simplistic an explanation of personality. Not only does cultural determinism fail to explain the uniqueness of personality, it also fails to recognize the complexity of modern societies, which have many subcultures—racial, religious, ethnic, occupational, and so on.

Sociologists refer to the overall process by which an individual's personality is formed as *socialization*. Socialization can be defined as the process whereby one internalizes the norms of his group so that a distinct "self" emerges. Although biological, cultural, and environmental factors provide needs and potentialities, it is the unique experience of each individual as he interacts with others that shapes his personality. A new-born infant lacks a concept of self. As he grows and matures he discovers that someone relieves his tensions caused by hunger, thirst, and pain. He soon comes to associate that someone as the mother. The child also learns to differentiate between various others by name—Daddy and Mommy. As the social experiences of the child accumulate, he becomes conscious of himself as a distinct human being which allows him to assume an identity—a self image —and an individuality of his own.

Socialization does not stop when an individual becomes an adult. The nature of adulthood in a complex and changing society requires continual reorientation. Most women and men, for example, were not prepared in their childhood for the changing status of women toward the new roles of economic self-reliance and equality. Also, because of new inventions and discoveries, many large organizations have developed elaborate retraining programs and expect their employees to keep abreast of changes in their particular occupation. In fact, some theorists feel that the rapid technological and social changes and the constant demand for relearning and reorientation are placing strain on personality development.

As the following articles demonstrate, personality and socialization—despite their complexities for sociologists and sociology students—are the basic aspects of sociology.

KINGSLEY DAVIS

Final Note on a Case of Extreme Isolation

The chief agents of socialization is the family. It influences the child in his earliest stages of development and remains a continuing influence throughout his life. Failure of the family in its role as agent of the socialization of a child can retard personality development. Attempts at compensatory socialization later in life are generally ineffective.

From time to time the media report on tragic instances of neglected children whose deranged parents have isolated their children from social contacts by locking them in attics, basements, or closets. These children, usually referred to as feral children, which literally means "untamed," offer a basis for judging the process of becoming human. The following article describes the conditions that produced a retarded and unsocial Anna and Isabelle.

Early in 1940 there appeared . . . an account of a girl called Anna. She had been deprived of normal contact and had received a minimum of human care for almost the whole of her first six years of life. At that time observations were not complete and the report had a tentative character. Now, however, the girl is dead, and, with more information available, it is possible to give a fuller and more definitive description of the case from a sociological point of view.

Reprinted from Kingsley Davis, "Final Note on a Case of Extreme Isolation," *The American Journal of Sociology*, Vol. III, No. 5 (March 1947), 432–437, by permission of the author and the University of Chicago Press.

Anna's death, caused by hemorhagic jaundice, occurred on August 6, 1942. Having been born on March 1 or 6, 1932, she was approximately ten and a half years of age when she died. The previous report covered her development up to the age of almost eight years; the present one recapitulates the earlier period on the basis of new evidence and then covers the last two and a half years of her life.

Early History

The first few days and weeks of Anna's life were complicated by frequent changes of domicile. It will be recalled that she was an illegitimate child, the second such child born to her mother, and that her grandfather, a widowed farmer in whose house her mother lived, strongly disapproved of this new evidence of the mother's indiscretion. This fact led to the baby's being shifted about.

Two weeks after being born in a nurse's private home, Anna was brought to the family farm, but the grandfather's antagonism was so great that she was shortly taken to the house of one of her mother's friends. At this time a local minister became interested in her and took her to his house with an idea of possible adoption. He decided against adoption, however, when he discovered that she had vaginitis. The infant was then taken to a children's home in the nearest large city. This agency found that at the age of only three weeks she was already in a miserable condition, being "terribly galled and otherwise in very bad shape." It did not regard her as a likely subject for adoption but took her in for a while anyway, hoping to benefit her. After Anna had spent nearly eight weeks in this place, the agency notified her mother to come to get her. The mother responded by sending a man and his wife to the children's home with a view to their adopting Anna, but they made such a poor impression on the agency that permission was refused. Later the mother came herself and took the child out of the home and then gave her to this couple. It was in the home of this pair that a social worker found the girl a short time thereafter. The social worker went to the mother's home and pleaded with Anna's grandfather to allow the mother to bring the child home. In spite of threats, he refused. The child, by then more than four months old, was next taken to another children's home in a near-by town. A medical examination at this time revealed that she had impetigo, vaginitis, umbilical hernia, and a skin rash.

Anna remained in this second children's home for nearly three weeks, at the end of which time she was transferred to a private foster-home. Since, however, the grandfather would not, and the mother could not, pay for the child's care, she was finally taken back as a last resort to the grandfather's house (at the age of five and a half months). There she remained, kept on the second floor in an attic-like room because her mother hesitated to incur the grandfather's wrath by bringing her downstairs.

The mother, a sturdy woman weighing about 180 pounds, did a man's work on the farm. She engaged in heavy work such as milking cows and tending hogs and had little time for her children. Sometimes she went out at night, in which case Anna was left entirely without attention. Ordinarily, it seems, Anna received only enough care to keep her barely alive. She appears to have been seldom moved from one position to another. Her clothing and bedding were filthy. She apparently had no instruction, no friendly attention.

It is little wonder that, when finally found and removed from the room in the grandfather's house at the age of nearly six years, the child could not talk, walk, or do anything that showed intelligence. She was in an extremely emaciated and undernourished condition, with skeleton-like legs and a bloated abdomen. She had been fed on virtually nothing except cow's milk during the years under her mother's care.

Anna's condition when found, and her subsequent improvement, have been described in the previous report. It now remains to say what happened to her after that.

Later History

In 1939, nearly two years after being discovered, Anna had progressed, as previously reported, to the point where she could walk, understand simple commands, feed herself, achieve some neatness, remember people, etc. But she still did not speak, and, though she was much more like a normal infant of something over one year of age in mentality, she was far from normal for her age.

On August 30, 1939, she was taken to a private home for retarded children, leaving the county home where she had been for more than a year and a half. In her new setting she made some further progress, but not a great deal. In a report of an examination made November 6 of the same year, the head of the institution pictured the child as follows:

> Anna walks about aimlessly, makes periodic rhythmic motions of her hands, and, at intervals, makes guttural and sucking noises. She regards her hands as if she had seen them for the first time. It was impossible to hold her attention for more than a few seconds at a time—not because of distraction due to external stimuli but because of her inability to concentrate. She ignored the task in hand to gaze vacantly about the room. Speech is entirely lacking. Numerous unsuccessful attempts have been made with her in the hope of developing initial sounds. I do not believe that this failure is due to negativism or deafness but that she is not sufficiently developed to accept speech at this time. . . . The prognosis is not favorable. . . .

More than five months later, on April 25, 1940, a clinical psychologist, the late Professor Francis N. Maxfield, examined Anna and reported the following: large for her age; hearing "entirely normal"; vision apparently normal; able to climb stairs; speech in the "babbling stage" and "promise for developing intelligible speech later seems to be good." He said further that "on the Merrill-Palmer scale she made a mental score of 19 months. On the Vineland social maturity scale she made a score of 23 months."

Professor Maxfield very sensibly pointed out that prognosis is difficult in such cases of isolation. "It is very difficult to take scores on tests standardized under average conditions of environment and experience," he wrote, "and interpret them in a case where environment and experience have been so unusual." With this warning he gave it as his opinion at that time that Anna would eventually "attain an adult mental level of six or seven years."

The school for retarded children, on July 1, 1941, reported that Anna had reached 46 inches in height and weighed 60 pounds. She could bounce and catch a ball and was said to conform to group socialization, though as a follower rather than a leader. Toilet habits were firmly established. Food habits were normal, except that she still used a spoon as her sole implement. She could dress herself except for fastening her clothes. Most remarkable of all, she had finally begun to develop speech. She was characterized as being at about the two-year level in this regard. She could call attendants by name and bring in one when she was asked to. She had a few complete sentences to express her wants. The report concluded that there was nothing peculiar about her, except that she was feeble-minded—"probably congenital in type."

A final report from the school, made on June 22, 1942, and evidently the last report before the girl's death, pictured only a slight advance over that given above. It said that Anna could follow directions, string beads, identify a few colors, build with blocks, and differentiate between attractive and un-attractive pictures. She had a good sense of rhythm and loved a doll. She talked mainly in phrases but would repeat words and try to carry on a conversation. She was clean about clothing. She habitually washed her hands and brushed her teeth. She would try to help other children. She walked well and could run fairly well, though clumsily. Although easily excited, she had a pleasant disposition.

Interpretation

Such was Anna's condition just before her death. It may seem as if she had not made much progress, but one must remember the condition in which she had been found. One must recall that she had no glimmering of speech, absolutely no ability to walk, no sense of gesture, not the least capacity to feed herself even when the food was put in front of her, and no comprehension of cleanliness. She was so apathetic that it was hard to tell whether or not she could hear. And all this at the age of nearly six years. Compared with this condition, her capacities at the time of her death seem striking indeed, though they do not amount to much more than a two-and-a-half-year mental level. One conclusion therefore seems safe, namely, that her isolation prevented a considerable amount of mental development that was undoubtedly part of her capacity. Just what her original capacity was, of course, is hard to say; but her development after her period of confinement (including the ability to walk and run, to play, dress, fit into a social situation, and, above all, to speak) shows that she had at least this much capacity—capacity that never could have been realized in her original condition of isolation.

A further question is this: What would she have been like if she had received a normal upbringing from the moment of birth? A definitive answer would have been impossible in any case, but even an approximate answer is made difficult by her early death. If one assumes, as was tentatively surmised in the previous report, that it is "almost impossible for any child to learn to speak, think, and act like a normal person after a long period of early isolation," it seems likely that Anna might have had a normal or near-normal capacity, genetically speaking. On the other hand, it was pointed out that Anna represented "a marginal case, [because] she was discovered before she had reached six years of age," an age "young enough to allow for some plasticity." While admitting, then, that Anna's isolation *may* have been the major cause (and was certainly a minor cause) of her lack of rapid mental progress during the four and a half years following her rescue from neglect, it is necessary to entertain the hypothesis that she was congenitally deficient.

In connection with this hypothesis, one suggestive though by no means conclusive circumstance needs consideration, namely, the mentality of Anna's forebears. Information on this subject is easier to obtain, as one might guess, on the mother's than on the father's side. Anna's maternal grandmother, for example, is said to have been college educated and wished to have her children receive a good education, but her husband, Anna's stern grandfather, apparently a shrewd, hard-driving, calculating farmowner, was so penurious that her ambitions in this direction were thwarted. Under the circumstances her daughter (Anna's mother) managed, despite having to do hard work on the farm, to complete the eighth grade in a country school. Even so, however, the daughter was evidently not very smart. "A schoolmate of [Anna's mother] stated that she was retarded in school work; was very gullible at this age; and that her morals even at this time were discussed by other students." Two tests administered to her on March 4, 1938, when she was thirty-two years of age, showed that she was mentally deficient. On the Standard Revision of the Binet-Simon Scale her performance was equivalent to that of a child of eight years, giving her an I.Q. of 50 and indicating mental deficiency of "middle-grade moron type."

As to the identity of Anna's father, the most persistent theory holds that he was an old man about seventy-four years of age at the time of the girl's birth. If he was the one, there is no indication of mental or other biological deficiency, whatever one may think of his morals. However, someone else may actually have been the father.

To sum up: Anna's heredity is the kind that *might* have given rise to innate mental deficiency, though not necessarily.

Comparison with Another Case

Perhaps more to the point than speculations about Anna's ancestry would be a case of comparison. If a child could be discovered who had been isolated about the same length of time as Anna but had achieved a much quicker recovery and a greater mental development, it would be a stronger indication that Anna was deficient to start with.

Such a case does exist. It is the case of a girl found at about the same time as Anna and under strikingly similar circumstances. A full description of the details of this case has not been published, but, in addition to newspaper reports, an excellent preliminary account by a speech specialist, Dr. Marie K. Mason, who played an important role in the handling of the child, has appeared. Also the late Dr. Francis N. Maxfield, clinical psychologist at Ohio State University, as was Dr. Mason, has written an as yet unpublished but penetrating analysis of the case. Some of his observations have been included in Professor Zingg's book on feral man. The following discussion is drawn mainly from these enlightening materials. The writer, through the kindness of Professors Mason and Maxfield, did have a chance to observe the girl in April, 1940, and to discuss the features of her case with them.

Born apparently one month later than Anna, the girl in question, who has been given the pseudonym Isabelle, was discovered in November, 1938, nine months after the discovery of Anna. At the time she was found she was approximately six and a half years of age. Like Anna, she was an illegitimate child and had been kept in seclusion for that reason. Her mother was a deaf-mute, having become so at the age of two, and it appears that she and Isabelle had spent most of their time together in a dark room shut off from the rest of the mother's family. As a result Isabelle had no chance to develop speech; when she communicated with her mother, it was by means of gestures. Lack of sunshine and inadequacy of diet had caused Isabelle to become rachitic. Her legs in particular were affected; they "were so bowed that as she stood erect the soles of her shoes came nearly flat together, and she got about with a skittering gait." Her behavior toward strangers, especially men, was almost that of a wild animal, manifesting much fear and hostility. In lieu of speech she made only a strange croaking sound. In many ways she acted like an infant. "She was apparently utterly unaware of relationships of any kind. When presented with a ball for the first time, she held it in the palm of her hand, then reached out and stroked my face with it. Such behavior is comparable to that of a child of six months." At first it was even hard to tell whether or not she could hear, so unused were her senses. Many of her actions resembled those of deaf children.

It is small wonder that, once it was established that she could hear, specialists working with her believed her to be feeble-minded. Even on nonverbal tests her performance was so low as to promise little for the future. Her first score on the Stanford-Binet was 19 months, practically at the zero point of the scale. On the Vineland social maturity scale her first score was 39, representing an age level of two and a half years. "The general impression was that she was wholly uneducable and that any attempt to teach her to speak, after so long a period of silence, would meet with failure."

In spite of this interpretation, the individuals in charge of Isabelle launched a systematic and skillful program of training. It seemed hopeless at first. The approach had to be through pantomime and dramatization, suitable to an infant. It required one week of intensive effort before she even made her first attempt at vocalization. Gradually she began to respond, however, and, after the first hurdles had at last been overcome, a curious thing happened. She went through the usual stages of learning characteristic of the years from one to six not only in proper succession but far more rapidly than normal. In a little over two months after her first vocalization she was putting sentences together. Nine months after that she could identify words and sentences on the printed page, could write well, could add to ten, and could retell a story after hearing it. Seven months beyond this point she had a vocabulary of 1,500–2,000 words and was asking complicated questions. Starting from an educational level of between one and three years (depending on what aspect one considers), she had reached a normal level by the time she was eight and a half years old. In short, she covered in two years the stages of learning that ordinarily require six. Or, to put it another way, her I.Q. trebled in a year and a half. The speed with which she reached the normal level of mental development seems analogous to the recovery of body weight in a growing child after an illness, the recovery being achieved by an extra fast rate of growth for a period after the illness until normal weight for the given age is again attained.

When the writer saw Isabelle a year and a half after her discovery, she gave him the impression of being a very bright, cheerful, energetic little girl. She spoke well, walked and ran without trouble, and sang with gusto and accuracy. Today she is over fourteen years old and has passed the sixth grade in public school. Her teachers say that she participates in all school activities as normally as other children. Though older than her classmates, she has fortunately not physically matured too far beyond their level.

Clearly the history of Isabelle's development is different from that of Anna's. In both cases there was an exceedingly low, or rather blank, intellectual level to begin with. In both cases it seemed that the girl might be congenitally feeble-minded. In both a considerably higher level was reached later on. But the Ohio girl achieved a normal mentality within two years, whereas Anna was still markedly inadequate at the end of four and a half years. This difference in achievement may suggest that Anna had less initial capacity. But an alternative hypothesis is possible.

One should remember that Anna never received the prolonged and expert attention that Isabelle received. The result of such attention, in the case of the Ohio girl, was to give her speech at an early stage, and her subsequent rapid development seems to have been a consequence of that. "Until Isabelle's speech and language development, she had all the characteristics of a feeble-minded child." Had Anna, who, from the standpoint of psychometric tests and early history, closely resembled this girl at the start, been given a mastery of speech at an earlier point by intensive training, her subsequent development might have been much more rapid.

The hypothesis that Anna began with a sharply inferior mental capacity is therefore not established. Even if she were deficient to start with, we have no way of knowing how much so. Under ordinary conditions she might have been a dull normal or, like her mother, a moron. Even after the blight of her isolation, if she had lived to maturity, she might have finally reached virtually the full level of her capacity, whatever it may have been. That her isolation did have a profound effect upon her mentality, there can be no doubt. This is proved by the substantial degree of change during the four and a half years following her rescue.

Consideration of Isabelle's case serves to show, as Anna's case does not clearly show, that isolation up to the age of six, with failure to acquire any form of speech and hence failure to grasp nearly the whole world of cultural meaning, does not preclude the subsequent acquisition of these. Indeed, there seems to be a process of accelerated recovery in which the child goes through the mental stages at a more rapid rate than would be the case in normal development. Just what would be the maximum age at which a person could remain isolated and still retain the capacity for full cultural acquisition is hard to say. Almost certainly it would not be as high as age fifteen; it might possibly be as low as age ten. Undoubtedly various individuals would differ considerably as to the exact age.

Anna's is not an ideal case for showing the effects of extreme isolation, partly because she was possibly deficient to begin with, partly because she did not receive the best training available, and partly because she did not live long enough. Nevertheless, her case is instructive when placed in the record with numerous other cases of extreme isolation. This and the previous article about her are meant to place her in the record. It is to be hoped that other cases will be described in the scientific literature as they are discovered (as unfortunately they will be), for only in these rare cases of extreme isolation is it possible "to observe *concretely separated* two factors in the development of human personality which are always otherwise only analytically separated, the biogenic and the sociogenic factors."

Discussion Questions

1. Briefly review what is similar and what is different about Anna's and Isabelle's infancy and early childhood socialization.

2. Why is Anna's case less conclusive than Isabelle's in demonstrating the negative effects of socialization patterns that are harmful to personality?

3. Discuss what goes into a child's learning to speak, walk, gesture, feed herself, practice cleanliness, and pay attention. How were Anna and Isabelle deprived in each of these areas of "learning"?

4. Why is it very difficult to develop a large body of scientific research on infants and young children who are deprived of "normal" childhood socialization?

HARRY L. GRACEY

Learning the Student Role: Kindergarten as Academic Boot Camp

As the previous article clearly demonstrates, the orderly maintenance of society requires that infants learn the cultural content of the society to become what is considered a "civilized" person. This civilizing and transforming process—a process sociologists call socialization—of infants, untamed creatures that yell and scream with abandon and urinate and defecate at will, depends upon social contacts with other socialized human beings. These contacts occur basically within the family, peer group, church, job, and school.

The tremendous importance of schools as primary agents of socialization is described by Harold Gracey in the following article. His description of the kindergarten at Wright School illustrates the content of the student role as well as the processes by which the children learn their roles through unquestioning obedience to class routines and the teacher's orders. As you read the article, pay special attention to the physical and social environment of the classroom and the way that such an environment prepares the children to cope with the large bureaucratic organizations they will face as adults.

Introduction

Education must be considered one of the major institutions of social life today. Along with the family and organized religion, however, it is a "secondary institution," one in which people are prepared for life in society as it is presently organized. The main dimensions of modern life, that is, the nature of society as a whole, is determined principally by the "primary institutions," which today are the economy, the political system, and the military establishment. Education has been defined by sociologists, classical and contemporary, as an institution which serves society by socializing people into it through a formalized, standardized procedure. At the beginning of this century Emile Durkheim told student teachers at the University of Paris that education "consists of a methodical socialization of the younger generation." He went on to add:

It is the influence exercised by adult generations on those that are not ready for social life. Its object is to arouse and to develop in the child a certain number of physical, intellectual, and moral states that are demanded of him by the political society as a whole and by the special milieu for which he is specifically des-

Reprinted from Readings in Introductory Sociology, 3rd ed., Dennis H. Wrong and Harry L. Gracey. Copyright © 1977, Macmillan Publishing Co., Inc.

tined. . . . To the egotistic and asocial being that has just been born, (society) must, as rapidly as possible, add another, capable of leading a moral and social life. Such is the work of education.

The educational process, Durkheim said, "is above all the means by which society perpetually recreates the conditions of its very existence." The contemporary educational sociologist, Wilbur Brookover, offers a similar formulation in his recent textbook definition of education:

> Actually, therefore, in the broadest sense education is synonymous with socialization. It includes any social behavior that assists in the induction of the child into membership in the society or any behavior by which the society perpetuates itself through the next generation.

The educational institution is, then, one of the ways in which society is perpetuated through the systematic socialization of the young, while the nature of the society which is being perpetuated—its organization and operation, its values, beliefs and ways of living—are determined by the primary institutions. The educational system, like other secondary institutions, *serves* the society which is *created* by the operation of the economy, the political system, and the military establishment.

Schools, the social organizations of the educational institution, are today for the most part large bureaucracies run by specially trained and certified people. There are few places left in modern societies where formal teaching and learning is carried on in small, isolated groups, like the rural, one-room schoolhouses of the last century. Schools are large, formal organizations which tend to be parts of larger organizations, local community School Districts. These School Districts are bureaucratically organized and their operations are supervised by state and local governments. In this context, as Brookover says:

> the term education is used . . . to refer to a system of schools, in which specifically designated persons are expected to teach children and youth certain types of acceptable behavior. The school system becomes a . . . unit in the total social structure and is recognized by the members of the society as a separate social institution. Within this structure a portion of the total socialization process occurs.

Education is the part of the socialization process which takes place in the schools; and these are, more and more today, bureaucracies within bureaucracies.

Kindergarten is generally conceived by educators as a year of preparation for school. It is thought of as a year in which small children, five or six years old, are prepared socially and emotionally for the academic learning which will take place over the next twelve years. It is expected that a foundation of behavior and attitudes will be laid in kindergarten on which the children can acquire the skills and knowledge they will be taught in the grades. A booklet prepared for parents by the staff of a suburban New York school system says that the kindergarten experience will stimulate the child's desire to learn and cultivate the skills he will need for learning in the rest of his school career. It claims that the child will find opportunities for physical growth, for satisfying his "need for self-expression," acquire some knowledge, and provide opportunities for creative activity. It concludes, "The most important benefit that your five-year-old will receive from kindergarten is the opportunity to live and grow happily and purposefully with others in a small society." The kindergarten teachers in one of the elementary schools in this community, one we shall call the Wilbur Wright School, said their goals were to see that the children "grew" in all ways: physically, of course, emotionally, socially, and academically. They said they wanted children to like school as a result of their kindergarten experiences and that they wanted them to learn to get along with others.

None of these goals, however, is unique to kindergarten; each of them is held to some extent by teachers in the other six grades at the Wright School. And growth would occur, but differently, even if the child did not attend school. The children already know how to get along with others, in their families and their play groups. The unique job of the kindergarten in the educational division of labor seems rather to be teaching children the student role. The student role is the repertoire of behavior and attitudes regarded by educators as appropriate to children in school. Observation in the kindergartens of the Wilbur Wright School revealed a great variety of activities through which children are shown and then drilled in the behavior and attitudes defined as appropriate for school and thereby induced to learn the role of student. Observations of the kindergartens and interviews with the teachers both pointed to the teaching and learning of classroom routines as the main element of the student role. The teachers expended most of their efforts, for the first half of the year at least, in training the children to follow the routines which teachers created. The children were, in a very real sense, *drilled* in tasks and activities created by the teachers for their own purposes and beginning and ending quite arbitrarily (from the child's point of view) at the command of the teacher. One teacher remarked that she hated September, because during the first month "everything has to be done rigidly, and repeatedly, until they know exactly what they're supposed to do." However, "by January," she said, "they know exactly what to do [during the day] and I don't have to be after them all the time." Classroom routines were introduced gradually from the beginning of the year in all the kindergartens, and the children were drilled in them as long as was necessary to achieve regular compliance. By the end of the school year, the successful kindergarten teacher has a well-organized group of children. They follow classroom routines automatically, having learned all the command signals and the expected responses to them. They have, in our terms, learned the student role. The following observation shows one such classroom operating at optimum organization on an afternoon late in May. It is the class of an experienced and respected kindergarten teacher.

An Afternoon in Kindergarten

At about 12:20 in the afternoon on a day in the last week of May, Edith Kerr leaves the teachers' room where she has been having lunch and walks to her classroom at the far end of the primary wing of Wright School. A group of five- and six-year-olds peers at her through the glass doors leading from the hall cloakroom to the play area outside. Entering her room, she straightens some material in the "book corner" of the room, arranges music on the piano, takes colored paper from her closet and places it on one of the selves under the window. Her room is divided into a number of activity areas through the arrangement of furniture and play equipment. Two easels and a paint table near the door create a kind of passageway inside the room. A wedge-shaped area just inside the front door is made into a teacher's area by the placing of "her" things there: her desk, file, and piano. To the left is the book corner, marked off from the rest of the room by a puppet stage and a movable chalkboard. In it are a display rack of picture books, a record player, and a stack of children's records. To the right of the entrance are the sink and clean-up area. Four large round tables with six chairs at each for the children are placed near the walls about halfway down the length of the room, two on each side, leaving a large open area in the center for group games, block building, and toy truck driving. Windows stretch down the length of both walls, starting about three feet from the floor and extending almost to the high ceilings. Under the windows are long shelves on which are kept all the toys, games, blocks, paper, paints and other equipment of the kindergarten. The left rear corner of the room is a play store with shelves, merchandise, and cash register; the right rear corner is a play kitchen with stove, sink, ironing board, and bassinette with baby dolls in it. This area is partly shielded from the rest of the room by a large standing display rack for posters and children's art work. A sandbox is found against the back wall between these two areas. The room is light, brightly colored and filled with things adults feel five- and six-year-olds will find interesting and pleasing.

At 12:25 Edith opens the outside door and admits the waiting children. They hang their sweaters on hooks outside the door and then go to the center of the room and arrange themselves in a semi-circle on the floor, facing the teacher's chair which she has placed in the center of the floor. Edith follows them in and sits in her chair checking attendance while waiting for the bell to ring. When she has finished attendance, which she takes by sight, she asks the children what the date is, what day and month it is, how many children are enrolled in the class, how many are present, and how many are absent.

The bell rings at 12:30 and the teacher puts away her attendance book. She introduces a visitor, who is sitting against the right wall taking notes, as someone who wants to learn about schools and children. She then goes to the back of the room and takes down a large chart labeled "Helping Hands." Bringing it to the center of the room, she tells the children it is time to change jobs. Each child is assigned some task on the chart by placing his name, lettered on a paper "hand," next to a picture signifying the task—e.g., a broom, a blackboard, a milk bottle, a flag, and a Bible. She asks the children who wants each of the jobs and rearranges their "hands" accordingly. Returning to her chair, Edith announces, "One person should tell us what happened to Mark." A girl raises her hand, and when called on says, "Mark fell and hit his head and had to go to the hospital." The teacher adds that Mark's mother had written saying he was in the hospital.

During this time the children have been interacting among themselves, in their semi-circle. Children have whispered to their neighbors, poked one another, made general comments to the group, waved to friends on the other side of the circle. None of this has been disruptive, and the teacher has ignored it for the most part. The children seem to know just how much of each kind of interaction is permitted—they may greet in a soft voice someone who sits next to them, for example, but may not shout greetings to a friend who sits across the circle, so they confine themselves to waving and remain well within understood limits.

At 12:35 two children arrive. Edith asks them why they are late and then sends them to join the circle on the floor. The other children vie with each other to tell the newcomers what happened to Mark. When this leads to a general disorder Edith asks, "Who has serious time?" The children become quiet and a girl raises her hand. Edith nods and the child gets a Bible and hands it to Edith. She reads the Twenty-third Psalm while the children sit quietly. Edith helps the child in charge begin reciting the Lord's Prayer, the other children follow along for the first unit of sounds, and then trail off as Edith finishes for them. Everyone stands and faces the American flag hung to the right of the door. Edith leads the pledge to the flag, with the children again following the familiar sounds as far as they remember them. Edith then asks the girl in charge what song she wants and the child replies, "My Country." Edith goes to the piano and plays "America," singing as the children follow her words.

Edith returns to her chair in the center of the room and the children sit again in the semi-circle on the floor. It is 12:40 when she tells the children, "Let's have boys' sharing time first." She calls the name of the first boy sitting on the end of the circle, and he comes up to her with a toy helicopter. He turns and holds it up for the other children to see. He says, "It's a helicopter." Edith asks, "What is it used for?" and he replies, "For the army. Carry men. For the war." Other children join in, "For shooting submarines." "To bring back men from space when they are in the ocean." Edith sends the boy back to the circle and asks the next boy if he has something. He replies "No" and she passes on to the next. He says "Yes" and brings a bird's nest to her. He holds it for the class to see, and the teacher asks, "What kind of bird made the nest?" The boy replies, "My friend says a rain bird made it." Edith asks what the nest is made of and different children reply, "mud," "leaves" and "sticks." There is also a bit of moss woven into the nest and Edith tries to describe it to the children. They, however, are more interested in seeing if anything is inside it, and Edith lets the boy carry it around the semi-circle showing the children its insides. Edith tells the children of some baby robins in a nest in her yard, and some of the children tell about baby birds they have seen. Some children are asking about a small object in the nest which they say looks like an egg, but all have seen the nest now and Edith calls on the next boy. A number of children say, "I know what Michael has, but I'm not telling." Michael brings a book to the teacher and then goes back to his place in the circle of children. Edith reads the last page of the book to the class. Some children tell of books which they have at home. Edith calls the next boy, and three children call out, "I know what David has." "He always has the same thing." "It's a bang-bang." David goes to his table and gets a box which he brings to Edith. He opens it and shows the teacher a scale-model of an old-fashioned dueling pistol. When David does not turn around to the class, Edith tells him, "Show it to the children," and he does. One child says, "Mr. Johnson [the principal] said no guns." Edith replies, "Yes, how many of you know that?" Most of the children in the circle raise their hands. She continues. Some children tell of books which they have at home. Edith calls the next boy, on the circle and he brings two large toy soldiers to her which the children enthusiastically identify as being from "Babes in Toyland." The next boy brings an American flag to Edith and shows it to the class. She asks him what the stars and stripes stand for and admonishes him to treat it carefully. "Why should you treat it carefully?" she asks the boy. "Because it's our flag," he replies. She congratulates him, saying, "That's right."

"Show and Tell" lasted twenty minutes and during the last ten one girl in particular announced that she knew what each child called upon had to show. Edith asked her to be quiet each time she spoke out, but she was not content, continuing to offer her comment at each "show." Four children from other classes had come into the room to bring something from another teacher or to ask for something from Edith. Those with requests were asked to return later if the item wasn't readily available.

Edith now asks if any of the children told their mothers about their trip to the local zoo the previous day. Many children raise their hands. As Edith calls on them, they tell what they liked in the zoo. Some children cannot wait to be called on, and they call out things to the teacher, who asks them to be quiet. After a few of the animals are mentioned, one child says, "I liked the spooky house," and the others chime in to agree with him, some pantomiming fear and horror. Edith is puzzled, and asks what this was. When half the children try to tell her at once, she raises her hand for quiet, then calls on individual children. One says, "The house with nobody in it"; another "The dark little house." Edith asks where it was in the zoo, but the children cannot describe its location in any way which she can understand. Edith makes some jokes but they involve adult abstractions which the children cannot grasp. The children have become quite noisy now, speaking out to make both relevant and irrelevant comments, and three little girls have become particularly assertive.

Edith gets up from her seat at 1:10 and goes to the book corner, where she puts a record on the player. As it begins a story about the trip to the zoo, she returns to the circle and asks the children to go sit at the tables. She divides them among the tables in such a way as to indicate that they don't have regular seats. When the children are all seated at the four tables, five or six to a table, the teacher asks, "Who wants to be the first one?" One of the noisy girls comes to the center of the room. The voice on the record is giving directions for imitating an ostrich and the girl follows them, walking around the center of the room holding her ankles with her hands. Edith replays the record, and all the children, table by table, imitate ostriches down the center of the room and back. Edith removes her shoes and shows that she can be an ostrich too. This is apparently a familiar game, for a number of children are calling out, "Can we have the crab?" Edith asks one of the children to do a crab "so we can all remember how," and then plays the part of the record with music for imitating crabs by. The children from the left table line up across the room, hands and feet on the floor and faces pointing toward the ceiling. After they have "walked" down the room and back in this posture they sit at their table and the children of the next table play "crab." The children love this; they run from their tables, dance about on the floor waiting for their turns and are generally exuberant. Children ask for the "inch worm" and the game is played again with the children squirming down the floor. As a conclusion Edith shows them a new animal imitation, the "lame dog." The children all hobble down the floor on three "legs," table by table, to the accompaniment of the record.

At 1:30 Edith has the children line up in the center of the room; she says, "Table one, line up in front of me," and children ask, "What are we going to do?" Then she moves a few steps to the side and says, "Table two over here, line up next to table one," and more children ask, "What for?" She does this for table three and table four and each time the children ask, "Why, what are we going to do?" When the children are lined up in four lines of five each, spaced so that they are not touching one another, Edith puts on a new record and leads the class in calisthenics, to the accompaniment of the record. The children just jump around every which way in their places instead of doing the exercises, and by the time the record is finished, Edith, the only one following it, seems exhausted. She is apparently adopting the President's new "Physical Fitness" program in her classroom.

At 1:35 Edith pulls her chair to the easels and calls the children to sit on the floor in front of her, table by table. When they are all seated she asks, "What are you going to do for work-time today?" Different children raise their hands and tell Edith what they are going to draw. Most are going to make pictures of animals they saw in the zoo. Edith asks if they want to make pictures to send to Mark in the hospital, and the children agree to this. Edith gives drawing paper to the children, calling them to her one by one. After getting a piece of paper, the children go to the crayon box on the right-hand shelves, select a number of colors, and go to the tables, where they begin drawing. Edith is again trying to quiet the perpetually talking girls. She keeps two of them standing by her so they won't disrupt the others. She asks them, "Why do you feel you have to talk all the time," and then scolds them for not listening to her. Then she sends them to their tables to draw.

Most of the children are drawing at their tables, sitting or kneeling in their chairs. They are all working very industriously and, engrossed in their work, very quietly. Three girls have chosen to paint at the easels, and having donned their smocks, they are busily mixing colors and intently applying them to their pictures. If the children at the tables are primitives and neo-realists in their animal depictions, these girls at the easels are the class abstract-expressionists, with their broad-stroked, colorful paintings.

Edith asks of the children generally, "What color should I make the cover of Mark's book?" Brown and green are suggested by some children "because Mark likes them." The other children are puzzled as to just what is going on and ask, "What book?" or "What does she mean?" Edith explains what she thought was clear to them already, that they are all going to put their pictures together in a "book" to be sent to Mark. She goes to a small table in the play-kitchen corner and tells the children to bring her their pictures when they are finished and she will write their message for Mark on them.

By 1:50 most children have finished their pictures and given them to Edith. She talks with some of them as she ties the bundle of pictures together—answering questions, listening, carrying on conversations. The children are playing in various parts of the room with toys, games and blocks which they have taken off the shelves. They also move from table to table examining each other's pictures, offering compliments and suggestions. Three girls at a table are cutting up colored paper for a collage. Another girl is walking about the room in a pair of high heels with a woman's purse over her arm. Three boys are playing in the center of the room with the large block set, with which they are building walk-ways and walking on them. Edith is very much concerned about their safety and comes over a number of times to fuss over them. Two or three other boys are pushing trucks around the center of the room, and mild altercations occur when they drive through the block constructions. Some boys and girl are playing at the toy store, two girls are serving "tea" in the play kitchen and one is washing a doll baby. Two boys have elected to clean the room, and with large sponges they wash the movable blackboard, the puppet stage, and then begin on the tables. They run into resistance from the children who are working with construction toys on the tables and do not want to dismantle their structures. The class is like a room full of bees, each intent on pursuing some activity, occasionally bumping into one another, but just veering off in another direction without serious altercation. At 2:05 the custodian arrives pushing a cart loaded with half-pint milk containers. He places a tray of cartons on the counter next to the sink, then leaves. His coming and going is unnoticed in the room (as, incidentally, is the presence of the observer, who is completely ignored by the children for the entire afternoon).

At 2:15 Edith walks to the entrance of the room, switches off the lights, and sits at the piano and plays. The children begin spontaneously singing the song, which is "Clean up, clean up. Everybody clean up." Edith walks around the room supervising the clean-up. Some children put their toys, the blocks, puzzles, games, and so on back on their shelves under the windows. The children making a collage keep right on working. A child from another class comes in to borrow the 45-rpm adaptor for the record player. At more urging from Edith the rest of the children shelve their toys and work. The children are sitting around their tables now and Edith asks, "What record would you like to hear while you have your milk?" There is some confusion and no general consensus, so Edith drops the subject and begins to call the children, table by table, to come get their milk. "Table one," she says, and the five children come to the sink, wash their hands and dry them, pick up a carton of milk and a straw, and take it back to their table. Two talking girls wander about the room interfering with the children getting their milk and Edith calls out to them to "settle down." As the children sit many of them call out to Edith the name of the record they want to hear. When all the children are seated at tables with milk, Edith plays one of the records called "Bozo and the Birds" and shows the children pictures in a book which go with the record. The record recites, and the book shows the adventures of a clown, Bozo, as he walks through a woods meeting many different kinds of birds, who, of course, display the characteristics of many kinds of people or, more accurately, different stereotypes. As children finish their milk they take blankets or pads from the shelves under the windows and lie on them in the center of the room, where Edith sits on her chair showing the pictures. By 2:30 half the class is lying on the floor on their blankets, the record is still playing and the teacher is turning the pages of the book. The child who came in previously returns the 45-rpm adaptor, and one of the kindergarteners tells Edith what the boy's name is and where he lives.

The record ends at 2:40. Edith says, "Children, down on your blankets." All the class is lying on blankets now, Edith refuses to answer the various questions individual children put to her because, she tells them, "it's rest time now." Instead she talks very softly about what they will do tomorrow. They are going to work with clay, she says. The children lie quietly and listen. One of the boys raises his hand and when called on tells Edith, "The animals in the zoo looked so hungry yesterday." Edith asks the children what they think about this and a number try to volunteer opinions, but Edith accepts only those offered in a "rest-time tone," that is, softly and quietly. After a brief discussion of animal feeding, Edith calls the names of the two children on milk detail and has them collect empty milk cartons from the tables and return them to the tray. She asks the two children on clean-up detail to clean up the room. Then she gets up from her chair and goes to the door to turn on the lights. At this signal the children all get up from the floor and return their blankets and pads to the shelf. It is raining (the reason for no outside play this afternoon) and cars driven by mothers clog the school drive and line up along the street. One of the talkative little girls comes over to Edith and pointing out the window says, "Mrs. Kerr, see my mother in the new Cadillac?"

At 2:50 Edith sits at the piano and plays. The children sit on the floor in the center of the room and sing. They have a repertoire of songs about animals, including one in which each child sings a refrain alone. They know these by heart and sing along through the ringing of the 2:55 bell. When the song is finished, Edith gets up and coming to the group says, "Okay, rhyming words to get your coats today." The children raise their hands and as Edith calls on them, they tell her two rhyming words, after which they are allowed to go into the hall to get their coats and sweaters. They return to the room with these and sit at their tables. At 2:59 Edith says, "When you have your coats on, you may line up at the door." Half of the children go to the door and stand in a long line. When the three o'clock bell rings, Edith returns to the piano and plays. The children sing a song called "Goodbye," after which Edith sends them out.

Training for Learning and for Life

The day in kindergarten at Wright School illustrates both the content of the student role as it has been learned by these children and the processes by which the teacher has brought about this learning, or, "taught" them the student role. The children have learned to go through routines and to follow orders with unquestioning obedience, even when these make no sense to them. They have been disciplined to do as they are told by an authoritative person without significant protest. Edith has developed this discipline in the children by creating and enforcing a rigid social structure in the classroom through which she effectively controls the behavior of most of the children for most of the school day. The "living with others in a small society" which the school pamphlet tells parents is the most important thing the children will learn in kindergarten can be seen now in its operational meaning, which is learning to live by the routines imposed by the school. This learning appears to be the principal content of the student role.

Children who submit to school-imposed discipline and come to identify with it, so that being a "good student" comes to be an important part of their developing identities, *become* the good students by the school's definitions. Those who submit to the routines of the school but do not come to identify with them will be adequate students who find the more important part of their identities elsewhere, such as in the play group outside school. Children who refuse to submit to the school routines are rebels, who become known as "bad students" and often "problem children" in the school, for they do not learn the academic curriculum and their behavior is often disruptive in the class-room. Today schools engage clinical psychologists in part to help teachers deal with such children.

In looking at Edith's kindergarten at Wright School, it is interesting to ask how the children learn this role of student—come to accept school-imposed routines—and what, exactly, it involves in terms of behavior and attitudes. The most prominent features of the classroom are its physical and social structures. The room is carefully furnished and arranged in ways adults feel will interest children. The play store and play kitchen in the back of the room, for example, imply that children are interested in mimicking these activities of the adult world. The only space left for the children to create something of their own is the empty center of the room, and the materials at their disposal are the blocks, whose use causes anxiety on the part of the teacher. The room, being carefully organized physically by the adults, leaves little room for the creation of physical organization on the part of the children.

The social structure created by Edith is a far more powerful and subtle force for fitting the children to the student role. This structure is established by the very rigid and tightly controlled set of rituals and routines through which the children are put during the day. There is first the rigid "locating procedure" in which the children are asked to find themselves in terms of the month, date, day of the week, and the number of the class who are present and absent. This puts them solidly in the real world as defined by adults. The day is then divided into six periods whose activities are for the most part determined by the teacher. In Edith's kindergarten the children went through Serious Time, which opens the school day, Sharing Time, Play Time (which in clear weather would be spent outside), Work Time, Clean-up Time, after which they have their milk, and Rest Time, after which they go home. The teacher has programmed activities for each of these Times.

Occasionally the class is allowed limited discretion to choose between proffered activities, such as stories or records, but original ideas for activities are never solicited from them. Opportunity for free individual action is open only once in the day, during the part of Work Time left after the general class assignment has been completed (on the day reported the class assignment was drawing animal pictures for the absent Mark). Spontaneous interests or observations from the children are never developed by the teacher. It seems that her schedule just does not allow room for developing such unplanned events. During Sharing Time, for example, the child who brought a bird's nest told Edith, in reply to her question of what kind of bird made it, "My friend says it's a rain bird." Edith does not think to ask about this bird, probably because the answer is "childish," that is, not given in accepted adult categories of birds. The children then express great interest in an object in the nest, but the teacher ignores this interest, probably because the object is uninteresting to her. The soldiers from "Babes in Toyland" strike a responsive note in the children, but this is not used for a discussion of any kind. The soldiers are treated in the same way as objects which bring little interest from the children. Finally, at the end of Sharing Time the child-world of perception literally erupts in the class with the recollection of "the spooky house" at the zoo. Apparently this made more of an impression on the children than did any of the animals, but Edith is unable to make any sense of it for herself. The tightly imposed order of the class begins to break down as the children discover a universe of discourse of their own and begin talking excitedly with one another. The teacher is effectively excluded from this child's world of perception and for a moment she fails to dominate the classroom situation. She reasserts control, however, by taking the children to the next activity she has planned for the day. It seems never to have occurred to Edith that there might be a meaningful learning experience for the children in re-creating the "spooky house" in the classroom. It seems fair to say that this would have offered an exercise in spontaneous self-expression and an opportunity for real creativity on the part of the children. Instead, they are taken through a canned animal imitation procedure, an activity which they apparently enjoy, but which is also imposed upon them rather than created by them.

While children's perceptions of the world and opportunities for genuine spontaneity and creativity are being systematically eliminated from the kindergarten, unquestioned obedience to authority and rote learning of meaningless material are being encouraged. When the children are called to line up in the center of the room they ask "Why?" and "What for?" as they are in the very process of complying. They have learned to go smoothly through a programmed day, regardless of whether parts of the program make any sense to them or not. Here the student role involves what might be called "doing what you're told and never mind why." Activities which might "make sense" to the children are effectively ruled out and they are forced or induced to participate in activities which may be "senseless," such as the calisthenics.

At the same time the children are being taught by rote meaningless sounds in the ritual oaths and songs, such as the Lord's Prayer, the Pledge to the Flag, and "America." As they go through the grades children learn more and more of the sounds of these ritual oaths, but the fact that they have often learned meaningless sounds rather than meaningful statements is shown when they are asked to write these out in the sixth grade; they write them as groups of sounds rather than as a series of words, according to the sixth grade teachers at Wright School. Probably much learning in the elementary grades is of this character, that is, having no intrinsic meaning to the children, but rather being tasks inexplicably required of them by authoritative adults. Listening to sixth grade children read social studies reports, for example, in which they have copied material from encyclopedias about a particular country, an observer often gets the feeling that he is watching an activity which has no intrinsic meaning for the child. The child who reads, "Switzerland grows wheat and cows and grass and makes a lot of cheese" knows the dictionary meaning of each of these words but may very well have no conception at all of this "thing" called Switzerland. He is simpling carrying out a task assigned by the teacher *because* it is assigned, and this may be its only "meaning" for him.

Another type of learning which takes place in kindergarten is seen in children who take advantage of the "holes" in the adult social structure to create activities of their own, during Work Time or out-of-doors during Play Time. Here the children are learning to carve out a small world of their own within the world created by adults. They very quickly learn that if they keep within permissible limits of noise and action they can play much as they please. Small groups of children formed during the year in Edith's kindergarten who played together at these times, developing semi-independent little groups in which they created their own worlds in the interstices of the adult-imposed physical and social world. These groups remind the sociological observer very much of the so-called "informal groups" which adults develop in factories and offices of large bureaucracies. Here too, within authoritatively imposed social organizations people find "holes" to create little subworlds which support informal, friendly, nonofficial behavior. Forming and participating in such groups seems to be as much part of the student role as it is of the role of bureaucrat.

The kindergarten has been conceived of here as the year in which children are prepared for their schooling by learning the role of student. In the classrooms of the rest of the school grades, the children will be asked to submit to systems and routines imposed by the teachers and the curriculum. The days will be much like those of kindergarten, except that academic subjects will be substituted for the activities of the kindergarten. Once out of the school system, young adults will more than likely find themselves working large-scale bureaucratic organizations, perhaps on the assembly line in the factory, perhaps in the paper routines of the white collar occupations, where they will be required to submit to rigid routines imposed by "the company" which may make little sense to them. Those who can operate well in this situation will be successful bureaucratic functionaries. Kindergarten, therefore, can be seen as preparing children not only for participation in the bureaucratic organization of large modern school systems, but also for the large-scale occupational bureaucracies of modern society.

Discussion Questions

1. Give three examples of how the kindergarten environment prepares children to cope with large bureaucratic organizations that they will face as adults.

2. Discuss what you see as positive and what you see as negative in this kind of role for kindergarten.

JACK O. BALSWICK, CHARLES W. PEEK

The Inexpressive Male: A Tragedy of American Society

Feminists have been very vocal in condemning modern child-rearing methods because they generate, among other things, a sense of inferiority in women. Social scientists such as Janet Lever (see previous article) and Margaret Mead have conducted a number of studies describing the primary influence of culture on the development of the female temperament. But what of the male temperament? Have the males been "helped" or "hurt" by the socialization patterns of our culture? Do young boys ever experience feelings of inferiority when they finally admit they can't grow babies the same way girls can? Some answers to these questions can be found in the following article, by Balswick and Peek.

The Creation of the Inexpressive Male

Children, from the time they are born both explicitly and implicitly are taught how to be a man or how to be a woman. While the girl is taught to act "feminine" and to desire "feminine" objects, the boy is taught how to be a man. In learning to be a man, the boy in American society comes to value expressions of masculinity and devalue expressions of femininity. Masculinity is expressed largely through physical courage, toughness, competitiveness, and aggressiveness, whereas femininity is, in contrast, expressed largely through gentleness, expressiveness, and responsiveness. When a young boy begins to express his emotions through crying, his parents are quick to assert, "You're a big boy and big boys don't cry." Parents often use the term, "he's all boy," in reference to their son, and by this term usually refer to behavior which is an expression of aggressiveness, getting into mischief, getting dirty, etc., but never use the term to denote behavior which is an expression of affection, tenderness, or emotion. What parents are really telling their son is that a real man does not show his emotions and if he is a real man he will not allow his emotions to be expressed. These outward expressions of emotion are viewed as a sign of femininity, and undesirable for a male.

Is it any wonder, then, that during the most emotional peak of a play or movie, when many in the audience have lumps in their throats and tears in their eyes, that the adolescent boy guffaws loudly or quickly suppresses any tears which may be threatening to emerge, thus demonstrating to the world that he is above such emotional feeling?

The Inexpressive Male as a Single Man

At least two basic types of inexpressive male seem to result from this socialization process: the cowboy and the playboy. Manville (1969) has referred to the *cowboy type* in terms of a "John Wayne Neurosis" which stresses the strong, silent, and two-fisted male as the 100 percent American he-man. For present purposes, it is especially in his relationship with women that the John Wayne neurosis is particularly significant in representing many American males. As portrayed by Wayne in any one of his many type-cast roles, the mark of a real man is that he does not show any tenderness or affection toward girls because his culturally-acquired male image dictates that such a show of emotions would be distinctly unmanly. If he does have anything to do with girls, it is on a "man to man" basis: the girl is treated roughly (but not sadistically), with little hint of gentleness or affection. As Manville puts it:

The on-screen John Wayne doesn't feel comfortable around women. He does like them sometimes—God knows he's not *queer*. But at the right time, and in the right place—which he chooses. And always with his car/horse parked directly outside, in/on which he will ride away to his more important business back in Marlboro country. (1969, 111)

Alfred Auerback, a psychiatrist, has commented more directly (1970) on the cowboy type. He describes the American male's inexpressiveness with women as part of the "cowboy syndrome." He quite rightly states that "the cowboy in moving pictures has conveyed the image of the rugged 'he-man,' strong, resilient, resourceful, capable of coping with overwhelming odds. His attitude toward women is courteous but reserved." As the cowboy equally loved his girlfriend and his horse, so the present day American male loves his car or motorcycle and his girlfriend. Basic to both these descriptions is the notion that the cowboy does have feelings toward women but does not express them, since ironically such expression would conflict with his image of what a male is.

The *playboy type* has recently been epitomized in *Playboy* magazine and by James Bond. As with the cowboy type, he is resourceful and shrewd, and interacts with his girlfriend with a certain detachment which is expressed as "playing it cool." While Bond's relationship with women is more in terms of a Don Juan, he still treats women with an air of emotional detachment and independence similar to that of the cowboy. The playboy departs from the cowboy, however, in that he is also "non-feeling." Bond and the playboy he caricatures are in a sense "dead" inside. They have no emotional feelings toward women, while Wayne, although unwilling and perhaps unable to express them does have such feelings. Bond rejects women as women, treating them as consumer commodities; Wayne puts women on a pedestal. The playboy's relationship with women represents the culmination of Fromm's description of a marketing-oriented personality in which a person comes to see both himself and others as persons to be manipulated and exploited. Sexuality is reduced to a packageable consumption item which the playboy can handle because it demands no responsibility. The woman, in the process, becomes reduced to a playboy accessory. A successful "love affair" is one in which the bed was shared, but the playboy emerges having avoided personal involvement or a shared relationship with the woman.

The playboy, then, in part is the old cowboy in modern dress. Instead of the crude mannerisms of John Wayne, the playboy is a skilled manipulator of women, knowing when to turn the lights down, what music to play on the stereo, which drinks to serve, and what topics of conversation to pursue. The playboy, however, is not a perfect likeness; for unlike the cowboy, he does not seem to care for the women from whom he withholds his emotions. Thus, the inexpressive male as a single man comes in two types: the inexpressive feeling man (the cowboy) and the inexpressive non-feeling man (the playboy).

The Inexpressive Male as a Married Man

When the inexpressive male marries, his inexpressiveness can become highly dysfunctional to his marital relationship *if* he continues to apply it across-the-board to all women, his wife included. The modern American family places a greater demand upon the marriage relationship than did the family of the past. In the typical marriage of 100 or even 50 years ago, the roles of both the husband and the wife were clearly defined as demanding, task-oriented functions. If the husband successfully performed the role of provider and protector of his wife and family and if the wife performed the role of homemaker and mother to her children, chances were the marriage was defined as successful, both from a personal and a societal point of view. The traditional task functions which in the past were performed by the husband and wife are today often taken care of by individuals and organizations outside the home. Concomitant with the decline of the task functions in marriage has been the increase in the importance of the companionship and affectionate function in marriage. As Blood and Wolfe (1960, 172) concluded in their study of the modern American marriage, "companionship has emerged as the most valued aspect of marriage today."

As American society has become increasingly mechanized and depersonalized, the family remains as one of the few social groups where what sociologists call the primary relationship has still managed to survive. As such, a greater and greater demand has been placed upon the modern family and especially the modern marriage to provide for affection and companionship. Indeed, it is highly plausible to explain the increased rate of divorce during the last

70 years, not in terms of a breakdown in marriage relationships, but instead, as resulting from the increased load which marriage has been asked to carry. When the husband and wife no longer find affection and companionship from their marriage relationship, they most likely question the wisdom of attempting to continue in their conjugal relationship. When affection is gone, the main reason for the marriage relationship disappears.

Thus, within the newly defined affectively-oriented marriage relationship male inexpressiveness toward *all* women, wife included, would be dysfunctional. But what may happen for many males is that through progressively more serious involvements with women (such as going steady, being pinned, engagement, and the honeymoon period of marriage), they begin to make some exceptions. That is, they may learn to be *situationally rather than totally inexpressive,* inexpressive toward women in most situations but not in all. As the child who learns a rule and then, through further experience, begins to understand the exceptions to it, many American males may pick up the principle of inexpressiveness toward women, discovering its exceptions as they become more and more experienced in the full range of man-woman relationships. Consequently, they may become more expressive toward their wives while remaining essentially inexpressive toward other women; they learn that the conjugal relationship is one situation that is an exception to the cultural requirement of male inexpressiveness. Thus, what was once a double *sexual* standard, where men had one standard of sexual conduct toward their fiancee or wife and another toward other women, may now be primarily a double *emotional* standard, where men learn to be expressive toward their fiancee or wife but remain inexpressive toward women in general.

To the extent that such situational inexpressiveness exists among males, it should be functional to the maintenance of the marriage relationship. Continued inexpressiveness by married males toward women other than their wives would seem to prohibit their forming meaningful relationships with these women. Such a situation would seem to be advantageous to preserving their marital relationships, since "promiscuous" expressiveness toward other women could easily threaten the stability of these companionship-oriented marital relationships.

In short, the authors' suggestion is that situational inexpressiveness, in which male expressiveness is essentially limited to the marital relationship, may be one of the basic timbers shoring up many American marriages, especially if indications of increasing extramarital sexual relations are correct. In a sense, then, the consequences of situational inexpressiveness for marital relationships do not seem very different from those of prostitution down through the centuries, where prostitution provided for extramarital sex under circumstances which discouraged personal affection toward the female partner strong enough to undermine the marital relationship. In the case of the situationally inexpressive husband, his inexpressiveness in relations with women other than his wife may serve as a line of defense against the possible negative consequences of such involvement toward marital stability. By acting as the cowboy or playboy, therefore, the married male may effectively rob extra-marital relationships of their expressiveness and thus preserve his marital relationship.

The inexpressiveness which the American male early acquires may be bothersome in that he has to partially unlearn it in order to effectively relate to his wife. However, if he is successful in partially unlearning it (or learning a few exceptions to it), then it can be highly functional to maintaining the conjugal relationship.

But what if the husband does not partially unlearn his inexpressiveness? Within the newly defined expressive function of the marriage relationship, he is likely to be found inadequate. The possibility of an affectionate and companionship conjugal relationship carries with it the assumption that both the husband and wife are bringing into marriage the expressive capabilities to make such a relationship work. This being the case, American society is ironically shortchanging males in terms of their ability to fulfill this role expectation. Thus, society inconsistently teaches the male that to be masculine is to be inexpressive, while at the same time, expectations in the marital role are defined in terms of sharing affection and companionship which involves the ability to communicate and express feelings. What exists apparently, is another example of a discontinuity in cultural conditioning of which Benedict (1938) spoke more than 30 years ago.

Conclusion and Summary

It has been suggested that many American males are incapable of expressing themselves emotionally to a woman, and that this inexpressiveness is a result of the way society socialized males into their sex role. However, there is an alternative explanation which should be explored, namely, that the learning by the male of his sex role may not actually result in his inability to be expressive, but rather only in his thinking that he is not supposed to be expressive. Granted, according to the first explanation, the male cannot express himself precisely because he was taught that he was not supposed to be expressive, but in this second explanation inexpressiveness is a result of present perceived expectations and not a psychological condition which resulted from past socialization. The male perceives cultural expectations as saying, "don't express yourself to women," and although the male may be capable of such expressiveness, he "fits" into cultural expectations. In the case of the married male, where familial norms do call for expressiveness to one's wife, it may be that the expectations for the expression of emotions to his wife are not communicated to him.

There has been a trickle of evidence which would lend support to the first explanation, which stresses the male's incapacity to be expressive. Several studies (Balswick, 1970; Hurvitz, 1964; Komarovsky, 1962; Rainwater, 1965) have suggested that especially among the lowly educated, it is the wife playing the feminine role who is often disappointed in the lack of emotional concern shown by her husband. The husband, on the other hand, cannot understand the relatively greater concern and emotional expressiveness which his wife desires, since he does not usually feel this need himself. As a result of her research, Komarovsky (1962, 156) has suggested that "the ideal of masculinity into which . . . (men are) . . . socialized inhibits expressiveness both directly, with its emphasis on reserve, and indirectly, by identifying personal interchange with the feminine role." Balswick (1970) found that males are less capable than females of expressing or receiving companionship support from their spouses. His research also supports the view that inadequacy of expressiveness is greatest for the less educated males. Although inexpressiveness may be found among males at all socioeconomic levels, it is especially among the lower class male that expressiveness is seen as being inconsistent with his defined masculine role.

There may be some signs that conditions which have contributed toward the creation of the inexpressive male are in the process of decline. The deemphasis in distinctiveness in dress and fashions between the sexes, as exemplified in the "hippy" movement can be seen as a reaction against the rigidly defined distinctions between the sexes which have characterized American society. The sexless look, as presently being advanced in high fashion, is the logical end reaction to a society which has superficially created strong distinctions between the sexes. Along with the blurring of sexual distinctions in fashion may very well be the shattering of the strong, silent male as a glorified type. There is already evidence of sharp criticism of the inexpressive male and exposure of him as constituting a "hangup." Marriage counselors, sensitivity group leaders, "hippies," and certainly youth in general, are critical of inexpressiveness, and candid honesty in interpersonal relations. Should these views permeate American society, the inexpressive male may well come to be regarded as a pathetic tragedy instead of the epitome of masculinity and fade from the American scene. Not all may applaud his departure, however. While those interested in more satisfactory male-female relationships, marital and otherwise, will probably gladly see him off, those concerned with more stable marital relationships may greet his departure less enthusiastically. Although it should remove an important barrier to satisfaction in all male-female relationships via an increase in the male's capacity for emotional response toward females, by the same token it also may remove a barrier against emotional entanglement in relations with females outside marital relationships and thus threaten the stability of marriages. If one finds the inexpressive male no longer present one of these days, then, it will be interesting to observe whether any gains in the stability of marriage due to increased male expressiveness *within* this relationship will be enough to offset losses in stability emanating from increasing displays of male expressiveness *outside* it.

References

Auerback, Alfred. The Cowboy Syndrome. Summary of research contained in a personal letter from the author, 1970.

Balswick, Jack O. The Effect of Spouse Companionship Support on Employment Success. *Journal of Marriage and the Family,* 1970, 32, 212–215.

Benedict, Ruth. Continuities and Discontinuities in Cultural Conditioning. *Psychiatry,* 1938, 1, 161–167.

Blood, Robert and Donald Wolfe. *Husbands and Wives: The Dynamic of Married Living.* Glencoe, Illinois: The Free Press, 1960.

Cox, Harvey. Playboy's Doctrine of Male. In Wayne H. Cowan (Ed.) *Witness to a Generation: Significant Writings from Christianity and Crisis (1941–1966).* New York: Bobbs-Merrill Company, 1966.

Hurvitz, Nathan. Marital Strain in the Blue Collar Family. In Arthur Shostak and William Gomberg (Eds.) *Blue-Collar World.* Englewood Cliffs, New Jersey: Prentice-Hall, 1964.

Komarovsky, M. *Blue-Collar Marriage.* New York: Random House, 1962.

Mead, Margaret. *Sex and Temperament in Three Primitive Societies.* New York: William Morrow and Company, 1935.

Manville, W. H. The Locker Room Boys. *Cosmopolitan,* 1969, 166 (11), 110–115.

Popplestone, John. The Horseless Cowboys. *Transaction,* 1966, 3, 25–27.

Rainwater, Lee. *Family Design: Marital Sexuality, Family Size, and Contraception.* Chicago: Aldine Publishing Company, 1965.

Discussion Questions

1. Review two or three patterns of socialization discussed by the authors that contribute to males' becoming inexpressive.
2. Does it seem to you that male inexpressiveness is caused by the way our society socializes males or by males' simply thinking that they are not supposed to be expressive? Discuss.

4 / Role and Status

Drawing by B. Tobey; in Look, 4-7-70.

"Albert, please! Can't you see Mommy is busy with the war!"

Every society has a system of statuses and accompanying roles. A *status* is an individual's social position relative to others. An individual's status can be identified by words and labels such as "mother," "chairman," "coach," "student," and "girlfriend." *Role* is the behavior expected of one who occupies a particular status. Each status gains meaning when its roles—the rights, duties, and obligations to other statuses—are clarified. The status of "girlfriend," for example, has meaning only when there is a reciprocal relationship with the status of "boyfriend." The status position of "student" similarly involves the role expectation that individual students will register, attend class, study, and take examinations.

Sociologists have classified statuses by the general concepts of ascribed status and achieved status. *Ascribed* status is assigned to an individual according to hereditary traits without regard to individual preference and ability. In all societies ascribed statuses include age, sex, race, and place of birth. Some of the ascribed statuses held by an individual can change. Age will change. As one matures from childhood to an "older" person, his status will change several times. Ascribed statuses can also be modified. Many women, for example, are dissatisfied with their ascribed status, which requires the roles of marriage, child rearing, and so forth. Some women argue for greater freedom to experiment, as men do, with the various statuses based on merit, skill, and achievement. Members of ethnic groups have also resented the status ascription that dictates their roles and denies them the right of individual choice. In a society that so frequently and passionately avows its dedication to freedom and equal opportunity, they argue, status ascription is both inconsistent and unjust. Whatever extent these ascribed statuses are modified to in the future, it is important to realize that few statuses are held entirely by ascription or entirely by achievement.

Achieved status is a position attained through individual choice, effort, and accomplishment. The most commonly recognized achieved statuses are education, occupation, income, and marital status. As societies have industrialized, the demand for specialized skills has increased the number of statuses based on achievement. Societies based on achieved statuses are generally extolled for providing their members with a high degree of choice. No longer is a young man required to learn his father's trade. He can choose among a variety of occupations. It is important to remember, however, that societies based on achieved statuses lead to insecurity and destroy alibis for failure to achieve a higher status.

It is also important to remember that a person who occupies a particular status is subject to many role expectations simultaneously. The concept *role set* refers to a complex set of role expectations associated with a particular status. Role set demonstrates the complex nature of roles. A businessman, for example, relates not only to his customers, but also to his employees, stockholders, and fellow businessmen. Similarly, a mother must relate to her child as well as other members of the family and groups in the community, such as the PTA. When a man marries, he does not marry the in-laws. Yet in-laws do become role partners and form a part of the role set associated with the newly acquired status of husband.

Because of many demands contained in a role set, an individual who occupies a status is subject to competing pressures. *Role strain* refers to the difficulty people have in meeting their role obligations. Role strain may arise out of role conflict. *Role conflict* may be built into a single role. The sex roles in our society offer a good example. Parents may remind a daughter in college that she is expected to study hard in preparation for a career, and at the same time inquire if she has been dating any nice young men, thereby implying the additional expectation that she also find a husband. The role strain produced by such a conflict can be reduced by a variety of ways such as focusing on one role at a time, denying that a conflict exists, or turning to a third party to make the decision on which role is most important.

The articles that follow indicate the pervasive influence on man's behavior in groups exercised by role and status.

ROBIN LAKOFF

Talking Like a Lady

In every society some roles are ascribed—assigned to an individual without regard to preference or ability. In our society women are ascribed roles that can be generally summarized by the term *feminine*. Being feminine requires conformity to certain forms of behavior regarding clothing, leisure time, and occupation. Very often this kind of ascription leads women to aspire to become nurses, teachers (of small children), and secretaries. They apparently don't want to become doctors, principals, or "the Boss." But being feminine also demands other less obvious forms of behavior, such as language that is appropriately "ladylike." In fact, argues Robin Lakoff in the following article, the language of women is one of the most important features of the role ascribed to women in our society.

"Women's language" shows up in all levels of the grammar of English. We find differences in the choice and frequency of lexical items; in the situations in which certain syntactic rules are performed; in intonational and other supersegmental patterns. As an example of lexical differences, imagine a man and a woman both looking at the same wall, painted a pinkish shade of purple. The woman may say (2):

(2) The wall is mauve,

with no one consequently forming any special impression of her as a result of the words alone; but if the man should say (2), one might well conclude he was imitating a woman sarcastically or was a homosexual or an interior decorator. Women, then, make far more precise discriminations in naming colors than do men; words like *beige, ecru, aquamarine, lavender,* and so on are unremarkable in a woman's active vocabulary, but absent from that of most men. I have seen a man helpless with suppressed laughter at a discussion between two other people as to whether a book jacket was to be described as "lavender" or "mauve." Men find such discussion amusing because they consider such a question trivial, irrelevant to the real world.

We might ask why fine discrimination of color is relevant for women, but not for men. A clue is contained in the way many men in our society view other "unworldly" topics, such as high culture and the Church, as outside the world of men's work, relegated to women and men whose masculinity is not unquestionable. Men tend to relegate to women things that are not of concern to them, or do not involve their egos. Among these are problems of fine color discrimination. We might rephrase this point by saying that since women are not expected to make decisions on important matters, such as what kind of job to hold, they are relegated the noncrucial decisions as a sop. Deciding whether to name a color "lavender" or "mauve" is one such sop.

If it is agreed that this lexical disparity reflects a social inequity in the position of women, one may ask how to remedy it. Obviously, no one could seriously recommend legislating against the use of the terms "mauve" and "lavender" by women, or forcing men to learn to use them. All we can do is give women the opportunity to participate in the real decisions of life.

Aside from specific lexical items like color names, we find differences between the speech of women and that of men in the use of particles that grammarians often describe as "meaningless." There may be no referent for them, but they are far from meaningless: they define the social context of an utterance, indicate the relationship the speaker feels between himself and his addressee, between himself and what he is talking about.

As an experiment, one might present native speakers of standard American English with pairs of sentences, identical syntactically and in terms of referential lexical items, and differing merely in the choice of "meaningless" particle, and ask them which was spoken by a man, which a woman. Consider:

(3) (a) Oh dear, you've put the peanut butter in the refrigerator again.
    (b) Shit, you've put the peanut butter in the refrigerator again.

It is safe to predict that people would classify the first sentence as part of "women's language," the second as "men's language." It is true that many self-respecting women are becoming able to use sentences like (3) (b) publicly without flinching, but this a relatively recent development, and while perhaps the majority of Middle America might condone the use of (b) for men, they would still disapprove of its use by women. (It is of interest, by the way, to note that men's language is increasingly being used by women, but women's language is not being adopted by men, apart from those who reject the American masculine image [for example, homosexuals]. This is analogous to the fact that men's jobs are being sought by women, but few men are rushing to become housewives or secretaries. The language of the favored group, the group that holds the power, along with its nonlinguistic behavior, is generally adopted by the other group, not vice versa. In any event, it is a truism to state that the "stronger" expletives are reserved for men, and the "weaker" ones for women.)

Now we may ask what we mean by "stronger" and "weaker" expletives. (If these particles were indeed meaningless, none would be stronger than any other.) The difference between using "shit" (or "damn," or one of many others) as opposed to "oh dear," or "goodness," or "oh fudge" lies in how forcefully one says how one feels—perhaps, one might say, choice of particle is a function of how strongly one allows oneself to feel about something, so that the strength of an emotion conveyed in a sentence corresponds to the strength of the particle. Hence in a really serious situation, the use of "trivializing" (that is, "women's") particles constitutes a joke, or at any rate, is highly inappropriate. (In conformity with current linguistic practice, throughout this work an asterisk (*) will be used to mark a sentence that is inappropriate in some sense, either because it is syntactically deviant or used in the wrong social context.)

(4) (a) * Oh fudge, my hair is on fire.
    (b) * Dear me, did he kidnap the baby?

As children, women are encouraged to be "little ladies." Little ladies don't scream as vociferously as little boys, and they are chastised more severely for throwing tantrums or showing temper: "high spirits" are expected and therefore tolerated in little boys; docility and resignation are the corresponding traits expected of little girls. Now, we tend to excuse a show of temper by a man where we would not excuse an identical tirade from a woman: women are allowed to fuss and complain, but only a man can bellow in rage. It is sometimes claimed that there is a biological basis for this behavior difference, though I don't believe conclusive evidence exists that the early differences in behavior that have been observed are not the results of very different treatment of babies of the two sexes from the beginning; but surely the use of different particles by men and women is a learned trait, merely mirroring nonlinguistic differences again, and again pointing out an inequity that exists between the treatment of men, and society's expectations of them, and the treatment of women. Allowing men stronger means of expression than are open to women further reinforces men's position of strength in the real world: for surely we listen with more attention the more strongly and forcefully someone expresses opinions, and a speaker unable—for whatever reason—to be forceful in stating his views is much less likely to be taken seriously. Ability to use strong particles like "shit" and "hell" is, of course, only incidental to the inequity that exists rather than its cause. But once again, apparently accidental linguistic usage suggests that women are denied equality partially for linguistic reasons, and that an examination of language points up precisely an area in which inequity exists. Further, if someone is allowed to show emotions, and consequently does, others may well be able to view him as a real individual in his own right, as they could not if he never showed emotion. Here again, then, the behavior a woman learns as "correct" prevents her from being taken seriously as an individual, and further is considered "correct" and necessary for a woman precisely because society does *not* consider her seriously as an individual.

Similar sorts of disparities exist elsewhere in the vocabulary. There is, for instance, a group of adjectives which have, besides their specific and literal meanings, another use, that of indicating the speaker's approbation or admiration for something. Some of these adjectives are neutral as to sex of speaker: either men or women may use them. But another set seems, in its figurative use, to be largely confined to women's speech. Representative lists of both types are below:

neutral	women only
great	adorable
terrific	charming
cool	sweet
neat	lovely
	divine

As with the color words and swear words already discussed, for a man to stray into the "women's" column is apt to be damaging to his reputation, though here a woman may freely use the neutral words. But it should not be inferred from this that a woman's use of the "women's" words is without its risks. Where a woman has a choice between the neutral words and the women's words, as a man has not, she may be suggesting very different things about her own personality and her view of the subject matter by her choice of words of the first set or words of the second.

(5) (a) What a terrific idea!
    (b) What a divine idea!

It seems to me that (a) might be used under any appropriate conditions by a female speaker. But (b) is more restricted. Probably it is used appropriately (even by the sort of speaker for whom it was normal) only in case the speaker feels the idea referred to to be essentially frivolous, trivial, or unimportant to the world at large—only an amusement for the speaker herself. Consider, then, a woman advertising executive at an advertising conference. However feminine an advertising executive she is, she is much more likely to express her approval with (5) (a) than with (b), which might cause raised eyebrows, and the reaction: "That's what we get for putting a woman in charge of this company."

On the other hand, suppose a friend suggests to the same woman that she should dye her French poodles to match her cigarette lighter. In this case, the suggestion really concerns only her, and the impression she will make on people. In this case, she may use (b), from the "woman's language." So the choice is not really free: words restricted to "women's language" suggest that concepts to which they are applied are not relevant to the real world of (male) influence and power.

One may ask whether there really are no analogous terms that are available to men—terms that denote approval of the trivial, the personal; that express approbation in terms of one's own personal emotional reaction, rather than by gauging the likely general reaction. There does in fact seem to be one such word: it is the hippie invention "groovy," which seems to have most of the connotations that separate "lovely" and "divine" from "great" and "terrific" excepting only that it does not mark the speaker as feminine or effeminate.

(6) (a) What a terrific steel mill!
    (b) * What a lovely steel mill! (male speaking)
    (c) What a groovy steel mill!

I think it is significant that this word was introduced by the hippies, and, when used seriously rather than sarcastically, used principally by people who have accepted the hippies' values. Principal among these is the denial of the Protestant work ethic: to a hippie, something can be worth thinking about even if it isn't influential in the power structure, or moneymaking. Hippies are separated from the activities of the real world just as women are—though in the former case it is due to a decision on their parts, while this is not uncontroversially true in the case of women. For both these groups, it is possible to express approval of things in a personal way—though one does so at the risk of losing one's credibility with members of the power structure. It is also true, according to some speakers, that upper-class British men may use the words listed in the "women's" column, as well as the specific color words and others we have categorized as specifically feminine, without raising doubts as to their masculinity among other speakers of the same dialect. (This is not true for lower-class Britons, however.) The reason may be that commitment to the work ethic need not necessarily be displayed: one may be or appear to be a gentleman of leisure, interested in various pursuits, but not involved in mundane (business or political) affairs, in such a culture, without incurring disgrace. This is rather analogous to the position of a woman in American middle-class society, so we should not be surprised if these special lexical items are usable by both groups. This fact points indeed to a more general conclusion. These words aren't, basically, "feminine"; rather, they signal "uninvolved," or "out of power." Any group in a society to which these labels are applicable may presumably use these words; they are often considered "feminine," "unmasculine," because women are the "uninvolved," "out of power" group *par excellence*.

Another group that has, ostensibly at least, taken itself out of the search for power and money is that of academic men. They are frequently viewed by other groups as analogous in some ways to women—they don't really work, they are supported in their frivolous pursuits by others, what they do doesn't really count in the real world, and so on. The suburban home finds its counterpart in the ivory tower: one is supposedly shielded from harsh realities in both. Therefore it is not too surprising that many academic men (especially those who emulate British norms) may violate many of these sacrosanct rules I have just laid down: they often use "women's language." Among themselves, this does not occasion ridicule. But to a truck driver, a professor saying, "What a lovely hat!" is undoubtedly laughable, all the more so as it reinforces his stereotype of professors as effete snobs.

When we leave the lexicon and venture into syntax, we find that syntactically too women's speech is peculiar. To my knowledge, there is no syntactic rule in English that only women may use. But there is at least one rule that a woman will use in more conversational situations than a man. (This fact indicates, of course, that the applicability of syntactic rules is governed partly by social context—the positions in society of the speaker and addressee, with respect to each other, and the impression one seeks to make on the other.) This is the rule of tag-question formation.[1]

[1] Within the lexicon itself, there seems to be a parallel phenomenon to tag-question usage, which I refrain from discussing in the body of the text because the facts are controversial and I do not understand them fully. The intensive *so,* used where purists would insist upon an absolute superlative, heavily stressed, seems more characteristic of women's language than of men's, though it is found in the latter, particularly in the speech of male academics. Consider, for instance, the following sentences:

(a) I feel *so* unhappy!
(b) That movie made me *so* sick!

A tag, in its usage as well as its syntactic shape (in English) is midway between an outright statement and a yes-no question: it is less assertive than the former, but more confident than the latter. Therefore it is usable under certain contextual situations: not those in which a statement would be appropriate, nor those in which a yes-no question is generally used, but in situations intermediate between these.

One makes a statement when one has confidence in his knowledge and is pretty certain that his statement will be believed; one asks a question when one lacks knowledge on some point and has reason to believe that this gap can and will be remedied by an answer by the addressee. A tag question, being intermediate between these, is used when the speaker is stating a claim, but lacks full confidence in the truth of that claim. So if I say

(7) Is John here?

I will probably not be surprised if my respondent answers "no"; but if I say

(8) John is here, isn't he?

instead, chances are I am already biased in favor of a positive answer, wanting only confirmation by the addressee. I still want a response from him, as I do with a yes-no question; but I have enough knowledge (or think I have) to predict that response, much as with a declarative statement. A tag question, then, might be thought of as a declarative statement without the assumption that the statement is to be believed by the addressee: one has an out, as with a question. A tag gives the addressee leeway, not forcing him to go along with the views of the speaker.

There are situations in which a tag is legitimate, in fact the only legitimate sentence form. So, for example, if I have seen something only indistinctly, and have reason to believe my addressee had a better view, I can say:

(9) I had my glasses off. He was out at third, wasn't he?

Sometimes we find a tag question used in cases in which the speaker

---

Men seem to have the least difficulty using this construction when the sentence is unemotional, or nonsubjective—without reference to the speaker himself:

(c) That sunset is *so* beautiful!
(d) Fred is *so* dumb!

Substituting an equative like *so* for absolute superlatives (like *very, really, utterly*) seems to be a way of backing out of committing oneself strongly to an opinion, rather like tag questions (cf. discussion below, in the text). One might hedge in this way with perfect right in making aesthetic judgments, as in (c), or intellectual, judgments, as in (d). But it is somewhat odd to hedge in describing one's own mental or emotional state: who, after all, is qualified to contradict one on this? To hedge in this situation is to seek to avoid making any strong statement: a characteristic, as we have noted already and shall note further, of women's speech.

knows as well as the addressee what the answer must be, and doesn't need confirmation. One such situation is when the speaker is making "small talk," trying to elicit conversation from the addressee:

(10) Sure is hot here, isn't it?

In discussing personal feelings or opinions, only the speaker normally has any way of knowing the correct answer. Strictly speaking, questioning one's own opinions is futile. Sentences like (11) are usually ridiculous.

(11) * I have a headache, don't I?

But similar cases do, apparently, exist, in which it is the speaker's opinions, rather than perceptions, for which corroboration is sought, as in (12):

(12) The way prices are rising is horrendous, isn't it?

While there are of course other possible interpretations of a sentence like this, one possibility is that the speaker has a particular answer in mind—"yes" or "no"—but is reluctant to state it baldly. It is my impression, though I do not have precise statistical evidence, that this sort of tag question is much more apt to be used by women than by men. If this is indeed true, why is it true?

These sentence types provide a means whereby a speaker can avoid committing himself, and thereby avoid coming into conflict with the addressee. The problem is that, by so doing, a speaker may also give the impression of not being really sure of himself, of looking to the addressee for confirmation, even of having no views of his own. This last criticism is, of course, one often leveled at women. One wonders how much of it reflects a use of language that has been imposed on women from their earliest years.

Related to this special use of a syntactic rule is a widespread difference perceptible in women's intonational patterns.[2] There is a peculiar sentence intonation pattern, found in English as far as I know only among women, which has the form of a declarative answer to a question, and is used as such, but has the rising inflection typical of a yes-no question, as well as being especially hesitant. The effect is as though one were seeking confirmation, though at the same time the speaker may be the only one who has the requisite information.

---

[2] For analogues outside of English to these uses of tag questions and special intonation patterns, ct. my discussion of Japanese particles in "Language in Context," *Language*, 48 (1972), 907–27. It is to be expected that similar cases will be found in many other languages as well. See, for example, M. R. Haas's very interesting discussion of differences between men's and women's speech (mostly involving lexical dissimilarities) in many languages, in D. Hymes, ed., *Language in Culture and Society* (New York: Harper & Row, 1964).

(13) (*a*) When will dinner be ready?
   (*b*) Oh . . . around six o'clock. . . ?

It is as though (*b*) were saying, "Six o'clock, if that's OK with you, if you agree." (*a*) is put in the position of having to provide confirmation, and (*b*) sounds unsure. Here we find unwillingness to assert an opinion carried to an extreme. One likely consequence is that these sorts of speech patterns are taken to reflect something real about character and play a part in not taking a woman seriously or trusting her with any real responsibilities, since "she can't make up her mind" and "isn't sure of herself." And here again we see that people form judgments about other people on the basis of superficial linguistic behavior that may have nothing to do with inner character, but has been imposed upon the speaker, on pain of worse punishment than not being taken seriously.

Such features are probably part of the general fact that women's speech sounds much more "polite" than men's. One aspect of politeness is as we have just described: leaving a decision open, not imposing your mind, or views, or claims on anyone else. Thus a tag question is a kind of polite statement, in that it does not force agreement or belief on the addressee. A request may be in the same sense a polite command, in that it does not overtly require obedience, but rather suggests something be done as a favor to the speaker. An overt order (as in an imperative) expresses the (often impolite) assumption of the speaker's superior position to the addressee, carrying with it the right to enforce compliance, whereas with a request the decision on the face of it is left up to the addressee. (The same is true of suggestions: here, the implication is not that the addressee is in danger if he does not comply—merely that he will be glad if he does. Once again, the decision is up to the addressee, and a suggestion therefore is politer than an order.) The more particles in a sentence that reinforce the notion that it is a request, rather than an order, the politer the result. The sentences of (14) illustrate these points: (14) (*a*) is a direct order, (*b*) and (*c*) simple requests, and (*d*) and (*e*) compound requests.[3]

(14) (*a*) Close the door.
   (*b*) Please close the door.
   (*c*) Will you close the door?
   (*d*) Will you please close the door?
   (*e*) Won't you close the door?

Let me first explain why (*e*) has been classified as a compound request. (A sentence like *Won't you please close the door* would then count as a doubly compound request.) A sentence like (14) (*c*) is close in sense to "Are you willing to close the door?" According to the normal rules of polite conversa-

---

[3] For more detailed discussion of these problems, see Lakoff, "Language in Context."

tion, to agree that you are willing is to agree to do the thing asked of you. Hence this apparent inquiry functions as a request, leaving the decision up to the willingness of the addressee. Phrasing it as a positive question makes the (implicit) assumption that a "yes" answer will be forthcoming. Sentence (14) (*d*) is more polite than (*b*) or (*c*) because it combines them: *please* indicating that to accede will be to do something for the speaker, and *will you*, as noted, suggesting that the addressee has the final decision. If, now, the question is phrased with a negative, as in (14) (*e*), the speaker seems to suggest the stronger likelihood of a negative response from the addressee. Since the assumption is then that the addressee is that much freer to refuse, (14) (*e*) acts as a more polite request than (14) (*c*) or (*d*): (*c*) and (*d*) put the burden of refusal on the addressee, as (*e*) does not.

Given these facts, one can see the connection between tag questions and tag orders and other requests. In all these cases, the speaker is not committed as with a simple declarative or affirmative. And the more one compounds a request, the more characteristic it is of women's speech, the less of men's. A sentence that begins *Won't you please* (without special emphasis on *please*) seems to me at least to have a distinctly unmasculine sound. Little girls are indeed taught to talk like little ladies, in that their speech is in many ways more polite than that of boys or men, and the reason for this is that politeness involves an absence of a strong statement, and women's speech is devised to prevent the expression of strong statements.

Discussion Questions

1. Find as many examples as possible of "women's language" and "men's language."
2. How does the author indicate that the situation seems to be changing? Do you believe this kind of change is positive or negative for U.S. society? Discuss.

MIRRA KOMAROVSKY

Cultural Contradictions and Sex Roles: The Masculine Case

None of us play our roles by ourselves. All roles involve interaction with others. This interaction is based on a clear set of expectations of how each person will behave. As a student, for example, you expect your teachers and professors to be knowledgeable, understandable, and fair in assigning work and awarding grades. Males and females likewise have expectations about how members of each sex will behave. Research indicates that females

Adapted from Mirra Komarovsky, *Dilemmas of Masculinity: A Study of College Youth.* New York: W. W. Norton & Company, Inc. Paperback edition 1976.

expect to marry males who are taller, more ambitious, and more intelligent than themselves. Males, on the other hand, expect about the opposite from the female they want to marry. However, given the recent social changes in our society males and females are experiencing some role strain. The specific causes and characteristics of this role strain are clearly described by Mirra Komarovsky in the following article.

In a rapidly changing society, normative malintegration is commonly assumed to lead to an experience of strain. Earlier research on cultural contradictions and the feminine sex role showed that women at an eastern college suffered uncertainty and insecurity because the norms for occupational and academic success conflicted with norms for the traditional feminine role. A replication at a western university reported agreement in the questionnaire data, but the interview material led the investigator to conclude that the problem was less important to the women than the earlier study had suggested. However, Wallin pointed out that, in his replication, the respondents were oriented to marriage, while the Komarovsky study had included an appreciable number of women oriented to careers. This finding tended to support the view that women who were satisfied with the traditional female role would show less strain when confronted with contrary expectations than women who hoped to have both a rewarding career and a rewarding marriage.

Men are also confronted with contradictory expectations. For example, the traditional norm of male intellectual superiority conflicts with a newer norm of intellectual companionship between the sexes. This research investigated the extent of masculine strain experienced by sixty-two college males randomly selected from the senior class of an Ivy League male college. The study included a variety of status relationships, but the results reported here deal with intellectual relationships with female friends and attitudes toward working wives.

Methods

Each of the sixty-two respondents contributed a minimum of three two-hour interviews and also completed a set of five schedules and two psychological tests, the California Personality Inventory and the Gough Adjective Check List. The psychological tests were interpreted by a clinical psychologist. The thirteen-page interview guide probed for data on actual role performance, ideal role expectations and limits of tolerance, personal preferences, perception of role partner's ideal expectations, and relevant attitudes of significant others. Direct questions on strains came only at the end of this sequence. Extensive use was made of quasi-projective tests in the form of brief episodes. The total response rate of the original sample ($N = 79$) was 78 per cent.

Intellectual Relationships with Female Friends

When fewer women attended college, the norm of male intellectual superiority might have had some validation in experience. But today college women are more rigorously selected than men in terms of high school academic performance. Nevertheless, social norms internalized in early childhood are resistant to change. The first question for this research was "How many men would show insecurity or strain in their intellectual relationships with women when confronted with both bright women and the traditional norm of male superiority?"

The Troubled Third. Of the fifty-three men for whom the data were available (six did not date, three could not be classified reliably), 30 per cent reported that intellectual insecurity or strain with dates was a past or current problem. This number included men who, having experienced stress, sought to avoid it by finding dates who posed no intellectual threat. The following excerpts from interviews illustrate the views of this troubled third:

> I enjoy talking to more intelligent girls, but I have no desire for a deep relationship with them. I guess I still believe that the man should be more intelligent.

> *   *   *

> I may be a little frightened of a man who is superior to me in some field of knowledge, but if a girl knows more than I do, I resent her.

> *   *   *

> Once I was seeing a philosophy major, and we got along quite well. We shared a similar outlook on life, and while we had some divergent opinions, I seemed better able to document my position. One day, by chance, I heard her discussing with another girl an aspect of Kant that just the night before she described to me as obscure and confusing. But now she was explaining it to a girl so clearly and matter-of-factly that I felt sort of hurt and foolish. Perhaps it was immature of me to react this way.

The mode of strain exemplified by these men might be termed "a socially structured scarcity of resources for role fulfillment." Apart from the ever present problem of lack of time and energy, some social roles are intrinsically more difficult to fulfill, given the state of technical skills, the inherent risks, or other scarcities of facilities. The strain of a doctor called upon to treat a disease for which modern medicine has no cure is another case in point.

Selective dating and avoidance of superior women solved the problem for some troubled youths, but this offered no solution for six respondents who yearned for intellectual companionship with women but dreaded the risk of invidious comparisons. The newly emerging norm of intellectual companionship with women creates a mode of strain akin to one Merton and Barber termed "sociological ambivalence." Universalistic values tend to replace sex-linked desiderata among some male undergraduates who now value originality and intelligence in female as well as in male associates. The conflict arises when, at the same time, the norm of masculine intellectual superiority has not been relinquished, as exemplified in the following case: "I am beginning to feel," remarked one senior about his current girl friend, "that she is not bright enough. She never says anything that would make me sit up and say, 'Ah, that's interesting!' I want a girl who has some defined crystal of her own personality and does not merely echo my thoughts." He recently met a girl who fascinated him with her quick and perceptive intelligence but this new girl made him feel "nervous and humble."

The problem of this youth is to seek the rewards of valued attributes in a woman without arousing in himself feelings of inferiority. It may be argued that in a competitive society this conflict tends to characterize encounters with males as well. Nonetheless, if similar problems exist between two males, the utility curve is shaped distinctively by the norm of male intellectual superiority because mere equality with a woman may be defined as a defeat or a violation of a role prescription.

The Adjusted Majority. The thirty-seven students who said that intellectual relationships with dates were not a problem represented a variety of types. Eleven men felt superior to their female friends. In two or three cases, the relationships were judged equalitarian with strong emphasis on the rewards of intellectual companionship. In contrast, several men—and their dates—had little interest in intellectual concerns. In a few instances the severity of other problems overwhelmed this one. Finally, some eight men were happily adjusted despite the acknowledged intellectual superiority of their women friends. What makes for accommodation to this still deviant pattern?

In seven of the eight cases, the female friend had some weakness which offset her intellectual competence, such as emotional dependence, instability, or a plain appearance, giving the man a compensating advantage. A bright, studious, but relatively unattractive girl may be acceptable to a man who is not as certain of his ability to win a sexually desirable female as he is of his mental ability. In only one of the eight cases the respondent admitted that his steady girl was "more independent and less emotional, actually a little smarter than I. But she doesn't make me feel like a dunce." Her superiority was tolerable because she provided a supportive relationship which he needed and could accept with only mild, if any, emotional discomfort.

Another factor which may account for the finding that 70 per cent of the sample reported no strain is the fact that intellectual qualities are no longer considered unfeminine and that the imperative of male superiority is giving way to the ideal of companionship between equals. This intrepretation is supported by responses to two standard questions and by the qualitative materials of the interviews. A schedule testing beliefs on sixteen psychological sex differences asked whether the reasoning ability of men is greater than that of women. Only 34 per cent of the respondents "agreed" or "agreed somewhat," while 20 per cent were "uncertain"; almost half "disagreed" or "disagreed somewhat."

Another question was put to all sixty-two respondents: what are for you personally the three or four most desirable characteristics in a woman (man) who is to be close to you? Of all the traits men desired in a woman, 33 per cent were in the "intellectual" cluster, in contrast with 44 per cent of such traits if the friend were male. The fact that the sex difference was not large seems significant. The major difference in traits desired in male and female intimates (apart from sexual attractiveness and love) was the relative importance of "social amenities and appearance" for women.

The qualitative data amply document the fact that the majority of the respondents ideally hoped to share their intellectual interests with their female as well as their male friends. To be sure, what men occasionally meant by intellectual rapport with women was having an appreciative listener: "I wouldn't go out," declared one senior, "with any girl who wasn't sharp and perceptive enough to catch an intellectual subtlety." But for the majority a "meaningful relationship" with a woman included also a true intellectual interchange and sharing. As one senior put it, "A guy leaving a movie with his date expects her to make a stimulating comment of her own and not merely echo his ideas." Another man wanted a date with whom he could "discuss things that guys talk about," and still a third man exclaimed: "What I love about this girl is that she is on my level, that I can never speak over her head."

It is this ideal of intellectual companionship with women, we suggest, that may explain the relative adjustment of the men in this sphere. As long as the expectation of male superiority persisted, anything near equality on the part of the woman carried the threatening message to the men: "I am not the intellectually *superior* male I am expected to be." But when the ideal of intellectual companionship between equals replaces the expectation of male superiority, the pressure upon the man eases and changes. Now he need only reassure himself that he is not inferior to his date, rather than that he is markedly superior to her. Once the expectation of clear superiority is relinquished, varieties of relationships may be accommodated. Given a generally similar intellectual level, comparative evaluations are blurred by different interests, by complementary strengths and weaknesses, and occasionally by rationalizations ("she studies harder") and other devices.

One final explanation remains to be considered. May the intellectual self-confidence of the majority be attributed in part to women's readiness to play down their intellectual abilities? That such behavior occurs is attested by a number of studies.

When respondents were asked to comment upon a projective story about a girl "playing dumb" on dates, the great majority expressed indignation at such "dishonest," "condescending" behavior. But some three or four found the behavior praiseworthy. As one senior put it, "Her intentions were good; she wanted to make the guy feel important."

Although we did not interview the female friends of our respondents, a few studies indicate that such playing down of intellectual ability by women is less common today than in the 1940s. Questionnaires filled out in 1970 and 1971 by eighty-seven members of two undergraduate classes in sociology at an eastern women's college duplicated earlier studies by Wallin and Komarovsky. The 1970 class was a course on the family, and the 1971 class probably recruited a relatively high proportion of feminists. Table 1 indicates that the occasional muting of intellectual competence by women may have played some role in the adjustment of the men, but it would appear to be a minor and decreasing role.

The hypothesis that the emerging ideal of intellectual companionship serves as a buffer against male strain needs a test which includes (as our study did not) some index of intellectual ability as well as indices of norms and of strain. Of the twenty-seven men who disagreed with the proposition that the reasoning ability of men is greater than that of women, only five reported intellectual insecurity with women, whereas of the thirty-four men who believed in masculine superiority or were uncertain, nine experienced strain. Most troubled were the twelve men who were "uncertain"; four of them were insecure with women. Case analyses suggests that the interplay between a man's experience, personality, and beliefs is complex. For example, one traditional man, having confessed feelings of intellectual insecurity on dates, clung all the more tenaciously to the belief in superior male reasoning ability.

Some men took the "liberal" position on sex differences as a matter of principle. Of the nine black students, eight rejected the belief in male superiority, perhaps because they opposed group comparisons in intelligence. Again,

Table 1/Readiness of Women to Play Down Intellectual Abilities (%)

	Wallin 1950 (N = 163)	Sociology class 1970 * (N = 33)	Advanced sociology class 1971 * (N = 55)
When on dates how often have you pretended to be intellectually inferior to the man?			
Very often, often, or several times. . . .	32	21	15
Once or twice.	26	36	30
Never	42	43	55
In general, do you have any hesitation about revealing your equality or superiority to men in intellectual competence?			
Have considerable or some hesitation.	35	21	13
Very little hesitation.	39	33	32
None at all.	26	46	55

* Mirra Komarovsky, unpublished study.

in some cases, the direction of the causal relation was the reverse of the one we posited: men who felt in fact intellectually superior were hospitable to the "liberal" ideology. In view of these complexities, our suggestive results as to the positive association between egalitarian norms and the absence of strain remain to be tested in larger samples.

Attitudes Toward Future Wives' Occupational Roles

The ethos on the campus of this study clearly demanded that men pay at least lip service to liberal attitudes toward working wives. If the initial responses to structured questions were accepted as final, the majority would have been described as quite feminist in ideology. But further probing revealed qualifications which occasionally almost negated the original response. For example, an affirmative answer to a proposition, "It is appropriate for a mother of a preschool child to take a full-time job," was, upon further questioning, conditioned by such restrictions as "provided, of course, that the home was run smoothly, the children did not suffer, and the wife's job did not interfere with her husband's career." The interview provided an opportunity to get an assessment of normative expectations, ideal and operative, as well as of actual preferences. The classification of attitudes to be presented in this report is based on the total interview. Preferences reported here assume that a wife's paycheck will not be an economic necessity. The overwhelming majority were confident that their own earnings would be adequate to support the family. Throughout the discussion of working, only two or three men mentioned the temptation of a second paycheck.

Four types of response to the question of wives' working may be identified. The "traditionalists," 24 per cent of the men, said outright that they intended to marry women who would find sufficient fulfillment in domestic, civic, and cultural pursuits without ever seeking outside jobs. "Pseudofeminists," 16 per cent of the men, favored having their wives work, at least when the question was at a high level of abstraction, but their approval was hedged with qualifications that no woman could meet.

The third and dominant response included almost half (48 per cent) of the respondents. These men took a "modified traditionalist" position which favored a sequential pattern: work, withdrawal from work for child rearing, and eventual return to work. They varied as to the timing of these stages and as to the aid they were prepared to give their wives with domestic and child-rearing functions. The majority saw no substitute for the mother during her child's preschool years. Even the mother of school-age children, were she to work, should preferably be at home when the children return from school. Though they were willing to aid their wives in varying degrees, they frequently excluded specific tasks, for instance, "not the laundry," "not the cleaning," "not the diapers," and so on. Many hoped that they would be "able to assist" their wives by hiring maids. The greater the importance of the wife's work, the more willing they were to help her. (One senior, however, would help only if his wife's work were "peripheral," that is, not as important to her as her home.)

The last, the "feminist" type, was the smallest, only 7 per cent of the total. These men were willing to modify their own roles significantly to facilitate their future wives' careers. Some recommended a symmetrical allocation of tasks—"as long as it is not a complete reversal of roles." In the remaining 5 per cent of the cases, marriage was so remote that the respondents were reluctant to venture any views on this matter.

The foregoing summary of types of male attitude toward working wives fails to reveal the tangled web of contradictory values and sentiments associated with these attitudes. We shall presently illustrate a variety of inconsistencies. But underlying them is one basic problem. The ideological support for the belief in sharp sex role differentiation in marriage has weakened, but the belief itself has not been relinquished. Increasing skepticism about the innate character of psychological sex differences and some convergence in the ideas of masculinity and femininity have created a strain toward consistency. The more similar the perceptions of male and female personalities, the more universalistic must be the principles of evaluation applied to both sexes. "If you could make three changes in the personality of the girl friend who is currently closest to you, what would they be?" we asked the seniors. Universalistic values were reflected in the following, as in many other responses: "I would like her to be able to set a goal for herself and strive to achieve it. I don't like to see people slacking off." Earlier cross-sex association in childhood and early adolescence has raised male expectation of enjoying an emotional and intellectual companionship with women. These expectations, however, coexist with the deeply rooted norm that the husband should be the superior achiever in the occupational world and the wife, the primary child rearer. One manifestation of this basic dilemma is the familiar conflict between a value and a preference. "It is only fair," declared one senior, "to let a woman do her own thing, if she wants a career. Personally, though, I would want my wife at home."

More interesting are the ambivalent attitudes manifested toward both the full-time homemaker and the career wife. The image of each contained both attractive and repellent traits. Deprecating remarks about housewifery were not uncommon, even among men with traditional views of women's roles. A conservative senior declared, "A woman who works is more interesting than a housewife." "If I were a woman," remarked another senior, "I would want a career. It must be boring sitting around the house doing the same thing day in, day out. I don't have much respect for the type of woman whom I see doing the detergent commercials on TV."

But the low esteem attached by some of the men to full-time homemaking coexisted with other sentiments and convictions which required just such a pattern for one's wife. For example, asked about the disadvantages of being a woman, one senior replied, "Life ends at forty. The woman has raised her children and all that remains is garden clubs and that sort of thing—unless, of course, she has a profession." In another part of the interview, this young man explained that he enjoyed shyness in a girl and detested aggressive and ambitious women. He could never be attracted to a career woman. It is no exaggeration to conclude that this man could not countenance in a woman who was to be his wife the qualities that he himself felt were necessary for a fulfilling middle age.

A similar mode of contradiction, incidently, was also disclosed by some seniors with regard to women's majors in college. "There are no 'unfeminine' majors," declared one senior. "I admire a girl who is premed or prelaw." But the universalistic yardstick which led this senior to sanction and admire professional goals for women did not extend to the means for their attainment, as he unwittingly revealed in another part of the interview. Questioned about examples of "unfeminine" behavior, this senior answered, "Excessive grade consciousness." If a premed man, anxious about admission to a good medical school, should go to see a professor about a C in chemistry, this senior would understand although he would disapprove of such preoccupation with grades. But in a woman premed he would find such behavior "positively obnoxious."

If the image of the full-time homemaker contained some alienating features, the main threat of a career wife was that of occupational rivalry, as illustrated in the following excerpt from the interviews. A senior speaks:

> I believe that it is good for mothers to return to full-time work when the children are grown, provided the work is important and worthwhile. Otherwise, housewives get hung up with tranquilizers, because they have no outlet for their abilities. . . . Of course, it may be difficult if a wife becomes successful in her own right. A woman should want her husband's success more than he should want hers. Her work shouldn't interfere with or hurt his career in any way. He should not sacrifice his career to hers. For example, if he is transferred, his wife should follow—and not vice versa.

In sum, work for married women with grown children is approved by this young man, provided that the occupation is of some importance. But such an occupation is precisely one which carries a threat to the husband's pride.

The expectation that the husband should be the superior achiever appears still to be deeply rooted. Even equality in achievement of husband and wife is interpreted as a defeat for the man. The prospect of occupational rivalry with one's wife seems intolerable to contemplate. "My girl friend often beats me in tennis," explained one senior. "Now, losing the game doesn't worry me. It in no way reduces my manhood. But being in a lower position than a woman in a job would hurt my self-esteem."

Another student, having declared his full support for equal opportunities for women in the occupational world, added a qualification: "A woman should not be in a position of firing an employee. It is an unpleasant thing to do. Besides, it is unfair to the man who is to be fired. He may be a very poor employee, but he is still a human being and it may be just compounding his unhappiness to be fired by a woman."

In sum, the right of an able woman to a career of her choice, the admiration for women who measure up in terms of the dominant values of our society, the lure but also the threat that such women present, the low status attached to housewifery but the conviction that there is no substitute for the mother's care of young children, the deeply internalized norm of male occupational superiority pitted against the principle of equal opportunity irrespective of sex—these are some of the revealed inconsistencies.

Such ambivalences on the part of college men are bound to exacerbate role conflicts in women. The latter must sense that even the men who pay lip service to the creativity of child rearing and domesticity reserve their admiration (if occasionally tinged with ambivalence) for women achievers who measure up in terms of the dominant values of our society. It is becoming increasingly difficult to maintain a system of values for women only.

Nevertheless, to infer from this account of male inconsistencies that this is an area of great stress for them would be a mistake. It is not. By and large, the respondents assumed that the women's "career and marriage" issue was solved by the sequential pattern of withdrawal and return to work. If this doomed women to second-class citizenship in the occupational world, the outcome was consistent with the conviction that the husband should be the superior achiever.

Men who momentarily worried about the fate of able women found moral anchorage in their conviction that today no satisfactory alternative to the mother's care of young children can be found. Many respondents expressed their willingness to help with child care and household duties. Similarly, many hoped to spend more time with their own children than their fathers had spent with them. But such domestic participation was defined as assistance to the wife who was to carry the major responsibility. Only two or three of the men approved a symmetrical, rather than a complementary, allocation of domestic and occupational roles. An articulate senior sums up the dominant view:

> I would not want to marry a woman whose only goal is to become a house-wife. This type of woman would not have enough bounce and zest in her. I don't think a girl has much imagination if she just wants to settle down and raise a family from the very beginning. Moreover, I want an independent girl, one who has her own interests and does not always have to depend on me for stimulation and diversion. However, when we both agree to have children, my wife must be the one to raise them. She'll have to forfeit her freedom for the children. I believe that, when a woman wants a child, she must also accept the full responsibility of child care.

When he was asked why it was necessarily the woman who had to be fully responsible for the children, he replied:

Biology makes equality impossible. Besides, the person I'll marry will want the child and will want to care for the child. Ideally, I would hope I'm not forcing her to assume responsibility for raising the children. I would hope that this is her desire and that it is the happiest thing she can do. After we have children, it will be her career that will end, while mine will support us. I believe that women should have equal opportunities in business and the professions, but I still insist that a woman who is a mother should devote herself entirely to her children.

The low emotional salience of the issue of working wives may also be attributed to another factor. The female partners of our respondents, at this particular stage of life, did not, with a few exceptions, force the men to confront their inconsistencies. Apparently enough women will freely make the traditional-for-women adjustments—whether scaling down their own ambitions or in other ways acknowledging the prior claims of the man's career. This judgment is supported by the results of two studies of female undergraduates done on the same campus in 1943 and 1971 (Table 2). The big shift in postcollege preferences since 1943 was in the decline of women undergraduates who opted for full-time homemaking and volunteer activities. In 1971, the majority chose the sequential pattern, involving withdrawal from employment for child rearing. The proportion of committed career women who hope to return to work soon after childbirth has remained constant among freshmen and sophomores.

Table 2/College Women's Attitudes Toward Work and Family Patterns (%)

	Random sample of sophomore class at women's liberal arts college 1943 ($N = 78$)	Class in introductory sociology. Same college 1971 ($N = 44$)
Assume that you will marry and that your husband will make enough money so that you will not have to work unless you want to. Under these circumstances, would you prefer:		
1. Not to work at all, or stop after childbirth and decide later whether to go back.	50	18
2. To quit working after the birth of a child but definitely go back to work.	30	62
3. To continue working with a minimum of interruption for childbearing.	20	20

Source.—Mirra Komarovsky, unpublished studies.

If women's attitudes have not changed more radically in the past thirty years, it is no doubt because society has failed to provide effective supports for the woman who wishes to integrate family life, parenthood, and work on much the same terms as men. Such an option will not become available as long as the care of young children is regarded as the responsibility solely of the mother. In the absence of adequate child-care centers, an acceptance of a symmetrical division of domestic and work responsibilities, or other facilitating social arrangements, the attitudes of the majority of undergraduates reflect their decision to make some kind of workable adjustment to the status quo, if not a heroic struggle to change it.

Summary

Role conflicts in women have been amply documented in numerous studies. The problem underlying this study was to ascertain whether recent social changes and consequent malintegration with regard to sex roles have created stressful repercussions for men as well as for women. In a randomly selected sample of sixty-two male seniors in an eastern Ivy League college, nearly one-third experienced some anxiety over their perceived failure to live up to the norm of masculine intellectual superiority. This stressful minority suffered from two modes of role strain: scarcity of resources for role performance and ambivalence. The absence of strain in the majority may be explained by a changed role definition. Specifically, the normative expectation of male intellectual superiority appears to be giving way on the campus of our study to the ideal of intellectual companionship between equals. Attitudes toward working wives abounded in ambivalences and inconsistencies. The ideological supports for the traditional sex role differentiation in marriage are weakening, but the emotional allegiance to the modified traditional pattern is still strong. These inconsistencies did not generate a high degree of stress, partly, no doubt, because future roles do not require an immediate realistic confrontation. In addition, there is no gainsaying the conclusion that human beings can tolerate a high degree of inconsistency as long as it does not conflict with their self-interest.

Discussion Questions

1. Review the traditional role definition of male-female intellectual capacity and male-female working patterns.
2. Does this article indicate that those traditional roles are changing? Do you believe this kind of change is positive or negative for U.S. society? Discuss.

SUSAN SONTAG

The Double Standard of Aging

This article discusses the different types of male-female anxiety regarding aging. The anxiety is related to feelings of achievement, sex, power, social class, and appearance. The author concentrates primarily upon the double standard as related to women and indicates they "have another option." Ms. Sontag's deceptively simple conclusion illustrates the complexity of role and status. The author says that in terms of the double standard of aging, "Women should tell the truth."

"How old are you?" The person asking the question is anybody. The respondent is a woman, a woman "of a certain age," as the French say discreetly. That age might be anywhere from her early twenties to her late fifties. If the question is impersonal—routine information requested when she applies for a driver's license, a credit card, a passport—she will probably force herself to answer truthfully. Filling out a marriage license application, if her future husband is even slightly her junior, she may long to subtract a few years; probably she won't. Competing for a job, her chances often partly depend on being the "right age," and if hers isn't right, she will lie if she thinks she can get away with it. Making her first visit to a new doctor, perhaps feeling particularly vulnerable at the moment she's asked, she will probably hurry through the correct answer. But if the question is only what people call personal—if she's asked by a new friend, a casual acquaintance, a neighbor's child, a co-worker in an office, store, factory—her response is harder to predict. She may side-step the question with a joke or refuse it with playful indignation. "Don't you know you're not supposed to ask a woman her age?" Or, hesitating a moment, embarrassed but defiant, she may tell the truth. Or she may lie. But neither truth, evasion, nor lie relieves the unpleasantness of that question. For a woman to be obliged to state her age, after "a certain age," is always a miniature ordeal.

If the question comes from a woman, she will feel less threatened than if it comes from a man. Other women are, after all, comrades in sharing the same potential for humiliation. She will be less arch, less coy. But she probably still dislikes answering and may not tell the truth. Bureaucratic formalities excepted, whoever asks a woman this question—after "a certain age"—is ignoring a taboo and possibly being impolite or downright hostile. Almost everyone acknowledges that once she passes an age that is, actually, quite young, a woman's exact age ceases to be a legitimate target of curiosity. After childhood the year of a woman's birth becomes her secret, her private property. It is something of a dirty secret. To answer truthfully is always indiscreet.

The discomfort a woman feels each time she tells her age is quite independent of the anxious awareness of human mortality that everyone has, from time to time. There is a normal sense in which nobody, men and women alike, relishes growing older. After thirty-five any mention of one's age carries with it the reminder that one is probably closer to the end of one's life than to the beginning. There is nothing unreasonable in that anxiety. Nor is there any abnormality in the anguish and anger that people who are really old, in their seventies and eighties, feel about the implacable waning of their powers, physical and mental. Advanced age is undeniably a trial, however stoically it may be endured. It is a shipwreck, no matter with what courage elderly people insist on continuing the voyage. But the objective, sacred pain of old age is of another order than the subjective, profane pain of aging. Old age is a genuine ordeal, one that men and women undergo in a similar way. Growing older is mainly an ordeal of the imagination—a moral disease, a social pathology—intrinsic to which is the fact that it afflicts women much more than men. It is particularly women who experience growing older (everything that comes *before* one is actually old) with such distaste and even shame.

The emotional privileges this society confers upon youth stir up some anxiety about getting older in everybody. All modern urbanized societies—unlike tribal, rural societies—condescend to the values of maturity and heap honors on the joys of youth. This revaluation of the life cycle in favor of the young brilliantly serves a secular society whose idols are ever-increasing industrial productivity and the unlimited cannibalization of nature. Such a society must create a new sense of the rhythms of life in order to incite people to buy more, to consume and throw away faster. People let the direct awareness they have of their needs, of what really gives them pleasure, be overruled by commercialized *images* of happiness and personal well-being; and, in this imagery designed to stimulate ever more avid levels of consumption, the most popular metaphor for happiness is "youth." (I would insist that it is a metaphor, not a literal description. Youth is a metaphor for energy, restless mobility, appetite: for the state of "wanting.") This equating of well-being with youth makes everyone naggingly aware of exact age—one's own and that of other people. In primitive and premodern societies people attach much less importance to dates. When lives are divided into long periods with stable responsibilities and steady ideals (and hypocrisies), the exact number of years someone has lived becomes a trivial fact; there is hardly any reason to mention, even to know, the year in which one was born. Most people in non-industrial societies are not sure exactly how old they are. People in industrial societies are haunted by numbers. They take an almost obsessional interest in keeping the score card of aging, convinced that anything above a low total is some kind of bad news. In an era in which people actually live longer and longer, what now amounts to the latter *two-thirds* of everyone's life is shadowed by a poignant apprehension of unremitting loss.

The prestige of youth afflicts everyone in this society to some degree. Men, too, are prone to periodic bouts of depression about aging—for instance, when feeling insecure or unfulfilled or insufficiently rewarded in their jobs. But men rarely panic about aging in the way women often do. Getting older is less profoundly wounding for a man, for in addition to the propaganda for youth that puts both men and women on the defensive as they age, there is a double standard about aging that denounces women with special severity. Society is much more permissive about aging in men, as it is more tolerant of the sexual infidelities of husbands. Men are "allowed" to age, without penalty, in several ways that women are not.

This society offers even fewer rewards for aging to women than it does to men. Being physically attractive counts much more in a woman's life than in a man's, but beauty, identified, as it is for women, with youthfulness, does not stand up well to age. Exceptional mental powers can increase with age, but women are rarely encouraged to develop their minds above dilettante standards. Because the wisdom considered the special province of women is "eternal," an age-old, intuitive knowledge about the emotions to which a repertoire of facts, worldly experience, and the methods of rational analysis have nothing to contribute, living a long time does not promise women an increase in wisdom either. The private skills expected of women are exercised early and, with the exception of a talent for making love, are not the kind that enlarge with experience. "Masculinity" is identified with competence, autonomy, self-control—qualities which the disappearance of youth does not threaten. Competence in most of the activities expected from men, physical sports excepted, increases with age. "Femininity" is identified with incompetence, helplessness, passivity, noncompetitiveness, being nice. Age does not improve these qualities.

Middle-class men feel diminished by aging, even while still young, if they have not yet shown distinction in their careers or made a lot of money. (And any tendencies they have toward hypochrondria will get worse in middle age, focusing with particular nervousness on the specter of heart attacks and the loss of virility.) Their aging crisis is linked to that terrible pressure on men to be "successful" that precisely defines their membership in the middle class. Women rarely feel anxious about their age because they haven't succeeded at something. The work that women do outside the home rarely counts as a form of achievement, only as a way of earning money; most employment available to women mainly exploits the training they have been receiving since early childhood to be servile, to be both supportive and parasitical, to be unadventurous. They can have menial, low-skilled jobs in light industries, which offer as feeble a criterion of success as housekeeping. They can be secretaries, clerks, sales personnel, maids, research assistants, waitresses, social workers, prostitutes, nurses, teachers, telephone operators—public transcriptions of the servicing and nurturing roles that women have in family life. Women fill very few executive posts, are rarely found suitable for large corporate or political responsibilities, and form only a tiny contingent in the liberal professions (apart from teaching). They are virtually barred from jobs that involve an expert, intimate relation with machines or an aggressive use of the body, or that carry any physical risk or sense of adventure. The jobs this society deems appropriate to women are auxiliary, "calm" activities that do not compete with, but aid, what men do. Besides being less well paid, most work women do has a lower ceiling of advancement and gives meager outlet to normal wishes to be powerful. All outstanding work by women in this society is voluntary; most women are too inhibited by the social disapproval attached to their being ambitious and aggressive. Inevitably, women are exempted from the dreary panic of middle-aged men whose "achievements" seem paltry, who feel stuck on the job ladder or fear being pushed off it by someone younger. But they are also denied most of the real satisfactions that men derive from work—satisfactions that often do increase with age.

The double standard about aging shows up most brutally in the conventions of sexual feeling, which presuppose a disparity between men and women that operates permanently to women's disadvantage. In the accepted course of events a woman anywhere from her late teens through her middle twenties can expect to attract a man more or less her own age. (Ideally, he should be at least slightly older.) They marry and raise a family. But if her husband starts an affair after some years of marriage, he customarily does so with a woman much younger than his wife. Suppose, when both husband and wife are already in their late forties or early fifties, they divorce. The husband has an excellent chance of getting married again, probably to a younger woman. His ex-wife finds it difficult to remarry. Attracting a second husband younger than herself is improbable; even to find someone her own age she has to be lucky, and she will probably have to settle for a man considerably older than herself, in his sixties or seventies. Women become sexually ineligible much earlier than men do. A man, even an ugly man, can remain eligible well into old age. He is an acceptable mate for a young, attractive woman. Women, even good-looking women, become ineligible (except as partners of very old men) at a much younger age.

Thus, for most women, aging means a humiliating process of gradual sexual disqualification. Since women are considered maximally eligible in early youth, after which their sexual value drops steadily, even young women feel themselves in a desperate race against the calendar. They are old as soon as they are no longer very young. In late adolescence some girls are already worrying about getting married. Boys and young men have little reason to anticipate trouble because of aging. What makes men desirable to women is by no means tied to youth. On the contrary, getting older tends (for several decades) to operate in men's favor, since their value as lovers and husbands is set more by what they do than how they look. Many men have more success romantically at forty than they did at twenty or twenty-five; fame, money, and, above all, power are sexually enhancing. (A woman who has won power in a competitive profession or business career is considered less, rather than more, desirable. Most men confess themselves intimidated or turned off sexually by such a woman, obviously because she is harder to treat as just a sexual "object.") As they age, men may start feeling anxious about actual sexual performance, worrying about a loss of sexual vigor or even impotence, but their sexual eligibility is not abridged simply by getting older. Men stay sexually possible as long as they can make love. Women are at a disadvantage because their sexual candidacy depends on meeting certain much stricter "conditions" related to looks and age.

Since women are imagined to have much more limited sexual lives than men do, a woman who has never married is pitied. She was not found acceptable, and it is assumed that her life continues to confirm her unacceptability. Her presumed lack of sexual opportunity is embarrassing. A man who remains a bachelor is judged much less crudely. It is assumed that he, at any age, still has a sexual life—or the chance of one. For men there is no destiny equivalent to the humiliating condition of being an old maid, a spinster. "Mr.," a cover from infancy to senility, precisely exempts men from the stigma that attaches to any woman, no longer young, who is still "Miss." (That women are divided into "Miss" and "Mrs.," which calls unrelenting attention to the situation of each woman with respect to marriage, reflects the belief that being single or married is much more decisive for a woman than it is for a man.)

For a woman who is no longer very young, there is certainly some relief when she has finally been able to marry. Marriage soothes the sharpest pain she feels about the passing years. But her anxiety never subsides completely, for she knows that should she re-enter the sexual market at a later date— because of divorce, or the death of her husband, or the need for erotic adventure—she must do so under a handicap far greater than any man of her age (*whatever* her age may be) and regardless of how good-looking she is. Her achievements, if she has a career, are no asset. The calendar is the final arbiter.

To be sure, the calendar is subject to some variations from country to country. In Spain, Portugal, and the Latin American countries, the age at which most women are ruled physically undesirable comes earlier than in the United States. In France it is somewhat later. French conventions of sexual feeling make a quasi-official place for the woman between thirty-five and forty-five. Her role is to initiate an inexperienced or timid young man, after which she is, of course, replaced by a young girl. (Colette's novella *Chéri* is the best-known account in fiction of such a love affair; biographies of Balzac relate a well-documented example from real life.) This sexual myth does make turning forty somewhat easier for French women. But there is no difference in any of these countries in the basic attitudes that disqualify women sexually much earlier than men.

Aging also varies according to social class. Poor people look old much earlier in their lives than do rich people. But anxiety about aging is certainly more common, and more acute, among middle-class and rich women than among working-class women. Economically disadvantaged women in this society are more fatalistic about aging; they can't afford to fight the cosmetic battle as long or as tenaciously. Indeed, nothing so clearly indicates the fictional nature of this crisis than the fact that women who keep their youthful appearance the longest—women who lead unstrenuous, physically sheltered lives, who eat balanced meals, who can afford good medical care, who have few or no children—are those who feel the defeat of age most keenly. Aging is much more a social judgment than a biological eventuality. Far more extensive than the hard sense of loss suffered during menopause (which, with increased longevity, tends to arrive later and later) is the depression about aging, which may not be set off by any real event in a woman's life, but is a recurrent state of "possession" of her imagination, ordained by society—that is, ordained by the way this society limits how women feel free to imagine themselves.

There is a model account of the aging crisis in Richard Strauss's senti-mental-ironic opera *Der Rosenkavalier,* whose heroine is a wealthy and glamorous married woman who decides to renounce romance. After a night with her adoring young lover, the Marschallin has a sudden, unexpected confrontation with herself. It is toward the end of Act I; Octavian has just left. Alone in her bedroom she sits at her dressing table, as she does every morning. It is the daily ritual of self-appraisal practiced by every woman. She looks at herself and, appalled, begins to weep. Her youth is over. Note that the Marschallin does not discover, looking in the mirror, that she is ugly. She is as beautiful as ever. The Marschallin's discovery is moral—that is, it is a discovery of her imagination; it is nothing she actually *sees.* Nevertheless, her discovery is no less devastating. Bravely, she makes her painful, gallant de-cision. She will arrange for her beloved Octavian to fall in love with a girl his own age. She must be realistic. She is no longer eligible. She is now "the old Marschallin."

Strauss wrote the opera in 1910. Contemporary operagoers are rather shocked when they discover that the libretto indicates that the Marschallin is all of thirty-four years old; today the role is generally sung by a soprano well into her forties or in her fifties. Acted by an attractive singer of thirty-four, the Marschallin's sorrow would seem merely neurotic, or even ridiculous. Few women today think of themselves as old, wholly disqualified from romance, at thirty-four. The age of retirement has moved up, in line with the sharp rise in life expectancy for everybody in the last few generations. The *form* in which women experience their lives remains unchanged. A moment ap-proaches inexorably when they must resign themselves to being "too old." And that moment is invariably—objectively—premature.

In earlier generations the renunciation came even sooner. Fifty years ago a woman of forty was not just aging but old, finished. No struggle was even possible. Today, the surrender to aging no longer has a fixed date. The aging crisis (I am speaking only of women in affluent countries) starts earlier but lasts longer; it is diffused over most of a woman's life. A woman hardly has to be anything like what would reasonably be considered old to worry about her age, to start lying (or being tempted to lie). The crises can come at any time. Their schedule depends on a blend of personal ("neurotic") vulnerability and the swing of social mores. Some women don't have their first crisis until thirty. No one escapes a sickening shock upon turning forty. Each birthday, but especially those ushering in a new decade—for round numbers have a special authority—sounds a new defeat. There is almost as much pain in the anticipation as in the reality. Twenty-nine has become a queasy age ever since the official end of youth crept forward, about a generation ago, to thirty. Being thirty-nine is also hard; a whole year in which to meditate in glum astonishment that one stands on the threshhold of middle age. The frontiers are arbitrary, but not any less vivid for that. Although a woman on her fortieth birthday is hardly different from what she was when she was still thirty-nine, the day seems like a turning point. But long before actually becoming a woman of forty, she has been steeling herself against the depression she will feel. One of the greatest tragedies of each woman's life is simply getting older; it is certainly the *longest* tragedy.

Aging is a movable doom. It is a crisis that never exhausts itself, because the anxiety is never really used up. Being a crisis of the imagination rather than of "real life," it has the habit of repeating itself again and again. The territory of aging (as opposed to actual old age) has no fixed boundaries. Up to a point it can be defined as one wants. Entering each decade—after the initial shock is absorbed—an endearing, desperate impulse of survival helps many women to stretch the boundaries to the decade following. In late adolescence thirty seems the end of life. At thirty, one pushes the sentence forward to forty. At forty, one still gives oneself ten more years.

I remember my closest friend in college sobbing on the day she turned twenty-one. "The best part of my life is over. I'm not young any more." She was a senior, nearing graduation. I was a precocious freshman, just sixteen. Mystified, I tried lamely to comfort her, saying that I didn't think twenty-one was *so* old. Actually, I didn't understand at all what could be demoralizing about turning twenty-one. To me, it meant only something good: being in charge of oneself, being free. At sixteen, I was too young to have noticed, and become confused by, the peculiarly loose, ambivalent way in which this society demands that one stop thinking of oneself as a girl and start thinking of oneself as a woman. (In America that demand can now be put off to the age of thirty, even beyond.) But even if I thought her distress was absurd, I must have been aware that it would not simply be absurd but quite unthinkable in a *boy* turning twenty-one. Only women worry about age with that degree of inanity and pathos. And, of course, as with all crises that are inauthentic and therefore repeat themselves compulsively (because the danger is largely fictive, a poison in the imagination), this friend of mine went on having the same crisis over and over, each time as if for the first time.

I also came to her thirtieth birthday party. A veteran of many love affairs, she had spent most of her twenties living abroad and had just returned to the United States. She had been good-looking when I first knew her; now she was beautiful. I teased her about the tears she had shed over being twenty-one. She laughed and claimed not to remember. But thirty, she said ruefully, that really is the end. Soon after, she married. My friend is now forty-four. While no longer what people call beautiful, she is striking-looking, charming, and vital. She teaches elementary school; her husband, who is twenty years older than she, is a part-time merchant seaman. They have one child, now nine years old. Sometimes, when her husband is away, she takes a lover. She told me recently that forty was the most upsetting birthday of all (I wasn't at that one), and although she has only a few years left, she means to enjoy them while they last. She has become one of those women who seize every excuse offered in any conversation for mentioning how old they really are, in a spirit of bravado compounded with self-pity that is not too different from the mood of women who regularly lie about their age. But she is actually fretting much less about aging than she was two decades ago. Having a child, and having one rather late, past the age of thirty, has certainly helped to reconcile her to her age. At fifty, I suspect, she will be ever more valiantly postponing the age of resignation.

My friend is one of the more fortunate, sturdier casualties of the aging crisis. Most women are not as spirited, nor as innocently comic in their suffering. But almost all women endure some version of this suffering: A recurrent seizure of the imagination that usually begins quite young, in which they project themselves into a calculation of loss. The rules of this society are cruel to women. Brought up to be never fully adult, women are deemed obsolete earlier than men. In fact, most women don't become relatively free and expressive sexually until their thirties. (Women mature sexually this late, certainly much later than men, not for innate biological reasons but because this culture retards women. Denied most outlets for sexual energy permitted to men, it takes many women *that* long to wear out some of their inhibitions.) The time at which they start being disqualified as sexually attractive persons is just when they have grown up sexually. The double standard about aging cheats women of those years, between thirty-five and fifty, likely to be the best of their sexual life.

That women expect to be flattered often by men, and the extent to which their self-confidence depends on this flattery, reflects how deeply women are psychologically weakened by this double standard. Added on to the pressure felt by everybody in this society to look young as long as possible are the values of "femininity," which specifically identify sexual attractiveness in women with youth. The desire to be the "right age" has a special urgency for a woman it never has for a man. A much greater part of her self-esteem and pleasure in life is threatened when she ceases to be young. Most men experience getting older with regret, apprehension. But most women experience it even more painfully: with shame. Aging is a man's destiny, something that must happen because he is a human being. For a woman, aging is not only her destiny. Because she is that more *narrowly* defined kind of human being, a woman, it is also her vulnerability.

To be a woman is to be an actress. Being feminine is a kind of theater, with its appropriate costumes, *décor,* lighting, and stylized gestures. From early childhood on, girls are trained to care in a pathologically exaggerated way about their appearance and are profoundly mutilated (to the extent of being unfitted for first-class adulthood) by the extent of the stress put on presenting themselves as physically attractive objects. Women look in the mirror more frequently than men do. It is, virtually, their duty to look at themselves—to look often. Indeed, a woman who is not narcissistic is considered unfeminine. And a woman who spends literally *most* of her time caring for, and making purchases to flatter, her physical appearance is not regarded in this society as what she is: a kind of moral idiot. She is thought to be quite normal and is envied by other women whose time is mostly used up at jobs or caring for large families. The display of narcissism goes on all the time. It is expected that women will disappear several times in an evening—at a restaurant, at a party, during a theater intermission, in the course of a social visit—simply to check their appearance, to see that nothing has gone wrong with their make-up and hairstyling, to make sure that their clothes are not spotted or too wrinkled or not hanging properly. It is even acceptable to perform this activity in public. At the table in a restaurant, over coffee, a woman opens a compact mirror and touches up her make-up and hair without embarrassment in front of her husband or her friends.

All this behavior, which is written off as normal "vanity" in women, would seem ludicrous in a man. Women are more vain than men because of the relentless pressure on women to maintain their appearance at a certain high standard. What makes the pressure even more burdensome is that there are actually several standards. Men present themselves as face-and-body, a physical whole. Women are split, as men are not, into a body and a face—each judged by somewhat different standards. What is important for a face is that it be beautiful. What is important for a body is two things, which may even be (depending on fashion and taste) somewhat incompatible: first, that it be desirable and, second, that it be beautiful. Men usually feel sexually attracted to women much more because of their bodies than their faces. The traits that arouse desire—such as fleshiness—don't always match those that fashion decrees as beautiful. (For instance, the ideal woman's body promoted in advertising in recent years is extremely thin: the kind of body that looks more desirable clothed than naked.) But women's concern with their appearance is not simply geared to arousing desire in men. It also aims at fabricating a certain image by which, as a more indirect way of arousing desire, women state their value. A woman's value lies in the way she *represents* herself, which is much more by her face than her body. In defiance of the laws of simple sexual attraction, women do not devote most of their attention to their bodies. The well-known "normal" narcissism that women display—the amount of time they spend before the mirror—is used primarily in caring for the face and hair.

Women do not simply have faces, as men do; they are identified with their faces. Men have a naturalistic relation to their faces. Certainly they care whether they are good-looking or not. They suffer over acne, protruding ears, tiny eyes; they hate getting bald. But there is a much wider latitude in what is esthetically acceptable in a man's face than what is in a woman's. A man's face is defined as something he basically doesn't need to tamper with; all he has to do is keep it clean. He can avail himself of the options for ornament supplied by nature: a beard, a mustache, longer or shorter hair. But he is not supposed to disguise himself. What he is "really" like is supposed to show. A man lives through his face; it records the progressive stages of his life. And since he doesn't tamper with his face, it is not separate from but is completed by his body—which is judged attractive by the impression it gives of virility and energy. By contrast, a woman's face is potentially separate from her body. She does not treat it naturalistically. A woman's face is the canvas upon which she paints a revised, corrected portrait of herself. One of the rules of this creation is that the face *not* show what she doesn't want it to show. Her face is an emblem, an icon, a flag. How she arranges her hair, the type of make-up she uses, the quality of her complexion—all these are signs, not of what she is "really" like, but of how she asks to be treated by others, especially men. They establish her status as an "object."

For the normal changes that age inscribes on every human face, women are much more heavily penalized than men. Even in early adolescence, girls are cautioned to protect their faces against wear and tear. Mothers tell their daughters (but never their sons): You look ugly when you cry. Stop worrying. Don't read too much. Crying, frowning, squinting, even laughing—all these human activities make "lines." The same usage of the face in men is judged quite positively. In a man's face lines are taken to be signs of "character." They indicate emotional strength, maturity—qualities far more esteemed in men than in women. (They show he has "lived.") Even scars are often not felt to be unattractive; they too can add "character" to a man's face. But lines of aging, any scar, even a small birthmark on a woman's face, are always regarded as unfortunate blemishes. In effect, people take character in men to be different from what constitutes character in women. A woman's character is thought to be innate, static—not the product of her experience, her years, her actions. A woman's face is prized so far as it remains unchanged by (or conceals the traces of) her emotions, her physical risk-taking. Ideally, it is supposed to be a mask—immutable, unmarked. The model woman's face is Garbo's. Because women are identified with their faces much more than men are, and the ideal woman's face is one that is "perfect," it seems a calamity when a woman has a disfiguring accident. A broken nose or a scar or a burn mark, no more than regrettable for a man, is a terrible psychological wound to a woman; objectively, it diminishes her value. (As is well known, most clients for plastic surgery are women.)

Both sexes aspire to a physical ideal, but what is expected of boys and what is expected of girls involves a very different moral relation to the self. Boys are encouraged to *develop* their bodies, to regard the body as an instrument to be improved. They invent their masculine selves largely through exercise and sport, which harden the body and strengthen competitive feelings; clothes are of only secondary help in making their bodies attractive. Girls are not particularly encouraged to develop their bodies through any activity, strenuous or not; and physical strength and endurance are hardly valued at all. The invention of the feminine self proceeds mainly through clothes and other signs that testify to the very effort of girls to look attractive, to their commitment to please. When boys become men, they may go on (especially if they have sedentary jobs) practicing a sport or doing exercises for a while. Mostly they leave their appearance alone, having been trained to accept more or less what nature has handed out to them. (Men may start doing exercises again in their forties to lose weight, but for reasons of health—there is an epidemic fear of heart attacks among the middle-aged in rich countries—not for cosmetic reasons.) As one of the norms of "femininity" in this society is being preoccupied with one's physical appearance, so "masculinity" means *not* caring very much about one's looks.

This society allows men to have a much more affirmative relation to their bodies than women have. Men are more "at home" in their bodies, whether they treat them casually or use them aggressively. A man's body is defined as a strong body. It contains no contradiction between what is felt to be attractive and what is practical. A woman's body, so far as it is considered attractive, is defined as a fragile, light body. (Thus, women worry more than men do about being overweight.) When they do exercises, women avoid the ones that develop the muscles, particularly those in the upper arms. Being "feminine" means looking physically weak, frail. Thus, the ideal woman's body is one that is not of much practical use in the hard work of this world, and one that must continually be "defended." Women do not develop their bodies, as men do. After a woman's body has reached its sexually acceptable form by late adolescence, most further development is viewed as negative. And it is thought irresponsible for women to do what is normal for men: simply leave their appearance alone. During early youth they are likely to come as close as they ever will to the ideal image—slim figure, smooth firm skin, light musculature, graceful movements. Their task is to try to maintain that image, unchanged, as long as possible. Improvement as such is not the task. Women care for their bodies—against toughening, coarsening, getting fat. They *conserve* them. (Perhaps the fact that women in modern societies tend to have a more conservative political outlook than men originates in their profoundly conservative relation to their bodies.)

In the life of women in this society the period of pride, of natural honesty, of unself-conscious flourishing is brief. Once past youth women are condemned to inventing (and maintaining) themselves against the inroads of age. Most of the physical qualities regarded as attractive in women deteriorate much earlier in life than those defined as "male." Indeed, they perish fairly soon in the normal sequence of body transformation. The "feminine" is smooth, rounded, hairless, unlined, soft, unmuscled—the look of the very young; characteristics of the weak, of the vulnerable; eunuch traits, as Germaine Greer has pointed out. Actually, there are only a few years—late adolescence, early twenties—in which this look is physiologically natural, in which it can be had without touching-up and covering-up. After that, women enlist in a quixotic enterprise, trying to close the gap between the imagery put forth by society (concerning what is attractive in a woman) and the evolving facts of nature.

Women have a more intimate relation to aging than men do, simply because one of the accepted "women's" occupations is taking pains to keep one's face and body from showing the signs of growing older. Women's sexual validity depends, up to a certain point, on how well they stand off these natural changes. After late adolescence women become the caretakers of their bodies and faces, pursuing an essentially defensive strategy, a holding operation. A vast array of products in jars and tubes, a branch of surgery, and armies of hairdressers, masseuses, diet counselors, and other professionals exist to stave off, or mask, developments that are entirely normal biologically. Large amounts of women's energies are diverted into this passionate, corrupting effort to defeat nature: to maintain an ideal, static appearance against the progress of age. The collapse of the project is only a matter of time. Inevitably, a woman's physical appearance develops beyond its youthful form. No matter how exotic the creams or how strict the diets, one cannot indefinitely keep the face unlined, the waist slim. Bearing children takes its toll: the torso becomes thicker; the skin is stretched. There is no way to keep certain lines from appearing, in one's mid-twenties, around the eyes and mouth. From about thirty on, the skin gradually loses its tonus. In women this perfectly natural process is regarded as a humiliating defeat, while nobody finds anything remarkably unattractive in the equivalent physical changes in men. Men are "allowed" to look older without sexual penalty.

Thus, the reason that women experience aging with more pain than men is not simply that they care more than men about how they look. Men also care about their looks and want to be attractive, but since the business of men is mainly being and doing, rather than appearing, the standards for appearance are much less exacting. The standards for what is attractive in a man are permissive; they conform to what is possible or "natural" to most men throughout most of their lives. The standards for women's appearance go against nature, and to come anywhere near approximating them takes considerable effort and time. Women must try to be beautiful. At the least, they are under heavy social pressure not to be ugly. A woman's fortunes depend, far more than a man's, on being at least "acceptable" looking. Men are not subject to this pressure. Good looks in a man is a bonus, not a psychological necessity for maintaining normal self-esteem.

Behind the fact that women are more severely penalized than men are for aging is the fact that people, in this culture at least, are simply less tolerant of ugliness in women than in men. An ugly woman is never merely repulsive. Ugliness in a woman is felt by everyone, men as well as women, to be faintly embarrassing. And many features or blemishes that count as ugly in a woman's face would be quite tolerable on the face of a man. This is not, I would insist, just because the esthetic standards for men and women are different. It is rather because the esthetic standards for women are much higher, and narrower, than those proposed for men.

Beauty, women's business in this society, is the theater of their enslavement. Only one standard of female beauty is sanctioned: the *girl*. The great advantage men have is that our culture allows two standards of male beauty: the *boy* and the *man*. The beauty of a boy resembles the beauty of a girl. In both sexes it is a fragile kind of beauty and flourishes naturally only in the early part of the life-cycle. Happily, men are able to accept themselves under another standard of good looks—heavier, rougher, more thickly built. A man does not grieve when he loses the smooth, unlined, hairless skin of a boy. For he has only exchanged one form of attractiveness for another: the darker skin of a man's face, roughened by daily shaving, showing the marks of emotion and the normal lines of age. There is no equivalent of this second standard for women. The single standard of beauty for women dictates that they must go on having clear skin. Every wrinkle, every line, every grey hair, is a defeat. No wonder that no boy minds becoming a man, while even the passage from girlhood to early womanhood is experienced by many women as their downfall, for all women are trained to want to continue looking like girls.

This is not to say there are no beautiful older women. But the standard of beauty in a woman of any age is how far she retains, or how she manages to simulate, the appearance of youth. The exceptional woman in her sixties who is beautiful certainly owes a large debt to her genes. Delayed aging, like good looks, tends to run in families. But nature rarely offers enough to meet this culture's standards. Most of the women who successfully delay the appearance of age are rich, with unlimited leisure to devote to nurturing along nature's gifts. Often they are actresses. (That is, highly paid professionals at doing what all women are taught to practice as amateurs.) Such women as Mae West, Dietrich, Stella Adler, Dolores Del Rio, do not challenge the rule about the relation between beauty and age in women. They are admired precisely because they *are* exceptions, because they have managed (at least so it seems in photographs) to outwit nature. Such miracles, exceptions made by nature (with the help of art and social privilege), only confirm the rule, because what makes these women seem beautiful to us is precisely that they do not look their real age. Society allows no place in our imagination for a beautiful old woman who does look like an old woman—a woman who might be like Picasso at the age of ninety, being photographed outdoors on his estate in the south of France, wearing only shorts and sandals. No one imagines such a woman exists. Even the special exceptions—Mae West & Co.—are always photographed indoors, cleverly lit, from the most flattering angle and fully, artfully clothed. The implication is they would not stand a closer scrutiny. The idea of an old woman in a bathing suit being attractive, or even just acceptable looking, is inconceivable. An older woman is, by definition, sexually repulsive—unless, in fact, she doesn't look old at all. The body of an old woman, unlike that of an old man, is always understood as a body that can no longer be shown, offered, unveiled. At best, it may appear in costume. People still feel uneasy, thinking about what they might see if her mask dropped, if she took off her clothes.

Thus, the point for women of dressing up, applying make-up, dyeing their hair, going on crash diets, and getting face-lifts is not just to be attractive. They are ways of defending themselves against a profound level of disapproval directed toward women, a disapproval that can take the form of aversion. The double standard about aging converts the life of women into an inexorable march toward a condition in which they are not just unattractive, but disgusting. The profoundest terror of a woman's life is the moment represented in a statue by Rodin called *Old Age:* a naked old woman, seated, pathetically contemplates her flat, pendulous, ruined body. Aging in women is a process of becoming obscene sexually, for the flabby bosom, wrinkled neck, spotted hands, thinning white hair, waistless torso, and veined legs of an old woman are felt to be obscene. In our direst moments of the imagination, this transformation can take place with dismaying speed—as in the end of *Lost Horizon,* when the beautiful young girl is carried by her lover out of Shangri-La and, within minutes, turns into a withered, repulsive crone. There is no equivalent nightmare about men. This is why, however much a man may care about his appearance, that caring can never acquire the same desperateness it often does for women. When men dress according to fashion or now even use cosmetics, they do not expect from clothes and make-up what women do. A face-lotion or perfume or deodorant or hairspray, used by a man, is not part of a disguise. Men, as men, do not feel the need to disguise themselves to fend off morally disapproved signs of aging, to outwit premature sexual obsolescence, to cover up aging as obscenity. Men are not subject to the barely concealed revulsion expressed in this culture against the female body—except in its smooth, youthful, firm, odorless, blemish-free form.

One of the attitudes that punish women most severely is the visceral horror felt at aging female flesh. It reveals a radical fear of women installed deep in this culture, a demonology of women that has crystallized in such mythic caricatures as the vixen, the virago, the vamp, and the witch. Several centuries of witch-phobia, during which one of the cruelest extermination programs in Western history was carried out, suggest something of the extremity of this fear. That old women are repulsive is one of the most profound esthetic and erotic feelings in our culture. Women share it as much as men do. (Oppressors, as a rule, deny oppressed people their own "native" standards of beauty. And the oppressed end up being convinced that they *are* ugly.) How women are psychologically damaged by this misogynistic idea of what is beautiful parallels the way in which blacks have been deformed in a society that has up to now defined beautiful as white. Psychological tests made on young black children in the United States some years ago showed how early and how thoroughly they incorporate the white standard of good looks. Virtually all the children expressed fantasies that indicated they considered black people to be ugly, funny looking, dirty, brutish. A similar kind of self-hatred infects most women. Like men, they find old age in women "uglier" than old age in men.

This esthetic taboo functions, in sexual attitudes, as a racial taboo. In this society most people feel an involuntary recoil of the flesh when imagining a middle-aged woman making love with a young man—exactly as many whites flinch viscerally at the thought of a white woman in bed with a black man. The banal drama of a man of fifty who leaves a wife of forty-five for a girl-friend of twenty-eight contains no strictly sexual outrage, whatever sympathy people may have for the abandoned wife. On the contrary. Everyone "understands." Everyone knows that men like girls, that young women often want middle-aged men. But no one "understands" the reverse situation. A woman of forty-five who leaves a husband of fifty for a lover of twenty-eight is the makings of a social and sexual scandal at a deep level of feeling. No one takes exception to a romantic couple in which the man is twenty years or more the woman's senior. The movies pair Joanne Dru and John Wayne, Marilyn Monroe and Joseph Cotton, Audrey Hepburn and Cary Grant, Jane Fonda and Yves Montand, Catherine Deneuve and Marcello Mastroianni; as in actual life, these are perfectly plausible, appealing couples. When the age difference runs the other way, people are puzzled and embarrassed and simply shocked. (Remember Joan Crawford and Cliff Robertson in *Autumn Leaves?* But so troubling is this kind of love story that it rarely figures in the movies, and then only as the melancholy history of a failure.) The usual view of why a woman of forty and a boy of twenty, or a woman of fifty and a man of thirty, marry is that the man is seeking a mother, not a wife; no one believes the marriage will last. For a woman to respond erotically and romantically to a man who, in terms of his age, could be her father is considered normal. A man who falls in love with a woman who, however attractive she may be, is old enough to be his mother is thought to be extremely neurotic (victim of an "Oedipal fixation" is the fashionable tag), if not mildly contemptible.

The wider the gap in age between partners in a couple, the more obvious is the prejudice against women. When old men, such as Justice Douglas, Picasso, Strom Thurmond, Onassis, Chaplin, and Pablo Casals, take brides thirty, forty, fifty years younger than themselves, it strikes people as remarkable, perhaps an exaggeration—but still plausible. To explain such a match, people enviously attribute some special virility and charm to the man. Though he can't be handsome, he is famous; and his fame is understood as having boosted his attractiveness to women. People imagine that his young wife, respectful of her elderly husband's attainments, is happy to become his helper. For the man a late marriage is always good public relations. It adds to the impression that, despite his advanced age, he is still to be reckoned with; it is the sign of a continuing vitality presumed to be available as well to his art, business activity, or political career. But an elderly woman who married a young man would be greeted quite differently. She would have broken a fierce taboo, and she would get no credit for her courage. Far from being admired for her vitality, she would probably be condemned as predatory, willful, selfish, exhibitionistic. At the same time she would be pitied, since such a marriage would be taken as evidence that she was in her dotage. If she had a conventional career or were in business or held public office, she would quickly suffer from the current of disapproval. Her very credibility as a professional would decline, since people would suspect that her young husband might have an undue influence on her. Her "respectability" would certainly be compromised. Indeed, the well-known old women I can think of who dared such unions, if only at the end of their lives—George Eliot, Colette, Edith Piaf—have all belonged to that category of people, creative artists and entertainers, who have special license from society to behave scandalously. It is thought to be a scandal for a woman to ignore that she is old and therefore too ugly for a young man. Her looks and a certain physical condition determine a woman's desirability, not her talents or her needs. Women are not supposed to be "potent." A marriage between an old woman and a young man subverts the very ground rule of relations between the two sexes, that is: whatever the variety of appearances, men remain dominant. Their claims come first. Women are supposed to be the associates and companions of men, not their full equals—and never their superiors. Women are to remain in the state of a permanent "minority."

The convention that wives should be younger than their husbands powerfully enforces the "minority" status of women, since being senior in age always carries with it, in any relationship, a certain amount of power and authority. There are no laws on the matter, of course. The convention is obeyed because to do otherwise makes one feel as if one is doing something ugly or in bad taste. Everyone feels intuitively the esthetic rightness of a marriage in which the man is older than the woman, which means that any marriage in which the woman is older creates a dubious or less gratifying mental picture. Everyone is addicted to the visual pleasure that women give by meeting certain esthetic requirements from which men are exempted, which keeps women working at staying youthful-looking while men are left free to age. On a deeper level everyone finds the signs of old age in women esthetically offensive, which conditions one to feel automatically repelled by the prospect of an elderly woman marrying a much younger man. The situation in which women are kept minors for life is largely organized by such conformist, unreflective preferences. But taste is not free, and its judgments are never merely "natural." Rules of taste enforce structures of power. The revulsion against aging in women is the cutting edge of a whole set of oppressive structures (often masked as gallantries) that kept women in their place.

The ideal state proposed for women is docility, which means not being fully grown up. Most of what is cherished as typically "feminine" is simply behavior that is childish, immature, weak. To offer so low and demeaning a standard of fulfillment in itself constitutes oppression in an acute form—a sort of moral neo-colonialism. But women are not simply condescended to by the values that secure the dominance of men. They are repudiated. Perhaps because of having been their oppressors for so long, few men really *like* women (though they love individual women), and few men ever feel really comfortable or at ease in women's company. This malaise arises because relations between the two sexes are rife with hypocrisy, as men manage to love those they dominate and therefore don't respect. Oppressors always try to justify their privileges and brutalities by imagining that those they oppress belong to a lower order of civilization or are less than fully "human." Deprived of part of their ordinary human dignity, the oppressed take on certain "demonic" traits. The oppressions of large groups have to be anchored deep in the psyche, continually renewed by partly unconscious fears and taboos, by a sense of the obscene. Thus, women arouse not only desire and affection in men but aversion as well. Women are thoroughly domesticated familiars. But, at certain times and in certain situations, they become alien, untouchable. The aversion men feel, so much of which is covered over, is felt most frankly, with least inhibition, toward the type of woman who is most taboo "esthetically," a woman who has become—with the natural changes brought about by aging—obscene.

Nothing more clearly demonstrates the vulnerability of women than the special pain, confusion, and bad faith with which they experience getting older. And in the struggle that some women are waging on behalf of all women to be treated (and treat themselves) as full human beings—not "only" as women—one of the earliest results to be hoped for is that women become aware, indignantly aware, of the double standard about aging from which they suffer so harshly.

It is understandable that women often succumb to the temptation to lie about their age. Given society's double standard, to question a woman about her age is indeed often an aggressive act, a trap. Lying is an elementary means of self-defense, a way of scrambling out of the trap, at least temporarily. To expect a woman, after "a certain age," to tell exactly how old she is— when she has a chance, either through the generosity of nature or the cleverness of art, to pass for being somewhat younger than she actually is—is like expecting a landowner to admit that the estate he has put up for sale is actually worth less than the buyer is prepared to pay. The double standard about aging sets women up as property, as objects whose value depreciates rapidly with the march of the calendar.

The prejudices that mount against women as they grow older are an important arm of male privilege. It is the present unequal distribution of adult roles between the two sexes that gives men a freedom to age denied to women. Men actively administer the double standard about aging because the "masculine" role rewards them the initiative in courtship. Men choose; women are chosen. So men choose younger women. But although this system of inequality is operated by men, it could not work if women themselves did not acquiesce in it. Women reinforce it powerfully with their complacency, with their anguish, with their lies.

Not only do women lie more than men do about their age but men forgive them for it, thereby confirming their own superiority. A man who lies about his age is thought to be weak, "unmanly." A woman who lies about her age is behaving in a quite acceptable, "feminine" way. Petty lying is viewed by men with indulgence, one of a number of patronizing allowances made for women. It has the same moral unimportance as the fact that women are often late for appointments. Women are not expected to be truthful, or punctual, or expert in handling and repairing machines, or frugal, or physically brave. They are expected to be second-class adults, whose natural state is that of a grateful dependence on men. And so they often are, since that is what they are brought up to be. So far as women heed the stereotypes of "feminine" behavior, they *cannot* behave as fully responsible, independent adults.

Most women share the contempt for women expressed in the double standard about aging—to such a degree that they take their lack of self-respect for granted. Women have been accustomed so long to the protection of their masks, their smiles, their endearing lies. Without this protection, they know, they would be more vulnerable. But in protecting themselves as women, they betray themselves as adults. The model corruption in a woman's life is denying her age. She symbolically accedes to all those myths that furnish women with their imprisoning securities and privileges, that create their genuine oppression, that inspire their real discontent. Each time a woman lies about her age she becomes an accomplice in her own underdevelopment as a human being.

Women have another option. They can aspire to be wise, not merely nice; to be competent, not merely helpful; to be strong, not merely graceful; to be ambitious for themselves, not merely for themselves in relation to men and children. They can let themselves age naturally and without embarrassment, actively protesting and disobeying the conventions that stem from this society's double standard about aging. Instead of being girls, girls as long as possible, who then age humiliatingly into middle-aged women and then obscenely into old women, they can become women much earlier—and remain active adults, enjoying the long, erotic career of which women are capable, far longer. Women should allow their faces to show the lives they have lived. Women should tell the truth.

Discussion Questions

1. Review the major differences in U.S. society between male and female aging.
2. What does the author mean by her deceptively simple last sentence?
3. In terms of this double standard of aging, do males or females have it harder in U.S. society? Discuss.

Runaway Wives

Role strain refers to the difficulty people have in meeting their role obligations. Role strain may arise out of role failure. In a rapidly changing and complex society a considerable amount of role failure is expected. Because of lack of experience, ability, or personality, many individuals fail to play the roles expected of them. A recent college graduate may be assigned a practical professional task for which he has only theoretical knowledge gleaned from books. An abnormally shy person trying to become a salesman may fail because the demands of the job are incompatible with his basic personality traits. Perhaps the most obvious example of role failure in our modren society is the failure of husbands and wives as marital partners. Does the following article suggest failure on the part of the wife? The husband? The institution of marriage?

Ginger's life was a round of Tupperware parties and baby showers. "I love it, I love it," she kept saying, until the day she caught a cross-country bus.

Ginger, like . . . most runaway wives, felt strapped by housework and child care. She broke three years ago, on Labor Day, while preparing a picnic supper for sixteen. "My beef Wellington crust wouldn't hold," she recalls, sitting now in a communal farmhouse where she lives with seven teen-age hippies. "It was too hot. The butter kept melting and the dough stuck to the board. By the time it stuck to the board six times, I got shaky . . . it was a real nightmare of mine . . . people come for dinner, and I'm not ready."

During that final hour of her marriage, Ginger tried to patch her crust over the foot-long log of beef fillet, stuff forty mushroom caps, mix a giant Caesar salad, and roll a confection called "crème de menthe balls."

By the time the guests begin to arrive, Ginger was a sticky mess, and she shooed everybody out onto the brick patio, where they drank with her husband, Peter. Peter, surprised that Ginger was not appearing with her famous *hors d'oeuvres,* walked into the kitchen to check. He found his distraught wife trying to do everything at once—mixing a salad with one hand, rolling candy balls with the other. He reached into the salad bowl and plucked out a lettuce leaf. "Too much dressing," he said. "What are you trying to do—drown the lettuce?"

That, as Ginger sees it, was her Moment of Truth. "There I was . . . shaking with exhaustion. And there *they* were—Peter, the guests, my kids— all waiting for me to get out there and serve them. I looked out the picture window and saw them all standing and chatting . . . it hit me: *They don't give a damn about me!"*

Reprinted from *Cosmopolitan* (February 1973) by permission of the author.

"Are you O.K.?" Peter had asked, but not as if he cared—he meant, *You better be O.K., baby.* Then an order: "Pull yourself together!"

Ginger did pull herself together. She ran upstairs and headed straight for Peter's wallet and the secret cache of big bills that he kept rolled in a sock. With ten crisp green twenties in her pocket, Ginger called a taxi service to come and get her . . . fast.

While Ginger reminisces, young people walk in and out of the barren farmhouse. One teen-age boy, whose denims are embroided with a patch that reads "Today is the First Day of the Rest of Your Life," hangs over Ginger's chair and fondles her long red hair as she speaks. He is seventeen. She is thirty-four. They are lovers.

"Isn't she cool?" the boy keeps saying. "She really got her head together. . . . Can you dig it?"

"I went from the West Coast to New York on a Greyhound bus," says Ginger. "I wanted to run as far from San Diego as I could. I hocked my wedding and engagement rings and used the cash for a stake. I went to the East Village, and it turned out I didn't really *need* money. There were people there who didn't care about furniture and money and things that had been my whole life. I could crash anywhere."

Ginger never redeemed her rings, says she doesn't want to see them ever again. But she still remembers the inscription: "P&G. April 1, 1960. Love forever."

"I was married ten whole years . . . doesn't that blow your mind?" she asks. "It took me ten years to get smart."

During those ten years, Ginger had experienced many warnings that her life was far from the *Family Circle* idea she had set out so studiously to copy. Now she recalls there were a series of "little accidents" suffered in the course of duty:

One morning, while mixing a chocolate torte, Ginger caught her finger between the blades of her electric mixer. Her left index finger was nearly severed, but a doctor sewed it back on. Although Ginger still cannot feel any sensation in that finger, it works perfectly.

Another time, Ginger deep-breathed gas fumes while cleaning her oven. She retched for nine hours, of which time, she says, "I felt sure I was dying . . ."

Peter finally noticed that Ginger was clumsy around the house—always bumping into things and cutting and burning herself. He chided her about it. "You're always black-and-blue. How can I make love to you when you're black-and-blue?"

"I can still remember him saying that . . . he actually said it . . . and he touched my hip. I had a bad bruise where I hit the steel sink. It had ulcerated. I had that one for months."

Ginger was crippled by housework—and almost killed by childbirth. Her children were born breech ("I did everything backward," she recalls). On the delivery table, struggling to push *à la Lamaze,* Ginger called her husband

and her obstetrician every dirty name she knew. The doctor, studying Ginger's dilating vagina, and equally dilating mouth, scolded her: "You ought to be ashamed of yourself, Mrs. Soltes."

And she was ashamed. After that, she tried so hard to be perfect. Ginger nursed the babies, knitted booties, tried 999 recipes for hamburger, started getting ready for Christmas in July, and moved faster under the sheets with Peter.

The ten years passed: an endless round of Tupperware parties. But Ginger herself felt sealed into a Tupperware world. And she felt stagnant, not fresh. "All the things that were supposed to be so great—kids, gardening, owning a big house, throwing parties—all they really meant was *more work.*"

Ginger Soltes ran away "to find her youth," she says. "I saw kids doing it . . . they were all so free . . . with their backpacks and no other hangups. I just wanted to join them."

She did. Now, with her teen-age lover ("He's sensational in a sleeping bag," she reports), Ginger says she "feels young for the first time in my life." As she relates this, the long-haired boy guides a skinny joint of marijuana to Ginger's lips. The former housewife sucks the joint, holding the sweet smoke inside her for a long minute. She releases her breath with a sigh. "Everything would be groovy, except Peter knows where I am. He found me two weeks ago—through a private eye. He wants to have me committed to a mental hospital . . . for shock treatments. He says that they worked for his sister-in-law. Who do you think is crazy—him or me?"

Discussion Questions

1. Peter obviously had role expectations for Ginger, his wife. Briefly describe them.
2. What caused Ginger to "get smart" and "run away" from those role expectations? What is her new status and what are some of her new role expectations?
3. How do you answer the question posed in the last sentence of this article?

5 / Social Deviation and Social Order

Berry's World. © by Newspaper Enterprise Association

"Don't give me any lip, Daddy—I'm TIME mag's 'Man of the Year'!"

Deviant behavior is behavior that varies significantly from the social norm for that behavior. A deviant act by itself does not make a person "deviant." To acquire this status, the label "deviant" must be applied by others. Thus, deviant behavior involves an *actor*, a *norm*, and an *audience* that defines the behavior of the actor as "deviant."

It has been said that deviant behavior is human behavior. After all, it is impossible for each of us to conform all of the time to every norm and expectation prescribed by our group. Deviance, however, is a matter of degree, since most norms have degrees of tolerance. Murder, for example, is punished very severely in most cases, but there is a tendency to be rather lenient with women who kill husbands and lovers who "cheated" on them. Limits of toler-ation are determined by the significance of the norm of the group, the situation within which the violation occurs, and the characteristics of the violator. Drunken-ness, for example, is tolerated on more festive occasions. A young slum-dweller might be defined as a lawbreaker if he wrote graffiti on a school building. If a young man from a well-to-do family performed the same act he might be con-sidered high-spirited.

No group, whether it is four college students sharing an apartment, a campus club, or a sociology class, can hope to achieve social order and function smoothly unless individual members conform to certain norms. While the social order of small, informal groups is usually achieved through techniques such as ridicule and ostracism, the achievement of social order in a large heterogenous society such as our own requires more formal sanctions such as fines and imprisonment. In order to administer these formal sanctions our society has developed an elaborate system of criminal justice and corrections.

When members of our society perceive that the social order is being threatened by a rising crime rate that includes the widespread use of drugs and the willful destruction of property, they can become preoccupied with simplistic solutions based on "law and order." Politicians, pundits, and citizens are free to use "law and order" in a rhetorical manner, but sociologists as social scientists must approach this concept with more systematic precision. While the rhetorical slogan "law and order" may create the expectation that if you have law you will automatically have order within society, the bitter fact is that many laws not only fail to achieve the desired social order, they unwittingly help to create disorder and to increase deviancy.

Since the prison riots that began with Attica, sociologists have begun to reappraise the system of criminal justice and the correctional system. To what degree do formal sanctions, especially imprisonment, actually serve to deter or rehabilitate deviants? To what degree does the correctional system actually encourage deviancy? A quick glance at the rate of recidivism and the unimpressive successes of rehabilitation programs provides little room for optimism. This condition gives increased urgency to the sociologist's task of evaluating the strengths and weaknesses of our present use of formal sanctions and, when possible, providing guidelines so that formal sanctions can be used in order to achieve a more ideal realization of "law and order."

D. L. ROSENHAN

On Being Sane in Insane Places

Over the years sociologists have developed a number of theories to explain deviant behavior. These theories are based on observations of the way people interact in different social settings. Some of the major sociological theories are found under the headings *social disorganization, differential association,* and *labeling.* Labeling theorists argue that deviance is not the result of an individual's committing a deviant act but rather of the *labeling* by others. So long as an individual can escape "detection," he can lead a rather normal, if not totally respectable, life. However, once the individual is caught committing the deviant act, he is then labeled a deviant. The importance of this labeling process is described in the following article by D. L. Rosenhan, who, with seven colleagues, contrived to have themselves admitted to several mental hospitals in 1973.

If sanity and insanity exist, how shall we know them?

The question is neither capricious nor itself insane. However much we may be personally convinced that we can tell the normal from the abnormal, the evidence is simply not compelling. It is commonplace, for example, to read about murder trials wherein eminent psychiatrists for the defense are contradicted by equally eminent psychiatrists for the prosecution on the

Reprinted from *Science,* vol. 179 (January 19, 1973), 250–58. Copyright © 1973 by the American Association for the Advancement of Science.

matter of the defendant's sanity. More generally, there are a great deal of conflicting data on the reliability, utility, and meaning of such terms as "sanity," "insanity," "mental illness," and "schizophrenia." Finally, as early as 1934, Benedict suggested that normality and abnormality are not universal. What is viewed as normal in one culture may be seen as quite aberrant in another. Thus, notions of normality and abnormality may not be quite as accurate as people believe they are.

To raise questions regarding normality and abnormality is in no way to question the fact that some behaviors are deviant or odd. Murder is deviant. So, too, are hallucinations. Nor does raising such questions deny the existence of the personal anguish that is often associated with "mental illness." Anxiety and depression exist. Psychological suffering exists. But normality and abnormality, sanity and insanity, and the diagnoses that flow from them may be less substantive than many believe them to be.

At its heart, the question of whether the sane can be distinguished from the insane (and whether degrees of insanity can be distinguished from each other) is a simple matter: do the salient characteristics that lead to diagnosis reside in the patients themselves or in the environments and contexts in which observers find them? From Bleuler, through Kretchmer, through the formulators of the recently revised *Diagnostic and Statistical Manual* of the American Psychiatric Association, the belief has been strong that patients present symptoms, that those symptoms can be categorized, and, implicitly, that the sane are distinguishable from the insane. More recently, however, this belief has been questioned. Based in part on theoretical and anthropological considerations, but also on philosophical, legal, and therapeutic ones, the view has grown that psychological categorization of mental illness is useless at best and downright harmful, misleading, and pejorative at worst. Psychiatric diagnoses, in this view, are in the minds of observers and are not valid summaries of characteristics displayed by the observed.

Gains can be made in deciding which of these is more nearly accurate by getting normal people (that is, people who do not have, and have never suffered, symptoms of serious psychiatric disorders) admitted to psychiatric hospitals and then determining whether they were discovered to be sane and, if so, how. If the sanity of such pseudopatients were always detected, there would be prima facie evidence that a sane individual can be distinguished from the insane context in which he is found. Normality (and presumably abnormality) is distinct enough that it can be recognized wherever it occurs, for it is carried within the person. If, on the other hand, the sanity of the pseudopatients were never discovered, serious difficulties would arise for those who support traditional modes of psychiatric diagnosis. Given that the hospital staff was not incompetent, that the pseudopatient had been behaving as sanely as he had been outside the hospital, and that it had never been previously suggested that he belonged in a psychiatric hospital, such an unlikely outcome would support the view that psychiatric diagnosis betrays little about the patient but much about the environment in which an observer finds him.

This article describes such an experiment. Eight sane people gained secret admission to twelve different hospitals.[1] Their diagnostic experiences constitute the data of the first part of this article; the remainder is devoted to a description of their experiences in psychiatric institutions. Too few psychiatrists and psychologists, even those who have worked in such hospitals, know what the experience is like. They rarely talk about it with former patients, perhaps because they distrust information coming from the previously insane. Those who have worked in psychiatric hospitals are likely to have adapted so thoroughly to the settings that they are insensitive to the impact of that experience. And while there have been occasional reports of researchers who submitted themselves to psychiatric hospitalization, these researchers have commonly remained in the hospitals for short periods of time, often with the knowledge of the hospital staff. It is difficult to know the extent to which they were treated as patients or as research colleagues. Nevertheless, their reports about the inside of the psychiatric hospital have been valuable. This article extends those efforts.

Pseudopatients and Their Settings

The eight pseudopatients were a varied group. One was a psychology graduate student in his twenties. The remaining seven were older and "established." Among them were three psychologists, a pediatrician, a psychiatrist, a painter, and a housewife. Three pseudopatients were women, five were men. All of them employed pseudonyms, lest their alleged diagnoses embarrass them later. Those who were in mental health professions alleged another occupation in order to avoid the special attentions that might be accorded by staff, as a matter of courtesy or caution, to ailing colleagues.[2] With the exception of myself (I was the first pseudopatient and my presence was known to the hospital administrator and chief psychologist and, so far as I can tell, to them alone), the presence of pseudopatients and the nature of the research program were not known to the hospital staffs.[3]

---

[1] Data from a ninth pseudopatient are not incorporated in this report because, although his sanity went undetected, he falsified aspects of his personal history, including his marital status and parental relationships. His experimental behaviors therefore were not identical to those of the other psuedopatients.

[2] Beyond the personal difficulties that the pseudopatient is likely to experience in the hospital, there are legal and social ones that, combined, require considerable attention before entry. For example, once admitted to a psychiatric institution, it is difficult, if not impossible, to be discharged on short notice, state law to the contrary notwithstanding. I was not sensitive to these difficulties at the outset of the project, nor to the personal and situational emergencies that can arise, but later a writ of habeas corpus was prepared for each of the entering pseudopatients and an attorney was kept "on call" during every hospitalization. I am grateful to John Kaplan and Robert Bartels for legal advice and assistance in these matters.

[3] However distasteful such concealment is, it was a necessary first step to examining these questions. Without concealment, there would have been no way to know how valid these experiences were; nor was there any way of knowing whether whatever

The settings were similarly varied. In order to generalize the findings, admission into a variety of hospitals was sought. The twelve hospitals in the sample were located in five different states on the East and West coasts. Some were old and shabby, some were quite new. Some were research-oriented, others not. Some had good staff-patient ratios, others were quite understaffed. Only one was a strictly private hospital. All of the others were supported by state or federal funds or, in one instance, by university funds.

After calling the hospital for an appointment, the pseudopatient arrived at the admissions office complaining that he had been hearing voices. Asked what the voices said, he replied that they were often unclear, but as far as he could tell they said "empty," "hollow," and "thud." The voices were unfamiliar and were of the same sex as the pseudopatient. The choice of these symptoms was occasioned by their apparent similarity to existential symptoms. Such symptoms are alleged to arise from painful concerns about the perceived meaninglessness of one's life. It is as if the hallucinating person were saying, "My life is empty and hollow." The choice of these symptoms was also determined by the *absence* of a single report of existential psychoses in the literature.

Beyond alleging the symptoms and falsifying name, vocation, and employment, no further alterations of person, history, or circumstances were made. The significant events of the pseudopatient's life history were presented as they had actually occurred. Relationships with parents and siblings, with spouse and children, with people at work and in school, consistent with the aforementioned exceptions, were described as they were or had been. Frustrations and upsets were described along with joys and satisfactions. These facts were important to remember. If anything, they strongly biased the subsequent results in favor of detecting sanity, since none of their histories or current behaviors was seriously pathological in any way.

Immediately upon admission to the psychiatric ward, the psuedopatient ceased simulating *any* symptoms of abnormality. In some cases, there was a brief period of mild nervousness and anxiety, since none of the pseudopatients really believed that he would be admitted so easily. Indeed, their shared fear was that they would be immediately exposed as frauds and greatly embarrassed. Moreover, many of them had never visited a psychiatric ward; even those who had nevertheless had some genuine fears about what might happen to them. Their nervousness, then, was quite appropriate to the novelty of the hospital setting, and it abated rapidly.

Apart from that short-lived nervousness, the pseudopatient behaved on the ward as he "normally" behaved. The psuedopatient spoke to patients and staff as he might ordinarily. Because there is uncommonly little to do on a psychiatric ward, he attempted to engage others in conversation. When

---

detections occurred were a tribute to the diagnostic acumen of the staff or to the hospital's rumor network. Obviously, since my concerns are general ones that cut across individual hospitals and staffs, I have respected their anonymity and have eliminated clues that might lead to their identification.

asked by staff how he was feeling, he indicated that he was fine, that he no longer experienced symptoms. He responded to instructions from attendants, to calls for medication (which was not swallowed), and to dining-hall instructions. Beyond such activities as were available to him on the admissions ward, he spent his time writing down his observations about the ward, its patients, and the staff. Initially these notes were written "secretly," but as it soon became clear that no one much cared, they were subsequently written on standard tablets of paper in such public places as the dayroom. No secret was made of these activities.

The pseudopatient, very much as a true psychiatric patient, entered a hospital with no foreknowledge of when he would be discharged. Each was told that he would have to get out by his own devices, essentially by convincing the staff that he was sane. The psychological stresses associated with hospitalization were considerable, and all but one of the pseudopatients desired to be discharged almost immediately after being admitted. They were, therefore, motivated not only to behave sanely, but to be paragons of cooperation. That their behavior was in no way disruptive is confirmed by nursing reports, which have been obtained on most of the patients. These reports uniformly indicate that the patients were "friendly," "cooperative," and "exhibited no abnormal indications."

The Normal Are Not Detectably Sane

Despite their public "show" of sanity, the pseudopatients were never detected. Admitted, except in one case, with a diagnosis of schizophrenia,[4] each was discharged with a diagnosis of schizophrenia "in remission." The label "in remission" should in no way be dismissed as a formality, for at no time during any hospitalization had any question been raised about any pseudopatient's simulation. Nor are there any indications in the hospital records that the psuedopatient's status was suspect. Rather, the evidence is strong that, once labeled schizophrenic, the pseudopatient was stuck with that label. If the pseudopatient was to be discharged, he must naturally be "in remission"; but he was not sane, nor, in the institution's view, had he ever been sane.

The uniform failure to recognize sanity cannot be attributed to the quality of the hospitals, for, although there were considerable variations among them, several are considered excellent. Nor can it be alleged that there was simply not enough time to observe the pseudopatients. Length of hospitalization ranged from seven to fifty-two days, with an average of nineteen days. The pseudopatients were not, in fact, carefully observed, but this failure

[4] Interestingly, of the twelve admissions, eleven were diagnosed as schizophrenic and one, with the identical symptomatology, as manic-depressive psychosis. This diagnosis has a more favorable prognosis, and it was given by the only private hospital in our sample.

clearly speaks more to traditions within psychiatric hospitals than to lack of opportunity.

Finally, it cannot be said that the failure to recognize the pseudopatients' sanity was due to the fact that they were not behaving sanely. While there was clearly some tension present in all of them, their daily visitors could detect no serious behavioral consequences—nor, indeed, could other patients. It was quite common for the patients to "detect" the pseudopatients' sanity. During the first three hospitalizations, when accurate counts were kept, 35 of a total of 118 patients on the admissions ward voiced their suspicions, some vigorously. "You're not crazy. You're a journalist, or a professor [referring to the continual note-taking]. You're checking up on the hospital." While most of the patients were reassured by the pseudopatient's insistence that he had been sick before he came in but was fine now, some continued to believe that the psuedopatient was sane throughout his hospitalization.[5] The fact that the patients often recognized normality when staff did not raises important questions.

Failure to detect sanity during the course of hospitalization may be due to the fact that physicians operate with a strong bias toward what statisticians call the type 2 error. This is to say that physicians are more inclined to call a healthy person sick (a false positive, type 2) than a sick person healthy (a false negative, type 1). The reasons for this are not hard to find: it is clearly more dangerous to misdiagnose illness than health. Better to err on the side of caution, to suspect illness even among the healthy.

But what holds for medicine does not hold equally well for psychiatry. Medical illnesses, while unfortunate, are not commonly pejorative. Psychiatric diagnoses, on the contrary, carry with them personal, legal, and social stigmas. It was therefore important to see whether the tendency toward diagnosing the sane as insane could be reversed. The following experiment was arranged at a research and teaching hospital whose staff had heard these findings but doubted that such an error could occur in their hospital. The staff was informed that at some time during the following three months, one or more pseudopatients would attempt to be admitted into the psychiatric hospital. Each staff member was asked to rate each patient who presented himself at admissions or on the ward according to the likelihood that the patient was a pseudopatient. A 10-point scale was used, with a 1 and 2 reflecting high confidence that the patient was a pseudopatient.

Judgments were obtained on 193 patients who were admitted for psychiatric treatment. All staff who had had sustained contact with or primary responsibility for the patient—attendants, nurses, psychiatrists, physicians, and psychologists—were asked to make judgments. Forty-one patients were al-

[5] It is possible, of course, that patients have quite broad latitudes in diagnosis and therefore are inclined to call many people sane, even those whose behavior is patently aberrant. However, although we have no hard data on this matter, it was our distinct impression that this was not the case. In many instances, patients not only singled us out for attention, but came to imitate our behaviors and styles.

leged, with high confidence, to be pseudopatients by at least one member of the staff. Twenty-three were considered suspect by at least one psychiatrist. Nineteen were suspected by one psychiatrist *and* one other staff member. Actually, no genuine pseudopatient (at least from my group) presented himself during this period.

The experiment is instructive. It indicates that the tendency to designate sane people as insane can be reversed when the stakes (in this case, prestige and diagnostic acumen) are high. But what can be said of the nineteen people who were suspected of being "sane" by one psychiatrist and another staff member? Were these people truly "sane," or was it rather the case that in the course of avoiding the type 2 error the staff tended to make more errors of the first sort—calling the crazy "sane"? There is no way of knowing. But one thing is certain: any diagnostic process that lends itself so readily to massive errors of this sort cannot be a very reliable one.

The Stickiness of Psychodiagnostic Labels

Beyond the tendency to call the healthy sick—a tendency that accounts better for diagnostic behavior on admission than it does for such behavior after a lengthy period of exposure—the data speak to the massive role of labeling in psychiatric assessment. Having once been labeled schizophrenic, there is nothing the pseudopatient can do to overcome the tag. The tag profoundly colors others' perceptions of him and his behavior.

From one viewpoint, these data are hardly surprising, for it has long been known that elements are given meaning by the context in which they occur. Gestalt psychology made this point vigorously, and Asch demonstrated that there are "central" personality traits (such as "warm" versus "cold") which are so powerful that they markedly color the meaning of other information in forming an impression of a given personality. "Insane," "schizophrenic," "manic-depressive," and "crazy" are probably among the most powerful of such central traits. Once a person is designated abnormal, all of his other behaviors and characteristics are colored by that label. Indeed, that label is so powerful that many of the pseudopatients' normal behaviors were overlooked entirely or profoundly misinterpreted. Some examples may clarify this issue.

Earlier I indicated that there were no changes in the pseudopatient's personal history and current status beyond those of name, employment, and, where necessary, vocation. Otherwise, a veridical description of personal history and circumstances was offered. Those circumstances were not psychotic. How were they made consonant with the diagnosis of psychosis? Or were those diagnoses modified in such a way as to bring them into accord with the circumstances of the pseudopatient's life, as described by him?

As far as I can determine, diagnoses were in no way affected by the relative health of the circumstances of a pseudopatient's life. Rather, the reverse occurred: the perception of his circumstances was shaped entirely by the diagnosis. A clear example of such translation is found in the case of a pseudopatient who had had a close relationship with his mother but was rather remote from his father during his early childhood. During adolescence and beyond, however, his father became a close friend, while his relationship with his mother cooled. His present relationship with his wife was characteristically close and warm. Apart from occasional angry exchanges, friction was minimal. The children had rarely been spanked. Surely there is nothing especially pathological about such a history. Indeed, many readers may see a similar pattern in their own experiences, with no markedly deleterious consequences. Observe, however, how such a history was translated in the psychopathological context, this from the case summary prepared after the patient was discharged.

> This white 39-year-old male . . . manifests a long history of considerable ambivalence in close relationships, which begins in early childhood. A warm relationship with his mother cools during his adolescence. A distant relationship to his father is described as becoming very intense. Affective stability is absent. His attempts to control emotionality with his wife and children are punctuated by angry outbursts and, in the case of the children, spankings. And while he says that he has several good friends, one senses considerable ambivalence embedded in those relationships also. . . .

The facts of the case were unintentionally distorted by the staff to achieve consistency with a popular theory of the dynamics of a schizophrenic reaction. Nothing of an ambivalent nature had been described in relations with parents, spouse, or friends. To the extent that ambivalence could be inferred, it was probably not greater than is found in all human relationships. It is true the pseudopatient's relationships with his parents changed over time, but in the ordinary context that would hardly be remarkable—indeed, it might very well be expected. Clearly, the meaning ascribed to his verbalizations (that is, ambivalence, affective instability) was determined by the diagnosis: schizophrenia. An entirely different meaning would have been ascribed if it were known that the man was "normal."

All pseudopatients took extensive notes publicly. Under ordinary circumstances, such behavior would have raised questions in the minds of observers, as, in fact, it did among patients. Indeed, it seemed so certain that the notes would elicit suspicion that elaborate precautions were taken to remove them from the ward each day. But the precautions proved needless. The closest any staff member came to questioning these notes occurred when one pseudopatient asked his physician what kind of medication he was receiving and began to write down the response. "You needn't write it," he was told gently. "If you have trouble remembering, just ask me again."

If no questions were asked of the pseudopatients, how was their writing interpreted? Nursing records for three patients indicate that the writing was seen as an aspect of their pathological behavior. "Patient engages in writing behavior" was the daily nursing comment on one of the pseudopatients who was never questioned about his writing. Given that the patient is in the hospital, he must be psychologically disturbed. And given that he is disturbed, continuous writing must be a behavioral manifestation of that disturbance, perhaps a subset of the compulsive behaviors that are sometimes correlated with schizophrenia.

One tacit characteristic of psychiatric diagnosis is that it locates the sources of aberration within the individual and only rarely within the complex of stimuli that surrounds him. Consequently, behaviors that are stimulated by the environment are commonly misattributed to the patients disorder. For example, one kindly nurse found a pseudopatient pacing the long hospital corridors. "Nervous, Mr. X?" she asked. "No, bored," he said.

The notes kept by pseudopatients are full of patient behaviors that were misinterpreted by well-intentioned staff. Often enough, a patient would go "beserk" because he had, wittingly or unwittingly, been mistreated by, say, an attendant. A nurse coming upon the scene would rarely inquire even cursorily into the environmental stimuli of the patient's behavior. Rather, she assumed that his upset derived from his pathology, not from his present interactions with other staff members. Occasionally, the staff might assume that the patient's family (especially when they had recently visited) or other patients had stimulated the outburst. But never were the staff found to assume that one of themselves or the structure of the hospital had anything to do with a patient's behavior. One psychiatrist pointed to a group of patients who were sitting outside the cafeteria entrance half an hour before lunchtime. To a group of young residents he indicated that such behavior was characteristic of the oral-acquisitive nature of the syndrome. It seemed not to occur to him that there were very few things to anticipate in a psychiatric hospital besides eating.

A psychiatric label has a life and an influence of its own. Once the impression has been formed that the patient is schizophrenic, the expectation is that he will continue to be schizophrenic. When a sufficient amount of time has passed, during which the patient has done nothing bizarre, he is considered to be in remission and available for discharge. But the label endures beyond discharge, with the unconfirmed expectation that he will behave as a schizophrenic again. Such labels, conferred by mental health professionals, are as influential on the patient as they are on his relatives and friends, and it should not surprise anyone that the diagnosis acts on all of them as a self-fulfilling prophecy. Eventually, the patient himself accepts the diagnosis, with all of its surplus meanings and expectations, and behaves accordingly.

The inferences to be made from these matters are quite simple. Much as Zigler and Phillips have demonstrated that there is enormous overlap in the symptoms presented by patients who have been variously diagnosed, so there is enormous overlap in the behaviors of the sane and the insane. The sane are not "sane" all of the time. We lose our tempers "for no good reason." We are occasionally depressed or anxious, again for no good reason.

And we may find it difficult to get along with one or another person—again for no reason that we can specify. Similarly, the insane are not always insane. Indeed, it was the impression of the pseudopatients while living with them that they were sane for long periods of time—that the bizarre behaviors upon which their diagnoses were allegedly predicated constituted only a small fraction of their total behavior. If it makes no sense to label ourselves permanently depressed on the basis of an occasional depression, then it takes better evidence than is presently available to label all patients insane or schizophrenic on the basis of bizarre behaviors or cognitions. It seems more useful, as Mischel has pointed out, to limit our discussions to *behaviors,* the stimuli that provoke them, and their correlates.

It is not known why powerful impressions of personality traits, such as "crazy" or "insane," arise. Conceivably, when the origins of and stimuli that give rise to a behavior are remote or unknown, or when the behavior strikes us as immutable, trait labels regarding the *behavior* arise. When, on the other hand, the origins and stimuli are known and available, discourse is limited to the behavior itself. Thus, I may hallucinate because I am sleeping, or I may hallucinate because I have ingested a peculiar drug. These are termed sleep-induced hallucinations, or dreams, and drug-induced hallucinations, respectively. But when the stimuli to my hallucinations are unknown, that is called craziness, or schizophrenia—as if that inference were somehow as illuminating as the others.

The Experience of Psychiatric Hospitalization

The term "mental illness" is of recent origin. It was coined by people who were humane in their inclinations and who wanted very much to raise the station of (and the public's sympathies toward) the psychologically disturbed from that of witches and "crazies" to one that was akin to the physically ill. And they were at least partially successful, for the treatment of the mentally ill *has* improved considerably over the years. But while treatment has improved, it is doubtful that people really regard the mentally ill in the same way that they view the physically ill. A broken leg is something one recovers from, but mental illness allegedly endures forever. A broken leg does not threaten the observer, but a crazy schizophrenic? There is by now a host of evidence that attitudes toward the mentally ill are characterized by fear, hostility, aloofness, suspicion, and dread. The mentally ill are society's lepers.

That such attitudes infect the general population is perhaps not surprising, only upsetting. But that they affect the professionals—attendants, nurses, physicians, psychologists, and social workers—who treat and deal with the mentally ill is more disconcerting, both because such attitudes are self-evidently pernicious and because they are unwitting. Most mental health professionals would insist that they are sympathetic toward the mentally ill, that they are neither avoidant nor hostile. But it is more likely that an exquisite ambivalence characterizes their relations with psychiatric patients, such that their avowed impulses are only part of their entire attitude. Negative attitudes are there too and can easily be detected. Such attitudes should not surprise us. They are the natural offspring of the labels patients wear and the places in which they are found.

Consider the structure of the typical psychiatric hospital. Staff and patients are strictly segregated. Staff have their own living space, including their dining facilities, bathrooms, and assembly places. The glassed quarters that contain the professional staff, which the pseudopatients came to call "the cage," sit out on every dayroom. The staff emerge primarily for caretaking purposes—to give medication, to conduct a therapy or group meeting, to instruct or reprimand a patient. Otherwise, staff keep to themselves, almost as if the disorder that afflicts their charges is somehow catching.

So much is patient-staff segregation the rule that, for four public hospitals in which an attempt was made to measure the degree to which staff and patients mingle, it was necessary to use "time out of the staff cage" as the operational measure. While it was not the case that all time spent out of the cage was spent mingling with patients (attendants, for example, would occasionally emerge to watch television in the dayroom), it was the only way in which one could gather reliable data on time for measuring.

The average amount of time spent by attendants outside the cage was 11.3 per cent (range, 3 to 52 per cent). This figure does not represent only time spent mingling with patients, but also includes time spent on such chores as folding laundry, supervising patients while they shaved, directing ward clean-up, and sending patients to off-ward activities. It was the relatively rare attendant who spent time talking with patients or playing games with them. It proved impossible to obtain a "per cent mingling time" for nurses, since the amount of time they spent out of the cage was too brief. Rather, we counted instances of emergence from the cage. On the average, daytime nurses emerged from the cage 11.5 times per shift, including instances when they left the ward entirely (range, 4 to 39 times). Late afternoon and night nurses were even less available, emerging on the average 9.4 times per shift (range, 4 to 41 times). Data on early morning nurses, who arrived usually after midnight and departed at 8:00 A.M., are not available because patients were asleep during most of this period.

Physicians, especially psychiatrists, were even less available. They were rarely seen on the wards. Quite commonly, they would be seen only when they arrived and departed, with the remaining time being spent in their offices or in the cage. On the average, physicians emerged on the ward 6.7 times per day (range, 1 to 17 times). It proved difficult to make an accurate estimate in this regard, since physicians often maintained hours that allowed them to come and go at different times.

The hierarchical organization of the psychiatric hospital has been commented on before, but the latent meaning of that kind of organization is worth noting again. Those with the most power have least to do with patients, and those with the least power are most involved with them. Recall, however, that the acquisition of role-appropriate behaviors occurs mainly through the observation of others, with the most powerful having the most influence. Consequently, it is understandable that attendants not only spend more time with patients than do any other members of the staff—that is required by their station in the hierarchy—but also, insofar as they learn from their superiors' behavior, spend as little time with patients as they can. Attendants are seen mainly in the cage, which is where the models, the action, and the power are.

I turn now to a different set of studies, these dealing with staff response to patient-initiated contact. It has long been known that the amount of time a person spends with you can be an index of your significance to him. If he initiates and maintains eye contact, there is reason to believe that he is considering your requests and needs. If he pauses to chat or actually stops and talks, there is added reason to infer that he is individuating you. In four hospitals, the pseudopatient approached the staff member with a request which took the following form: "Pardon me, Mr. [or Dr. or Mrs.] X, could you tell me when I will be eligible for grounds privileges?" (or ". . . when I will be presented at the staff meeting?" or ". . . when I am likely to be discharged?"). While the content of the question varied according to the appropriateness of the target and the pseudopatient's (apparent) current needs the form was always a courteous and relevant request for information. Care was taken never to approach a particular member of the staff more than once a day, lest the staff member become suspicious or irritated. In examining these data, remember that the behavior of the pseudopatients was neither bizarre nor disruptive. One could indeed engage in good conversation with them.

Minor differences between these four institutions were overwhelmed by the degree to which staff avoided continuing contacts that patients had initiated. By far, their most common response consisted of either a brief response to the question, offered while they were "on the move" and with head averted, or no response at all.

The encounter frequently took the following bizarre form:

PSEUDOPATIENT: Pardon me, Dr. X. Could you tell me when I am eligible for grounds privileges?
PHYSICIAN: Good morning, Dave. How are you today? [*Moves off without waiting for a response.*]

It is instructive to compare these data with data recently obtained at Stanford University. It has been alleged that large and eminent universities are characterized by faculty who are so busy that they have no time for students. For this comparison, a young lady approached individual faculty members who seemed to be walking purposefully to some meeting or teaching engagement and asked them the following six questions.

1. "Pardon me, could you direct me to Encina Hall?" (at the medical school: ". . . to the Clinical Research Center?").
2. "Do you know where Fish Annex is?" (there is no Fish Annex at Stanford).
3. "Do you teach here?"
4. "How does one apply for admission to the college?" (at the medical school: ". . . to the medical school?").
5. "Is it difficult to get in?"
6. "Is there financial aid?"

Without exception all of the questions were answered. No matter how rushed they were, all respondents not only maintained eye contact, but stopped to talk. Indeed, many of the respondents went out of their way to direct or take the questioner to the office she was seeking, to try to locate "Fish Annex," or to discuss with her the possibilities of being admitted to the university.

Similar data were obtained in the hospital. Here too, the young lady came prepared with six questions. After the first question, however, she remarked to eighteen of her respondents, "I'm looking for a psychiatrist," and to fifteen others, "I'm looking for an internist." Ten other respondents received no inserted comment. The general degree of cooperative responses is considerably higher for these university groups than it was for pseudopatients in psychiatric hospitals. Even so, differences are apparent within the medical school setting. Once having indicated that she was looking for a psychiatrist, the degree of cooperation elicited was less than when she sought an internist.

Powerlessness and Depersonalization

Eye contact and verbal contact reflect concern and individuation; their absence, avoidance and depersonalization. The data I have presented do not do justice to the rich daily encounters that grew up around matters of depersonalization and avoidance. I have records of patients who were beaten by staff for the sin of having initiated verbal contact. During my own experience, for example, one patient was beaten in the presence of other patients for having approached an attendant and told him, "I like you." Occasionally, punishment meted out to patients for misdemeanors seemed so excessive that it could not be justified by the most radical interpretations of psychiatric canon. Nevertheless, they appeared to go unquestioned. Tempers were often short. A patient who had not heard a call for medication would be roundly excoriated, and the morning attendants would often wake patients with, "Come on, you m——f——s, out of bed!"

Neither anecdotal nor "hard" data can convey the overwhelming sense of powerlessness which invades the individual as he is continually exposed to the depersonalization of the psychiatric hospital. It hardly matters *which* psychiatric hospital—the excellent public ones and the very plush private hospital were better than the rural and shabby ones in this regard, but, again, the features that psychiatric hospitals had in common overwhelmed by far their apparent differences.

Powerlessness was evident everywhere. The patient is deprived of many of his legal rights by dint of his psychiatric commitment. He is shorn of credibility by virtue of his psychiatric label. His freedom of movement is restricted. He cannot initiate contact with the staff, but may only respond to such overtures as they make. Personal privacy is minimal. Patient quarters and possessions can be entered and examined by any staff member, for whatever reason. His personal history and anguish is available to any staff member (often including the "gray lady" and "candy striper" volunteer) who chooses to read his folder, regardless of their therapeutic relationship to him. His personal hygiene and waste evacuation are often monitored. The water closets may have no doors.

At times, depersonalization reached such proportions that pseudopatients had the sense that they were invisible, or at least unworthy of account. Upon being admitted, I and other pseudopatients took the initial physical examinations in a semipublic room, where staff members went about their own business as if we were not there.

On the ward, attendants delivered verbal and occasionally serious physical abuse to patients in the presence of other observing patients, some of whom (the pseudopatients) were writing it all down. Abusive behavior, on the other hand, terminated quite abruptly when other staff members were known to be coming. Staff are credible witnesses. Patients are not.

A nurse unbuttoned her uniform to adjust her brassiere in the presence of an entire ward of viewing men. One did not have the sense that she was being seductive. Rather, she didn't notice us. A group of staff persons might point to a patient in the dayroom and discuss him animatedly, as if he were not there.

One illuminating instance of depersonalization and invisibility occurred with regard to medications. All told, the psuedopatients were administered nearly 2100 pills, including Elavil, Stelazine, Compazine, and Thorazine, to name but a few. (That such a variety of medications should have been administered to patients presenting identical symptoms is itself worthy of note.) Only two were swallowed. The rest were either pocketed or deposited in the toilet. The pseudopatients were not alone in this. Although I have no precise records on how many patients rejected their medications, the pseudo-patients frequently found the medications of other patients in the toilet before they deposited their own. As long as they were cooperative, their behavior and the pseudopatients' own in this matter, as in other important matters, went unnoticed throughout.

Reactions to such depersonalization among pseudopatients were intense. Although they had come to the hospital as participant observers and were fully aware that they did not "belong," they nevertheless found themselves caught up in and fighting the process of depersonalization. Some examples: a graduate student in psychology asked his wife to bring his textbooks to the hospital so he could "catch up on his homework"—this despite the elaborate precautions taken to conceal his professional association. The same student, who had trained for quite some time to get into the hospital, and who had looked forward to the experience, "remembered" some drag races that he had wanted to see on the weekend and insisted that he be discharged by that time. Another pseudopatient attempted a romance with a nurse. Subsequently, he informed the staff that he was applying for admission to graduate school in psychology and was very likely to be admitted, since a graduate professor was one of his regular hospital visitors. The same person began to engage in psychotherapy with other patients—all of this as a way of becoming a person in an impersonal environment.

The Sources of Depersonalization

What are the origins of depersonalization? I have already mentioned two. First are attitudes held by all of us toward the mentally ill—including those who treat them—attitudes characterized by fear, distrust, and horrible expectations on the one hand, and benevolent intentions on the other. Our ambivalence leads, in this instance as in others, to avoidance.

Second, and not entirely separate, the hierarchical structure of the psychiatric hospital facilitates depersonalization. Those who are at the top have least to do with patients, and their behavior inspires the rest of the staff. Average daily contact with psychiatrists, psychologists, residents, and physicians combined ranged from 3.9 to 25.1 minutes, with an over-all mean of 6.8 (six pseudopatients over a total of 129 days of hospitalization). Included in this average is time spent in the admissions interview, ward meetings in the presence of a senior staff member, group and individual psychotherapy contacts, case presentation conferences, and discharge meetings. Clearly, patients do not spend much time in interpersonal contact with doctoral staff. And doctoral staff serve as models for nurses and attendants.

There are probably other sources. Psychiatric installations are presently in serious financial straits. Staff shortages are pervasive, staff time at a premium. Something has to give, and that something is patient contact. Yet, while financial stresses are realities, too much can be made of them. I have the impression that the psychological forces that result in depersonalization are much stronger than the fiscal ones and that the addition of more staff would not correspondingly improve patient care in this regard. The incidence of staff meetings and the enormous amount of record-keeping on patients, for example, have not been as substantially reduced as has patient contact. Priorities exist, even during hard times. Patient contact is not a significant priority in the traditional psychiatric hospital, and fiscal pressures do not account for this. Avoidance and depersonalization may.

Heavy reliance upon psychotropic medication tacitly contributes to de-personalization by convincing staff that treatment is indeed being conducted and that further patient contact may not be necessary. Even here, however, caution needs to be exercised in understanding the role of psychotropic drugs. If patients were powerful rather than powerless, if they were viewed as interesting individuals rather than diagnostic entities, if they were socially significant rather than social lepers, if their anguish truly and wholly com-pelled our sympathies and concerns, would we not *seek* contact with them, despite the availability of medications? Perhaps for the pleasure of it all?

The Consequences of Labeling and Depersonalization

Whenever the ratio of what is known to what needs to be known approaches zero, we tend to invent "knowledge" and assume that we understand more than we actually do. We seem unable to acknowledge that we simply don't know. The needs for diagnosis and remediation of behavioral and emotional problems are enormous. But rather than acknowledge that we are just em-barking on understanding, we continue to label patients schizophrenic, manic-depressive, and insane, as if in those words we had captured the essence of understanding. The facts of the matter are that we have known for a long time that diagnoses are often not useful or reliable, but we have nevertheless continued to use them. We now know that we cannot distinguish insanity from sanity. It is depressing to consider how that information will be used.

Not merely depressing, but frightening. How many people, one wonders, are sane but not recognized as such in our psychiatric institutions? How many have been needlessly stripped of their privileges of citizenship, from the right to vote and drive to that of handling their own accounts? How many have feigned insanity in order to avoid the criminal consequences of their behavior, and, conversely, how many would rather stand trial than live interminably in a psychiatric hospital—but are wrongly thought to be mentally ill? How many have been stigmatized by well-intentioned, but never-theless erroneous, diagnoses? On the last point, recall again that a "type 2 error" in psychiatric diagnosis does not have the same consequences it does in medical diagnosis. A diagnosis of cancer that has been found to be in error is cause for celebration. But psychiatric diagnoses are rarely found to be in error. The label sticks, a mark of inadequacy forever.

Finally, how many patients might be "sane" outside the psychiatric hos-pital but seem insane in it—not because craziness resides in them, as it were, but because they are responding to a bizarre setting, one that may be unique to institutions which harbor nether people? Goffman calls the process of socialization to such institutions "mortification"—an apt metaphor that in-cludes the processes of depersonalization that have been described here. And while it is impossible to know whether the pseudopatients' responses to these processes are characteristic of all inmates—they were, after all, not real patients—it is difficult to believe that these processes of socialization to a psychiatric hospital provide useful attitudes or habits of response for living in the "real world."

Summary and Conclusions

It is clear that we cannot distinguish the sane from the insane in psychiatric hospitals. The hospital itself imposes a special environment in which the meanings of behavior can easily be misunderstood. The consequences to patients hospitalized in such an environment—the powerlessness, depersonalization, segregation, mortification, and self-labeling—seem undoubtedly countertherapeutic.

I do not, even now, understand this problem well enough to perceive solutions. But two matters seem to have some promise. The first concerns the proliferation of community mental health facilities, of crisis intervention centers, of the human potential movement, and of behavior therapies that, for all of their own problems, tend to avoid psychiatric labels, to focus on specific problems and behaviors, and to retain the individual in a relatively nonpejorative environment. Clearly, to the extent that we refrain from sending the distressed to insane places, our impressions of them are less likely to be distorted. (The risk of distorted perceptions, it seems to me, is always present, since we are much more sensitive to an individual's behaviors and verbalizations than we are to the subtle contextual stimuli that often promote them. At issue here is a matter of magnitude. And, as I have shown, the magnitude of distortion is exceedingly high in the extreme context that is a psychiatric hospital.)

The second matter that might prove promising speaks to the need to increase the sensitivity of mental health workers and researchers to the *Catch 22* position of psychiatric patients. Simply reading materials in this area will be of help to some such workers and researchers. For others, directly experiencing the impact of psychiatric hospitalization will be of enormous use. Clearly, further research into the social psychology of such total institutions will both facilitate treatment and deepen understanding.

I and the other pseudopatients in the psychiatric setting had distinctly negative reactions. We do not pretend to describe the subjective experiences of true patients. Theirs may be different from ours, particularly with the passage of time and the necessary process of adaptation to one's environment. But we can and do speak to the relatively more objective indices of treatment within the hospital. It could be a mistake, and a very unfortunate one, to consider that what happened to us derived from malice or stupidity on the part of the staff. Quite the contrary, our overwhelming impression of them was of people who really cared, who were committed and who were uncommonly intelligent. Where they failed, as they sometimes did painfully, it would be more accurate to attribute those failures to the environment in which they, too, found themselves than to personal callousness. Their perceptions and behavior were controlled by the situation, rather than being motivated by a malicious disposition. In a more benign environment, one that was less attached to global diagnosis, their behaviors and judgments might have been more benign and effective.

Discussion Questions

1. Based on this article, discuss the problems of defining such terms as
   sanity
   insanity
   mental illness
   schizophrenia

2. How does the author describe the people he met who were responsible for caring for the "insane"? What caused their shortcomings and how can this be remedied?

HOWARD S. BECKER

Becoming a Marihuana User

Many forms of deviance such as prostitution, homosexuality, and drug addiction require more than one person: the prostitute and the homosexual need a partner and the drug addict a supplier. As a result, much of the deviance in our society is associated with established subcultures. One of the most basic functions of deviant subcultures is the socialization of recruits. Novices must learn the skills, beliefs, values, and norms of the subculture. In the following article, Howard S. Becker describes how the process of socialization works with first-time marihuana users.

The novice does not ordinarily get high the first time he smokes marihuana, and several attempts are usually necessary to induce this state. One explanation of this may be that the drug is not smoked "properly," that is, in a way that insures sufficient dosage to produce real symptoms of intoxication. Most users agree that it cannot be smoked like tobacco if one is to get high:

> Take in a lot of air, you know, and . . . I don't know how to describe it, you don't smoke it like a cigarette, you draw in a lot of air and get it deep down in your system and then keep it there. Keep it there as long as you can.

Reprinted from Howard S. Becker, "Becoming a Marihuana User," with permission of Macmillan Publishing Co., Inc., from *Outsiders: Studies in the Sociology of Deviance* (pp. 46–58) by Howard S. Becker. © The Free Press of Glencoe, a Division of Macmillan Publishing Co., Inc.

Without the use of some such technique [1] the drug will produce no effects, and the user will be unable to get high:

> The trouble with people like that [who are not able to get high] is that they're just not smoking it right, that's all there is to it. Either they're not holding it down long enough, or they're getting too much air and not enough smoke, or the other way around or something like that. A lot of people just don't smoke it right, so naturally nothing's gonna happen.

If nothing happens, it is manifestly impossible for the user to develop a conception of the drug as an object which can be used for pleasure, and use will therefore not continue. The first step in the sequence of events that must occur if the person is to become a user is that he must learn to use the proper smoking technique so that his use of the drug will produce effects in terms of which his conception of it can change.

Such a change is, as might be expected, a result of the individual's participation in groups in which marihuana is used. In them the individual learns the proper way to smoke the drug. This may occur through direct teaching:

> I was smoking like I did an ordinary cigarette. He said, "No, don't do it like that." He said, "Suck it, you know, draw in and hold it in your lungs till you . . . for a period of time."
> I said, "Is there any limit of time to hold it?"
> He said, "No just till you feel that you want to let it out, let it out." So I did that three or four times.

Many new users are ashamed to admit ignorance and, pretending to know already, must learn through the more indirect means of observation and imitation:

> I came on like I had turned on [smoked marihuana] many times before, you know. I didn't want to seem like a punk to this cat. See, like I didn't know the first thing about it—how to smoke it, or what was going to happen, or what. I just watched him like a hawk—I didn't take my eyes off him for a second because I wanted to do everything just as he did it. I watched how he held it, how he smoked it, and everything. Then when he gave it to me I just came on cool, as though I knew exactly what the score was. I held it like he did and took a poke just the way he did.

No one I interviewed continued marihuana use for pleasure without learning a technique that supplied sufficient dosage for the effects of the drug to appear. Only when this was learned was it possible for a conception of the drug as an object which could be used for pleasure to emerge. Without such a conception marihuana use was considered meaningless and did not continue.

[1] A pharmacologist notes that this ritual is in fact an extremely efficient way of getting the drug into the blood stream. See R. P. Walton, *Marihuana: America's New Drug Problem* (Philadelphia: J. B. Lippincott, 1938), p. 48.

Learning to Perceive the Effects

Even after he learns the proper smoking technique, the new user may not get high and thus not form a conception of the drug as something which can be used for pleasure. A remark made by a user suggested the reason for this difficulty in getting high and pointed to the next necessary step on the road to being a user:

> As a matter of fact, I've seen a guy who was high out of his mind and didn't know it.
> [How can that be, man?]
> Well, it's pretty strange, I'll grant you that, but I've seen it. This guy got on with me, claiming that he'd never got high, one of those guys, and he got completely stoned. And he kept insisting that he wasn't high. So I had to prove to him that he was.

What does this mean? It suggests that being high consists of two elements: the presence of symptoms caused by marihuana use and the recognition of these symptoms and their connection by the user with his use of the drug. It is not enough, that is, that the effects be present; alone, they do not automatically provide the experience of being high. The user must be able to point them out to himself and consciously connect them with having smoked marihuana before he can have this experience. Otherwise, no matter what actual effects are produced, he considers that the drug has had no effect on him: "I figured it either had no effect on me or other people were exaggerating its effect on them, you know. I thought it was probably psychological, see." Such persons believe the whole thing is an illusion and that the wish to be high leads the user to deceive himself into believing that something is happening when, in fact, nothing is. They do not continue marihuana use, feeling that "it does nothing" for them.

Typically, however, the novice has faith (developed from his observation of users who do get high) that the drug actually will produce some new experience and continues to experiment with it until it does. His failure to get high worries him, and he is likely to ask more experienced users or provoke comments from them about it. In such conversations he is made aware of specific details of his experience which he may not have noticed or may have noticed but failed to identify as symptoms of being high:

> I didn't get high the first time . . . I don't think I held it in long enough. I probably let it out, you know, you're a little afraid. The second time I wasn't sure, and he [smoking companion] told me, like I asked him for some of the symptoms or something, how would I know, you know. . . . So he told me to sit on a stool. I sat on—I think I sat on a bar stool—and he said, "Let your feet hang," and then when I got down my feet were real cold, you know.

And I started feeling it, you know. That was the first time. And then about a week after that, sometime pretty close to it, I really got on. That was the first time I got on a big laughing kick, you know. Then I really knew I was on.

One symptom of being high is an intense hunger. In the next case the novice becomes aware of this and gets high for the first time:

They were just laughing the hell out of me because like I was eating so much. I just scoffed [ate] so much food, and they were just laughing at me, you know. Sometimes I'd be looking at them, you know, wondering why they're laughing, you know, not knowing what I was doing. [Well, did they tell you why they were laughing eventually?] Yeah, yeah, I come back, "Hey, man, what's happening?" Like, you know, like I'd ask, "What's happening?" and all of a sudden I feel weird, you know. "Man you're on, you know. You're on pot [high on marihuana]." I said, "No, am I?" Like I don't know what's happening.

The learning may occur in more indirect ways:

I heard little remarks that were made by other people. Somebody said, "My legs are rubbery," and I can't remember all the remarks that were made because I was very attentively listening for all these cues for what I was supposed to feel like.

The novice, then, eager to have this feeling, picks up from other users some concrete referents of the term "high" and applies these notions to his own experience. The new concepts make it possible for him to locate these symptoms among his own sensations and to point out to himself a "something different" in his experience that he connects with drug use. It is only when he can do this that he is high. In the next case, the contrast between two successive experiences of a user makes clear the crucial importance of the awareness of the symptoms in being high and re-emphasizes the important role of interaction with other users in acquiring the concepts that make this awareness possible:

[Did you get high the first time you turned on?] Yeah, sure. Although, come to think of it, I guess I really didn't. I mean, like that first time it was more or less of a mild drunk. I was happy, I guess, you know what I mean. But I didn't really know I was high, you know what I mean. It was only after the second time I got high that I realized I was high the first time. Then I knew that something different was happening.

[How did you know that?] How did I know? If what happened to me that night would of happened to you, you would've known, believe me. We played the first tune for almost two hours—one tune! Imagine, man! We got on the stand and played this one tune, we started at nine o'clock. When we got finished I looked at my watch, it's a quarter to eleven. Almost two hours on one tune. And it didn't seem like anything.

I mean, you know, it does that to you. It's like you have much more time or something. Anyway, when I saw that, man, it was too much. I knew I must really be high or something if anything like that could happen. See, and then they explained to me that that's what it did to you, you had a different sense of time and everything. So I realized that that's what it was. I knew then. Like the first time, I probably felt that way, you know, but I didn't know what's happening.

It is only when the novice becomes able to get high in this sense that he will continue to use marihuana for pleasure. In every case in which use continued, the user had acquired the necessary concepts with which to express to himself the fact that he was experiencing new sensations caused by the drug. That is, for use to continue, it is necessary not only to use the drug so as to produce effects but also to learn to perceive these effects when they occur. In this way marihuana acquires meaning for the user as an object which can be used for pleasure.

With increasing experience the user develops a greater appreciation of the drug's effects; he continues to learn to get high. He examines succeeding experiences closely, looking for new effects, making sure the old ones are still there. Out of this there grows a stable set of categories for experiencing the drug's effects whose presence enables the user to get high with ease.

Users, as they acquire this set of categories, become connoisseurs. Like experts in fine wines, they can specify where a particular plant was grown and what time of year it was harvested. Although it is usually not possible to know whether these attributions are correct, it is true that they distinguish between batches of marihuana, not only according to strength, but also with respect to the different kinds of symptoms produced.

The ability to perceive the drug's effects must be maintained if use is to continue; if it is lost, marihuana use ceases. Two kinds of evidence support this statement. First, people who become heavy users of alcohol, barbiturates, or opiates do not continue to smoke marihuana, largely because they lose the ability to distinguish between its effects and those of the other drugs.[2] They no longer know whether the marihuana gets them high. Second, in those few cases in which an individual uses marihuana in such quantities that he is always high, he is apt to feel the drug has no effect on him, since the essential element of a noticeable difference between feeling high and feeling normal is missing. In such a situation, use is likely to be given up completely, but temporarily, in order that the user may once again be able to perceive the difference.

[2] "Smokers have repeatedly stated that the consumption of whiskey while smoking negates the potency of the drug. They find it very difficult to get 'high' while drinking whiskey and because of that smokers will not drink while using the 'weed.' " (New York City Mayor's Committee on Marihuana, *The Marihuana Problem in the City of New York,* Lancaster, Pa.: Jacques Cattell Press, 1944, p. 13.)

Learning to Enjoy the Effects

One more step is necessary if the user who has now learned to get high is to continue use. He must learn to enjoy the effects he has just learned to experience. Marihuana-produced sensations are not automatically or necessarily pleasurable. The taste for such experience is a socially acquired one, not different in kind from acquired tastes for oysters or dry martinis. The user feels dizzy, thirsty; his scalp tingles; he misjudges time and distances. Are these things pleasurable? He isn't sure. If he is to continue marihuana use, he must decide that they are. Otherwise, getting high, while a real enough experience, will be an unpleasant one he would rather avoid.

The effects of the drug, when first perceived, may be physically unpleasant or at least ambiguous:

> It started taking effect, and I didn't know what was happening, you know, what it was, and I was very sick. I walked around the room, walking around the room trying to get off, you know; it just scared me at first, you know. I wasn't used to that kind of feeling.

In addition, the novice's naïve interpretation of what is happening to him may further confuse and frighten him, particularly if he decides, as many do, that he is going insane:

> I felt I was insane, you know. Everything people done to me just wigged me. I couldn't hold a conversation, and my mind would be wandering, and I was always thinking, oh, I don't know, weird things, like hearing music different. . . . I get the feeling that I can't talk to anyone. I'll goof completely.

Given these typically frightening and unpleasant first experiences, the beginner will not continue use unless he learns to redefine the sensations as pleasurable:

> It was offered to me, and I tried it. I'll tell you one thing. I never did enjoy it at all. I mean it was just nothing that I could enjoy. [Well, did you get high when you turned on?] Oh, yeah, I got definite feelings from it. But I didn't enjoy them. I mean I got plenty of reactions, but they were mostly reactions of fear. [You were frightened?] Yes. I didn't enjoy it. I couldn't seem to relax with it, you know. If you can't relax with a thing, you can't enjoy it, I don't think.

In other cases the first experiences were also definitely unpleasant, but the person did become a marihuana user. This occurred, however, only after a later experience enabled him to redefine the sensations as pleasurable:

> [This man's first experience was extremely unpleasant, involving distortion of spatial relationships and sounds, violent thirst, and panic produced by these

symptoms.] After the first time I didn't turn on for about, I'd say, ten months to a year. . . . It wasn't a moral thing; it was because I'd gotten so frightened, bein' so high. An' I didn't want to go through that again, I mean, my reaction was, "Well, if this is what they call bein' high, I don't dig [like] it." . . . So I didn't turn on for a year almost, accounta that. . . .

Well, my friends started, an' consequently I started again. But I didn't have any more, I didn't have that same initial reaction, after I started turning on again.

[In interaction with his friends he became able to find pleasure in the effects of the drug and eventually became a regular user.]

In no case will use continue without a redefinition of the effects as enjoyable.

This redefinition occurs, typically, in interaction with more experienced users who, in a number of ways, teach the novice to find pleasure in this experience which is at first so frightening.[3] They may reassure him as to the temporary character of the unpleasant sensations and minimize their seriousness, at the same time calling attention to the more enjoyable aspects. An experienced user describes how he handles newcomers to marihuana use:

Well, they get pretty high sometimes. The average person isn't ready for that, and it is a little frightening to them sometimes. I mean, they've been high on lush [alcohol], and they get higher that way than they've ever been before, and they don't know what's happening to them. Because they think they're going to keep going up, up, up till they lose their minds or begin doing weird things or something. You have to like reassure them, explain to them that they're not really flipping or anything, that they're gonna be all right. You have to just talk them out of being afraid. Keep talking to them, reassuring, telling them it's all right. And come on with your own story, you know: "The same thing happened to me. You'll get to like that after awhile." Keep coming on like that; pretty soon you talk them out of being scared. And besides they see you doing it and nothing horrible is happening to you, so that gives them more confidence.

The more experienced user may also teach the novice to regulate the amount he smokes more carefully, so as to avoid any severely uncomfortable symptoms while retaining the pleasant ones. Finally, he teaches the new user that he can "get to like it after awhile." He teaches him to regard those ambiguous experiences formerly defined as unpleasant as enjoyable. The older user in the following incident is a person whose tastes have shifted in this way, and his remarks have the effect of helping others to make a similar redefinition:

A new user had her first experience of the effects of marihuana and became frightened and hysterical. She "felt like she was half in and half out of the room" and experienced a number of alarming physical symptoms. One of the more experienced users present said, "She's dragged because she's high

[3] Sol Charen and Luis Perelman, "Personality Studies of Marihuana Addicts," *American Journal of Psychiatry,* CII (March, 1946), p. 679.

like that. I'd give anything to get that high myself. I haven't been that high in years."

In short, what was once frightening and distasteful becomes, after a taste for it is built up, pleasant, desired, and sought after. Enjoyment is introduced by the favorable definition of the experience that one acquires from others. Without this, use will not continue, for marihuana will not be for the user an object he can use for pleasure.

In addition to being a necessary step in becoming a user, this represents an important condition for continued use. It is quite common for experienced users suddenly to have an unpleasant or frightening experience, which they cannot define as pleasurable, either because they have used a larger amount of marihuana than usual or because the marihuana they have used turns out to be of higher quality than they expected. The user has sensations which go beyond any conception he has of what being high is and is in much the same situation as the novice, uncomfortable and frightened. He may blame it on an overdose and simply be more careful in the future. But he may make this the occasion for a rethinking of his attitude toward the drug and decide that it no longer can give him pleasure. When this occurs and is not followed by a re-definition of the drug as capable of producing pleasure, use will cease.

The likelihood of such a redefinition occurring depends on the degree of the individual's participation with other users. Where this participation is in-tensive, the individual is quickly talked out of his feeling against marihuana use. In the next case, on the other hand, the experience was very disturbing, and the aftermath of the incident cut the person's participation with other users to almost zero. Use stopped for three years and began again only when a combination of circumstances, important among which was a resumption of ties with users, made possible a redefinition of the nature of the drug:

It was too much, like I only made about four pokes, and I couldn't even get it out of my mouth, I was so high, and I got real flipped. In the basement, you know, I just couldn't stay in there anymore. My heart was pounding real hard, you know, and I was going out of my mind; I thought I was losing my mind completely. So I cut out of this basement, and this other guy, he's out of his mind, told me, "Don't, don't leave me, man. Stay here." And I couldn't.

I walked outside, and it was five below zero, and I thought I was dying, and I had my coat open; I was sweating, I was perspiring. My whole insides were all . . . , and I walked about two blocks away, and I fainted behind a bush. I don't know how long I laid there. I woke up, and I was feeling worst, I can't describe it at all, so I made it to a bowling alley, man, and I was trying to act normal, I was trying to shoot pool, you know, trying to act real normal, and I couldn't lay and I couldn't stand up and I couldn't sit down, and I went up and laid down where some guys that spot pins lay down, and that didn't help me, and I went down to a doctor's office. I was going to go in there and tell the doctor to put me out of my misery . . . because my heart was pounding so hard, you know. . . . So then all week end I started flipping, seeing things there and going through hell, you know, all kinds of abnormal things. . . . I just quit for a long time then.

[He went to a doctor who defined the symptoms for him as those of a nervous breakdown caused by "nerves" and "worries." Although he was no longer using marihuana, he had some recurrences of the symptoms which led him to suspect that "it was all his nerves."] So I just stopped worrying, you know; so it was about thirty-six months later I started making it again. I'd just take a few pokes, you know. [He first resumed use in the company of the same user-friend with whom he had been involved in the original incident.]

A person, then, cannot begin to use marihuana for pleasure, or continue its use for pleasure, unless he learns to define its effects as enjoyable, unless it becomes and remains an object he conceives of as capable of producing pleasure.

In summary, an individual will be able to use marihuana for pleasure only when he goes through a process of learning to conceive of it as an object which can be used in this way. No one becomes a user without (1) learning to smoke the drug in a way which will produce real effects; (2) learning to recognize the effects and connect them with drug use (learning, in other words, to get high); and (3) learning to enjoy the sensations he perceives. In the course of this process he develops a disposition or motivation to use marihuana which was not and could not have been present when he began use, for it involves and depends on conceptions of the drug which could only grow out of the kind of actual experience detailed above. On completion of this process he is willing and able to use marihuana for pleasure.

He has learned, in short, to answer "Yes" to the question: "Is it fun?" The direction his further use of the drug takes depends on his being able to continue to answer "Yes" to this question and, in addition, on his being able to answer "Yes" to other questions which arise as he becomes aware of the implications of the fact that society disapproves of the practice: "Is it expedient?" "Is it moral?" Once he has acquired the ability to get enjoyment by using the drug, use will continue to be possible for him. Considerations of morality and expediency, occasioned by the reactions of society, may interfere and inhibit use, but use continues to be a possibility in terms of his conception of the drug. The act becomes impossible only when the ability to enjoy the experience of being high is lost, through a change in the user's conception of the drug occasioned by certain kinds of experience with it.

Discussion Questions

1. Describe the techniques and skills a novice must learn in order to get the "proper" effect from smoking marihuana.
2. In order for an individual to acquire the status of "deviant," his behavior must be perceived and defined as deviant, the label of "deviant" must be applied to him, and he must incorporate this status into his self-conception. Given this definition of a deviant, do you think most marihuana smokers are deviants? Discuss.

JAMES Q. WILSON

Lock 'Em Up and Other Thoughts on Crime

Some students of crime and punishment argue that we ought to replace the prison system or face a violent and terribly costly revolution. Others argue that notwithstanding the failure of prisons to correct and reform criminals, prisons are still needed to protect the innocent in our society from the criminally wicked. This point of view is based on the assumption, supported by a growing body of scientific knowledge, that there is a *criminal personality* not readily amenable to reform. In the following article, James Q. Wilson argues why he believes we should "lock 'em up."

As much as anything, our futile efforts to curb or even understand the dramatic and continuing rise in crime have been frustrated by our optimistic and unrealistic assumptions about human nature. Considering that our society is in the grip of a decade-old crime wave despite a decade-long period of prosperity, it is strange that we should persist in the view that we can find and alleviate the "causes" of crime, that serious criminals can be rehabilitated, that the police can somehow be made to catch more criminals faster, and that prosecutors and judges have the wisdom to tailor sentences to fit the "needs" of the individual offender.

I argue for a sober view of man and his institutions that would permit reasonable things to be accomplished, foolish things abandoned, and utopian things forgotten. A sober view of man requires a modest definition of progress. A 20 per cent reduction in robbery would still leave us with the highest robbery rate of almost any Western nation but would prevent about 60,000 robberies a year. A small gain for society, a large one for the would-be victims. Yet a 20 per cent reduction is unlikely if we concentrate our efforts on dealing with the causes of crime or even if we concentrate on improving police efficiency. But were we to devote those resources to a strategy that is well within our abilities—to incapacitating a larger fraction of the convicted serious robbers—then not only is a 20 per cent reduction possible, even larger ones are conceivable.

Most serious crime is committed by repeaters. What we do with first offenders is probably far less important than what we do with habitual offenders. A genuine first offender (and not merely a habitual offender caught for the first time) is in all likelihood a young person who, in the majority of cases, will stop stealing when he gets older. This is not to say we should forgive first offenses, for that would be to license the offense and erode the moral judgments that must underlie any society's attitude toward crime. The gravity of the offense must be appropriately impressed on the first offender, but the effort to devise ways of re-educating or uplifting him in order to insure that he does not steal again is likely to be wasted—both because we do not know how to re-educate or uplift and because most young delinquents seem to re-educate themselves no matter what society does.

After tracing the history of nearly 10,000 Philadelphia boys born in 1945, Marvin Wolfgang and his colleagues at the University of Pennsylvania found that more than one-third were picked up by the police for something more serious than a traffic offense but that 46 per cent of these delinquents had no further police contact after their first offense. Though one-third started on crime, nearly half seemed to stop spontaneously—a good thing, because otherwise the criminal justice system in that city, already sorely taxed, would in all likelihood have collapsed. Out of the 10,000 boys, however, there were 627—only 6 per cent—who committed five or more offenses before they were 18. Yet these few chronic offenders accounted for *more than half* of all the recorded delinquencies and about *two-thirds* of all the violent crimes committed by the entire cohort.

Only a tiny fraction of all serious crimes leads immediately to an arrest, and only a slightly larger fraction is ultimately "cleared" by an arrest, but this does not mean that the police function is meaningless. Because most serious crime is committed by repeaters, most criminals eventually get arrested. The Wolfgang findings and other studies suggest that the chances of a persistent burglar or robber living out his life, or even going a year, with no arrest are quite small. Yet a large proportion of repeat offenders suffers little or no loss of freedom. Whether or not one believes that such a penalty, if inflicted, would act as a deterrent, it is obvious that it could serve to incapacitate these offenders, and thus, for the period of the incapacitation, prevent them from committing additional crimes.

We have a limited (and declining) supply of detention facilities, and many of those that exist are decrepit, unsafe, and overcrowded. But as important as expanding the supply and improving the decency of the facilities is the need to think seriously about how we wish to allocate those spaces that exist. At present, that allocation is hit or miss. A 1966 survey of more than 15 juvenile correctional institutions disclosed that about 30 per cent of the inmates were young persons who had been committed for conduct that would have been judged criminal were it committed by adults. They were runaways, "stubborn children," or chronic truants—problem children, to be sure, but scarcely major threats to society. Using scarce detention space for them when in Los Angeles more than 90 per cent of burglars with a major prior record receive no state prison sentence seems, to put it mildly, anomalous.

In a joint study, Prof. Reuel Shinnar of City College of New York and his son Shlomo have estimated the effect on crime rates in New York State of a judicial policy other than that followed during the last decade or so. Given the present level of police efficiency and making some assumptions about how many crimes each offender commits per year, they conclude that the rate of serious crime would be only *one-third* what it is today if every person convicted of a serious offense were imprisoned for three years. This reduction would be less if it turned out (as seems unlikely) that most serious crime is committed by first-time offenders, and it would be much greater if the proportion of crimes resulting in an arrest and conviction were increased (as also seems unlikely). The reduction, it should be noted, would be solely the result of incapacitation, making no allowance for such additional reductions as might result from enhanced deterrence or rehabilitation.

The Shinnar estimates are based on uncertain data and involve assumptions that can be challenged. But even assuming they are overly optimistic by a factor of two, a sizable reduction in crime would still ensue. In other countries such a policy of greater incapacitation is in fact followed. A robber arrested in England, for example, is more than three times as likely as one arrested in New York to go to prison. That difference in sentencing does not account for all the difference between English and American crime rates, but it may well account for a substantial fraction of it.

That these gains are possible does not mean that society should adopt such a policy. One would first want to know the costs, in additional prison space and judicial resources, of greater use of incapacitation. One would want to debate the propriety and humanity of a mandatory three-year term; perhaps, in order to accommodate differences in the character of criminals and their crimes, one would want to have a range of sentences from, say, one to five years. One would want to know what is likely to happen to the process of charging and pleading if every person arrested for a serious crime faced a mandatory minimum sentence, however mild. These and other difficult and important questions must first be confronted. But the central fact is that *these are reasonable questions* around which facts can be gathered and intelligent arguments mustered. To discuss them requires us to make few optimistic assumptions about the malleability of human nature, the skills of officials who operate complex institutions, or the capacity of society to improve the fundamental aspects of familial and communal life.

Persons who criticize an emphasis on changing the police and courts to cope with crime are fond of saying that such measures cannot work so long as unemployment and poverty exist. We must acknowledge that we have not done very well at inducting young persons, especially but not only blacks, into the work force. Teen-age unemployment rates continue to exceed 20 per cent and show little sign of abating. Nor should we assume that declining birth rates will soon reduce either the youthful demand for jobs or the supply of young criminals. The birth rates are now very low; it will not be until the mid- or late-nineteen-eighties that these low rates will affect the proportion of the population that is entering the job-seeking and crime-prone ages of 16 through 26.

In the meantime, while anticrime policies may be hampered by the failure of employment policies, it would be equally correct to say that so long as the criminal-justice system does not impede crime, efforts to reduce unemployment will not work. If legitimate opportunities for work are unavailable, many young persons will turn to crime; but if criminal opportunities are profitable, many young persons will not take those legitimate jobs that exist. The benefits of work and the costs of crime must be increased simultaneously; to increase one but not the other makes sense only if one assumes that young people are irrational.

One rejoinder to this view is the argument that if legitimate jobs are made absolutely more attractive than stealing, stealing will decline even without any increase in penalties for it. That may be true provided there is no practical limit on the amount that can be paid in wages. Since the average "take" from a burglary or mugging is quite small, it would seem easy to make the income from a job exceed the income from crime.

But this neglects the advantages of a criminal income: One works at crime at one's convenience, enjoys the esteem of colleagues who think a "straight" job is stupid and skill at stealing is commendable, looks forward to the occasional "big score" that may make further work unnecessary for weeks, and relishes the risk and adventure associated with theft. The money value of all these benefits—that is, what one who is not shocked by crime would want in cash to forego crime—is hard to estimate but is almost certainly far larger than what either public or private employers could offer to unskilled or semiskilled young workers. The only alternative for society is so to increase the risks of theft that its value is depreciated below what society can afford to pay in legal wages, and then take whatever steps are necessary to insure that those legal wages are available.

Another rejoinder to the "attack poverty" approach to crime is this: The desire to reduce crime is the worst possible reason for reducing poverty. Most poor persons are not criminals; many are either retired or have regular jobs and lead conventional family lives. The elderly, the working poor, and the willing-to-work poor could benefit greatly from economic conditions and government programs that enhance their incomes without there being the slightest reduction in crime—indeed, if the experience of the nineteen-sixties is any guide, there might well be, through no fault of most such beneficiaries, an increase in crime. Reducing poverty and breaking up the ghettos are desirable policies in their own right, whatever their effects on crime. It is the duty of government to devise other measures to cope with crime: not only to permit antipoverty programs to succeed without unfair competition from criminal opportunities, but also to insure that such programs do not inadvertently shift the costs of progress, in terms of higher crime rates, onto innocent parties, not the least of whom are the poor themselves.

One cannot press this economic reasoning too far. Some persons will commit crimes whatever the risks; indeed, for some, the greater the risk, the greater the thrill, while others—the alcoholic wife beater, for example—are only dimly aware that there are any risks. But more important than the insensitivity of certain criminal offenders to changes in risks and benefits is the impropriety of casting the crime problem wholly in terms of a utilitarian calculus. The most serious offenses are crimes not simply because society finds them inconvenient, but because it regards them with moral horror. To steal, to rape, to rob, to assault—these acts are destructive of the very possibility of society and affronts to the humanity of their victims. It is my experience that parents do not instruct their children to be law-abiding merely by pointing to the risks of being caught, but by explaining that these acts are wrong whether or not one is caught. I conjecture that those parents who simply warn their offspring about the risks of crime produce a disproportionate number of young persons willing to take those risks.

Even the deterrent capacity of the criminal-justice system depends in no small part on its ability to evoke sentiments of shame in the accused. If all it evoked were a sense of being unlucky, crime rates would be even higher. James Fitzjames Stephens, the 19th-century British jurist, makes the point by analogy. To what extent, he asks, would a man be deterred from theft by the knowledge that by committing it he was exposing himself to 1 chance in 50 of catching a serious but not fatal illness—say, a bad fever? Rather little, we would imagine—indeed, all of us regularly take risks as great as or greater than that: when we drive after drinking, when we smoke cigarettes, when we go hunting in the woods. The criminal sanction, Stephens concludes, "operates not only on the fears of criminals, but upon the habitual sentiments of those who are not criminals. [A] great part of the general detestation of crime . . . arises from the fact that the commission of offenses is associated . . . with the solemn and deliberate infliction of punishment wherever crime is proved."

Much is made today of the fact that the criminal-justice system "stigmatizes" those caught up in it, and thus unfairly marks such persons and perhaps even furthers their criminal careers by having "labeled" them as criminals. Whether the labeling process operates in this way is as yet unproved, but it would indeed be unfortunate if society be unfortunate if society treated a convicted offender in such a way that he had no reasonable alternative but to make crime a career. To prevent this, society ought to insure that one can "pay one's debt" without suffering permanent loss of civil rights, the continuing and pointless indignity of parole supervision, and frustration in being unable to find a job. But doing these things is very different from eliminating the "stigma" from crime. To destigmatize crime would be to lift from it the weight of moral judgment and to make crime simply a particular occupation or avocation which society has chosen to reward less (or perhaps more!) than other pursuits. If there is no stigma attached to an activity, then society has no business making it a crime. Indeed, before the invention of the prison in the late 18th and early 19th centuries, the stigma attached to criminals was the major deterrent to and principal form of protection from criminal activity. The purpose of the criminal-justice system is not to expose would be criminals to a lottery in which they either win or lose, but to expose them in addition and more importantly to the solemn condemnation of the community should they yield to temptation.

Anyone familiar with the police stations, jails and courts of some of our larger cities is keenly aware that accused persons caught up in the system are exposed to very little that involves either judgment or solemnity. They are instead processed through a bureaucratic maze in which a bargain is offered and a haggle ensues at every turn—over the amount of bail, the degree of the charged offense and the nature of the plea. Much of what observers find objectionable about this process could be alleviated by devoting many more resources to it, so that an ample supply of prosecutors, defense attorneys and judges was available. That we do not devote those additional resources in a country obsessed with the crime problem is one of the more interesting illustrations of the maxim, familiar to all political scientists, that one cannot predict public policy simply from knowing popular attitudes. Whatever the cause, it remains the case that in New York County (Manhattan) there were, in 1973, 31,098 felony arrests to be handled by only 125 prosecutors, 119 public defenders and 59 Criminal Court judges. The result was predictable: Of those arrested, only 4,130 pleaded guilty to or were convicted on a felony charge; 81 per cent of the felony arrests were disposed of by pleading guilty to a misdemeanor or by discharging the case.

One wonders whether the stigma properly associated with crime retains much deterrent or educative value. My strong inclination is to resist explanations for rising crime that are based on the alleged moral breakdown of society, the community or the family. I resist in part because most of the families and communities I know have not broken down, and in part because, had they broken down, I cannot imagine any collective action we could take consistent with our civil liberties that would restore a moral consensus, and yet the facts are hard to ignore. Take the family: More than one-third of all black children and 1 in 14 of all white children live in single-parent families. More than two million children live in single-parent households (usually the father absent), almost *double* the number of 10 years ago. In 1950, 18 per cent of black families were headed by females; in 1969 the proportion had risen to 27 per cent; by 1973 it exceeded 35 per cent. The average income for a single-parent family with children under 6 years of age was, in 1970, only $3,100, well below the official "poverty line."

Studies done in the late nineteen-fifties and the early nineteen-sixties showed that children from broken homes were more likely than others to become delinquent. In New York State, 58 per cent of the variation in pupil achievement in 300 schools could be predicted by but three variables—broken homes, overcrowded housing and parental educational level. Family disorganization, writes Prof. Urie Bronfenbrenner of Cornell University, has been shown in thousands of studies to be an "omnipresent overriding factor" in behavior disorders and social pathology. And that disorganization is increasing.

These facts may explain some elements of the rising crime rate that cannot be attributed to the increased number of young persons, high teen-age unemployment or changed judicial policies. The age of persons arrested has been declining for more than 15 years and the median age of convicted defendants (in jurisdictions for which data are available) has been declining for the last six years. Apparently, the age at which persons begin to commit serious crime has been falling. For some young people, thus, whatever forces weaken their resistance to criminal activity have been increasing in magnitude, and these forces may well include the continued disorganization of the family and the continued deterioration of the social structure of inner-city communities.

One wants to be objective, if not optimistic. Perhaps single-parent families today are less disorganized—or have a different significance—than such families in the past. Perhaps the relationship between family structure and social pathology will change. After all, for at least a brief while, the heroin epidemic on the East Coast showed signs of abating as law enforcement reduced the supply of narcotics, treatment programs took many addicts off the streets and popular revulsion against addiction mounted. Perhaps other aspects of the relationship among family, personality and crime will change. Perhaps. But even as this is being written, and after the book from which it is taken went to press, there have appeared ominous signs that the East Coast heroin shortage may be ending and the use of heroin once again increasing.

No one can say how much of crime results from its increased profitability and how much from its decreased shamefulness. But one or both factors must be at work, for population changes alone simply cannot account for the increases. Crime in our cities has increased far faster than the number of young people, or poor people, or black people, or just plain people who live in those cities. In short, objective conditions alone, whether demographic or economic, cannot account for the crime increases; ideas, attitudes, values have played a great part, though in ways hard to define and impossible to measure. An assessment of the effect of these changes on crime would provide a partial understanding of changes in the moral structure of our society.

But to understand is not to change. If few of the demographic factors contributing to crime are subject to planned change, virtually none of the subjective ones are. Though intellectually rewarding, from a practical point of view it is a mistake to think about crime in terms of its "causes" and then to search for ways to alleviate those causes. We must think instead of what it is feasible for a government or a community to do, and then try to discover, by experimentation and observation, which of those things will produce, at acceptable costs, desirable changes in the level of criminal victimization.

There are, we now know, certain things we can change in accordance with our intentions, and certain ones we cannot. We cannot alter the number of juveniles who first experiment with minor crimes. We cannot lower the recidivism rate, though within reason we should keep trying. We are not yet certain whether we can increase significantly the police apprehension rate. We may be able to change the teen-age unemployment rate, though we have learned by painful trial and error that doing this is much more difficult than once supposed. We can probably reduce the time it takes to bring an arrested person to trial, even though we have as yet made few serious efforts to do so. We can certainly reduce the arbitrary and socially irrational exercise of prosecutorial discretion over whom to charge and whom to release, and we can most definitely stop pretending that judges know, any better than the rest of us, how to provide "individualized justice." We can confine a larger proportion of the serious offenders and repeaters and fewer of the common drunks and truant children. We know that confining criminals prevents them from harming society, and we have grounds for suspecting that some would-be criminals can be deterred by the confinement of others.

Above all, we can try to learn more about what works, and in the process abandon our ideological preconceptions about what *ought* to work. Nearly 10 years ago I wrote that the billions of dollars the Federal Government was then preparing to spend on crime control would be wasted and indeed might even make matters worse if they were merely pumped into the existing criminal-justice system. They were, and they have. In the next 10 years I hope we can learn to experiment rather than simply spend, to test our theories rather than fund our fears. This is advice, not simply or even primarily to government—for governments are run by men and women who are under irresistible pressures to pretend they know more than they do—but to my colleagues: academics, theoreticians, writers, advisers. We may feel ourselves under pressure to pretend we know things, but we are also under a positive obligation to admit what we do not know and to avoid cant and sloganizing. The Government agency, the Law Enforcement Assistance Administration, that has futilely spent those billions was created in consequence of an act passed by Congress on the advice of a Presidential commission staffed by academics, myself included.

It is easy and popular to criticize yesterday's empty hopes and mistaken beliefs, especially if they seemed supportive of law enforcement. It is harder, and certainly most unpopular, to criticize today's pieties and pretensions, especially if they are uttered in the name of progress and humanity. But if we were wrong in thinking that more money spent on the police would bring down crime rates, we are equally wrong in supposing that closing our prisons, emptying our jails and supporting "community-based" programs will do any better. Indeed, there is some evidence that these steps will make matters worse, and we ignore it at our peril.

Since the days of the crime commission we have learned a great deal, more than we are prepared to admit. Perhaps we fear to admit it because of a new-found modesty about the foundations of our knowledge, but perhaps also because the implications of that knowledge suggest an unflattering view of man. Intellectuals, although they often dislike the common person as an individual, do not wish to be caught saying uncomplimentary things about humankind. Nevertheless, some persons will shun crime even if we do nothing to deter them, while others will seek it out even if we do everything to reform them. Wicked people exist. Nothing avails except to set them apart from innocent people. And many people, neither wicked nor innocent, but watchful, dissembling and calculating of their opportunities, ponder our reaction to wickedness as a cue to what they might profitably do. We have trifled with the wicked, made sport of the innocent and encouraged the calculators. Justice suffers, and so do we all.

Discussion Questions

1. According to the author, why should society take those with a "criminal personality" and "lock 'em up"?
2. The author concludes with the statement that "justice suffers, and so do we all." What does he mean by this and why does he believe this is so?

WILLIAM OVEREND

Ex-con a Success as Rehabilitator

Perhaps the most remarkable kind of success story concerning deviancy is of an ex-con who is rehabilitated. The following is one such account. John Maher's success suggests that we might look to the ex-cons themselves rather than the social sciences to develop new methods of behavior modification necessary to rehabilitate criminals.

They were society's trash, but now they have a chance to start again and be something better. Many of them won't make it in this tough, communal society of former drug addicts and convicts known as Delancey Street. There isn't any easy cure for these people, because nobody can really solve what's wrong with them except themselves.

The discipline is harsh. They are forced to work hard at their jobs and made to confront every character defect and personality flaw. They will have two years at Delancey Street to toughen themselves and understand that they have been weak and stupid in the past. If they can do that, they will be able to survive in the even tougher world outside. If they can't, Delancey Street will only be another rest stop for them on the same old road to nowhere.

They will get a little stronger every day they stick it out. For every failure, there has been a miracle here for someone else. One thing that helps the newcomers make it through the first weeks and months in this strange new world is that so many of the miracles, their own lives already changed by their experience here, are working and living beside them, a constant reminder that even the most wretched human beings can change their lives if they try hard enough and get enough help from others who care.

"We haven't turned out any Albert Einsteins yet," says John Maher, the 36-year-old former addict and thief who founded Delancey Street seven years ago. "But now that we've got our businesses firmly established and have a lot of our residents going to school, it's getting easier for them to see the possibilities.

"Most of these people never made it past the eighth grade," he adds. "We get 'em a high school equivalency first, and we've got 60 to 70 of 'em going to the universities. We have four residents in law school now, and we've put dozens through computer school."

Sylvester Herring is one of Delancey Street's more dramatic success stories. Born in Los Angeles 41 years ago, he is a former heroin addict who spent a total of eight years in prison on burglary and armed robbery charges.

"I was at a point in my life where everything had gone wrong," Herring says. "I had tried other programs, including methadone, but they hadn't worked for me. I thought from the beginning that Delancey Street would be different, mainly because it wasn't in the ghetto and I knew some people who had been helped."

Herring came to Delancey Street five years ago. He says he was always interested in helping others as well as himself, and with that purpose he founded the activist Peoples Democratic Club, one of San Francisco's many political groups. A supporter of George Moscone's successful campaign for mayor two years ago, he was selected as one of 15 members of San Francisco's Human Rights Commission last year. He is the first black ex-convict and heroin addict in that position.

Crucial Transition

Success at Delancey Street, however, isn't simply a matter of achieving outside status. What counts more is making the transition from weakness and worthlessness to strength and self-respect.

Rene Shenessky, 27, falls into that category. A heroin user at 12 and a street prostitute at 13, she had been in a dozen other drug programs before she came to Delancey Street 23 months ago. She had also spent three years in jail and tried to kill herself twice.

"Women like me, when they come here, all they know is how to use their bodies to get things," she says. "Only two things had ever made me feel good—drugs and men. At Delancey Street, there is absolutely no sex for the first three months, and it gives the women a chance to start establishing their own identities.

"When I first came here, I didn't really have any plans to stay," she adds. "I was doing what a lot of addicts do, just looking for a program where I could clean up for a month or so. But this place blew my mind. I'd never been talked to that way before. I'd never been ridiculed for living the way I had lived. I'd never realized how pitiful my life was."

For Ms. Shenessky, that realization was the first step toward rehabilitation. Although her two-year commitment ends in another month, she plans to remain at Delancey Street for at least another year. Her jobs have involved screening disciplinary problems of the residents and interviewing other women in jails and prisons who are potential residents, but ultimately she would like to be a television or movie camerawoman. Another step in her personal development is that she realizes that is impractical now because she has no experience.

"There will be a day when I am ready to try it outside, but I'm not in any hurry," she says. "Women are sort of placed on a pedestal here. That's never happened to me before, and I like the feeling. To tell you the truth, it's a joy to be here."

For many Delancey Street residents, the turning point comes in weekend encounter sessions known as "dissipations" designed to force them to admit their failures, confront their guilt directly and convince them that they really can be different if they try.

These are tricky sessions. Maher and the others who preside must be tough enough to force the guilt out, but also gentle enough to offer some hope. Charles Hampden-Turner, a British sociologist, spent a year living in Delancey Street and wrote a book titled "Sane Asylum" describing the process. In it, he reveals the subtleties behind the sledgehammer psychological blows that are part of Maher's therapy.

Licia is a 35-year-old Latin woman and former heroin addict whose son has been charged with double murder, accused of robbing a married couple, then murdering them in front of their 8-year-old daughter and sexually assaulting the child's mother as she was dying. In the following passage, a 1974 confrontation when a conviction meant a possible death sentence, Maher and Willie Harper, a senior resident, attempt to force her to confront the horror.

" 'Now you have to consider, lady, what it was about you as a mother and role model that could have turned this kid into a killer,' Willie begins. 'So you have to ask yourself what *you* did to raise a MONSTER like this . . . Let's talk about *your* position and *your* responsibility.'

"But she is still not 'hearing' and John's voice breaks in angrily . . .

Face the Reality

" 'We're telling you, Licia, *the death penalty is back in California* . . . Is *this* the time you want a fix, Licia? You want to run an' help your kid and perhaps *fortify* yourself on the way! Or are you gonna be a woman and *face reality?* . . . When the jury hears that kid get up in court and say, "That man killed my mommy and daddy . . . I was there," they're going through the roof! You can't even *cross-examine* the kid in that situation. Your son's gonna be sentenced *to the gas*, lady, he's *gonna get the pellet*. And I'm surprised they didn't gun him down the day they brought him in, considering that repulsive crime!'

"A long, shrill scream breaks from Licia. John pauses—and speaks more gently . . .

" 'Listen! I'm telling you, WE CAN BEAT THE PELLET. We got the best lawyers in town. Chances are he'll get gas from the jury; *then* we'll knock it down to a five-to-life on appeal. The *real* question is whether he'll ever see the street again in his lifetime, and *that* depends on you. Ten years from now, *if* you're clean and got your life together, we can say to the parole board, "Here's his mama. She's someone he can look up to. She's held responsible positions for years." And we can get your kid paroled into our custody.

" 'You really want to help that kid? Well, it's gonna be a 10-to-15 YEAR JOB, with a LOT OF HARD WORK, no fixes and no fantasies, and a capacity for courage you ain't shown so far! Because right now you couldn't help your kid if you wanted to! You go down to court and do your weepy-whiney dope-fiend act and they'll put him away forever!'

"There is another scream from Licia. She hides her face and sobs, 'I wanta die! I wanta die! I'll kill myself!'

" 'YOU AIN'T GOT NO RIGHT TO DIE! Not until you get the man *you* brought into this world *out* of that jail!' John is implacable. 'I *know* what you're thinking, Licia. I've seen it a thousand times. You're babbling to yourself, "He's gonna get out! He's gonna get out! . . ." You mothers want to buy your kids back with one bad check and a quick fix! You don't *like* work, sister? TOO BAD! 'Cause when you make a baby that's A LIFE'S WORK!' "

"John has reached the end of the room in his walking disquisition. Now he comes up to Licia, places a hand on her shoulder and speaks with measured intensity.

" 'So get it into your mind that you and your son can come out of this only with great nerve and great realism and great dignity—and no weaseling out on a cheapo catharsis like this one and false hope. To get this boy out we *first* have to get his mama well—only mama keeps fantasizing. You'll kill yourself? What happens to him *then?* Ain't difficult for you to die, lady. You been dying for years. It's difficult to *live*.' "

It is early evening and the Delancey Street Club across from San Francisco's Golden Gate Park is filled with residents who are finishing their dinners and chatting at tables while they wait for the evening encounter sessions called "games," a shorter and milder version of the longer dissipations, to begin.

Although only about a third of the Delancey Street residents live in this particular facility, they all eat their meals and hold their meetings here. It is the social center for the foundation, a place to sit and drink coffee and relax between the long hours of work and therapy that take up most of the day.

These are the faceless people who are almost always collectively dismissed as "ex-convicts and ex-addicts," overshadowed in large part by the very dynamics of the program they are in and the personality of the man who founded it. But, in a real sense, they *are* Delancey Street, and it is time to meet some of them. . . .

Bob Simpson, 49, born in Nebraska, a pipe-smoker and jazz pianist, also an alcoholic and "qualified as a downer freak." He is a quiet man, a former salesman, divorced now, the children grown. He has been here for 10 months.

"You get the feeling of belonging here, doing some really great things," he says. "I like the life-style. This place gears you to getting outside. I don't want to live like a monk the rest of my life, but as long as I stay here I'll never be bored. An older guy like me, we act more as a supportive function. I can have an exciting life there, watching the young people change their lives."

A Day at a Time

Dee Nicholson, 28, an attractive brunette with dimples and an almost-innocent seductive charm, married three times, two children living with relatives, a former blackjack dealer in Reno, a heroin addict for almost 10 years, probated by the courts to Delancey Street on a sentence for the sale of heroin. She has slept with men for a bag of heroin, she says, but not for money. She has been here only 30 days, and she's not sure yet what she really thinks about it.

"Right now I'm just taking it a day at a time," she says. "I like the feeling of concern. I got a game played on me last night for playing innocent, using men. I guess nobody wants to know about themselves as others see them, but you can't even talk to men for the first 90 days, and that's difficult for me. My (third) husband and I are very close. I won't be able to see him for my first year here, and that will be hard."

Pat Yadlosky, 33, a former factory worker in Detroit, addicted to morphine and heroin for 10 years. In Delancey Street for three years, he now manages one of the two dormitories leased by Delancey Street to house its residents in converted mansions in San Francisco's Pacific Heights area.

"The first thing that struck me here was the pace, people traveling fast and working hard," he says. "In my first year I had a chance to work with senior citizens, handicapped children. Then I was a salesman for our plants and glassware business, going door to door to businesses, calling on bankers and real estate people. It was the first time in my life I was encouraged to be a more social person. It's incredible how many people I talk to every day. I've also worked as a bodyguard for Cesar Chavez. I'm not the same person I was. Now I'm entertaining the idea of operating my own facility to help people. It's very intense here. Before you realize the changes, you have changed."

Six nights a week, the Delancey Street residents break into groups of 16 for the "games" in which they release their pent-up frustrations and hostilities and attempt to force their fellow residents to look honestly at their own defects. The games are about to begin now, and in a few minutes some of the people who have been chatting quietly will be screaming at each other, some of them because they are basically vicious people, others because they think it will do some good.

As the game progresses, almost everyone becomes the target at one point or another. Pat Lavelle, a 60-year-old woman who has been sitting quietly all night, suddenly bursts into an emotional tirade when the game turns on Oral Nelson, 27, a resident for almost five years. She had been upset by a personal problem the day before, she says, but Nelson, who needed to talk to her about some Delancey Street project, had insisted on seeing her even though she wanted to be alone.

Defense for Actions

"You're insensitive," she shouts, almost sobbing. "You don't care about people. You think you're important. You didn't need to talk to me that very second. You could have waited. . . ."

Nelson, whose basic problem was a self-destructive compulsion to gamble, is one of the few residents without a criminal record, which permitted him to recently qualify to take and pass the examinations necessary to become a San Francisco deputy sheriff. Clearly surprised, he defends himself and soon the real reasons for Mrs. Lavelle's emotion come pouring out. Although she looks like somebody's grandmother, it turns out that Mrs. Lavelle is an embezzler, and she had been notified by the Internal Revenue Service just the day before that because there was no way to collect taxes on almost $117,000 she had embezzled, she most likely will never receive a penny in Social Security benefits.

"I have no home to go to," she tells the others. "You will be able to leave here. But I will have to die here now. . . ."

"So what if you have nowhere to go," one resident shouts. "Big deal! None of us really has anywhere to go. You're 60. So what! The trouble with you is you don't feel you're one of us. You never really try to get to know any of us. All you talk about is what you do. This is the first time you've ever even tried to share your problems."

She sits there, accepting the criticisms, seemingly without resentment. As the game continues, she seems more composed. For Mrs. Lavelle, it was the first time she had managed to pour her feelings out to the others, and she seems to be feeling better now. . . .

There is a special sadness to some of the stories, and Mrs. Lavelle's is one of them. A graduate in accounting from Northwestern University, she had much more going for her at the beginning than many of her fellow residents.

A gray-haired matronly widow who looks like she's probably a volunteer at Delancey Street from some church group, Mrs. Lavelle first got into trouble in 1942 when she embezzled $3,500 from a Chevrolet dealer in Milwaukee. She spent three years in prison, then worked for the next 25 years as an accountant in Kansas and California without stealing a penny from anyone.

Her husband, however, suffered from congestive heart failure. In 1967, Mrs. Lavelle embezzled $35,000 from a potato rancher in Burlingame, using the money to pay her husband's medical bills. She was finally caught two years later, served another 18 months in prison, then returned immediately to another accountant's job. Her husband died in 1974. Working at that time for a manufacturing company in Burlingame, Mrs. Lavelle embezzled $117,-000 during the following two years. This time it was for herself.

"I was lonely and trying to buy friends," Mrs. Lavelle says. "I took some cruises to the Caribbean and Hawaii and gambled away a lot of it. Then they caught me, and I had my choice of coming here or serving a 1 to 10-year sentence. I thought I would only be here two years, but now that they're going to take my Social Security away I will have to stay here the rest of my life. I feel very frustrated and afraid of being lonely."

There are others at Delancey Street whose backgrounds and personalities seem to set them apart from the others. Richard Kleiner, 29, is a millionaire's son, a graduate from Beverly Hills School in 1966. He was also a heroin addict and he managed to spend every cent of $20,000 given to him for his Bar Mitzvah to support his habit.

"I remember one time I cashed in $2,000 worth of AT&T to buy a couple of ounces of heroin," Kleiner says. "I was a comparative literature major and I wanted to be a writer. But I was bored and terrified by the outside world. I like Delancey Street, but I don't know if I will stick it out. If I leave it will be because I've decided I'd rather dissipate my life."

Rome Dennis, 38, a black ex-con with poise and obvious potential for leadership, is another special case. His problem, other residents say, is that he is so smooth and so attractive as an individual that the others at Delancey Street have a problem reaching him. More than most, the job of changing himself is something only Dennis can do.

A heroin addict for 20 years, Dennis has spent 15 years in state and federal prisons. He was facing a 20-year sentence for bank robbery when he was probated to Delancey Street. In many respects it would have been easier for him simply to have returned to prison.

"Time had become easy for me," Dennis says. "This has been a lot harder. Being in the pen, emotions aren't allowed and there ain't no problem getting nothing in the pen. I mean nothing, I could get fixed (with heroin) in the pen quicker than on the street."

Dennis says he feels he is becoming more involved with Delancey Street every day. He has lasted six months, and he wants very much to change his life. His problems now are troubles only he can deal with—learning how to care enough and learning how to give.

"I felt I was just another old junkie who's been in the pen when I first came here," he says. "Then I started trying to figure out what this place is all about. I'd like to be able to care. I really would, because there's lots of things to care about. I could see myself with a little more polish going into juvenile halls and kids' facilities and speaking all day long. There's lots of things I'd like to do, and it's slowly beginning to happen."

Dennis smiles. He has been told that despite his obvious potential he is the type who is frequently most difficult to reach. He is struggling now to convince himself that the doubters are wrong.

Delancey Street has been operating in San Francisco since 1970, and John Maher has seen it grow to an organization with assets worth more than $2 million. He plans to have a branch in the Los Angeles area by early summer, and the advance guard is already at work.

For the past two weeks, two Delancey Street residents, Henry Schwank, a former heroin addict, and John Barber, have been making the rounds of Los Angeles businesses, primarily looking for pledges of furniture and other useful goods that might be donated to the foundation. "We've already received a lot of pledges," Barber says. "A lot of these people want to help."

In San Francisco, Charlie Brown, a 40-year-old former addict who spent almost 20 years in prisons, has been supervising the search for a suitable location. He has inspected 30 possible sites and feels he is getting close to finding either a hotel or ranch that could house at least 75 to 100 people.

Meanwhile, it is business as usual at Delancey Street. On a Wednesday morning, a 28-year-old addict and burglar sits in a tiny office at the Delancey Street Club, waiting for the interview that will determine whether he will be accepted as a resident.

His story is typical. He started shooting speed in 1966, switched to heroin three years later and has been a junkie and a thief ever since. His last job was three years ago. He has been in jail nine times and presently faces charges on possession of heroin and an illegal gun. He is here this morning not because of any overwhelming desire to change his life. It's just that he doesn't want to go back to jail.

The two people who will decide whether Steve will be admitted are Jack and Clare Behan. They have both been at Delancey Street for five years, and this will be their life from now on. Behan is as tough as they come. Born in the South Bronx like Maher, he spent 16 years in prison, 10 of them in Sing Sing for a robbery committed when he was 19. His wife, 27, grew up in orphanages, and says her major reason for coming to Delancey Street was "scrambled brains."

"You guys are making it very hard for us to exist," Behan tells the applicant. "You keep coming here when your back's against the door. You never say what am I doing. . . . We're not the Salvation Army, you know. This isn't easy time. We'll shave your head when you come in, you'll work 18 hours a day, no alcohol, no drugs, no talking to girls for 90 days, no outside contact for a year."

It is a game. Eventually Steve will be accepted. Delancey Street tries to discourage the people who ask for admission, but if they are desperate enough there will always be room.

"It took me getting shot in a fight to come here," says Behan, who married Clare in a wedding on Alcatraz three years ago. "I had a bullet wound two days old in my shoulder when I came in here. I understand your position, but we can't do it for you. It will be up to you."

Steve shakes his head, as if he understands. But he really doesn't. At the moment Delancey Street is simply an easy way of avoiding jail. In the months ahead, he will learn that the job of changing his life will be the toughest challenge he has ever faced.

Discussion Questions

1. Review this excon's prescription for rehabilitation. Do you tend to agree with it? Discuss.
2. In your opinion is there a contradiction between punishment for criminal behavior and rehabilitation? Discuss, reflecting as much as possible the last two articles.

6 / Political Institutions

"O, say can you see, by the dawn's early light: corruption in government, with no end in sight!"

Editorial cartoon by Frank Interlandi. Copyright Los Angeles Times. Reprinted with permission.

While sociologists differ in their use of the term *institution,* it is usually seen as a basic system of organized behavior designed to meet the needs that arise out of man's efforts to cope with his environment. Every society must provide its members with acceptable ways of satisfying needs and desires for recreations, self-expression, and a system of values and beliefs that define the meaning and purpose of life. The reproduction and socialization of new members are necessary. Every society also needs a system of production and distribution of goods and services as well as a system to maintain order within society and protect its members from those who attempt to destroy that order. The most important institutions that have developed to satisfy these needs are the family, the economy, politics, education, and religion.

When sociologists study the political system they share an interest with po-litical scientists. However, while political scientists are especially interested in the development and use of power to control the policy-making process, sociologists are concerned with the nature of the groups that are involved in that process. Sociologists are not only interested in describing the groups that tend to participate in the political process, they also try to explain why these groups are involved and the conditions in other institutions which tend to generate involvement or apathy.

It is important to remember that an institution is not a group; you do not belong to it in the same way you belong to a group. The term *institution* is a higher level of sociological abstraction which attempts to describe areas of social life that have become organized into discernible patterns which *include* groups with common values, procedures, and a system of relationships involving a network of statuses. An institution of politics, for example, includes a set of common values about liberty and justice, a set of common procedures such as campaigns and elections, and a network of roles and statuses such as President, citizen, and the Chief Justice of the Supreme Court.

Harold Lasswell defines politics as "who gets what, when, and how." Robert Dahl defines politics as "any persistent pattern of human relationships that involves, to a significant extent, power, rule, and authority." Politics, as these definitions indicate, would seem so general as to include the behavior found in all social institutions and associations. It is not uncommon, for example, to talk of "playing politics" within a church, corporation, college, or fraternity. Sociologists recognize that private disputes such as those between labor and management may eventually become public disputes involving the interests of the entire society. Therefore, while the line between public and private politics is difficult to draw precisely, sociologists are primarily interested in the more formal agencies of the government and the various associations such as political parties and pressure groups, which are organized with the explicit objective of influencing, if not determining, policy-making.

It is important for every member of society to realize politics can also involve force and coercion. The government agencies, which hold a predominance of power, have been characterized by the inclination to "play favorites" by making decisions favoring certain groups over others, yet binding on all. This fact raises a fundamental political problem: Why should those who do not fare well in the struggle for favoritism in the government's use of power abide by its decisions? The overly simplistic answer of "might makes right" is insufficient for the long-run stability of the institution of politics and all too often brings on rebellion and revolution with all of their attendant evils. In order to achieve the desired stability, the exercise of power must be recognized by its citizens to be the exercise of *legitimate authority* which they feel a moral obligation to obey rather than the sheer imposition of power.

All modern governments have sought legitimacy by appealing to philosophies that justify their use and allocation of power. In America the philosophy can be generally referred to as *democracy.* Democracy sets norms describing *how* political decisions ought to be made, *who* ought to make them, and *what* limits ought to be placed on the exercise of political power. Democratic philosophy is itself subject to numerous interpretations, and its implementation in America is often criticized and disparaged as impotent, ineffectual, and the cause of many of our social ills. It must be remembered, however, that the awesome task of maintaining the delicate balance between liberty and authority, and unity and diversity involves the interrelationship of all social institutions and not simply that of politics alone.

WILLIAM L. RIORDAN

Honest Graft and Dishonest Graft

As the cities of the United States grew in size during the late nineteenth and early twentieth centuries, they desperately needed the service of fire and police protection, transportation, utilities, and various kinds of financial aid. Such needs created opportunities for public service and private profit on a vast scale. Franchises for water and gas came to be worth millions. Quite often providing the services of justice, education, and fire protection was a

Reprinted from William L. Riordan, *Plunkitt of Tammany Hall* (New York: E. P. Dutton, 1963) by permission of the publisher.

lucrative enterprise rather than a public obligation. These conditions opened the way for corrupt bargains between venal public servants and businessmen seeking special favors.

These kinds of situations brought about alliances between the political and financial interests. Some of the most noteworthy examples of these alliances are found in the political machines of George Plunkitt of Tammany Hall in New York, Mayor Curley of Boston, and "Big Bill" Thompson of Chicago.

George Plunkitt was one of the influentials of Tammany Hall, the Democratic machine that had governed New York for twenty years. What some citizens and journalists referred to as a "machine," however, was devoutly referred to by the machine-style professional politician as *the organization.* At its peak influence Tammany Hall numbered thirty-two thousand individuals committed to nominating candidates, getting out the vote, winning elections, and generally maintaining power and influence for their people and their programs (by whatever means necessary!). Victory at the polls provided the rewards of patronage and various spoils described in the article below. The sociology student will devote special attention to the *institutionalized role* and *institutional traits* of the Tammany machine professional politician.

Everybody is talkin' these days about Tammany men growin' rich on graft, but nobody thinks of drawin' the distinction between honest graft and dishonest graft. There's all the difference in the world between the two. Yes, many of our men have grown rich in politics. I have myself. I've made a big fortune out of the game, and I'm gettin' richer every day, but I've not gone in for dishonest graft—blackmailin' gamblers, saloonkeepers, disorderly people, etc.—and neither has any of the men who have made big fortunes in politics.

There's an honest graft, and I'm an example of how it works. I might sum up the whole thing by sayin': "I seen my opportunities and I took 'em."

Just let me explain by examples. My party's in power in the city, and it's goin' to undertake a lot of public improvements. Well, I'm tipped off, say, that they're going to lay out a new park at a certain place.

I see my opportunity and I take it. I go to that place and I buy up all the land I can in the neighborhood. Then the board of this or that makes its plan public, and there is a rush to get my land, which nobody cared particular for before.

Ain't it perfectly honest to charge a good price and make a profit on my investment and foresight? Of course, it is. Well, that's honest graft.

Or supposin' it's a new bridge they're goin' to build. I get tipped off and I buy as much property as I can that has to be taken for approaches. I sell at my own price later on and drop some more money in the bank.

Wouldn't you? It's just like lookin' ahead in Wall Street or in the coffee or cotton market. It's honest graft, and I'm lookin' for it every day in the year. I will tell you frankly that I've got a good lot of it, too.

I'll tell you of one case. They were goin' to fix up a big park, no matter where. I got on to it, and went lookin' about for land in that neighborhood.

I could get nothin' at a bargain but a big piece of swamp, but I took it fast enough and held on to it. What turned out was just what I counted on. They couldn't make the park complete without Plunkitt's swamp, and they had to pay a good price for it. Anything dishonest in that?

Up in the watershed I made some money, too. I bought up several bits of land there some years ago and made a pretty good guess that they would be bought up for water purposes later by the city.

Somehow, I always guessed about right, and shouldn't I enjoy the profit of my foresight? It was rather amusin' when the condemnation commissioners came along and found piece after piece of the land in the name of George Plunkitt of the Fifteenth Assembly District, New York City. They wondered how I knew just what to buy. The answer is—I seen my opportunity and I took it. I haven't confined myself to land; anything that pays is in my line.

For instance, the city is repavin' a street and has several hundred thousand old granite blocks to sell. I am on hand to buy, and I know just what they are worth.

How? Never mind that. I had a sort of monopoly of this business for a while, but once a newspaper tried to do me. It got some outside men to come over from Brooklyn and New Jersey to bid against me.

Was I done? Not much. I went to each of the men and said: "How many of these 250,000 stones do you want?" One said 20,000, and another wanted 15,000, and another wanted 10,000. I said: "All right let me bid for the lot, and I'll give each of you all you want for nothin'."

They agreed, of course. Then the auctioneer yelled: "How much am I bid for these 250,000 fine pavin' stones?"

"Two dollars and fifty cents," says I.

"Two dollars and fifty cents!" screamed the auctioneer. "Oh, that's a joke! Give me a real bid."

He found the bid was real enough. My rivals stood silent. I got the lot for $2.50 and gave them their share. That's how the attempt to do Plunkitt ended, and that's how all such attempts end.

I've told you how I got rich by honest graft. Now, let me tell you that most politicians who are accused of robbin' the city get rich the same way.

They didn't steal a dollar from the city treasury. They just seen their opportunities and took them. That is why, when a reform administration comes in and spends a half million dollars in tryin' to find the public robberies they talked about in the campaign, they don't find them.

The books are always all right. The money in the city treasury is all right. Everything is all right. All they can show is that the Tammany heads of departments looked after their friends, within the law, and gave them what opportunities they could to make honest graft. Now, let me tell you that's never goin' to hurt Tammany with the people. Every good man looks after his friends, and any man who doesn't isn't likely to be popular. If I have a good thing to hand out in private life, I give it to a friend. Why shouldn't I do the same in public life?

Another kind of honest graft. Tammany has raised a good many salaries. There was an awful howl by the reformers, but don't you know that Tammany gains ten votes for every one it lost by salary raisin'?

The Wall Street banker thinks it shameful to raise a department clerk's salary from $1500 to $1800 a year, but every man who draws a salary himself says: "That's all right. I wish it was me." And he feels very much like votin' the Tammany ticket on election day, just out of sympathy.

Tammany was beat in 1901 because the people were deceived into believin' that it worked dishonest graft. They didn't draw a distinction between dishonest and honest graft, but they saw that some Tammany men grew rich, and supposed they had been robbin' the city treasury or levyin' blackmail on disorderly houses, or workin' in with the gamblers and lawbreakers.

As a matter of policy, if nothing else, why should the Tammany leaders go into such dirty business, when there is so much honest graft lyin' around when they are in power? Did you ever consider that?

Now, in conclusion, I want to say that I don't own a dishonest dollar. If my worst enemy was given the job of writin' my epitaph when I'm gone, he couldn't do more than write:

"George W. Plunkitt. He Seen His Opportunities, and He Took 'Em."

Discussion Questions

1. Plunkitt's institutionalized political role differs from the idealized role of a "good" politician. Discuss this difference. What would Plunkitt say about this difference?
2. Should the role of a politician be one where "He seen his opportunities, and he took 'em"? If not, what should his role be?
3. What do you think of Plunkitt's description of "honest" and "dishonest" graft?

ROBERT SHERRILL

Pawning Off the Pennsy: Taken—by Train

A quick, superficial reading of this article might reinforce belief that public policy in Washington is controlled by powerful "elites" who work in a cooperative and even conspiratorial fashion as the "establishment" to promote the economic interests of the favored few. On the other hand, a *careful* reading will indicate that the political decision to "help our friends at the Pennsy" was not based on the command "Give us money!" Rather, the decision to subsidize the Penn Central Railroad was much more complex

Reprinted from Robert Sherrill, "Pawning off the Pennsy: Taken—by Train," *The Nation*, June 29, 1970, pp. 786–88. © 1970 by Nation Associates, Inc. Reprinted by permission of the publisher.

and subtle, involving such features as a combination of appeals designed to obtain support from the congressional leadership. One appeal invoked the prevailing conventional wisdom: "You men hold the entire free enterprise system in your hands." Other equally convincing appeals involved the public welfare and national security. Obviously the author of this article does not agree with the government's decision to subsidize the Penn Central Railroad because such a subsidization would favor the vested economic interests of men like Treasury Under Secretary Paul A. Volcker. This article, however, demonstrates many other complex and subtle power relationships involved in the politics of government decision making.

Out of respect for Richard K. Mellon, who had for years been a director of the Pennsylvania Railroad, other board members attended his funeral in Pittsburgh on June 5. Not wanting to spend all their time frivolously, they used the graveside get-together to plan how they might persuade the federal government to bail the nation's largest railroad out of it present financial difficulties.

Sen. Hugh Scott, the Republican minority leader, was also at the funeral, and the directors agreed to meet the following Tuesday in his Washington office. By the time this august group of businessmen assembled in the Senate Office Building on June 9, they had the procedure well arranged, for shortly after leaving Mellon's mortal remains, they were on the telephone to David Rockefeller at Chase Manhattan Bank, and shortly thereafter David was on the telephone to brother Nelson, and he quickly passed the word on to the White House.

So the meeting in Scott's office went off like clockwork. At 9:30 the Congressional fall guys trooped in: Mike Mansfield; Wright Patman, and John Sparkman, chairmen of the banking committees; Warren Magnuson and Harley Staggers, chairmen of the commerce committees. Transportation Secretary John Volpe and his Under Secretary James M. Beggs were ostensibly in charge of the meeting, and they did participate with a passion, but the fellow who *really* ran the show was Treasury Under Secretary Paul A. Volcker.

The purpose of the meeting was to sell everyone present on the idea that the Pennsylvania Railroad—or rather the Pennsylvania Central, as it became with the merger in 1968—should be given a $200 million loan under the Defense Production Act. Now, inasmuch as the Treasury Department has nothing whatsoever to do with the Defense Production Act, you may wonder what business this was of Treasury Under Secretary Volcker. On a sentimental basis, if nothing else, he had every reason not only to be there but to dominate the meeting: he was a vice-president of Chase Manhattan before he came to the Treasury Department, and Chase Manhattan owns 5.6 percent of the stock of Penn Central—believed to be the biggest bloc of that stock held by any person or corporation, except for the 7.2 percent held by Morgan Guaranty Trust Co.

Using some large colored flip cards (supplied by Penn Central) to lecture from, Volcker ran swiftly through a maze of statistics to prove that the railroad was very probably on its deathbed. One who was there said: "I noticed that Volcker seldom had to look at the flip cards. He seemed to know the Penn Central data by heart." Volcker's tone was panicky. Without exactly saying it, he told his audience: "You men hold the entire free enterprise system in your hands. You can walk out of here having said 'no' to us, and the system will crumble." He topped that requiem by saying, "Unless we can go back to the banks with some kind of agreement this afternoon, the Penn Central will have to take bankruptcy by the end of the week."

It was clear that the White House and the Defense Department had agreed to "help our friends at the Pennsy," and had ordered their underlings to "find some law we can use." The law dredged up for the occasion was the Defense Production Act, which normally has been used to give loans to small businesses that are needed for defense work and can't float large enough loans through normal channels. Never before has the Defense Production Act been used to salvage one of the corporate giants.

On cue from Volcker, Assistant Secretary of Defense Barry Shillito sprang to his feet and delivered a lecture on what absolutely essential defense work the Pennsy did for the nation. But an observer of the session said later that Senator Magnuson interrupted at that point and got Shillito to admit that actually the Penn Central earned only about $100 million a year from the Pentagon, or about 5 percent of the railroad's $2 billion income, which hardly would qualify the Penn Central to call itself a major cog in the Pentagon machinery.

The bank-controlled Treasury Department's interest in Penn Central is much broader than merely Chase and Morgan. Seventy-seven banks have in recent years loaned a total of $500 million to the Penn Central management, and of course they all would much prefer to get paid in full rather than take 60¢ on the dollar, which is what they would get if Penn Central went into bankruptcy.

To understand just how fully this is a banker problem—not a railroad problem—one should scan the interlocking ties between the Penn Central and financial institutions at the time of these negotiations. For example, these are Penn directors:

- S. T. Saunders, director of Chase Manhattan, First National Exchange Bank of Virginia, Philadelphia Savings Fund, First Pennsylvania Banking and Trust Co. and its holding company.
- A. E. Perlman, a director of Marine Midland Grace Trust Co.
- D. C. Bevan, director of Provident National Bank.
- P. A. Gorman, Bankers Trust Co., and its holding company.
- L. W. Cabot, New England Merchants National Bank and Suffolk Franklin Savings Bank.
- W. L. Day, Philadelphia Savings Fund and First Pennsylvania Corp.

- J. T. Dorrance Jr., Morgan Guaranty Trust Co., and its holding company.
- S. H. Knox, Marine Midland Grace Trust Co., and its holding company.
- W. A. Marting, Bankers Trust Co., and its holding company, and National City Bank of Cleveland.
- R. S. Odell, Wells Fargo Bank.
- T. L. Perkins, Morgan Guaranty Trust Co.
- R. G. Rincliffe, Philadelphia National Bank and Philadelphia Savings Fund.
- R. S. Rauch, Girard Trust Bank and Philadelphia Savings Fund.
- J. M. Seabrook, director of Provident National Bank.

Three directors—Cabot, Perkins and Dorrance—subsequently resigned from Penn Central on the ground that they wanted to allay public suspicion of "dividend interests." (It isn't good business to be too obvious.)

With banker clout like that on its board, one would think Penn Central could float another loan, or as many loans as it needed, whenever it needed them. But at the skull session in Scott's office, Volcker claimed that the railroad had actually gone into the market the week before with debentures carrying 10.5 percent interest and couldn't raise a measly $120 million loan.

As Rep. William A. Barrett later observed: "The very fact that the big banks were beginning to cut Penn Central off from credit should have given the Nixon administration reason to doubt the advisability of backing new loans to the corporation. When banks won't lend to a $7-billion corporation, then something is drastically wrong and I question whether it is proper for the federal government to become involved in an apparently open-ended guarantee of credit in such a situation."

The mechanics of the loan as agreed on will see the same 77 banks already into Pennsy supplying the railroad with the $200 million at 8 percent interest, the loan guaranteed by the government. That means a saving of at least 2.5 percentage points over what the railroad would have had to pay for a normal commercial loan—if it had found one. Other loans of $300 million are anticipated in the next few months at the same interest rate and with the same government guarantee. At first glance the lower interest may seem to be a disadvantage to the lending banks. But if the rail line *should* go bust at some future time, the government—you and I—will have to pay off the half-billion-dollar bank loans at face value, rather than at the bankruptcy percentage that would hold for a normal commercial loan. Thus the public is lifting that much burden of risk from Chase and Morgan and the other fat cats who own this road.

There are other ways the Penn Central directors could have taken care of their problem, if they had wanted to go the free-enterprise route rather than come crying to the government. They could have sold off some of their assets and paid their loans as they fell due. The Penn Central doesn't own just railroad equipment and roadbeds. It owns many millions of dollars worth of oil wells, real estate property (including some of the choicest in New York

City), pipelines, hotels and amusement parks, and other Americana. When *you* get hopelessly in debt, you sell your second car and pay up. But not the Pennsy. It doesn't like to do anything that might disturb the luxurious atmosphere in which its immediate past president, Stuart T. Saunders, and its new president, Paul T. Gorman, earn quarter-million-dollar incomes. Rather than tighten up on that kind of expenditure, it runs to the government.

Another thing that these great believers in the free-enterprise system could have done, if they had wanted to play by the rules they demand of everyone else, was to have gone bankrupt like good sports. Volcker kept wailing that the bankruptcy of the line "would mean no coal would be delivered to utility companies in critical areas," and "needed chemicals would not be delivered to industry in critical areas." Everyone who was listening knew that was nonsense.

Railroads that go bankrupt don't stop running. The New Haven line, bankrupt and in receivership for years, kept rolling along. A number of lines were bankrupt during the depression of the 1930s, but they kept rolling— until the big free-enterprise champions like the Pennsy gobbled them up.

There might be some argument for using public funds to save the Pennsy if it were a power for good, but it isn't. It has done everything it could to suppress needed competition. For example, Ben Heineman, perhaps the most imaginative railroad man of this generation, tried to put together a line that would bypass Chicago and St. Louis, offering an alternate east-west railroad that would get away from those notable traffic bottlenecks. Although it would not have posed damaging competition to rail networks in which the Pennsylvania had an interest, it would have offered competition of a sort, and the management of the Pennsylvania and of the Santa Fe joined forces with the Morgan Guaranty Trust and other major money interests to block Heineman.

The Pennsy has not survived because it was the most efficient road; it has survived and prospered out of financial bullying. As a matter of fact, its reputation for the last 10 or 15 years has been that of one of the least competent railroads, and it has got progressively worse since its merger with the New York Central. Its annual financial statements—symptomatic of the sickness that besets the line—have become notorious in the railroad industry for their inaccuracies and what appears to be outright deception.

On this point *Forbes* magazine, May 15, noted sarcastically: "If there were a prize for the annual report that goes furthest in trying to put a good face on a bad situation, the prize would go to Penn Central. The company had a simply disastrous year in 1969. Nevertheless, it managed to report a small ($4 million) net profit before an extraordinary loss of $125 million. It did so by imaginative bookkeeping and tax offsets."

The financial difficulties of the Penn Central have been talked about by railroad men for years. A. Scheffer Lang, who was Federal Railroad Administrator in the Department of Transportation (DOT) under the Johnson administration and now is on the faculty at MIT, says that the present crisis was anticipated and discussed by DOT officials in his day and that they agreed the railroad should receive no federal help and should be allowed to go bankrupt.

Shortly after leaving that office, Lang said in an interview with *Railway Age* that while "in the early years, the Pennsylvania Railroad was by all odds the best managed and most progressive railroad in the world," now "in almost any technical or management area you want to name, you can find one or more roads that do a better job." He said the Penn Central was operating simply with a caretaker philosophy, the ultimate and most disastrous example of which would be found in the New Haven line (owned by the Penn Central).

Asked if he meant that the Pennsylvania was taking itself and the rest of the industry down the New Haven path, Lang answered: "Not exactly. I'm sure none of the responsible people in Penn Central management are consciously willing to take the industry as a whole, let alone their own company, down the kind of road the New Haven has traveled. That would mean, of course, nationalization—because while you can pawn the New Haven off on Penn Central, you can't pawn Penn Central off on anybody except the federal government."

A year after Lang made that observation the Penn Central is being pawned off on the federal government; not, however, with any honest admission of nationalization.

Discussion Questions

1. What is similar and what is different between the "friends" of this article and Plunkitt's "friends" in the previous article?
2. This article discusses "interlocking ties." The ties are among economic and political groups. List as many of these groups as you can. What does this list teach you about politics and sociology?

LOUISE BROWN

The IRS: Taxation with Misrepresentation

Additional sources of the power that is at the base of political institutions are secrecy, inconsistency, and complexity. These are qualities of the many administrative agencies of the federal government. The Internal Revenue Service (IRS), for example, often forces a higher tax on individuals by providing complex and confusing tax laws that defy logical reckoning. At the very least, the tax laws defy the reckoning of the average taxpayer unaided by expensive tax consultants. The IRS is inconsistent in the application of its laws and 90 per cent of its rulings are kept from the public. This means the

Reprinted by permission from *The Progressive,* 408 West Gorham Street, Madison, Wisconsin 53703. Copyright © 1973, The Progressive, Inc.

"IRS can treat different taxpayers unequally." Although the celebrated loopholes and benefits in the federal tax code are estimated at $91 billion, a significant dent into that figure could be made if low- and middle-income taxpayers received the same sophisticated tax advice as the wealthy.

While the IRS is perhaps the easiest government agency to criticize for the inequitable use of its power, virtually all government agencies maintain, enhance, and exercise power by secrecy, inconsistency, and especially complexity. Complexity can be readily observed through the proliferation of rules, regulations, "wafflepaper," and red tape. Of course, such complexity may be interpreted simply as inefficiency. However, because the complexity may cause *you* to pay money to the government that others don't pay, it must be recognized as a very important source of power.

Got a tax problem? Don't call H&R Block or the IRS. Call the White House. Unless, of course, you're an "enemy."

In the shambles of American totems blasted to pieces at the Watergate hearings, it is disheartening to see the reputation of one of our most trusted (however grudgingly) Federal agencies crumble with the rest—especially since the Internal Revenue Service affects the lives, pocketbooks, and well-being of more than 75,000,000 individual taxpayers every year.

Yet Washington tax lawyers are not surprised at the allegations of special tax treatment for White House "friends" like John Wayne and the Reverend Billy Graham, nor at the reported "political" audits of White House enemies.

The White House reportedly even tried to use IRS against bothersome organizations. For instance, back in September, 1970, White House aide Tom Charles Huston sent a memo to H. R. Haldeman which said: "Nearly eighteen months ago, the President indicated a desire for IRS to move against leftist organizations taking advantage of tax shelters. I have been pressing IRS since that time to no avail." And, Huston continued, "What we cannot do in a courtroom via criminal prosecutions to curtail the activities of some of these groups, IRS could do by administrative action."

But IRS was more cooperative than Huston thought. In exactly the same month and year that Huston wrote his memo, the public interest–minded Center on Corporate Responsibility applied to IRS for tax-exempt status vital to its funding program. The Center waited two and one half years for IRS to act. Finally, its funds nearly gone, the Center took its case to court on May 2, 1973. Alleging that IRS had deliberately held off acting on the request, the Center introduced a photocopy of its application, which bore the handwritten words "pressure from the White House." The lawsuit stung IRS into belated action, and two weeks later it turned the Center's application down. The Center is seeking a reversal of the IRS action.

Tax lawyers have always known that the question is not whether IRS hands out special treatment, but how much. The other major questions are: While IRS has been giving prominent taxpayers special treatment, how fairly has it been treating average taxpayers? What happens, for instance, to taxpayers who cannot afford professional tax counsel, let alone political favors? How well does IRS serve the ordinary citizen?

Spurred by mounting citizen complaints, a subcommittee headed by Senator Joseph Montoya, New Mexico Democrat, held hearings this past spring to dig out some answers. Although reports of the hearings were largely lost in the swirl of Watergate revelations, the testimony was significant. It revealed that average taxpayers are generally defenseless in IRS audits and collections. The Service often gives them incorrect or contradictory tax advice. They face problems never dreamed of by wealthy taxpayers and large corporations served by skilled counsel.

For three days a parade of witnesses outlined the problems for the Montoya Subcommittee. Testimony confirmed complaints the Subcommittee had been receiving for months: that some overzealous IRS employes harassed and threatened taxpayers; that some IRS employes, pressured by their superiors to bring in more revenue, made unjustified assessments against taxpayers; that some agents failed to tell taxpayers their rights; that taxpayers were intimidated and confused by appeal procedures, and most failed to appeal their cases; and that IRS refused to honor its own tax advice when it assisted taxpayers.

One of the more shocking complaints by witnesses was that IRS refused to let the public see most of its private rulings, which are, in effect, agreements it makes with wealthy taxpayers and big businesses, even though similar rulings might benefit other taxpayers if only they knew about them. A U.S. District Court judge declared such refusal illegal on June 6, 1973, but IRS still does not publish most of its rulings. The Service may decide to appeal the court's decision.

Tax attorneys and accountants make a career of coping with such problems for their clients, but average taxpayers cannot afford such help. They must rely upon the services IRS provides for them, and the services are not always good or fair.

The first hurdle for the average taxpayer is figuring out how much he owes —that is, filling out the return. IRS will help, but taxpayers take IRS advice at their own risk. Consider the case of a Pennsylvania housewife whose husband went to their local IRS office for tax help. She wrote:

". . . he had supreme confidence in the IRS. . . . My husband . . . paid what the man at IRS said was the right amount and forgot about it. One year and a half later we got a bill from the IRS. . . . I couldn't believe it. Not only had their man made the mistake, but we had to pay interest for eighteen months on his mistake. . . . We had to borrow the money from a bank and pay interest on that, and then in order to pay the bank we had to sell an insurance policy, which we had been paying on for some time for one of our children. . . . It made me a lifelong enemy of the IRS."

Like the Pennsylvania housewife, many taxpayers do not realize that the Service will not honor its own employes' advice. The taxpayer who relies on an IRS employe's tax guidance gets no guarantee that IRS will not demand more taxes later.

Just how reliable is IRS advice? In April, 1972, *Wall Street Journal* reporter Tom Herman asked five different IRS offices for help. Each time he presented the same relatively simple tax problem. The five IRS offices gave him five different opinions on how much tax refund he had coming. The amounts ranged from $177 to $448. The IRS officials even disagreed on the number of tax forms he should fill out.

Affluent taxpayers need not rely on such poor IRS advice. Their high-priced lawyers know how to get ironclad agreements from the IRS on exactly how much tax their clients owe. These lawyers ask the Service to make a "private ruling" on their clients' problems. In effect, the IRS provides a free tax consulting service, with results guaranteed, for a special group—even though *all* taxpayers pay for the service with their tax dollars.

These private rulings can hide big tax breaks for powerful people. In a classic 1964 case, an IRS ruling saved millions of dollars for wealthy DuPont stockholders (mainly DuPont family members). The chronology follows: In an antitrust action, a U.S. District Court directed DuPont and its Christiana Securities holding company to distribute their General Motors stock (63.5 million shares valued at $3.5 billion) to their stockholders. Congress passed a special law to lighten the DuPont stockholders' tax load on this GM stock windfall by making it subject to the capital gains rate of taxation, which is lower than the rate they would have paid if the stocks distributed had been treated as dividends subject to regular income tax rates. However, the price of GM stock doubled over the three-year distribution period, and the DuPonts, no longer satisfied with the break Congress had already given them, looked for a way to escape even the capital gains taxes. So they quietly asked IRS for a private ruling. In a ruling that delighted the DuPonts, the IRS permitted the DuPonts to exchange GM stocks for Christiana stock held in their tax-exempt foundations, and these exchanges would be totally tax free. The new ruling allowed them to escape $56 million in taxes.

The IRS estimates that it makes about 30,000 rulings a year. Of all these decisions, it publishes only six to seven hundred annually. The Service refuses to let the public—the same taxpaying public that paid for the rulings in the first place—even see the rest. This means IRS can treat different taxpayers unequally, and such injustice can be concealed.

The Montoya Senate Subcommittee hearings highlighted the contrast between the IRS tax guarantees for the rich and its unreliable advice to average taxpayers. The Pennsylvania housewife and her husband did not get DuPont-style service from IRS. Instead of honoring its own advice, IRS audited the Pennsylvania family's return and demanded about $500 in additional taxes and interest.

Each year the Service chooses for audit more than one million individual returns of the 75,000,000 filed. This means the audited taxpayers must produce records and accounts to prove the claims on their returns. Average taxpayers usually face audit without tax counsel. Why? First, most may not even realize that they need professional help. Those who do seek it find they cannot afford to pay the $30 an hour—or more—that the tax professionals charge. Instead, taxpayers confront the IRS frightened and alone, like the woman who wrote: "I spent the whole morning at the tax office in Brooklyn and when my time came for the 'explaining' of my ways, I was treated with sullen contempt. . . . I was absolutely terrified by their attitude. . . ."

Other taxpayers may trust the IRS man, assuming he knows the law and that he will be impartial, open, and above board. But L. Hart Wright, Michigan University Law School professor, points out that "these assumptions are often not justified." Wright should know. On and off, for almost twenty years, he has taught tax law at the IRS training center and has served as a member of the IRS Commissioner's Advisory Group and as a consultant to the Commissioner. In addition, he has written two IRS tax law manuals.

What happens when average taxpayers face an audit without professional help? Unable to defend themselves, some sixty-three per cent wind up with an increased tax bill averaging about $150. In 1972, that was almost half a million taxpayers. About thirty-four per cent get no increase, and three per cent receive refunds. The high "no change" rate—one in three—suggests that IRS may spend too much time subjecting small taxpayers to expensive and unnecessary investigations. One woman reported that IRS audited her returns for five consecutive years, although her annual salary never reached $4,000. She wrote:

"It was my church donations which they questioned. You see, I am a Seventh Day Adventist and believe in paying ten per cent of all my income to the church. The church treasurer gives receipts for donations paid into the church. I kept all my receipts. Their investigation finds out that my internal revenue reports come out right to the penny with receipts to prove same. I had to take off from my job to appear in Des Moines for the investigation, which meant loss of pay for that day. . . ."

When the audit begins, the taxpayer faces a system which, in a real sense, is out to get him. First, the IRS agent *expects* to find that the taxpayer owes Uncle Sam more than he paid—ordinarily that is why the taxpayer's return was chosen for audit in the first place. The examiner himself is under pressure to bring in extra revenue. The Service rates him, in large part, by his "productivity"—the amount of money he brings in from taxpayers. Senator Montoya questioned Vincent Connery, former IRS agent and president of the National Association of Internal Revenue Employes, on whether he felt he had to "produce" in order to sustain his standing as an efficient revenue agent. Replied Connery, "The simple answer to that is 'yes.' "

In their eagerness to bring in money, IRS examiners are not always candid with taxpayers. They may not explain what kinds of proof of the taxpayer's claim IRS will accept, or whether the taxpayer's case has merit. Many ordinary taxpayers have a hard time supporting their deduction claims. A secretary wrote of her difficulties when IRS demanded she prove that she actually supported her dependent mother:

"I was only making around $5,500 or $6,000. I was told . . . [to] report all the money I spent on my mother in the last year . . . food, clothing, etc. I had to return the next day with a detailed account . . . I accounted for every penny . . . because I didn't want to go to jail—or so they made me feel."

Even sophisticated newspaper reporters have trouble supporting their claims. Syndicated columnist Tom Braden recently wrote:

"You have to be able to prove everything. For example, if you're a newspaperman and do a great deal of traveling, you'll have to produce the airline stubs which prove that you did indeed go to Los Angeles to write a story about Los Angeles which bears a Los Angeles dateline. Sometimes foolish people like me or people without secretaries—also like me—lose their airline stubs. It is expensive."

Sometimes IRS examiners will omit facts that might help the taxpayer. One former IRS agent has pointed out: "The overzealous examiner does not have to disclose to the taxpayer anything about the cases the Government has lost . . . They just state IRS' position as [an] amount of tax . . . and the poor taxpayer most of the time will pay. . . ."

Agents may even threaten to raise taxes without reason. Rudolph J. Passero of the National Society of Public Accountants told Senator Montoya about one time when an IRS agent, frustrated because he could not find any errors in a return, said, "I know there is something here. Now, how much do you want to pay to settle the case?" Passero reported the agent to his IRS superiors, but few unrepresented taxpayers are as willing to stand up for their rights against abusive IRS officials.

The well-represented taxpayers do much better by appealing the IRS agents' claims. Examination of the IRS' annual reports discloses that wealthy taxpayers, over the past five years, have protested more than $6.7 billion in examiners' demands before the Service's conference officials at the highest level. The IRS reviewers overruled the examiners and reduced the demands by an incredible seventy per cent of this amount—by $4.7 billion. Thus, these taxpayers actually had to pay, on the average, only thirty per cent of the amounts that overzealous agents had tried to claim. Big money was at stake in these settlements. The figures in one IRS document reveal that approximately eighty-four per cent of the money in dispute involved claims of $100,000 or more. Clearly, IRS is more willing to bend in favor of big taxpayers than smaller ones.

By comparison, average taxpayers fare poorly at the appellate level. For example, in 1971, according to IRS records, taxpayers with cases under $1,000 ended up paying an average of sixty-eight cents on the dollar, while those with tax cases of $1 million or more settled for an average of only twenty-four cents on the dollar.

But almost none—only two per cent—of the average taxpayers who have gone through the IRS audit ever appeal their increased taxes at all. Why not? Because appeals procedures are confusing, frightening, and expensive. Taxpayers can go to court, or can try to explain their side to Internal Revenue superiors at an IRS district conference. If that fails, they can trudge on still higher to an IRS appellate conference. Wherever they turn, average taxpayers find the procedures too much to cope with. It is so much easier to pay than to fight. Worse yet, many average taxpayers may not even know of their right to appeal. IRS does not routinely give taxpayers written notice of appeal procedures until *after* the taxpayer has formally disagreed with an examiner's findings and refused to pay an increased tax.

While most average taxpayers agree to pay what IRS says they owe, some fail to make the actual payment, and then the IRS Collection Division steps in. The IRS collection officer has the power to seize and sell almost all the taxpayer's goods. He can clean out bank accounts. He can seize paychecks. He can even sell a taxpayer's home.

Like the IRS examiner, the collector is under pressure to bring in money. Until this year, the IRS district office in San Francisco had a unique way of applying this pressure—the "point system." Employes seeking promotion had to fill out a five-page "work experience statement" which assigned points to some thirty-four different kinds of collection actions. Vincent Connery of the IRS employes' union described how the system worked. He said it was just like a contest:

"You get a point for going out and seizing somebody's money who is either on relief or Social Security or a pension. . . . You also get a point for notice . . . served on someone's life insurance policy. . . . It is more than a couple of points if you are regarded as a 'seizure man.' If an American businessman owed money, you go out and seize his business and you get points. Those points translate into promotion."

William L. Lefbom, chief of the San Francisco district collection and taxpayer service division, eliminated the "work experience" point system this year. IRS said it was "administratively cumbersome." But the pressure to bring in money goes on. Jerry Klepner, communications director of the IRS employes' union, has pointed out, "Supervisors know how much a man collects and how many cases he has closed. If the employe does not meet the standards, he loses his job or his promotion."

Most tax lawyers are skilled at keeping such IRS officials from their clients' doors. If tax appeals fail, they advise their clients how best to settle. They know, for example, how to arrange to pay back taxes over a number of years. And they know what kinds of compromises IRS might make. Even if these lawyers get a case after IRS has threatened to collect, they know where to go—in the agency or outside it—for help. Inside, successful tax lawyers talk to their collection division contacts. Outside, White House and other political connections might be effective. Or tax lawyers with clients friendly to Senator Russell Long of Louisiana or Representative Wilbur Mills of Arkansas might find either one helpful. Mills and Long, both Democrats, co-chair the powerful Joint Committee on Internal Revenue Taxation. IRS answers their letters within twenty-four hours. It was Mills' intervention, *The Wall Street Journal* recently reported, that called off an IRS tax investigation of shoe corporations, saving them, a former agent estimates, some $100 million in taxes.

Most of us do not fare so well. Once started, there is almost no way the average taxpayer can stop a collection action. A collector can simply move in and make the seizure. An angry trucker in the household moving business reported that IRS officers took his only moving van (worth $33,740) to satisfy a tax debt of $1,500, while he frantically sought help. He wrote, "Now I have no truck and no money." And, incidentally, no way to earn the money IRS says he owes.

Sometimes taxpayers suddenly discover that the IRS has seized their paychecks—even though they have paid their taxes and can prove it. A Midwestern certified public accountant described a common case. A black laborer had his paycheck seized even though he had two receipts which showed he had paid the tax due in full. Yet, wrote the CPA, the IRS collection department in Cincinnati was indifferent and simply said the man would get a refund in six weeks. "They never admitted," he wrote, "that they had made a mistake and never apologized for denying this man and his children food, clothing, and lodging, for at least one week."

Most average taxpayers have no place to turn for help when IRS seizes their pay. Even if the Service refunds the money in a few weeks, the hapless taxpayer has been deprived of his income, and his reputation with his employer has probably been hurt.

What can be done to give average taxpayers something like the help the rich (and their professional counsel) get from IRS? Senator Montoya has suggested that the Government provide a system of taxpayer advocates representing taxpayers with small claims. Ralph Nader has urged that IRS give those taxpayers facing audit or collection a short written notice that would outline, in plain language, the taxpayer's rights and duties, how he can appeal, and the names of IRS officials to whom he can complain. Nader also called for an "oversight" body, responsible to Congress, which would investigate citizen complaints, study IRS operations, and report its recommendations to Congress.

IRS, for its part, could keep track of the questions taxpayers ask most frequently at IRS offices. This would help Congress decide which parts of the tax laws need to be simplified.

Much can be done in the way of reform. The tax system does not have to be a dense, dangerous jungle for the average taxpayer. But tax justice will not come by itself. Taxpayers will have to push their representatives in Congress hard, particularly those who put special treatment for a few ahead of tax justice for all the American people.

The best time to improve IRS practices is *before* you have a tax dispute with IRS. Your word to Congress can make a difference.

Discussion Questions

1. Group power relationships are discussed by both this and the previous article. "Friends" are involved in both articles. List the "friends" mentioned in this article.

2. From the above list, discuss in some detail two of the "friendship" relationships that resulted in preferential treatment for some taxpayers.

7/ *Religious Institutions*

Drawing by H. Martin; © 1973 The New Yorker Magazine, Inc.

"You notice how he's quoting the Times *more and the Bible less?"*

Some social scientists have treated religion as a passing fancy, a relic of man's ignorance, used by primitive and insecure men to explain the unexplainable and to rationalize the predicament of a harsh, brutish, and short life. Surely, these social scientists argued, educated and enlightened individuals would turn from the magic and superstitions of religion to the reliable findings and insights of science. Despite these expectations, and despite vast twentieth-century scientific and technological achievements, there are many signs that Americans are turning more and more to dependence on various forms of religion.

Religious institutions are the organized patterns of beliefs, symbols, and behavior devoted to a relationship between people and what they believe to be ultimate reality. As a social institution, religion can be considered a relatively permanent property of groups which include orthodox religions, organized humanists, and social philosophies such as Communism. All of these groups provide answers to questions about the purpose, origin, and fate of the world: Where did we come from? What should we be doing here? What happens after death?

Religion performs a variety of individual as well as social functions which make it as indispensable for modern man as it was for primitive man. It provides the individual with a sense of security, explanations for mysteries, solace in death, principles of relationship with his fellow man, and a sense of individual dignity. Religion provides the society with a means of social control. The priests, ministers, rabbis, and other leaders elucidate moral guidelines which they encourage their followers to obey.

Religious institutions support and interrelate with other institutions. A key example of this is the reciprocal involvement of the *Protestant Ethic* and the *Spirit of Capitalism.* The Protestant Ethic was implanted in the American culture by the Puritans. They stressed individual achievement, hard work, scholarship, honesty, thrift, and social responsibility. By emphasizing these qualities in Sunday morning services, churchmen are providing norms that support a bourgeois capitalist economy. The following readings indicate how the institution of religion, like politics, is intertwined with economic and other institutions.

WILLIAM C. MARTIN

The God-Hucksters of Radio

Will Herberg, a noted Social and Religious Historian, recently lamented the secularization of Judaism and the emergence of what he called the "Cultural Jew" whose only religious experience was the gastronomical effect of cream cheese and bagels! In this spirit, it seems that our culture, especially in its bureaucratic and commercialized aspects, has often so secularized and commercialized religion as to emasculate it. In order to fill the needs for *sacred* elements which answer questions about ultimate meaning, a variety of substitutes for bureaucratized commercialized religion have developed. One of these substitutes is the Evangelical movement. The following article describes how certain forms of Evangelism use modern technology to carry their message. More important, these forms of Evangelism show an understanding for the difficulties faced by many people and offer symbolized solutions that serve these people in ways often ignored by the more established religions. The sociology student might reflect on where the line is drawn between man's social and religious needs.

You have heard them, if only for a few seconds at a time. Perhaps you were driving cross-country late at night, fiddling with the radio dial in search of a signal to replace the one that finally grew too weak as you drew away from Syracuse, or Decatur, or Amarillo. You listened for a moment until you recognized what it was, then you dialed on, hoping to find *Monitor* or *Music Till Dawn*. Perhaps you wondered if, somewhere, people really listen to these programs. The answer is, they do, by the tens and hundreds of thousands. And they not only listen; they believe and respond. Each day, on local stations that cater to religious broadcasting and on the dozen or so "super-power" stations that can be picked up hundreds of miles away during the cool nighttime hours, an odd-lot assortment of radio evangelists proclaims its version of the gospel to the Great Church of the Airwaves.

Not all who produce religious broadcasts, of course, are acceptable to the scattered multitude for whom "gospel radio" is a major instrument of instruction and inspiration. Denominational programs and Billy Graham are regarded as too Establishment. Billy James Hargis and his Christian Anti-Communist Crusade are too political. Even faith healer Oral Roberts, once a favorite out there in radioland, has become suspect since he founded a university and joined the Methodist Church. For these believers, the true vessels of knowledge, grace, and power are people like Brother Al ("That's AL, Brother Al"); the Reverend Frederick B. Eikerenkoetter II, better known to millions as "Reverend Ike"; C. W. Burpo ("Spelled 'B,' as in Bible . . ."); Kathryn Kuhlman ("Have . . . you . . . been . . . waiting . . . for me?"); and the two giants of radio religion, healer A. A. Allen (of Miracle Valley, Arizona) and teacher Garner Ted Armstrong, who can be heard somewhere at this very moment proclaiming The Plain Truth about The World Tomorrow.

The format of programs in this genre rarely makes severe intellectual demands on either pastor or flock. C. W. Burpo (Dr. Burpo accents the last syllable; local announcers invariably stress the first) and Garner Ted Armstrong usually give evidence of having thought about the broadcast ahead of time, though their presentations are largely extemporaneous. Some of the others seem simply to turn on the microphone and shout. Occasionally there is a hint of a sermon. J. Charles Jessup of Gulfport, Mississippi, may cite Herodias' directing her daughter to ask for the head of John the Baptist as illustrating how parents set a bad example for their children, David Terrell may, in support of a point on the doctrine of election, note that God chose Mary for his own good reasons, and not because she was the only virgin in Palestine—"There was plenty of virgins in the land. Plenty of 'em. Mucho virgins was in the land." Evangelist Bill Beeny of St. Louis, Missouri (Period. Beeny regards the Zip Code as a plot to confuse the nation), may point to the flea's ability to jump 200 times his own length as proof that God exists. Often, however, a program consists of nothing more than a canned introduction, a taped segment from an actual "healing and blessing" service (usually featuring testimonials to the wondrous powers of the evangelist), and a closing pitch for money.

The machinery for broadcasting these programs is a model of efficiency. A look at station XERF in Ciudad Acuña, Coahuila, Mexico, just across the border from Del Rio, Texas, illustrates the point. Freed from FCC regulations that restrict the power of American stations to 50,000 watts, XERF generates 250,000 watts, making it the most powerful station in the world. On a cold night, when high-frequency radio waves travel farthest, it can be heard from Argentina to Canada. Staff needs are minimal; less than a dozen employees handle all duties, from the front office to equipment maintenance. The entire fourteen hours of programming, from 6:00 P.M. to 8:00 A.M., are taped. Each week the evangelists send their tapes to the station, with a check for the air time they will use.

All announcing is done by Paul Kallinger, "Your Good Neighbor along the way." A peasant, gregarious man, Kallinger has been with XERF since 1949.

In the fifties, he performed his duties live. At present he operates a restaurant in Del Rio and tapes leads and commercials in a small studio in his home; he has not been to the station in years. A lone technician switches back and forth between the preachers and Kallinger from dusk till dawn. Kallinger recognizes the improbability of some of the claims made by the ministers and acknowledges that their motives may not be entirely altruistic. Still, he figures that, on balance, they do more good than harm, and he does his best to impress listeners with the fact that "these are faith broadcasts and need your tithes and love offerings if they are to remain on the air with this great message."

Who listens to these evangelists, and why? No single answer will suffice. Some, doubtless, listen to learn. Garner Ted Armstrong discusses current problems and events—narcotics, crime, conflict, space exploration, pollution —and asserts that biblical prophecy holds the key to understanding both present and future. C. W. Burpo offers a conservative mixture of religion, morals, and politics. Burpo is foursquare in favor of God, Nixon, and constitutional government, and adamantly opposed to sex education, which encourages the study of materials "revealing the basest part of human nature."

Others listen because the preachers promise immediate solutions to real, tangible problems. Although evidence is difficult to obtain, one gets the definite impression, from the crowds that attend the personal appearances of the evangelists, from the content and style of oral and written testimonials, from studies of storefront churches with similar appeals, and from station executives' analyses of their listening population, that the audience is heavily weighted with the poor, the uneducated, and others who for a variety of reasons stand on the margins of society. These are the people most susceptible to illness and infirmity, to crippling debts, and to what the evangelists refer to simply as "troubles." At the same time, they are the people least equipped to deal with these problems effectively. Some men in such circumstances turn to violence or radical political solutions. Others grind and are ground away, in the dim hope of a better future. Still others, like desperate men in many cultures, succumb to the appeal of magical solutions. For this group, what the preachers promise is, if hardly the Christian gospel, at least good news.

The "healers and blessers," who dominate the radio evangelism scene, address themselves to the whole range of human problems: physical, emotional, social, financial, and spiritual. Like their colleagues in the nonmiraculous healing arts, some evangelists develop areas of special competence, such as the cure of cancer or paralysis. Brother Al is something of a foot specialist— "God can take corns, bunions, and tired feet, and massage them with his holy love and make them well." A. A. Allen tells of disciples who have received silver fillings in their teeth during his meetings and asks, sensibly enough, "Why not let God be your dentist?" But most are general practitioners. On a single evening's set of programs, hope is extended to those suffering from alcoholism, arthritis, asthma, birth defects, blindness, blood pressure (high and low), bunions, calluses, cancer (breast, eye, lung, skin, stomach, and throat), corns, death, diabetes, dope, eye weakness, gallstones, heart disease, insomnia, kidney trouble, leukemia, mental retardation, mononucleosis, nervous breakdown, nervous itch, nicotine addition, obesity, pain, paralysis, polio, pregnancy, respiratory problems, rheumatic fever, tuberculosis, tumors (brain, abdominal, and miscellaneous), ulcers, useless limbs, and water in the veins.

The continually fascinating aspect of the healing and blessing ministries is that they do produce results. Some of the reported healings are undoubtedly fraudulent. One station canceled a healer's program after obtaining an affidavit from individuals who admitted posing as cripples and being "healed" by the touch of the pastor's hand. Police officers have occasionally reported seeing familiar vagrants in the healing lines of traveling evangelists, apparently turning newly discovered disorders into wine. But these blatant frauds are probably rare, and a faith healer need not depend on them to sustain his reputation. He can rely much more safely on psychological, sociological, and psychotherapeutic mechanisms at work among his audience.

The testimonials that fill the broadcasts and publications of the healers point to two regularities in a large percentage—not all—of the reported cures. First, the believer had suffered from his condition for some time, and had been unable to gain relief from medical or other sources. Long illness or disability can weaken emotional and mental resistance to sources of help that one would not consider in other circumstances. Second, most of the cures occur at actual healing services, when the deep desire to be made whole is transformed into eager expectation by a frenzied whirl of noise, anxiety, and promise, and the pervasive power of the gathered group of true believers.

In recent years, the miracle-workers have turned their attention to financial as well as physical needs. They promise better jobs, success in business, or, in lieu of these, simple windfalls. A. A. Allen urges listeners to send for his book *Riches and Wealth, the Gift of God.* Reverend Ike fills his publications and broadcasts with stories of financial blessings obtained through his efforts— "This Lady Blessed with New Cadillac," "How God Blessed and Prospered Mrs. Rena Blige" (he revealed to her a secret formula for making hair grow). "Sister Rag Muffin Now Wears Mink to Church," and "Blessed with New Buick in 45 Minutes." Forty-five minutes is not, apparently, unusually fast for Reverend Ike. He regularly assures his listeners, "The moment you get your offering [and] your prayer requests into the mail, start looking up to God for your blessing because it will be on the way."

These men of God realize, of course, that good health and a jackpot prize on the Big Slot Machine in the Sky are not all there is to life. They promise as well to rid the listener of bad habits, quiet his doubts and fears, soothe his broken heart, repair his crumbling marriage, reconcile his fussing kinfolk, and deliver him from witches and demons. No problem is too trivial, too difficult, or past redemption. Brother Al will help women "that wants a ugly mouth cleaned out of their husband." A. A. Allen claims to have rescued men from the electric chair. Glenn Thompson promises "that girl out there 'in trouble' who's trying to keep it from Dad and Mother" that if she will "believe and doubt not, God will perform a miracle."

The radio evangelists do not cast their bread upon the waters, however, without expecting something in return. Though rates vary widely, a fifteen-minute daily program on a local radio station costs, on the average, about $200 per week. On a superpower station like XERF the rate may run as high as $600. The evangelists pay this fee themselves, but they depend upon their radio audience to provide the funds. For this reason, some take advantage of God's Precious Air Time to hawk a bit of sacred merchandise. Much of it is rather ordinary—large-print Bibles, calendars, greeting cards, Bible-verse yo-yos, and ball-point pens with an inspirational message right there on the side. Other items are more unusual. Bill Beeny, who tends to see the darker side of current events, offers $25-contributors a Riot Pack containing a stove, five fuel cans, a rescue gun, a radio, and the marvelous Defender, a weapon that drives an attacker away and covers him with dye, making him an easy target for police. Ten dollars will buy a blue-steel, pearl-handled, tear-gas pistol, plus the informative and inspirational Truth-Pac #4. Or, for the same price, Evangelist Beeny will send his own album of eighteen songs about heaven, together with the Paralyzer, "made by the famous Mace Company." Presumably, it is safer to turn the other cheek if one has first paralyzed one's enemy.

The most common items offered for sale, however, are the evangelist's own books and records. Brother Al's current book is *The Second Touch:* "It's wrote in plain, down-to-earth language, and has big print that will heal any weak eyes that reads it." For a $5 offering C. W. Burpo will send his wonderful recording of "My America," plus a bonus bumper sticker advertising his program, The Bible Institute of the Air—"Be a moving billboard for God and Country." Don and Earl, "two young Christian singers from Forth Worth, Texas," offer for only $3 "plus a extra quarter to pay the postage back out to your house," albums of heart-touching songs and stories that include such old favorites as "Just One Rose Will Do," "A Tramp on the Streets," "Lord, Build Me a Cabin in Heaven," "Streamline to Glory," "Remember Mother's God," "A Soldier's Last Letter," "That Little Pair of Half-worn Shoes," "Just a Closer Walk with Thee" (featuring the gospel whistling of Don), and that great resurrection hymn, "There Ain't No Grave Gonna Keep My Body Down."

In keeping with St. Paul's dictum that "those who proclaim the gospel should get their living by the gospel," the radio ministers do not always offer merchandise in return for contributions. In fact, the books and records and magazines probably function primarily as a link that facilitates the more direct appeals for money almost sure to follow.

Brother Al, sounding like a pathetic Andy Devine, asks the faithful to send "God's Perfect Offering—$7.00. Not $6.00, nor $8.00, but $7.00." An offering even more blessed is $77, God's two perfect numbers, although any multiple of seven is meritorious. "God told me to ask for this. You know I don't talk like this. It's got to be God. God told me he had a lot of bills to pay. Obey God—just put the cash inside the envelope." In addition to cash, Brother Al will also accept checks, money orders, and American Express—surely he means traveler's checks. Seven's perfection stems from its prominence in the Bible: the seven deadly sins, the seven churches of Asia, and so forth. Radio Pastor David Epley also believes God has a perfect number, but he has been reading about the apostles and the tribes of Israel. Quite understandably, he seeks a $12 offering, or the double portion offering of $24.

Brother Glenn Thompson, who also names God as his co-solicitor, claims that most of the world's ills, from crabgrass and garden bugs to Communism and the Bomb, can be traced to man's robbing God. "You've got God's money in your wallet. You old stingy Christian. No wonder we've got all these problems. You want to know how you can pay God what you owe? God is speaking through me. God said, 'Inasmuch as you do it unto one of these, you do it unto me.' God said, 'Give all you have for the gospel's sake.' My address is Brother Glenn, Paragould, Arkansas."

In sharp contrast, Garner Ted Armstrong makes it quite clear that all publications offered on his broadcasts are absolutely free. There is no gimmick. Those who request literature never receive any hint of an appeal for funds unless they specifically ask how they might contribute to the support of the program. Garner Ted's father, Herbert W. Armstrong, began the broadcast in 1937, as a vehicle for spreading a message that features a literalistic interpretation of biblical prophecy. The program has spawned a college with campuses in California, Texas, and London, and a church of more than 300,-000 members. Characteristically, the ministers of the local churches, which meet in rented halls and do not advertise, even in the telephone book, will not call on prospective members without a direct invitation. This scrupulous approach has proved quite successful. *The World Tomorrow,* a half-hour program, is heard daily on more than four hundred stations throughout the world, and a television version is carried by sixty stations.

• • •

To become a disciple of one of these prophet-preachers is, by the evangelist's own admission, to obtain a guide without peer to lead one over life's uneven pathway. Though few of them possess standard professional credentials, they take pains to assure their scattered flocks that they have divine recognition and approval. Some associate themselves with leading biblical personalities, as when A. A. Allen speaks of the way "God has worked through his great religious leaders, such as Moses and myself," or when C. W. Burpo intones, "God loves you and I love you." Several report appearances by heavenly visitors. According to David Terrell, Jesus came into his room on April 17, about eight-thirty at night and told him there was too much junk going around. "Bring the people unto me." Though some receive angels regularly, they do not regard their visits lightly. "If you don't think that it'll almost tax your nervous system to the breaking point," says the Reverend

Billy Walker, Jr., "let an angel come to you." Other evangelists simply promise, as does Brother Al, "I can get through to God for you." In support of such claims, they point to the testimony of satisfied disciples and to their own personal success; the flamboyance in dress affected by some of the men obviously capitalizes on their followers' need for a hero who has himself achieved the success denied them.

In the fiercely competitive struggle for the listener's attention and money, most of the evangelists have developed a novel twist or gimmick to distinguish them from their fellow clerics. C. W. Burpo does not simply pray; he goes into the "throne room" to talk to God. The door to the throne room can be heard opening and shutting. David Epley's trademark is the use of the gift of "discernment." He not only heals those who come to him, but "discerns" those in his audience who need a special gift of healing, in the manner of a pious Dunninger. A. A. Allen emphasizes witchcraft on most of his current broadcasts, blaming everything from asthma to poverty on hexes and demons. In other years he has talked of holy oil that flowed from the hands of those who were being healed, or crosses of blood that appeared on their foreheads. David Terrell frequently calls upon his gift of "tongues." Terrell breaks into ecstatic speech either at the peak of an emotional passage or at points where he appears to need what is otherwise known as "filler." Certain of his spirited words tend to recur repeatedly. *Rapha, nissi,* and *honda bahayah* are three favorites. The first two may be derived from the Hebrew words for healing and victory. Unless the third is a Hebrew term having to do with motorcycles, its meaning is known only to those with the gift of interpretation. Terrell defends his "speaking in the Spirit" over the radio on the grounds that he is an apostle—"not a grown-up apostle like Peter or Paul; just a little boy apostle that's started out working for Jesus."

Once one has made contact with a radio evangelist, preferably by a letter containing a "love offering," one is usually bombarded with letters and publications telling of what God has recently wrought through his servant, asking for special contributions to meet a variety of emergencies, and urging followers to send for items personally blessed by the evangelist and virtually guaranteed to bring the desired results. One runs across holy oil, prosperity billfolds, and sacred willow twigs, but the perennial favorite of those with talismaniacal urges is the prayer cloth.

Prayer cloths come in several colors and sizes, and are available in muslin, sackcloth, terrycloth, and, for a limited time only, a revival-tent cloth. As an optional extra, they can be anointed with water, oil, or ashes. My own model is a small ($2\frac{1}{2} \times 3\frac{1}{2}$ inches) unanointed rectangle of pinked cloth. The instructions state that it represents the man of God who sent it, and that it can be laid upon those with an ailment, hidden in the house to bring peace and blessings, carried in the purse or pocketbook for financial success, and even taken to court to assure a favorable outcome. One woman told Reverend Ike that she had cut her cloth in two and placed a piece under the separate beds of a quarreling couple. She declared the experiment an unqualified success, to the delight of Reverend Ike—"You did that? You rascal, you! Let's all give God a great big hand!"

These scraps of paper and cloth serve to bind preacher and people together until the glorious day when a faithful listener can attend a live service at the civic auditorium or the coliseum, or under the big tent at the fairgrounds. It is here, in the company of like-minded believers, that a person loses and perhaps finds himself as he joins the shouting, clapping, dancing, hugging, weeping, rejoicing throng. At such a service, a large Negro lady pointed into the air and jiggled pleasantly. Beside her, a sad, pale little woman, in a huge skirt hitched up with a man's belt, hopped tentatively on one foot and looked for a moment as if she might have found something she had been missing. On cue from the song leader, all turned to embrace or shake hands with a neighbor and to assure each other that "Jesus is *all right!*" Old men jumped about like mechanical toys. Two teen-age boys "ran for Jesus." And in the aisles a trim, gray-haired woman in spike heels and a black nylon dress, danced sensuously all over the auditorium. She must have logged a mile and a half, maybe a mile and three quarters, before the night was over. I couldn't help wondering if her husband knew where she was. But I was sure she liked where she was better than where she had been.

If a radio evangelist can stimulate this kind of response, whether he is a charlatan (as some undoubtedly are) or sincerely believes he is a vessel of God (as some undoubtedly do) is secondary. If he can convince his listeners that he can deliver what he promises, the blend of genuine need, desperate belief, reinforcing group—and who knows what else?—can move in mysterious ways its wonders to perform. And, for a long time, that will likely be enough to keep those cards and letters coming in.

Discussion Questions

1. What needs are fulfilled by "gospel radio"? Which of these needs are more social and which are more religious? What does your answer tell you about the role of religion in man's life?

2. Reread the last paragraph. Is Dr. Martin critical of these "God-Hucksters of Radio"? Discuss.

KENNETH AND ELIZABETH WOODWARD
Why Are Teens Turning to Religion?

Individual religious activity in the United States is characterized by complex and contradicting patterns. There is a notable decline in the membership and participation in such large churches as the Catholic, Methodist, and

Episcopal; on the other hand there are notable increases in membership and participation in such churches as the Baptist, Seventh Day Adventist, and Mormon churches. What is particularly puzzling to many sociologists is the tremendous surge of religious activity on the part of the "sophisticated" kids at the colleges and universities who seem to be seeking a more intense form of Christianity. An effort to explain this religious revival among the youth of America is provided in the article below.

For a young woman nineteen years old, Jennifer Webb has made a lot of "trips" in her life. There was the drug trip at sixteen, the sex trip at seventeen and several trips to a family counselor before Jennifer discovered what she calls "the ultimate trip." "It's God," says Jennifer, casually tossing her long blond hair back from her radiant face.

Jennifer is a freshman at a junior college in upstate New York, but if you ask her what she's into, she'll tell you it's religion. For more than a year now, she has been meeting three times a week and twice on weekends with a group of some fifty "born-again Christians," as they call themselves, for Bible study, intense prayer and cheerful spiritual counseling. Jennifer's bearded boy friend, Lenny, is in the group. So are all of her best campus friends. When she finishes her studies in speech therapy, Jennifer plans to devote her entire life to God, her family and her career—in that order.

Jennifer is one of millions of young Americans who have made the search for God in the 1970s what civil rights and the antiwar movement were to millions of equally restless, questioning students in the 1960s. Not all these young people are turning to Christianity or Judaism. Unlike their parents, they have a whole spiritual smorgasbord to choose from—various forms of Buddhism, Islam, Hinduism, as well as a host of minor sects and exotic cults. In fact, where missionaries from the United States once went abroad to convert others to Christianity, this country has itself become missionary territory for hundreds of gurus, self-proclaimed messiahs and other religious zealots anxious to feed many of the young people who have developed a genuine hunger for God.

To put the current religious scene into perspective, it is useful to remember that ten years ago a group of Protestant theologians shocked religious Americans with their dramatic announcement, "God is dead." What they meant was that the very idea of God had become irrelevant, unnecessary and uninspiring. At the same time, public opinion polls showed that increasing numbers of Americans were, in fact, staying away from church and losing confidence in organized religion.

Today, however, opinion polls seem to tell a different story. In its 1975 report on religion in America the Gallup poll discloses that religion, after a decade of decline, is regaining some of its influence—particularly among America's youth. Compared with 1970, the poll shows, twice as many young people between the ages of eighteen and twenty-four (37 per cent) now believe that religion is "increasing its influence" in American society. Fully 55 per cent of those surveyed told Gallup pollsters that they have a "great deal" or "quite a lot" of confidence in organized religion, while only 17 per cent expressed "very little" or "none at all." And in a special comparative survey of young people from nine industrial nations throughout the world, American youth turned out to be the most frequent churchgoers; some 35 per cent of them told Gallup pollsters that they usually attend religious services on week-ends.

Even so, the youth movements of the sixties have produced enormous changes in the kind of religious services conventional Christian churches now offer the young. The Jesus Movement, which began outside the churches among college and high school students, has found a home in the seventies among Baptist and other conservative Protestant denominations, where ministers in long hair and modish clothes encourage young people to pour out their newfound faith through informal rap sessions and country-western spirituals like *Gospel Road.* A similar youth orientation is evident in the popular folk masses which have become a Sunday feature in many Roman Catholic parishes, and in the use of guitars, dancing and unusual visual art forms in many Episcopal and Lutheran churches. Among transplanted mid-westerners in California, Mormon missionaries find whole families anxious to join the Church of Jesus Christ of Latter-Day Saints because of its emphasis on family togetherness. Meanwhile, some young Jews are rediscovering their own traditions in the synagogue and through roving bands of singing, dancing Hassids (members of a mystical orthodox sect) who often visit college campuses.

Going to church, of course, is not the only or even the most useful measure of religious attitudes, especially among the young. "Young people are interested in ritual, but only if it helps them feel closer to God," says Father Andrew Greeley, the noted Catholic sociologist. According to a recent—and highly revealing—survey for the National Opinion Research Center, Father Greeley and his fellow sociologists found that a third of those surveyed have had at least one mystical experience in their lives—a religious experience that has nothing to do with going to church. Moreover, those under twenty were more willing to talk about those experiences than their elders. "Unlike a lot of older people," Greeley reports, "teens have not given up on a God who will make His presence felt in their lives. They think that is what religion is all about."

This search for religious *experience,* then, appears to be the main reason why so many teens are interested in religion. It also helps to explain why more than four million Americans, most of them young people, have turned to various forms of Hinduism, Buddhism and other oriental religions which emphasize spiritual techniques for developing a new consciousness of self, the world and God.

Perhaps the easiest of these techniques to understand is Transcendental Meditation. TM is a simple mental exercise taught by the Maharishi Mahesh Yogi, the bearded Indian guru who has counted among his disciples such well-known figures as the Beatles, football quarterback Joe Namath and cover girl Samantha Jones. Although the Maharishi does not call it a religion, TM is in fact a form of yoga, long practiced by Hindu holy men, which the Maharishi has packaged and presented (for a fee) through organizations such as the Students International Meditation Society (SIMS). In a ceremony redolent with incense and flowers, each initiate is given a personal mantra—a word picked from the Sanskrit language purely for its sound—and told never to reveal it to anyone else. Disciples are then instructed to sit comfortably, close their eyes and repeat the mantra silently to themselves.

The initial purpose of Transcendental Meditation is to relax the body so the mind can "naturally" ascend to higher levels of spiritual awareness. Merely by meditating for twenty minutes twice each day, the Maharishi promises, the mind will eventually transcend ordinary consciousness and rise to a level of "pure awareness," which the guru claims is the source of all creative energy and intelligence. What the Maharishi does *not* say—at least right away—is that this technique is based on classic Hindu theology and requires many years of devoted practice (and often thousands of dollars for advanced meditative training) in order to achieve the highest state of "cosmic consciousness."

Most young people, it seems, are initially attracted to TM as a way of combating physical and emotional stress. That's how Laura Pierce, seventeen, first got involved with TM two years ago, but that's not why she is still meditating today. "At first I was just looking for an easy way to calm myself after big hassles at home or in school," says the thin brunette from a San Francisco suburb. "But then it got to be an energy thing, like spiritual jogging. The more I meditated, the more I found my whole life changing." After a summer spent mostly on weekend meditation retreats where she joined other students in studying the Maharishi's books, meditating and eating only vegetarian meals, Laura has decided to enroll at the Maharishi International University in Fairfield, Iowa, where students follow a regular schedule of studies augmented by daily meditation exercises.

What often surprises American parents is the willingness—and eagerness —of so many young religion seekers to give up the freedoms and comforts considered essential to the good life, American-style. Nowhere is this self-denial more evident than among the youthful devotees of the International Society for Krishna Consciousness (ISKON), a rigid Buddhist sect founded ten years ago by His Divine Grace A. C. Bhaktivedanta Swami Prabuhpada, a retired Indian businessman from Bengali.

The sect's essential spiritual exercise is not much different from that of TM: instead of meditating silently, members chant their mantra ("Hare

Krishna, Hare Krishna, Krishna Krishna, Hare Hare"), usually to the accompaniment of hand cymbals, clay drums and bare dancing feet. The chant is a form of "worship yoga" dedicated to Lord Krishna, a classic Hindu manifestation of God. The purpose of the chant, and of all the sect's rites and rules, is to develop Krishna's divine consciousness of "absolute reality" among all the sect's members.

What first strikes outsiders about the young followers of Krishna is their unusual costumes. The women wear multicolored saris and the men dress in saffron robes. All males, even infants, have the head shaved except for a single tuft of hair on the back of the skull which, so the legend goes, Lord Krishna may someday grab to yank them up to heaven.

When they are not out chanting and begging in the streets, devotees of Lord Krishna live frugally in their ashrams, or communes. Most are celibates. Those who do marry are permitted to have sexual intercourse only once a month at precisely the optimum time for conception, and even married couples must cease all sexual activity by the age of thirty. Couples who do produce children must give them up when they reach the age of five. At that point, all Krishna children are sent to the sect's Gurukula, a special boarding school housed in a former Christian church in East Dallas, Texas, where they are raised as wards of the entire community.

Why do some young Americans choose such an ascetic life? "To serve God and dwell in his consciousness," says Belinda, a shy young woman who refused to give her family name or exact age. "Once you realize Krishna Consciousness, you want it for your children too. We teach them to love God and avoid contaminated environments," she says, meaning most of the attractions of the conventional American way of life.

Along with mystical experience, many young people today also want religion to provide them with a total philosophy of life (something they apparently cannot find at home or in school) and an authority figure they can trust to show them what is right and wrong.

"I think this interest in religion has a lot to do with a rejection of parental permissiveness," says George Williamson, a college professor who has seen both his son and daughter leave home to live in separate religious communes. "I must admit that we raised our children without much religion," he acknowledges. "We left it pretty much up to them to decide what, if anything, to believe in. But what we really did, I guess, is train them perfectly for a religious guru who could give them all the answers."

For Williamson's daughter, Margaret, that guru turned out to be the Maharaj-Ji, the seventeen-year-old Perfect Master of the Divine Light Mission. Margaret lives in one of the Mission's fifty-odd ashrams in the United States, where she scrubs floors beneath a sign which reads "God is great, but greater is Guru because he holds the key to God." Like most gurus, the Maharaj-Ji teaches his devotees a special spiritual technique, which he calls The Knowledge. In a secret rite, initiates learn to see a dazzling white light, hear celestial music and feel ecstatic vibrations—a total religious experience called "blessing out."

In appreciation for what The Knowledge has given them, the guru's disciples devote their time and money to winning more followers for the Maharaj-Ji. But while his followers live simply in their ashrams, shunning sex, meat and most of the normal comforts of life, the Perfect Master enjoys chauffered limousines, three separate estates and two airplanes which he uses to fly his "divine family" from one religious rally to another.

A third reason young people are turning to religion is the close family feeling they get from living in a religious group. Indeed, the newest and most bizarre religion in America is called The United Family, a strange mixture of oriental family piety and Protestantism that stresses a good marriage (including lots of children) as the only road to spiritual happiness. Instead of forming congregations, the sect's members (few of the estimated 500,000 United States members are over thirty) form interlocking family units, each devoted to promulgating the gospel of the sect's leader, Dr. Sun Myung Moon.

Dr. Moon is a mysterious South Korean evangelist who has somehow collected enough money to purchase three luxurious estates in New York, including a palatial mansion on the Hudson River for his own family. Wherever Dr. Moon preaches, he busses in thousands of young people who dutifully stand on street corners drumming up an audience for him. Every few years, Dr. Moon stages a mass wedding ceremony, where as many as 750 young couples come from all over the world to exchange marriage vows. This United Family, Dr. Moon teaches, is the advance guard for a new messiah who is to come soon to save the world. And in his lectures, the oriental evangelist makes it rather clear that this world savior could turn out to be Dr. Moon himself.

How can young people distinguish between genuine holy men and cunning rip-offs? Obviously, it isn't easy. But two warnings are worth keeping in mind: true spiritual growth takes a lifetime to achieve; perfect fulfillment is an illusion. What's more, traditional holy men have never lived handsomely off the devotion and offerings of their disciples but have set an example of disdain for creature comforts.

Despite competition from Eastern sects, the religion of most young Americans is still some form of Christianity. The search for mystical experience, a total philosophy of life and a family-style sense of community is also evident among today's young Christians. This is particularly true within the Charismatic, or Pentecostal, movement which is spreading rapidly among both Protestants and Roman Catholics. These Christians call themselves Pentecostals because they believe that the Holy Spirit will fill their souls with His spiritual powers, just as, according to the Bible, He filled the souls of Jesus' apostles on the Day of Pentecost.

The chief characteristic of Pentecostals is their habit of speaking in tongues, a form of ecstatic prayer using strange words and sounds. At a recent Pentecostal prayer meeting in Washington, D.C., for example, some four hundred people, ranging in age from ten to sixty-five, gathered in a Georgetown University building for a typical service. Several young people picked away at guitars; gradually, their attention was focused on a group leader who read a passage from the Bible. Then all fell into silent meditation, awaiting the Holy Spirit. "Praise Jesus," someone said from the back of the room, and the chant was picked up by others. Another moment of silence fell over the crowd and then it began: "Hum-ra-tom-kum" a woman said, and soon nearly everyone began speaking in tongues. Their eyes were shut, their faces wore expressions of intense joy, their hands were raised, palms upward, toward the ceiling.

"Speaking in tongues is a special kind of love language," says Martha McGee, a high school senior from suburban Alexandria, Virginia. "It just wells up inside of you when you can no longer find normal words to express how you feel about God's power and presence. The Holy Spirit just takes over and you feel this overwhelming sense that God loves you."

Most Pentecostals are not satisfied with this personal experience of God's love. They want to share it with others, and often do by laying their hands on those among them who are ill and asking the Holy Spirit for a cure. In fact, during a massive weekend rally staged last year by some thirty thousand Pentecostals at the University of Notre Dame campus, several hundred such miraculous cures were reported.

Outsiders may be rightly skeptical of miraculous claims, but few who have spent time with Pentecostals doubt their spiritual sincerity. This is especially evident in "the household movement," in which groups of Pentecostals live together and share their work, hopes, prayers and income. The household movement is particularly strong in big cities, like Atlanta, Georgia, where members work among the poor, and in university towns, such as Ann Arbor, Michigan, where some six hundred Catholic and Protestant Pentecostals are involved in the Community of the Holy Spirit.

Just how far the spiritual revolution of the seventies will spread or how long it will last are questions no one can answer. If past history is any guide, the religious enthusiasm so many young people now display will eventually give way to spiritual flabbiness and another period of secular-life-as-usual. A brighter hope is that their fresh sense of God's presence will invigorate conventional church life and give a new sense of community to those who have grown cool in their faith.

No doubt spiritual awareness is something that every generation must discover for itself, and it apparently has fallen to this generation of Americans to waken others to the fact that God is far from dead. They remind us all that even in the midst of wars, poverty and terrible hunger in large parts of the world, the greatest evil of all is the failure to find God's love. Perhaps there is a constant pressure on the human spirit, which St. Augustine has beautifully described in one simple prayer: "Thou has made us for Thyself, O Lord, and our hearts are restless until they rest in Thee."

Discussion Questions

1. Why would a revived interest in religion among college students have a lot to do with a rejection of parental permissiveness?
2. How do recent public opinion polls demonstrate a revived interest in religion in American society?
3. What accounts for the increasing popularity among youth for Oriental religion?

U.S. NEWS & WORLD REPORT

Religion in the U.S.—Where It's Headed

Interview with Dr. Will Herberg

Dr. Herberg, addresses himself to the state of religion in the United States today in this interview. His statements go beyond statistics and analytical descriptions to probe the gaps between theoretical and practiced religion in the United States. This probing describes the interrelationship of religion and other social institutions. His treatment of the concept of "civil religion" should be of special concern to the sociology student. In the same vein, the sociology student will find food for thought in Dr. Herberg's reflections on affluence and its effects on man's religious needs.

Q   Dr. Herberg, what is the state of religion in the United States today?

A   In numbers, the mass of American people are immersed in religiousness.

Ninety-five per cent identify themselves as being Protestant, Catholic or Jew. About 70 per cent say they're members of churches. In 1972, the Gallup Poll reports, 40 per cent of American adults said they attended church or synagogue in a typical week.

In content, however, this religiousness is becoming more and more vacuous, because religion has come to serve a new role in this country—a nonreligious role, essentially. I mean religious "belonging" has now become a primary form of self-identification and social location, the way of being an American. It defines one's place in the totality of American life.

Nevertheless, in numbers at least, the American people are probably the most religious of all Western nations.

Q   Has that always been true?

A   No. Available figures indicate that about 1800 America was the least churched of all Western countries. Maybe 10 to 15 per cent of all Americans then belonged to churches. Even by 1900 the figure came to about 35 per cent. Today America is the most churched nation in the West—a tremendous revolution.

Reprinted from *U.S. News & World Report,* "Religion in the U.S.—Where It's Headed" (Interview with Dr. Will Herberg), *U.S. News & World Report* (June 4, 1973), 54–60. Copyright © 1973 U.S. News & World Report, Inc.

Q Is this giving churchmen a new and powerful voice in national affairs, as suggested by their role in promoting civil rights, antiwar and other campaigns?

A Not at all. The noise you hear coming out of churches is from the leaders—not from the masses of members. You say "churchmen." You mean top leaders in denominations like the Presbyterian Church, the United Church of Christ, the Methodist Church and some Jewish and Roman Catholic clergymen—yes, they're generally ultraliberal, but they have no influence whatever among rank-and-file members, who belong to the ordinary mass of Americans.

A large number of these church members are annoyed and embarrassed by the liberal and radical statements of their leaders. They don't know how to replace this leadership, and it would take centuries, anyway. Do you know what these ordinary Americans are doing? They're staging a "pocketbook rebellion." They just won't send money to the central offices of their denominations. Religious giving has not diminished. It's a little higher this year than last year. But it's going to local churches and for local purposes. Increasingly, rank-and-file members of the churches refuse to send money to the central offices, and the top leaders are raising Cain about it, but they can't help it.

Q Does this disaffection involve ecumenical bodies such as the National Council of Churches?

A Of course. The National Council is practically nonexistent in its impact on America. I mean, people hear the name, but I doubt if half the church members in America would know how to identify it. That's a very, very generous estimate—maybe three quarters wouldn't be able to identify it. The National Council of Churches has no influence whatever in this country except on top church leaders—and they have no influence on anybody else.

Q Does this mean that a sharp division is developing between church leaders and ordinary members?

A That has existed for decades. But it has become more pronounced in recent years, because the top leadership in some of the big Protestant denominations has become more and more separated in sentiment from the mass of people. Honestly, they live on different planets.

Q Yet some church leaders insist that churches must take a more-active hand in political and social issues in order to survive—

A Nonsense. That's one of the fancy ploys of the intellectual leadership. What they're doing, actually, is pushing church membership more and more toward conservatism.

Look, here's a book called "Why Conservative Churches Are Growing." It's by Dean Kelley, a Methodist scholar, and he provides evidence that all conservative churches are growing and all liberal churches are stagnant or declining. Without question. Some of the figures are sensational. You have the Methodist Church membership, under social-action leadership, plummeting—while Southern Baptists, the least oriented of the big denominations to social action, have been rising strongly over recent years. The same is true of the Mormons.

Q Are the "Jesus people" a reflection of this conservative reaction to liberal leadership in major denominations?

A Yes, but it's part of a much broader cultural movement in America today—a turn to inwardness instead of social causes, arm-waving and argument.

Here's something else about the "Jesus people."

First, they're emerging from inside the counterculture of youth rebellion to break through it. The "Jesus people" are definitely part of the counterculture, you know. But they're breaking through it on drugs, sexual morality and religion.

Secondly—and this is very important—the "Jesus people" are a recurrence of a tendency toward pietism that has been endemic in American Protestantism for centuries. You had it in New England in colonial times—the Great Awakening initiated by Jonathan Edwards spread over the colonies. You had it along the frontier. Pietism really churched America through one revivalist movement after another. The "Jesus people" are a recent manifestation of this pietism, only now it's among youth that it's taking place, while before it was primarily among the middle-aged.

Q Aren't the "Jesus people" also rebelling against conventional religion —or what you call "religiousness"?

A Yes. So did the nineteenth-century pietists. To the older churches then, camp meetings were obviously what we would call a "counterculture," which attacked the older churches because they were in a rut.

Q Would that mean that churches today, generally, aren't meeting the religious needs of members?

A Well, I don't think most churches ever did, in the sense of their one legitimate religious function: preaching the Gospel, which conveys conviction of sin and assurance of grace. I didn't invent this definition. It's from St. Augustine.

Q Are you saying that churches are getting bogged down in too many other activities—putting up bigger and better buildings, getting into all kinds of recreational and social activities, and so forth?

A Not necessarily. This is neither new nor especially wrong. I know of a group of Jews in Chicago who wanted to form a "companionship" in the old style, and get away from the usual synagogue. These were rich people, and they were going to do away completely with all of the trappings of the synagogue. They could afford all of these extra activities, but they didn't want them.

But what would happen to their children? Who would give them religious education? Other needs came up. In five years, these Jews had established on a much more extensive scale all of the various elaborations of the synagogue.

You see, it's unavoidable. Who joins churches? People. So you have men's clubs, women's clubs, youth clubs, basketball courts—a church, in America, necessarily has to be a kind of settlement house. Otherwise, you know what will happen? The young people will go to more-sinister places for their recreation. This sort of thing happens in every institution—churches, labor unions, or whatever.

Every institution goes through the process described by Charles Péguy, a Catholic publicist at the turn of this century, in these words: "It all begins with *mystique,* it ends with *politique.*" That's the logic of institutions; but without institutions, you can't live.

Q How do churchgoers themselves feel about institutional churches?

A It's completely untrue that there is a widespread desire to get away from the institutional church.

Certainly the "Jesus people" say they don't like the institutional church. In its very nature, pietism or revivalism is anti-institutional—not in principle, however, but simply because so many of the established churches are felt to be in a rut.

What do you suppose "revivalism" wants? Revival. Whom is it going to revive? The spiritually dead. Who are the spiritually dead? Members of churches that are in a rut.

The pietists aren't out to destroy the institutional church, but to revive it. By their own logic, furthermore, they sometimes grow into established churches themselves.

Q Will that happen to the "Jesus people"?

A I'll tell you what I think will happen with the "Jesus people." There are two general elements. One is composed of "Jesus freaks" who become converted individually. The other consists of the "Children of God"—highly organized, highly centralized and fairly authoritarian.

Now the Jesus freaks, as they grow up and settle down, will join the established churches and reminisce about the good old days when they were excited over the discovery of Jesus. I'm not saying that their experience today won't have some effect on their future. It will. But they won't remain Jesus freaks forever. They will drop out, or join the established churches.

The "Children of God" are different. You mark my words: They're going to form a tiny Protestant denomination, like the Campbellites who broke away from the Presbyterian Church in the 1830s. They became the "Disciples of Christ," you know, but they began like the "Children of God."

Q Do you think that this will affect developments within the major churches?

A It's already affecting them. There's this growing stress on inwardness I mentioned. The mass of people in the pews now want the preacher to preach the Gospel—however they may define the Gospel—not social causes.

One of my graduate students, a young professor now in Michigan, tells me: "This minister of ours reads 'The New York Times' book reviews, and makes a sermon out of them." People don't like that sort of thing today. They want to hear things like the Sermon on the Mount. It makes them feel religious. If they hear a sermon about a social cause, they grumble—or just tune it out.

That's one way they protect themselves from what they don't want to hear.

Q Is the inwardness mood behind the reported growth of interest in Oriental religions?

A What growth? It's very minor. Not even minor—it's a bubble of a bubble of a bubble. There are 205 million or so people in the United States, and if all the Oriental cults put together gross 100,000 people, it would be a great achievement.

A Demand for "Richer" Ritual—

Q Does inwardness mean less interest in outward manifestations, such as ritual?

A Definitely not—not among the mass of churchgoers, anyway. They want what they call "richer" liturgy and more affecting ritual.

Q What about Roman Catholic congregations? Aren't they moving toward simpler—almost Protestantized—services?

A The great mass of Catholics in this country have pretty much retained the old ritual—except on one point. The bishops have gone ahead with a vernacular Mass. But that has aroused considerable resistance. First of all, it uses a vile translation. You don't really know what vile English is until you hear that translation. Secondly, it's unfamiliar. They're jabbering in English, and the real religious vitality comes from Latin.

Don't judge what most Catholics want by a few articulate "progressives," as they call themselves.

Q Are Catholic churchgoers rebelling?

A They can't rebel through the pocketbook, because the financial system is different in the Catholic Church. But they do grumble. You need leadership to organize a protest, but grumbling is a very important sociological indicator. Never mind if it doesn't sound like an organized rebellion. If there is any kind of rebellion in the Catholic Church today, it's against the attempt to change the ages-old pattern of worship.

Q What seems to be the net result on U.S. Catholics of the Vatican Council "updating" a decade ago?

A When the propaganda about updating (*aggiornamento*) was in the headlines, Catholic membership growth slowed down a little and there was a brief decline. Now it's rising again slowly.

The impact differs according to what part of the Catholic Church we're talking about. For the mass of the faithful, Vatican II was a glamorous event —but it had no impact on them to any real purpose. They're still thoroughly loyal to Rome and to the Pope. Nearly all the bishops are traditional in their views, too.

So that accounts for the top hierarchy and the mass of churchgoers. In between are the priests, where you'll find a fairly strong element of progressives.

But don't take too seriously the figures of those leaving the priesthood as though this was something new. We know that about the same proportion of priests left the clergy 50 years ago, with or without permission, but they did not get any publicity. Nowadays they get lots of publicity, and it gives a false impression of a sudden growth in defections.

Still, there are strong elements of antitraditionalism among the priests. Strong? Well, maybe 10 to 15 per cent. Actually, you'll find the problem is bigger among the sisters—the nuns.

Some years ago, I was lecturing in Los Angeles at a time when the Immaculate Heart community and college had come into conflict with Cardinal James Francis McIntyre. I warned them: "Better be careful—if you continue on your course, it'll mean breaking with the Church." They laughed. Now they've broken with the Church.

I would say that maybe 25 per cent of the sisters in this country find themselves on the margin. This is a large figure. It may be because they have taken their vocations without adequate preparation. They're brought into vocations too young to know what it's about. In the past, there was enough pressure on them, so generally they stayed in. Now the pressure has been relaxed and they can just get out.

Q Will birth control continue to be a troublesome issue for Catholic leaders?

A Well, it's becoming clear that Catholic parishioners practice birth control in the same proportion as other Americans in their socio-cultural class. But priests have devised a way for loyal Catholics to practice birth control, yet receive the sacraments. How? The confessor listens as the woman—usually it's women who confess, not their husbands—tells about using birth control. She says: "Either I do that, or the marriage will break up. It's just going to be terrible." Her confessor knows she has committed a sin but absolves her because, if she hadn't committed that particular sin, she would have precipitated a greater evil, namely, breakup of the marriage. It's casuistry, of course, but casuistry is perfectly proper. It means applying a moral principle to particular cases.

You know, a fourteenth-century canonist, Nicolas DeLyra, raised a similar question. Prostitution, he said, was forbidden by the moral law. But all Christian governments then not only permitted it but regulated it. Why? Because it was one of the *minora mala*—one of the lesser evils. That is, if prostitution were not permitted, man's natural sexual vitality would burst all bounds and destroy society. Therefore, prostitution had to be permitted in order to preserve society, the highest requirement of any social law.

On the same principle, you can permit contraception—and confessors do. The Church will continue preaching against it, but also, in confession and spiritual guidance, permit it.

Q In the last year or so, there's been a spate of newspaper articles quoting Jewish religious leaders on their concern over the "alienation" of the young from Judaism—

A Sure, you'll read it. People who make news about this are rabbis who feel insecure or who want to prove to everyone that they're doing their work.

The fact is, there's much more identification of the young with Judaism today than a generation or two ago. When I was in college, I didn't say I was Jewish. I said I was of Jewish origin, just as Walter Reuther said he was of German origin. Today the large majority of Jewish students say they're Jewish.

Q How do they mean that—religiously, culturally or what?

A Well, in the heyday of Zionism a generation ago, "Jewishness" had a national meaning for most Jews, though some thought of it as cultural.

Today, about 85 per cent of Jewish youth say they're Jewish, and if you ask them what that means, they say, "Oh, it's like being a Protestant or a Catholic." I'm not vouching for the fervor of their faith. I'm just describing how they understand their position—nothing else.

Q Does the Jewish community as a whole relate to the faith the same way it did when immigrants were pouring in at the turn of the century?

A It's a different relationship—that's obvious—just as it's different for Lutherans of German origin or Catholics of Italian origin. All immigrant groups have gone through a kind of cycle. Immigrants themselves were concerned first of all with their churches—or synagogues—which were the center of their lives in Europe, and provided a kind of continuity between their old life and the new.

For the second generation, or for many of them, the religion of their fathers was just another item of "foreignness" to be overcome or played down so they could become real Americans.

The third generation is sufficiently American, but there is the problem of self-identification, the need to belong to some defined group. So you have what Marcus L. Hansen formulated in his classic studies of immigrants: "What the son wishes to forget, the grandson wishes to remember."

Q What is happening as Jews move out of the cities into suburbs? Is that breaking up the Jewish community?

A No, because most still want to live among their own kind, so you get "gilded ghettos" in the suburbs. At least half of those leaving the city, I would say, go to this kind of "Jewish neighborhood"—today the word isn't "ghetto," it's "neighborhood." It's a good word. "Ghetto" is an unpleasant-sounding word.

In religious affiliation, it's the same story. A generation or two ago, Jews who were moving up became "refugees from the Bronx" and moved to other parts of the city or elsewhere. Especially intellectuals. Professors ceased to be Jews and became Unitarians. Why? They wanted to get rid of their foreignness. To them, being Jewish was like being German or Polish—a foreign "nationality." But not any more. Today the sons of the "refugees from the Bronx" are Jews again.

Q Didn't Jewish faith and community gain in strength and cohesiveness from centuries of persecution?

A Right. That means that today they need more inner strength. At present American Jews are held together not by inner religious bonds primarily, but by the fact that in America you have to be something—a Protestant, Catholic or Jew. And they're Jews.

Q How will they achieve real cohesion?

A I don't know how—well, I'll try to tell you how:

In an automobile factory I know about, come the Jewish High Holy Days and if the Jewish workers don't stay away, the Catholic and Protestant workers look at them as scum. "What do you mean?" they ask. "You're Jewish, aren't you?" Imagine that—that Protestant and Catholic workers put pressure on Jewish workers to be Jews. That's America for you.

Q How does the religious picture in the U.S. compare with that of other countries in over-all strength?.

A Certainly the proportion of Americans who say they belong to churches is very much higher than anywhere else in the Western world. Attendance is probably higher here than anywhere else except, maybe, Greece.

England doesn't have this upsurge of religiousness we have here. In France, the Roman Catholic Church is just barely holding its own. In the Scandinavian countries, there's a real crisis. Sweden is probably the least religious of all Western nations.

Q Does this mean that religion abroad tends to occupy a different place in national life than it does here?

A Definitely. Almost nowhere else will you find the national life religionized—where national culture and religion become intermingled into a kind of civil religion.

Q By civil religion, do you mean a state religion?

A No, no. Civil religion is a term first used by Jean-Jacques Rousseau in his "Social Contract," when he said that a perfect society would have its civil religion—it's in the last chapter of his book.

Not long ago I delivered an address on civil religion and I described it—I quote—as "an organic structure of ideas, ideals, values and beliefs that constitutes a faith common to Americans as Americans, and is genuinely operative in their lives; a faith that markedly influences, and is influenced by, their professed religions." Civil religion religionizes national values, national heroes, national history, national ideals.

Q Could you give some examples?

A They're all over the place. Look at your dollar bill, and you see on the Great Seal of the United States an unfinished pyramid under the eye of God, with the Latin motto, *"Annuit Coeptis"*—"He, God, has smiled upon our beginnings"—and with it another motto, *"Novus Ordo Seclorum"*—"A new order of the ages." This fuses national and religious visions.

We give virtually superhuman status to George Washington and Abraham Lincoln. The popular imagination sees them as virtually free of sin, and sometimes they have even been compared to Jesus Christ.

The national holidays all tend to be invested with religious significance—Thanksgiving, of course, is the prime example.

Look at our history and literature describing America. Much of it sees America as a nation peculiarly under Divine Providence and with a religious mission on earth. In his book "White-Jacket," Herman Melville proclaims: "God has predestined, mankind expects great things from our race," and goes on to describe America as the coming of the "political Messiah." More recently you have had Americans describing President Eisenhower as the spiritual leader of the nation.

Did you watch the recent Inaugural ceremony? There you saw—just as in the ancient Athenian processions—the warriors and the priests participating in powerful enactment of civil religion's traditional role.

For contrast, look at France—there the presidential inaugural has no religious functionary officiating.

Israel's President is sworn in without any suggestion of religion in the ceremony.

"Spreading the American Way"—

Q   How does civil religion affect our dealings abroad?

A   It's very obvious to foreigners. Americans can't conceive of anything good without seeing themselves as missionaries. Now that they've burned their fingers in Vietnam, they don't want to get involved in remote wars, but they're all in favor of spreading the American way all over the world.

The American way is not seen as limited to Americans. It's the right way of life for everybody. So we speak of our "mission" in the world and launch "crusades" on behalf of the American way.

Q   What does this religion preach, specifically?

A   Well, it preaches national unity. Politically it exalts the Constitution much as Socrates deified the laws of Athens. Economically it stands for free enterprise. Socially it exalts egalitarianism. And it places a very high value on religious "belonging."

President Eisenhower, you know, was quoted as saying that "our Government makes no sense unless it is founded in a deeply felt religious faith—and I don't care what it is." Of course, he did care; he would have been much worried if Americans had turned Shintoist or Buddhist. What he didn't care was whether they were Protestants, or Catholics or Jews. Why didn't he care? Because they all say the same thing. What do they say? The American way of life. Simple enough?

Sanctified: "All Kinds of Things"—

Q   Is civil religion's impact confined to broad issues?

A   Not at all. We religionize all kinds of things.

One day, in a restaurant in Evanston, Ill., I saw a printed placard—I made inquiries and found out it had been distributed to 22,000 restaurants in the Midwest. Anyway, here's what it said: "Sanitation is a way of life. As a way of life, it must be nourished from within and grow as a spiritual ideal in human relations."

So, you see, cleanliness is not just next to godliness. It becomes a sort of coequal.

Q   Do many Americans themselves see their national ideals to be religious in this sense?

A   Of course not. Most Americans wouldn't use the word "religion" to describe how they feel about America, because they almost all have a professed religion. They're Methodists, Baptists, Catholics, Jews or whatever. But if you tell an ordinary rank-and-file American about civil religion, he'll say: "Why, that's what religion was always about."

Q   How did it originate?

A   In America, it's really a secularized version of Puritanism and revivalism, combined. From the Puritans, it gets its idealism and moralism—minus the Puritan sense of sin and judgment. From the revivalists, it gets its practical, optimistic and promotional character. It started with Protestantism identifying itself with the great national virtues. The Catholics and Jews came in later—there was nothing they could object to, and it was a good way of identifying yourself as a genuine American.

Q   Has any nation in the past religionized its values and goals to this extent?

A   The Greeks and Romans did in ancient times. The French historian, Numa Denis Fustel de Coulanges, described it in his great work, "The Ancient City." Here's what he says: "Every city had its city religion; a city was a little church, all complete, with its gods, its dogmas and its worship."

Rome, with its Pantheon, had an overarching civil religion based on Roman citizenship and Roman destiny. But Rome had to deal with a variety of religious faiths that ranged from Greco-Roman deities in the West to ancestral worship and "mystery" religions of the East; there was never the broad consensus that has enabled civil religion in America to identify itself with the three major faiths.

Q   Has civil religion helped or hurt professed religions in this country?

A   In some ways, it is very supportive. Civil religion stresses belief in God, and places high value on belonging to a church or synagogue. So most people believe in God, and most people belong to a church. A great majority believe in heaven, too, but only a minority believe in hell. Why? First, God is too good to consign anyone to hell. Second, we ourselves are too good to be consigned to hell. You see, hell doesn't fit comfortably into the American way of life.

Now, it's also very possible that increasing devotion to civil religion—which is a genuine religion—may weaken somewhat the pressure to attend church as time goes on.

Q Is Dr. Billy Graham a good example of the close interplay between civil religion and organized religion?

A Yes, but he's also the point of contact between established religion and the "Jesus people." Established religion and the "Jesus people" alike value him very highly. He plays a very important and a very interesting role.

Q You spoke of our national life being religionized. Does it also work the other way—so that national life secularizes religion?

A Yes. The late Bruce Barton [advertising executive] called Jesus Christ the "supreme salesman." Pragmatism turns faith into something useful, a kind of miracle drug. Dr. Norman Vincent Peale [of Marble Collegiate Church in New York City] gets a big response with this approach, telling about all the wonderful things God can do for you if you have faith—make you a success, or help you think positively. It becomes a faith in faith.

Q Does it make people more intensely devout?

A About half of the people in this country can't even locate a book in the Bible. And yet about 80 per cent believe that the Bible is the revealed word of God, even if they don't know what's in it. They like to hear the Ten Commandments or the Sermon on the Mount. It warms their hearts. But if you ask them, "Do you love your neighbor as yourself?" the honest answer probably would be: "Do you know *my* neighbor? My God, who'd love *him?*"

People's values, you see, are determined by the general structure of the American way. Sanitation ranks very high. Education ranks very high. Belief in God ranks very high. But the particulars of religious teaching enter the popular consciousness only as they enter into the American way.

Q Does this mean that civil religion tends to drain the content of professed religion?

A Well, that's what I meant when I said religiousness was becoming more and more vacuous. Of course it also exalts noble virtues, and it strengthens some elements of professed religion.

But when civil religion is elevated alongside the Biblical faiths, or supersedes them—that's idolatry. These Biblical faiths can't allow any secular idea or institution to claim ultimate and absolute status, no matter how noble its ideals and values. That would be idolatry, and idolatry to the man of faith is the worst possible sin—the very worst.

In ancient Israel, the people of Jerusalem boasted that no harm could come to them, no one could seize the city, because it was the site of God's House, the Temple. But the prophet warned them that the city would be destroyed, and they with it, because they were placing their ultimate confidence not in God, but in something short of God, even if it was holy.

Q Would religious faith be stronger in the United States if there were not separation of church and state?

A No. On the contrary, I think that voluntarism—meaning that people have to support their church if it is going to survive—strengthens their bonds with the church. The greatest laxity is found where a church is "established" by law and all that is required of members is to get born, baptised, die and be buried in that church—and, in between, get married by the church.

Q Will churches, and perhaps the three faiths, tend to lose their identity and merge?

A They won't merge. Never. Just because each sees the others as different versions of a common faith, each insists on maintaining its own identity with greater force. Each wants its own brand name—that's how it is identified in American life.

The church-union movement was a movement of the top leaders, that's all.

Q Judaism and Christianity, in the past, flourished in societies where poverty was the common lot, and their message was addressed—in large part —to the poor. Are they having problems in adjusting to a more affluent society?

A Yes. Their followers used to be mainly poor; now they're mainly middle class.

Some of the churches go through the verbal motions of the old message on poverty. But the problem today is affluence, not poverty, and affluence is a much more difficult problem to handle. Poverty, you see, is something nobody likes, so you can oppose it. But affluence—well, everybody wants to be affluent.

Can you mount a campaign against affluence? Who wants to be told to look for the worm in the apple he's eating? Nobody. He's interested in the apple, not the worm.

Q Do you think that Biblical faith will survive?

A If you're talking about inner religious content, it will probably become more and more vacuous as real emphasis on the sense of sin declines. But there will be periods of vitality and search for inner meaning.

However, the survival of Judaism and Christianity depends on God. Speaking as a theologian, I must say they are instruments in God's hands.

About 30 years ago I was editor of a quarterly magazine called "Judaism," and in those days they worried a great deal about the survival of Judaism. They're worried about it now—everybody is always worrying. Anyway, I wrote then that the survival of Jewry was a matter of Divine Providence, not of a "strategy for survival." And that's true.

If God has no purpose for Judaism and Christianity, why should they survive?

If God has a purpose for them, all the forces of the world won't be able to destroy them.

Discussion Questions

1. What is the sociological significance of the "sharp division . . . developing between church leaders and ordinary members"?
2. Dr. Herberg has a less pessimistic perspective on churches "getting bogged down in too many other activities—putting up bigger and better buildings, getting into all kinds of recreational and social activities, and so forth"—than the two previous articles in this chapter. With which perspective do you tend to agree? Why?
3. Discuss Dr. Herberg's idea of "civil religion" in the United States. In your opinion, is "civil religion" more or less beneficial to the United States? Why?

GARY E. KESSLER

The Occult Today: Why?

What many sociologists have noted as a "religious revival" is not restricted to Christianity or the Eastern sects discussed in the previous article. The occult is also experiencing growth in membership and activity. Most of us are familiar with the Hollywood versions of the occult through such movies as *Race With the Devil* and *The Exorcist,* and consequently tend to view it as superstitious hocus-pocus, or emotional nonsense. But the occult can involve a sophisticated form of religious behavior, and according to the following article it requires attention and study by social scientists. This article attempts to provide a systematic view of the occult as a part of religious behavior in America today.

Time Magazine does a cover story on "The Occult Revival." "The New Alchemy" is the subject of a two-part series in the *Los Angeles Free Press*. Sunday supplements and flashy national magazines run feature stories with titles like "Satanism in the Suburbs." It is estimated that $150,000,000 a year is spent on horoscopes in America. Small stores spring up across the country selling everything a witch needs to work a few spells. Blood-chilling tales of ritual murders make headlines. Courses on the occult multiply in universities. Churches of Satan and of Wicca dismay and alarm Establishment preachers. Need I mention movies such as "The Exorcist" and "Rosemary's Baby?" What is going on, and why?

The occult has always been with us. Its roots go back to the dim preliterate past, finding expression in the visions and the magic of the shaman. Anyone familiar with Western history knows that no age has ever been devoid of interest in the occult. So why should there be surprise at finding it once again in 20th-century America?

The surprise is due not only to a lack of historical perspective, but even more to the naive assumption, shared by many intellectuals, that science has

Reprinted from Gary E. Kessler, "The Occult Today: Why?" *Intellect* (November 1975), 171–174. Reprinted with permission of the publisher.

banished once and for all that superstition known as occultism. We can understand how "ignorant" peasants or "superstitious" natives could be taken in by hocus-pocus. We can dismiss with a smile the well-intentioned, but uninformed, little old ladies who attend seances, or movie stars who dabble in astrology, or the uneducated lower class who believe in magical healings. However, the interest in—and practice of—the occult cuts across all classes, educated or not. Indeed, the recent interest seems to stem precisely from that segment of society which is college-educated, middle-class, and relatively affluent. These are the people who ought to know better!

Science has not banished the supernatural and man's interest in the arcane and the occult. To assume that it should have shows not only a woefully narrow view of science, but also an ignorance of what occultism is. In this essay, I shall offer some reflections on the "why" of this contemporary interest. I hope to be able to convince the reader that, if he or she has been surprised by the recent rise of occultism, sober reflection will dispell some fears and, perhaps, even convince him or her that occultism is not merely superstition.

Occult and Gnosis

Occultism is a much-abused word. So many diverse phenomena, from mysticism to parapsychology, have been associated with it, that it is almost impossible to define. For some, it boils down to Satanism, pure and simple; for others, it embodies a lofty and wise metaphysics; while, for still others, it smacks of sex and violence. The word itself means that which is esoteric, hidden, or secret. Historically, the term has been used to classify a wide and varying group of phenomena which purport to give esoteric knowledge through practices and experiences aimed at securing greater power than is available to man in his ego state of consciousness. This esoteric knowledge is not what we call scientific knowledge nor even information in the ordinary sense. It is knowledge in the sense of gnosis—that is, a nondiscursive understanding of the unity and interrelationships of all the various levels of reality. It consists of the personal and immediate realization of the unity of opposites, usually articulated metaphysically by the doctrine of the microcosm-macrocosm. This gnosis is hidden or esoteric not in the sense that a secret is not publically known but could be, but in the sense that its object is hidden behind the appearances of things.

In respect to this element of gnosis, occultism can be viewed as part of what Ellwood has termed the "alternative reality" tradition of the West, and which others refer to as the perennial philosophy.[1] It is attractive to mystics and philosophers alike who are interested in the possibility of a unitative gnosis.

[1] Robert S. Ellwood, Jr., *Religious and Spiritual Groups in Modern America* (Englewood Cliffs, N.J.: Prentice-Hall, 1973), p. 42.

Magic

Occultism also consists of certain practices and experiences aimed at gaining power, and it is this element which is usually responsible for its popular appeal, as well as its rejection by mystic, philosopher, and intellectual. The practices of occultism are known as magic, and consist of individual or group rituals designed either to gain gnosis or exercise its power (gnosis is power). Magic comes in many varieties, ranging from simple healing rituals to complex conjurings and a bewildering variety of divinatory techniques. The Tarot, astrology, Ouija, and I-Ching are but a few examples.

The commercial exploitation of occultism emphasizes this element exclusively, usually in a very superficial manner. Almost everyone is tempted to spend a few dollars for the power to make beautiful women or handsome men fall in love with them. Promises of "telecult" powers or the "secret health remedies of the ancients" always will appeal to people, especially to the relatively powerless. In an age when more and more areas of an individual's life are being taken from his personal control by ever-increasing government and technology, magic becomes for many almost the only alternative they have left in attempting to regain personal power and control. Freud offered his theory of the individual fixating at the stage of development he called the "omnipotence of thought" to explain man's fascination with magic. When reality gets too harsh, adults, like children, retreat into a fantasy world, where events and people can be controlled by the mind.

We are constantly being reminded that we live in an age of science and technology. While this fact would seem, on the surface, to make the turn to magic improbable, Claude Levi-Strauss has pointed out that magic itself is a kind of technology. Indeed, magic presupposes a completely deterministic universe of cause and effect. For some, technology may appear to be little more than our society's form of magic. The control of scientific technology is open to only a highly educated few, but magical technology is more readily available and, from this perspective, does not at all appear as an illogical means to combat the loss of power at the hands of scientific technology.

Insofar as some magic really seems to "work" for some people, many have turned to parapsychology and various forms of ESP for a "scientific" explanation. If ESP exists, and if, by chance, magical techniques have discovered ways of utilizing it, this would make the occult all the more appealing to the technologically powerless.

We must also note that contemporary subatomic technology and astrophysics seem to be destroying many scientific "myths" with a vision of new possibilities which sound more occult than scientific. This creates an atmosphere which makes some occult ideas almost "scientific" to the speculatively bold. Philosophical speculation on the limits of reason and anthropologically generated cultural relativism also contribute to this atmosphere in which anything seems possible.

The magical practices of occultism can never be separated from the quest for gnosis without distortion. Behind pop magic stands the hope for gnosis and a sophisticated metaphysical view of the ultimate unity of opposites. The serious student of the occult realizes that magical techniques embody and concretely illustrate a fairly complex gnosis which is not apparent on the surface. For the serious occultist, magical rituals are symbolic embodiments of deeper levels of reality. The difference between the popular and commercial view of magic and that of the serious occultist is like the difference between regarding alchemy only as a means to make gold and regarding it as a concrete symbolic embodiment of a highly spiritual gnosis and psychology.

Carl Jung has been largely responsible for teaching us this fact about alchemy, and his views can be extended to other occult practices. However, Jung is not only helpful in revealing the symbolic richness of occultism—he also helps us to understand why magical practices and ideas appeal to those unaware of their symbolic depth. Jung's views on archtypes and the collective unconscious illuminate how even the most debased and popularized magical ritual can communicate unconsciously to the very depths of our humanity. The ankh, which is an ancient occult symbol consisting of a tau cross with a circle above, symbolizes the union of male (the phallic tau) and female (the circle). It stands for fertility and life. The ritual magical circle divided by a cross into four parts symbolizes the unification of opposites. These and similar symbols which abound in occultism speak, according to Jung, directly and intuitively to our unconscious, arousing emotions and responses of which we may be only half conscious.[2]

Occult Power

The power or force with which the occultist seeks contact and over which he seeks control has been conceived in a variety of ways. Most often, it has been thought of in terms of the supernatural. This power, while regarded as ultimately unitary, is believed to be manifested in a great variety of forms. It is ethically neutral in the sense that it transcends good and evil, being itself the unification of all opposites. However, its manifestations may be termed good or evil from a lesser viewpoint. It is a notorious fact that, with the triumph of Christianity, the gods of the pagans became the demons of Christianity. Because occultism contains a good deal of "pagan" mythology and symbolism, it is not surprising to find Christians associating occult power with evil and Satan. A more objective viewpoint recognizes that this power is closer to the primitive idea of mana, an ethically neutral form of energy which manifests itself as sheer overwhelming power. Rudolph Otto's concept of the

[2] See Lee W. Gibbs, "Religions, Devils, and Contemporary Crosses," *Ohio Journal of Religious Studies,* 2:53–62, April, 1974, for a discussion of the ankh and other symbols from a Jungian viewpoint.

"mysterium tremendum," which he finds at the heart of all religious experience, comes closer to characterizing this force than either the terms supernatural or evil.

Ironically, many modern would-be occultists have bought the Christian viewpoint, and actively seek to worship and obey what the Christians have called Satan. It should be noted, however, that some serious magicians like Aleister Crowley actively seek out debased and "evil" methods precisely because of their belief in the unification of opposites. If this power does unify good and evil, then the "lefthanded" or sinister path ought to lead there as well as the "righthanded" path. Indeed, some occultists maintain that the sinister route is the shortest, although also the most dangerous. Those who actively seek this lefthanded or "black" magical route may be consciously or unconsciously reacting against an established religious tradition and a puritanism which have, from the occult viewpoint, overstressed the righthanded way, and thereby made it practically useless.

More recently, it has become fashionable, even in occult circles, to regard this power and its many manifestations as "higher" states of consciousness transcending our ego states. Metzner has argued that the various occult and magical practices ought to be understood as "maps" to higher and better states of human awareness.[3] As such, they are of interest to psychology, especially psychoanalysis, humanistic psychology, and transpersonal psychology, which are deeply interested in the human potential to achieve greater states of consciousness and being.

Ecstatic Experience

Occultism has always, to a certain degree, offered its followers the opportunity to achieve ecstatic experiences. These experiences are often directly related to magical practices, and hold out the possibility of a radically empirical or experiential unification with the power which reconciles opposites. Ralph Metzner was an associate of Timothy Leary at Harvard and, for a while, was very much into the psychedelic scene. Here, we have the link between the interest in occultism today, and what people like Theodore Roszak have termed the "counter culture," others the "youth culture," and still others the "hippie" movement. Whatever the label, there can be little doubt that this movement, which broke upon the American scene in the 1960's, is an important factor in the rise of popular interest in occultism.

Their route to occultism was via the psychedelic experience and a youthful opposition to the evils of technocratic society. The psychedelic experience gave thousands a brief glimpse at a land of expanded consciousness that few had dreamed was there. They found these ecstatic experiences echoed in

[3] Ralph Metzner, *Maps of Consciousness* (New York: Collier-Macmillan, 1971), *Introduction.*

primitive shamanistic religions, Eastern mysticism, occultism, and even in Christian pentecostalism and evangelical revivalism. John B. Orr and others have developed the image of Protean and expansive man to grasp a new form of the American character which has developed out of this experience.[4] Expansive man seeks experiences which will expand his conscious horizons. The occultistic promise of an ecstatic experience appeals to him.

Max Weber distinguished between two forms of prophecy. One he called emissary, the other exemplary. A charismatic religious founder can be understood as a person who has gained wisdom and knowledge through some ecstatic experience. An emissary prophet is one whose followers seek to utilize his teachings as the prime ideal to be realized. Most Western religion has been of this type. If, on the other hand, it is the ecstatic experience itself which is considered central and which the followers are urged to realize, the prophet is of an exemplary type. Much of Eastern religion is exemplary. Occultism may be regarded as fitting Weber's exemplary model. If one has come to see, through a series of ego-shattering ecstatic experiences, the hypocrisy, narrow-mindedness, ego-ridden, Appollianian character of modern technocratic society and all its institutions, including the church, the expansive promise, Dionysian abandon, and greater awareness promised by an exemplary type of movement like occultism become very appealing indeed.

Rapid Social Change

Of course, not everyone who is "into" occultism has gone through the counter culture or the psychedelic experience. However, many Americans interested in occultism have experienced what Durkheim called "anomie," most recently popularized as "Future Shock." In times of rapid social change, traditional values and ideals tend to break down. This causes a feeling of helplessness, bewilderment, fear, anxiety, and the like. It causes individuals and groups to enter a kind of random search for new values or ways to shore up the old.

If one couples this concept of anomie with Weber's notion of the routinization of charisma and what some have called the "death of God" and others His absence, one has most of the ingredients necessary to understand, at least in part, why many turn to the occult. Weber taught us that all attempts to preserve the charisma of a religious founder lead to institutions which, of necessity, must destroy, in time, that very charisma they seek to preserve. Dostoyevsky's *The Grand Inquisitor* is a masterful dramatic enactment of this idea. We know from our study of the history of religions that, when "high" gods or "sky" gods become so remote that they are no longer per-

---

[4] Robert Jay Lifton, "Protean Man," in Donald Cutler, ed., *The Religious Situation: 1969* (Boston: Beacon, 1969), p. 816; and John B. Orr and F. Patrick Nichelson, *The Radical Suburb: Soundings in Changing American Character* (Philadelphia: Westminster, 1970).

ceived as directly available to the believers, magical rituals and rites centering around lesser, but more accessible, deities gain ascendency. It appears the case that established Western religion of a primarily emissary type has routinized itself to the point of death, and its "sky god" has become very remote indeed. This has left a religious vacuum or void which is rapidly being filled by religions and occult groups which seem far less routinized, and which offer gods more accessible to man.

Catastrophic and Eschatological History

In articulating some of the possible reasons for the "revival" (perhaps it is more accurate to say resurfacing) of the occult today, I have neglected to mention the reasons the occultists might cite, and those reasons given by their most vocal opponents, fundamentalistic Christians. Occultists generally subscribe to both a catastrophic and a cyclical view of history. History repeats itself, so the occult claims, insofar as societies evolve from simple to complex and then some misuse of power causes the destruction of the complex civilization. The last great civilization to be destroyed by the misuse of power was Atlantis. Western civilization now stands at the same place Atlantis did before its fall. We have the opportunity to prevent another Atlantis, and thereby to cause a shift from sheer repetition to a higher state of civilized, indeed, cosmic evolution. The gnosis made available by the occult is the key that can save us. The occult has resurfaced today precisely to present us with that opportunity.

This is something of an eschatological vision and is, in that respect, similar to the fundamentalistic Christian claim that we stand at the brink of the second coming of Christ. The last days are upon us and, as the Bible foretold, in these days, Satan will gain more and more ground, roaming as a beast over the face of the earth, turning as many from Christ as he can. The occult today confirms, for these Christians, those Biblical prophecies.

The reader may be surprised that I mention these ideas as "reasons" for the interest in the occult today. Surely, they are too bizarre and unscientific to be taken seriously. However, following the good occult principle that appearances are deceiving, we may find more in these unscientific ideas than meets the eye. Myth often contains a truth our science can not see. William Irwin Thompson, in his book, *At the Edge of History,* has taken such ideas seriously, at least in their symbolic depth.[5] The result is a fascinating speculation on the transformations of cultures and an illuminating insight into the trials and tribulations of our age. I do not have the space to fully explicate his ideas, so I will merely commend the book and close with a few of my own speculations, inspired by Thompson.

A plausible model for the evolution of society can be constructed around the idea that, as complexity increases, the conflict between values increases.

[5] See, especially, Chapter 4 in Thompson, *At the Edge of History* (New York: Harper & Row, 1971).

This complexity and conflict reach a point where culture itself becomes transformed. Such times of radical transformation are experienced as "eschatological ages." They are typified by anxiety in the face of an unknown future and by an intensification of value conflict to the point where something has to give. The occult can be viewed as a kind of underground esoteric value system which stands in conflict with the exoteric traditions of society. It is like a mirror image of established values, reflecting them in a reversed manner. In times of transformation, this underground esoteric stream emerges, intensifying the conflict of values and offering what appears to many as a real alternative route into a better future. We live, I think, in such a time, "at the edge of history," when the desire for the unification of opposites makes any kind of gnosis, magical or otherwise, a power to be sought after and prized.

Discussion Questions

1. Why does there seem to be a more pronounced interest in the occult today than in other periods of American history?

2. Do you agree or disagree with the author's contention that the occult should be viewed as a part of religious behavior in America today? Discuss.

8 / Education

Peanuts cartoon by Charles M. Schultz. © 1974 by United Feature Syndicate, Inc.

Every society is challenged by the need to teach and train each new generation in the knowledge and skills necessary for survival. In primitive societies the knowledge and skills were transmitted by the family. As societies became more complex and the need for specialized skills increased, the process of transmitting these skills required the more formal structure of the educational institution. Although formal schools and academies have always existed in the United States, it was not until the development of the public school system that virtually all children could attend.

The development of the public school system has closely paralleled technological developments. The initial emphasis of the public schools on learning the "three R's" has given way to an emphasis on specialized skills usually obtained through the elaborate process of college education that embraces an increasing portion of an individual's lifespan. Well over a quarter of the American population is either enrolled in, teaching in, or staffing a school of some kind. As a result of this growth, education is considered America's largest industry.

The American institution of education serves a variety of functions for both the society and its individual members. From the standpoint of the individual, education is the primary determinant of occupational skills, social status, opportunities for upward mobility, and personal development. From the vantage point of the society, some of the most important contributions of the institution of education involve the transmission of values, symbols, and beliefs to help implement the social integration of a heterogeneous society by teaching a common language and fostering standardized expectations of all children irrespective of cultural or ethnic background, and to serve as a source of innovation and change.

While the development of the American educational system is often recalled with pride, it is important to note that over the past decade it has been increasingly subjected to indictments for its lack of both *equality* and *quality*. As a result of judicial decrees and unprecedented financial investment, the government has become an intimate partner of the educational system. The criticisms, however, remain. Not only are many black Americans, Indians, and Spanish-speaking Americans critical of receiving a generally poor education, but many of the teachers and students of middle-class high schools and the nation's best colleges express dissatisfaction with courses, rules and procedures that are seen as bureaucratic, impersonal, and irrelevant to their needs.

The following articles illustrate some of the demands made on the institution of education in the United States and some of the resulting problems when these demands are not met.

GENE LYONS

The Higher Illiteracy

Failure to educate children in elementary and high schools, schools that are plagued by the lack of parental support, low teacher morale, and discipline problems that approximate the *Blackboard Jungle* are often-heard criticisms of the U.S. educational system. But the failure to teach college students to read and write is a much more fundamental and disturbing criticism. Examples of basic reading and writing inabilities among college graduate abound. Recently an elementary school principal received a student bearing the following note from a new teacher who had just been awarded a masters degree by a large accredited state university: "Carmen needs to understant my authority. She was asked to set at at another tabel. There was alread 4 at her tabel." If this teacher is typical, there is little hope for her students. The more pertinent sociological and educational issue, however, is not the pervasive character of illiteracy in this ostensibly "educated" society, but the *causes* of this illiteracy. Is it poor teaching? "Dumb" students? Anachronistic teaching methods? An attempt to answer these questions is provided by Gene Lyons, who has taught English at several state universities and contributed articles to many publications, including the *New York Times Book Review*.

The idea of a "literacy crisis" fits so conveniently the current mood of cultural reaction that one inclines to doubt its validity. Contemporary students, we are told, display a growing inability to read and write the English language. College freshmen now read at what used to be considered the junior-high-school level; they write in fragments and cannot think at all. It is hard not to suspect hyperbole and to conclude that if we just wait a while this latest threat to civilized values, existing only in the metaphysical netherworld of the weekly newsmagazine feature, shall also pass.

But even those of us who would perfer to disregard the coming of a plague of semiliteracy must find the evidence persuasive. Consider, for example, the steady drop in the average national score on the verbal section of the Scholastic Aptitude Test; the fact that nearly half of the entering class at the University of California at Berkeley, a fairly selective school which takes only the top eighth of California high-school graduates, failed placement exams and had to be enrolled in remedial composition courses; the news that applicants to journalism programs at Wisconsin, Minnesota, Texas, and North Carolina flunk basic spelling, punctuation, and usage tests at rates that vary between 30 and 50 per cent; a survey by the Association of American Publishers showing that college freshmen *really do* read on what used to be considered a high-school freshman level.

"The great majority of American high-school pupils," wrote H. L. Mencken in 1926, "when they put their thoughts on paper, produce only a mass of confused and puerile nonsense. . . . They express themselves so clumsily that it is often quite impossible to understand them at all." Similar evaluations of the graceless muck churned out by the average student have been frequent ever since. The principal difference now, one might say, is that inarticulateness seems to be, in sociological terms, "upwardly mobile." No one expects very much more than gibberish from high-school students these days; it is the colleges, the universities, and even the graduate schools that make the loudest moan. Bearing in mind the usual qualifications about the reliability and consistency of the SAT, the changing admissions standards, and other variables, it still appears that the language is in trouble.

Art for Art's Sake

One thing that is going on is business as usual in American higher education. Mencken, at least, was consistent. He blamed bad writing on bad thinking and bad thinking on faulty genes. Only a tiny minority of the human race, he thought, was fit to be educated. Of the rest, he said that "trying to teach them to think is as vain an enterprise as trying to teach a streptococcus the principles of Americanism." But although our schools, colleges, and universities are theoretically dedicated to the notion that Mencken was wrong, in practice they are agreeing with him. American students are not learning to write because nobody bothers to teach them how.

Teaching individual students to read, write, and think is surely not what the American university is about. Like many other bureaucracies our universities have become in large measure ingrown, so self-contained that most of their faculties believe, without ever pausing to think about it, that what is good for them is good for the culture at large. In English departments, where one would expect a concern for literacy to be located, the attitude of self-interest appears to be all but universal. Far from resisting the general dissolution, English professors as a group pay almost no attention at all to such mundane topics as literate writing. If they have the misfortune to get stuck in a school that forces them to teach that horror beyond contemplation, freshman composition, they teach it against their will.

The business of the American English department is not the teaching of literacy; it is the worship of literature. After eight years' experience as a student and seven more as a faculty member at five state universities, I am every day more astonished by the increasing distance between most English departments and the everyday concerns of the society that pays their bills. So accustomed have they become to thinking of themselves as the very vanguard, if not the salvation, of Western culture, that the average member of "The Profession," as it likes to call itself, believes that society exists to serve literary scholarship rather than the other way around. Consider the answer to the question "Why study English?" in a 1959 pamphlet distributed under the auspices of the Modern Language Association, the National Council of Teachers of English, and the American Studies Association, three groups which comprise virtually the entire academic literary Establishment:

> [The] literary part of our cultural heritage is rich in the past and alive in the present. Ignorance of it would leave one a barbarian, in the sense that he would have no real connection with the culture of the past which produced him, or with the deep and significant currents of feeling and thought in his own time.

With so lofty an ideal it is no wonder that the profession of teaching English has developed a rhetoric of transcendence very nearly resembling that of a priestly sect. Like all academics, English teachers have no objective standards for measuring books or each other. So it has been but a logical progression from an infatuation with the Joycean religion of art to the existence of an elaborate hierarchy that devotes most of its time to the intricacies of caste. The miseducation of the majority of American students thus confirms the academy in its monasticism. If the barbarians are at the walls, then the last thing the monk is about to do is take up his prayer book and reason with them. What he must do is see about protecting the holy texts.

This is particularly true in the higher reaches of the profession, in those universities with graduate programs. The survey *College Composition and Communication* (published in 1974 by the National Council of Teachers of English) showed that, among four-year state colleges with an enrollment of more than 9,000, the percentage using regular full-time faculty members to teach freshman composition was 7 per cent; for state schools of more than 14,000 students the figure was 4 per cent. At least one, and frequently two, semesters of composition are generally required of nearly all entering freshmen in such institutions. Figures are less dramatic for other kinds of colleges because the survey does not provide a breakdown for private institutions. But, in general, if a university, public or private, has a graduate program in English, a freshman student will be very unlikely to be taught by a full-time member of the English department. Indeed, unless he or she becomes an English major or takes junior- or senior-level electives, which a sharply declining number are doing these days, the likelihood that the student will ever see a regular member of the English department inside a classroom is quite low.

Remember, too, that this is the kind of school in which virtually all of the teachers at other colleges get their training and presumably form their professional values.

Before proceeding further, I should offer a modest disclaimer. What I am saying applies in varying degree to every academic discipline that I know anything about, particularly those in the humanities, arts, and social sciences. Only the metaphors of self-justification vary. "English" merely states them in their purest form. The subject at hand is literacy, for which English departments presumably bear direct responsibility, and the profession has assumed the status of a small industry in this country. In 1970–71, the most recent academic year for which figures are available, more than 20 per cent of all public secondary-school teachers and roughly 15 per cent of all college faculty members were English teachers. Because of the composition requirement, the English department is usually far and away the largest academic unit on any given campus. (Quite a political factor when it comes to changing things from within, incidentally.) But in its failure, even its refusal, to concern itself with the fundamental needs of its students it is far from unique.

Exactly why persons will fight like proverbial Turks to be allowed to teach *Moby Dick* or *The Dunciad* for twenty consecutive semesters is beyond my power to conceive. The teachers who do so nevertheless count themselves among the company of the elect, with the result that they look with condescension upon lowly teachers of basic writing skills. This attitude of disdain is communicated to the graduate students who teach most of the freshmen and to undergraduate English majors, who in turn carry it to the high schools, where it thrives. Except in those many school districts where they are given upward of 150 students at a time, high-school English teachers apparently have come to think of themselves as transmitters of the civilizing arts. They seldom stoop to lessons about complete sentences and coherent paragraphs. As things stand now, it is rare to find more than half-a-dozen college students out of a class of twenty-five who say that they were given regular instruction in writing in secondary school. (And that is as true, for those readers who still cherish regional prejudices, in Massachusetts as it is in Arkansas and Texas, the three states in which I have taught recently.)

The goal, the end, and ultimately the cause of all this is the practically universal demand made by American culture that every person "fulfill himself" at the "highest" level of activity that his calling offers. When it comes to the question of the relationship between what he *thinks* he is and what he *does,* the average literary academic can be as self-righteous as Henry David Thoreau. He expects, however, to be paid a good deal better, and by the rest of us. Far from being outside of, or even in opposition to, the consumer society, such a pedagogue is in fact its ideal end product, almost its archetype. For, besides sharing the customary intellectual and class biases of the trade (e.g., that driving, say, a Pontiac station wagon is evidence of vulgar materialism, while a Volvo station wagon, which costs more, is not), what the kind of academic I am talking about consumes is *himself*. He doesn't work, in the ordinary sense of the word. He has a career.

Most persons in a healthy society need to regard their work, at some level, as a *job,* a useful social task which they agree to perform for money. Most jobs are not "fulfilling" most of the time if one views them from the perspective of the nineteenth-century romantic artist, which, it seems, is the way many academics see their work. In living the life of the artist without any art (most do not in fact do very much of the "research" they are given free time for), they are living one of the most personally and socially destructive forms of life known to middle-class man. The more perceptive students see such teachers less as dedicated practitioners of their disciplines than as persons whose good fortune it has been to convince the government or the trustees to underwrite their hobbies. And what students are learning from these teachers is that learning to write is simply not very important.

The Academic Elite

An example of what I mean can be examined in a controversy over the teaching of writing that took place at the University of Texas in the spring of 1975. Eighty-five per cent of the freshman composition classes there, along with half of the sections of a required sophomore literature class, are taught by "teaching assistants." Together, the two courses make up 75 per cent of the department's total enrollment, and 332 of its 452 classes. Yet, when it came time to cut the money, teaching assistants were getting $607,096 of a departmental salary budget of $2,237,450 and were being reimbursed at rates of $3,200 to $4,000 a year for half-time work. Half-time for them is two courses each semester (many carry a full-time course load as students). Full-time for a regular faculty member is three undergraduate courses. Yet the department voted down by a heavy margin a proposal that would have required all full-time faculty members to teach one section of freshman composition *every one-and-a-half years.* A report on the question written by a departmental committee stated:

> *Not every English professor is suited to teaching Freshman Composition, just as not every English professor is suited to teaching linguistics. Doing a competent job in FC requires two skills: the ability to teach composition, and the ability to reach freshmen. Some of us have one skill but not the other; some of us have neither skill and openly acknowledge the fact.*

The report goes on to say that students would be made unhappy and the life of the director of composition difficult by teachers who were forced to teach a course they disliked. Passing over the specious equation of teaching composition (which any literate person, with some training, ought to be able to do) with teaching a specialized body of knowledge, such as linguistics, one wonders about the logic of teachers who use incompetence and unwilling-ness to perform a task being paid for by public funds to justify their elevation to a "higher" level of activity.

Given the order of priorities in the academic world, the sort of persons who "acknowledge" so openly that they cannot reach freshmen are in fact boasting that they are incapable of descending to the freshman level. The answer to that claim, of course, is that an English professor who could not teach composition probably could not teach anything at all. I singled out the University of Texas because the squabbling of its English department pro-duced a document giving facts and figures very difficult to come by most of the time. Both the figures cited and the results of such a vote would most likely be similar at any parallel institution anywhere in the United States.

The simple truth is that academic ethics today, like those of journalism, are very like those of the entertainment industry. Professors are paid and otherwise rewarded less for what they *do* as teachers than for *who they are*. Who they are is in turn decided almost entirely by "publications," of which the only judges deemed competent are other members of their particular specialty. The reader will recognize this as an aged issue that has been much discussed in the past, but the tired fact remains that the scarcity of jobs for college teachers has driven the frenzy for learned books, monographs, articles, bibliographies, and "scholarly editions" ever wider and deeper into the profession. The rebelliousness that characterized the academics during the Vietnam war years was, for the most part, directed against the society at large. Many of the junior faculty who let their scholarly publications slide while indulging in political and cultural protest were very unpleasantly surprised when they were denied tenure and let go. This was particularly true of persons who entered the profession in the latter half of the Sixties. When I took my first job as an assistant professor at the University of Massachusetts in 1969, for example, one demonstrated one's competence and goodwill to the English department by spending Sunday mornings on the Amherst Town Common protesting the war. Besides politics, the only other important factor in making tenure decisions seemed to be duration; for all our collective fears of persecu-tion, times were good in academia. Only an admitted Republican, or maybe a Jackson Democrat, should such an unlikely specimen have materialized, would have had any good reason to suspect that he would be denied a lifetime sinecure.

Then came the time of troubles. Enrollments dropped, money got tight, and administrations began to look very hard at departments in which 75 per cent or more of the faculty was already tenured and no one had been "non-renewed" within recent memory. Except for one man who wrote a book on Alexander Pope, everyone who hired on in 1969 at the University of Massa-chusetts either has been fired or left on his own account. Things are pretty much the same everywhere else. Even marginal institutions of dubious repute which, as recently as five years ago, had difficulty hiring Ph.D.s now demand pedantry. Generally, a person teaching at such a place need not publish unless he gives the administration some other reason not to like him, but the fear is always there, and with it all the accompanying snobbery and posturing. For all the quibbling of the majority of literary scholars, one hears the word "brilliant," or the slightly more modest "first-rate," in the halls of an English department almost as often as variants of the verb "to hit" at a convention of football coaches.

If this behavior prevailed among Egyptologists at private institutions, it would be of no concern to the public. But what is at issue is the transmission of literacy and literary culture within our society. And while those skills and values appear to many observers to be going the way of sand painting, literary academia indulges itself even more than ever in hobbyhorse "research" of a kind that used to be done primarily by potty Church of England vicars when it was too rainy for croquet. In the nine years between 1964 and the most recently available Modern Language Association bibliography (now running two years behind, because of what one might call "the footnote explosion") the number of scholarly articles and books indexed in one category, "Twentieth-Century American Literature," jumped from 778 to 1,986. In 1973 there were 457 publications on Shakespeare. Among the 133 items concerning Faulkner in the same year were two called "Community and the Country Store in *The Hamlet*" and "A Word List of Southern Farm Terms from Faulkner's *The Hamlet*." One university press published a book on Irving Wallace.

The evidence suggests that this is only a fraction of the pedantry being produced. *American Literature,* one of the more prestigious journals, reports that it accepted only 50 out of 530 submissions in 1973. *College English* took 160 out of 800, and *Publications of the Modern Language Association,* a stuffy periodical which, as Edmund Wilson put it, "contains for the most part unreadable articles on literary problems and discoveries of very minute or no interest," printed 52 of 526 submissions. This is what professors are doing while accepting between $12,000 and $35,000 a year for eight or nine months of work and refusing to teach freshmen.

What is the point of all this stuff besides advancing the careers of the people who write it? Except for a veneer of truly fine and intellectually adventurous work, it is in the main devoted to two topics: the justification of its own existence and what Frederick Crews calls "hopeful guesses about the uplifting value of literature." Although literary critics, like historians, sometimes compete for the honorable designation of being "scientific," almost no one can agree that genuine progress has been made. In the sense of generating falsifiable hypotheses which may be tested against the evidence, ordinary scholarship is about as "scientific" as the weather predictions in the *Farmer's Almanac.* Frederick Crews makes a similar point in an essay called "Anaesthetic Criticism":

The history of literary study is transparently a history of intellectual and political fashion, never more so than in recent formalism and neo-religious moralism. Critics have arrived at no agreement whatever about the meaning of beauty, the criteria of value, or even the grossest facts about books and authors, such as whether Shakespeare was or wasn't stoical, whether Milton was or wasn't of the Devil's party, whether Blake was crazy or visionary or both, whether The Golden Bowl *is an example of self-transcendence or of colossal arrogance and evasion. Unless one had decided in advance to find criticism "coherent and progressive," he would be hard pressed to justify calling it an intellectual discipline at all.*

What is even more remarkable to the average educated person is that academic criticism rarely concerns itself with deciding the relative importance of books and writers. As Crews points out, it is impolite to favor one theoretical approach or even one author over another. Why this is so is not hard to imagine when one considers that the stakes are often lifetime employment. Professor X is completing a study of, say, Hemingway, whom Professor Y privately considers a ham-witted boasthard. But X will be voting on Y's promotion, and Y is himself engrossed in Faulkner, whom X thinks of as a dipsomaniacal obscurantist. The last one to say anything unpleasant is Z. He is doing a scholarly edition of the works of a long-forgotten poet whom all three recognize to be justifiably out of print.

An even sadder irony is that a reasonable case can be made for the proposition that pedantry and illiteracy are between them contributing as heavily as any other factors to the declining prestige of imaginative literature. Confronted as early as junior high school with the notion that reading fiction and poems is a moral exercise in the decoding of abstruse symbols and the unearthing of Deep Hidden Meanings, the majority of students these days either become fearful of literature, lest they miss too much, or grow disgusted and conclude that it is all worthless. I am often reminded in this connection of a friend who admitted to me once that when he read fiction, whether it was Bellow or Mailer or Graham Greene, it was generally for entertainment and pleasure. He was greatly relieved when I said that I thought most normal people did.

The role of the teaching assistant, who has most of the responsibility for writing courses at most large schools, is that of acolyte. That he is no longer an "assistant" at teaching the classes for which he is given sole responsibility is rarely remarked upon. Typically he has no training in teaching writing at all. How could he? Most English professors take only one course in the subject, when they are freshmen. That the terminology itself is every bit as dishonest and evasive as "protective reaction strikes" and "inoperative statements" is also unmentioned. Nor does one hear much protest against the almost universal practice of setting up dummy "research" courses that do not exist and registering teaching assistants and other graduate students into them for the purpose of falsifying faculty teaching loads and generating more funds for salaries. No doubt many teaching assistants do an excellent job, but, if so, they do it almost purely by accident. Other departments commonly complain that the composition course they want their students to take is often turned into a literature class by teaching assistants.

My point in all this has not been to say that academic politics are any lower than those of the surrounding community. As nearly as one can determine these kinds of things, they would seem to be about the same as those at Lockheed, Gulf, and the United States Congress, with the exception that academics rarely have direct opportunities for laying their hands on other people's cash. But for many years the American people have been sold the idea that quality education is their primary assurance that they and their children can get a fair share in society. For the most part it has worked; higher education, especially the public variety, has served as well as anything else as an agency of class mobility. As the first person in my family to attend, much less to teach in, a college of any kind, I am not about to turn against education. But it seems to me that the Vietnam years exacerbated the already unfortunate tendency of many academics to see themselves as apart from and superior to the rest of American culture. With the costs of education rising so dramatically, and with performance standards dropping all around them, it is time for academics to cease pretending that criticisms of *us* can only be couched in *their* (i.e. in anti-intellectual) terms. What we all share—Left and Right, businessman, plumber, artist—is an interest in seeing that persons paid out of public funds to perform a task that society wants done be held accountable for performing it. The swindling of the public interest should be seen as objectionable no matter what the motives of the swindlers.

Experience suggests that such abuses will never be altered from within the academy without a vast change in the society as a whole. "Academic freedom" has become so identified with self-interest and the profession so dominated by its hierarchical structure that many academics have come to believe that an English department deserves the unquestioning support of the state.

Most of the things that can be done by persons outside the universities entail self-evident dangers. No one who has watched members of the average state legislature in action can feel entirely at ease about recommending that they involve themselves in the internal affairs of universities, but there are things that can be done. Funding can be cut off for useless and superfluous "scholarly" publishing ventures; laws can be passed requiring that senior faculty teach a certain number of basic courses in all disciplines; funding formulas can be altered, particularly in overcrowded fields, so that it stops being so profitable for universities to exploit underqualified graduate students as teachers in order to fatten departmental budgets. Job categories can be written that will allow faculty members to identify themselves and be evaluated primarily as *teachers*. This would have three advantages: those who chose to be scholar-teachers would have to do the work and be evaluated on its worth or give up the free time; the costs of that research would be made visible and therefore manageable; and the reduction in hypocrisy might prevent many of the best young students from leaving graduate school as soon as they understood academic politics.

A final note: I have not mentioned those persons within academia who agree with what I have been saying. The controversy at Texas, I am told, was fierce, protracted, and acrimonious. There is a subdued minority within the universities that disagrees with what I have described as the prevailing ethos. It consists of people who feel trapped, often worried that their suspicions are a sign of an inability to make the grade as scholars. Quite correctly, they worry that if they announced or acted upon their convictions, they would soon find themselves unemployed. The "higher" one goes up the academic ladder, the more likely it becomes that an interest in teaching writing courses, particularly to freshmen, will be taken as a confession of intellectual inferiority.

As long as there are books there will be pedants, most of them arrogant, but teachers accepting public money should be required to do the job for which they are paid.

Discussion Questions

1. List the main causes of "the higher illiteracy" in American educational society. Discuss which of these you think is the most important.
2. What does the author mean by this statement? "If the barbarians are at the walls, then the last thing the monk is about to do is take up his prayer book and reason with them. What he must do is see about protecting the holy texts."
3. How does the phenomenon described in the above quotation contribute to "the higher illiteracy"?

MALCOLM COWLEY

Sociological Habit Patterns in Linguistic Transmogrification

Some scholars consider the declining literacy rates among college students as partially caused by the artificiality of much that they are forced to read and write in order for them to earn their A's. A great deal of the vocabulary used by teachers and texts is confusing, misleading, and pseudoscientific. The result is that the student's mind—including his ability to write—degenerates. Examples of this kind of jargon as found within the discipline of sociology are provided in the following article.

I have a friend who started as a poet and then decided to take a postgraduate degree in sociology. For his doctoral dissertation he combined his

Reprinted from Malcolm Cowley, "Sociological Habit Patterns in Linguistic Transmogrification," *The Reporter* (September 20, 1956), 41–43. Copyright © by Malcolm Cowley 1956.

two interests by writing on the social psychology of poets. He had visited poets by the dozen, asking each of them a graded series of questions, and his conclusions from the interviews were modest and useful, though reported in what seemed to me a barbarous jargon. After reading the dissertation I wrote and scolded him. "You have such a fine sense of the poet's craft," I said, "that you shouldn't have allowed the sociologists to seduce you into writing their professional slang—or at least that's my judgmental response to your role selection."

My friend didn't write to defend himself; he waited until we met again. Then dropping his voice, he said: "I knew my dissertation was badly written, but I had to get my degree. If I had written it in English, Professor Blank"—he mentioned a rather distinguished name—"would have rejected it. He would have said it was merely belletristic."

From that time I began to study the verbal folkways of the sociologists. I read what they call "the literature." A few sociologists write the best English they are capable of writing, and I suspect that they are the best men in the field. There is no mystery about them. If they go wrong, their mistakes can be seen and corrected. Others, however—and a vast majority—write in a language that has to be learned almost like Esperanto. It has a private vocabulary which, in addition to strictly sociological terms, includes new words for the commonest actions, feelings, and circumstances. It has the beginnings of a new grammar and syntax, much inferior to English grammar in force and precision. So far as it has an effect on standard English, the effect is largely pernicious.

Sometimes it misleads the sociologists themselves, by making them think they are profoundly scientific at points where they are merely being verbose. I can illustrate by trying a simple exercise in translation, that is, by expressing an idea first in English and then seeing what it looks like in the language of sociology.

An example that comes to hand is the central idea of an article by Norman E. Green, printed in the February, 1956, issue of the *American Sociological Review*. In English his argument might read as follows:

"Rich people live in big houses set farther apart than those of poor people. By looking at an aerial photograph of any American city, we can distinguish the richer from the poorer neighborhoods."

I won't have to labor over a sociological expression of the same idea, because Mr. Green has saved me the trouble. Here is part of his contribution to comparative linguistics. "In effect, it was hypothesized," he says—a sociologist must never say "I assumed," much less "I guessed"—"that certain physical data categories including housing types and densities, land use characteristics, and ecological location"—not just "location," mind you, but "ecological location," which is almost equivalent to locational location—"constitute a scalable content area. This could be called a continunum of residential desirability. Likewise, it was hypothesized that several social data categories, describing the same census tracts, and referring generally to the social stratification system of the city, would also be scalable. This scale could be called a continuum of socio-economic status. Thirdly, it was hypothesized that there would be a high positive correlation between the scale types on each continuum."

Here, after ninety-four words, Mr. Green is stating, or concealing, an assumption with which most laymen would have started, that rich people live in good neighborhoods. He is now almost ready for his deduction, or snapper:

"This relationship would define certain linkages between the social and physical structure of the city. It would also provide a precise definition of the commonalities among several spatial distributions. By the same token, the correlation between the residential desirability scale and the continuum of socio-economic status would provide an estimate of the predictive value of aerial photographic data relative to the social ecology of the city."

Mr. Green has used 160 words—counting "socio-economic" as only one—to express an idea that a layman would have stated in thirty-three. As a matter of fact, he has used many more than 160 words, since the whole article is an elaboration of this one thesis. Whatever may be the virtues of the sociological style—or Socspeak, as George Orwell might have called it—it is not specifically designed to save ink and paper. Let us briefly examine some of its other characteristics.

Fuzzing Up the Obvious

A layman's first impression of sociological prose, as compared with English prose, is that it contains a very large proportion of abstract words, most of them built on Greek or Latin roots. Often—as in the example just quoted—they are used to inflate or transmogrify a meaning that could be clearly expressed in shorter words surviving from King Alfred's time.

These Old English or Anglo-Saxon words are in number less than one-tenth of the entries in the largest dictionaries. But they are the names of everyday objects, attributes, and actions, and they are also the pronouns, the auxiliary verbs, and most of the prepositions and conjunctions, so that they form the grammatical structure of the language. The result is that most novelists use six Anglo-Saxon words for every one derived from French, Latin, or Greek, and that is probably close to the percentage that would be found in spoken English.

For comparison or contrast, I counted derivations in the passage quoted from the *American Sociological Review,* which is a typical example of "the literature." No less than forty-nine per cent of Mr. Green's prose consists of words from foreign or classical languages. By this standard of measurement, his article is more abstruse than most textbooks of advanced chemistry and higher mathematics, which are said to contain only forty per cent of such words.

In addition to being abstruse, the language of the sociologists is also rich in neologisms. Apparently they like nothing better than inventing a word, deforming a word, or using a technical word in a strange context. Among their favorate nouns are "ambit," "extensity" (for "extent"), "scapegoating," "socializee," "ethnicity," "directionality," "cathexis," "affect" (for "feeling"), "maturation" (for both "maturing" and "maturity"), and "commonalities" (for "points in common"). Among their favorite adjectives are "processual," "prestigeful," and "insightful"—which last is insightful to murder—and perhaps their favorite adverb is "minimally," which seems to mean "in some measure." Their maximal pleasure seems to lie in making new combinations of nouns and adjectives and nouns used as adjectives, until the reader feels that he is picking his way through a field of huge boulders, lost among "universalistic-specific achievement patterns" and "complementary role-expectation-sanction systems," as he struggles vainly toward "ego-integrative action orientation," guided only by "orientation to improvement of the gratification-deprivation balance of the actor"—which last is Professor Talcott Parsons's rather involved way of saying "the pleasure principle."

But Professor Parsons, head of the Sociology Department at Harvard, is not the only delinquent recidivist, convicted time and again of corrupting the language. Among sociologists in general there is a criminal fondness for using complicated terms when there are simple ones available. A child says "Do it again," a teacher says "Repeat the exercise," but the sociologist says "It was determined to replicate the investigation." Instead of saying two things are alike or similar, as a layman would do, the sociologist describes them in being either isomorphic or homologous. Instead of saying that they are different, he calls them allotropic. Every form of leadership or influence is called a hegemony.

A sociologist never cuts anything in half or divides it in two like a layman. Instead he dichotomizes it, bifurcates it, subjects it to a process of binary fission, or restructures it in a dyadic conformation—around polar foci.

The New Grammar

So far I have been dealing with the vocabulary of sociologists, but their private language has a grammar too, and one that should be the subject of intensive research by the staff of a very well-endowed foundation. I have space to mention only a few of its more striking features.

The first of these is the preponderance of nouns over all the other parts of speech. Nouns are used in hyphenated pairs or dyads, and sometimes in triads, tetrads, and pentads. Nouns are used as adjectives without change of form, and they are often used as verbs, with or without the suffix "ize." The sociological language is gritty with nouns, like sanded sugar.

On the other hand, it is poor in pronouns. The singular pronoun of the first person has entirely disappeared, except in case histories, for the sociologist never comes forward as "I." Sometimes he refers to himself as "the author" or "the investigator," or as "many sociologists," or even as "the best sociologists," when he is advancing a debatable opinion. On rare occasions he calls himself "we," like Queen Elizabeth speaking from the throne, but he usually avoids any personal form and writes as if he were a force of nature.

The second-personal pronoun has also disappeared, for the sociologist pretends to be speaking not to living persons but merely for the record. Masculine and feminine pronouns of the third person are used with parsimony, and most sociologists prefer to say "the subject," or "X=," or "the interviewee," where a layman would use the simple "he" or "she." As for the neuter pronoun of the third person, it survives chiefly as the impersonal subject of a passive verb. "It was hypothesized," we read, or "It was found to be the case." Found by *whom?*

The neglect and debasement of the verb is another striking feature of "the literature." The sociologist likes to reduce a transitive verb to an intransitive, so that he speaks of people's adapting, adjusting, transferring, relating, and identifying with no more of a grammatical object than if they were coming or going. He seldom uses transitive verbs of action, like "break," "injure," "help," and "adore." Instead he uses verbs of relation, verbs which imply that one series of nouns and adjectives, used as the compound subject of a sentence, is larger or smaller than, dominant over, subordinate to, causative of, or resultant from another series of nouns and adjectives.

Considering this degradation of the verb, I have wondered how one of Julius Caesar's boasts could be translated into Socspeak. What Caesar wrote was *"Veni, vidi, vici"*—only three words, all of them verbs. The English translation is in six words: "I came, I saw, I conquered," and three of the words are first-person pronouns, which the sociologist is taught to avoid. I suspect that he would have to write: "Upon the advent of the investigator, his hegemony became minimally coextensive with the areal unit rendered visible by his successive displacements in space."

The whole sad situation leads me to dream of a vast allegorical painting called "The Triumph of the Nouns." It would depict a chariot of victory drawn by the other conquered parts of speech—the adverbs and adjectives still robust, if yoked and harnessed; the prepositions bloated and pale; the conjunctions tortured; the pronouns reduced to sexless skeletons; the verbs dichotomized and feebly tottering—while behind them, arrogant, over-fed, roseate, spilling over the triumphal car, would be the company of nouns in Roman togas and Greek chitons, adorned with laurel branches and flowering hegemonies.

Discussion Questions

1. What rebuttal might be offered by the educators Cowley is criticizing?
2. Is the problem of "Socspeak," as Cowley characterizes it, inevitable in the field of sociology? Discuss.

TOM WICKER

America and Its Colleges:
An End of an Affair

The great boom of higher education in the United States reflects the expectation that a college degree is the ticket to upward mobility and the good life. The land of opportunity for many Americans has been and still is linked to education. While there is no doubt of the importance of education to many Americans, sociologists contend that there are other factors involved in educational success such as place of residence, income, family background, teacher's expectations, and race. Also, with more and more of the recent college graduates finding it difficult if not impossible to get a job in the area of their education, the luster of the degree has been dimmed. The following article traces the rise of bureaucracy, the lack of a guiding philosophy or purpose, and the lack of meaningful learning. It is important to note that the author also suggests possible reforms for the future.

My daughter has just become a senior in high school, and is therefore well into the agonizing rituals of getting into college. First test scores. (Who can keep straight all those SATs, PSATs, achievements, National Merits, etc.?) were registered in blood and tears well over a year ago. We got two entrance interviews over with last spring, I am making plane and train reservations for more this fall, and if all goes well in this year's testing, I know a banker who might swing the financing.

It was not ever thus. Back in the thirties and early forties in small-town North Carolina, nobody felt much pressure about college. The chances were you didn't want it and your family couldn't afford it. Only the real brains were willing or had any need to wait tables and wash dishes in lieu of paying tuition. I never took any entrance tests and the only interview I can recall was with an earnest old party in baggy pants who was offering cut rates at a one-horse teachers' college. If you did happen to be going off to college, the choice was simple and ordained: Baptist to Wake Forest, girls to N.C.C.W. at Greensboro, and everybody else to the University at Chapel Hill or to N.C. State at Raleigh, then the state's Cow College. There was no trouble in getting into any of them; you could show up on registration day without advance notice. Wake Forest needed the money and the state schools had to take anybody who could show them a high school diploma.

The change from these simple folkways to today's dazzling landscape of higher education, with its vast mushroom field of crowded campuses, its tor-

Reprinted from Tom Wicker, "America and Its Colleges," *Change Magazine*, Vol. 3, No. 5 (September 1971), 22–25. Reprinted with permission of the publisher and the author.

turous selection processes, its maniacal pressures on the tender young, its assembly line teaching techniques (one of the nagging grievances at Kent State was being graded by number instead of name), its world wide array of research and development enterprises, and its ruinous costs—this great metamorphosis of higher education is the consequence of a quarter century of ever-expanding size and affluence more in the onward and upward style of American business than the quieter tradition of the campus. But the great boom now appears to be ending in a fog of uncertainties, and to at least this layman's eyes, it is high time.

Like one of those rich but rickety conglomerates thrown together overnight by some high stepping wheeler dealer, today's high-powered colleges and universities were bound to reach some practical limit to the upward spiral. They did, and now they don't seem quite to know whether to spin off, wind down or dig in.

It's no wonder. Forced draft growth is not the same as putting together a cathedral stone by stone over the ages. In its great boom era, higher education and its administrators and priests could have had little time or opportunity to develop a philosophy or even a practical analysis of the situation after the boom; they were able to do little more than meet public demand.

After all, the easygoing world of higher education that I remember—no doubt, with a bit of good-old-days delusion—was only a generation ago. Even then, of course, parents scrimped and slaved expressly to send their children to college, and poor students (one of whom is in the White House today) eked out a degree on black coffee, hard work and an "iron butt."

But a good many other Americans at that time could take a college education or leave it alone. Most jobs didn't require a degree. There was no social stigma to being without one—in fact, "book learning" beyond the Three R's was historically considered somewhat impractical. While there was a recognition, particularly among some immigrant groups, that education was a key to upward mobility, there was a deeper Honest Abe tradition in prewar America —that if a man worked hard, saved his pennies, paid cash and went to church, he'd get ahead without wasting time on formal education. Hadn't Lincoln and John D. Rockefeller? Of course, the Depression had disabused a lot of people of that notion by the time World War II came along.

So it is really only since the G.I. Bill of Rights caused the first jam-packed campuses after the war that we have had the boom era of higher education. Postwar affluence provided the first major building programs; the wartime baby boom made it necessary to think big for the future; Cold War pressures drew the government into the field, with financial aid and research contracts. Campuses expanded, new ones sprang up; that one-horse teachers' college whose recruiter failed to sway me thirty years ago is now a state university with a graduate school and a well-ranked football team.

Parallel, perhaps prior, change was taking place in society. There had always been, even in the immigrant family's sacrifice for the bright young chemistry major or in the incredible labors of the self-help student working all day and studying all night, something a little suspect in the American attitude toward the blessings of higher learning. No generation of Americans can fairly be accused of having sought to develop a cultural elite—scarcely even a culture.

In the fifties and sixties, in the boom days of American society, economy and higher education, the problem became more than suspect. It became plain that Americans generally had come to consider a college degree as a necessary ticket-of-entry—a passport to higher income, higher status, greater security. Just as an immigrant grandfather had needed a strong back, his grandson needed a sheepskin; and that attitude became the treacherous base on which the education boom was built.

Exactly how and why the ticket-of-entry concept flamed so fiercely after the war may be disputed—it probably stemmed from the complexity of a new technological economy—but by the early fifties, it was being strongly enforced. Major corporations granted only menial, assembly line or secondary jobs to persons without degrees; noting this well, fathers and mothers so condemned began pushing children—no matter what the children thought or wanted—toward college. So did the lower schools influenced by the parents' taxes and PTAs. Not to be college educated became a business and social handicap; the label "college dropout" became stigmatic, virtually an entry on police records. Even on women, whose place so lately had been the home, college pressures increased—largely because a man with a degree needed a wife with a degree, and some corporations even required it of him. And above all, if you were going for a degree, you could not be drafted—the ultimate enforcement.

Inevitably, ticket-of-entry attitudes influenced education itself, perhaps most seriously in the bigness of its institutions and the mass-produced techniques, with all that meant in impersonality and monotony.

The campus also became a great operational talent pool—for private companies and the government, if less so for undergraduates. The mushrooming of military-oriented research is well-known. But beyond that, by the end of 1970, there were 120 American universities holding 318 contracts from AID alone, for overseas developmental work, at a price of something like $50 million annually. From fishpond research at Auburn to family planning by Columbia University in Costa Rica, such projects are big business. Louisiana State is even providing South Vietnam with a program of no doubt needed legal assistance services.

Supplying the burning public demand that it did, higher education was bound to seek and receive vast public support. President Johnson's Administration, typically grandiose, ultimately promised a college education to every child capable of it. By the fall of 1969, as a result of the 20-year boom, there were 2,525 American "institutions of higher education"—an average of 50 per state—of all varieties; they enrolled 7.9 million students.

Twenty-six of those institutions enrolled *more than 30,000 students;* 39 more boasted of more than 20,000 students. By 1966, the annual income of this educational juggernaut, from all sources and for all the individual institutions, was nearly $18 billion; in 1940, by the best available figures, it had been less than $1 billion. Obviously, a nation that believed in universal public education had moved on to mass higher education. But, ominously, as taxes and contributions and tuition and enrollment went up, so did expectations.

Out in California, an unemployed physicist becomes a policeman and finds himself a happier man. In Pennsylvania, a faculty-student-administration committee reduces a $285,000 college budget deficit to only $13,000. There is a shortage of plumbers and a glut of history PhDs. Columbia University drops linguistic studies, Congress debates—and approves—a comprehensive higher education subsidy bill, and here and there state legislatures begin to pass bills regulating the number of hours college professors are supposed to teach.

In one way or another, each of those disconnected events reflects the new uncertainties of higher education as its boom levels off. The combination of a general economic crisis and a sharp loss of public confidence—the two are not unrelated—appears to have brought the whole field under the most searching public, political and internal scrutiny.

"The atmosphere of the seventies isn't going to be as favorable for higher education as it was in the fifties and sixties," says Logan Wilson of the American Council of Education. Again, a layman must wonder whether that is necessarily bad.

Public confidence in higher education appears to be shaken. There is at least one sound reason why. Suddenly the ticket-of-entry is not working well. Unemployment is remarkably high—for the first time in history—among degree-bearing people, particularly the technically educated in the aerospace and allied industries.

It has been shocking to discover, given the American degree fixation, that many of these college graduates were essentially glorified factory workers earning maybe $12,000 a year; their fathers on assembly lines were doing about as well, but with less status and more union.

Robert Hansen, a physicist, was laid off from his aerospace job in 1970. He became a policeman in Van Nuys, Calif., for $889 a month as against the $1,000 a month he had received from North American Rockwell, and recently told Robert Wright of *The New York Times* that he was "more enthusiastic" about working than he had been for years; all along he had found aerospace work monotonous.

College degrees are not generally required of policemen. Mr. Hansen is not necessarily typical, but his experience suggests that the degree pressures of recent years may have pushed unknown numbers of Americans into work they don't like, and might not normally have chosen. In any case, Mr. Hansen's physics degree didn't protect him from the economic ax when it began swinging.

Reports from the campus today are that the big corporations' recruiters are not waiting as eagerly as in the past to pounce on the graduate clutching his or her sure-fire degree; nor are the beginning salaries of 1971 what they were a year or so ago.

It is clear enough that we have overproduced certain definable types for which there is a measurable demand—physics, chemistry and history PhDs, for example. But to what extent have we overproduced less identifiable types of white-collar workers—who, despite the prized degree framed on the wall of the den, either can't get a white-collar job, or can't replace one when they lose it. Worse, how many such people feel stultified and sullen in work that does not suit them? Two cars in a suburban garage are a meager compensation for hating one's work.

There is another reason, also fundamentally encouraging, for loss of confidence in the ticket-of-entry. Not only are degree holders, and those who paid the tuition and tax bills the degrees required, becoming more aware that diplomas won't necessarily open the door to the millennium; but more and more young people are refusing to become degree fodder in the first place. . . .

This appears to be primarily because no school, higher or lower, teaches a child as much about life as he learns in the home; and a lot of American children have been learning in the home that they do not like the great postwar American suburban affluent two-car two-martini two-TV corporate heart attack rat race. If it is a ticket-of-entry to *that* that they are expected to earn through all those SATs, interviews, amphitheater courses, grades by the numbers and lockstep routines—well, no thanks, Dad.

If, on the other hand, some young person today is genuinely interested in public service work, getting back to nature, doing something with his hands, art—what is his need for the lengthy routine of degree production, let alone the degree itself? The argument can be made that every policeman and carpenter ought to be as educated and cultivated as possible, but that is not the ticket-of-entry thesis—which holds that the degree keeps one from having to be a carpenter in the first place.

But those who rebel against contemporary society are not the only ones resisting the degree pressure. Probably even more young people—the two groups overlap—more sharply resist the mass-production, interchangeable-part approach to higher education that dominates the American campus.

The "four-year straitjacket," the "lockstep" of required courses, classroom hours, exam grades; the vastness of it all—computerized registration, huge classes, platooning professors—and the resulting impersonality; the increasing homogeneity of instruction and institutions (even the old distinction between public and private universities has been eroded, and will disappear further as federal support for higher education becomes dominant, which federal support always does); the "relevance" or lack of it that courses have to life beyond the campus; the dependence of the university on the government, particularly the military, and the big corporations—hence its supposedly stand-pat establishment nature; all these, real, imagined and in-between, are causing wholesale unrest, resentment and refusal among the younger brothers and sisters of those who, ten years ago, marched in docility through the degree mill to the suburbs:

> And the children go to school,
> and the children go to summer camp,
> and then to the university
> where they are put in boxes
> and they all come out the same . . .
> and they're all made out of ticky-tacky
> and they all look just the same.

So, as some youngsters dropped out and others demonstrated, hard working American parents could easily wonder if it was not the university that somehow had created the Woodstock Nation and the Chicago marchers. It seemed clear to them that if the kids themselves prized the ticket-of-entry so little, there must be something wrong with what they were being taught up there at that place of intellectualism and effete snobbery; faculties suddenly seemed to bristle with the likes of Marcuse and Angela Davis.

After all, typical American boys and the girls next door left the suburb, didn't they, went to college, shacked up, sat in, turned on and derided football? Quarterbacks even quit the team rather than cut their hair, which was *too much*. The anti-rationalism of much of the youthful peace-and-protest movement found its counterpart in the anti-rationalism of reaction.

Even what the more enlightened universities tried to do to win back the support of their students—work-study programs, years off for travel or work, three-year programs, political action leaves, co-ed dorms, real student participation in governance—could seem to a two-car Middle American druggist like permissive egghead coddling of a bunch of kids too spoiled to appreciate the advantage he himself had never had. And anyway, everybody knows it takes four years on campus and in class to get a degree; at least, it always has.

So the great degree chase, if it is by no means over, is suddenly being questioned by those whom it has duped or disappointed, those to whom it smacks of subversion, those who resist its pressures to make them like everyone else, those who have to foot the bills, those who have to cope with these attitudes.

As one direct result, legislators are tightening budgets, or at least checking them more closely, and private contributors are more reluctant to come through. The Council for Financial Aid to Education has just reported that in 1969–70, private giving to higher education suffered its first decline in more than a decade—down $20 million from 1968–69 to $1.78 billion for public and private institutions. Politicians find the permissive university a fat target; the reaction against the upheavals at Berkeley led straight to the imposition of tuition in the University of California.

These are not entirely disastrous trends. If, for instance, the effort in some legislatures to impose minimum teaching hours on professors stems mostly from a know-nothing stab at their supposed political involvements, it might also bring some of the university's best brains back from the government laboratory to the classroom and seminar.

As for money, boom days are profligate days; if they are at an end, the university will no longer simply be able to add students, buildings and faculty to sate public demand. It may be forced to discover more innovative and creative means of spending its money, both in an educational and an administrative sense.

Thus President Howard Rubendall of Dickinson College found that two students, two administrators, and three faculty members—the budget subcommittee of the college's Institutional Priorities and Resources Committee—had gone over his $7 million budget with pruning shears and reduced its deficit by $272,000—cutting as ruthlessly into student services and faculty salaries and prerequisites as into administrative expenses.

Rubendall values the savings little more than the "community effort" that he thinks has to be an integral part of a university today—the antidote, perhaps to its inevitable elements of impersonality and routine.

But it is surely not the accompanying shortages of money and public support—which may well be short run difficulties anyway—that make it a good thing for the boom era in higher education to have leveled off. To a layman, at least two other developments seem more important and to offer greater long term possibilities.

The first is the likelihood that the crest has been reached and the tide is receding in the fervent conviction of a suburban society and a corporate economy that only the college degree is a guaranteed ticket-of-entry to the good life. Every indication is that a healthy skepticism about mass higher education is replacing the admiring indulgence of the postwar years.

Moreover, there has been an explosion of competition for the traditional university—community colleges, technical institutes, junior colleges, two-year colleges, "external degrees" earned by doing academic work rather than enrolling at a college, "open universities," and the like. If there is an easing of social pressures to force a baccalaureate degree on every individual, the means appear far more nearly at hand for young people to choose more freely that kind of higher education—including none—that truly suits their tastes and ambitions.

The other development is a longer shot. It seems possible that the combination of technology and affluence will give Americans more leisure than ever before.

If that is the case, then it may also be supposed that more Americans than ever before will be turning to the life of the mind in order to develop the useful and fruitful way of living that is becoming ever harder to find in work. Work ultimately is satisfying only when it is productive, which it used to be in America; but productive work is almost the hardest thing to find in the technological society of created demand that we have today.

That prospect—if it is one—would mean that the true university might at last come into its own in America, as a place where people come to contemplate and inquire and learn, from which they derive a sense of oneness with nature, history, and their fellow men.

Such a university is a long way down the road from the degree mill. But as demand produced the latter, so it might the former; and whatever else it did, the great boom at least made higher education a prominent part of American life. If it did not, in the end, manage to package the good life in sheepskin, it might be that disillusionment will be the beginning of enlightenment.

Discussion Questions

1. Review the reasons Wicker offers for the development of "the boom era of higher education" in the United States. How many of these are "educational" reasons? What does your answer tell you about the institution of higher education in the United States?
2. Do you agree with this statement by Wicker? "[N]o school, higher or lower, teaches a child as much about life as he learns in the home. . . ." Discuss.
3. In one of his concluding paragraphs Wicker speaks of "the great degree chase, if . . . by no means over, is suddenly being questioned by those whom it has duped or disappointed, those to whom it smacks of subver-

sion, those who resist its pressures to make them like everyone else, those who have to foot the bills, those who have to cope with these attitudes." Give examples of persons who would fit these categories. Are there any others who will fill these ranks and continue "the great degree chase"?
4. Review the competitive higher educational institutions Wicker discusses at the conclusion of this article. Do you think that they will be successful? Related to this, do you think—as Wicker suggests—that "the true university might at last come into its own in America" because of the factors in his article? Discuss.

THOMAS J. COTTLE

The Integration of Harry Benjamin

In the United States, race is one of the most important measurable determinants of an individual's chances for educational advancement. As previously indicated, other factors such as family background and teacher's expectations also serve to help or hinder a student's educational progress regardless of his natural ability. All students experience some degree of boredom, frustration, and tension. However, a student in the United States with its "middle-class culture," if he is non "middle class," is likely to be overwhelmed by the frustrations of different and contradictory norms and expectations. Such a student survives by developing defense mechanisms (and, in many instances, by simply "dropping out"). The following article describes Harry Benjamin's frustrations and defense mechanisms.

For several years in Boston, a school busing operation has been employed to increase racial integration. A small number of black students from Boston's

Reprinted from Thomas J. Cottle, "The Integration of Harry Benjamin," *New York Times Magazine* (April 23, 1972).

inner city are transported each school day to rather opulent suburban high schools, some of them as many as 25 miles away. Not all the suburban school systems have accepted the busing program, and hence all-white schools, or schools with less than 1 per cent nonwhite populations, still exist.

Harry Benjamin is a black youth, 16 years old, from Boston's Roxbury district. I rode the school bus with him quite a few days, mornings and afternoons, hoping that I might come to know a few of the feelings attached to this recent attempt to integrate schools. What follows is a portion of a conversation I had with this young man after knowing him almost two years. We were together at the suburban school he attended, he being one of 70 black students among some 1,500 white students.

"My problem," Harry Benjamin was saying one morning after English class, "is that I just don't know what the hell I'm supposed to make of all this b—— they're teachin' me. Man, they go throwin' some of this stuff around like it's supposed to mean something."

"What were they discussing in there?" I asked him as we marched down the halls of the large suburban school. "Any books in particular?"

"Yeah. Greek tragedy. Now what do I know or care about Greek tragedy? I ask you that, Man, I don't even know where Greece *is*. And that's another thing. Before they go to speaking about this play or that play, like 'Oedipus Rex,' they show us this map of Greece and then they got one of the Roman Empire. I can't get it in my mind where these places are in the world. I ain't even traveled nowhere. I'd like to maybe, though . . . ," and he started to dream: "I'd like to go to Africa someday."

The halls between 9:14 and 9:20 were filled with students running, walking, whistling, moping their way to second-period class. That feeling of school. Everyone knows it. It has anxiety and reactions to authority and giddiness and depression, all the world and all the feelings of the world tied up with it. When I think of that word, "microcosm"; which some inevitably apply to the nature of schools, I have to wonder whether they mean a collection of feelings more than anything else. Surely no one would say society is like this, an easy extension of, and an elaborated form of, school. Harry interrupted my thoughts:

"You know, strange thing about this place, you know, you were askin' me before?"

"Yes?"

"School's kinda like the whole world, only in miniature."

"It *is?*" I questioned him, somewhat surprised.

"Sure. Look. This place is doin' its best to teach us who we are. School stinks a lot of the time but that's the way life is. That's what my father always says to me. 'You gotta learn the hard knocks there,' he says, ' 'cause you're gonna find out there is no perfect smooth sailing anywhere.' He says that all the time. I don't want to conform, you know, be like all the rest of the kids, but you can't always start out and be different. That ain't the way to be. you gotta learn to take orders and give orders."

"But you make it sound a bit like the Army," I replied.

"Yeah, maybe I do." One could see him thinking about his own words. "But school ought to be a little like that. You gotta do things you don't like."

"Even like Greek tragedy?"

"Yeah. Even that. You surprised to hear me say that?"

"Yeah. I am a little, truthfully."

"Well, don't be. See, here's the thing you can't dig, so I'm gonna make you understand."

"I'm ready." I smiled at him.

"Seriously," he started. "I'm black. Right?"

"Right."

"Everybody knows that, right?"

"Right."

"Don't need to tell anybody, right?"

"Right."

"See," he began to giggle although his teeth were closed tightly, "you're gettin' all the answers right."

"You watch me, man," I blurted out unthinkingly, "I'm gonna get straight A's."

"Well, that'll be good, too. 'Least one of us is passing."

"I'm sorry, Harry. Go on."

"Yeah. Yeah. O.K. See, I gotta learn about what the white kids are learning, otherwise I'm always going to be behind them. I'm going to have to work harder at all of this stuff, no matter what happens. I don't dig it most of the time but I'm going to stick it out. Man, there's no one in this school hates it more than I do when some sonofabitch teacher, white or black . . . That's another thing. Don't make no difference, you know. Some of them black teachers can be just as bad or worse on us black kids.

"Like, you know, I'd take Levy over Henkle anytime. Boy, he's a mean s——, that guy Henkle. He ain't been no friendly cat to me, whereas Levy, he's been a good friend, or you know, straight with me. A regular guy."

We were heading now down the main stairs of the building, caught in a trafficking of bodies and a swirl of language, conversations, pinching, smells of high school. Harry Benjamin was the single black person I could see in this entire swarm of persons. I was checking for this as he spoke his piece, but not he. He just kept poking and shoving his way downward, his words flying out for anyone to hear. It wasn't as though he had rehearsed his sentiments exactly; it was merely that nothing he was saying was meant for me alone to hear.

"O.K. So that's the race part of it. Now, like I was saying, they got horrible cats teaching here. They boss us here, they boss us there; don't even give us a chance to listen to ourselves think and figure out what we are or who we'd like to be. But it ain't no matter. I'm going to take it so I can make it like all the families of these kids have made it. I don't want my children to have to be bused out to no white suburb someday. This s—— gonna have to stop. Damn thing which near drives me crazy is how the white kids all think we're something so special or something. They really think we got something on 'em. They should only know."

The crowd of white students was slamming up against us as our feet hunted first for one step and then the next. We had reached the landing above the ground floor. Suddenly, my anxiety of getting trampled to death—actually, a highly unlikely fate—was supplanted by a more intense anxiety connected with the thought that this tide of adolescents might inadvertently sweep me into some classroom from which I would not be able to escape before making an utter fool of myself. And still, as we began the last descent from the landing, I saw no other black faces in the crowd.

"Part I don't like about this school I guess more than any other is how they keep looking at you and pushin' you. It's like they gotta always control us, keep us under wraps or something." For the first time he looked about at the swarm of noisy students making their way toward the various first-floor classrooms. "Now you dig this scene?"

"Man, I've been jostled around in it seems like days," I said.

"Yeah, it's a sonofabitch, ain't it?"

"Yup," I said. He laughed.

"Well," he went on, "who's going to make trouble in a setup like this with all these people starin' at you all the time. Ain't no place to even move an inch, much less get out of line. Man. You hear what I'm saying? Get out of line. They got me talking their way now."

"Matthew [a friend of ours] says that school pressures him like I pressure him," I responded. "The phrase he used which I like is that I give him no corners to hide in and no windows to jump out of."

"I can dig it. I can dig it." Harry nodded assent and pleasure. "Someday there's gonna be one great revolution. All the kids of this country are going to slug the s—— out of their teachers. O-o-o-e-e-e that's gonna be one beautiful day for us. You know, at one designated time all the clocks in all the schools gonna hit their chimes and very slowly, very slowly mind you, all these cats gonna get outta their little chairs and walk up to the front of the classrooms and s-o-o-W-A-N-G, they're gonna knock their teachers right through the blackboards. I can dig it. I can dig it."

"That means some of the good teachers that you like are going to go under with the bad ones, right?" Always my fears about a revolution come back to me.

"That's it. Sorry about that, man, but that's the way it's gotta be in times of revolution." He was smiling broadly. "S-o-o-W-A-N-G and they'll drop like flies. Got to do something about this overpopulation problem we got here in these halls. You just said it yourself. Too many goddamn people here. So we'll start first with the teachers, then, maybe if everything all goes according to plan, we'll knock out the administration too. Then we'll really be running the show."

"You know," I started to say timidly, "it almost sounds like you've done a lot of thinking about this already."

"You better believe I have. I think about it every day in class." He laughed. "Every day I'm sitting in this class or that class rackin' my poor mind as to how to get school to be more the way I want it. Now you take math here. I got math coming up, right?"

"You'll think about this vision in math too, eh?"

"Sure. Got to, man. Got to. Can't let the dream die, not now before we've gotten something underway. You'll see. Well, you won't see, but I'll be in there and Oates will be crankin' on 'bout math and I'll turn on my revolutionary dream."

"Your what?" I hadn't heard his words properly.

"My revolutionary dream, man. My revolutionary dream." I had heard his words properly. "I'll be sitting in there figuring out just how we get to organize the entire country and get all the kids involved so that they can take over every school. I mean every school, man. Not just these suburban deals. All of 'em. In every state as well as Alaska and Hawaii. Even the school where you once went."

"Five hundred years ago," I muttered, trying to get him to have a little tolerance for an old man, should a revolution come. He wouldn't have any of it.

"C'mon, man," he came back, looking at me as we neared the math class. Only a few minutes to go before that bell would ring, then there would be silence. "You know what? You got a thing about age. You know that? You ain't so old that you can't remember school and your desires to explode it, or take it over. Or were you one of those nice little well-behaved dudes?"

As he said these words two thoughts struck me, almost as arrows might. First, I remembered a vision I once had of blowing up a chemistry lab when I was a high-school junior. A group of boys had gotten together to laugh over the teacher's absentmindedness and misperceptions of the perfectly obvious. We thought we would take the laboratory door off its hinges and get everybody inside and then put the door back before the teacher came in for class. This procedure would be necessary because the door was always locked. What kept us from doing it, we reasoned, and probably rightly so, was that the teacher would never have noticed that we had gotten in without his opening the door for us. So, later on, we thought of total annihilation. I remember the anxiety I had felt then as we spoke of, well, revolution.

The second thought was how much Harry Benjamin had changed as we had moved from the last seconds of first-period English to the minutes just before second-period mathematics. His resolute way, his willingness to adapt to a trying situation whose payoff in 30 years was as visible now as the kids who milled in the halls, and his conformity, all were being altered. His language too, and his resentment of the rules of the game that ultimately constituted his schooling, had undergone tremendous transformations in these few minutes. The fact was, he even seemed more handsome now than he had five minutes before; and if this were only my imagination, then surely he had grown several inches in this time.

"What you thinkin' about?" he asked me.

"About students and schools," I answered him. "Basically what you were saying."

"Yeah. Well, don't take it all too seriously, man."

"Well, I do, I suppose."

"You don't have to. It's only a dream, my stuff. I ain't about to get into any trouble here. If I did, my father would draw the belt on me. I'd have to run away from here rather than face that."

"Well, that may be true," I said, "but you know, school must be terrible if all you're doin' is sittin' in class thinking about ways to overthrow it."

"School s——!" Harry Benjamin looked at me, straight on. Now, at last I believed him to be as close to what he really was, or would be that one day. "It s——! Ain't no one gonna give you any argument there. Very few kids dig it. Every once in while something good might happen. Might be in class or outside of class. But man, when you gotta take it this way, day in, day out, you gotta be mighty strong or mighty dumb not to be defeated by it. That's kind of why I plot to take it over. 'Cause I ain't so strong and I ain't so dumb neither."

"That's about the way I felt when I went to school, Harry, years and beers ago." He smiled when he heard me use his father's expression. "I never thought I was dumb, but I also didn't seem to have the strength to do it the way it was supposed to have been done." He was deeply interested in what I was divulging. But it had taken his wild, melodramatic fantasy to get me to dredge up my meager little left-over feelings about school—the feelings which come back to me like an old girl friend's name the moment I step on school grounds, any school grounds, anywhere.

"You know what, dad?" He was about to enter the mathematics classroom. "This has been a groove. You're one of the few people that has leveled with me about this school jazz." But I haven't, I thought. I haven't leveled with you at all, Harry Benjamin. I'm giving you rehearsed, well-baked bits of my childhood that I don't mind parting with at all to anyone. I got millions more like them. Don't you know that they don't mean a thing? "Yup," he was saying, "You're an honest dude, so I'll give you an honest ticket back. In return, like."

"I'd like to hear it," I said, half expecting to hear something like a parade of the raw bits of my history that I give only rarely, and even then reluctantly —and never, never once gave to any teacher that I can think of.

"My dreams about overthrow are extremist and all that. No one needs to tell me that." He switched his books to his left hand in preparation for opening the door with his right. For the first time he looked about wearily, making certain that no one else would hear him. Then he waited for a girl to go into the room. "Hi, Harry," she said softly, the two words brimming full of feeling.

"Hey, what d'you say, mamma." Then he looked the mustard-colored linoleum floor and began.

"I'm scared, man. I'm scared s—— in this place. Almost two years now I been coming here and I still get the flies in my stomach every day. Every morning before we leave. Every day. I don't belong here, man. Not just 'cause I'm black and everyone's white. It's just that it's all over my head. They got lots of teachers here tellin' me my talents are fine and I'm, you know, gonna be all right. But they're jivin' me. It's gonna be one helluva cold day in hell 'fore I get to makin' it here like you're supposed to. The thing is, no matter how hard I try it ain't never enough. I work harder than any of 'em and I can't do it. I just can't do it. I just can't do it, and I . . . I . . . don't know who to talk to 'cause it just ain't easy to tell someone you're failing and you know they're keeping you practically no matter what 'cause you're black or you're poor or your father's an alcoholic or your mother's a whore."

The class bell blared in the hall and everywhere around me I heard doors slam. Quickly the noise diminished. A few stragglers dashed about, along with those who were free this one period. "They're doin' the best they can. So am I. I'm doin' the best I can but it just ain't workin' out and *you* can't say a thing or figure out anything to do neither, 'cause you know it's true. Every last word I say."

And just like that he was gone.

Discussion Questions

1. Harry describes his "revolutionary dream" in the following terms: "Someday there's gonna be one great revolution. All the kids of this country are going to slug the s—— out of their teachers." Mr. Cottle, the article's author, had "a vision . . . of blowing up a chemistry lab when (he) was a high school junior." How are these dreams similar and how are they different? Discuss.

2. Discuss this defense mechanism of Harry's: "I work harder than any of 'em and I can't do it. I just can't do it. I just can't do it. . . ." What does this attitude tell you about the difference between the individual and the social demands of the institution of education in the United States?

3. Referring to his "revolutionary dream," Harry says ". . . don't take it all too seriously . . ." Should it be taken seriously? Discuss.

9 / Economic Institutions

"Complications have developed; his check bounced."

Pepper . . . and Salt cartoon by Tom Zib. From The Wall Street Journal.

Every society requires that its members find ways to make a living. The basic elements of this process are *production, distribution,* and *consumption.* In an industrial society such as our own this process involves the organization of work by such groups as unions, professions, and bureaucracies. In fact, all statuses, groups and organizations primarily concerned with production, distribution, and consumption constitute economic institutions.

The economic institutions of America had their beginning in the Industrial Revolution and development of commercialism. Industrial development depended on the existence of free labor unfettered by feudal restrictions, investment capital, and machinery driven by a productive and reliable power source. It began with the *putting-out system* in the late Middle Ages. The work and production of this system was done in the homes of individual artisans instead of in the shop of a master craftsman. Although the scale of production was small, the organization was basically capitalistic. Over time the organization of production developed into the *factory system* which brought laborers together in large central shops where they worked under a fixed routine. From this system emerged large *corporations* and the concentration of economic power in a few hands. These corporations are organized on the basic bureaucratic principles of a division of labor and hierarchy of supervision. As a result, distinct groups such as labor unions and management have emerged to protect the interest of their members in the rewards that result from their investment of capital or labor as well as the conditions under which the labor is performed.

Because of the great power wielded

by corporations and unions, government agencies have become involved in regulating, subsidizing, and assisting the production and distribution of goods. As a result, sociologists have begun to look at the governmental and economic institutions together. Since 1932 the government has been moving toward more control of the economy. The history of controls, however, reflects favoritism for established interests. One of the most pressing modern problems is the balancing of public interest, economic efficiency, and ecological considerations.

The readings that follow demonstrate the difficulties of achieving ideal relationships among the various organizations that compromise the economic institutions of the United States.

KATHERINE CARLSON

Reciprocity in the Marketplace: Tipping in an Urban Nightclub

All economic activity is based on reciprocal obligations. This is true of a simple barter economy or of a sophisticated credit economy. Occasionally, however, we must be reminded of our obligations and duties. In the following article Katherine Carlson describes how a cocktail waitress develops strategies to remind customers of their responsibility—their economic duty—to provide tips for service. Since she depends largely on tips for a living, her skill at reminding customers becomes very important.

A man and a woman enter a busy Waikiki nightclub. Led to a table by a doorman, they are soon approached by a waitress who greets them and takes their order for drinks. The waitress returns in a few minutes with their order, a bourbon and water and a margarita. After placing the drinks in front of them, she says, "That will be four dollars, please," and waits as the man fishes in his wallet for a five-dollar bill. "Here," he says, handing her the money, "Keep the change." As she takes the cash she thanks him, knowing the extra dollar is meant for her. She has received a tip.

This example of tipping is familiar to most Americans. The custom is an integral part of several economic transactions in which one person serves another. Whenever we drink at a club, ride in a taxicab, eat at a restaurant, or face a bellman who has just opened the door to our hotel room, we expect to give a gratuity to the person who has served us. For most people, tipping is a regular, though sometimes burdensome, obligation.

To the people who serve others—waitresses, waiters, coat check girls, porters, cab drivers—tips are both a blessing and a curse. They are a blessing because they provide extra, usually undertaxed, income occasionally in substantial amounts. They are a curse because employers tend to underpay employees who receive tips, assuming that workers can derive an adequate living from gratuities. The end result for service personnel is a potentially large income subject to extreme fluctuation and instability. There are customers who regularly fail to live up to their tipping obligation, or who are at best unpredictable as tippers. There are also seasonal fluctuations, and unlike most salaried workers, the service employee is directly and immediately affected by a decline in business.

The problem is particularly acute for cocktail waitresses who work in busy clubs and have a minimum of contact with their customers. Ideally, a customer should tip the waitress at a rate amounting to no less than 15 percent of his bill. On a good night, many customers will live up to this expectation, and some may even tip as high as 50 percent. When tips are large, the waitress will make far more from them than she does from her wages. A large volume of business should increase tip income.

But many nights are bad. Customers may regularly depart without leaving a tip, or may give an amount far short of the customary sum. Several factors can contribute to a bad night. In Waikiki, where research for this paper was conducted, one of the slowest business periods for both tourists and local tradesmen is between Thanksgiving and Christmas. This season delivers few customers and those who do go to bars seem to be less generous. Accordingly, income from tips is low and the waitress's income drops substantially. The type of tourist is also important. Canadians, for example, are reputed to be heavy drinkers but poor tippers. Canadian tourists appear in large numbers during certain times of year, contributing to the waitress's work load but not to her income.

For the waitress, tips are income; regular wages are "extra." This view may stem from the fact that her working shift is short, usually no more than four or six hours a night. Although she considers herself employed full time, a waitress may work only twenty or thirty hours a week and receive an hourly wage set at the legal minimum. As a consequence, she feels that if she is not tipped, she is not being paid. It is not surprising, therefore, that she resents customers who undertip or fail to leave a tip at all, and that she attempts to do something about them. To obtain a desired minimum level of tipping income, she employs a set of strategies that can be called *tipping practices.*

Tipping practices are a complex set of strategies that play on the customer's personal reputation and sense of obligation. Practices may simply remind someone who has bought drinks that he is a customer and hence should tip, or they may amount to a public confrontation in which the customer loses face if he fails to leave a gratuity. In either case the waitress attempts to heighten the customer's awareness, and sometimes the awareness of those around him, that he has a particular kind of relationship with her that involves tipping. To understand the special nature of tipping practices, it is important to look at the reciprocal nature of tipping itself.

Reciprocity

When the couple in our opening example entered the Waikiki nightclub and ordered drinks, they really assumed two kinds of economic obligation. First, they contracted with the waitress for two drinks, a bourbon and water and a margarita, which had stated prices; by doing so they assumed the obligation to pay for the drinks. Anthropologists usually refer to this kind of economic transaction as market exchange. It fits the Western economic model based on price, supply, and demand and resembles the usual kind of buying and selling that Americans are familiar with in the marketplace.

But the couple, or more accurately the man, for it is males who generally pay bills and tip in nightclubs, also assumed a second kind of economic obligation. By ordering drinks he assumed the identity of customer, which is paired with the identity of waitress. One requirement of being a customer is to tip the waitress at the accepted rate. Economic transactions of this sort, which require exchange on the basis of one's role obligations, are called reciprocal exchange. Christmas and birthday gifts, dinner parties for friends, and tipping all fall into this category.

The sense of obligation associated with reciprocal exchange as opposed to that associated with market exchange limits the options open to the waitress who wishes to ensure adequate tips. Failure to pay for something in the market is prohibited by law. If a customer attempts to leave a nightclub without paying for his drinks, he will be stopped by a doorman, asked to pay, and eventually turned over to the police if he refuses to comply.

Reciprocal exchange is a different matter. Because his role obligates him to do so, the customer is expected to tip the waitress. But if he fails in this duty he cannot be arrested or even pressured by a doorman, for his obligation to tip is not buttressed by law. As in so many other roles we play in daily life, proper behavior can be enforced only through public pressure or can result from a sense of personal obligation to follow social norms.

The waitress must act within these limits when attempting to influence her customers. In fact, her approach can never be entirely direct. She is in the same position as the person who wishes to be invited to dinner at a friend's house or the man who wants his wife to buy him an expensive set of golf clubs for his birthday. She cannot simply state her desire for a tip just as these people cannot ask for what they want. To do so would threaten or even destroy the reciprocal relationship. Instead, she must communicate her desires and the customer's duty more subtly, a constraint that sets limits on the tipping practices she may use.

Tipping Practices

Tipping practices are the strategies used by waitresses to communicate their desire for tips and to ensure that customers leave an acceptably large gratuity. Not all tipping practices carry the same weight; some confront the customer with his duty more directly than others. Let us examine these different tipping strategies.

Personalizing the service. Personalizing the service is the most obvious route open to the waitress who wishes to ensure an acceptably large tip. Theoretically, the waitress's obligation in her relationship with a customer is to provide service. The more personal the service, the more likely the customer will recognize the reciprocal nature of the relationship and feel the need to fulfill his end of the bargain. There are a number of things the waitress can do to make the customer feel that he has received personal and special attention. To begin with, she greets him with a smile and a welcome before she asks for his drink order. She may also ask where he is from or find something else to talk with him about. But the amount of personal conversation is limited by demands on her time when the club is busy. She will probably engage in less small talk when business is heavy, for under busy conditions, stopping to talk to some may lead to unreasonable and resented delays for other customers.

The waitress may also improve the quality of her interaction with customers by being prompt with orders, emptying ashtrays regularly, and being attentive to their needs for new drinks. Again, she must be careful not to cross the line between good service and pushiness. Although the first may be rewarded, the second is likely to cause resentment and decrease the size of her tips. Instead, she combines a personal touch with efficiency, remembering which drink goes to which customer and the entire order for parties of several people who want another round. Although her ability to memorize large drink orders comes primarily from repeating them and inspecting empty glasses from the previous round, it makes each customer feel he is an individual, distinct within the crowd of people the waitress is serving. Her real feelings, of course, may be quite different as summed up by her comment to the bartender, "Here's scotch and water again."

Unfortunately for the waitress, personalized service is not always possible nor does it always work. When this strategy fails, she must resort to other tactics which tell the customer more clearly that he is expected to tip.

Reminders. Reminders symbolize the tipping transaction. To convey their message, all reminders depend in some way on the manipulation of the customer's change. Most customers do not have the correct change when they come to pay their bills. The act of giving the customer his change provides the waitress with an opportunity to remind him of his obligation to her. These reminders fall into three basic categories: laying the money on the table, using a tip tray, and using a tip tray with some change in quarters.

The simplest way to return change is by laying the money on the table. This act may seem relatively innocent but actually it contains some hints for the customer. Instead of placing the money in his hand, the waitress puts it on a surface that is part of her property or is at least her responsibility. She cleans the table, sets it up, and clears it off. Things left on it unclaimed will come to her. When a customer picks up his change from the table and places it in his pocket, he removes the money from her jurisdiction. Thus, he must consciously decide how much money to pick up from the table, a process that reminds him of an obligation to tip.

Knowing this, the waitress will even try to ignore a customer's action when he reaches out to take his change, for experience tells her that once he has his money in hand, he is much less likely to give any of it to her. Placing the money on the table also makes it easier for the customer to tip, because it gives him a surface from which to draw. Otherwise, he has to juggle the change in his hands.

One refinement associated with laying the change on the table involves the order in which the change is returned. The coins are put on the table first, and the bills placed on top of them. To retrieve his change, the customer must use two motions. First he must pick up the bills, and when he does, the coins are left to remind him that he should tip. If he decides to retrieve them, too, he must use a second or even a third motion, each symbolizing his unwillingness to live up to his responsibilities.

Laying the money on the table sometimes has a special advantage. The table top may be messy and wet from the remains of many drinks. Customers do not like to put wet money in their pockets so the waitress may put the money down where she is sure it will become damp. She does not care if her tips are wet and sticky.

In Hawaii, it is the custom in many bars for persons to place a "pool" of money on the table. When the waitress brings drinks, she draws money from this pool to pay for them and returns change to the same spot. On reorders, the waitress continues to draw bills from the pool, but will try to avoid taking any coins. After an evening of drinking, a considerable pile of change will have accumulated. The great number of coins may be seen as a burden by the customer, and because it looks like a minor sum of money, may be left as part of the waitress's tip. However, the pile may add up to a large amount of money.

Use of a tip tray represents a more insistent reminder to the customer. The tray is not only a receptacle designed for the return of change, it is, as its name signifies, an artifact that serves notice on the customer that he is expected to tip. Some hints associated with placing the customer's change on the table can be used with the tip tray as well—for example, change may be returned with the coins under the bills.

The tip tray can also be used with a practice that involves giving the customer ready-made tipping money. Called a *quarter break,* this practice involves dividing one dollar of the change into four quarters. Again, the extra change reminds the customer that he is expected to tip and provides him with the means to do so. The quarters make it easier for the customer by permitting him to tip less than a dollar when that amount would be too much. The practice of breaking change may be extended in the case of large bills. If a bill is fourteen dollars, for example, and the customer gives the waitress a twenty-dollar bill, she will return his change in the form of four quarters and five one-dollar bills. Breaking the five-dollar bill into ones makes a more definite statement that tipping is expected.

Most waitresses feel that the way coins are arranged on the tip tray also works to remind the customer to tip. They often place quarters in each corner of the tray or at least in some regular pattern. By this arrangement the customer is put on notice that the waitress is aware of the money on the tray and that she knows the customer has enough change to tip her. When tips have been especially bad, waitresses may experiment with different arrangements of quarters, trying to hit on the one that yields the best results. In one club, a waitress even bought a bag of Hershey "kisses" and began leaving them on the tip tray along with the change. She hoped that this additional "gift" would lead to larger tips, but she discontinued the practice when customers began to recover their change and leave her the candy.

Use of a tip tray may help counteract other problems. When money is left on the table, the waitress must wait for the customer to leave before she can collect it. Sometimes a prudent wife, more conservative with the family budget and perhaps a bit jealous of a gratuity meant for another woman who is attractive and revealingly dressed, will pick up the coins. As she sees the woman follow her husband out of the club, the waitress can only stand by and watch, helpless as her tip slips away from her. With the use of the tip tray the money is a bit safer. Once the customer has signaled his intention to tip her by taking some of his change, the waitress may be able to pick up the tray before he leaves. Such immediate tipping is preferable in clubs where customers leave the table to dance or where they move from one table to another.

Confrontations. When the waitress lays the money on the table or uses a tip tray, there is still the possibility that a customer will ignore the messages these acts communicate and will fail to tip her. Under these circumstances she may resort to more direct measures by confronting the customer. Confrontation requires the waitress's presence, which renders the customer's tipping behavior public. In using confrontation, the waitress takes full advantage of the customer's presumed uncertainty about tipping and of his embarrassment at being caught failing to reciprocate in his relationship with her. Aware of the customer's possible reluctance, the waitress attempts to convey the consequences of his failure to tip before it is too late. She does this by subjecting him to both visual and verbal embarrassment in the form of four strategies: making a fast pickup, using the cocktail tray, hiding the change, and lowering the cocktail tray.

Making a fast pickup is used in conjunction with the tip tray. If the amount of money on the tray is fairly small and can reasonably be given as a tip, the waitress will wait only a short time before she retrieves it. In one small club, waitresses have been known to make one circle of the room after returning the customer's change, then to return, pick up the tray, thank the customers, and walk off as if the money in the tray is meant for them. Some customers do intend to leave all the money on the tray for the waitress, but many simply have not had time to pick up their change. Once the waitress has left with the money, the only way a customer can retrieve change is by calling her back and publicly announcing that she has gotten away with his money.

Should she be called back, the waitress will apologize, saying that she thought the money on the tray was her tip. Unless he wishes to look like a cheapskate the customer will have to let the waitress keep the money.

The cocktail tray is also used to confront the reluctant customer. The waitress uses her cocktail tray as a kind of personal tip tray, holding it out with the change on it for the customer to retrieve. She will complicate this process by using a quarter break and by placing the bills on top of the coins. The customer is faced with the task of picking up a pile of bills and change while the waitress looks on. She watches as he decides how much to tip her, and by her gaze she exerts considerable pressure. If he is uncertain about what is correct or expected, or even if he would prefer to leave a small gratuity, her presence is likely to make him opt for the role of big spender rather than that of cheapskate.

The cocktail tray offers another advantage. It is supported only by a woman's forearm providing a very unstable surface from which to pick up change. As the customer pushes down on the tray to pick up his change, it will move and wobble, giving the impression that he is overanxious to retrieve the money. In addition, the cocktail tray is usually wet. As a result, coins tend to stick to it. If he wants his change, the customer must painstakingly slide each coin off the tray separately, looking and presumably feeling like a penny pincher with each successful recovery. Rather than suffer this embarrassment and loss of esteem, which is made worse by the presence of the waitress, the customer will usually leave one or two quarters as a tip. He often does so with a sigh of exasperation, having given up in the battle for the change and waving the waitress away with a surly "Keep it." Again, she politely thanks him.

The waitress can make it even more embarrassing for the customer by lowering the tray, thus effectively exaggerating the instability of the tray's surface. If she moves her tray down just slightly as the customer reaches for his change, he will appear to grab for his money rather than pick it up. This will be apparent to others, and although the customer may suspect the waitress is behind his problem, he will also be affected by the way he has acted. Again, this may be sufficient to convince him that he should leave the change for the waitress.

A final variation in the use of the cocktail tray is a little like the fast pickup described above. Called *hiding the change,* it is a deliberate attempt to coerce the customer. To effect the strategy, the waitress places the coins very close to the lip of the tray under the bills. Because a cocktail tray has an edge that obscures part of its surface, it may be impossible for the customer to see the coins, causing him to retrieve only the bills. The waitress may exaggerate this problem by holding the tray above the seated customer's eye level. After he removes his hand and begins to put his bills away, the waitress dips the tray to show him the coins, says "Thank you," and walks away. By the time the customer realizes that his change amounted to more than just bills, and that the coins he has just seen and for which he has just been thanked have been taken as a tip, the waitress is gone. The only way he can get the money back is to call out to the waitress, announcing his cheapness to her and to everyone else within earshot.

Customer Response

Of course, customers are not entirely helpless in their exchanges with waitresses. They have at their disposal several techniques that interfere with the waitress's tipping practices. A customer may, for example, deny the waitress a medium for action by paying with the exact change or by using a credit card. Without the change as an operating tool, the waitress can do very little. Customers with exact change, however, are rare because it requires that their pockets be stuffed with coins.

The customer may also make specific requests to the waitress that deny her the use of tipping practices. He may require her to place the money on the table, for example, when she would like to give it to him on the cocktail tray. Or he may ask that she avoid giving him silver. The waitress can counter this request by claiming that she has no bills with which to make change, but there may be no point in doing so if it is clear that the customer will pick up his money in any form it is given to him. Customers may also ask the waitress to steady her cocktail tray, or more forcefully, reach out and stabilize it themselves. Customers who do this are often impervious to the impression it makes on those around them and will not succumb to any practice the waitress can employ.

In fact, a customer may ignore American cultural rules about tipping and the exchange of money without any sign of embarrassment. He may simply refuse or fail to recognize the existence of tipping practices when they are directed at him by the waitress. A surprising number of customers, for example, will methodically pick quarters off a sticky, unstable tray without worrying about the meaning that others may attribute to their actions. Such resistance may occur relatively frequently; it represents a response to pressure from the waitress. High-pressure techniques often lead to negative feelings between the two, for in using them, the waitress demands that the customer meet his obligations or pay a high social cost.

Finally, a customer may respond to the waitress by putting her off. He may say, "I'll tip you later," in an effort to reassure her that she is in his mind. Waitresses, however, are well aware that people who say this seldom do tip, or tip less than a reasonable amount. All the waitress can do is hope that a tip will come and be as attentive as possible to the customer's needs.

Club Atmosphere

In larger perspective, the way tipping practices are employed says something about human relationships in public places. Waitresses do not regularly use all the practices available to them. Instead, certain practices seem to be used by most waitresses in particular nightclubs, indicating that there is something about the club environment itself that favors particular techniques.

The feature of clubs that seems most important in this respect is intimacy. Some nightclubs are felt to be intimate either because they are small, or because their space and activity give an illusion of intimacy. Other clubs seem impersonal because they are large or crowded. Noise level, busy activity, and sexual display also contribute to the degree of intimacy or impersonality a club achieves. Even small clubs may appear impersonal if they are noisy, frantically busy, or marked by a live sex display, striptease show, or topless waitresses.

Although customers may not be conscious of the quality of their surroundings, their tipping behavior seems to conform to it. In intimate clubs they feel closer to the waitress. A regular relationship between the two is easily established. In impersonal clubs the reverse is true. Customers are likely to think of themselves as part of a faceless crowd. They may hardly notice the waitress, or they think of her merely as an employee of the establishment, paid for her work by the management, and having no special relationship with them.

It is not surprising, therefore, to discover that tipping practices are not usually employed by waitresses in very intimate clubs, or if used at all, they constitute reminders rather than confrontations. In impersonal nightclubs, on the other hand, confrontations are common. In fact, tipping practices may be part of a club's policy. New waitresses are told in some establishments to use their cocktail tray to return change, or engage in some other variety of confrontation with the customer.

Another feature of nightclubs that seems to affect customers is quality of service and entertainment. If a customer feels he is getting his money's worth because the quality of the drinks, the service, and the show is high, he is more likely to tip the waitress. But if the club offers a second-rate show, watery drinks, and poor service, a customer is likely to take his resentment out on the waitress by tipping her poorly or not at all. The situation may be made worse if the management wants waitresses to press drinks on customers or to rush them in any way. This sense of pressure can be found in many Waikiki nightclubs that boast exorbitant prices for drinks and poor shows. When customers are pleased with the nightclub, waitresses generally need not use tipping practices that confront the customer. But in nightclubs that dissatisfy the customer, confrontation practices are common and probably add to the customer's overall dislike of his surroundings.

Conclusion

As we have seen, two kinds of economic transaction operate between a waitress and her customer in a nightclub. In one, market exchange, the customer orders and pays for a commodity, the drinks. In the other, reciprocity, he tips the waitress because he must as part of his customer role. The first transaction is underwritten by legal sanctions and is almost always carried on without incident. The second transaction, reciprocity, is maintained only by informal obligation. What the waitress thinks she should receive as a tip may not coincide with what the customer feels he should give her. Because she depends on tips to make her living, the waitress uses tipping practices to remind the customer of his obligations. The simplest of these merely reminds the customer that he is expected to tip; more complex practices confront him with his duty.

The growth of impersonal public settings in the American hotel and entertainment industry may spell the end of tipping altogether. Perhaps because it is impossible to maintain the illusion of personal service and thus reciprocal obligation under these circumstances, there is more and more talk of abolishing tipping. A recent solution, however, has changed the nature of tipping as an economic transaction. In some clubs a service charge is automatically added to the customer's bill, making the tip part of the regular market transaction. In some clubs where the service charge is not included on the bill, a reminder that "tips are not included," is printed instead. In such cases the establishment itself uses a reminder to help the waitress get her tips.

As our mass society becomes less personal, reciprocal exchange becomes something of an anachronism within the larger market economy. In those reciprocal exchanges that remain, the market aspect of goods is downplayed by emphasizing the nonmonetary nature of the exchange and stressing "It's the thought, not the price of the gift, that counts." Although we tend to put a financial value on gifts, and expect to receive gifts of appropriate value in return, we downplay price in favor of emotion.

For tipping there is no such alternative. Travel and dining-out publications may advise customers about the extent of their tipping obligation, and some customers may even laboriously figure out the precise percentage of their bill as a basis for their tip, but the feeling of personal association between the customer and waitress is difficult to sustain. It seems impossible for the custom of tipping to last forever in large, impersonal settings. Nevertheless, waitresses, who are both recipients and enforcers of the reciprocal obligation as it is now defined, will continue to employ and adjust their tipping practices according to the necessities of the situation.

Discussion Questions

1. Review the strategies of economic cooperation discussed in this article.
2. How does this article clarify the economic and sociological behavior of paying for a commodity and role playing?
3. The author believes the practice of tipping is fading. Why? Do you agree? Discuss.

Self-Images for Everybody

The consumption of goods and services is an important element of our society's economic institutions. Through the use of modern advertising the
potential consumer is often stimulated in exaggerated ways. An example of
this kind of exaggerated stimulation through certain kinds of advertising is
a deodorant advertisement which passes off a particular brand of deodorant
as a cure for loneliness! In the selection below, Vance Packard gives his
version of how the motivational researchers of the advertising world appeal
to our "hidden" thoughts, fears, and dreams, and how they are making us
an increasingly consumption-oriented society.

*"People have a terrific loyalty to their brand of cigarette and yet in tests cannot
tell it from other brands. They are smoking an image completely."*
—Research director, New York advertising agency
(name withheld upon request).

The subconscious salesmen, in groping for better hooks, deployed in several directions. One direction they began exploring in a really major way was
the molding of images; the creation of distinctive, highly appealing "personalities" for products that were essentially undistinctive. The aim was to build
images that would arise before our "inner eye" at the mere mention of the
product's name, once we had been properly conditioned. Thus they would
trigger our action in a competitive sales situation.

A compelling need for such images was felt by merchandisers, as I've indicated, because of the growing standardization of, and complexity of, ingredients in most products, which resulted in products that defied reasonable
discrimination. Three hundred smokers loyal to one of three major brands of
cigarettes were given the three brands to smoke (with labels taped) and asked
to identify their own favorite brand. Result, 35 per cent were able to do so;
and under the law of averages pure guesses would have accounted for a third
of the correct identifications. In short, something less than 2 per cent could
be credited with any real power of discrimination. Somewhat comparable results were obtained when merchandisers tried "blindfold" tests on beer and
whisky drinkers.

If people couldn't discriminate reasonably, marketers reasoned, they should
be assisted in discriminating *unreasonably,* in some easy, warm, emotional
way.

Pierre Martineau, a high apostle of image building, analyzed the problem with startling candor in talking to Philadelphia advertising men in early 1956. Advertising, he admonished them, is no longer just a neat little discussion of your product's merits.

"Basically, what you are trying to do," he advised, "is create an illogical situation. You want the customer to fall in love with your product and have a profound brand loyalty when actually content may be very similar to hundreds of competing brands." To create this illogical loyalty, he said, the first task "is one of creating some differentiation in the mind—some individualization for the product which has a long list of competitors very close to it in content."

While a competitor can often successfully imitate your product as to ingredients and claims of quality, a vivid personality image is much more difficult to imitate and so can be a more trustworthy sales factor.

A fairly simple, straightforward use of nonrational symbolism in image building was Louis Cheskin's transformation of the Good Luck margarine package. The package originally contained several elements, including a picture of the margarine. In one corner was a little four-leaf clover. Mr. Cheskin found from his depth probing that the four-leaf clover was "a wonderful image" so in three successive changes he brought it into more and more prominence until finally he had a simple foil package completely dominated by a large three-dimensional four-leaf clover. Mr. Cheskin reports that sales rose with each change.

A chief of research for a major advertising agency was showing me many dozens of drawings people had made of cars when they were asked by his investigators to "draw a car." He said casually, "You can just about predict from the way a person draws a car the brand of gasoline he will buy." I expressed astonishment and said I thought people bought gasoline because of the dealer's location or because they liked him or because of the supposed quality of his gasoline. He agreed those all had some bearing, but not as much as we assume, and cited a study showing that where there were four dealers at an intersection and one dealer changed his brand his business would suddenly go up or down as much as 30 per cent as a result of the change in image.

This man said his staff had classified the drawings as to the kind of personality they revealed in the drawer and then had checked the findings against the kind of gasoline the drawer constantly bought. They found a startling correlation between the way a person draws a car and the gasoline image that will attract him. He explained:

"In buying a gasoline you get played back to you who you are. Each gasoline has built up an image or personality. Each helps a buyer answer the question 'Who am I?' Your aim is to find the people who have an affinity for your gasoline."

He showed me a series of car drawings made by people who consistently buy the particular brand his agency handles. The agency has deliberately sought to give its gasoline an image of bigness, authority. The cars drawn by users of the gasoline clearly showed a tendency to be long, streamlined, big. And he said that an analysis of the personal characteristics of these users showed they tended to be either local successes in their community (merchants, doctors, lawyers, etc.) or else were people frustrated in yearnings for bigness.

Then he showed me another series of drawings of cars. These tended to be done not in any grand style but with loving detail. They were all done by people who prefer brand B gasoline, which has built up an image of being a friendly gasoline. Its image reminds people of outdoors, small towns, warm colors. Even its TV show presents an image of folksiness. The people who buy this gasoline, my informant said, are the chatty type who like to get out of the car and talk with the station attendant while the car is being serviced.

A third series of drawings was like Rube Goldberg cartoons, flamboyant. The car might not run but it had an aerial and a host of other gadgets on it. Typically the artist thinks of his car as a wonderful plaything. The gasoline he consistently buys has sought to build an image of itself, on TV and elsewhere, as an exciting, dramatic, flamboyant gasoline. My informant explained:

"By understanding these personalities we are not only in a better position to maintain our present customers, but to know where to make gains from our competitors. Of these five brands I can say, 'Where am I going to get increases? Which is the gasoline most vulnerable to us?' Actually the brand B buyer is most vulnerable to us because, although he is folksy, he wants bigness. By warming up our image of brand A we can appeal to this brand B buyer."

A little later this research director got to talking about the images of cigarettes. Roughly 65 per cent of all smokers are absolutely loyal, and 20 per cent more relatively loyal to one brand of cigarette. Even though in tests they cannot identify that cigarette, they will walk down five flights of stairs to buy their brand rather than accept a substitute. He cited an experiment his chief psychologist performed in the early fifties. This psychologist chose a group of eighty smokers known to have a strong loyalty for some brand of cigarette and gave these eighty smokers the Rorschach ink-blot test. Later the psychologist, who had not been advised what brand each favored, went through the Rorschach results and from the emotional make-ups indicated named with only a few misses the brand of cigarette that each of the eighty smokers *had* to favor!

This agency has built a comprehensive personality profile of the typical smoker of each major brand of cigarette. This material is confidential. However, the type of material in it resembles to a large degree profiles assembled by other investigators. Social Research, for instance, profiled several of the leading cigarettes for *The Chicago Tribune*. It found, for example, that Camels were regarded as masculine, and strong, and for the ordinary working people. Lucky Strikes had a similar reputation—strong and for men, too; for ordinary people, but less for the workingman. Chesterfields were thought to be for both men and women and on the mild side and not bound by class.

This study was made shortly before the cigarette industry was thrown into its tizzy by the now famous cancer scare, which in the words of one spokesman of the advertising agencies put the "cigarette industry in one hell of a fix." Some of the old leaders who had built themselves images as rough, tough cigarettes found themselves losing customers. There was turmoil as the cigarettes groped for more reassuring images. Retailers were flooded with new brands all claiming to be safer than others. As a result of the cancer scare virtually every major tobacco marketer brought out a filter-tip brand, and in four years filter-tip sales rose 1800 per cent. By 1957 the filter tips, too, were, by skilled image building, developing distinctive personalities, the old brands were developing more "gentle" personalities, and cigarette sales as a whole began trending upward again, starting in 1955.

Perhaps the most spectacularly successful image building has been done by the automobile industry. The automobile has become far more than a mere means of conveyance. In the words of Pierre Martineau, "The automobile tells who we are and what we think we want to be. . . . It is a portable symbol of our personality and our position . . . the clearest way we have of telling people of our exact position. [In buying a car] you are saying in a sense, 'I am looking for the car that expresses who I am.' "

Buick, in fact, suggested this in its ad when it offered this promise to the public: "It makes you feel like the man you are."

One of the most remarkable documents I came across in my investigation was a pamphlet called "Automobiles, What They Mean to Americans." It reports on a study made for *The Chicago Tribune* by Social Research, Inc. The major merchandising journals have discussed its findings in great detail. The study was conducted by a team of social scientists who used a variety of probing techniques on 352 car owners in the Chicago area.

The investigators found that only a minority of the population, mostly men in the lower class, have any real interest in the technical aspect of cars. And the major finding that stands out in the survey is that automobiles are heavily laden with social meanings and are highly esteemed because they "provide avenues for the expression . . . of the character, temperament and self concept of the owner and driver. . . . The buying process is an interaction between the personality of the car and the personality of the individual."

The report indicated the personality of one sort of owner of various major makes of car by presenting a series of circles. Each circle contained words written in to indicate the dominant traits of this owner and their relative importance. Here are some of the owner profiles that were indicated:

Cadillac: "Proud . . . flashy . . . salesman . . . middle-aged . . . social mobility . . . good income level . . . responsible."

Ford: "Speed demon . . . good income . . . young man . . . proud . . . upper lower class . . . drives to work . . . practical."

DeSoto: "Conservative . . . responsible . . . matron . . . upper middle class . . . good income . . . proud."

Studebaker: "Neat look . . . sophisticated . . . intellectual . . . mobile . . . professional . . . young man."

Pontiac: "Stable class outlook . . . middle of road . . . married woman . . . mother . . . sincere . . . conventional . . . busy."

Mercury: "Salesman . . . assertive . . . mobile . . . modern . . . substantial . . . lower middle . . . father . . . quick."

The report stated that "people buy the cars they think are especially appropriate for them" and then made these points:

People who want to seem conservative, to tell the world they are very serious and responsible tend to buy Plymouth, Dodge, DeSoto, Packard, four-door sedans, dark colors, minimum accessories and gadgets.

People who want to seem sociable and up-to-date but in a middle-of-the-road sort of way tend to favor Chevrolet, Pontiac, Buick, Chrysler, two-door coupés, light colors, moderate accessories and gadgets.

People who want to express some showiness, to assert their individualism and modernity, tend to buy Ford, Mercury, Oldsmobile, Lincoln, hardtops, two tones, bright shades and hues, a range of extras, gadgets, fads.

People who need to express unusual status or individual needs favor Cadillac (ostentation, high status), Studebaker, Hudson, Nash, Willys, convertibles (impulsiveness), very bright colors, red, yellow, white, latest gadgets and accessories.

Discussion Questions

1. Why is the consumption function of the economic institution less logical and rational than the production and distribution functions? How does this selection demonstrate this relative lack of logic and rationality?
2. Review the products discussed in this selection and their respective "self-images." Do you tend to agree with Packard and the authorities he cites that the advertising of these products attempts to stimulate "illogical loyalty" and "nonrational symbolism"? Discuss.

ROGER RAPOPORT

A Candle for St. Greed's

Many members of the medical profession argue that the norms of their professional culture qualify them as an independent institution. The norms reflected in the following article, however, seem to indicate that the medical profession has pronounced characteristics of the economic institutions, especially profit motivation. Medical care has traditionally been dispensed on a "fee-for-service" basis. The best medical care is currently produced and

Reprinted from Roger Rapoport, "A Candle for St. Greed's," *Harper's Magazine* (December 1972), 70–75. Copyright © 1972 by Roger Rapoport. Reprinted by permission of The Sterling Lord Agency, Inc.

distributed as a luxury to be consumed according to an individual's ability to pay for it. The high costs of medical care, the reasons for it, and related attitudes might be viewed as what the sociologist terms the *latent functions* of a medical profession resulting from the "fee-for-service" concept.

As many times as he has passed the nursery, Charles Heath has never wearied of looking in on the latest output of the Palm Harbor Stork Club. Eventually the children will grow up to become paying customers, and as the administrator of the Palm Harbor Hospital in Garden Grove, California (two miles south of Disneyland), Charles Heath has an abiding interest in profit. He is a mild-mannered and unobtrusive man who happens to like babies even though the Palm Harbor obstetrics department never breaks out of the red. During the first ten months of fiscal 1972 the maternity ward lost his hospital $102,000.

"Every face you see in there costs our hospital $75, but we really don't mind it," Heath says: "We like to look on our obstetrics operation as a loss leader; it's really a way of introducing families to Palm Harbor. During pregnancy mothers learn about the hospital through our Stork Club teas. After the baby is born they tend to think of Palm Harbor as their medical home away from home. You just know the mothers will bring these kids back to us when it's time for the old tonsils to come out. Then we'll make it all back and probably come out ahead."

Heath walks downstairs to his surgical suite where he greets a rumpled woman lying nervously on a metal cart. She is waiting her turn to be anesthetized upon a table. Heath nods to the nurses, waves to the doctors, and checks the surgical schedule for this department that netted $225,000 during the first ten months: "You know it's too bad we couldn't just do tonsillectomies, D and Cs, appendectomies, and hernias; we could really make out like bandits."

Heath goes through his other big moneymaking departments like central supply ($331,000), the lab ($62,000), X ray ($49,000) and EKG ($36,-000). These revenues easily offset money losers like obstetrics and give the hospital a ten-month net of $364,000 on a gross business of $5,905,000.

Profit is not a dirty word at Palm Harbor or any of the 350 other proprietary hospitals (i.e., hospitals run for profit) bought and built by thirty corporate chains during the past five years. With roughly 35,000 beds in thirty states (representing 5 per cent of the nation's nonfederal hospitals), these new institutions have become a big business in California, Florida, and Texas.

The coterie of insurance men, lawyers, accountants, hotel managers, dairymen, fried-chicken salesmen, and wine merchants who have acquired the proprietary hospitals will net about $90 million in 1973 on a $1.5 billion gross. A 15 per cent annual growth in earnings has brought hotel names like Ramada Inn, Hyatt House, and Sheraton into the management of hospital and related convalescent facilities. The chairman and president of Holiday Inns have jointly started Medicenters of America, which will sell you your very own hospital franchise equipped with everything from "sign to pills." No previous medical management experience is required.

The advent of chain hospitals is the logical culmination of America's fran-. chising boom. Soon you will be able to visit anywhere in the country and breakfast at International House of Pancakes, lunch at Kentucky Fried Chicen, snack at Orange Julius, dine at McDonald's, and top it all off with a little Dairy Queen, Stuckey's pecan pie, and Shakey's pizza. Should you subsequently fall ill, you may climb into your Hertz car and drive to the nearest emergency room of Hospital Corporation of America, Beverly Enterprises, American Medicorp, American Medical International, Hyatt Medical Enterprises, Extendicare, General Health Services, National Medical, or Ramada Medical. These giants of the proprietary-hospital industry already operate in over 150 cities, primarily smaller cities in newly populous states.

Despite this heady success, industry leaders feel they've only just begun. In Nashville multimillionaire Jack C. Massey has resigned from the chairmanship of Kentucky Fried Chicken to become chairman of Hospital Corporation of America (HCA), where business is finger lickin' good. Since 1968 HCA has opened forty hospitals with 5,250 beds in twelve states. Another 2,000 beds are under construction. Mr. Massey believes "the growth potential in hospitals is unlimited; it's even better than Kentucky Fried Chicken."

Capitalistic thinking of this sort explains why one proprietary hospital in Southern California has come to be known as "St. Greed's." Although the operators of such hospitals readily admit that the hope of gain attracted them to the business, they also think of themselves as public servants. They point out that with their capital resources they can build desperately needed modern medical facilities in small or remote communities. Their economies of scale can reduce overhead costs, and, of course, corporate management can relieve doctors from administrative concerns, thus leaving them free to concentrate their energies on the practice of medicine.

All these companies are sensitive to accusations of profiteering from the ills of others. Many respond by presenting fiscal information in euphemistic ways. Typically, the 1971 annual report of Community Psychiatric Centers, which operates ten mental hospitals on the West Coast, began as follows:

TO OUR SHAREHOLDERS
Questions Freud never asked but, nevertheless, questions and answers we assume will be of interest to you as a CPC shareholder.

Actually it was doctors, not management experts, who discovered hospital capitalism. Over the past forty years local physicians have made many attempts to build and run their own hospitals on a free-enterprise basis. In some instances the physicians were not good enough to be admitted to the staffs of existing hospitals. Surgeons who liked to cut right and left needed a place to practice. Some doctors resented their work being overseen by community hospital medical staffs. Others perceived big profit potential in the simple expedient of excluding charity cases and not providing money-losing facilities for obstetrics and emergencies. A few built themselves hospitals because their communities didn't have one.

These doctor-owned hospitals often became medical fiefdoms, with patients being emptied out on Friday so the physicians could spend their weekend fishing. By 1950 more than 1,200 profit-oriented facilities were in business. Although some were perfectly reputable, they became generally known as the mom and pop hospitals of America. Stories of doctors propping up their own medical facilities with needless surgery and unnecessary hospitalizations hurt their reputation. Good physicians soon kept their patients away, and by the end of the 1950s more than 360 of these hospitals had closed, primarily for financial reasons.

About this time a number of hospital contractors, suppliers, accountants, and lawyers began to notice an opportunity. One of the first was Uranus Appel, a former Pittsburgh hotel and restaurant man who started operating hospital laboratories in Southern California after World War II. One of his lab contracts was at Westlake Hospital in Los Angeles. The hospital was about to go bankrupt in 1959 when Appel bought it: "I was making $1,800 a month on the lab and couldn't afford to lose the contract." The following year he bought another hospital under similar circumstances; thus appeared the first corporate hospital chain, know today as American Medical International (AMI).

Growth was slow in the early years because AMI was primarily limited to taking over hospitals in bad financial shape and struggling to turn them around. But in the late 1960s a major stock issue helped generate enough capital for AMI to begin acquiring healthier hospitals. Among the acquisitions were several nonprofit hospitals run by local governments and religious organizations. Rather than fight inflation, spiraling wage demands, and soaring equipment costs, these public hospitals elected to let AMI assume the management headaches. The firm also began building hospitals from scratch, particularly in small towns and booming suburban areas of the South and West. At present the firm operates forty hospitals, among them Palm Harbor, in ten states and in England. AMI shares are traded on the New York Stock Exchange, where, having split twice, the issue sells for $45 a share; 100 shares bought for $225 during the firm's first offering twelve years ago would now be worth $15,600.

Today Uranus Appel works out of an aging central Los Angeles headquarters building, soon to be traded in for plush new offices in Beverly Hills. At fifty-five Appel is a buoyant, sunburned man who speaks with the verve of Hubert Humphrey on campaign. Although given to conservative suits and drab ties, he runs an informal office; during long conferences his subordinates feed on crunchy granola. Appel himself works from behind a desk cluttered with computer printouts. He is happy to share his trade secrets:

"When I got into this field I could see many similarities between running a hotel and running a hospital. In hotels the profit center is in bars. In hospitals it's in ancillary medical services.

"The crucial difference is that most hospitals lose money on room and board. To offset this they must maximize profitable units like the lab, pharmacy, operating room, and medical supplies. They can also save by merging nursing stations, using more part-time personnel, and working everyone a little harder. Computerized cost control and centralized purchasing help too.

"But the key profit factor is turnover. Unlike a hotel you are trying to cut down the average length of stay. In a typical hospital the patient stays about 8.2 days. At the average proprietary unit it's about 6.8 days, and we have it down to 5.6. We do this because most of the patient profit is generated during his first three days in the hospital. That's when all the lucrative sides of your operation like lab, X ray, and the operating room are busy. Why, in the first few days it's not uncommon for the patient to run up a $1,000 bill. After that the patient is merely recuperating and we are lucky to break even on his room-and-board bill.

"Of course, to keep the hospital viable you usually have to offer certain unprofitable services like emergency, maternity, and hemodialysis [in which an expensive machine clears waste from the blood of patients suffering from kidney disease]. What else can you do? If you don't offer hemodialysis, your kidney patients will die. That's why we subsidize them."

Appel turns to one of his thick computer printouts and flips through the numbers: "Here, let's see what we lost on the hemodialysis unit at our Glendora hospital." He runs down a list of figures and frowns: "Well, I guess I didn't pick such a good example; our kidney unit there made $58,000 for the first ten months of fiscal 1972. Let me look at Palm Harbor. No, their unit made $74,000 for the same period. That can't be right. Let me check another place here for a second. Maybe they've accounted wrong." Appel turns to a different page, squints for a minute, and then scratches his head: "Well, I'll be damned. You know, this is the first time I realized we were making money off hemodialysis."

Profit and Loss

The proprietary hospitals have come up with many other ways of turning red ink to black. They often try to close money-losing services and foist them off on nearby nonprofit hospitals. For example, when Extendicare took over St. Joseph's Infirmary in Louisville, it promised to expand the hospital's nursing school. After the acquisition was completed, the unprofitable nursing school was closed, much to the community's dismay. (Extendicare has tried to make amends by paying for scholarships and two professorships at a nearby nursing school.) When Hospital Corporation of America took over a Selma, Alabama, hospital, it shut down the obstetrics department and persuaded the town's other (nonprofit) hospital to accept all the maternity patients. At the same time HCA built Selma's first coronary-care facility, and the other hospital sent over its heart patients. This way the corporation replaced an unprofitable obstetrics department with a profitable coronary-care unit.

These cost-cutting techniques put the proprietaries far behind the nonprofits in terms of available facilities and teaching programs. Although all profit and nonprofit hospitals are regulated by state health departments, a 1971 American Hospital Association study places the proprietary hospitals below the national average for thirty-five out of thirty-eight major hospital services. Just six proprietaries have residency programs, five have nursing schools, and only two have internship and medical school affiliations. Another study of 200 Southern California community hospitals shows the average nonprofit charging $112.96 per day and offering 13.1 services while the proprietaries average $128.05 per day and provide 8.9 services.

When they do offer unprofitable services, proprietary hospitals keep their losses at a minimum. Consider how Palm Harbor's Stork Club reduces the traditional maternity deadbeat problem. "We operate the Stock Club pretty much like a Christmas savings club," says administrator Charles Heath. "Each pregnant mother makes monthly payments that are recorded in a pink ledger book. They are guaranteed a hospital charge of $350, a $75 discount off the normal rate. If they run into complications like a Cesarean, then their $350 is applied to the $700 bill. Frankly, I'd rather have 100 prepaid births at $350 than fifty regular ones at $425. On the $425 births we always get stuck with bad debts and have to hire expensive collection agencies. You know, I just couldn't conceive of running a hospital without a Stork Club."

Another key to profits is giving doctors a financial stake in the hospital. Many chains do this by simply buying doctor-owned hospitals with stock. Others have encouraged physicians to buy shares in their corporations. Either way the doctors end up with a clear financial interest in the hospital. The medical men do their best to keep up on the financial health of their parent firms. Physicians at Beverly Enterprises' Encino, California, hospital keep a television in a lounge adjacent to their surgical suite tuned to a UHF business news channel. Administrator Max Weinberg explains: "They like to see how their stock is doing. I usually come down every morning to find out myself."

Many nonprofit hospital administrators believe it unethical for a doctor to hold stock in his own medical facility. They worry that physicians might be tempted to recruit patients to inflate hospital occupancy rates. Some also fear that physicians might be tempted to schedule expensive and unnecessary lab tests for such patients. John R. Gadd, executive director of Lee Memorial Hospital in Fort Meyers, Florida, says the chains find it "nice to have as hospital stockholders the doctors who can keep the beds full of choice patients . . . It is also very convenient and profitable for the stockholder doctor to have staff privileges . . . in a nearby nonprofit hospital where he can dump the financially undesirable patients."

Most proprietary hospital administrators find nothing wrong with their doctors owning stock in the company. In fact some encourage their patients to buy into the firm. They feel this is an excellent way to build up community loyalty to the hospital. AMI's Charles Heath talked about this from the driver's seat of his blue Cadillac on the way to lunch one day in Garden Grove: "Some of our regular patients are always telling me they've been in here so much they've paid for an entire wing. I always tell 'em, 'Hell, you can buy yourself a share of this place for $44.' A lot of them take me up on it. In fact patients are always stopping me during my rounds to ask what AMI stock is trading at."

Heath points ahead at the roadway: "You know we're kind of lucky to be in this sort of a community. The people are behind us. We've got Disneyland generating a lot of emergency business for us, as well as the Garden Grove, Santa Ana, and Newport freeways. Man, there are a lot of wrecks out here. We lose on the emergency, but it's a good loss leader for us, just like obstetrics."

Most stockholders want to know how their companies plan to restrain soaring medical costs. Several of the latest cost-cutting techniques have been initiated by the medical subsidiaries of hotel firms. Chains like Hyatt Medical and Ramada Medical save by purchasing everything from sheets to blueberry pies from the parent firm. Hyatt's hotel-construction division is building two new hospitals for the medical unit. Hyatt medical chairman Maurice Lewitt talked about this recently at his Encino, California, headquarters: "There are a lot of similarities between putting up hotels and hospitals. The big difference is where they have a bar we have a surgical suite. Operating-wise they also have a lot in common. Both are basically service oriented. Face it, you go into a hospital and the surgery could be terrible, but you'll probably never know. But what you do know and care about are the same things that matter to the hotel guest: good food, clean floors, and a big color TV."

Despite the close relationship between Hyatt Medical and Hyatt House hotels, there are certain limitations. Lewitt says, "If someone gets sick in one of our Hyatt hotels, we would never send him to a Hyatt hospital. It wouldn't look very good if he didn't turn out. Know what I mean?"

New Markets

Not all the new proprietary hospitals provide acute care. Medicenters of America has built forty-four intermediate-care hospitals that tend recuperating patients in twenty-four states. Each unit looks like a Holiday Inn without the swimming pool and call itself "a nice place to get well." Illustrating this theme is the Memphis Medicenter where arriving patients get a choice of four room decors: green, blue-green, gold or beige. Every room comes equipped with scenic murals, television, Muzak, and a direct intercom link to the nurse. There is live entertainment in the dining hall and a stereo-equipped station wagon that can run patients back to the hospital in case of a relapse.

Medicenter franchises remain open in many parts of the country. The licensee must demonstrate sufficient capital reserves and then pay an initial fee of $100 per bed or $5,000, whichever is greater. Subsequent royalties are 3 per cent on gross room, board, and nursing revenue, plus 1 per cent of all other revenue. In return the company provides the licensee such benefits as an operating manual and a discount on malpractice insurance.

The only trouble with Medicenters is their loss of nearly $1 million during fiscal 1972. The federal government has delayed reimbursement of $5.4 million worth of Medicare patient charges because of a disagreement over federal regulations. Local doctors have decided to keep most of their Medicare patients away from Medicenters until the dispute is resolved. As a result, the company's occupancy rate has dropped to 32 per cent. Currently the firm is trying to boost revenues by converting space in several Medicenters to more lucrative eye, ear, nose, and throat hospitals. Profitable psychiatric care is also being expanded.

Several psychiatric chains distinguish themselves by pushing a particular line of therapy. One is the Raleigh Hills Hospitals, which operates three West Coast units and will add five more across the country during the next two years. This growing enterprise treats alcoholics exclusively at a cost of $1,400 to $1,800 for a ten- to twelve-day stay. Raleigh Hills is run by Peter Tighe, a reformed alcoholic who used to develop cultured cottage cheese, sour cream, and buttermilk for Carnation.

Some psychiatrists wince at Tighe's hospitals because they treat every patient the same way. But the Raleigh Hills president predicts his Pavlovian cure will work for nearly 75 per cent of his annual patient load of 1,100. Exactly how does Tighe's staff achieve these astonishing results? The technique is called aversion therapy, which should be familiar to anyone who has seen the motion picture *Clockwork Orange*. The patient is taken into a treatment room and injected with Emitine, which shuts off the pyloric valve to the stomach for twenty minutes. Then the nurse gives him a choice of premium bourbon, Scotch, gin, vodka, beer, or wine. The patient is also handed a pan, because he will throw up as soon as he takes a drink. This treatment is repeated four more times during the visit.

Tighe indicates: "There's a good profit in this if you can keep the patient census up. Of course we'll never make as much as some hospitals. Our overhead is terrific. We have a big staff. And every one of the treatment rooms is stocked with several hundred dollars worth of booze."

While some free-enterprise hospitals work to wipe out alcoholism, some liquor companies are out building hospitals. In Los Angeles the Batik Wine and Spirits Company merged with a chain of five hospitals when its wine sales began to flag. Batik's first medical facility was purchased in 1970, just one month after the firm's chairman, California State Senator Mervyn Dymally, pushed through legislation authorizing nonmedical firms to own hospitals.

The company subsequently acquired a string of hospitals, changed its name to Comprehensive Health Systems, Inc. and phased out the wine business. Although Senator Dymally resigned as board chairman before Batik decided to merge with the hospital chain, he did not dispose of his 6,500 shares in the firm until after the *Los Angeles Times* exposed the Batik story in August 1972. The firm remains a prime candidate for a $14.4 million California contract to provide health-care services for 60,000 MediCal recipients in low-income sections of Los Angeles. The firm's records were recently subpoenaed by Senator Edward Kennedy's health subcommittee as part of an investigation into the medical-care business.

Despite this kind of public-relations setback, the proprietary-hospital industry remains confident of meteoric growth. General Health Services vice-president Leon Hamlin explained why over breakfast at a Copper Penny restaurant not long ago: "Financial analysts are always asking if the advent of more miracle drugs and better preventive care are going to hurt our earnings. I tell them not to worry. People will always need us. There are just too many uncontrollable things like car crashes and bathtub falls."

At Palm Harbor Hospital, Charles Heath couldn't agree more: "Sure you don't see smallpox anymore, but we've got new things going for us today. Thanks to all the smog our inhalation-therapy business is picking up beautifully. Inhalation-therapy; now there's a moneymaker."

Discussion Questions

1. In your view, is "an abiding interest in profit" compatible with the traditional concept of medical service embodied in the Hippocratic Oath? Or, on the other hand, should these "proprietary hospitals" be looked upon as purely part of the American economic institutions? Discuss.
2. Does this article leave you optimistic or pessimistic about the compatibility of the profit motive and medical service motivations? Why?
3. Discuss the significance of the following statement from the perspective of the American economic institutions and public health: "There are a lot of similarities between putting up hotels and hospitals." Do you agree with this statement?

10 / The Family

Drawing by W. Miller; © 1973 The New Yorker Magazine, Inc.

"What's up? That's Harv Fliedner's ex-wife Doris's car, and that's Harv, but those aren't Harv's kids, and they aren't Jenny Beckworth's, and that isn't Jenny, but that's Jenny's dog, Mitra."

In all known societies, the family serves as the basic social institution. The family can be defined as a kinship grouping which provides for the rearing of children and certain other needs such as the regulation of sexual behavior, parental obligation, transmission of material goods, social status, and companionship. While the family provides for many human needs, a most important reason for its existence is the regulation of sex. Sex is a significant factor precisely because it involves the conception and birth of children. Not only have pregnant women needed help during and after pregnancy, but because an infant matures slowly, it requires both protection and socialization. Despite the fact that modern societies have other social institutions that can help with the protection and socialization functions, only the family can ensure that the individual is given the chance to learn the knowledge and skills necessary for survival.

A chief element of family life is marriage. The process of getting married offers some fascinating alternatives which range from individual determination to wife capture. Historically the most popular alternative seems to have been marriages arranged by either a matchmaker or the parents themselves. In America, getting married involves an elaborate series of rituals which begins with dating, progresses to courtship, and culminates in marriage.

The family also takes many forms of organization in different societies. In America the most common form is the *conjugal,* or *nuclear,* family which is characterized by a married couple, their children, and occasionally a relative. Another form of family organization is the *consanguine,* or *extended,* family which also includes grandparents and perhaps other relatives.

The development of the nuclear family is usually associated with the developments of urbanism and a sophisticated economy that demands a labor force that is geographically and occupationally mobile. While the nuclear family does have the benefit of being consistent with the American ethos of individuality and self-reliance by allowing individuals to choose place of residence and kind of jobs, it also suffers from relative instability. Many sociologists argue that some or all of the following conditions have caused the instability. (1) Women entering the labor force are less dependent economically on the husbands, thereby undermining traditional male dominance. (2) Effective contraceptive devices enable women to devote fewer years to child rearing or escape it altogether. (3) The family has lost many of its functions to other social institutions. The educational system, for example, now assumes a significant portion of the socializing task. As a result, parental control of children is becoming increasingly difficult. (4) The freedom and isolation of the members of a nuclear family from group pressure and constraints usually found in the extended family make social control more difficult and increase the possibility and incidence of deviance. (5) The isolation of the nuclear family leaves individual members lonely and insecure. This is especially obvious in the estrangement of the elderly from the mainstream of social life.

Whatever the causes or combination of causes may be, it is obvious that the structure of the American family has experienced some far-reaching changes. The size of the family has decreased, the status of divorce has changed, along with the division of labor and authority. However, many of the basic functions of the family remain. While there seems to be greater incidence of premarital sexual relations, the sex-regulating function remains relatively unchanged. The reproduction and status functions also remain intact. The socializing function claims increased attention. Dr. Benjamin Spock's guidelines for child rearing, for example, were widely read as mothers sought help in socializing their children. The companionship function, however, has emerged as the most valued aspect of marriage in the United States. While married couples are *less* dependent on each other economically, they are *more* dependent on each other for companionship and affection. The protection function has also changed. The aged and the sick are often shuttled off to nursing homes and "retirement centers." The greatest change, however, is the economic function. Whereas the traditional family was a producing unit it has become a consuming unit.

What these changes spell for the future is difficult to say. Some sociologists predict that the family is an archaic structure that cannot survive the forces of modernity. Others predict an evolution, the beginnings of which can be seen in alternate life-styles found in communes and among the unmarried marrieds, contractual marriages, and group marriages. However, despite these experiments and the shortcomings of the nuclear family, there is little evidence to suggest that it will be abandoned in the near future.

JOHN FINLEY SCOTT

Sororities and the Husband Game

Choosing a mate for marriage in our society is a serious business. Before couples marry in our society they are supposed to fall in love. Although falling in love implies freedom of choice in a vast marriage market, there are numerous informal but very effective controls to insure that children

Reprinted from John Finley Scott, "Sororities and the Husband Game," *Society,* Vol. 2, No. 6 (Sept.–Oct. 1965). Copyright © 1965 by Transaction Inc. Reprinted with permission.

marry the "right" person. For example, we find that most Americans are homogamous (like marries like) on the dimensions of race, religion, and social class. That is, blacks marry blacks, whites marry whites, Protestants marry Protestants, rich marry rich, and so on. The social structures that facilitate such homogamous patterns are usually not consciously considered by young couples as they date and fall in love. Such lack of awareness, however, does not deny the existence of these social structures. In the following article, John Finley Scott describes how the structure and function of the university sorority control and facilitate marriage within the class structure of our society.

Marriages, like births, deaths, or initiations at puberty, are rearrangements of structure that are constantly recurring in any society; they are moments of the continuing social process regulated by custom; there are institutionalized ways of dealing with such events.
—*A. R. Radcliffe-Brown*, African Systems of Kinship and Marriage.

In many simple societies, the "institutionalized ways" of controlling marriage run to diverse schemes and devices. Often they include special living quarters designed to make it easy for marriageable girls to attract a husband: the Bontok people of the Philippines keep their girls in a special house, called the *olag,* where lovers call, sex play is free, and marriage is supposed to result. The Ekoi of Nigeria, who like their women fat, send them away to be specially fattened for marriage. Other peoples, such as the Yao of central Africa and the aborigines of the Canary Islands, send their daughters away to "convents" where old women teach them the special skills and mysteries that a young wife needs to know.

Accounts of such practices have long been a standard topic of anthropology lectures in universities, for their exotic appeal keeps the students, large numbers of whom are sorority girls, interested and alert. The control of marriage in simple societies strikes these girls as quite different from the freedom that they believe prevails in America. This is ironic, for the American college sorority is a pretty good counterpart in complex societies of the fatting houses and convents of the primitives.

Whatever system they use, parents in all societies have more in mind than just getting their daughters married; they want them married to the *right* man. The criteria for defining the right man vary tremendously, but virtually all parents view some potential mates with approval, some with disapproval, and some with downright horror. Many ethnic groups, including many in America, are *endogamous,* that is, they desire marriage of their young only to those within the group. In *shtetl* society, the Jewish villages of eastern Europe, marriages were arranged by a *shatchen,* a matchmaker, who paired off the girls and boys with due regard to the status, family connections, wealth, and personal attractions of the participants. But this society was strictly endogamous—only marriage within the group was allowed. Another rule of endogamy relates to social rank or class, for most parents are anxious that their children marry at least at the same level as themselves. Often they hope the children, and especially the daughters, will marry at a higher level. Parents of the *shtetl,* for example, valued *hypergamy*—the marriage of daughters to a man of higher status—and a father who could afford it would offer substantial sums to acquire a scholarly husband (the most highly prized kind) for his daughter.

The marriage problem, from the point of view of parents and of various ethnic groups and social classes, is always one of making sure that girls are available for marriage with the right man while at the same time guarding against marriage with the wrong man.

The University Convent

The American middle class has a particular place where it sends its daughters so they will be easily accessible to the boys—the college campus. Even for the families who worry about the bad habits a nice girl can pick up at college, it has become so much a symbol of middle-class status that the risk must be taken, the girl must be sent. American middle-class society has created an institution on the campus that, like the fatting house, makes the girls more attractive; like the Canary Island convent, teaches skills that middle-class wives need to know; like the *shtetl,* provides matchmakers; and without going so far as to buy husbands of high rank, manages to dissuade the girl from making alliances with lower-class boys. That institution is the college sorority.

A sorority is a private association which provides separate dormitory facilities with a distinctive Greek letter name for selected female college students. Membership is by invitation only, and requires recommendation by former members. Sororities are not simply the feminine counterpart of the college fraternity. They differ from fraternities because marriage is a more important determinant of social position for women than for men in American society, and because standards of conduct associated with marriage correspondingly bear stronger sanctions for women than for men. Sororities have much more "alumnae" involvement than fraternities, and fraternities adapt to local conditions and different living arrangements better than sororities. The college-age sorority "actives" decide only the minor details involved in recruitment, membership, and activities; parent-age alumnae control the important choices. The prototypical sorority is not the servant of youthful interests; on the contrary, it is an organized agency for controlling those interests. Through the sorority, the elders of family, class, ethnic, and religious communities can continue to exert remote control over the marital arrangements of their young girls.

The need for remote control arises from the nature of the educational system in an industrial society. In simple societies, where children are taught the culture at home, the family controls the socialization of children almost completely. In more complex societies, education becomes the province of special agents and competes with the family. The conflict between the family and outside agencies increases as children move through the educational system and is sharpest when the children reach college age. College curricula are even more challenging to family value systems than high school courses, and children frequently go away to college, out of reach of direct family influence. Sometimes a family can find a college that does not challenge family values in any way: devout Catholic parents can send their daughters to Catholic colleges; parents who want to be sure that daughter meets only "Ivy League" men can send her to one of the "Seven Sisters"—the women's equivalent of the Ivy League, made up of Radcliffe, Barnard, Smith, Vassar, Wellesley, Mt. Holyoke and Bryn Mawr—if she can get in.

The solution of controlled admissions is applicable only to a small proportion of college-age girls, however. There are nowhere near the number of separate, sectarian colleges in the country that would be needed to segregate all the college-age girls safely, each with her own kind. Private colleges catering mostly to a specific class can still preserve a girl from meeting her social or economic inferiors, but the fees at such places are steep. It costs more to maintain a girl in the Vassar dormitories than to pay her sorority bills at a land-grant school. And even if her family is willing to pay the fees, the academic pace at the elite schools is much too fast for most girls. Most college girls attend large, tax-supported universities where the tuition is relatively low and where admissions policies let in students from many strata and diverse ethnic backgrounds. It is on the campuses of the free, open, and competitive state universities of the country that the sorority system flourishes.

When a family lets its daughter loose on a large campus with a heterogenous population, there are opportunities to be met and dangers to guard against. The great opportunity is to meet a good man to marry, at the age when the girls are most attractive and the men most amenable. For the girls, the pressure of time is urgent; though they are often told otherwise, their attractions are in fact primarily physical, and they fade with time. One need only compare the relative handicaps in the marital sweepstakes of a thirty-eight-year-old single male lawyer and a single, female teacher of the same age to realize the urgency of the quest.

The great danger of the public campus is that young girls, however properly reared, are likely to fall in love, and—in our middle-class society at least—love leads to marriage. Love is a potentially random factor, with no regard for class boundaries. There seems to be no good way of preventing young girls from falling in love. The only practical way to control love is to control the type of men the girl is likely to encounter; she cannot fall dangerously in love with a man she has never met. Since kinship groups are unable to keep "undesirable" boys off the public campus entirely, they have to settle for control of counter-institutions within the university. An effective counter-institution will protect a girl from the corroding influences of the university environment.

There are roughly three basic functions which a sorority can perform in the interest of kinship groups:

It can ward off the wrong kind of men.

It can facilitate moving-up for middle-status girls.

It can solve the "Brahmin problem"—the difficulty of proper marriage that afflicts high-status girls.

Kinship groups define the "wrong kind of man" in a variety of ways. Those who use an ethnic definition support sororities that draw an ethnic membership line; the best examples are the Jewish sororities, because among all the ethnic groups with endogamous standards (in America at any rate), only the Jews so far have sent large numbers of daughters away to college. But endogamy along class lines is even more pervasive. It is the most basic mission of the sorority to prevent a girl from marrying out of her group (exogamy) or beneath her class (hypogamy). As one of the founders of a national sorority artlessly put it in an essay titled "The Mission of the Sorority":

> There is a danger, and a very grave danger, that four years' residence in a dormitory will tend to destroy right ideals of home life and substitute in their stead a belief in the freedom that comes from community living . . . culture, broad, liberalizing, humanizing culture, we cannot get too much of, unless while acquiring it we are weaned from home and friends, from ties of blood and kindred.

A sorority discourages this dangerous weaning process by introducing the sisters only to selected boys; each sorority, for example, has dating relations with one or more fraternities, matched rather nicely to the sorority on the basis of ethnicity and/or class. (A particular sorority, for example, will have dating arrangements not with all the fraternities on campus, but only with those whose brothers are a class-match for their sisters.) The sorority's frantically busy schedule of parties, teas, meetings, skits, and exchanges keep the sisters so occupied that they have neither time nor opportunity to meet men outside the channels the sorority provides.

Marrying Up

The second sorority function, that of facilitating hypergamy, is probably even more of an attraction to parents than the simpler preservation of endogamy. American society is not so much oriented to the preservation of the *status quo* as to the pursuit of upward mobility.

In industrial societies, children are taught that if they study hard they can get the kind of job that entitles them to a place in the higher ranks. This incentive actually is appropriate only for boys, but the emphasis on using the most efficient available means to enter the higher levels will not be lost on the girls. And the most efficient means for a girl—marriage—is particularly attractive because it requires so much less effort than the mobility through hard work that is open to boys. To the extent that we do socialize the sexes in different ways, we are more likely to train daughters in the ways of attracting men than to motivate them to do hard, competitive work. The difference in motivation holds even if the girls have the intelligence and talent required for the status climbing on their own. For lower-class girls on the make, membership in a sorority can greatly improve the chances of meeting (and subsequently marrying) higher-status boys.

Now we come to the third function of the sorority—solving the Brahmin problem. The fact that hypergamy is encouraged in our society creates difficulties for girls whose parents are already in the upper strata. In a hypergamous system, high status *men* have a strong advantage; they can offer their status to a prospective bride as part of the marriage bargain, and the advantages of high status are often sufficient to offset many personal drawbacks. But a *woman's* high status has very little exchange value because she does not confer it on her husband.

This difficulty of high status women in a hypergamous society we may call the Brahmin problem. Girls of Brahmin caste in India and Southern white women of good family have the problem in common. In order to avoid the horrors of hypogamy, high status women must compete for high status men against women from all classes. Furthermore, high status women are handicapped in their battle by a certain type of vanity engendered by their class. They expect their wooers to court them in the style to which their fathers have accustomed them; this usually involves more formal dating, gift-giving, escorting, taxiing, etc., than many college swains can afford. If upperstratum men are allowed to find out that the favors of lower class women are available for a much smaller investment of time, money, and emotion, they may well refuse to court upper-status girls.

In theory, there are all kinds of ways for upper-stratum families to deal with surplus daughters. They can strangle them at birth (female infanticide); they can marry several to each available male (polygyny); they can offer money to any suitable male willing to take one off their hands (dowries, groom-service fees). All these solutions have in fact been used in one society or another, but for various reasons none is acceptable in our society. Spinsterhood still works, but marriage is so popular and so well rewarded that everybody hopes to avoid staying single.

The industrial solution to the Brahmin problem is to corner the market, or more specifically to shunt the eligible bachelors into a special marriage market where the upper stratum women are in complete control of the bride-supply. The best place to set up this protected marriage-market is where many suitable men can be found at the age when they are most willing to marry—in short, the college campus. The kind of male collegians who can be shunted more readily into the specialized marriage-market that sororities run, are those who are somewhat uncertain of their own status and who aspire to move into higher strata. These boys are anxious to bolster a shaky self-image by dating obviously high-class sorority girls. The fraternities are full of them.

How does a sorority go about fulfilling its three functions? The first item of business is making sure that the girls join. This is not as simple as it seems, because the values that sororities maintain are more important to the older generation than to the college-age girls. Although the sorority image is one of membership denied to the "wrong kind" of girls, it is also true that sororities have quite a problem recruiting the "right kind." Some are pressured into pledging by their parents. Many are recruited straight out of high school, before they know much about what really goes on at college. High school recruiters present sorority life to potential rushees as one of unending gaiety; life outside the sorority is painted as bleak and dateless.

A membership composed of the "right kind" of girls is produced by the requirement that each pledge must have the recommendation of, in most cases, two or more alumnae of the sorority. Membership is often passed on from mother to daughter—this is the "legacy," whom sorority actives have to invite whether they like her or not. The sort of headstrong, innovative, or "sassy" girl who is likely to organize a campaign inside the sorority against prevailing standards is unlikely to receive alumnae recommendations. This is why sorority girls are so complacent about alumnae dominance, and why professors find them so bland and uninteresting as students. Alumnae dominance extends beyond recruitment, into the daily life of the house. Rules, regulations, and policy explanations come to the house from the national association. National headquarters is given to explaining unpopular policy by an available stratagem; a favorite device (not limited to the sorority) is to interpret all nonconformity as sexual, so that the girl who rebels against wearing girdle, high heels, and stockings to dinner two or three times a week stands implicitly accused of promiscuity. This sort of argument, based on the shrewdness of many generations, shames into conformity many a girl who otherwise might rebel against the code imposed by her elders. The actives in positions of control (house manager, pledge trainer, or captain) are themselves closely supervised by alumnae. Once the right girls are initiated, the organization has mechanisms that make it very difficult for a girl to withdraw. Withdrawal can mean difficulty in finding alternative living quarters, loss of prepaid room and board fees, and stigmatization.

Sororities keep their members, and particularly their flighty pledges, in line primarily by filling up all their time with house activities. Pledges are required to study at the house, and they build the big papier-mâché floats (in collaboration with selected fraternity boys) that are a traditional display of "Greek Row" for the homecoming game. Time is encompassed completely; activities are planned long in advance, and there is almost no energy or time available for meeting inappropriate men.

The girls are taught—if they do not already know—the behavior appropriate to the upper strata. They learn how to dress with expensive restraint, how to make appropriate conversation, how to drink like a lady. There is some variety here among sororities of different rank; members of sororities at the bottom of the social ladder prove their gentility by rigid conformity in dress and manner to the stereotype of the sorority girl, while members of top houses feel socially secure even when casually dressed. If you are born rich you can afford to wear Levi's and sweatshirts.

Preliminary Events

The sorority facilitates dating mainly by exchanging parties, picnics, and other frolics with the fraternities in its set. But to augment this the "fixer-uppers" (the American counterpart of the *shatchen*) arrange dates with selected boys; their efforts raise the sorority dating rate above the independent level by removing most of the inconvenience and anxiety from the contracting of dates.

Dating, in itself, is not sufficient to accomplish the sorority's purposes. Dating must lead to pinning, pinning to engagement, engagement to marriage. In sorority culture, all dating is viewed as a movement toward marriage. Casual, spontaneous dating is frowned upon; formal courtship is still encouraged. Sorority ritual reinforces the progression from dating to marriage. At the vital point in the process, where dating must be turned into engagement, the sorority shores up the structure by the pinning ritual, performed after dinner in the presence of all the sorority sisters (who are required to stay for the ceremony) and attended, in its classic form, by a choir of fraternity boys singing outside. The commitment is so public that it is difficult for either partner to withdraw. Since engagement is already heavily reinforced outside the sorority, pinning ceremonies are more elaborate than engagements.

The social columns of college newspapers faithfully record the successes of the sorority system as it stands today. Sorority girls get engaged faster than "independents," and they appear to be marrying more highly ranked men. But what predictions can we make about the system's future?

All social institutions change from time to time, in response to changing conditions. In the mountain villages of the Philippines, the steady attacks of school and mission on the immorality of the *olag* have almost demolished it. Sororities, too, are affected by changes in the surrounding environment. Originally they were places where the few female college students took refuge from the jeers and catcalls of men who thought that nice girls didn't belong on campus. They assumed their present, endogamy-conserving form with the flourishing of the great land-grant universities in the first half of this century.

On the Brink

The question about the future of the sorority system is whether it can adapt to the most recent changes in the forms of higher education. At present, neither fraternities nor sororities are in the pink of health. On some campuses, there are chapter houses which have been reduced to taking in nonaffiliated boarders to pay the costs of running the property. New sorority chapters are formed, for the most part, on new or low-prestige campuses (where status-anxiety is rife); at schools of high prestige fewer girls rush each year and the weaker houses are disbanding.

University administrations are no longer as hospitable to the Greeks as they once were. Most are building extensive dormitories that compete effectively with the housing offered by sororities; many have adopted regulations intended to minimize the influence of the Greeks on campus activities. The campus environment is changing rapidly: academic standards are rising, admission is increasingly competitive and both male and female students are more interested in academic achievement; the proportion of graduate students seriously training for a profession is increasing; campus culture is often so obviously pluralist that the Greek claim to monopolize social activity is unconvincing.

The sorority as it currently stands is ill-adapted to cope with the new surroundings. Sorority houses were built to provide a setting for lawn parties, dances, and dress-up occasions, and not to facilitate study; crowding and noise are severe, and most forms of privacy do not exist. The sorority songs that have to be gone through at rushing and chapter meetings today all seem to have been written in 1915 and are mortifying to sing today. The arcane rituals, so fascinating to high school girls, grow tedious and sophomoric to college seniors.

But the worst blow of all to the sorority system comes from the effect of increased academic pressure on the dating habits of college men. A student competing for grades in a professional school, or even in a difficult under-graduate major, simply has not the time (as he might have had in, say, 1925) to get involved in the sorority forms of courtship. Since these days almost all the "right kind" of men *are* involved in demanding training, the traditions of the sorority are becoming actually inimical to hypergamous marriage. Increasingly, then, sororities do not solve the Brahmin problem but make it worse.

One can imagine a sorority designed to facilitate marriage to men who have no time for elaborate courtship. In such a sorority, the girls—to start with small matters—would improve their telephone arrangements, for the fraternity boy in quest of a date today must call several times to get through the busy signals, interminable paging, and lost messages to the girl he wants. They might arrange a private line with prompt answering and faithfully recorded messages, with an unlisted number given only to busy male students with a promising future. They would even accept dates for the same night as the invitation, rather than, as at present, necessarily five to ten days in advance, for the only thing a first-year law student can schedule that far ahead nowadays is his studies. Emphasis on fraternity boys would have to go, for living in a fraternity and pursuing a promising (and therefore competitive) major field of study are rapidly becoming mutually exclusive. The big formal dances would go (the fraternity boys dislike them now); the football floats would go; the pushcart races would go. These girls would reach the hearts of their men not through helping them wash their sports cars but through typing their term papers.

But it is inconceivable that the proud traditions of the sororities that compose the National Panhellenic Council could ever be bent to fit the new design. Their structure is too fixed to fit the changing college and their function is rapidly being lost. The sorority cannot sustain itself on students alone. When parents learn that membership does not benefit their daughters, the sorority as we know it will pass into history.

Discussion Questions

1. What are the three functions of sororities the author discusses?

2. Review how the sororities go about fulfilling these functions.

JUDITH VIORST

Just Because I'm Married, Does It Mean I'm Going Steady?

The most obvious feature about the process of getting married and staying married in the seventies is the diversity. Many couples, for example, are living as unmarried marrieds. When they do marry—and generally they do—it is often a new-styled wedding "for as long as we dig it" rather than "till death do us part."

The love Judith Viorst refers to in this article is not breathless, trembling love, but the kind of love that provides intimacy, emotional support, and a special sense of belonging. It is the type of love that fulfills the affectional and companionship needs—a set of needs that appears to be more fundamental than even sex.

Mrs. Viorst's article recognizes the subtle ongoing nature of these needs for companionship. The article also questions, in a lighthearted manner, the blessings of "new," "open," and "more mature" forms of marital relationships.

As my husband and I look forward to our 13th anniversary I am hoping that it's not an unlucky number. Wherever I turn, the world's most blissful couples are getting divorced and people are writing books called *Marriage Is Hell.*

All of a sudden I'm feeling insecure. Will my marriage make it?

There seems to be no certainty that if we've survived our first hard year of marriage, we're bound to survive the following 49. Or that once I've smoothly negotiated my husband's seven-year itch, he won't get even itchier later on.

All of a sudden I'm feeling awfully nervous. Will my marriage last?

Some of the marriage experts are saying it may be that *marriage* won't last, because, they claim, the institution is dead. Men and women, their argument goes, no longer need marriage for economic survival, for love or sex or self-fulfillment or children. Furthermore, we now live too long to live with one partner for life. "Till death us do part" should become "until it's a drag."

I'm feeling unstrung.

I'm feeling unstrung because the current wisdom seems to be that it's hard for marriage *not* to be a drag. We compromise. We settle for less. We're disappointed. We're bored. "Is this all there is?" we wonder, wanting more.

"On a scale of one to ten," I asked my husband the other day, "how would you honest and truly rate our marriage?"

"I honest and truly wouldn't answer that question," Milton replied, "if you offered me a lifetime pass to the Redskins' games or a weekend with Candy Bergen and Raquel Welch."

I'm getting depressed.

I'm getting depressed because I'm looking over our life together and I'm suddenly noticing Marriage Danger Signs. As in:

Q Do you and your husband share many common interests?

A No. My husband enjoys skiing, canoe trips, hiking and adventure. I enjoy sun bathing, movies, Scrabble and being careful.

Q Do you and your husband find each other intellectually stimulating?

A No. We find strangers at cocktail parties intellectually stimulating because with them we talk about psychiatry, literature and the future of mankind. With each other we talk about getting the car inspected. And head colds. And why shouldn't I buy that dress I saw at Saks.

Q Do you and your husband ever think of other men and women in what you'd have to call a "carnal" way?

A Isn't there something nicer we could call it?

Q Do you and your husband feel that, in this age of changing sex roles, your marriage suffers from certain unresolved tensions?

A Plenty.

Q Do you and your husband recognize and accept each other's frailties and limitations?

A Recognize, yes. Accept, no.

Q Do you and your husband fight about (a) money, (b) children, (c) relatives, (d) vacations, (e) turning off lights, (f) nothing, (g) everything?

A (g).

I think I'm going to cry.

And then I think I'm going to take some steps to save our marriage before my husband notices it's doomed. There are plenty of brave new notions around about how to make marriage work. I'm planning to investigate them all.

One of the bravest new notions, of course, is simply "Don't get married." Live in what formerly was known as sin. Do not succumb to the pressures of convention or of mothers' swearing to leap from the Brooklyn Bridge. For insecure in the knowledge that he can leave me any time (and also vice versa), I will try harder to like canoe trips and he will try harder to like Scrabble.

But not getting married poses a bit of a problem for people like me who've already said, "I do." I guess I could go out and get a divorce and see if my marriage improved, but maybe I ought to consider less drastic solutions.

Like, for instance, having a broad-minded marriage. Or as some of the broad-minded people might put it, just because you happen to be married doesn't really mean you're going steady.

In old-fashioned marriage, the broad-minded people explain, a wife is supposed to be everything to her husband, a husband is supposed to be everything to his wife. And when they discover that no human being can be everything to another, well . . . that's life. Friends, of course, can help fill needs unmet by our own spouses. But friendship in old-fashioned marriage is never co-ed. Married folks deal with the opposite sex only as couple to couple. And this, say the broad-minded, doesn't make sense.

So why can't a husband go skiing with some other woman? Why can't a wife see a movie with some other man? Why can't a man have women for friends even after he's married? Why can't married women have friendships with men?

I think I've got an answer to those questions, but maybe all I've got is a dirty mind. I've also got some statements (from Nena and George O'Neill's book *Open Marriage*) on the benefits of the broad-minded point of view.

Frank: "If Janet goes out of an evening, I want her to have a good time, to have an interesting time. She shares her experiences with me and I gain enrichment in my life. . . ."

(I can see it now. "Wake up, Milton," I'll say. "Sorry I'm so late, but you know how fascinating Arnie is. And wait until I tell you this incredible story he told me—it'll enrich your life.")

Another happy husband told the O'Neills: "It's a great feeling to walk down the street . . . and know that if I meet someone, male or female, that I want to know, I can do it without feeling guilty—we can have a drink, take advantage of the spontaneity of the moment—and I don't have to worry about how I'm going to explain it all when I get home."

Well, he's lucky he isn't married to someone like me, because, let me guarantee you, he'd *have* to feel guilty. And explain it all. Especially the part that goes "take advantage of the spontaneity of the moment."

But mine, the O'Neills would point out, is—alas!—a closed marriage, which augurs ill for my future married life. The grass, they say, is greener on the other side of the fence only when you've bothered building fences. Lead us not into temptation, I say back.

The theory of the broad-minded view is that freedom is healthy for marriage, even if freedom involves certain sexual risks. There's no point sitting there chewing our nails and wondering what *else* they're doing. We've got to have trust.

Or else we've got to go further and have a *very* broad-minded marriage. And then we won't have to wonder. Then we'll know. We'll know because we'll be swapping, or having orgies, or having *ménages à trois,* or my husband will bring his girl friends to the house, or I'll phone my husband at work and say, "Hi, dear. Mark and I have just finished making love, so could you pick up two heads of lettuce, six lemons and a carton of skim milk on your way home?"

The very broad-minded people say fidelity in marriage is narrow, exclusive and other unwholesome things. Or as John and Mimi Lobell explain in their book *John and Mimi,* "We often work, and socialize and pursue friendships independently of each other. There is no reason why sex should be considered more of a threat to marriage than any of these other contacts."

Now, I can think of a couple of reasons—like jealousy and divorce—but John and Mimi claim that that's absurd.

"We understand our marriage," says John, "in terms of an adventure, not in terms of sexual exclusiveness."

As for divorce over sex—why, that's inconceivable, for it's thanks to their free and honest infidelities that John and Mimi have discovered the "beautiful, self-sustaining bedrock in our relationship." If they ever broke up, says Mimi, it would not be because she attended a meeting where John had slept with everyone in the room. (Heavens, no! Indeed, that very situation has occurred, and what it gave her was "a warm feeling of appreciation for him.") They could, however, separate, says Mimi, if "our consciousness had changed to a point where, for example, I might want to enter a Zen monastery or John might want to live with a primitive New Guinea tribe."

Well, such are the risks of freedom.

Now, I would like to state right here that Milton and I will never split up over primitive New Guinea tribes or Zen monasteries. I would also like to state that—jealous, possessive lady that I am—a meeting room full of women my husband had slept with couldn't possibly give a lift to our marriage.

No, a very broad-minded marriage isn't going to solve our problems. But maybe writing a marriage contract would. And, of course, it would have to be a Women's Lib marriage contract, which casts aside traditional male-female roles and insists that spouses relate as full human beings.

"A Marriage Agreement," written by Alix Shulman (see *Redbook,* August, 1971), is an effort to do exactly that. What she sets forth is a point-by-point contract—devised by her husband and her—to share completely all child-care and household chores.

From cooking to shopping to cleaning to laundry to answering children's questions, these chores are divided—by hour, by day and by week. Allowances are made for deals "by mutual agreement," but the contract clearly stipulates that "changes must be formally agreed upon" and that "if one party works overtime in any domestic job, she/he must be compensated by equal extra work by the other."

How's that for fair?

Well, I guess it was fair enough for Alix Shulman, who within two years after signing was not only the editor of one book and the author of five others, but also much more happily married than before. Which seems to prove that the divvying up of all domestic chores can lessen the tensions and pressures of married life.

Except . . . it wouldn't happen that way with us. With us, I'm afraid, it would go something like this:

Milton: I'll trade you five days of beds and two trips to the pediatrician for a week of dinner dishes. Is that mutually agreed?

Me: Of course not! What kind of chintzy deal are you trying to make? Throw in cooking Sunday brunch and waxing the dining-room chairs, and I'll consider it.

Milton: You must be joking. You already owe me compensatory work for the overtime I put in the other night. It was your turn to answer Anthony's questions, and I wound up answering them all.

Me: That kid has got to learn to ask about baseball on your answer-questions night. Why don't you straighten him out on that right now?

Milton: Because I have to straighten him out only on Mondays, Wednesdays, Fridays and alternate Sundays—and today is Tuesday.

No, all that a marriage contract could give us is something new to fight about, and new things to fight about we really don't need. New *ways* to fight about old things we've fought about—known as Constructive Aggression—could, however, lead to marital bliss.

The Intimate Enemy (written by Peter Wyden and Dr. George Bach) expounds the Constructive Aggression point of view: that unexpressed anger causes estrangement between a husband and wife. So let it all out. Go on—fight! Only fight fair.

Those who are trained in Constructive Aggression (and yes, people actually are) learn, for instance, to fight by appointment only. As in: "Okay, Milton, you nasty, vicious, self-absorbed, bestial fiend, we'll deal with this at nine fifteen in the breakfast nook, but right now let's enjoy our cocktail hour."

Constructive Aggressionists also learn to state—in a rational way—the aims of their fighting, some possible solutions and, quite important, their nonnegotiable limits. As in: "My aim is a car with a functioning heater. The solutions are to buy a new heater or buy a new car. My nonnegotiable limit is if I don't have a working heater by noon tomorrow, I'm driving the car off a cliff."

In addition, Constructive Aggressionists do not "gunny-sack" (store up grievances) or "drop the bomb on Luxembourg" (overreact) or stage a "Virginia Woolf" (you know what that is) because they are too busy "leveling with each other," "fighting above the belt" and trying to get good grades on their intimate-fights test. (Yes, there actually is an intimate-fights test, though "more intuitive types," say the authors, can skip it.)

And some of us "more intuitive types" may just have to skip the whole thing, since Constructive Aggression relies on good will and restraint. I can't deny that good will and restraint—and a wish to resolve, not defeat—could lead to better fights and a better marriage. But while I can't deny it, I also can't do it.

But wait—perhaps we wouldn't have to fight so very much if we learned to understand each other better. Perhaps all we really need to do is . . . communicate.

For communication—or, rather, the lack thereof—appears on every marriage-killer list. She says something. He doesn't listen. She says something. He listens but doesn't really hear. She says something. He listens, he hears, but he doesn't grasp the meaning behind her words. She says something. He listens, he hears, he even grasps the meaning, but, alas, he doesn't give her "feedback."

Are you still with me?

For instance, I say, "It's a nice day," at which point Milton (a) continues watching TV, (b) looks up with glazed eyes and then goes back to watching TV, or (c) replies, "Yeah, it is," but (d) does not say, "Yes, I recognize and sympathize with the fact that you'd hoped we could go on a picnic this afternoon, but what I plan to do is watch this ball game."

Now, *that's* feedback.

But it's not, as yet, ideal communication, since ideally I should have relayed my true feelings more clearly. (As in: "It's a perfect day for a picnic, so why the hell are you watching that stupid ball game?")

No, that's not quite it either.

For communication entails, in addition, tact and a sense of timing. (In other words: Change "why the hell" to "why in heaven's name," drop "stupid" altogether and wait until half time.)

That certainly is better, but it is also recommended that I recognize my husband's limitations. And frailties. And that I accept them. Warped and juvenile though they are. (Suggestion: Toss in something warm and understanding on this subject before proceeding.)

Now, *that's* communication. But who has the strength?

And I haven't even got to nonverbal communication, or what is often referred to as "body language"—those wordless gestures and facial expressions and wriggles and toe taps and twitches that signal how we really, really feel.

The Mirages of Marriage (by William J. Lederer and Don D. Jackson, M.D.) provides some examples:

"When Mary sleeps in pajamas instead of her silk nightgown, I know she's annoyed. I wonder if she realizes this is how I know not to approach her sexually on certain nights."

"When John simply slides his eyes around at me without moving any part of his body and says nothing, I know that he is disagreeing with what I have said."

"When John has little wrinkles by the side of his eyes and tugs at the end of his ear, I know he's about to play a practical joke."

"When Mary sits up straight in the chair and stares right at me when I'm telling her something important, I know she has something else on her mind and isn't even listening."

To each, I guess, his own body language. For when I sleep in pajamas instead of my silk nightgown, it's because the furnace has conked out and I'm freezing. And when Milton has little wrinkles by the side of his eyes and tugs at the end of his ear, it's because his ear itches.

Of course, we too have our own nonverbal signals, and maybe we ought to understand them better. And yet, now that I think of it, maybe not.

For if I'm on the phone long distance and Milton starts clearing his throat and slamming doors, do I really want to know that he's telling me, "Hang up!"?

No, I don't.

And if Milton's having a glorious time at a party and I start grinding my teeth and tapping my foot, does he want to know that I'm telling him, "Let's go!"?

No, he doesn't.

Communication, it seems, can be overdone.

But then, what's the answer, what shall I do, to ensure that we remain man and wife? I'm running out of ideas. Will our marriage survive?

Well, let's see:

Q Can you and your husband turn to each other in sorrow and in joy?

A Yes, we can.

Q Would you or would he be happier with somebody else?

A Probably not.

Q If you were getting married today, do you think you would still choose each other?

A I do.

Perhaps we're going to make it after all.

Discussion Questions

1. Contrast the approach to marriage of the sources Mrs. Viorst reviews in this article and the "Viorst approach." In your view, which approach is more desirable?

2. What is the significance of the title of this article? What is the author's answer to the question posed in the title?

MARGARET MEAD

Can the American Family Survive?

Everyone agrees that the family is undergoing important changes, even though few can agree on the direction of these changes. Will the family as we know it survive? There are those today who doubt it. They paint a grim picture of rising rates of divorce, desertion, child abuse, and the unhappy relationship of continuing marriage in an unhappy family for the benefit of

Reprinted from Margaret Mead, "Can the American Family Survive?" *Redbook* (Feb. 1977) pp. 93, 154–161. Reprinted with permission.

children, relatives, religion, or social pressure. This indictment of the family is discussed by Margaret Mead in the following article, in which she looks bluntly at the major problems that plague the modern family and offers some thoughtful and provocative suggestions about what individuals can do to restore family stability.

All over the United States, families are in trouble.

It is true that there are many contented homes where parents are living in harmony and raising their children responsibly, and with enjoyment in which the children share. Two out of three American households are homes in which a wife and husband live together, and almost seven out of ten children are born to parents living together in their first marriage.

However, though reassuring, these figures are deceptive. A great many of the married couples have already lived through one divorce. And a very large number of the children in families still intact will have to face the disruption of their parents' marriage in the future. The numbers increase every year.

It is also true that the hazards are much greater for some families than for others. Very young couples, the poorly educated, those with few skills and a low income, Blacks and members of other minority groups—particularly if they live in big cities—all these are in danger of becoming high-risk families for whose children a family breakdown is disastrous.

But no group, whatever its status and resources, is exempt. This in itself poses a threat to all families, especially those with young children. For how can children feel secure when their friends in other families so like their own are conspicuously lost and unhappy? In one way or another we all are drawn into the orbit of families in trouble.

Surely it is time for us to look squarely at the problems that beset families and to ask what must be done to make family life more viable, not only for ourselves now but also in prospect for all the children growing up who will have to take responsibility for the next generation.

The Grim Picture

There are those today—as at various times in the past—who doubt that the family can survive, and some who believe it should not survive. Indeed, the contemporary picture is grim enough.

- Many young marriages entered into with love and high hopes collapse before the first baby is weaned. The very young parents, on whom the whole burden of survival rests, cannot make it entirely on their own, and they give up.
- Families that include several children break up and the children are uprooted from the only security they have known. Some children of divorce, perhaps the majority, will grow up as stepchildren in homes that, however

loving, they no longer dare to trust fully. Many—far too many—will grow up in single-parent homes. Still others will be moved, rootless as rolling stones, from foster family to foster family until at last they begin a rootless life on their own.

- In some states a family with a male breadwinner cannot obtain welfare, and some fathers, unable to provide adequately for their children, desert them so that the mothers can apply for public assistance. And growing numbers of mothers, fearful of being deserted, are leaving their young families while, as they hope and believe, they still have a chance to make a different life for themselves.

- As divorce figures have soared—today the proportion of these currently divorced is more than half again as high as in 1960, and it is predicted that one in three young women in this generation will be divorced—Americans have accepted as a truism the myth that from the mistakes made in their first marriage women and men learn how to do it better the second time around. Sometimes it does work. But a large proportion of those who have resorted to divorce once choose this as the easier solution again and again. Easily dashed hopes become more easily dashed.

- At the same time, many working parents, both of whom are trying hard to care for and keep together the family they have chosen to bring into being, find that there is no place at all where their children can be cared for safely and gently and responsibly during the long hours of their own necessary absence at their jobs. They have no relatives nearby and there is neither a day-care center nor afterschool care for their active youngsters. Whatever solution they find, their children are likely to suffer.

The Bitter Consequences

The consequences, direct and indirect, are clear. Thousands of young couples are living together in some arrangement and are wholly dependent on their private, personal commitment to each other for the survival of their relationship. In the years from 1970 to 1975 the number of single persons in the 25-to-34-year age group has increased by half. Some couples living together have repudiated marriage as a binding social relationship and have rejected the family as an institution. Others are delaying marriage because they are not sure of themselves or each other; still others are simply responding to what they have experienced of troubled family life and the effects of divorce.

At the end of the life span there are the ever-growing numbers of women and men, especially women, who have outlived their slender family relationships. They have nowhere to turn, no one to depend on but strangers in public institutions. Unwittingly we have provided the kind of assistance that, particularly in cities, almost guarantees such isolated and helpless old people will become the prey of social vultures.

And at all stages of their adult life, demands are made increasingly on women to earn their living in the working world. Although we prefer to interpret this as an expression of women's wish to fulfill themselves, to have the rights that go with money earned and to be valued as persons, the majority of women who work outside their homes do so because they must. It is striking that ever since the 1950s a larger proportion of married women with children than of married but childless women have entered the labor force. According to recent estimates some 14 million women with children—four out of ten mothers of children under six years of age and more than half of all mothers of school-age children—are working, the great majority of them in full-time jobs.

A large proportion of these working women are the sole support of their families. Some 10 million children—more than one in six—are living with only one parent, generally with the mother. This number has doubled since 1960.

The majority of these women and their children live below the poverty level, the level at which the most minimal needs can be met. Too often the women, particularly the younger ones, having little education and few skills, are at the bottom of the paid work force. Though they and their children are in great need, they are among those least able to demand and obtain what they require merely to survive decently, in good health and with some hope for the future.

But the consequences of family trouble are most desperate as they affect children. Every year, all over the country, over 1 million adolescents, nowadays principally girls, run away from home because they have found life with their families insupportable. Some do not run very far and in the end a great many come home again, but by no means all of them. And we hear about only a handful whose terrifying experiences or whose death happens to come into public view.

In homes where there is no one to watch over them, elementary-school children are discovering the obliterating effects of alcohol; a growing number have become hard-case alcoholics in their early teens. Other young girls and boys, wanderers in the streets, have become the victims of corruption and sordid sex. The youngsters who vent their rage and desperation on others by means of violent crimes are no less social victims than are the girls and boys who are mindlessly corrupted by the adults who prey on them.

Perhaps the most alarming symptom of all is the vast increase in child abuse, which, although it goes virtually unreported in some groups, is not limited to any one group in our population. What seems to be happening is that frantic mothers and fathers, stepparents or the temporary mates of parents turn on the children they do not know how to care for, and beat them—often in a desperate, inarticulate hope that someone will hear their cries and somehow bring help. We know this, but although many organizations have been set up to help these children and their parents, many adults do not know what is needed or how to ask for assistance or whom they may expect a response from.

And finally there are the children who end their own lives in absolute despair. Suicide is now third among the causes of death for youngsters 15 to 19 years old.

What Has Gone Wrong?

In recent years, various explanations have been suggested for the breakdown of family life.

Blame has been placed on the vast movement of Americans from rural areas and small towns to the big cities and on the continual, restless surge of people from one part of the country to another, so that millions of families living in the midst of strangers, lack any continuity in their life-style and any real support for their values and expectations.

Others have emphasized the effects of unemployment and underemployment among Blacks and other minority groups, which make their families peculiarly vulnerable in life crises that are exacerbated by economic uncertainty. This is particularly the case where the policies of welfare agencies penalize the family that is poor but intact in favor of the single-parent family.

There is also the generation gap, particularly acute today, when parents and their adolescent children experience the world in such very different ways. The world in which the parents grew up is vanishing, unknown to their children except by hearsay. The world into which adolescents are growing is in many ways unknown to both generations—and neither can help the other very much to understand it.

Then there is our obvious failure to provide for the children and young people whom we do not succeed in educating, who are in deep trouble and who may be totally abandoned. We have not come to grips with the problems of hard drugs. We allow the courts that deal with juveniles to become so overloaded that little of the social protection they were intended to provide is possible. We consistently underfund and understaff the institutions into which we cram children in need of re-education and physical and psychological rehabilitation, as if all that concerned us was to get them—and keep them—out of our sight.

Other kinds of explanations also have been offered.

There are many people who, knowing little about child development, have placed the principal blame on what they call "permissiveness"—on the relaxing of parental discipline to include the child as a small partner in the process of growing up. Those people say that children are "spoiled," that they lack "respect" for their parents or that they have not learned to obey the religious prohibitions that were taught to their parents, and that all the trouble plaguing family life have followed.

Women's Liberation, too, has come in for a share of the blame. It is said that in seeking self-fulfillment, women are neglecting their homes and children and are undermining men's authority and men's sense of responsibility. The collapse of the family is seen as the inevitable consequence.

Those who attribute the difficulties of troubled families to any single cause, whether or not it is related to reality, also tend to advocate panaceas, each of which—they say—should restore stability to the traditional family or, alternatively, supplant the family. Universal day care from birth, communal living, group marriage, contract marriage and open marriage all have their advocates.

Each such proposal fastens on some trouble point in the modern family—the lack of adequate facilities to care for the children of working mothers, for example, or marital infidelity, which, it is argued, would be eliminated by being institutionalized. Others, realizing the disastrous effect of poverty on family life, have advocated bringing the income of every family up to a level at which decent living is possible. Certainly this must be one of our immediate aims. But it is wholly unrealistic to suppose that all else that has gone wrong will automatically right itself if the one—but very complex—problem of poverty is eliminated .

A Look at Alternatives

Is there, in fact, any viable alternative to the family as a setting in which children can be successfully reared to become capable and responsible adults, relating to one another and a new generation of children as well as to the world around them? Or should we aim at some wholly new social invention?

Revolutionaries have occasionally attempted to abolish the family, or at least to limit its strength by such measures as arranging for marriages without binding force or for rearing children in different kinds of collectives. But as far as we know, in the long run such efforts have never worked out satisfactorily.

The Soviet Union, for instance, long ago turned away from the flexible, impermanent unions and collective child-care ideals of the early revolutionary days and now heavily emphasizes the values of a stable family life. In Israel the kibbutz, with its children's house and carefully planned, limited contact between parents and children, is losing out to social forms in which the family is both stronger and more closely knit. In Scandinavian countries, where the standards of child care are very high, serious efforts have been made to provide a viable situation for unmarried mothers and the children they have chosen to bring up alone; but there are disturbing indices of trouble, expressed, for example, in widespread alcoholism and a high rate of suicide.

Experience suggests that we would do better to look in other directions. Two approaches may be rewarding. First we can look at other kinds of societies—primitive societies, peasant societies and traditional complex but unindustrialized societies (prerevolutionary China, for example)—to discover whether there are ways in which families are organized that occur in all societies. This can give us some idea of needs that must be satisfied for families to survive and prosper.

Second we can ask whether the problems that are besetting American families are unique or are instead characteristic of families wherever modern industrialization, a sophisticated technology and urban living are drawing people into a new kind of civilization. Placing our own difficulties within a wider context can perhaps help us to assess what our priorities must be as we attempt to develop new forms of stability in keeping with contemporary expressions of human needs.

Looking at human behavior with all that we know—and can infer—about the life of our human species from earliest times, we have to realize that the family, as an association between a man and a woman and the children she bears, has been universal. As far as we know, both primitive "group" marriage and primitive matriarchy are daydreams—or nightmares, depending on one's point of view—without basis in historical reality. On the contrary, the evidence indicates that the couple, together with their children, biological or adopted, are everywhere at the core of human societies, even though this "little family" (as the Chinese called the nuclear family) may be embedded in joint families, extended families of great size, clans, manorial systems, courts, harems or other institutions that elaborate on kin and marital relations.

Almost up to the present, women on the whole have kept close to home and domestic tasks because of the demands of pregnancy and the nursing of infants, the rearing of children and the care of the disabled and the elderly. They have been concerned primarily with the conservation of intimate values and human relations from one generation to another over immense reaches of time. In contrast, men have performed tasks that require freer movement over greater distances, more intense physical effort and exposure to greater immediate danger; and everywhere men have developed the formal institutions of public life and the values on which these are based. However differently organized, the tasks of women and men have been complementary, mutually supportive. And where either the family or the wider social institutions have broken down, the society as a whole has been endangered.

In fact, almost everywhere in the world today societies *are* endangered. The difficulties that beset families in the United States are by no means unique. Families are in trouble everywhere in a world in which change—kinds of change that in many cases we ourselves proudly initiated—has been massive and rapid, and innovations have proliferated with only the most superficial concern for their effect on human lives and the earth itself. One difference between the United States and many other countries is that, caring so much about progress, Americans have moved faster. But we may also have arrived sooner at a turning point at which it becomes crucial to redefine what we most value and where we are headed.

Looking to the past does not mean that we should return to the past or that we can undo the experiences that have brought us where we now are. The past can provide us only with a base for judging what threatens sound family life and for considering whether our social planning is realistic and inclusive enough. Looking to the past is not a way of binding ourselves but of increasing our awareness, so that we are freer to find new solutions in keeping with our deepest human needs.

So the question is not whether women should be forced back into their homes or should have an equal say with men in the world's affairs. We urgently need to draw on the talents women have to offer. Nor is there any question whether men should be deprived of a more intimate family role. We have made a small beginning by giving men a larger share in parenting, and I believe that men and children have been enriched by it.

What we need to be sure of is that areas of caretaking associated in the past with families do not simply drop out of our awareness so that basic human needs go unmet. All the evidence indicates that this is where our greatest difficulties lie. The troubles that plague American families and families all over the industrialized world are symptomatic of the breakdown of the responsible relationship between families and the larger communities of which they are part.

For a long time we have worked hard at isolating the individual family. This has increased the mobility of individuals; and by encouraging young families to break away from the older generation and the home community, we have been able to speed up the acceptance of change and the rapid spread of innovative behavior. But at the same time we have burdened every small family with tremendous responsibilities once shared within three generations and among a large number of people—the nurturing of small children, the emergence of adolescents into adulthood, the care of the sick and disabled and the protection of the aged. What we have failed to realize is that even as we have separated the single family from the larger society, we have expected each couple to take on a range of obligations that traditionally have been shared within a larger family and a wider community.

So all over the world there are millions of families left alone, as it were, each in its own box—parents faced with the specter of what may happen if either one gets sick, children fearful that their parents may end their quarrels with divorce, and empty-handed old people without any role in the life of the next generation.

Then, having pared down to almost nothing the relationship between families and the community, when families get into trouble because they cannot accomplish the impossible we turn their problems over to impersonal social agencies, which can act only in a fragmented way because they are limited to patchwork programs that often are too late to accomplish what is most needed.

Individuals and families do get some kind of help, but what they learn and what those who work hard within the framework of social agencies convey, even as they try to help, is that families should be able to care for themselves.

What Can We Do?

Can we restore family stability? Can we establish new bonds between families and communities? Perhaps most important of all, can we move to a firm belief that living in a family is worth a great effort? Can we move to a new expectation that by making the effort, families can endure? Obviously the process is circular. Both optimism and action are needed.

We shall have to distinguish between the things that must be done at once and the relations between families and communities that can be built up only over time. We shall have to accept willingly the cost of what must be done, realizing that whatever we do ultimately will be less costly than our present sorry attempts to cope with breakdown and disaster. And we shall have to care for the failures too.

In the immediate future we shall have to support every piece of Federal legislation through which adequate help can be provided for families, both single-parent families and intact poor families, so that they can live decently and safely and prepare their children for another kind of life.

We shall have to support Federal programs for day care and afterschool care for the children of working mothers and working parents, and for facilities where in a crisis parents can safely leave their small children for brief periods; for centers where the elderly can be cared for without being isolated from the rest of the world; for housing for young families and older people in communities where they can actually interact as friendly grandparents and grandchildren might; and for a national health program that is concerned not with fleecing the Government but with health care. And we must support the plea of Vice-President Walter F. Mondale, who, as chairman of the Senate Subcommittee on Children and Youth, called for "family impact" statements requiring Government agencies to account for what a proposed policy would do for families—make them worse off or better able to take care of their needs.

Government-funded programs need not be patchwork, as likely to destroy as to save. We need to realize that problems related to family and community life—problems besetting education, housing, nutrition, health care, child care, to name just a few—are interlocked. To solve them, we need awareness of detail combined with concern for the whole, and a wise use of tax dollars to accomplish our aims.

A great deal depends on how we see what is done—whether we value it because we are paying for it and because we realize that the protection given families in need is a protection for all families, including our own. Committing ourselves to programs of care—instead of dissociating ourselves from every effort—is one step in the direction of reestablishing family ties with the community. But this will happen only if we accept the idea that each of us, as part of a community, shares in the responsibility for everyone, and thereby benefits from what is done.

The changes that are needed cannot be accomplished by Federal legislation alone. Over a longer time we must support the design and building of communities in which there is housing for three generations, for the fortunate and the unfortunate, and for people of many backgrounds. Such communities can become central in the development of the necessary support system for families. But it will take time to build such communities, and we cannot afford just to wait and hope they will happen.

Meanwhile we must act to interrupt the runaway belief that marriages must fail, that parents and children can't help but be out of communication, that the family as an institution is altogether in disarray. There still are far more marriages that succeed than ones that fail; there are more parents and children who live in trust and learn from one another than ones who are out of touch; there are more people who care about the future than we acknowledge.

What we need, I think, is nationwide discussion—in magazines, in newspapers, on television panel shows and before Congressional committees—of how people who are happily married can help those who are not, how people who are fortunate can help those who are not and how people who have too little to do can help those who are burdened by too much.

Out of such discussions can come a heightened awareness and perhaps some actual help, but above all, fresh thought about what must be done and the determination to begin to do it.

It is true that all over the United States, families are in trouble. Realizing this should not make us cynical about the family. It should start us working for a new version of the family that is appropriate to the contemporary world.

Discussion Questions

1. How does Margaret Mead answer the question in the title?
2. Review the problems of "the grim picture" for today's American family.
3. What are Ms. Mead's suggestions for restoring family stability?

CARLFRED B. BRODERICK

Damn Those Gloomy Prophets— The Family Is Here to Stay

The nuclear family has been severely criticized as overly isolated from a larger network of relationships and the cause of loneliness and estrangement. Some psychologists see the nuclear family as the cause of fearful, neurotic personalities. Women's Liberation indicts the family as a stifling trap, pro-

Reprinted from Carlfred B. Broderick, "Damn Those Gloomy Prophets—The Family Is Here to Stay," *Los Angeles Times* (June 17, 1973), Part VII, p. 4, by permission of the author.

ducing stunted growth and frustrations. Some sociologists argue that the family is an anachronistic relic in its death throes. A contrary perspective is offered by the article below which claims the besieged nuclear family "is here to stay."

Perhaps it is insensitive to mention this on Father's Day, but general opinion has it that families may be on their way out and fathers with them. Nearly every social prophet these days seems to get the same picture in his crystal ball—a world in which men and women relate to each other mostly on a short-term basis.

These observers see the state replacing the father as the backup for the mother, with government agencies providing child care so that she can work, and financial support when she cannot.

The idea is that this arrangement will be far better suited to rapid social change, that it will provide children with a more rational upbringing and will place everyone in a happier, more varied and rewarding situation.

As a father myself, I am determined not to die out without a struggle and as a family sociologist I cannot help noting that not all the indicators are gloomy for the family.

For example, one of the most frequently noted indicators that marriage is increasingly passé is the tendency of young people these days to live together, without marriage, frequently with a great deal of rhetoric about marriage being too confining, possessive and inhibiting to growth.

If that were the only criterion, it would be easy to conclude that our Father's Days are indeed numbered (since children of such unions nearly always go with the mother when the couple splits).

However, other facts cast a different light on the matter. Take the marriage rate, for instance. If the prophets of family doom were right, it should be going down. But it is going up. The marriage rate was higher in the 1960s than in the 1950s, and it is higher in the 1970s than it was in the 1960s.

More than 95% of us now get married before age 40. That means that more people are getting married today than watch television. It means that over half of all preferential homosexuals must be heterosexually married (since about 10% of the population is estimated to be preferential homosexuals). It means that even Roman Catholic priests and nuns are leaving holy orders in substantial numbers to get married.

Probably no other country in the Western world has as high a marriage rate. So what about all those young persons who are living together without getting married? It turns out that after a year or two, most of them either give up their rhetoric and marry each other or break up and marry someone else. The same thing happens to people in communes. The half-life of most communes is under 18 months. And what do those leaving communes drop out into? Marriage.

When all is said and done, it appears that living together is less a substitute for marriage than it is a substitute for living alone or with a same-sex roommate.

But what about the divorce rate? Already 50% of all marriages end in divorce and it looks as though it will soon be 60% or even 70%, critics of the family argue. If marriage is here to stay, they say, you'd better tell those millions of Americans who tried it and are voting with their feet.

I admit that the divorce rate is going up. It is not skyrocketing, but is climbing slowly and steadily, although it is only within the last five years that it passed the 1946 level. Both postwar peaks probably reflected the number of returning servicemen who found that their marriages did not survive the rigors of extended separation and uncertainties.

However, the scare statistic of one out of two marriages currently ending in divorce is extremely misleading. It is based on a comparison between the number of people getting married in a given year and the number of people getting divorced that year.

But those are not very sensible numbers to compare. Statisticians never use that index. Instead they compare the number of marriages with the number of people eligible to marry in a given year. Likewise, statisticians compare the number of divorces to the number of people eligible to get a divorce in any given year—namely, all those who are married.

If you look at these more meaningful figures you discover that only about 1% of all marriages end in divorce in any given year in California. The average length of marriage is a little more than 20 years and almost three-fourths of all marriages end only when one or the other spouse dies.

Even stronger evidence against the argument that the divorce rate shows a negative attitude toward marriage is the fact that, age for age, no group has a higher marriage rate than divorcees. At a given age, say 35, the divorcee is most likely to marry, the widow next, and the never-married person last likely. Apparently it is not marriage that is disapproved but that detestable ex-spouse. Despite a painful experience, marriage itself is highly valued.

As for fatherhood, a recent random sample of all families with children under 18 in San Diego County found only 15% headed by mothers and 10% headed by stepfathers. The remaining 75% were headed by natural fathers. It may be premature to sell your stock in greeting card companies on the grounds that Father's Day is on its way out.

But those skeptical of the future of the conventional marriage and family turn for ammunition to sex and the enormous shift in sexual behavior in the last 10 years.

Girls are admitting to more sex before marriage than ever before, they argue. Even colleges in conservative sections of the country like Georgia and Utah are showing increases of up to 300% in the number of nonvirgins. My own studies of random samples of newly married couples in Illinois and Pennsylvania show that over three-fourths of them had had sex with each other before marriage compared with only 50% in the Kinsey studies 20 years earlier.

After marriage, it is estimated that between 2 million and 10 million Americans are involved in swinging or mate swapping or group sex, skeptics say. That may be marriage, but it's not the old-fashioned sexually exclusive marriage that we see slipping into oblivion. Future marriage, they add, will be transformed from the possessive, stultifying mutual incarceration it has been to the open, growth-sponsoring association of two mature, nonpossessive adults.

Critics of marriage have a point there. There is no question that more girls are coming to marriage with sexual experience than ever before. Whatever one thinks of the desirability or undesirability of this, however, the question is whether the exclusivity of the marital contract itself is seriously threatened by it. The institution seems to have survived millenia of premarital sexual experience by males without sinking.

The matter of swinging is a special case. Most swingers do not feel they are being disloyal to their spousal commitments since they swing together, and by mutual consent. Swinging is an attempt to take advantage of the cultural shift toward more permissiveness in sex without endangering the marriage. It is interesting to note that the one big study of swinging tended to show that the average couple tired of this pattern after two years and dropped back into a monogamous pattern.

Sexual variety does appeal to a deep human instinct for a new experience and risk, but it is often overlooked that there are even more fundamental instincts for security and stability. I do not believe, as some have suggested, that marriage evolved because men wanted slaves to tend to their domestic and sexual needs. I believe, rather, that men and women found (and find) marriage to be a sensible and satisfying arrangement for two adults whereby they divide the labor and share resources and responsibilities for each other and their children. To the extent that sexual variety threatens that basic arrangement, I believe it will yield to more exclusive and stable sexual contract as it always has.

Many persons believe that traditional family commitment not only will disappear, but ought to disappear. Their point is that a major commitment to a spouse and children is a real obstacle to personal growth and individual fulfillment.

There is a growing feeling in some quarters that having children is not only bad for the environment but also blocks a person (and especially a woman) from pursuing opportunities for developing her fullest potential.

I have no argument against this because it is true that if a woman sacrifices some part of her career for her family she may indeed give up the achievement of some potentially rewarding alternatives.

Both men and women feel the impact of children on their income, expenses, mobility, resources and privacy. Children extract a number of significant costs, and many adults will decide to forego both the children and the cost.

But I believe that people will go on having children in the face of improved contraceptives, more easily available abortions, better career opportunities for women and the pressures from the environmentalists, because having and raising children remains one of the most challenging and fulfilling experiences available to men and women.

Time will tell, but the evidence I see fails to convince me that the family or the role of father in it is in any danger of extinction.

So happy Father's Day and many happy returns.

Discussion Questions

1. What differences do you see in Mr. Broderick's views about the future of the family and Margaret Mead's views?
2. Do you tend to agree with this author that "having and raising children remains one of the most challenging and fulfilling experiences available to men and women"? Discuss.

11 / Formal Organizations

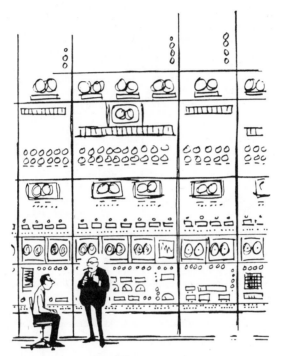

"I decided we're not having an office Christmas party this year."

In the small towns and villages of a traditional rural society, one-man shops and family enterprises such as those of the blacksmith and carpenter fulfilled virtually all of the local residents' economic needs. Production and services of goods occurred primarily in small, informal groups. The development of a modern industrial-urban society, however, rendered such methods of production inefficient and obsolete. Now most of the production and services are carried out through large, formally organized groups.

A *formal organization* is a social group created by a number of individuals to further their objectives. These objectives can vary from making money, influencing the decisions of government agencies, or simply enjoying the camaraderie of one's fellows. These types of groups do not just happen; they are explicitly organized and given a name such as the Rotary Club, the Republican Party, or the University of California. General Motors is an example of a formal organization dedicated to making, among other things, a profit. It is worth more than $13 billion dollars, employs well over half a million individuals, and has three-quarters of a million stockholders.

Formal organizations are one of the most dominant factors of modern urban life. They not only include large-scale organizations such as corporations, labor unions, and political parties, they also include *voluntary associations* such as sports clubs, country clubs, lodges, alumni associations, and various civic groups. All of these groups have a formal structure consisting of a hierarchy of authority which facilitates leadership and a chain of command. Each group also has a program of action such as fund raising for charity or campaigning for a political candidate.

The most characteristic pattern of large-scale organizations is *bureaucracy*. Because these organizations have specific objectives and involve many individuals, the allocation and supervision of duties must be *rationally* organized in order to maximize *efficiency*. The ideal bureaucracy is characterized by specialization, merit appointments and job tenure, formalistic impersonality, and chain of command.

Despite the avowed efficiency of a bureaucracy, it is usually associated in the popular mind with a cumbersome, bungling, and inefficient machinery. Although sociologists generally admire the goals of bureaucratic organizations, they have been very critical of their failures and defects. These failures and defects are described by the concept of *bureaupathology. Some of the aspects of bureaupathology* are the depersonalization resulting from a formalistic chain of command, emphasis on the rules as ends rather than as means with the result of "waffle-paper," red tape, and the toll on individuals in the form of frustrations, boredom, and unsatisfied work experiences. As a result, many bureaucrats have developed skills in areas such as buck-passing, a technique designed to keep one's "nose" clean and out of trouble until the next promotion or retirement. This practice has in turn caused many individuals to bypass the formal structure of command and responsibility and rely on the *informal structure* of "string-pulling" and reciprocal obligations. A continued reliance on the informal structure serves to undermine the formal structure even more.

In spite of bureaupathology, bureaucracy in large-scale organizations will continue to exist and grow as long as this nation and its organizations are dedicated to serving all of its citizens. What is needed is an understanding of techniques of administration that will enable these organizations to achieve their goals in a way that will also prove beneficial to the individuals involved.

KEN McKENNA

If Creeping Boredom Is Your Work Problem . . .

Most Americans are employed by large-scale organizations whose most prevailing pattern is bureaucracy. The bureaucratic structure of these organizations was not designed to provide individual participants with feelings of satisfaction, fulfillment, or the development of personal potentialities. As a result, dissatisfaction, boredom, and alienation all too often characterize the attitudes of many workers.

You may have discovered that being bored with your job is one of the troubles of your life.

You may be asking yourself such questions as: "Why am I bored at work?" "Is it my fault?" "My boss's?" "The company's?" "Does the problem lie with my work itself?" "What can I do to stop being bored with my work?"

Reprinted from *Today's Health* (August 1972), 45, 69–70, by permission of the author.

To find answers to these questions, *Today's Health* interviewed psychologists, scientists and experts in personnel management, including Dr. Sol Warren, a psychologist at the New York State Office of Vocational Rehabilitation. He says, "First of all, I'd like to say that being bored on the job is a common complaint. Many of the job dissatisfaction surveys reveal that between 60 and 80 per cent of workers are dissatisfied with what they are doing and would change jobs if they could."

The reasons why any particular employee, from file clerk to secretary or assembly line worker to foreman or executive, say, is a victim of job ennui vary with the individual. "For some people, work is a sentence they serve each week to get the reward of their weekend freedom. Such a man or woman has outside interests that are the motivational mainstay of his existence."

Take as an example a man we'll call Joe Smith. He works in the computer processing department of a major life insurance company 12 hours a day from seven in the morning until eight o'clock at night—with a half-hour break for lunch and another half-hour for dinner—three days a week. Then he has four consecutive days off. Even with such lengthy weekends, most people would find Joe's job boring: he transports the program tapes to and fro from the files to the computer. But Joe says, "I'm never bored because I keep my mind on the nice trip my wife and I and the kids will be taking in just a few days. I bought a new car and we're seeing the country."

Or listen to Mary Brown who works in a typing pool at a bank from 8:30 in the morning until 5 at night with 45 minutes for lunch in the company cafeteria. "Sure, I'm bored to tears from Monday until Friday and so are the other girls. But I have my own apartment where I can entertain my friends, I go dancing two or three times a week, I go shopping on the week-ends so my clothes are really nice, there are parties and things—and then I won't have to work forever. Someday I'll meet Mr. Right and get married and have a family."

For such people, job boredom is the price to pay to get the things you want. "They'll submit to any routine, short of what they despise," says Dr. Warren. But for countless others, job boredom is so painful it becomes destructive of the rest of their lives. An assembly-line worker in Detroit may toil eight hours a day welding auto bodies, then drive through rush hour traffic to his home, where he will wolf his dinner and blur reality in front of his TV set. Here the work itself is clearly at fault, but so, too, is the worker's lack of constructive outside interests. "If the individual regards his job as a sentence to serve and has nothing enriching to look forward to after work is done, he will be unhappy and make others unhappy," the psychologist says.

It is not only assembly-line workers or typists who yawn their way through days of tedium. At a time when computers supply the nuts and bolts for an increasing number of jobs and management is concentrating on making employees more efficient, the needs of the individual are often ignored. In many cases the man no longer controls the job: the job controls the man.

A corporate vice president, Edward Status III, is proud of his title and success, yet he is disconcerted to learn that despite his apparent executive responsibility he is a mere channel for decisions made by his superiors who are, themselves, only implementing policy laid down by the board of directors in response to stockholder pressure.

"Such an individual would answer the question 'Do you find your job less interesting than when you first started?' with an unqualified 'Yes.' He is in a quandary. He doesn't like his position, though he does like the salary, the apparent status, the fringe benefits and the pension to which he can look forward. But he feels hollow, because he lacks the dignity that would come, he believes, with meaningful responsibilities," says Dr. Warren.

Here the fault probably lies with company policy. Also, not only this corporate executive, but many types of employees suffer from the loss of the sense of accomplishment. An auto assembly-line worker queried about the scandalous list of new-car defects that have caused every major company to recall hundreds of thousands of autos, replies: "Sure, we read how the working man today has no pride in his work, and it's true. But what you don't read is how the company has broken down the work into smaller and smaller units so that no man can feel pride in what he's doing. If they'd just let me build a car occasionally. Just one."

"The degree of the individual's alienation from his work depends on his philosophy of life," Dr. Warren points out. "The time-server simply turns off his mind while he's on the job. The over-qualified skilled worker, or executive cannot do the same.

What can such a worker do? "He can do what he can to enrich himself within the setting of the job."

The answer in many cases of job ennui may be to drop out. "Sometimes the loss of income, of fringe benefits, the insecurity about finding another job, even a possible readjustment of one's way of life to a lower economic scale, are worth it if they lead to job satisfaction," says the psychologist. Again it depends on the individual's philosophy. If he is unhappy at his work and he is making his family unhappy, then finding a career which will make him feel that what he is doing is worthwhile will restore human values not only to himself but also to his family.

If a person sees his job each day as just another day's drudgery, he finds it increasingly difficult to face his family each morning. "Workers in general want to avoid jobs that are monotonous, repetitive, over-controlled and isolated from interaction with others," comments Michael Maccoby of Harvard's Institute of Policy Studies.

As Manhattan psychologist Dr. Harold Greenwald suggests about many union grievances—typically a long recital of niggling complaints—they represent, he says "a cry for recognition that the complainer is a man and not a machine."

Too often, worker gripes are misdirected because the individuals themselves do not understand the root of their discontent.

Lee A. Parent, director of personnel and office services of the American

Medical Association, agrees with Dr. Greenwald. "Often personnel knows before the employee's supervisor that the individual is bored on the job. We will receive complaints that there is too much noise in the office. Or a secretary will come in and say she doesn't like her typewriter and needs a new one of this or that kind. Or sometimes an employee will say 'My supervisor doesn't like me.'

"These complaints are indications that the employee is completely unchallenged in the position. The solution is a promotion or a resignation.

"Of course, individuals differ. Many employees are passive and only want to do what they are told to do. Others are ambitious and will tend to do their jobs in their own way. It is important to take the difference between the passive and aggressive type of employee into account when evaluating and working to alleviate job boredom."

The individual and his supervisor are encouraged to sit down and discuss his job. The employee is asked to consider and decide what is the most critical area of his work in terms of getting top results. The supervisor, in his turn, tells the employee what he hopes to accomplish.

"This is called management by objectives," says Mr. Parent. "Under such a program of job enrichment a task is never assigned to an employee until he and the supervisor sit down and discuss this job. The supervisor listens to the employee's ideas of how the objective can best be accomplished. When I'm the supervisor, the employee may end up doing it my way, but I will have considered his way. It takes longer but it results in a better quality of work."

Another means of alleviating job boredom, Mr. Parent points out, is to modify jobs by allotting special responsibility outside of the regularly assigned responsibilities. This gives the employee a change of pace.

Employees' attitudes toward work—even the same kind of work—are as variable as the surplus of dull jobs now available. A clerk with a Bronx drug distribution company reacted to a newspaper article about job boredom with immediate recollection of a former employer. One of his clerk's duties was to sweep the center aisle of the company warehouse. The first time his boss glanced at the clean floor, he exclaimed, "Hey! Nice job you did there."

"That's all, nothing else, but every day or every time I swept the floor he would say something nice about it," the clerk remembered. Once, the boss elaborated, "If it weren't for you sweeping the floor, it would be a lot tougher working here."

The sweeper's reaction: "Simple words like these can make a person feel that he or she has achieved something. Somebody cares about what you are doing and that what you are doing is important. So, every time you do it, you do it better."

That boredom can be of a person's own making is emphasized by the experience of Mrs. Thelma Stackpole, who is on the staff of the Community Service Society of New York, a leading social welfare agency. She works with Chinese immigrants from Hong Kong and Taiwan and has been impressed with their ability to handle stoically jobs that are far beneath their abilities.

"Many are skilled workers and professional people who are unable to follow their field in this country," she said. "One ex-school teacher is working as a waiter. A great number have lowly jobs in the garment center. Among trained people, work like this can produce boredom, but they have the strength of purpose that makes them able to resist it."

On the other hand, she is currently trying to help a seasoned skilled worker who was disabled in an accident. He has been reduced to a job as a dishwasher. "He's had to have psychiatric help. His attitude interferes with his family and social relations," Mrs. Stackpole said.

As Dr. Frederick Herzberg, a prominent psychologist and one of the pioneers in studies of job ennui, wrote: "Motivation means he (the worker) wants to do the job. He's not doing it just because he needs the money. . . ."

For years, employers shrugged off the findings of psychologists who pointed out that work without personal involvement breeds apathy. Management officials argued that wage scales are higher each year and "fringe" benefits beyond the wildest expectations of a decade ago. In effect, they were saying that an employee—whether an executive or a security guard assigned to stand on his feet eight hours a day—was being well paid for being bored.

But behavioral scientist Dr. A. H. Maslow points out that there has been a shift in the priorities of mid-20th century man. His primitive needs for food, shelter and security have been satisfied. Now higher-level needs have emerged.

Increasingly, companies have found they cannot buy off a work force that mainly finds their jobs a dull grind. A. J. Schiavetti, a top personnel executive at New York City's Chemical Bank, admits that "salary will only buy you a short-run benefit. It's the intrinsic value of the work that a person performs and what that work means to him that is going to give us any sustained drive as far as productivity is concerned."

Dr. Chris Argysis, a Yale scientist who has probed deeply into job motivation, contends, "The employee must be provided more 'power' over his own work environment and therefore he must be given responsibility, authority and increased control over the decision-making that affects his immediate work environment. He must become self-responsible."

Discussion Questions

1. Must bureaucracy produce the kind of boredom being discussed in this article? Discuss.
2. Do you agree with this statement by A. H. Maslow? "[T]here has been a shift in the priorities of mid-20th century man. His primitive needs for food, shelter and security have been satisfied. Now higher-level needs have emerged." In your view, can these "higher-level needs" and bureaucratic efficiency be compatible? Discuss.

MATTHEW P. DUMONT

Down the Bureaucracy!

Although bureaucracy is a method employed by individuals to achieve effi-ciency, it is usually associated in the popular mind with a cumbersome, bungling, and inefficient machinery. While the ideals of bureaucratic methods continue to be admired, the reality of most functioning bureaucracies, such as the federal government bureaucracy, have been severely criticized. The following article by Dumont describes some of the causes of bureaucratic inefficiency. The author also suggests a model for reform.

There has been a certain tension among the people of our federal city lately. I am not talking about the black population of the district, which be-comes visible to the rest of the world only when its rage boils over. I am referring to the public servants who ooze across the Maryland and Virginia lines each day to manipulate the machinery of government.

It has never been a particularly gleeful population, but in the last year or so it has developed a kind of mass involutional melancholia, a peculiar mix-ture of depression, anxiety and senescence.

As in similarly depressed communities, the young, the healthy and those with good job prospects have tended to migrate. Among those who have de-parted are a large proportion of that scarce supply of idealistic and pragmatic people who try to work for social change "within the system." They are leaving because they feel unwanted and ineffectual. Let me describe what they are turning their backs on.

Washington is a malaria swamp covered over with buildings of neofascist design and ringed with military bases.

Do you remember Rastignac shaking his fist at Paris from Goriot's grave site? Washington is a city made for fists to be shaken at. Shaken at, not bloodied on. Federal buildings are especially constructed to be impervious to blood. You can rush headlong into a marble balustrade smearing brains and blood and bile three yards wide. But as the lady does on television, with a smile and a few whisks of a damp cloth, the wonderful material will come up as clean and white and sparkling as before.

Some people have tried burning themselves into the concrete. That doesn't work either.

And, as you might have guessed, all that urine on the Pentagon was gone within minutes after the armies of the night retreated.

No, you may, individually or en masse, descend upon the Federal Triangle. You may try to impale and exsanguinate yourselves, flay, crucify and castrate yourselves. You may scream shrill cries or sing "Alice's Restaurant" or chant "Om," but it won't help. The buildings were made to last forever and to forever remain shining and white, the summer sun glaring off their walls, stunning the passerby.

Inside, one might spend eternity hearing the sounds of his own footsteps in the corridors of these buildings and never see his sun-cast shadow. If you took all the corridors in all of the federal buildings in Washington and laid them end to end, and inclined one end slightly and started a billiard ball rolling down, by the time it reached the lower end, the ball would have attained such a velocity that it would hurtle on through space while approaching an infinite mass and thereby destroy the universe. This is not likely to happen because such coordination is unheard of among federal agencies. But we will get to that later.

Off the corridors are offices and conference rooms. (There is also a core of mail chutes, telephone lines, elevator shafts, sewer pipes, trash cans and black people, but these are all invisible.) The offices have desks—wooden ones for important people and steel ones for unimportant people. (Otherwise, the distinction is impossible to make unless you could monitor their telephone calls to each other and determine the relative hierarchy depending on whose secretary manages to keep the other party waiting before putting her boss on.)

The offices also contain file cabinets that are filled with paper. The paper is mainly memos—the way people in the federal government communicate to one another. When communication is not necessary, memos "for the record" are written and filed. It has been estimated that the approximate cost on labor and supplies for the typing of a memo is 36¢. The cost in professional time for its preparation is incalculable.

The conference rooms are for conferences. A conference is for the purpose of sharing information among a group of federal officials who have already been apprised of the information to be shared, individually, by memo. Coffee and cigarettes are consumed. By prior arrangement, each participant is, in turn, interrupted by his secretary for an urgent phone call. After the conference additional memos are exchanged.

But let me describe the people who work in the federal government because some mythology must be laid to rest.

They are good people, which is to say that they are no less good than anyone else, which is to say that we are all pretty much cut from the same material and most of it is pretty rotten. I do not wish to be cavalier about the problem of evil, but I will ask you to accept as a premise for this thesis that the differences between the "best of us" and the "worst of us" are no greater than the differences *within* each of us at varying times.

I have been and will be more sober and precise about this issue in other writings, but what I am attempting to convey is a conviction that the great evils of mankind, the genocides and holy wars, the monstrous exploitations and negligences and injustices of societies have less to do with the malice of individuals than with unexamined and unquestioned institutional practices.

I am talking about the Eichmannism—a syndrome wherein individual motives, consciences or goals become irrelevant in the context of organizational behaviors. This can be seen in pure culture in the federal government. There are a host of written rules for behavior for the federal civil servants, but these are rarely salient. It is the unwritten rules, tacit but ever present, subtle but overwhelming, unarticulated but commanding, that determine the behavior of the men and women who buzz out their lives in the spaces defined by the United States government.

These rules are few in number. Rule number one is to *maintain your tenure*. This is at the same time the most significant and the easiest rule to abide by. If you desire to keep a job for several decades and retire from it with an adequate pension, and if you have the capacity to appear at once occupied and inconspicuous, then you can be satisfied as a "fed."

Appearing occupied means walking briskly at all times. It means looking down at your desk rather than up into the distance when thinking. It means always having papers in your hands. Above all, it means, when asked how things are, responding "very hectic" rather than "terrific" or "lousy."

Being inconspicuous means that your competence in appearing occupied should be expressed quietly and without affect. The most intolerable behavior in a civil servant is psychotic behavior. Being psychotic in the federal government is looking people directly in the eye for a moment too long. It is walking around on a weekday without a tie. It is kissing a girl in an elevator. (It doesn't matter whether she is a wife, mistress, secretary or daughter.) It is writing a memo that is excessively detailed, or refusing to write memos. It is laughing too loud or too long at a conference. It is taking a clandestine gulp of wine in a locker room rather than ordering two martinis over lunch. (This explains why there are more suspensions for alcoholism among lower level workers than higher level ones.)

In short, there is no more sensitive indicator of deviant behavior than personnel records of the federal government.

This does not mean that federal officials never vary their behavior. Currently, for example, it is modish to sport sideburns and a moustache. The specter of thousands of civil servants looking like Che Guevara may seem exciting, but it has no more significance than cuffless trousers.

You may or may not wish to follow the fashions, but do not initiate them. In general, follow a golden mean of behavior, that is, do what most people seem to be doing. Do it quietly. And if you are not sure how to behave, take annual leave.

The second rule of behavior in the government, and clearly related to the sustenance of your own tenure, is to *keep the boss from getting embarrassed*. That is the single, most important standard of competence for a federal official. The man who runs interference effectively, who can anticipate and obviate impertinent, urgent or obvious demands from the boss's boss, or from the press, or from the public, or from Congress, will be treasured and rewarded. This is so pervasive a desideratum in a civil servant that the distinction between line and staff activities becomes thin and artificial in the face of it. Your primary function in the hierarchy (after the protection of your own tenure) is the protection of your superior's tenure rather than the fulfillment of assigned responsibilities. (Obvious exceptions to this rule are J. Edgar Hoover and certain elements in the Department of Defense, who, like physicians and priests, respond to a higher authority.)

The third unwritten rule of federal behavior is to *make sure that all appropriated funds are spent by the end of the fiscal year*. Much of the paper that stuffs the orifices of executive desks has to do with justifications for requests for more money. For money to be returned after such justifications are approved is to imply that the requester, his supervisor and Congress itself were improvident in their demands on the taxpayer's money. It would be like a bum asking for a handout for a cup of coffee. A passerby offers a quarter and the bum returns 15¢ saying, "Coffee is only a dime, schmuck."

Contract hustlers, who abound in Washington, know that their halcyon days are in late spring when agencies are frequently panicked at the realization that they have not exhausted their operating funds and may be in the black by the fiscal year's end. Agencies that administer grant-in-aid programs celebrate end-of-fiscal-year parties with Dionysian abandon when instead of having a surplus of funds they cannot pay all of their obligations.

The only effective way to evaluate a federal program is the rapidity with which money is spent. Federal agencies, no less than purveyors of situation comedies, cigarettes and medical care, are dominated by a marketplace mentality which assumes that you have a good product if the demand exceeds the supply.

The fourth unwritten rule of behavior in government is to *keep the program alive*. It is not appropriate to question the original purposes of the program. Nor is it appropriate to ask if the program has any consonance with its original purposes. It is certainly not appropriate to assume that its purposes have been served. It is only appropriate to assume that once a program has been legislated, funded and staffed it must endure. An unstated and probably unconscious blessing of immortality is bestowed upon the titles that clutter organizational charts in federal agencies.

Congress, with its control of funds, is perceived as a nurturant breast with a supply of vital fluids that may at any time run dry and thus starve the program to death. Such a matter must be looked upon with intense ambivalence, a state of mind associated with schizophrenia in the hostile-dependent offspring. And, indeed, Congress is perceived by federal executives with a mixture of adulation and rage, and, indeed, federal programming is schizophrenic. Like the schizophrenic, federal programs have the capacity to assume pseudomorphic identities, having the outline and form of order and direction and vitality but actually being flat, autistic and encrusted with inorganic matter. Like the schizophrenic, federal programs develop a primitive narcissism that is independent of feedback from the environment other than the provision of life-sustaining funds.

Even programs that are conceived with some imagination as relatively bold and aggressive attempts to institutionalize change, such as Model Cities or Comprehensive Community Mental Health Centers or Community Action Programs, become so preoccupied with survival that compromises in the face of real or imagined criticism from Congress very quickly blunt whatever cutting edges the program may have had.

The fifth and final unwritten rule of federal behavior is to *maintain a stable and well-circumscribed constituency*. With so great a concern for survival in the government, it is necessary to have friends outside of it. One's equity within an agency and a program's equity in Congress are a function of equity with vested interests outside. The most visible and articulate vestedness is best to cultivate. Every agency and every department knows this, as does every successful executive. The constituency not only represents survival credits but has the quality of a significant reference group. The values, purposes and rewards of the federal agent must mesh with those of his program's constituents.

It is easy to see how this works between the Defense Department and the military-industrial complex; between Agriculture and the large, industrialized farming interests; between Labor and the unions; between Commerce and big business. It is obvious that the regulatory commissions of government have a friendly, symbiotic relationship with the organizations they were meant to monitor. It is less clear, however, that the good guys in government, the liberals who run the "social programs," have their exclusive constituents as well. The constituents of welfare programs are not welfare recipients, but social workers. The constituents of educational programs are not students, but educators. The constituents of health programs are the providers of health care, not their consumers. The mental health programs of the government are sensitive to the perturbations of mental health professionals and social scientists, not so much to the walking wounded.

In the latter case, for example, to suggest that nonprofessionals should have something to say about the expenditure of millions of research, training and service dollars is to threaten a constituency. And a threatened one is an unfriendly one, which is not good for the program in Congress or for the job possibilities of the executive in the marketplace. As long as the constituency is stable and circumscribed, credits can be counted.

These, then, are the rules of behavior for functionaries in the federal bureaucracy. If they sound familiar, they should. They are not by any means unique to this system. With minor alterations, they serve as the uncodified code of conduct in any organization. They are what sustained every arch-bureaucrat from Pilate to Eichmann. They explain in large part why the United States government is such a swollen beast, incapable of responding to the unmet needs of so many people.

But only in part. One other feature of the Washington scene must be described before we can say we know enough of it to elaborate a strategy of assault. This has to do with power.

There is a lot of nonsense about power in the government. One sees a black Chrysler with a vinyl top speeding by. A liveried chauffeur, determined and grim, operates the vehicle. In the rear, a gooseneck, high-intensity lamp arched over his shoulder, sits a man studying the *Washington Post*. One is tempted to say, "There goes a man of power."

It is a vain temptation. Power in the government does not reside within gray eminences in black Chryslers. It is a soft, pluralistic business shared by a large number of middle managers. Organizational charts in federal agencies read as if there is a rigid line of authority and control from the top down. It would appear that the secretary of each department with his designated assistants and deputies would control the behavior of the entire establishment. In fact, there is a huge permanent government that watches with covert bemusement as the political appointees at the top come and go, attempting in their turn to control the behavior of the agencies "responsible to them."

This does not mean that there is not a good deal of respect and deference paid by middle managers to their superiors. But, as in many organizations, this deference can have an empty and superficial quality to it that amounts to mockery. In most hospitals, for example, it is not the doctors who determine what happens to patients, but nurses. Nurses may appear as subordinate to physicians as slaves to their masters, but as soon as the doctor has left the ward the nurses does what she wants to do anyway.

Similarly, in federal agencies, it is the great army of middle managers that controls the show. There is not even the built-in accountability of a dead patient for the boss to see.

Power in the government resides less in position and funds than it does in information, which is the medium of exchange. The flow of information is controlled not at the top, but at the middle. There is very little horizontal flow between agencies because of the constant competition for funds, and all vertical flow must be mediated by the GS 14 to GS 17 bureaucrats who make up the permanent government.

This concentration of power in the middle, controlled by masses of managers who subscribe to the unwritten code of behavior described above, is the reason why the national government is essentially unresponsive. It does not respond to the top or the bottom; it does not respond to ideology. It is a great, indestructible mollusk that absorbs kicks and taunts and seductions and does nothing but grow.

But it's worse than that. The government is righteous. The people who man the bastions of the executive branch (like the rest of us) have the capacity to invest their jobs with their personal identities. Because it is theirs, their function must be defended. Their roles become, in the language of psychiatry, ego-syntonic. Their sense of personal integrity, their consciences, their self-esteem begin to grow into the positions they hold. It is as if their very identities partake of the same definition as their organizationally defined function.

Can you imagine trying to fight a revolution against a huge, righteous marshmallow? Even if you had enough troops not to be suffocated by it, the best you can hope for is to eat it. And, as you all know, you become what you eat. And that is the point. For a revolution to be meaningful it must take into account the nature of organizational life. It must assume that the ideologically pure and the ideologically impure are subject to the same Eichmannesque forces. If a revolution harbors the illusion that a reign of terror will purify a bureaucracy of scoundrels and exploiters, it will fail. It matters little whether bureaucrats are Royalist or Republican, Czarist or Bolshevik, Conservative or Liberal, or what have you. It is the built-in forces of life in a bureaucracy that result in the bureaucracy being so indifferent to suffering and aspiration.

Does this mean that radical change is not possible? No. It means that intelligence and planning must be used, as well as rhetoric, songs, threats, uniforms and all the other trappings of a "movement." The intelligence and planning might orient themselves around a concept of nonalienated revolution that relies on a strategy of guerrilla administration.

This is not meant to be an exclusive strategy. Social change, radical and otherwise, has to be a pluralistic phenomenon. It needs to allow for foxes as well as hedgehogs. This represents one attempt, then, to approach the Great White Marshmallow in such a way that victories are neither impossible nor terrible.

Assuming that power in the federal government is controlled by a vast cadre of middle managers who are essentially homeostatic, and assuming the softness and purposelessness of the system in which they operate, it is conceivable that a critical mass of change agents working within that system may be effective in achieving increasingly significant ad hoc successes.

This requires a group of people who are prepared to work as civil servants but who have little or no concern with the five unwritten rules of behavior of such service. Specifically, their investment in their own jobs carries a very limited liability. The ultimate sanction, being fired, is no sanction at all. Either because they command credentials which will afford them the security they need wherever they work or because they emerge from a generation that has not been tainted by the depression and so have fewer security needs, they are not afraid of being fired.

While they may like the boss, and one may hope they do, they do not see themselves as primarily concerned with saving him from embarrassment.

Spending the program money by the end of the fiscal year and the related rule—keeping the program alive—are significant to them only insofar as the program's purposes mesh with their social consciences, and then only insofar as the program is demonstrating some fealty to those purposes.

Most important, however, is that this critical mass of change agents *not* abide by the rule of maintaining a stable and circumscribed constituency. This is at the same time a liberating principle of behavior and a major strategy of change. It is precisely by broadening the base of the constituencies of federal programs that they will become more responsible to the needs of more people.

This network of communication and collaboration shares as its purpose the frustration of the bureaucracy. But it is the homeostatic, self-serving and elitist aspects of bureaucratic life that are to be frustrated. And this can only be accomplished through the creative tension that emerges from a constant appreciation of unmet needs.

The network of change agents represents a built-in amplifier of those needs either because the agents are, themselves, among the poor, the colored and the young or because they are advocates of them.

It is not critical that the guerrilla administrators who compromise this network be in a position to command funds or program directions. They must simply have access to information, which, you recall, is the medium of exchange in government.

This network, in order to avoid the same traps as the bureaucracy it is meant to frustrate, should never become solidified or rigidified in structure and function. It may have the form of a floating crap game whose location and participation are fluid and changing, but whose purposes and activities are constant. The contacts should remain informal, nonhierarchical and task-oriented. The tasks chosen should be finite, specific, salient and feasible. The makeup of each task force is an ad hoc, self-selected clustering of individuals whose skills or location or access to information suggests their roles. This network of change agents becomes a reference group, but not a brotherhood. There need not be a preoccupation with loyalty, cordiality or steadfastness. They do not even have to be friendly.

This is a rather dry and unromantic strategy of social change. It does not stir one's heart or glands. Where is the image of Parnell pulling his cap low on his forehead as he points his gallant band to the General Post Office? Or Lenin approaching the borders of a trembling Russia in a sealed train? Or Fidel or Che? Or Spartacus, or Mao? Where are the clasped hands and the eyes squinting into a distant line of troops? Where are the songs, the flags, the legends? Where is the courage? Where is the glory?

Such a revolutionary force has nothing of the triumphal arch in it. Nor has it anything of the gallows. It lives without the hope of victory or the fear of defeat. It will yearn for saints and despair of scoundrels, but it will see as its eternal mission the subversion of those systems that force both saints and scoundrels into a common, faceless repression of the human spirit.

Discussion Questions

1. Review the author's list of causes for bureaucratic inefficiency.

2. Review the author's proposed reforms.

MELVIN SEEMAN

Antidote to Alienation:
Learning to Belong

Alienation is a popular term that is commonly used in such phrases as "alienation from politics," "alienation from the system," and "alienation from society." The subject of alienation has been discussed by nineteenth-century social scientists who warned against the evils of industrialization, urbanization, and the development of a massive, faceless society. More recently, however, sociologists have tried to explain the specific social conditions underlying alienation from work when individuals become dissatisfied and alienated in reaction to the monotony, boredom, inflexible rules, lack of opportunity, overbearing bosses, and powerlessness of their occupations. The following article is one such study. Moreover, this article offers a prescription to remedy the alienation: learning to belong.

Most of us in the United States now live in the great, faceless conglomerates of population—the large metropolitan areas with their strung-out suburban belts—where who one's neighbors are is largely a matter of accident, and it usually doesn't pay to get closely involved with them, because they keep changing. Parents and children are close—perhaps even closer than before—as long as they live in the same house; but older generations and other relatives drift away, take jobs in other cities, go to retirement homes, have their own interests and associates. Often, it seems painful but realistic to conclude that, in the last analysis, you and your family are alone, and the only ones you can really count on for help and support are yourselves. No one else cares.

The American legend has it that not much more than a generation ago it used to be very different. Our fathers lived, mostly, in a golden age of belonging, in the traditional tree-shaded small town or closely-knit neighborhood (complete with the *Saturday Evening Post* version of a colonial-style church at the end of the block). Everyone was friendly and solicitous, and, in the case of need, neighbors by the tens and cousins by the dozens would come running.

For most of us, this dream, to the extent that it ever was real, is dead.

It is the dominant theme of "mass theory" in social psychology that such social and personal ties cannot be cut or seriously weakened without major damage—both to us and to the democratic process. Torn loose from so many of our emotional supports and roots—from the guidelines that remind us who we are and what we are worth—we must, so the theme goes, become prey increasingly to feelings of isolation, helplessness, and alienation.

But a theme is not yet a theory. It becomes a theory by being specific about processes—by describing the step-by-step development from cause to effect. How do the feelings of isolation, helplessness, and alienation come about, and what is their consequence? Mass theory becomes useful when it combines (1) history and social structure with (2) a description of the psychological effects of that structure, those alienative effects that, in turn, lead to (3) predicted behavior. *Alienation* is the center and the key to mass theory—it is produced by the structure of society, and it produces distinctive behavior.

To describe this process in greater detail:

- *Historically and structurally,* the old roots and close relationships have practically disappeared and have been replaced by anonymity and impersonality in social and personal life and by bureaucracy and mechanization at work.
- *Psychologically,* this must result in *alienation*. Alienation can take a number of forms: feelings of powerlessness, rootlessness, lack of standards and beliefs, and "self-estrangement" (having no clear idea of your personality or place, not even "belonging" to yourself).
- Alienation, in turn, results in *alienated behavior,* such as political passivity, racial and religious prejudice, taking part in movements that promise to usher in the millenium (but have little immediate or practical effects), and the like.

Since personal alienation is the key element, psychological theory is crucial to its understanding. In trying to understand and explain these psychological processes, I have found the social-learning theory of Julian B. Rotter very helpful (*Social Learning and Clinical Psychology,* Prentice-Hall, 1954). Rotter's principal contention is that human behavior depends on (1) the degree to which a person *expects* that the behavior will have a successful outcome, and (2) the *value* of that success to the person trying to achieve it. If these factors are powerful, separately or together, the behavior is most likely to occur. Specifically, if a person expects that learning something will help him achieve some goal, or he values that goal, he is more likely to learn.

Rotter's theory helps clarify the different meanings of alienation. Let us concentrate on what is probably the most important aspect of alienation in mass society—feelings of *powerlessness,* a person's belief that there is little he can do to bring about what he wants. People conceive of success and failure as being not only due to *external* factors—those that work on a man essentially from the outside and are usually considered beyond his control (luck, fate, "city hall," or "they")—but also *internal* factors, coming from within, which often do give him some control (skills, motives, determination, work).

Rotter and his co-workers argue that most experimental studies in learning usually unwittingly emphasize *external* control—the experimenter himself controls most of the pressures and conditions of the situation, and the subject is really not independent at all. If the subject could feel that he had some personal control over the learning, could relate it to his own needs and self-respect, then the patterns and amounts of learning might be very different.

A number of recent studies have supported this principle. These studies show that, when the same learning task is performed in two separate ways, with two sets of instructions—one, for instance, emphasizing the skill and energy required from the learner, and the other stressing the luck or chance aspect of the task (*internal* versus *external* control)—there are striking differences in learning and retention. A person will definitely learn *less* from experiences he conceives to be dominated by others, or by chance, which he feels he cannot influence.

This finding parallels the argument of the followers of mass theory that the isolated individual in "the lonely crowd," subordinated to, and intimidated by, bureaucracy, becomes convinced of his powerlessness and gives up learning about those things that might affect his future. As a specific example, he becomes apathetic and indifferent to politics—"You can't fight city hall."

Thus, mass-society theory and Rotter's social-learning theory agree that those persons with greater feelings of powerlessness will not learn as much or as well as those who feel they exercise some control over the factors that influence their lives.

The statement that feelings of powerlessness inhibit knowledge is a basic conclusion about human beings. If true, it should be true not only of a few people but of many; not only of those in our country but in other nations as well. It should be true not only about one type of learning but throughout a wide spectrum of learning situations. Providing always, of course, that the learning is *relevant to control*—that it seems to the learner to be giving him a tool he can use to change his condition. Thus, an unemployed man learning how and where best to apply for a job is acquiring *control-relevant* information—while one learning baseball batting averages is not. The alienated can presumably learn escapist and irrelevant information as quickly as anyone—perhaps more quickly.

To test the hypothesis that the connection between feelings of powerlessness and inhibition of learning was generally true of mankind, we conducted several studies on powerlessness and alienation:

- in different institutions (a hospital and a reformatory);
- with different degrees of belonging to a work organization (unorganized versus unionized workers in Columbus, Ohio);
- and in different nations (Sweden and the United States).

Although specific items used in the several studies (hospital, reformatory, Columbus, and Sweden) varied somewhat, in all cases the person was offered a choice between an expression of mastery and one of powerlessness. For example:

- "Many times I feel that I have little influence over the things that happen to me," or, "I do not believe that chance and luck are very important in my life";
- "Becoming a success is a matter of hard work; luck has little or nothing to do with it," or, "Getting a job depends mainly on being in the right place at the right time."

The study of the hospital, published by John W. Evans and myself in the *American Sociological Review* (1962), and of the reformatory in *American Journal of Sociology* (1963), may be considered as a pair. They were both done in the United States. They sought to find out how feelings of powerlessness are related to lack of knowledge and information, in places where knowledge and information might give the individual some understanding and control of his fate. The hospital study dealt with tuberculosis patients; we found that those with the strongest feelings of powerlessness knew less about health matters than those not so alienated. In the reformatory study, inmates with greater feelings of helplessness learned relatively little when given information about parole, even though it might have helped shorten their confinement.

A third American study with Arthur G. Neal (*American Sociological Review*, 1964), was designed to test whether, as predicted, members of a formal occupational organization, such as a union or professional association, would feel less powerless than nonmembers. In form and feeling (if not always in fact) joining a vocational association apparently dedicated to a common goal should give a member some feeling of control over his job destiny and perhaps over broader socio-economic matters as well. Mass theory postulates that the great centers of power—government and the major corporations—are rapidly increasing in size and impersonality. At the same time, and as a consequence, jobs are becoming more specialized, more interchangeable, and the workers are moving more and more from job to job and city to city. This breakdown of personal identification with his work is supposed to make the worker feel more insignificant, expendable, and isolated ("just another cog"). The labor organizations that mediate between him and the great bureaucracies should therefore become more and more important to him, especially as a means of providing him with some sense of control.

Organized for Power

We picked at random about 800 adult male names from the Columbus, Ohio, city directory, and mailed questionnaires to them designed to explore this relationship between union membership and feelings of powerlessness. About 57 per cent answered—245 manual workers and 216 nonmanuals.

The results of the Columbus study were definite. When factors such as age, income, education, and type of job are equal, unorganized workers *do* feel more powerless. This was true of both manual and nonmanual workers. (The powerlessness was a little greater for workers who changed jobs most often.) Further, these results were *specific* to powerlessness; that is, a test of the workers' generalized unhappiness (anomie) showed that the unorganized do not feel significantly more despairing about everything (or even most things) than the organized—it is apparently a rather specific sense of *mastery,* but not of well-being in general, that organization membership provides.

On the basis of the Columbus study, we could state that feelings of powerlessness do arise among unorganized workers in the United States. But a further demonstration seemed necessary, one that could combine all three elements—organization, powerlessness, and knowledge—into a single study; that could show whether these findings were peculiar to America; and that could concentrate on a broader field than health or corrections—the field of politics and international affairs.

Accordingly, a study was designed for Sweden to fulfill these needs and was carried out by interview (in Swedish) with a sample of the male work force in Malmo. (Malmo is Sweden's third largest ctiy, population about 240,000, with a heavy concentration of commercial and seaport occupations.) A random sample of males aged twenty to seventy-nine was drawn from the official register maintained by government authorities. A total of 558 workers were interviewed.

The interview contained questions on three major variables:

- *Feelings of powerlessness:* (The individual's expectations of control), proffering the usual choice between items expressing mastery and powerlessness.
- *Organization membership:* Apart from simple membership in a union or other work organization, evidence was gathered on (1) the person's *degree* of participation and (2) his *involvement* in organizations outside of work.
- *Political knowledge:* A sixteen-item information test dealt with both Swedish politics and international affairs.

When the Swedish data had been collected, checked, and evaluated, the differences were found to be consistently and significantly as predicted: *High feelings of powerlessness and low political knowledge were found together among the unorganized workers.* Second, there was a relatively small but predictable difference between those who were officials and those who were simply members of unions.

Master of the Political Ship

These results are clearly consistent with the learning- and mass-society theses. But, before they can be accepted without question, other complicating factors must be eliminated. What about education? Could differences in education be the real underlying cause of the differences in feelings of powerlessness? What about other factors, such as age or job prestige? A close examination of the data, correcting for education and other elements, makes the result even more emphatic. In Sweden, as in the United States, neither education nor other differences obliterated the trend. High powerlessness among the workers appeared to flow from lack of union membership and was intimately related to low political knowledge.

The officers of unions were shown to have the lowest feelings of powerlessness and to be highest in political knowledge. But was this due to the fact that they were *officers* and, therefore, a special kind of member (and also, perhaps, a special breed of cat with different personality characteristics); or was it primarily because they were more involved—"more engaged" —in the affairs of the union and, therefore, more capable of exerting control? Would other "more engaged" members (who were nonofficers) also be less alienated and have greater capacity for learning control-relevant information?

"Engaged" members, we decided, would be those who attended meetings regularly, considered the union to be important in their lives, and thought individual members were important and influential in the union. Pitting the scores of such rank-and-file members against the "less engaged," we found a parallel with the over-all comparison of organized versus unorganized workers. The relationship is modest but consistent: The greater the personal involvement in union meetings and affairs, the less the feelings of powerlessness; and, for the manual workers (who would generally tend to have less education), involvement and amount of political knowledge go together as well. (This picture calls to mind the old socialist ideal of the politically wise proletarian who spent much time in study and discussion of the political and economic factors that controlled his life and then organized to do something about them.)

We found, too, that the person's *interest* in political affairs is part of the same picture. Of course, those with more interest in politics have greater knowledge of it; but more important here is the fact that strong feelings of powerlessness go along with low interest. Those who do not feel mastery do not develop interest and do not learn.

This interest, or lack of it, is directly related to union membership—to belonging to an organization that could exert job control. Organized workers were significantly more interested in political affairs than the nonunion workers. And this interest, again, was *specific* to what we call *control-relevant* information. The unorganized were *not* totally withdrawn or apathetic; they were just as interested as the organized workers in personal and local affairs and in discussing their work. But the unorganized felt powerless to control their larger destinies—and politics and international affairs represented these larger destinies.

So far, these conclusions agree with both learning theory and mass theory. Men with little hope for success feel powerless; lose interest in, and have difficulty learning, control-relevant information.

However, it must be recalled that Rotter's learning theory made a distinction between a person's *expectation* that he can achieve a goal and the *value* he places on that goal. Theoretically, at least, a person will not try very earnestly for a goal he does not value, no matter how sure he is he can get it; contrariwise, he may try very hard, even with little hope of achievement, if he wants the goal badly enough.

In the American reformatory study, knowledge that might have helped the inmate have some control over his future (parole information) and non-control knowledge (descriptive information about the institution) were both offered to the inmates tested. We split the subjects into two groups—those who tended to conform to what prison authorities wanted of them, who seemed to value the officially approved goals and behavior set for them (working hard, obeying regulations, making no trouble, trying to meet parole requirements), and those who would not conform. We reasoned that, if the inmate did not value parole (as part of the prison system) very highly, then whether or not he believed he could achieve it was not very important in determining whether he would learn parole information; however, if he did value parole, his expectation (or lack of it) that he could determine his own life should affect how much he would study and learn about parole. The results were consistent with this view: Generally, those inmates who valued the conventional standards of how to get ahead in the reformatory world, who "conformed," learned more of the parole information than did the "unconventionals." But even in this conforming group, those who felt powerless learned less. We may conclude, then, that both the *value* of the goal and the *expectation* of achieving it will be reflected in how much learning a man will acquire that relates to the goal.

Rising Expectations

Summarizing the over-all conclusions of all four studies:

- *Powerlessness and organization:* A person's feelings of self-reliance and power are tied up with whether he belongs to an organization that has some control over his occupational destiny. If he does belong to such an organization—union, business, or professional association—his further feelings of mastery are directly tied up with how actively he works in it—whether he has some control over *its* destiny.

- *Powerlessness and learning:* The ability to learn and retain knowledge that has some connection with control over an individual's future (politics, parole, or health information) is also directly affected by belonging to a union or other relevant organization, and to a person's alienation. To the extent that he feels powerless to affect his future, he will not learn as well what he needs to know to affect it. And he will not be as interested in it—he may even reject it.

  To the degree that he *expects* to achieve his goal, he will attend to the associated learning; to the degree that he *values* the goal, he will also be oriented to learn.

- The connection between organization membership and powerlessness holds true from nation to nation—it is as true in Sweden, for example, as in the United States.

- The connection between powerlessness and learning holds true through many different kinds of organizations (reformatories, hospitals, unions) and many different kinds of control information (parole and health information, politics, international affairs).

These studies are perhaps more important for what they promise than for what they presently accomplish. The promise is that controlled studies of this kind, carried out in various cultures and settings, can establish the validity of arguments and theories about contemporary life that depend upon the idea of alienation. There is much literature of this kind, both inside and outside of social science; and it deals with a wide range of subjects—for example, mass movements, intergroup prejudice, mass communication, and politics. It is a literature that touches a powerful array of basic human values: normlessness and trust, meaninglessness and understanding, self-estrangement and integrity.

The promise is that we can concern ourselves with such large questions about the individual in modern society and test long-held theories that have highly practical consequences—learning what it really means, under various circumstances, to exert control, to sink roots, to find understanding, or even to be oneself.

Discussion Questions

1. Give a brief review to the author's prescription for remedying alienation.
2. This article discusses two kinds of powerlessness. Review them and the author's suggestions to remedy them.

12 / Social Class and Social Mobility

"No—I can't remember if we got a card from the Coles last year! Why?"

A basic ethos of American society is "that all men are created equal." The belief in a classless society would appear to be supported by recent research which has shown that over 90 per cent of Americans identified themselves somewhere in the broad range of the middle class. Recent research also indicates, however, that most Americans are aware of a class structure and that "some are more equal than others." Researchers have concluded, therefore, that many Americans misperceive their social position within the class structure. Awareness by Americans of a class structure is also indicated by the terms commonly used to differentiate and distinguish individuals and groups—for example: "jet set," "social climber," "the wrong side of the tracks," "rich and poor," and the "establishment."

Just as a student is ranked according to grades, and a professor according to his teaching and research skills, so are individuals and families of modern society ranked according to their wealth, power, and prestige. In fact all known societies have developed a system of *social stratification* whereby individuals and families are ranked into categories, strata, or social classes according to their share of "scarce commodities." *Social class,* therefore, can be viewed as a classification of individuals and families who share a common position in a system of stratification. As a result, sociologists have classified families by concepts such as "upper-middle class," and "lower-middle class," or "blue-collar" and "white-collar" workers. While such classifications suffer from shortcomings and are not acceptable to all sociologists, they do assist us in dealing with differences in life-style that result from the unequal distribution of wealth, power, and prestige.

Sociologists have also identified the factors that contribute to an individual's social class: (1) family prestige; (2) occupation or profession; (3) possession of wealth; (4) possession of power; (5) educational background and achievement; (6) possession of leisure; (7) location of residence and standard of living; (8) taste preferences; (9) identification and acceptance. It should be noted from this list that an individual's social class is based as much on nonrational factors as it is on objective factors.

An individual's social class has been found to be especially significant because of its overwhelming influence on his way of life. It influences his values, attitudes, and colors his personality and informal mode of behavior. Social class also determines life opportunities, assigns social responsibilities, defines the conventional morality, and explains group differences often simplistically assigned to race, religion, and ethnic differences.

An individual may move to higher or lower social class by the process of *social mobility*. The history of the United States with its expanding economy and relatively low reproduction rates has been characterized by a steady increase in the percentages of individuals enjoying a greater distribution of wealth, power, and prestige. The children and grandchildren of European immigrants have gained political power, wealth, and prestige. The percentage of Americans living below the poverty line has dropped by more than half since 1947. Such gains toward equality, however, should not hide the fact that social mobility has eluded many Americans. Members of certain racial, ethnic, and religious groups have often experienced little if any mobility. Mobility is also hampered by the demands for specialization, the rigid education requirements of many high-level professions, and economic recessions, which influence the supply and demand for labor.

SHEILA K. JOHNSON

Sociology of Christmas Cards

History is replete with examples of class attitudes and prejudice. Human beings, it seems, have long been preoccupied with their social standing. In this context it must be remembered that status and prestige require at least two persons: one to claim it and another to recognize it. Claims to prestige are usually based on such considerations as property, birth, occupation, and education. Actually, almost anything can be used to distinguish one person from another. As Sheila K. Johnson has concluded, even Christmas cards can serve as the basis for claims to prestige and status.

Anyone who has ever composed a Christmas card list has pondered the inclusion and exclusion of names on the basis of a variety of fairly explicit considerations. Shall I send so-and-so a card this year, since he didn't send me

Reprinted from Sheila K. Johnson, "Sociology of Christmas Cards," *Society*, Vol. 8, No. 3 (Jan. 1971). Copyright © 1971 by Transaction Inc. Reprinted with permission.

one last year? Or, I *must* send so-and-so a card this year, even though he probably won't send me one, because I want to be remembered by him. Like the decisions we make about whom to vote for, we like to think of these choices as purely individual, rational matters. Nevertheless, sociologists have demonstrated that, regardless of how and why we choose a candidate, voting behavior can be analyzed as a function of one's socioeconomic status, mobility aspirations, ethnicity and religious affiliation. Similarly, it seems likely that the patterns in which people send and receive Christmas cards can also be explained in terms of certain social characteristics, especially their social status and mobility aspirations.

This proposition first occurred to me several years ago, as I was opening some Christmas cards and noticed that there was a strange disjunction between the cards we were receiving and the ones we had sent out. About half of the cards we received were from people to whom we had also sent cards, but the other half came from people to whom we had not sent cards and to whom we had had no intention of sending cards, and we ourselves had sent half of our cards to people from whom we had not expected to receive (and did not receive) a card in return. When I studied the names that fell into each of these three categories, it dawned on me that the people with whom we had exchanged cards reciprocally were either relatives or people with whom we were on an equal social footing—professional friends of my husband or personal friends in different but nevertheless comparable occupations. The cards we had sent but to which we had received no reply, I discovered, went invariably to individuals whom *we* wanted to cultivate—people with regard to whom we were, in sociological terms, "upwardly mobile," such as professional acquaintances who might someday prove useful or important or social acquaintances whom we wished we knew better. By the same token, the cards we received and to which we did not reply came from individuals who wanted to cultivate us—some of my husband's graduate students and office employees, the liquor store, the hairdresser and foreign scholars who obviously expected to visit the United States at some time in the future.

In order to test out my theory I telephoned several friends shortly after Christmas and asked them to sort the cards they had received into two piles—reciprocals and those to whom they had not sent cards—and also to count up the number of cards they had sent "upward." (Some of the incensed replies to this request would indicate that the nature of Christmas card sending is a very touchy subject indeed.) Those of my friends who continued to speak to me and who complied with my request corroborated my theory. Several couples in their late thirties or early forties who, although in different professions, were rather similar to ourselves in their mobility aspirations and in the number of people they knew who were upwardly mobile with regard to them found that their Christmas cards could be grouped into equal thirds (one-third sent and not received, one-third sent and received and one-third received but not sent). However, a young graduate student reported that about

70 percent of his cards were reciprocal, with 30 percent sent upward and none received from people who were trying to curry favor with him. This is clearly the pattern for those with their foot on the bottom rung of the status ladder. At the other end, several retired people reported that 90 percent of their cards were reciprocal, with only 5 percent sent upward and 5 percent received from people who still regarded them as important. A man who had retired but taken a second job, however, reported that 70 percent of his cards were reciprocal but that 10 percent had been sent upward and 20 percent had come from people trying to cultivate him.

While the percentages of cards an individual sends and receives tell us a good deal about his mobility aspirations, the fact that he sends Christmas cards at all places him rather firmly in the middle class. Members of the upper class—particularly a closed upper class to which one gains admission by birth rather than through the acquisition of wealth—have no need to send cards upward, and sending cards to other members of the upper class is a formality that many are dispensing with. In England, for example, it is increasingly common for upper-class families to place an ad in the personal columns of the London *Times* stating that Lord and Lady So-and-So send warm greetings to all their friends for Christmas and the New Year as they will not be sending cards. (Several years ago an upper-class English wit poked fun at these ads by placing one asking *his* friends to send him Christmas cards as he would not be able to read the *Times* columns during December.) In the United States, because the upper class is more fluid than in England, and because the country is simply too large for all one's upper-class friends to read the same daily newspaper, the custom of sending cards among upper-class individuals has not died out. One would predict, however, that most of the private card sending of the upper class is reciprocal and that only its business Christmas cards are sent upward, since there is always room for upward mobility in the business world.

Lower-class and working-class individuals also send few or no Christmas cards, but for entirely different reasons. Sociologists have demonstrated that lower- and working-class individuals tend to rely upon tightly knit family networks and neighbors for their friendships and that they are less geographically mobile than the middle class. Thus a skilled union man will probably have a large number of relatives living in the same town or same general area as he does, and he will be on friendly terms with many of his neighbors. There is no need to send these people Christmas cards, however, since he sees them nearly every day. He may be upwardly mobile in terms of his job, but this is handled by the union, and a Christmas card to the front office is not likely to do the trick. Only if he is upwardly mobile to the extent of trying to leave his stratum and become a white-collar worker may he take to sending Christmas cards to people who can help him. In that case he may adopt other middle-class behavior patterns, such as joining various clubs and lodges, in which he will make a broader range of friends to whom he will also want to send cards at Christmas.

Senders and Recipients

It is the middle class—particularly the upper middle class, consisting of high managerial and professional people—who are the Christmas card senders par excellence. These are the people who are both geographically and socially mobile—growing up in one place, going to college somewhere else and then moving about as success in one's firm or profession seems to dictate. Kinship ties tend to be far-flung and tenuous, since it would not be advantageous to be tied down to a given area by one's aging parents or embarrassed by the sudden appearance of a lower-class cousin. Friendships are formed among social equals—at school, at work, in professional or social organizations—but these, too, change as one moves up the ladder of success or to a different section of the country. Such are the ideal conditions for the exchange of Christmas cards. Friends and relatives are scattered widely, but one wants to keep "in touch," and there are vast sources of upward mobility to be tapped.

I realize that some people will object strenuously to this analysis of their Christmas card sending and receiving. While I was attempting to collect data on the subject, several of my friends declined to cooperate on the grounds that they did not fit into the pattern I had just described to them. "Really," one of them said self-righteously, "I keep an up-to-date Christmas list, and the only people I send cards to are people who send me cards. There is no upward sending or downward receiving in our family; it's strictly reciprocal." This is pure propaganda, nurtured by the myth of absolute social equality that exists in this country. Everyone can think of some acquaintances to whom he simply *has* to send cards, regardless of whether he gets one in return. The obligatory nature of the act is the real tip-off to the social pressures at work. As for people who receive cards they were not expecting—that is, cards being sent upwards to them—and who then shamefacedly rush out on Christmas Eve to mail the forgotten sender one of theirs, they are simply insecure in their status position. Imagine the president of Chase Manhattan Bank receiving a Christmas card from the janitor and saying remorsefully, "Oh, my God, and I didn't send *him* one." Yet thousands of people do roughly the same thing when they receive a card from someone who looks up to them. What should they do instead? The answer is nothing, except sit back and enjoy it. Of course, if the upward sender shows other indications of increased social status, it might be wise to send him a Christmas card next year, but that would depend on circumstances ranging far beyond the scope of this article.

In a recent film, "Diary of a Mad Housewife," the husband is shown counting the family's Christmas cards and remarking to his wife "One-hundred-and-fifty-three. That's fine. Three more weeks to go until Christmas and we've already reached the half-way mark . . . We sent out 300." He then goes on to instruct his wife to note carefully who has sent cards to them, since there's "no point" in sending cards the following year to people who have not sent them one this year. Here the authors of the film have missed a bet, however, since the husband is depicted as a social climber of the first water who would clearly insist on sending Christmas cards to certain "important" people—the same people whom he invites to his abysmal party and tries to cultivate in other ways.

In addition to scrutinizing the number of Christmas cards people send and receive for signs of social status and mobility aspirations, one can also tell a good deal about the personality of the sender by the kind of card he chooses. There may still be a few rare individuals who choose every Christmas card individually to suit the *recipient* but for the most part those days went out with the advent of boxed cards. Somewhat more common is the tendency for people with two radically different constituencies—for example, businessmen who keep their business and private acquaintances well compartmentalized—to choose two different sets of cards. However, in such cases it is not at all clear whether the two sets of cards are chosen to suit the different sets of recipients or to reflect the different personality that the businessman wishes to convey to each group—sober and elegant cards for his business acquaintances and mod, swingerish cards for his personal friends. In general one may assume that cards reflect the sender rather than the reciever, and that a Madison Avenue executive would no more receive a museum card from his Aunt Emma in Vermont than he would send her a Hallmark Santa Claus with a rhymed poem inside.

How can one classify some of the cards that people consciously or subconsciously select to convey not only their Christmas wishes but also their personality? Among university types, whom I know best, there seem to be several distinct patterns. Well-established WASP professors tend to send museum cards or rather small studio cards of abstract design. Usually, the more powerful the professor, the smaller the card. (This appears to be a snobbish, willful inversion of the usual business pattern: the more important the executive, the bigger and more lavish the card. An academic friend argues that there are exceptions to this rule and cites Professor Henry Kissinger, from whom last year he received an absolutely gigantic Christmas card portraying both sides of the globe. I would maintain, however, that this Christmas card merely illustrates Professor Kissinger's defection from the academic ranks and his adoption of the big-business ethos of the Nixon administration.) Jewish and youngish, slightly left-of-center professors tend to send UNICEF cards, often choosing a design that reflects their area of academic interest—India specialists send the Indian-designed card, Africa specialists send the African-designed card and so forth. A similar tendency may be observed among government officials.

From professors who have (or think they have) artistic wives we get hand-screened, hand-blocked or otherwise handcrafted Christmas cards. From professors who have just had their first child we get (you guessed it) baby photographs, and from professors who are doing research abroad we often get photos of their children in native dress. From professors abroad sans children, or from those who've been there before, we get interesting Chinese, Japanese or Thai renderings of the nativity. (The most fascinating Thai card we ever received, from a high-ranking Thai army officer, was a photograph of the gentleman himself posed proudly beside his now Jaguar XKE. *Joyeux Noel* indeed!)

People with strong political convictions tend to remind us of these at Christmas time. Thus we get our share of CORE and CND cards. From less political but equally morally outraged friends we get a strange assortment of messages: cards that say on them "printed by spastics" or "designed by the deaf" and cards depicting felled redwood trees or oil-stained beaches. From our wealthier, nonacademic friends we get cards supporting the Symphony Association and the Junior League.

In addition to all of these types of cards, we get, every year, a couple of photographs of houses. These are never from the academic world—although some professors I know live in very nice houses—because the houses displayed on Christmas cards have a special status significance. Most of the houses that I have seen on Christmas cards belonged to friends who had just retired to Florida or Hawaii, or they were the dream-come-true of people who had finally bought that acre in the country. Whatever the occasion, the house depicted is usually the visible sign of a major change in social status, and it is certainly no accident that the president's Christmas card almost always features the White House.

Finally, and perhaps hardest of all to pin down sociologically, there is the category of Christmas card known as the mimeographed Christmas letter. I would like to hold a contest sometime for the most fatuous Christmas letter, but I'm afraid I'd be deluged with entries. It is hard to attribute the Christmas letter to a particular type of person or a particular station in life, because almost everyone who has ever had an eventful year, taken an exciting trip, or accomplished a great deal has felt the urge to compose one. I have received them from internationally famous professors who were attempting to describe their world travels, from graduate students describing their Ph.D. research in the field and from relatives recounting the latest family gossip. Perhaps mimeographed Christmas letters should be used as a vanity indicator, since they expose those among us who yielded to, rather than resisted, the pervasive temptation to blow one's own horn.

A Matter of Tone

The chief defect of the Christmas letter is its tone—that peculiar half-personal, half-distant note that makes most of them sound as if they were addressed to mentally defective 13-year-olds. This tone is the inevitable result of trying to address a single letter to a score or more of different friends. As any letter writer knows, one usually manipulates the tone of a letter to convey a certain personal image to a specific correspondent. If it is often difficult to send the same *card* to business as well as personal acquaintances because of the image to be conveyed to each group, how much more difficult to compose a letter that will ring true to a variety of recipients.

Not only is the tone of Christmas letters muddled by the lack of a clearly defined recipient, but it also often lacks the unifying voice of a single sender. Most Christmas cards can convey the status and life style of a couple or a family as readily as they can those of an individual. But this is because cards deal in visual symbols, whereas letters traffic in words. It is always hard to believe that a mimeographed letter from "Betty and Bob" is really a joint verbal product, and so one looks for telltale "I's" and "he's" or "she's" to pin down the author. In a genuine Christmas letter, however, such slips never occur, and one is left to figure out for himself who is being the more sanctimonious from sentences that announce: "While Bob worked like a demon interviewing local politicians and village chiefs, Betty spent her time learning how to cook native dishes and teaching English to some of the wives and children." (For the full effect, one must try substituting "I" for each of the proper nouns in turn.)

There are doubtless still other sociological and psychological facets to the sending and receiving of Christmas cards. However, having said all this, I would not want readers to conclude that I am trying to denigrate Christmas cards or that I personally am above sending them. Far from it. Having already passed through my family photograph, foreign and UNICEF phases, I may even succumb to sending a Christmas letter one of these years. My card this year was a small, high-status museum number depicting a medieval knight being hoisted on his own petard. The motto on his banner reads: *Honi soit qui mal y pense.* I think it suits me rather well.

Discussion Questions

1. State Sheila Johnson's hypothesis for her "Christmas card study." From what she says, is this a scientific sociological study? Discuss.
2. Review your own last Christmas card sendings and receivings. Does your experience confirm or disconfirm Mrs. Johnson's findings?
3. What do the last three sentences of this article tell you about this Christmas card study?

WALTER E. SCHAFER, CAROL OLEXA, KENNETH POLK

Programmed for Social Class: Tracking in High School

Virtually everybody in America believes that a "good education" is absolutely essential to obtain the "good" things of life and to experience

Reprinted from Walter E. Schafer, Carol Olexa, and Kenneth Polk, "Programmed for Social Class: Tracking in High School," *Society,* Vol. 7, No. 2 (Oct. 1970). Copyright © 1970 by Transaction Inc. Reprinted with permission.

upward social mobility. However, contrary to popular belief, the schools of our nation do not create social mobility. Mobility is determined largely by the attitudes of the family and the economic-political factors of the larger society, which provides job opportunities.

These factors have generally assigned each child to a class position before he or she even graduates from high school. The following article provides evidence that describes exactly how the "tracking system" of American high schools not only *prevents* social mobility but also helps to *maintain* the existing social divisions.

If, as folklore would have it, America is the land of opportunity, offering anyone the chance to raise himself purely on the basis of his or her ability, then education is the key to self-betterment. The spectacular increase in those of us who attend school is often cited as proof of the great scope of opportunity that our society offers: 94 per cent of the high school age population was attending school in 1967, as compared to 7 per cent in 1890.

Similarly, our educational system is frequently called more democratic than European systems, for instance, which rigidly segregate students by ability early in their lives, often on the basis of nationally administered examinations, such as England's "11-plus." The United States, of course, has no official national policy of educational segregation. Our students, too, are tested and retested throughout their lives and put into faster or slower classes or programs on the basis of their presumed ability, but this procedure is carried out in a decentralized fashion that varies between each city or state.

However, many critics of the American practice claim that, no matter how it is carried out, it does not meet the needs of the brighter and duller groups, so much as it solidifies and widens the differences between them. One such critic, the eminent educator Kenneth B. Clark, speculates: "It is conceivable that the detrimental effects of segregation based upon intellect are similar to the known detrimental effects of schools segregated on the basis of class, nationality, or race."

Patricia Cayo Sexton notes that school grouping based on presumed ability often reinforces already existing social divisions:

> Children from higher social strata usually enter the "higher quality" groups and those from lower strata the "lower" ones. School decisions about a child's ability will greatly influence the kind and quality of education he receives, as well as his future life, including whether he goes to college, the job he will get, and his feelings about himself and others.

And Arthur Pearl puts it bluntly:

> . . . "special ability classes," "basic track," or "slow learner classes" are various names for another means of systematically denying the poor adequate access to education.

In this article, we will examine some evidence bearing on this vital question of whether current educational practices tend to reinforce existing social class divisions. We will also offer an alternative aimed at making our public schools more effective institutions for keeping open the opportunities for social mobility.

Education Explosion

Since the turn of the century, a number of trends have converged to increase enormously the pressure on American adolescents to graduate from high school: declining opportunity in jobs, the upgrading of educational requirements for job entry, and the diminishing needs for teen-agers to contribute to family income. While some school systems, especially in the large cities, have adapted to this vast increase in enrollment by creating separate high schools for students with different interests, abilities, or occupational goals, most communities have developed comprehensive high schools serving all the youngsters within a neighborhood or community.

In about half the high schools in the United States today, the method for handling these large and varied student populations is through some form of tracking system. Under this arrangement, the entire student body is divided into two or more relatively distinct career lines, or tracks, with such titles as college preparatory, vocational, technical, industrial, business, general, basic, and remedial. While students on different tracks may take some courses together in the same classroom, they are usually separated into entirely different courses or different sections of the same course.

School men offer several different justifications for tracking systems. Common to most, however, is the notion that college-bound students are academically more able, learn more rapidly, should not be deterred in their progress by slower, noncollege-bound students, and need courses for college preparation that noncollege-bound students do not need. By the same token, it is thought that noncollege-bound students are less bright, learn more slowly, should not be expected to progress as fast or learn as much as college-bound students, and need only a general education or work-oriented training to prepare themselves for immediate entry into the world of work or a business or vocational school.

In reply, the numerous critics of tracking usually contend that, while the college-bound are often encouraged by the tracking system to improve their performance, noncollege-bound students, largely as a result of being placed in a lower-rated track, are discouraged from living up to their potential or from showing an interest in academic values. What makes the system especially pernicious, these critics say, is that noncollege-bound students more often come from low-income and minority group families. As a result, high schools, through the tracking system, inadvertently close off opportunities for large numbers of students from lower social strata, and thereby contribute to the low achievement, lack of interest, delinquency, and rebellion that school men frequently deplore in their noncollege-track students.

If these critics are correct, the American comprehensive high school, which is popularly assumed to be the very model of an open and democratic institution, may not really be open and democratic at all. In fact, rather than facilitating equality of educational opportunity, our schools may be subtly denying it and, in the process, widening and hardening existing social divisions.

Tracks and Who Gets Put On Them

During the summer of 1964, we collected data from official school transcripts of the recently graduated senior classes of two Midwestern three-year high schools. The larger school, located in a predominantly middle-class, academic community of about 70,000, had a graduating class that year of 753 students. The smaller school, with a graduating class of 404, was located in a predominantly working-class, industrial community of about 20,000.

Both schools placed their students into either a college prep or a general track. We determined the positions of every student in our sample by whether he took tenth-grade English in the college prep or the general section. If he was enrolled in the college-prep section, he almost always took other college-prep sections or courses, such as advanced mathematics or foreign languages, in which almost all enrollees were also college prep.

Just how students in the two schools were assigned to—or chose—tracks is somewhat of a mystery. When we interviewed people both in the high schools and in their feeder junior highs, we were told that whether a student went into one track or another depended on various factors, such as his own desires and aspirations, teacher advice, achievement test scores, grades, pressure from parents, and counselor assessment of academic promise. One is hard put to say which of these weighs most heavily, but we must note that one team of researchers, Cicourel and Kitsuse, showed in their study of *The Educational Decision-Makers* that assumptions made by counselors about the character, adjustment, and potential of incoming students are vitally important in track assignment.

Whatever the precise dynamics of this decision, the outcome was clear in the schools we studied: socio-economic and racial background had an effect on which track a student took, quite apart from either his achievement in junior high or his ability as measured by I.Q. scores. In the smaller, working-class school, 58 per cent of the incoming students were assigned to the college-prep track; in the larger, middle-class school, 71 per cent were placed in the college-prep track. And, taking the two schools together, whereas 83 per cent of students from white-collar homes were assigned to the college-prep track, this was the case with only 48 per cent of students from blue-collar homes. The relationship of race to track assignment was even stronger: 71 per cent of the whites and only 30 per cent of the blacks were assigned to the college-prep track. In the two schools studied, the evidence is plain: Children from low-income and minority-group families more often found themselves in low-ability groups and noncollege-bound tracks than in high-ability groups or college-bound tracks.

Furthermore, this decision-point early in the students' high school careers was of great significance for their futures, since it was virtually irreversible. Only 7 per cent of those who began on the college-prep track moved down to the noncollege-prep track, while only 7 per cent of those assigned to the lower, noncollege track moved up. Clearly, these small figures indicate a high degree of rigid segregation within each of the two schools. In fact, greater mobility between levels has been reported in English secondary modern schools, where streaming—the British term for tracking—is usually thought to be more rigid and fixed than tracking in this country. (It must be remembered, of course, that, in England, the more rigid break is between secondary modern and grammar schools.)

Differences Between Tracks

As might be expected from the schoolmen's justification for placing students in separate tracks in the first place, track position is noticeably related to academic performance. Thirty-seven per cent of the college-prep students graduated in the top quarter of their class (measured by grade-point average throughout high school), while a mere 2 per cent of the noncollege group achieved the top quarter. By contrast, half of the noncollege-prep students fell in the lowest quarter, as opposed to only 12 per cent of the college prep.

Track position is also strikingly related to whether a student's academic performance improves or deteriorates during high school. The grade-point average of all sample students in their ninth year—that is, prior to their being assigned to tracks—was compared with their grade-point averages over the next three years. While there was a slight difference in the ninth year between those who would subsequently enter the college and noncollege tracks, this difference had increased by the senior year. This widening gap in academic performance resulted from the fact that a higher percentage of students subsequently placed in the college-prep track improved their grade-point average by the senior year, while a higher percentage of noncollege prep experienced a decline in grade-point average by the time they reached the senior year.

Track position is also related strongly to dropout rate. Four per cent of the college-prep students dropped out of high school prior to graduation, as opposed to 36 per cent of the noncollege group.

Track position is also a good indication of how deeply involved a student will be in school, as measured by participation in extracurricular activities.

Out of the 753 seniors in the larger school, a comparatively small number of college-prep students—21 per cent—did not participate in any activities, while 44 per cent took part in three or more such activities. By contrast, 58 per cent, or more than half, of the noncollege group took part in no extra-curricular activities at all, and only 11 per cent of this group took part in three or more activities.

Finally, track position is strikingly related to deviance, both in and out of school. Out of the entire student body of the larger school who committed one or more serious violations of school rules during the 1963–64 year, just over one-third were college-bound, while just over one-half were noncollege-bound. (The track position of the remaining one-tenth was unknown.) Among those who committed three or more such violations, 19 per cent were college-bound compared with 70 per cent who were noncollege-bound. Among all those suspended, over one-third were college-bound while just over half were noncollege-bound. In short, the noncollege-bound students were considerably more often caught and sanctioned for violations of school rules, even though they comprised less than one-third of the student body.

Furthermore, using juvenile court records, we find that, out of the 1964 graduating class in the larger school, 6 per cent of the college-prep and 16 per cent of the noncollege-bound groups were delinquent while in high school. Even though 5 per cent of those on the noncollege track had already entered high school with court records, opposed to only 1 per cent of the college-prep track, still more noncollege-bound students became delinquent during high school than did college-prep students (11 per cent compared with 5 per cent). So, the relation between track position and delinquency is further supported.

We have seen, then, that, when compared with college-prep students, noncollege-prep students show lower achievement, great deterioration of achievement, less participation in extracurricular activities, a greater tendency to drop out, more misbehavior in school, and more delinquency outside of school. Since students are assigned to different tracks largely on the basis of presumed differences in intellectual ability and inclination for further study, the crucial question is whether assignment to different tracks helped to meet the needs of groups of students who were already different, as many educators would claim, or actually contributed to, and reinforced, such differences, as critics like Sexton and Pearl contend.

The simplest way to explain the differences we have just seen is to attribute them to characteristics already inherent in the individual students, or —at a more sophisticated level—to students' cultural and educational backgrounds.

It can be argued, for example, that the difference in academic achievement between the college and noncollege groups can be explained by the fact that college-prep students are simply brighter; after all, this is one of the reasons they were taken into college-prep courses. Others would argue that noncollege-bound students do less well in school work because of family background: They more often come from blue-collar homes, where less value is placed on grades and college, where books and help in schoolwork are less readily available, and [where] verbal expression [is] limited. Still others would contend that lower-track students get lower grades because they performed less well in elementary and junior high, have fallen behind, and probably try less hard.

Fortunately, it was possible with our data to separate out the influence of track position from the other suggested factors of social-class background (measured by father's occupation), intelligence (measured by I.Q.—admittedly not a perfectly acceptable measure), and previous academic performance (measured by grade-point average for the last semester of the ninth year). Through use of a weighted percentage technique known as test factor standardization, we found that, even when the effects of I.Q., social class, and previous performance are ruled out, there is still a sizable difference in grade-point average between the two tracks. With the influence of the first three factors eliminated, we nevertheless find that 30 per cent of the college prep, as opposed to a mere 4 per cent of the noncollege group, attained the top quarter of their class; and that only 12 per cent of the college prep, as opposed to 35 per cent of the noncollege group, fell into the bottom quarter. These figures, which are similar for boys and girls, further show that track position has an independent effect on academic achievement that is greater than the effect of each of the other three factors—social class, I.Q., and past performance. In particular, assignment to the noncollege track has a strong negative influence on a student's grades.

Looking at dropout rate, and again controlling for social-class background, I.Q., and past performance, we find that track position in itself has an independent influence that is higher than the effect of any of the other three factors. In other words, even when we rule out the effect of these three factors, noncollege-bound students still dropped out in considerably greater proportion than college-bound students (19 per cent vs. 4 per cent).

When Forecasters Make the Weather

So our evidence points to the conclusion that the superior academic performance of the college-bound students, and the inferior performance of the noncollege students, is partly caused by the tracking system. Our data do not explain how this happens, but several studies of similar educational arrangements, as well as basic principles of social psychology, do provide a number of probable explanations. The first point has to do with the pupil's self-image.

Stigma. Assignment to the lower track in the schools we studied carried with it a strong stigma. As David Mallory was told by an American boy, "Around here you are *nothing* if you're not college prep." A noncollege-prep girl in one of the schools we studied told me that she always carried her "general"-track books upside down because of the humiliation she felt at being seen with them as she walked through the halls.

The corroding effect of such stigmatizing is well known. As Patricia Sexton has put it, "He [the low track student] is bright enough to catch on very quickly to the fact that he is not considered very bright. He comes to accept this unflattering appraisal because, after all, the school should know."

One ex-delinquent in Washington, D.C., told one of us how the stigma from this low track affected him.

It really don't have to be the tests, but, after the tests, there shouldn't be no separation in the classes. Because, as I say again, I felt good when I was with my class, but when they went and separated us—that changed us. That changed our ideas, our thinking, the way we thought about each other, and turned us to enemies toward each other—because they said I was dumb and they were smart.

When you first go to junior high school you do feel something inside—it's like ego. You have been from elementary, to junior high, you feel great inside. You say, well daggone, I'm going to deal with the *people* here now, I am in junior high school. You get this shirt that says Brown Junior High, or whatever the name is, and you are proud of that shirt. But then you go up there and the teacher says—"Well, so-and-so, you're in the basic section, you can't go with the other kids." The devil with the whole thing—you lose—something in you—like it just goes out of you.

Did you think the other guys were smarter than you?

Not at first—I used to think I was just as smart as anybody in the school—I knew I was smart. I knew some people were smarter, and I *wanted* to go to school, I wanted to get a diploma and go to college and help people and everything. I stepped into there in junior high—I felt like a fool going to school—I really felt like a fool.

Why?

Because I felt like I wasn't a part of the school. I couldn't get on special patrols, because I wasn't qualified.

What happened between the seventh and ninth grade?

I started losing faith in myself—after the teachers kept downing me. You hear "a guy's in basic section, he's dumb," and all this. Each year—"you're ignorant—you're stupid."

Considerable research shows that such erosion of self-esteem greatly increases the chances of academic failure, as well as dropping out and causing "trouble" both inside and outside of school.

Moreover, this lowered self-image is reinforced by the expectations that others have toward a person in the noncollege group.

The self-fulfilling prophecy. A related explanation rich in implications comes from David Hargreaves' *Social Relations in a Secondary School,* a study of the psychological, behavioral, and educational consequences of the student's position in the streaming system of an English secondary modern school. In "Lumley School," the students (all boys) were assigned to one of five streams on the basis of ability and achievement, with the score on the "11-plus" examination playing the major role.

Like the schools we studied, students in the different streams were publicly recognized as high or low in status and were fairly rigidly segregated, both formally in different classes and informally in friendship groups. It is quite probable, then, that Hargreaves' explanations for the greater anti-school attitudes, animosity toward teachers, academic failure, disruptive behavior, and delinquency among the low-stream boys apply to the noncollege-prep students we studied as well. In fact, the negative effects of the tracking system on noncollege-bound students may be even stronger in our two high schools, since the Lumley streaming system was much more open and flexible, with students moving from one stream to another several times during their four-year careers.

Streamed Schools

As we noted, a popular explanation for the greater failure and misbehavior among low-stream or noncollege-bound students is that they come from homes that fail to provide the same skills, ambition, or conforming attitude as higher-stream or college-bound students. Hargreaves demonstrates that there is some validity to this position: In his study, low-stream boys more often came from homes that provided less encouragement for academic achievement and higher-level occupations, and that were less oriented to the other values of the school and teachers. Similar differences may have existed among the students we studied, although their effects have been markedly reduced by our control for father's occupation, I.Q., and previous achievement.

But Hargreaves provides a convincing case for the position that, whatever the differences in skills, ambition, self-esteem, or education commitment that the students brought to school, they were magnified by what happened to them in school, largely because low-stream boys were the victims of a self-fulfilling prophecy in their relations with teachers, with respect to both academic performance and classroom behavior. Teachers of higher-stream boys expected higher performance and got it. Similarly, boys who wore the label of stream "C" or "D" were more likely to be seen by teachers as limited in ability and troublemakers and were treated accordingly.

In a streamed school, the teacher categorizes the pupils not only in terms of the inferences he makes of the child's classroom behavior but also from the child's stream level. It is for this reason that the teacher can rebuke an "A" stream boy for being like a "D" stream boy. The teacher has learned to *expect* certain kinds of behavior from members of different streams. . . . It would be hardly surprising if "good" pupils thus became "better," and the "bad" pupils become "worse." It is, in short, an example of a self-fulfilling prophecy. The negative expectations of the teacher reinforce the negative behavioral tendencies.

A recent study by Rosenthal and Jacobson in an American elementary school lends further evidence to the position that teacher expectations influence student's performance. In this study, the influence is a positive one. Teachers of children randomly assigned to experimental groups were told at the beginning of the year to expect "unusual intellectual" gains, while teachers of the control group children were told nothing. After eight months, and again after two years, the experimental group children, the "intellectual spurters," showed significantly greater gains in I.Q. and grades. Further, they were rated by the teachers as being significantly more curious, interesting, and happy and more likely to succeed in the future. Such findings are consistent with theories of interpersonal influence and with the interactional or labeling view of deviant behavior.

If, as often claimed, American teachers underestimate the learning potential of low-track students and expect more negative attitudes and greater trouble from them, it may well be that they partially cause the very failure, alienation, lack of involvement, dropping out, and rebellion they are seeking to prevent. As Hargreaves says of Lumley, "It is important to stress that, if this effect of categorization is real, it is entirely unintended by the teachers. They do not wish to make low streams more difficult than they are!" Yet, the negative self-fulfilling prophecy was probably real, if unintended and unrecognized, in our two schools as well as in Lumley.

Two further consequences of the expectation that students in the noncollege group will learn less well are differences in grading policies and in teacher effectiveness.

Grading policies. In the two schools we studied, our interviews strongly hint at the existence of grade ceilings for noncollege-prep students and grade floors for college-bound students. That is, by virtue of being located in a college preparatory section or course, college-prep students could seldom receive any grade lower than "B" or "C," while students in noncollege-bound sections or courses found it difficult to gain any grade higher than "C," even though their objective performance may have been equivalent to a college-prep "B." Several teachers explicitly called our attention to this practice, the rationale being that noncollege-prep students do not deserve the same objective grade rewards as college-prep students, since they "clearly" are less bright and perform less well. To the extent that grade ceilings do operate for noncollege-bound students, the lower grades that result from this policy, almost by definition, can hardly have a beneficial effect on motivation and commitment.

Teaching effectiveness. Finally, numerous investigations of ability grouping, as well as the English study by Hargreaves, have reported that teachers of higher ability groups are likely to teach in a more interesting and effective manner than teachers of lower ability groups. Such a difference is predictable from what we know about the effects of reciprocal interaction between teacher and class. Even when the same individual teaches both types of classes in the course of the day, as was the case for most teachers in the two schools in this study, he is likely to be "up" for college-prep classes and "down" for noncollege-prep classes—and to bring out the same reaction from his students.

A final, and crucial, factor that contributes to the poorer performance and lower interest in school of noncollege-bound students is the relation between school work and the adult career after school.

Future payoff. Noncollege-bound students often develop progressively more negative attitudes toward school, especially formal academic work, because they see grades—and, indeed, school itself—as having little future relevance or payoff. This is not the case for college-prep students. For them, grades are a means toward the identifiable and meaningful end of qualifying for college, while among the noncollege-bound grades are seen as far less important for entry into an occupation or a vocational school. This difference in the practical importance of grades is magnified by the perception among noncollege-bound students that it is pointless to put much effort into school work, since it will be unrelated to the later world of work anyway. In a study of *Rebellion in a High School* in this country, Arthur Stinchcombe describes the alienation of noncollege-bound high school students:

> The major practical conclusion of the analysis above is that rebellious behavior is largely a reaction to the school itself and to its promises, not a failure of the family or community. High school students can be motivated to conform by paying them in the realistic coin of future advantage. Except perhaps for pathological cases, any student can be motivated to conform if the school can realistically promise something valuable to him as a reward for working hard. But for a large part of the population, especially the adolescent who will enter the male working class or the female candidates for early marriage, the school has nothing to offer. . . . In order to secure conformity from students, a high school must articulate academic work with careers of students.

Being on the lower track has other negative consequences for the student that go beyond the depressing influence on his academic performance and motivation. We can use the principles just discussed to explain our findings with regard to different rates of participation in school activities and acts of misbehavior.

Tracks Conformity and Deviance

For example, the explanations having to do with self-image and the expectations of others suggest that assignment to the noncollege-bound track has a dampening effect on commitment to school in general, since it is the school that originally categorized these students as inferior. Thus, assignment to the lower track may be seen as independently contributing to resentment, frustration, and hostility in school, leading to lack of involvement in all school activities, and finally ending in active withdrawal. The self-exclusion of the noncollege group from the mainstream of college student life is probably enhanced by intentional or unintentional exclusion by other students and teachers.

Using the same type of reasons, while we cannot prove a definite causal linkage between track position and misbehavior, it seems highly likely that assignment to the noncollege-prep track often leads to resentment, declining commitment to school, and rebellion against it, expressed in lack of respect for the school's authority or acts of disobedience against it. As Albert Cohen argued over a decade ago in *Delinquent Boys,* delinquency may well be largely a rebellion against the school and its standards by teen-agers who feel they cannot get anywhere by attempting to adhere to such standards. Our analysis suggests that a key factor in such rebellion is noncollege-prep status in the school's tracking system, with the vicious cycle of low achievement and inferior self-image that go along with it.

This conclusion is further supported by Hargreaves' findings on the effect of streaming at Lumley:

> There is a real sense in which the school can be regarded as a generator of delinquency. Although the aims and efforts of the teachers are directed toward deleting such tendencies, the organization of the school and its influence on subcultural development unintentionally foster delinquent values. . . . For low stream boys . . . , school simultaneously exposes them to these values and deprives them of status in these terms. It is at this point they may begin to reject the values because they cannot succeed in them. The school provides a mechanism through the streaming system whereby their failure is effected and institutionalized, and also provides a situation in which they can congregate together in low streams.

Hargreaves' last point suggests a very important explanation for the greater degree of deviant behavior among the noncollege-bound.

The student subculture. Assignment to a lower stream at Lumley meant a boy was immediately immersed in a student subculture that stressed and rewarded antagonistic attitudes and behavior toward teachers and all they stood for. If a boy was assigned to the "A" stream, he was drawn toward the values of teachers not only by the higher expectations and more positive rewards from the teachers themselves but from other students as well. The converse was true of lower-stream boys, who accorded each other high status for doing the opposite of what teachers wanted. Because of class scheduling, little opportunity developed for interaction and friendship across streams. The result was a progressive polarization and hardening of the high- and low-stream subcultures between first and fourth years and a progressively greater negative attitude across stream lines, with quite predictable consequences.

> The informal pressures within the low streams tend to work directly against the assumption of the teachers that boys will regard promotion into a higher stream as a desirable goal. The boys from the low streams were very reluctant to ascend to higher streams because their stereotypes of "A" and "B" stream boys were defined in terms of values alien to their own and because promotion would involve rejection by their low stream friends. The teachers were not fully aware that this unwillingness to be promoted to a higher stream led the high informal status boys to depress their performance in examinations. This fear of promotion adds to our list of factors leading to the formation of anti-academic attitudes among low stream boys.

Observations and interviews in the two American schools we studied confirmed a similar polarization and reluctance by noncollege-prep students to pursue the academic goals rewarded by teachers and college-prep students. Teachers, however, seldom saw the antischool attitudes of non-college-prep students as arising out of the tracking system—or anything else about the school—but out of adverse home influences, limited intelligence, or psychological problems.

Implications. These, then, are some of the ways the schools we studied contributed to the greater rates of failure, academic decline, uninvolvement in school activities, misbehavior, and delinquency among noncollege-bound students. We can only speculate, of course, about the generalization of these findings to other schools. However, there is little reason to think the two schools we studied were unusual or unrepresentative, and, despite differences in size and social-class composition, the findings are virtually identical in both. To the extent that findings are valid and general, they strongly suggest that, through their tracking system, the schools are partly causing many of the very problems they are trying to solve and are posing an important barrier to equal educational opportunity to lower-income and black students, who are disproportionately assigned to the noncollege-prep track.

The notion that schools help cause low achievement, deterioration of educational commitment and involvement, the dropout problem, misbehavior, and delinquency is foreign and repulsive to many teachers, administrators, and parents. Yet, our evidence is entirely consistent with Kai Erikson's observation that "deviant forms of conduct often seem to derive nourishment from the very agencies devised to inhibit them."

What, then, are the implications of this study? Some might argue that, despite the negative side effects we have shown, tracking systems are essential for effective teaching, especially for students with high ability, as well as for adjusting students early in their careers to the status levels they will occupy in the adult occupational system. We contend that, however reasonable this may sound, the negative effects demonstrated here offset and call into serious question any presumed gains from tracking.

Others might contend that the negative outcomes we have documented can be eliminated by raising teachers' expectations and noncollege-track students, making concerted efforts to reduce the stigma attached to noncollege classes, assigning good teachers to noncollege-track classes, rewarding them for doing an effective job at turning on their students, and developing fair and equitable grading practices in both college-prep and noncollege-prep classes.

Attractive as they may appear, efforts like these will be fruitless so long as tracking systems, and indeed schools as we now know them, remain unchanged. What is needed [is] wholly new, experimental environments of teaching-learning-living, even outside today's public schools, if necessary. Such schools of the future must address themselves to two sets of problems highlighted by our findings: ensuring equality of opportunity for students now "locked out" by tracking, and offering—to all students—a far more fulfilling and satisfying learning process.

One approach to building greater equality of opportunity, as well as fulfillment, into existing or new secondary schools is the New Careers model. This model, which provides for fundamentally different ways of linking up educational and occupational careers, is based on the recognition that present options for entering the world of work are narrowly limited: One acquires a high school diploma and goes to work, or he first goes to college and perhaps then to a graduate or professional school.

The New Careers model provides for new options. Here, the youth who does not want to attend college, or would not qualify according to usual criteria, is given the opportunity to attend high school part time while working in a lower-level position in an expanded professional career hierarchy (including such new positions as teacher aide and teacher associate in education). Such a person would then have the options of moving up through progressively more demanding educational and work stages, and moving back and forth between the work place, the high school, and then the college. As ideally conceived, this model would allow able and aspiring persons ultimately to progress to the level of the fully certified teacher, nurse, librarian, social worker, or public administrator. While the New Careers model has been developed and tried primarily in the human-service sector of the economy, we have pointed out elsewhere that it is applicable to the industrial and business sector as well.

This alternative means of linking education with work has a number of advantages: Students can try different occupations while still in school; they can earn while studying; they can spend more time outside the four walls of the school, learning what can best be learned in the work place; less stigma will accrue to those not immediately college bound, since they, too, will have a future; studying and learning will be inherently more relevant, because it will relate to a career in which they are actively involved; teachers of such students will be less likely to develop lower expectations, because these youth, too, will have an unlimited, open-ended future; and antischool subcultures will be less likely to develop, since education will not be as negative, frustrating, or stigmatizing.

Changes of this kind imply changes in the economy as well and, therefore, are highly complicated and far-reaching. Because of this, they will not occur overnight. But they are possible, through persistent, creative, and rigorously evaluated educational, economic, and social experimentation.

Whatever the future, we hope teachers, administrators, and school boards will take one important message from our findings: What they do to students makes a difference. Through the kind of teaching-learning process they create, the schools can screen out and discourage large numbers of youth, or they can develop new means for serving the interests and futures of the full range of their students.

Discussion Questions

1. Contrast the myth that American education contributes to upward social economic mobility with the educational reality as this article describes it.
2. How does educational tracking relate to this myth?

3. The article quotes the point of view that "there is a real sense in which the school can be regarded as a generator of delinquency." How can this be so? Discuss.

STEPHEN BIRMINGHAM

The Dying Art of Social Climbing

While social mobility is not guaranteed every American, the fact that our society tends toward an *open-class* system provides those individuals with "guts, determination, and a knowledge of the ground rules" an opportunity to improve their status. From a sociologist's vantage point, anyone who desires to elevate his social class status must begin by acquiring the education and occupation to fit his ambitions. Then he must skillfully change his standard of living, cultivate behavior of the desired class, manipulate associations, and even marry "properly." In the article below, Stephen Birmingham outlines specific guidelines for the would-be successful social climber.

Reprinted from Stephen Birmingham, "The Dying Art of Social Climbing," from *The Right Places (For the Right People)*. Copyright © 1969 by Stephen Birmingham. Reprinted by permission of Little, Brown and Co.

It used to be that an upper crust could not exist in the United States without the thousands of persons clambering to penetrate its shell from underneath. Certainly, if this had not been the case, the crust would not have been as cohesive and recognizable as it was and would simply have been an amorphous collection of rich people looking worried. "Blessed be the social climbers," those who considered themselves to have been better than others must —or should—have murmured to themselves from time to time as they contemplated their lot; "without them, we would be unwanted."

In Europe, it was always different. Those who were of the aristocracy knew who they were, and so did everyone else, and that was that. You couldn't *climb* into European aristocracy, not even by marrying into it. In the United States, something more than a title was always required to be of the topmost social level, which was probably why the topmost social level in America often ended up resembling very much what a European would consider the middle class—moored there like a kite in a tree. Old Mrs. Vanderbilt, "Queen of Newport Society," repaired to her pantry after every dinner party and painstakingly counted her linens and her silver. Henriette Seligman, doyenne of New York's Jewish society during the early part of this century, entertained like a mad thing in her Manhattan town house—with meals that were always catered by Schrafft's.

In the United States, the social climber's relationship to society was the opposite of the mountaineer's to Everest. The social climber didn't climb simply because society was *there*. The social climber created his own mountain, and the best social climbers met at the top, at ringside tables, with all the people they moved out of Brooklyn to avoid.

With these facts in mind, social climbing has never been a difficult art. Essentially, all the successful social climber needed—like any other aerialist— was guts, determination, skin the thickness of rhinoceros hide, and a knowledge of the ground rules. Social climbing was not for the faint of heart or the easily discouraged. Even so, there were always some who were better at it than others. It helped, for example, if the climber was reasonably good-looking. If he or she had dandruff, chronic halitosis, a wooden leg, or was hopelessly overweight, his or her rise was less swift. It was, on the other hand, always helpful to look well in clothes, to have an easy smile, to be able to dance, play tennis or at least backgammon, to be witty—but not *too* funny, which was off-putting—to enjoy gossip, to be able to drink well, not to make a big thing about a person's morals, to be able to remember names and faces quickly, and to know at any given moment just who it was whom everybody hated. It went without saying, if you were interested in social climbing, that you were rich. All this was true as recently as a decade ago. But today, social climbing is becoming a dying art, and it has become so for a simple reason: Nowadays it's so easy. One cannot consider as a true art form what has become as simple as a childish exercise in finger-painting.

For example, it used to be that the kiss of death for any social climber was to be caught at it. The social climber used to have to affect an air of indifference towards his goal, to pretend not to care whether or not he achieved it, to insinuate himself gradually and oh-so-gently into the perfumed waters of the people he wanted to get to know. The social climber used the traditional avenues—hard work (or at least the appearance of hard work) for charities, hospitals, churches, and worthy civic causes, and from there into the better clubs and dinner parties. It was a climb, in other words, within the social framework that prevailed in any given city.

Today, all that has changed. Now the social climber seldom beats around the bush. If he cares at all, he simply lays his cards on the table and says, in effect, "Look, here I am. I want to get in, and if it costs I'm willing to pay." Needless to say, this makes for a cut-and-dried situation, but one that is not without a certain amount of excitement. It may be exciting for others to know that here, now, is a person nobody had heard of a year ago—with money, or at least some money, from God knows where—willing to put himself on the line to get to mix with whoever are supposed to be the right people in town.

Today, the main thing the climber needs is recognition. Someone should say, "Here comes So-and-So," when So-and-So enters the room or the restaurant door. Recognition means the press, the name or the photograph, or both, in the social columns. It used to be that this could best be achieved through the use of a social publicist who, for a fee ranging from five hundred to a thousands dollars a month, "placed" items in columns about his clients. The publicist could also arrange for his clients' names to appear on certain lists, on the committees for certain benefits, and for them to be invited to certain art and theater openings as well as to parties given by people the clients would like to know. The publicist is still a climbing tool of sorts. "They dress them up in a David Webb pin, put them in Sarmi pants and trot them around," says one public relations man. Marianne Strong, who has taken on socially ambitious clients in the past, now says, "All we can do is take them around to parties and introduce them to people. After that, they're on their own."

Today's climber, however—in today's less constrained, less selfconscious mood—has discovered that the social publicist may have become superfluous. If you want publicity, you can do it yourself. If you want your party written up in Leonard Lyons's column, why not just invite Leonard Lyons to your party? In a recent, and brilliant, example of the dexterity with which this can be handled, an attractive woman had a large dinner party in her New York apartment with three important columnists present—three powerful and competitive women who do not really like each other. It was all right; they stayed in different corners of the room, and the hostess was mentioned in three newspapers in the morning.

If climbers take on this task for themselves there are a few simple basics to bear in mind. Here, then, are ten easy rules for today's upstart:

1. Find something about yourself to promote, get a label. That way, people will say, "Oh yes, I've heard of her," even when they haven't. The label can be based on anything, no matter how tenuous. Have a gimmick, an identifying fetish. Be "Mrs. Anne Kerr Slater, whose inevitable blue-tinted glasses

and huge diamond solitaire . . . etc." or "Mrs. Reed Albee, who wears nothing but white in winter, nothing but black in summer," or anything equally silly. People, including the columnists, will learn to spot you.

2. Be generous to your friendy society columnist at Christmas time. "I used to pay a publicist once a month, now I pay just once a year," says one woman, obviously pleased with the results of her economy. Cash gifts, however, are frowned upon. A hand-me-down designer dress, on the other hand, is not.

3. Find a designer and spend a bit on his clothes. When asked, "Whose dress is that?" don't look puzzled and say, "Mine." Designers employ publicists too, and if you spend enough their publicists will publicize you—for free. They will feed your picture to *Women's Wear Daily* and make sure that it is a picture of you looking your loveliest.

4. Latch on to, by all means—up to, if not including, threat of bodily harm—someone *big,* preferably from out of town, even more preferably from out of the country, certainly from out of your league, whom everyone will flock to your house in droves to see. Mr. Robert R. Young built a whole house just to entertain the Windsors in, and when they were in residence, her parties were the most popular in Palm Beach. Royalty still carries weight down there, at least. Once you have made your Very Important Friend, cherish and cosset her. Lavish her with gifts and flattery and she will serve you well. Don't be shy. Zero in on the top people around. Remember that quite often the top people are sitting around twiddling their thumbs on a Saturday evening. Often they are the easiest to get because everyone else is too in awe of them to ask them to dinner. Splendor can create isolation.

In Washington, once upon a time, Mrs. Gwen Cafritz discovered that Supreme Court justices and their wives were so loftily regarded that they were being socially shortchanged. She fixed all that, made them her special property, and decorated her parties with justices again and again. Mrs. Cafritz's technique lives on. There is also the old but still workable technique of calling one Important Friend to say you're having a party for another Important Friend, and then calling the second one to say you're having a party for the first one. Then you hold your breath and hope that at least one of your guests of honor shows up.

5. Be Jewish. Many of the most publicized "new" names recently have been Jewish, and this has nothing to do with anything in the so-called Jewish character. It is simply that it is better, in big-city society, to be Jewish today than it has ever been before. Never has social anti-Semitism been so unfashionable, nor have so many people been out to prove that they are liberal-liberal-liberal. If you can't be Jewish, sprinkle your guest list liberally with fashionable Jews and—even more important—with blacks. This is more than your social conscience at work if you are climber. It is because you know that most reporters of metropolitan newspapers nowadays are liberal in their outlook. Your mixed racial and religious gathering will get more attention and more praise and sympathy than if you confine yourself to old-hat WASPs.

6. Pay for the photographs that come to you in the mail unsolicited. Increasingly, at social gatherings—openings, benefits, private parties—photographers roam about the premises, shutters clicking. The pictures, when they arrive—often handsomely displayed in leather frames—can become a costly item (the bill enclosed with the pictures always urges you to return them, and no hard feelings). But the photographers feed society columns, and if you don't buy their wares they have ways of taking their revenge. "They get very skillful at taking your picture while you're scratching yourself," one woman has said.

7. If you're a woman, lunch out selectively—both as to restaurant and as to luncheon companion. It's not a bad idea, for instance, to lunch with a man other than your husband. This helps create talk, and might even become a column item. If you go to the "in" restaurants, be sure to tip your captain, as well as your waiter, handsomely, until you have successfully worked your way up to the best tables and are greeted, when you come in, by name. Be willing to withstand the humiliation of rebuffs, blank stares, and placement in "Siberia" as you progress toward your goal. In New York, the five most "in" restaurants are La Grenouille, La Côte Basque, La Caravelle, Le Pavillon, and Lafayette, in more or less that order. But even more "in" than lunching at one of the above, which are all French, is having a corned beef sandwich in the workroom of a pet designer, such as Halston, so there you are. Perhaps this is why several of the formerly "in" restaurants—Chauveron, the Colony—have closed, for lack of interest.

8. Knock, for all they're worth, all the old traditional society institutions—the Colony Club, Newport, coming-out parties, the Junior League, fox-hunting, Foxcroft, beagling, billiards, the *Social Register*. These institutions are hopelessly out of date, at least as topics of conversation. This does not mean that if asked to go to something involving one of them you should not treat the invitation seriously.

9. Become involved with Art. Art has become one of the most effective avenues and the most rewarding for the social climber. Also, as far as Art goes, anything goes for Art these days, which makes it all the easier. Go to gallery openings. You do not even need an invitation to most of these, where gate-crashers are expected. Sign the guest book and the gallery concerned will promptly invite you to its next opening. An evening's roam of galleries can be, according to one art expert, "the easiest free drunk in town"—that is, if you like the least expensive brands of domestic champagne. Start a collection of art. Give your art away to museums or send it on tour. Get on the board of directors of a major art museum, and you will have arrived.

Aside from the importance of art, how you decorate your house matters less today than ever before. It is not considered smart to admit to using an interior decorator (interior decorators today try to be called "designers," but the old label sticks). In your house, order an atmosphere of cultivated clutter and, as soon as the decorator is out of ear shot, claim to have done it all yourself.

10. When you entertain, serve good food. Remember that not just women but men too have a say in which invitations are accepted and which are not. His wife may call you "that silly little climber," but if he knows that you will reward him with a spectacular meal at your table, they will more than likely both show up. (Superb food is, after all, available in only a handful of restaurants and clubs in the world.) In most cities, the most fashionable night to entertain is Monday. Next comes Thursday. No one knows why. Friday and Saturday nights are for entertaining in the country. Sunday is for cocktail parties. Think twice before giving a cocktail party.

Go, if you must, to charity balls—but go selectively, favoring only the best ones, that is, those for the best charities. Go to these by making up a table, which, being a climber, you'll want to be ringside, up front. Go, and don't be too surprised if you spot, at the ringside table next to yours, a few of the old crowd from Brooklyn. After all, it's a fact of life that social climbers meet mostly other social climbers. You will also see, at other nearby tables, numberless nameless faces, which is because these tables have been purchased by large corporations and filled up with their employees and friends.

Where, then, are real society, the Old Guard, the founding families of our cities, the great names to conjure with? Well, some of them have moved out of town—to Arizona, to a ranch in Wyoming, or just to Manhasset. Others have simply tired of the sort of thing you're having so much fun doing, and you'd find them very boring. The rest have simply died.

But don't worry. Now that you've been climbing, and have made it up so far, you've undergone certain important changes. Social climbing is supposed to be self-improving, and the new you is much more happy than the old. And if you take another look at that old Brooklyn crowd, they're looking better too.

Not long ago, New York's famous old El Morocco—which had fallen upon sorry days under a series of different managers—was reopened as a strictly private, members-only club by that prince (real Russian title and all) of publicists, Serge Obolensky. Everyone from the Onassises on down turned out for the opening, and the club has been a huge popular success with what passes for society in New York today. Exclusivity has been the club's keynote and touted cornerstone. In addition to the ability to pay five hundred dollars a month dues, new members must be sponsored by at least two older members, plus two members of the august Board of Governors. When, the other day, a public relations man had a client who wanted to join El Morocco, he spent an hour or so on the telephone calling members and governors, asking them to sponsor his client. By the end of the afternoon, the client had all the sponsorship he needed. Not one of the sponsors knew, or had even heard of, the prospective member before that afternoon. One sponsor even let the prospective member sign the sponsor's name on the application; it seemed like too much trouble to send the application over to his office. The new member went sailing in.

And so, having mastered the simple rules of modern social climbing, you must ask yourself: Was it worth the candle? Or wasn't there some point you missed? Wasn't the point that today's society, where the right people get together in the right places, is everywhere and everyone? Perhaps, without knowing it, you are *there* already. Mr. Fitzgerald might have found the present-day situation confusing, or even disappointing. But now that the rich *are* you and me, there are really no more places that are closed to life on earth.

Discussion Questions

1. How does this article on "social climbing" contrast with the previous article?
2. How much of a put-on do you find in this article? For example, do any or all of the ten basic rules for social climbing in this article seem to you to be valid?

BURTON N. WIXEN

Children of the Newly Rich: The Dangers of Growing Up in a World Apart

Our democratic ethos argues that social mobility is both necessary and good. It not only provides every individual with the opportunity to experiment in the direction of self-fulfillment, it also stabilizes the social order by providing discontented individuals with outlets other than social revolution. Social mobility, however, also has its costs. The newly acquired status breeds insecurity, emotional strain, and the disruption of patterns of friendships and family ties. In the following article Burton Wixen describes and discusses the impact social mobility can have on children.

There are people with great potential who are leading meaningless lives. They are very wealthy, but their wealth gives them very little pleasure. On the contrary, the life-styles made possible by their affluence have turned out to be traps from which too few manage to escape. Many could be creative and productive. They and their wealth are a wasted resource for our country.

In spite of unforgivable bigotry and injustice, our country has the most mobile class structure the world has ever known. As great numbers of people move upward in their social status, they encounter problems in themselves and their children that they are unprepared for.

They find themselves at crossroads which represent crucial stages for the future history of their families. A failure to recognize what is happening as life-styles begin to change may sentence an entire family to dead-end lives.

Reprinted from *Children of the Rich* by Burton N. Wixen, M.D. © 1973 by Burton N. Wixen. Used by permission of Crown Publishers, Inc.

As a psychiatrist and psychoanalyst, I have known and tried to help some of these disadvantaged rich. I have also worked with many people caught in crises produced by rapid changes in their social positions. Usually it is the children and young adults who suffer the most and for whom the most can be done.

A typical situation: Matt, an only child, has grown up in Brentwood and led "the good life." His father worked his way from a real estate salesman to president of a large investment firm. When Matt is 16 his parents rather suddenly become alarmed by his late hours and poor grades. A series of serious fights, interspersed with chronic tension, persists between him and his parents for the next year. Drugs are added to the cauldron, and there are a number of LSD trips and regular use of marijuana. There is one attempt at psychotherapy, but Matt refuses to continue after meeting with me once.

By his 17th birthday he has dropped out of high school and stays in his room all day. He goes out every night or has friends over to smoke grass and listen to music. His family tries everything—pleading, threats, bribery—but feels completely defeated. Matt warns them to quit bugging him or he will leave home. They don't and he does.

Matt is not heard from for the next year and a half. A private detective engaged by the family locates him in a commune in New Mexico. He now has a full beard, a black wife given to Hindu readings and an infant daughter.

"Come home?" A long, not forced, laugh. "I am home. My wife and family are here."

His mother is crying, "Oh, Matt, I don't know where we failed but we're sorry! Please, please! Bring your wife and baby and come back with us."

"Why?"

"Why?—because this shack isn't fit to live in. You have no toilets, the place must leak like a shower in the rain. There are no schools—and everyone here looks high on dope."

"Some of them are," Matt says. "Each of us here is free to live as he sees fit. Man survived for eons without marble toilets. We have our own school where we teach the children what we feel is important, in our own way. We teach the importance of the earth and of love. We do without color television —or radio, for that matter—and we grow our own healthy food. Your smog-filled, insecticide-polluted city isn't fit to live in."

The discussion goes on for several hours but ends up at the same impasse. Matt refuses to accept any money from them and refuses to promise to write. "I can't write you. The post office in town is 20 miles away and we have no cars. The sheriff hassles us when we come to town, so we stay away. Anyway, we have nothing to say to each other."

"But you're our son—we're your parents. We love you . . ." Mother and Father try desperately to make contact, but there is none.

They leave, heartbroken.

I can't tell you in detail what motivated Matt to adopt this new life-style. I saw him only that once, when he was 17. He was very bright and well-read.

He had an almost analytical detachment from his parents, whose life-style he discussed freely and critically.

"They are having fits because I don't want to go into Dad's business," he told me at the time. "I've had it with school because it's all Establishment brainwashing. I have a list of great books of the world—and not just the white man's world. I study them in my room or at the library. The East has much to teach us. So do those outside the Establishment."

I tried to probe for areas of conflict.

He understood and answered, "I went through the spoiled-brat scene. Then something happened. My parents started hassling me. I met some really wise friends and started reading a lot. Then they started hassling me even more. If you're a spoiled brat you get hassled, and if you become concerned with the rest of the world you get hassled."

"You seem angry with your parents," I said.

"You're damn right I am. But lately I've begun to feel sorry for them, too. They're so caught up in the country club business. And making money. And making more money. That means nothing to me. If they don't stop hassling me, I'll split."

He showed some anger at them, but there was also a touch of pity.

I made no effort to debate the value of his family's way of life with him, nor the accuracy of his view of it. I did urge him to come back to talk more about his feelings, and he said simply, "No."

Matt seemed to have gone through a more or less typical identity crisis seen in the children of families who have made major jumps in social position. Instead of resolving it after a period of turbulence—often admixed with the more usual features of adolescent rebellion—as is the most frequent outcome, he took a different path. He did not become neurotic; there were no symptoms, no depression—only an increasing alienation from his family. Finally he made a complete break and adopted a radically new life-style.

I can tell you more about the family background from another source: his mother came to me for a few visits after her trip to New Mexico. She was suffering from a moderate depression. The therapy amounted to helping her through a period of mourning; for her, her son was dead.

One facet from the parents' background may have some bearing on the direction that Matt's identity crisis resolution took. They had both been "revolutionaries" in college. After their disenchantment with communism, they actively supported liberal causes, especially civil rights. At the same time, they had servants and were actively seeking status. I detected more than a touch of disgust with their less liberal neighbors and, on the wife's part, a touch of guilt about her own wealth.

Much of Matt's new life-style was built on a reversal, a negative identification with his parents. But a number of questions nagged me:

- Was there something more than a new identity built upon repudiating the old?

- Did he in some way identify with his parents' old revolutionary zeal?
- Did their old idealism somehow get transmitted to him and blossom to a fruition they never dared dream of?
- Did the parents unconsciously sanction and encourage his dropping out?
- Did they vicariously fulfill their frustrated idealism at his expense?

There are no answers to these questions—only a history of a past idealism lost in the parents' new materialism.

Matt and the family from which he came are like many people who have accumulated great sums of wealth and who have seen tremendous shifts in their social status. Values, ideals, role images—the components of one's sense of identity—have met with changes in a few decades that are greater than the changes of preceding centuries.

I feel there is a waste in Matt's case, a tragedy. But I recognize that he could answer all the arguments one could muster, and there is no evidence of neurotic suffering. He may turn out to be among the lucky ones.

Time will tell; my guess is he'll come back.

Discussion Questions

1. Review what Dr. Wixen describes as "a more or less typical identity crisis seen in the children of families who have made major jumps in social position." How "typical" do you believe Matt's identity crisis is?
2. Do you see a relationship between the parents' general background and Matt's identity crisis, or would you explain the identity crisis primarily in terms of the upward move in social and economic status of Matt's parents? Discuss.
3. Do you agree with Dr. Wixen's guess that Matt will "come back"? Why or why not?

13 / Race and Ethnic Relations

SHINE
35¢

Throughout history and in all societies, people have been intensely conscious of racial, religious, cultural, and nationality differences. This consciousness has been the cause of a variety of forms of intergroup conflict, many of which have become persistent features of American life. Such conflict is not confined to the United States alone. It reaches out to engulf other societies characterized by two or more identifiable categories of people. Some of the more obvious examples are Arab vs. Jew, Catholic vs. Protestant in Ulster, and African vs. Asian in Uganda. In the United States the most persistent conflicts have been between whites and blacks, but the heterogeneity of American racial and ethnic groups—unparalleled in other nations—has engendered many other conflicts.

The relationship between the various racial and ethnic groups in the United States was initially shaped by the dominant group—the whites of northern Eu-

ropean heritage. In its most outright form, dominant vs. minority relationship is characterized by aggression, segregation, and discrimination. *Aggression,* in its most blatant form, is exemplified by the genocidal policy of the Nazis toward the Jews. Open conflict, however, is not the most common form of aggression. Forms of *symbolic aggression,* such as the dominant group's use of jokes and epithets to perpetuate its prejudice against the minority group, is more common. *Covert aggression,* which is illustrated by the circumvention of civil rights legislation, is another form of symbolic aggression. This kind of aggression can also be employed by the minority group in the form of jokes that ridicule the dominant group. *Segregation,* when practiced by the dominant group, involves the requirement, in a direct or an indirect form, that the minority group live or use facilities in isolation from the dominant group. **Discrimination** is behavior that excludes the minority group from access to certain facilities and activities such as education, employment, housing, parks, and so forth.

There are some equalitarian patterns of relationships between the dominant and minority groups. Sociologists define the most common of these patterns as cultural pluralism, assimilation, integration, and amalgamation. *Cultural pluralism* permits minority groups to retain and practice differences in customs and traditions while the minority group members cooperate with the dominant group in politics, education, and other aspects of social relationships. *Assimilation* occurs when newcomers adopt the language, values, and cultural patterns of the dominant group. *Amalgamation* comes about through intermarriage and biological mixing. *Integration* has been invoked in the United States by judicial decisions and federal as well as state laws.

While the dominant group initially dictates the patterns of society, it is important to remember that the minority group can also influence the character of intergroup conflict. *Submissive manipulation* occurs when the minority group accepts a lower position by becoming, for example, a "good nigger," or an "Uncle Tom." *Marginal adaptation* is exemplified by the minority group's finding business opportunities neglected by the dominant group because these kinds of opportunities are relatively unappealing. *Riots and collective violence* are conditions that Americans have become familiar with during the 1960s. Watts, Newark, and Detroit, among others, are witnesses to property destruction, death, and brutality. The past roots for these minority-group reactions include dominant-group violence such as lynchings as well as direct or indirect discriminations against the minority group.

In the post–World War II era America's black population has made significant political, social, and economic gains. To the dismay of many whites, however, many blacks seem to have become more rather than less militant and discontented. Moreover, American Indians and Mexican Americans are also expressing their resentment against historical inequities and the slow rate at which promised remedies are delivered. Despite the problems, recent trends are toward greater equality among the various racial and ethnic groups in the United States.

The following readings discuss some of the troubled racial and ethnic interrelationships among dominant and minority groups in this country.

HENRY LOUIS GATES, JR.

Portraits in Black

Racism is the organizing principle of a society that is structured on the basis of racial ancestry and one race occupies a position superior to other races. Subordination is achieved through segregation, discrimination, prejudice, and stereotyping. All of these forms of racism have been openly advocated and practiced in the past. However, as a result of the civil rights movement, most forms of legal discrimination and segregation have ended. Yet the cry of *racism* is still to be heard throughout the land. After the combined efforts of the Congress, the Supreme Court, and the Presidency, how can our society still be considered racist by so many blacks, especially those who have been the apparent benefactors of recent changes? The following article by a black professor at Yale University offers an answer to this question.

He argues that while racism is still very real, the cry of racism all too often becomes an *opiate* of the black elite. He describes how the media has subtly maintained racist attitudes by fostering stereotypical images of blacks and how the media still fails to recognise that the numerous separate and distinct black groups defy a simple portrait that describes the behavior of all blacks.

"I say dere, Brother Andy!"
"Yeah, Brother Kingfish?"
"Let us simonize our watches."

Not too long ago, a black face on television gathered a black audience larger than even the regular, predawn assortment congregated to discover what the day's daily double had been. I can remember as a child sitting upstairs in my back bedroom and hearing my mother shout at the top of her voice that someone *"colored . . . colored!"* was on the screen and we'd all best come down right away. And we would. As we ran down the stairs, momma shot to the front porch to let all the neighbors know, while daddy let the folks downtown know by way of the telephone. *"Colored, colored, on channel five!"* he'd shout to be heard over the commercial, while momma's echo sounded from the street: *"Colored, colored."* We were so starved for images of ourselves that we'd all sit in that living room, nervous, expectant, praying that our home boy would not let the race down.

That, of course, was a while ago; a lot has changed since then. Today, there are as many blacks and "black shows" on TV as all of us combined then would ever have dreamed of, back in the late Fifties in Piedmont, West Virginia. Then the tension, the awful terror we felt as we watched and waited for our immediate symbol of racial equality to save the day, made us susceptible to an acute embarrassment should our hero not prevail. More often than not our heroes did *not* prevail. Yet, there was ample occasion when embarrassment for a fallen hero was not an uncomfortable embarrassment, projected onto ourselves; frequently, it was sympathetic, projected onto a duped character whom we managed, quite nicely, to avoid confusing with the race or with our living room. Into this category fell the misadventures of Andy Brown (Spencer Williams), the perennial victim of that urban Br'er Fox, George "Kingfish" Stevens (Tim Moore), who managed to convince Andy that Central Park was Yosemite, that a stage set was a "railroad apartment" (after Andy asked incredulously why his just-rented house had no middle or back), and that little white rabbits would make Andy's fortune in the "rare chinchilla trade"—all this three weeks in a row!

There were, however, embarrassing occasions, when our representative of the race, we were convinced, had set back by at least two centuries our quest to be regarded as equal. There was the night when Joe Louis, one of the two guest celebrities on *Name That Tune* (Sugar Ray Robinson was the other), unable all evening to identify correctly even *one* song title despite loud cues from our living room, hauled all 200-plus bronze pounds down that narrow alleyway (leaving an alarmed Robinson, mouth open, aghast, far in his tracks), only to shout out in a huffing, puffing voice with all the strength of his and our frustrations that the name of *"Tweedlee Dee"* was *"Tiddly Winks"!* The stopper, I suppose, was the night when *Imitation of Life* (1934) was televised. Aunt Delilah (Louise Beavers) was informed by her employer and friend, Miss Bea (Claudette Colbert), that her remarkable pancake mix (long a secret, passed down through untold generations from matriarch to matriarch) was to bring both of them fortune. "Now, Delilah," Claudette Colbert said, "you're going to be rich. You'll be able to move away and buy yourself a nice house." "My own house?" a confused Louise Beavers asked. "You gonna send me away? Don't do that to me. How I gonna take care of you and Miss Jesse if I's away? I's yo' cook. You kin have it. I makes you a present of it." To which Ned Sparks could only reply deadpan, and much to our agreement: "Once a pancake, always a pancake."

We accepted Tarzan as King of the Jungle without too many doubts. It was not until much, much later that anything even remotely "political" about Tarzan ever crossed our greased-down, stocking-capped minds. But the *National Geographic*-type documentaries, with bare-chested black women and grass-skirted tribesmen who spoke funny mumbo-jumbo talk, were the source of *real* embarrassment, and I'm sure that we all silently thanked some nameless Dutch sea captain for carting us up and out of the Heart of Darkness into the good ole U.S.A.

Our feelings, as subconscious and undeveloped as they were then, have characterized black aesthetic arguments for the past hundred years. The novels of Charles Chestnutt, for instance, abound with "refined Afro-American doctors" who could understand why white people kept most blacks confined to Jim Crow sections on trains, but who couldn't for the life of them understand why these same white folks couldn't see *they* were *different* from the herd. Further, the aesthetic arguments of the Harlem Renaissance during the 1920s centered on the controversy "How Shall the Negro Be Portrayed?" and fierce debates raged over the projection of the proper "elevating" cultural images, which would ameliorate the social conditions of the race. This confusion of the realms of art and propaganda was a mutation of Matthew Arnold's notion of culture and anarchy, simplified thirty years later into Brooker T. Washington's "toothbrush and a bar of soap" as supremely pressing concerns for the reconstructed black man.

The "New Negro" movement, which contained the Harlem Renaissance, was the logical extension, not only of Washington's ideas on social mobility, but also of W.E.B. DuBois's notion of a "talented tenth," the intellectual and professional "natural" aristocracy, whose prime task was to lead the sheltered masses up and out of the psychological effects of slavery. Every artistic creation by the black men of the 1920s was held to be a "revelation"; through art, the black man would be free. Heywood Broun told the New York Urban League on January 25, 1925, that "a supremely great negro artist, who could catch the imagination of the world, would do more than any other agency to remove the disabilities against which the negro now labors." Broun went on to say that this artist-redeemer could come at any time, and asked his audience to remain silent for ten seconds to imagine his coming. DuBois summarized this line of thinking. "We want," he said, "everything that is said about us to tell of the best and highest and noblest in us. We insist that our Art and Propaganda be one. We fear that evil in us will be called racial while in others it is viewed as individual. We fear that our shortcomings are not merely human but foreshadowings and threatenings of disaster and failure." If the "truth," or even an aspect of the "truth" about black people was held to be in any manner pejorative, then it must be censored, for images of "the lowly life" would hamper the quest for civil rights.

By the mid-sixties, this kind of thinking had been displaced by a much more sophisticated analysis of black images as projected by the news media. The image, it was held, is not only message but massage. Control of the American news media, for instance, allows for control of projected images of spontaneous events, and these images, in turn, control response to the original event. Thus the image itself becomes the event, as far as millions of media consumers are concerned. Shadow becomes substance; the reflection of reality is taken to be reality itself.

This process gives the media the power to mold perceptions. Reality assumes secondary significance to its reporting, and what is "true" is to be found somewhere between the pages of *Time* and *Reader's Digest,* for the bulk of American readers.

Black Americans contribute very little to the reporting of an event of their own making, and thus white reporters are forced to conjure up their own perceptions of a "black" event. Often this distance allows for a certain objectivity; but, more often cultural and social gaps prevail against it. Since white reporters write for a white audience, a black event is reflected in a gray image to be consumed by white Americans. Reality as perceived replaces reality as experienced. What's more, should that reality, subsequently encountered, fail to conform with its image, it is not recognized as "valid." Suspicious, both blacks and whites disavow these "imitations."

Not only through its capacity for emphasis, but (and often more significantly) through its powers of deletion, the media can make a nonevent meaningful or a significant event insignificant. "Black power," for instance, with all its concomitant negative associations, was largely a phenomenon of the white press.

Black power was "born" during the James Meredith march through Mississippi in June 1966. Suddenly, literally overnight, a symbolic march was transformed into the handwriting on the wall: black people, it was said, were at long last giving vent to a new-found militancy and hate, based on reverse racism. In a few hours, black power became a vicious, violent, and sinister focus of the shared hate of blacks for whites.

Black militants, sensing the tremendous energy dormant in this slogan, played upon the media-created, media-reinforced fears of the whites. Rhetorical threats of annihilation and retaliation became prerequisites for "validity" (and adequate press coverage). But means became ends: the rhetoric remained in peoples' minds, while its deeper aspects were underreported, if reported at all. A slogan that had invoked social development through individual and collective pride came to mean a coming orgy of violence, blacks against whites.

About a year-and-a-half after the Meredith march, the white press gave black power a face-lift. After the November 1967 elections, the radio commentator Paul Harvey, for one, said that the validity of black power lay in the electoral process. Joseph Alsop uncharacteristically exclaimed that "Mayors-elect Stokes and Hatcher represent 'Black Power' in the best American tradition—and thank God for it." *Time* entitled its cover story on Carl Stokes "The Real Black Power." As Columbus discovered America, so did the press discover the political aspect of black power.

The paragon of journalistic reversal in image creation was the *New York Times's* treatment of black power between July and November 1967. On July 22, a *Times* editorial, "Black Pheonix," suggested that a phoenix of an expanded conception of black power could arise from the ashes of Newark. "The words 'black power' suggest chauvinism and militancy for some dark purpose," the editorial said. "They need not."

Two days later, the *Times* changed its mind. The ongoing conference on back power in Newark was characterized as "racist." Then, on November 12, black power and the *Times* reconciled their differences. In a lead editorial entitled "Black Power and the Elections," the *Times* argued that, at long last, the election of black officials in Cleveland, Gary, and throughout the South had miraculously transformed black power—"that mischievous and opaque slogan"—into "the only meaningful terms it can have: political success achieved through democratic process." By this time, nature had been made to imitate art, and art to imitate nature, much to the detriment of whatever it was "black power" was intended to be. Many black-power advocates had become what they beheld, in the same way that the Panthers would.

Since 1967, much has changed in the relationship between blacks and the media, at least on the surface. In part because of governmental pressures, as well as a growing black consumer market for white media, blacks in major cities are just as likely as women to be announcers and reporters. More blacks are writing under their own by-lines than ever before. And all major newspapers, network news programs, and magazines claim at least a "representative influence" on their editorial boards. On occasion, this "representative influence" is telling: Walter Cronkite just this past spring eulogized Elijah Muhammad as the man who made of the term "black" a description suggesting dignity and self-respect. Yet, fifteen or so years ago, it had been Mike Wallace, in a documentary called *The Hate That Hate Produced,* who had done so much to create a false picture of the Nation of Islam as a violence-prone group of ex-convicts and lower-class blacks.

Prime-time television, too, is replete with situation comedies that depict black people who laugh and cry, who share middle-class aspirations and harbor middle-class prejudices, who live on the East Side of New York and the South Side of Chicago. Blacks fill other TV slots and polka-dot just about every program from soap operas and soap commercials to the Sammy Davis, Jr., show.

Against this background we must place the death of the civil-rights era, and the financial demise of those organizations whose *raison d'être* was the integration of American institutions, in the style of Martin Luther King, Jr. This collapse is partly due to the lack of public and private funding; but it is also a result of the failure of these organizations to adapt their strategies and ideologies (where there *are* ideologies) to the new world, which they, ironically, helped to create. The disease from which these groups suffer—the lack of an incisive, coherent approach—can be seen in the pattern of protest that recently arose against Ralph Bakshi's satiric fable, *Coonskin,* and Lars Ulvenstam and Tomas Dillen's documentary, *Harlem: Voices, Faces.*

While the projection of the images of black people was to have become the preoccupation of the major networks, the "quality" of these reflections has become the preoccupation of a tiny coterie of "concerned" black people, determined to protect the black community from images of itself. In part, this loose federation consists of exhausted civil-rights leaders searching for that simple answer to social problems that will, overnight, elevate them to national prominence and national funding. To this group of politicos add a dash of black media types, scorned for years by white media and anxious to substitute their view of the black man not only for the white man's view but often for the view of blacks who have infiltrated the white media.

The collective veto of this motley band has such a prescriptive right that to air a program despite their protests is not merely to ignore their opinion, but to reject it. This veto was supposed to be a tool to argue the supremacy of a new media elite. However, after a plethora of polemics and pressures over image projection and the black community, it has become patently clear that our Black Oracle is fallible. Sometimes it has been dumb, and sometimes it has lied.

Harlem: Voices, Faces is a three-hour documentary shot in the summer of 1973 by Lars Ulvenstam and Tomas Dillen of the state-controlled Swedish broadcasting system. Shown in its original version in Sweden, East Germany, Canada, Finland, Denmark, and Norway, it won a prestigious prize in Sweden as the best TV documentary of 1974.

About a year-and-a-half ago, Robert Kotlowitz, WNET's vice-president of programming, saw the film and liked it. It was approved by nine members each of the programming staffs and the Corporation for Public Broadcasting, including one black viewer on each staff, and CPB provided $23,000 for WNET to buy the film.

Bernette Golden, a young black producer at WNET, assembled a panel of blacks who would appear at the end of the screening to comment on its assumptions. When the station put out a press release on April 23, however, its inept and unfortunate wording ("In Harlem, children learn to use the needle at age 9 or 10. It is considered normal and, to some, a mark of adulthood, which comes early in the ghetto") caused an unprecedented roar of protest, mostly from people who had not seen the film.

Tony Brown, producer and host of the PBS series, *Black Journal,* protested formally in two letters to Hartford Gunn, president of PBS; Irma Norris, WNET's engineering coordination manager, circulated a petition calling for the film's suppression, signed by forty-three of the station's seventy-one blacks; Emma Bowen, president of the Black Citizens for Fair Media, sent hundreds of photocopies of the press release to black elected officials and similar organizations around the country; and pressure mounted from the National Urban League, Operation Breadbasket, the National Black Media Coalition, and the Harlem Congress on Racial Equality. One objector, Bill Cherry, national director of communications for Jesse Jackson's PUSH, "writing on behalf of Reverend Jesse Jackson," urged suppression of "the type of interviews it is alleged you have in this film." The original panel resigned; Percy Sutton decided, after seeing the film, that he didn't like it, and on May 13 WNET president John Jay Iselin cancelled the film. A few months later, after a postmortem panel had been assembled, the film finally was approved.

I sat through *Harlem: Voices, Faces* twice at New Haven, and found it one of the most remarkable documentaries done to date on black Americans. In fact, I am only sorry that black filmmakers didn't do it first. David Denby, writing in the *Times,* summarized it this way: "The Swedes see America as a cruelly competitive capitalist system, a consumption-happy nightmare-land in which blacks have been defined and maintained as the losers by a racist white majority. Their environment a shambles, their homes disorderly and unsupportive, Harlem's children barely stand a chance at school and are seen as doomed to suffer the crushing disappointments of America's outsiders; the people of Harlem are further trapped by a series of destructive illusions: TV advertising, Shaft-Superfly fantasies, get-rich-quick schemes, and the false consolations of religion. The way out is booze and dope." Denby's summary is correct, and so is the documentary's analysis of Harlem's pathology. Two separate groups of black people—a group of children from Harlem, and a group of older Harlem residents for whom Hilton Clark (the only Harlem resident on the original panel) screened the film—recognized this, and opposed the film's cancellation. "Calling the film detrimental to blacks," an ad hoc committee formed by Clark wrote to the station, "is much akin to blaming the messenger for the bad news he brings."

If the attempt to censor *Harlem: Voices, Faces* was lame, the panel discussion after its showing was pathetic. Marjorie Henderson, of the NAACP in New York, protested loudly about showing "the sinned against, not the sinners," about "exploiting the misery of blacks," and "projecting all the vices in the world on us," and about showing the "perpetrators and purveyors."

James McCullen, of the National Black Media Coalition, called the film "racially inflammatory," and said that it "attacks and assaults black intelligence, dignity, integrity, and self-respect." McCullen said that he urged censorship before he even saw the film. He wanted "to show who was responsible" for the conditions depicted in the film. Yet the whole film showed *precisely* who, and what was responsible: slum landlords, police graft, corruption, and other systemic ills, not whores and winos. Only Hilton Clark made sense. It was, he said slowly, "an aspect we so often try to sweep under the rug."

The protest against *Harlem: Voices, Faces* is a significant as the documentary itself. What emerges from the polemics, once the smoke has cleared, is this: we are no longer an organic community. Stratification accompanying the economic advances for the few, for which we fought so hard for so long, has created separate and distinct black groups, each with its own ideological and economic interests to protect.

Coonskin is Ralph Bakshi's best film. (His previous films were *Fritz the Cat* and *Heavy Traffic.*) It is a satiric fable about the American city as hell. Bakshi uses straight animation mixed with photography to embody an old convict's fantasy. The story he tells is of three Southern rural black men who go to New York, become leaders of black organized crime, then destroy the white gangsters who control Harlem. Although nearly everyone in the film is the object of satire, Bakshi's real targets are those he holds responsible for ghetto life; his most telling blows are aimed at a white policeman and an Italian Mafia family. Again, I wish a black filmmaker had done this. I hope it makes impossible the one-dimensional portrayals of black people found in such films as *Shaft, Superfly,* and *Cleopatra Jones.*

This time, censorship cries came largely from CORE, East Coast and West. Elaine Parker, former chairman of the Harlem of CORE, said after a screening, "It depicts blacks as slaves, hustlers, and whores." CORE picketed the New York headquarters of Gulf and Western, which owns Paramount and which had put up the money for *Coonskin.* Paramount, after much pressure, decided not to distribute the film. Fortunately, Bryanston Films, a small independent distributor, worked out an agreement with Albert S. Ruddy, and now the film has been released, much to the protests of Charles Cook, the Los Angeles regional chairman of CORE, who said, in rhetoric reminiscent of the Panthers', "We hold Bakshi, Ruddy, and Bryanston responsible for what happens. We charge them with high crimes against black people—stereotyping and degrading blacks." Cook went on to say that "the black community does not need people like Bakshi who want to make clowns out of us. Every movie and TV show depicts blacks as comics, whores, pushers, or pimps," he said, hyperbolically. Gene Garvin, director of the Los Angeles chapter of CORE agreed. "We consider the black actors who appeared in this film as traitors to their race." To which Charles Gordone who plays the preacher in the film (and wrote the Pulitzer Prize-winning *No Place to Be Somebody*) responded, "These organizations like CORE make me angry. If they didn't have something to bitch about, they'd be out of business."

If this sort of analysis is what the Congress of Racial Equality and the NAACP stand for, then it is time for us to hold the mirror to their nostrils and perform the postmortem.

I do not mean to imply that the media have no racist tendencies, or even that I am happy with the way they project black images. But I am saying that the CORE-NAACP arguments outlined above are not adequate anymore, if they ever were. The effect of image distortion on "the black psyche" is complex, and black people can no longer be content to call something "racist" without being able to defend that view, in all its complexity. For what we are speaking of is *censorship,* a practice almost as abhorrent to art as lynching is to justice. Ubiquitous cries of racism serve no real purpose, other than to mask complex problems. Indeed, racism is the opiate of the black elite.

There are, however, questions we can demand answers to. We must oppose the sort of censorship that precludes access to the media by black filmmakers. We must ask ourselves why it is easier to see, say, *The Harder They Come,* at Harvard than in Harlem. Just as we must defend the rights of Ulvenstam and Dillen to make a Marxist analysis of Harlem, we must also defend and demand the right of black filmmakers to produce documentaries full of positive black images, as well as to analyze, say, a day in the life of the residents of Scarsdale. We must question the admissions procedures of film and journalism schools, and must continue to press for more and more black editors and reporters on white publications and networks. We must demand equal access to financing and distribution of films and articles. Our voices must be heard beyond the situation comedy and the one-hour talk show.

But there is an even more urgent consideration. We must begin to understand why public outrage over the ghetto as a place of exile, as a living hell in the national imagination, has diminished since the ghetto situation comedies appeared. This sort of thinking is very subtle, and our own black oracle has yet to make its subtleties of thought public. By making ghetto life palatable, TV is defusing its sheer *horror.* Ironically, the decision to portray ghetto life in this way in large measure stems from the standard, simpleminded criticisms that only our seamy side is emphasized publicly. So Harlem and the South Side of Chicago become livable.

We must come to understand that all the "violence" in the "blaxploitation" films only serves to create another form of escapism. Real violence shapes reality; it limits our choices almost as much as do economic pressures. To see what makes people act, what makes them not act, and what creates different value systems—these are the educative functions of black films and TV programs. These could increase understanding between ethnic groups, where only confusion, hate, and distrust reign. One wonders how many whites in South Boston, for example, watch *The Jeffersons, Good Times,* or *Sanford and Son.*

By projecting the semblances of motivating social forces, the media encouraged the dehumanization of our society. We are allowed to escape reality. This problem must become the preoccupation of those who work in the media, and of black media-watchers concerned with the effects of images on "the black psyche."

If this happened, then the simplemindedness of protest against the old stereotypes, such as *Amos 'n' Andy,* would be unnecessary. For there is enough of *Amos 'n' Andy* that is "true" for black folks from Harlem to Harvard to crack Kingfish jokes with instant empathy and humor the result. In the exaggerated chorus of American stereotypes and satire is found a remarkable amount of observation that is accurate. We must learn to laugh at ourselves again, without the worry of the nouveau riche, black or white, who long to forget even a satiric rendition of the land from whence they came. We cannot simply toss Mantan Moreland and Stepin Fetchit into the garbage can of history. Is the portrayal of these awkward or ignorant stock characters to be censored entirely, now that we are Black? Did these caricatures have a more insidious or harmful effect on our lives than Pearl Bailey did, when she played the fool on a recent session of *Meet the Press?* No one laughed when Miss Bailey argued (demonstrating as she explained) that African delegates "strutted" down the aisles at the U.N. and hence weren't to be taken seriously. Do these stereotypes injure us as much as the censorship Motown has long practiced over its artists (which Stevie Wonder broke only by threatening to sign a new contract with another, *white* recording company)? We must begin the systematic criticism of our own institutions, and develop sophisticated criticisms of "white" media.

Ultimately, we must return to Du Bois's final word on censorship of the "lowly" side of black life. "The more highly trained we become, the less we can laugh at Negro comedy," he wrote in 1921. "We will have it all tragedy and the triumph of dark Right over pale villains." I hope that we are sophisticated enough to realize that to laugh at *Amos 'n' Andy* is not to believe that all black people fit into one of the stereotypes it portrays. I would like to be able to laugh at the antics of the Kingfish again.

Discussion Questions

1. Review the two kinds of racism this article discusses. In your opinion which is worse? Discuss.
2. How does the author review the dilemma of whether American society should laugh at "Amos 'n' Andy"? Should it?

STEPHEN JAY GOULD

Racist Arguments and I.Q.

One of the most enduring causes of racial segregation has been the widely held belief that members of minority groups were inherently incapable, with few exceptions, of working and competing in our highly sophisticated and competitive society. Support for such myths was provided by so-called scientific evidence. For example, Professor Arthur Jensen argued that the reason blacks scored so low on IQ tests was the direct result of inferior "black" genes. He also argued that the more "white" genes a black person possessed—which of course could only be acquired by crossbreeding with a white person—the higher the intelligence. Although such "scientists" have been severely criticized and their numerous scientific failings exposed in the academic journals, the public is often unaware of such refutations. The following article is an attempt to remedy this oversight by providing a clear description of the scientific failings of such arguments.

Louis Agassiz, the greatest biologist of mid-nineteenth-century America, argued that God had created blacks and whites as separate species. The defenders of slavery took much comfort from this assertion, for biblical proscriptions of charity and equality did not have to extend across a species boundary. What could an abolitionist say? Science had shone its cold and dispassionate light upon the subject; Christian hope and sentimentality could not refute it.

During the Spanish-American War, a great debate raged over whether we had the right to annex the Philippines. Imperialists again took comfort from science, for social Darwinism proclaimed a hierarchy in racial ability. When antiimperialists cited Henry Clay's contention that God would not create a race incapable of self-government, Rev. Josiah Strong answered: "Clay's contention was formed before modern science had shown that races develop in the course of centuries as individuals do in years, and that an underdeveloped race, which is incapable of self-government, is no more of a reflection on the Almighty than is an underdeveloped child, who is incapable of self-government."

I cite these examples not merely because they expose science at its most ridiculous, but because they illustrate a far more important point: statements that seem to have the sanction of science have been continually invoked in attempts to equate egalitarianism with sentimental hope and emotional blindness. People who are unaware of this historical pattern tend to accept each recurrence at face value: that is, they assume each such statement arises from the "data" actually presented rather than from the social conditions that truly inspire it.

We have never, I shall argue, had any hard data on genetically based differences in intelligence among human groups. Speculation, however, has never let data stand in its way; and when men in power need such an assertion to justify their actions, there will always be scientists available to supply it.

The racist arguments of the nineteenth century were primarily based on craniometry, the measurement of human skulls. Today, these contentions stand totally discredited. What craniometry was to the nineteenth century, intelligence testing has been to the twentieth. The victory of the eugenics movement in the Immigration Restriction Act of 1924 signaled its first unfortunate effect—for the severe restrictions upon non-Europeans and upon southern and eastern Europeans gained much support from the results of the first extensive and uniform application of intelligence tests in America—the Army Mental Tests of World War I. These tests were engineered and administered by psychologist Robert M. Yerkes, who concluded that "education alone will not place the negro race [sic] on a par with its Caucasian competitors." It is now clear that Yerkes and his colleagues knew no way to separate genetic from environmental components in postulating causes for different performances on the tests.

The latest episode of this recurring drama began in 1969, when Arthur Jensen published his article entitled, "How Much Can We Boost I.Q. and Scholastic Achievement?" in the *Harvard Educational Review*. Again, the claim was made that new and uncomfortable information had come to light, and that science had to speak the "truth" even if it refuted some cherished notions of a liberal philosophy. But again, I shall argue, Jensen had no new data; and what he did present was flawed beyond repair by inconsistencies in the data themselves and by illogical claims in his presentation.

Jensen assumes that I.Q. tests adequately measure something we may call "intelligence." He attempts to tease apart the genetic and environmental factors causing differences in performance on these tests. He does this by relying upon the one natural experiment we possess: identical twins reared apart— for here the differences can only be environmental. The average difference in I.Q. for such twins is less than the difference for two unrelated individuals raised in similarly varied environments. From the data on twins, he obtains an estimate of the magnitude of environmental influence and estimates the genetic component from the additional differences in I.Q. between unrelated individuals. He concludes that I.Q. has a heritability of about 0.8 (or 80 percent) *within* the population of American and European whites. The average difference between American whites and blacks is 15 I.Q. points (one standard deviation). He asserts that this difference is too big to attribute to environment, given the high heritability of I.Q. Lest anyone think that he writes in the tradition of abstract scholarship, I merely quote the first line of his famous work: "Compensatory education has been tried, and it apparently has failed."

I believe that this argument can be refuted in a "hierarchical" fashion—that is, we can discredit it at one level and then show that it would fail at a more inclusive level even if we allowed Jensen's argument for the first two levels:

Level 1: The equation of I.Q. with intelligence. Who knows what I.Q. measures? It is a good predictor of "success" in school, but is such success a result of intelligence, apple polishing, or the assimilation of values that the leaders of society prefer? Some psychologists get around this argument by defining intelligence operationally as the scores attained on "intelligence" tests. A neat trick. But at this point, the technical definition of intelligence has strayed so far from the vernacular that we no longer can define the issue. But let me allow (although I don't believe it), for the sake of argument, that I.Q. measures some meaningful aspect of intelligence in its vernacular sense.

Level 2: The heritability of I.Q. Here again, we encounter a confusion between vernacular and technical meanings of the same word. "Inherited," to a layman, means "fixed," "inexorable," or "unchangeable." To a geneticist, "inherited" refers to an estimate of similarity between related individuals based on genes held in common. It carries no implication of inevitability or of immutable entities beyond the reach of environmental influence. Eyeglasses correct a variety of inherited problems in vision; insulin can check diabetes.

Jensen insists that I.Q. is 80 percent heritable. Princeton psychologist Leon J. Kamin has recently done the dog-work of meticulously checking through details of the twin studies that form the basis of this estimate. He has found an astonishing number of inconsistencies and downright inaccuracies. For example, the late Sir Cyril Burt, who generated the largest body of data on identical twins reared apart, pursued his studies of intelligence for more than forty years. Although he increased his sample sizes in a variety of "improved" versions, some of his correlation coefficients remain unchanged to the third decimal place—a statistically impossible situation. Other studies did not standardize properly for age and sex. Since I.Q. varies with these properties, an improper correction may produce higher values between twins not because they hold genes for intelligence in common, but simply because they share the same sex and age. The data are so flawed that no valid estimate for the heritability of I.Q. can be drawn at all. But let me assume (although no data support it), for the sake of argument, that the heritability of I.Q. is as high as 0.8.

Level 3: The confusion of within- and between-group variation. Jensen draws a causal connection between his two major assertions—that the within-group heritability of I.Q. is 0.8 for American whites, and that the mean difference in I.Q. between American blacks and whites is 15 points. He assumes that the black "deficit" is largely genetic in origin because I.Q. is so highly heritable. This is a *non sequitur* of the worst possible kind—for there is no necessary relationship between heritability within a group and differences in mean values of two separate groups.

A simple example will suffice to illustrate this flaw in Jensen's argument. Height has a much higher heritability within groups than anyone has ever claimed for I.Q. Suppose that height has a mean value of five feet two inches and a heritability of 0.9 (a realistic value) within a group of nutritionally deprived Indian farmers. This high heritability simply means that short farmers will tend to have short offspring, and tall farmers tall offspring. It says nothing whatever against the notion that proper nutrition could raise the mean height to six feet (taller than average white Americans). It only means that, in this improved status, farmers shorter than average (they may now be five feet ten inches) would still tend to have shorter than average children.

I do not claim that intelligence, however defined, has no genetic basis— I regard it as trivially true, uninteresting, and unimportant that it does. The expression of any trait represents a complex interaction of heredity and environment. Our job is simply to provide the best environmental situation for the realization of valued potential in all individuals. I merely point out that a specific claim purporting to demonstrate a mean genetic deficiency in the intelligence of American blacks rests upon no new facts whatever and can cite no valid data in its support. It is just as likely that blacks have a genetic advantage over whites. And, either way, it doesn't matter a damn. An individual can't be judged by his group mean.

If current biological determinism in the study of human intelligence rests upon no new facts (actually, no facts at all), then why has it arisen from so many quarters of late? The answer must be social and political—and the sooner we realize how much of science is so influenced, the sooner we will demythologize it as an inexorable "truth-making machine." Why now? The 1960s were good years for liberalism; a fair amount of money was spent on poverty programs and relatively little happened. Enter new leaders and new priorities. Why didn't the earlier programs work? Two possibilities are open: (1) we didn't spend enough money, we didn't make sufficiently creative efforts, or (and this makes any established leader jittery) we cannot solve these problems without a fundamental social and economic transformation of society; or (2) the programs failed because their recipients are inherently what they are—blaming the victims. Now, which alternative will be chosen by men in power in an age of retrenchment?

I have shown, I hope, that biological determinism is not simply an amusing matter for clever cocktail party comments about the human animal. It is a general notion with important philosophical implications and major political consequences. As John Stuart Mill wrote, in a statement that should be the motto of the opposition: "Of all the vulgar modes of escaping from the consideration of the effect of social and moral influences upon the human mind, the most vulgar is that of attributing the diversities of conduct and character to inherent natural differences."

Discussion Questions

1. The author alleges, "And, either way, it doesn't matter a damn. An individual can't be judged by his group mean." What does the author mean by this? Discuss.
2. Although this article is in the "Race and Ethnic Relations" chapter, it could be used to illustrate problems of "Science and Sociology." Discuss the most significant points about sociology as a science being made here.

TOM ENGELHARDT

Ambush at Kamikaze Pass

Aggression is one of the most distinctive characteristics of dominant–minority group relationships. While it has taken the form of genocide, it is more typically expressed in *symbolic forms*. The dominant group maintains a culture of jokes, epithets, and other symbolic devices that serve to perpetuate its prejudices against the minority. In the following article, Tom Engelhardt describes how the motion picture industry has helped to maintain and perpetuate this culture of prejudice and discrimination.

I was visiting an Indian school and a movie was being shown in the auditorium about the cavalry and the Indians. The cavalry was, of course, outnumbered and holding an impossible position where the Indians had chased them into the rocks. The Indians, attempting to sneak up on the cavalry, were being killed, one every shot. When it finally appeared that the Indians were going to overrun the army position, the ubiquitous cavalry appeared on the far horizon with their bugle blowing, and charged to save the beleaguered few. The whole auditorium full of Indian students cheered.—*Our Brother's Keeper: The Indian in White America*

*   *   *

It was a thrilling drama of love and death they saw silently reeled off; the scenes, laid at the court of an oriental despot, galloped past, full of gorgeousness and naked bodies, thirst of power and raving religious self-abnegation, full of cruelty, appetite and deathly lust, and slowing down to give a full view of the muscular development of the executioner's arms. Constructed, in short, to cater to the innermost desires of an onlooking, international civilization.—Thomas Mann, *Magic Mountain*

"Westerns" may have been America's most versatile art form. For several generations of Americans, Westerns provided history lessons, entertainment, and a general guide to the world. They created or recreated a flood of Ameri-

Reprinted from *Bulletin of Concerned Asian Scholars,* Vol. 3, No. 1 (Winter-Spring 1971), by permission of the author. Copyright © 1971 by Tom Engelhardt.

can heroes, filled popcorned weekends, and overwhelmed untold imaginations. It's as difficult today to imagine movies without them as to think of a lunch-eonette without Coca-Cola. In their folksy way, they intruded on our minds. Unobtrusively they lent us a hand in grinding a lens through which we could view the whole of the nonwhite world. Their images were powerful; their structure was satisfying; and at their heart lay one archetypal scene which went something like this:

> *White canvas-covered wagons roll forward in a column. White men, on their horses, ride easily up and down the lines of wagons. Their arms hang loosely near their guns. The walls of the buttes rise high on either side. Cakey streaks of yellow, rusty red, dried brown enclose the sun's heat boiling up on all sides. The dust settles on their nostrils, they gag and look apprehensively towards the heights, hostile and distant. Who's there? Sullenly, they ride on.*
> *Beyond the buttes, the wagon train moves centrally into the flatlands, like a spear pointed at the sunset. The wagons circle. Fires are built; guards set. From within this warm and secure circle, at the center of the plains, the white-men (-cameras) stare out. There, in the enveloping darkness, on the peripheries of human existence, at dawn or dusk, hooting and screeching, from nowhere, like maggots, swarming, naked, painted, burning and killing, for no reason, like animals, they would come. The men touch their gun handles and circle the wagons. From this strategically central position, with good cover, and better machines, today or tomorrow, or the morning after, they will simply mow them down. Wipe them out. Nothing human is involved. It's a matter of self-defense, no more. Extermination can be the only answer.*

There are countless variations on this scene. Often the encircled wagon train is replaced by the surrounded fort; yet only the shape of the object has changed. The fort, like the wagon train, is the focus of the film. Its residents are made known to us. Familiarly, we take in the hate/respect struggle between the civilian scout and the garrison commander; the love relations between the commander's daughter and the young first lieutenant who-has-yet-to-prove-himself; the comic routines of the general soldiery. From this central point in our consciousness, they sally forth to victory against unknown besiegers with inexplicable customs, irrational desires, and an incomprehensible language (a mixture of pig-latin and pidgin Hollywood).

What does this sort of paradigm do to us? Mostly, it forces us to flip history on its head. It makes the intruder exchange places in our eyes with the intruded upon. (Who ever heard of a movie in which the Indians wake up one morning to find that, at the periphery of their existences, in their own country, there are new and aggressive beings ready to make war on them, incomprehensible, unwilling to share, out to murder and kill, etc.?) It is the Indians, in these films, who must invade, intrude, break in upon the circle—a circle which contains all those whom the film has already certified as "human." No wonder the viewer identifies with those in the circle, not with the Indians left to patrol enigmatically the bluffs overlooking humanity. In essence, the viewer is forced behind the barrel of a repeating rifle and it is from that position, through its gunsights, that he receives a picture history of Western colonialism and imperialism. Little wonder that he feels no sympathy for the enemy as they fall before his withering fire—within this cinematic structure, the opportunity for such sympathy simply ceases to exist.

Such an approach not only transforms invasion into an act of self-defense; it also prepares its audiences for the acceptance of genocide. The theory is simple enough: We may not always be right (there are stupid commanders, etc.), but we are human. By any standards (offered in the film), "they" are not. What, then, are they? They are animate, thus they are, if not human, in some sense animals. And, for animals facing a human onslaught, the options are limited. Certain of the least menacing among them can be retained as pets. As a hunter trains his dog, these can be trained to be scouts, tracking down those of their kind who try to escape or resist, to be porters, to be servants. Those not needed as pets (who are nonetheless domesticable) can be maintained on preserves. The rest, fit neither for house training nor for cages, must be wiped out.[1]

From the acceptance of such a framework flows the ability to accept as pleasurable, a relief, satisfying, the mass slaughter of the "nonhuman"—the killing, mowing down of the nonwhite, hundreds to a film and normally in the scene which barely precedes the positive resolution of the relationships among the whites. Anyone who thinks the body count is a creation of the recent Indochinese war should look at the movies he saw as a kid. It was the implicit rule of those films that no less than ten Indian (Japanese, Chinese, . . .) warriors should fall for each white, expendable, secondary character.[2]

Just as the style and substance of the Indian wars was a prototype for many later American intrusions into the Third World (particularly the campaigns in the Philippines and Indochina), so movies about those wars provided the prototype from which nearly every American movie about the Third World derived. That these Third World movies are pale reflections of the framework, outlook, and even conventions of the cowboy movie is easy enough to demonstrate. Just a few examples, chosen almost at random from the thirty or forty films I've caught on TV in the last few months. Pick your country: the Mexico of toothy Pancho Villan bandits, the North Africa of encircled Foreign Legionaires, the India of embattled British Lancers, or even South Africa. One would think treatment of South Africa might be rather special, have its own unique features. But lo! We look up and already the Boers are trekking away, in (strange to say) wagons, and, yep, there's, no . . . let's see . . . Susan Hayward. Suddenly, from nowhere, the Zulus appear, hooting and howling, to surround the third-rate wagons of this third-rate movie. And here's

[1] The men who historically advocated or pursued such a policy in the American West openly and unashamedly referred to it at the time as an "extermination" policy.

[2] One must at least credit John Ford, the director, with keeping the carnage down in several of his films (for example, *She Wore a Yellow Ribbon,* 1950) and for allowing the Indians (*Fort Apache,* 1948) to emerge victorious, if no more comprehensible, from at least one movie in the history of the Western film.

that unique touch we've all been waiting for. It seems to be the singular quality of the Zulus that they have no horses and so must circle the wagon train on foot, yelling at the tops of their voices and brandishing their spears . . . but wait . . . from the distance . . . it's the Transvaal cavalry to the rescue. As they swoop down, one of the Boers leaps on a wagon seat, waving his hat with joy, and calls to his friend in the cavalry, "You've got 'em running, Paul. Keep 'em running, Paul! Run 'em off the end of the earth!" (*Untamed*, 1955)

Or switch to the Pacific. In any one of a hundred World War II flicks, we see a subtle variation on the same encirclement imagery. From the deck of our flagship, amidst the fleet corraled off the Okinawa coast, we look through binoculars. The horizon is empty; yet already the radar has picked them up. Somewhere beyond human sight, unidentified flying objects. The sirens are howling, the men pouring out of their bunks and helter-skelter into battle gear. At their guns, they look grimly towards the empty sky: the young ensign too eager for his first command, the swabby who got a date with that pretty Wave, the medic whose wife just sent him a "Dear John" letter (he's slated to die heroically). A speck on the horizon, faces tense, jokes fall away, it's the Kamikaze! Half-man, half machine, an incomprehensible human torpedo bearing down from the peripheries of fanatical animate existence to pierce the armored defenses of the forces of Western democracy. The result? Serious damage to several ships, close calls on more, several secondary characters dead, and an incredible number of Japanese planes obliterated from the sky.[3]

That there is no feeling of loss at the obliteration of human torpedoes is hardly surprising. Even in those brief moments when you "meet" the enemy, movies like this make it immaculately clear that he is not only strange, barbarous, hostile, and dangerous, but has little regard for his own life. Throwing himself on the gatling guns of the British with only spear in hand, or on the ack-ack guns of the Americans with only bomb in portal, he is not acting out of any human emotion. It is not a desire to defend his home, his friends, or his freedom. It has no rational (i.e., "human") explanation. It is not even "bravery" as we in the West know it (though similar acts by whites are portrayed heroically). Rather, it is something innate, fanatical, perverse—an inexplicable desire for death, disorder, and destruction.

When the enemy speaks a little English, he often explains this himself. Take, for instance, the captured Japanese officer in *Halls of Montezuma* (1951). The plot is already far advanced. On an island in the Pacific, hours before the big attack, Marines are pinned down by Japanese mortars whose position they cannot locate. Yet if they do not locate them, the attack will fail. The Japanese officer obstinately refuses to help them. Richard Widmark pleads with him, appealing to his life force. "You have a future—to rebuild Japan—to live for . . . ." But the officer replies: "Captain, you seem to have forgotten, my people for centuries have thought not of living well but dying well. Have you not studied our Judo, our science. . . . We always

[3] The land equivalent of the Kamikaze onslaught is the Banzai! charge (as in Fuller's *Merrill's Marauders,* 1962).

take the obvious and reverse it. Death is the basis of our strength." Suddenly a mortar shell explodes above the bunker. Everybody ducks. Rafters fall; dust billows; slowly the air clears; a shocked voice yells out: "My God, the Jap's committed hari-kari!" Fortunately the idiot gave it all away. He reminded the Americans of the quirks in the nonwhite mind. As any schoolboy should have known, orientals think backwards. The Japs put their rockets on the front slope of the mountain, not the protected rear slopes as an American would have done. The attack, to the tune of the Marine Hymn, moves forward, preparing to wipe the Japs off the face of the island.

If, in print, such simple idiocy makes you laugh, it probably didn't when you saw the film; nor is it in any way atypical of four decades of action films about Asia. The overwhelmingly present theme of the nonhumanness of the nonwhite prepares us to accept, without flinching, the extermination of our "enemies" (as John Wayne commented in *The Searchers,* 1956, there's "humans" and then there's "Commanches") and just as surely it helped prepare the ideological way for the leveling and near-obliteration of three Asian areas in the course of three decades.

It is useful, in this light, to compare the cinematic treatment of the European front in World Wars I and II with that of the Pacific front. From *The Big Parade* (a silent film) on, a common and often moving convention of movies about the wars against Germany went something like this: The allied soldier finds himself caught in a foxhole (trench, farmhouse, etc.) with a wounded German soldier. He is about to shoot when the young, begrimed soldier holds up his hand in what is now the peace symbol, but at the time meant "Do you have a cigarette?" Though speaking different languages, they exchange family pictures and common memories.[4]

The scene is meant to attest to man's sense of humanity and brotherhood over and above war and national hatred. Until very recently, such a scene simply did not appear in movies about the Japanese front. Between the American and his nonwhite enemy, a bond transcending enmity was hardly even considered. Instead, an analogous scene went something like this: A group of Japanese, shot down in a withering crossfire, lie on the ground either dead or severely wounded. The American soldiers approach, less from humanitarian motives than because they hope to get prisoners and information.[5] One of the Japanese, however, is just playing possum. As the American reaches down to give him water (first aid, a helping hand), he suddenly pulls out a hand grenade (pistol, knife) and, with the look of a fanatic, tries to

[4] While somewhat harder to find in Nazi war flicks, see *The Enemy Below* (1958) for the World War II (and naval version) of the same scene. The last shot is of the opposing American and Nazi commanders who have disabled each other's ships and saved each other's lives, standing at the stern, sharing a cigarette and looking out together over the endless sea.

[5] This is not to say that Americans are portrayed as lacking generosity. Quite the opposite, humanitarian gestures are second nature to them; however, those gestures tend to be directed towards humans. As in the scene where Merrill's Marauders, having smashed through a mass of Japs, are confronted with a wounded comrade. "You wouldn't leave me?" he asks. "We never leave anybody" is the reply.

blow them *all* to smithereens. He is quickly dispatched. (See, for instance, *In Love and War,* 1959.)

The theme of alien intruders descending on embattled humans and being obliterated from an earth they clearly are not entitled to is most straightforwardly put in science-fiction movies; for monsters turn out to be little more than the metaphysical wing of the Third World. These movies represent historically events which have taken place only in the Western imagination. Thus, the themes of the cowboy (-Third World) movie come through in a more primeval way. An overlay of fear replaces the suspense. Metaphorically, the world is the wagon train; the universe, the horizon. (Or, alternately, the earth spaceship is the wagon train; an alien planet, the horizon.) From that horizon, somewhere at the peripheries of human existence, from the Arctic icecap (*The Thing,* 1951), the desert (*Them,* 1954), the distant past (*The Beast from 20,000 Fathoms,* 1953), the sky (*War of the Worlds,* 1953), at dawn or dusk, hooting and beeping come the invaders. Enveloping whole armies, they smash through human defenses, forcing the white representatives of the human race to fall back on their inner defense line (perhaps New York or Los Angeles). Imperiling the very heartland of civilized life, they provide only one option—destroy THEM before THEM can destroy us.

In this sort of a movie, the technical problems involved in presenting the extinction of a race for the enjoyment of an audience are simplified.[6] Who would even think about saving the Pod People (*Invasion of the Body Snatchers,* 1956)? Ordinarily the question of alternatives to elimination barely comes to mind. If it does, as in that prototype "modern" sci-fi film *The Thing* (James Arness of Matt Dillon fame played the monster), usually the man who wants to save Them, "talk to Them," is the bad mad scientist as opposed to the good, absent-minded scientist (who probably has the pretty daughter being wooed by the cub reporter).[7]

[6] Extermination has, however, been spoken of quite bluntly in certain Third World movies. This was particularly true of those movies made during the war against Japan. Take, for example, *The Purple Heart* (1944), about Japanese attempts to try the Doolittle flyers for "war crimes." At the trial, the leader of the American flyers tells the Japanese judge: "We'll come by night and we'll come by day. We'll blacken your skies and burn your cities to the ground until you get down on your knees and beg for mercy. . . . This was your war. You asked for it. You started it . . . and now we won't stop until your crummy little empire is wiped off the face of the earth." The Japanese chief prosecutor immediately commits hara-kiri because of loss of face in failing to break the American prisoners. Or again, *Objective Burma* (1945): the American journalist sees tortured and dead American prisoners. In anger, he says, "This was done in cold blood by a people who claim to be civilized . . . stinking little savages. Wipe 'em out. Wipe 'em off the face of the earth, I say. Wipe 'em off the face of the earth!"

[7] Of all the forms discussed, only science-fiction films exhibit certain themes which run against this grain. It seems to me there are two sources for this opening toward "deviation." First, in the particularly chilly years of the fifties, antinuclear, antimilitary freaks flocked to this form whose very fantastical nature provided an allegorical legitimacy for their questionable messages. Thus, even the monster-eradication movies often hide a plea for "peace"/deliverance from incompetent military defenders and their nuclear disasters, whose by-products are sci-fi's ubiquitous radioactive creatures. Second, a traditional tie-in with the sky, heaven, and God led to a semi-religious countertheme of "divine intervention" and human (implicitly white) inferiority. This conception of wisdom

Unfortunately for American moviemakers, Asians and others could not simply be photographed with three heads, tentacles, and gelatinaceous bodies. Consequently, other conventions had to be developed (or appropriated) that would clearly differentiate them from "humanity" at large. The first of these was invisibility. In most movies about the Third World, the nonwhites provide nothing more than a backdrop for all-white drama—an element of exotic and unifying dread against which to play out the tensions and problems of the white world. Sometimes, even the locales seem none-too-distinguishable, not to speak of their black, brown, or yellow inhabitants. It is not surprising, for instance, that the Gable-Harlow movie *Red Dust* (1932), set on an Indochinese rubber plantation (Gable is the foreman), could be transported to Africa without loss two decades later as the Gable-Kelly *Mogambo*. It could as well have been set in Brazil on a coffee plantation, or in Nevada with Gable a rancher.

As George Orwell commented of North Africa in 1939,

> All people who work with their hands are partly invisible, and the more important the work they do, the less visible they are. Still, a white skin is always fairly conspicuous. In northern Europe, when you see a labourer ploughing a field, you probably give him a second glance. In a hot country, anywhere south of Gibraltar or east of Suez, the chances are that you don't even see him. I have noticed this again and again. In a tropical landscape one's eye takes in everything except the human beings. It takes in the dried-up soil, the prickly pear, the palm tree and the distant mountains, but it always misses the peasant hoeing at his patch. He is the same colour as the earth, and a great deal less interesting to look at. It is only because of this that the starved countries of Asia and Africa are accepted as tourist resorts.[8]

Theoretically, it should have been somewhat more difficult since the Chinese and Vietnamese revolutions and other uprisings of the oppressed and nonwhite around the world, to ignore the people for the scenery. Yet we can't fault Hollywood for its valiant attempt. Generally, American films have hewed with unsurpassed tenacity to this framework—reproducing the white world whole in the Orient, with Asians skittering at the edges of sets as servants or scenic menace (as in the recent horrific extravaganza, *Krakatoa, East* [sic] *of Java,* 1969, where a volcano takes over the Lassie role and the Asian female pearl divers go under in the final explosions). This is even more true in films on Africa, where for generations whites have fought off natives and lions, not necessarily in that order.

A second convention of these films concerns the pecking order of white

---

descending from above to straighten out the stupid problems of blundering, incapable humanity is basic to *The Day the Earth Stood Still* (1952), in which "Klaatu" appears from space to tour Washington and plead for nuclear peace (and a fascist robot-police force to patrol the world); or *The Next Voice You Hear* (1950), in which God intervenes in person—via radio.

[8] George Orwell, "Marrakech," in *Essays* (Doubleday, 1954), pp. 189–190.

and nonwhite societies when they come into conflict. It is a "united front" among whites. Often the whites portrayed are the highly romanticized third-rate flotsam and jetsam of a mythologized American society—adventurers, prostitutes, opportunists, thieves (just as the films themselves, particularly when about Asia, tend to represent the brackish backwater of the American film industry). Yet no matter how low, no matter what their internal squabbles, no matter what their hostilities towards each other, in relation to the Third World the whites stand as one: Missionary's daughter and drunken ferryboat captain ("I hate the Reds," he says to her, "because they closed a lot of Chinese ports where they have dames. Chinese, Eurasian, and White Russian. . . . Somebody pinned the bleeding heart of China on your sleeve but they never got around to me."—*Blood Alley,* 1956); soldier of fortune and adventurer-journalist, natural enemies over The-Woman-They-Both-Love (they escape Canton together, avoiding the clutches of the Reds in a stolen boat—*Soldier of Fortune,* 1955); sheriff, deputies, and captured outlaws (they are surrounded by Mexican bandits—*Bandolero!,* 1968); or on a national level, the British, Americans, and Russians (they must deal with "the chief enemy of the Western world," Mao Tse-tung—*The Chairman,* 1969). This theme is, of course, simply a variation on a more home-grown variety— the Confederates and Yankees who bury their sectional hatreds to unite against the Indians; the convicts on their way to prison who help the wagon train fight off the Sioux, bringing the women and children to safety, etc. (See, for example, *Ambush at Cimarron Pass,* 1958, which combines everything in one laughable mess—a Yankee patrol and its prisoner team up with a Confederate rancher to fight off an Apache attack.)

The audience is expected to carry two racial lessons away from this sort of thing. The first is that the presence of the incomprehensible and nonhuman brings out what is "human" in every man. Individual dignity, equality, fraternity, all that on which the West theoretically places premium value, are brought sharply into focus at the expense of "alien" beings. The second is the implicit statement that, in a pinch, any white is a step up from the rest of the world. They may be murderers, rapists, and mother-snatchers, but they're ours.

When the inhabitants of these countries emerge from the ferns or mottled huts, and try to climb to the edges of the spotlight, they find the possibilities limited indeed. In this cinematic pick-up-sides, the whites already have two hands on the bat handle before the contest begins. The set hierarchy of roles is structured something like this: All roles of positive authority are reserved for white characters. Among the whites, the men stand triumphantly at the top; their women cringe, sigh, and faint below; and the Asians are left to scramble for what's left, like beggars at a refuse heap.

There is only one category in which a nonwhite is likely to come out top dog—villain. With their stock of fanatical speeches and their propensity for odd tortures, Third World villains provided the American film-maker with a handy receptacle for his audience's inchoate fears of the unknown and inhuman. Only as the repository for Evil could the nonwhite "triumph" in films. However, this is no small thing; for wherever there is a Third World country, American scriptwriters have created villain slots to be filled by otherwise unemployable actors (though often even these roles are monopolized by whites in yellowface). From area to area, like spirits, their forms change: the Mexican bandit chief with his toothy smile, hearty false laugh, sombrero and bushy eyebrows (see, f.i., the excellent *Treasure of the Sierra Madre*, 1948, or the awful *Bandolero*); the Oriental warlord with his droopy mustache and shaven head (see *Left Hand of God*, 1955; *The General Died at Dawn*, 1936; *Shanghai Express*, 1932; *Seven Women*, 1966, etc. ad nauseam); the Indian "khan" or prince with his little goatee and urbane manner (*Khyber Patrol*, 1955; *Charge of the Light Brigade*, 1936). Yet their essence remains the same.

Set against their shiny pates or silken voices, their hard eyes and twitching mouths, no white could look anything but good. In *Left Hand of God*, Humphrey Bogart, the pilot-turned-opportunist-warlord-advisor-turned-fraudulent-priest becomes a literal saint under the leer of Lee J. Cobb's General Yang. Gregory Peck, an "uninvolved" scientist-CIA spy, becomes a boy wonder and living representative of humanity when faced with a Ping-Pong-playing Mao Tse-tung in *The Chairman*. How can you lose when the guy you want to double-deal represents a nation which has discovered an enzyme allowing pineapples to grow in Tibet and winter wheat in Mongolia, yet (as one of the Russian agents puts it) is holding it so that the rest of the "underdeveloped" world, "90% poor, 90% peasant . . . will crawl on their hands and knees to Peking to get it." All in all, these nonwhite representatives of evil provide a backboard off which white Western values can bounce in, registering one more cinematic Score for Civilization.

The other group of roles open to nonwhites are roles of helplessness and dependence. At the dingy bottom of the scale of dependence crouch children. Nonwhite children have traditionally been a favorite for screenwriters and directors. Ingrid Bergman helped them across the mountains to safety (*The Inn of the Sixth Happiness*, 1959); Deborah Kerr taught them geography (*The King and I*, 1956); Humphrey Bogart helped them to memorize "My Old Kentucky Home" (*Left Hand of God*); Carroll Baker went with them on a great trek back to their homelands (*Cheyenne Autumn*, 1965); Richard Widmark took one (a little half-breed orphan girl—sort of the black, one-eyed Jew of the tiny tot's universe) back to the States with him (*55 Days at Peking*). And so on.

Essentially, nonwhite children fulfill the same function and have the same effect as nonwhite villains. They reflect to the white audience just another facet of their own humanity. Of course, if you ignore W. C. Fields, children have a traditionally cloying place in American films; but in the Third World movie they provide a particularly strong dose of knee-jerk sentiment, allowing the white leads to show the other side of Western civilization. It is their duty not just to exterminate the world's evil forces, but to give to those less capable (and more needy) than themselves. And who more closely fits such a description than the native child who may someday grow up to emulate us.

While it is children who demonstrate the natural impulses of the white authorities towards those who do not resist them, but are helpless before them or dependent upon them, it is women who prove the point. Even within the cinematic reflection of the white world, women have seldom held exalted positions. Normally they are daughters of missionaries, sweethearts of adventurers, daughters, nurses, daughters of missionaries, wives on safari, schoolmarms, daughters of missionaries, or prostitutes. (The exceptions usually being when women come under a "united front" ruling—that is, they confront Asian men, not white men. Then, as with Anna in *The King and I*, while their occupations may not change they face society on a somewhat different footing.) Several rungs down the social ladder, nonwhite women are left mainly with roles as bargirls, geishas, belly dancers, nurse's aids, missionary converts, harem girls, prostitutes. In such positions, their significance and status depends totally on the generosity (or lack of generosity) of those white men around whom the movies revolve.

However "well-intentioned" the moviemaker, the basic effect of this debased dependency is not changeable. Take that classic schmaltz of the 1950's, *The World of Suzie Wong*. William Holden, a dissatisfied architect-businessman, has taken a year's sabbatical in Hong Kong to find out if he can "make it" as an artist. (It could have been Los Angeles, but then the movie would have been a total zilch.) He meets . . . Suzie Wong . . . , a bargirl who is cute as a Walt Disney button and speaks English with an endearing "Chinese" accent. ("Fo' goo'niss sakes" she says over and over at inappropriate moments.) He wants her to be his model. She wants to be his "permanent girlfriend." Many traumas later, the moviemakers trundle out their good intentions towards the world's ill-treated masses. They allow Holden to choose Susie over Kay, the proper, American, upper-class woman who is also chasing him. This attempt to put down the upper classes for their prejudices towards Chinese and bargirls, however, barely covers over the basic lesson of the movie: a helpless, charming Chinese bargirl *can* be saved by the right white man, purified by association with him, and elevated to dependency on him. (Her bastard child, conveniently brought out for his pity quotient, is also conveniently bumped off by a flash flood, avoiding further knotty problems for the already overtaxed sensibilities of the scriptwriters.) It all comes across as part act of God, part act of white America.

Moving upwards towards a peak of Third World success and white condescension, we discover the role of "sidekick." Indispensable to the sidekick is his uncanny ability to sacrifice his life for his white companion at just the right moment. In this, he must leave the audience feeling that he has repaid the white man something intangible that was owed to him. And, in this, we find the last major characteristic of Third World roles—expendability. Several classic scenes come to mind. In this skill, the otherwise pitiful Gunga Din excelled (*Gunga Din,* 1939). Up there on a craggy ledge, already dying, yet blowing that bugle like crazy to save the British troops from ambush by the fanatic Kali-worshipers. Or, just to bring up another Third World group, the death of the black trainer in *Body and Soul* (1948), preventing his white World Heavyweight Champion (John Garfield) from throwing the big fight. Or even, if I remember rightly, Sidney Poitier, Mau Mau initiate, falling on the Punji sticks to save the white child of his boyhood friend Rock Hudson (*Something of Value,* 1957). The parts blend into each other: the Filipino guide to the American guerrillas, the Indian pal of the white scout, that Mexican guy with the big gut and sly sense of humor. In the end, Third World characters are considered expendable by both moviemakers and their audiences because they are no more a source of "light" than the moon at night. All are there but to reflect in differing mirrors aspects of white humanity.

While extermination, dependency, and expendability have been the steady diet of these movies over the decades, American moviemakers have not remained totally stagnant in their treatment of the Third World and its inhabitants. They have, over the last forty years, emerged ponderously from a colonial world into a neocolonial one. In the 1930's, the only decade when anything other than second-rate films were made about Asia, moviemakers had no hesitation about expressing an outright contempt for subjugated and/or powerless Asians; nor did they feel self-conscious about proudly portraying the colonial style in which most Westerners in Asia lived. The train in *Shanghai Express* (1932) is shown in all its "colonial" glory; the Chinese passengers crammed into crude compartments; the Westerners eating dinner in their spacious and elegant dining room. Here was the striking contrast between the rulers and the ruled and nobody saw any reason to hide it.

During this period, with the European imperial structure in Asia still unbroken, colonial paternalism abounded. No one blinked an eye when Shirley Temple asked her Grandfather, the British Colonel (*Wee Willie Winkie,* 1937), why he was mad at "Khoda Khan," leader of the warlike tribes on India's northeast border; and he replied, "We're not mad at Khoda Khan. England wants to be friends with all her peoples. But if we don't shoot him, he'll shoot us. . . . (They've been plundering for so many years) they don't realize they'de be better off planting crops" [a few poppy seeds maybe?]. Nor were audiences taken aback when Cary Grant called his Indian sidekick a "beastie" (or alternately the "regimental beastie") in *Gunga Din;* nor when Clark Gable kicked his Indochinese workers out of a ditch (to save them from a storm, of course), calling them similar names (*Red Dust*).

A decade later such scenes and lines would have been gaffes.[9] In the wake of the World War and its flock of anti-Japanese propaganda flicks (whose progeny were still alive in the early 1960's), the destruction of the British, French, and Dutch empires, the success of the Communist revolution in China,

[9] There were, of course, some holdovers from the '30's. Particularly junk like *Khyber Patrol* (1955), in which British Lancer Richard Egan, getting ready to capture rebel leaders in a village, tells a fellow officer: "I don't want any of those devils to escape us."

the birth and death of dreaded "neutralism," and the rise of the United States to a position of preeminence in the world, new cinematic surfaces were developed to fit over old frames. In their new suits, during the decade of the 1950's, cowboy-Third World movies flourished as never before. A vast quantity of these low-budget (and not-so-low-budget) films burst from Hollywood to flood the country's theaters. In the more "progressive" of them, an India in chains was replaced by a struggling, almost "independent" country; the "regimental beastie" by a Nehru (-Gandhi) type "rebel" leader; the Kali-worshipping, loinclothed fanatic by Darvee, the Maoist revolutionary ("You cannot make omelettes without breaking eggs."). Yet this sort of exercise was no more than sleight of hand. The Nehru character looked just as ridiculously pompous and imitative as did Gunga Din when he practiced his bugle; nor did the whites any less monopolize center stage (holding, naturally, the key military and police positions); nor could the half-breed woman (Ava Gardner) any less choose light (the British officer) over darkness (Darvee and his minions). Soon, all this comes to seem about as basic a change in older forms as was the "independence" granted to many former colonies in the real world (*Bhowani Junction,* 1956).

If any new elements were to enter these movies in the 1950's (and early '60's), it was in the form of changes in relations within the white world, not between the white and nonwhite worlds. These changes, heralded by the "adult westerns" of the late fifties, have yet to be fully felt in films on Asia; yet a certain early (and somewhat aborted) move in this direction could be seen in some of the films that appeared about the Korean war (not a particularly popular subject, as might be imagined)—a certain tiredness ("Three world wars in one lifetime"—*Battle Circus,* 1953) and some doubts. The WWII flick's faith in the war against the "Japs," in a "civilian" army, and in "democracy" comes across tarnished and tired. The "professional" soldier (or flyer) takes center stage. ("We've gotta do a clean, professional job on those [North Korean] bridges."—*The Bridges at Toko-ri,* 1954.) There is, for instance, no analogue in your WWII movies to the following conversation in *The Bridges at Toko-ri.* Mickey Rooney (a helicopter rescue pilot) and William Holden (a flyer) are trapped (shot down) behind the North Korean lines. Surrounded, they wait in a ditch for help to arrive. During a lull in the shooting, they begin to talk:

Holden: "I'm a lawyer from Denver, Colorado, Mike. I probably couldn't hit a thing [with this] . . . ."
Rooney: "Judas, how'd you ever get out here in a smelly ditch in Korea?"
Holden: "That's just what I've been asking myself . . . the wrong war in the wrong place and that's the one you're stuck with. . . . You fight simply because you are here."

Within minutes, they are both killed by the advancing Korean soldiers.

Yet though the white world might seem tarnished, its heroes bitter, tired, and ridden with doubts, its relationship to the nonwhite world had scarcely changed. If anything, the introduction of massive air power to Asian warfare had only further reduced the tangential humanity of Asian peoples. For in a movie like *Toko-ri* (as at Danang today), you never even needed to see the enemy, only charred bodies.

This attempt, particularly in Westerns, to introduce new attitudes in the white world, increasingly muddied the divisions between stock characters, brought to the fore the hero-as-cynic, and called into question the "humanity" of the whites vis-à-vis each other. Such adjustments in a relatively constant cinematic structure represented an attempt to update a form which the world's reality put in increasing danger of unbelievability. By the early 1960's, the "adult western" had reached a new stage—that of elegy (see, for instance, *The Man Who Shot Liberty Valence,* 1962). Superficially, such movies seem to be in a state of sentimental mourning for the closing of the frontier and the end of a mythical white frontier life. However, Westerns as a form were originally created amidst industrial America partially to mourn just such a loss. The elegiac Western of the 1960's was, in fact, mourning the passing of itself. Today, this form has come to what may be its terminal fruition in America, the "hip" Western—*Butch Cassidy and the Sundance Kid* (1970), which is a parody not of the Western, but of the elegiac Western, since not even that can be taken totally straight any more.[10]

However, even in this extension of the Western, one thing has not changed —attitudes towards the Third World. When, for instance, Butch and Sundance cannot make a go of it in a hemmed-in West, they naturally move on, "invading" Bolivia. In Bolivia, of course, it's the same old local-color scene again, with one variation: instead of the two of them killing off hundreds of Bolivians in that old wagon-train scene, hundreds of unidentified Bolivians band together to kill them. It all boils down to the same thing.

Whatever *Butch Cassidy* may be the end of, I think we stand at the edge of a totally new, but nonetheless yawning, abyss—the "sympathetic" film. The first of what I expect will be an onslaught of these are appearing now. They have at least pretensions toward changing how we see relationships not only within the white world itself, but between the white and Indian worlds. And what is appearing in Westerns today may be the transmuted meat of Asian or African films within the next decade.

The recent *A Man Called Horse* (1970) is a good example. It seems to have been a sincere and painstaking attempt to make a large-scale, commercially successful movie about the Sioux (before they were overrun by the whites), to show from an Indian point of view their way of life, their rituals (recreated from Catlin's paintings) and beliefs, their feelings and fears. Yet, at every turn, the film betrays the edges of older and more familiar frameworks.

It concerns an English lord hunting in the American West early in the nineteenth century. Captured by a Sioux raiding party, he is brought back to their village (where the rest of the film takes place). There he becomes a slave (horse) for an Indian woman (Dame Judith Anderson). Already a white

[10] Even John Wayne, the last of the cowboy superstars still in the saddle, is forced to mourn his own passing in *True Grit* (1969).

"hero" has been slipped into this movie about Indians, betraying an assumption that American audiences could not sustain interest in a film without whites. Given the way we look at these films, he immediately becomes the center of our attention; thus, in the end, you are forced to relate to the Sioux village through his eyes; and to relate to the Sioux as they relate to him (aiding him or mistreating him). Second, by following the travails of this lord-turned-beast-of-burden as he assimilates to the tribe, the movie seems to prove that old adage, "put a white man among even the best of savages and you have a natural chief." (He kills enemy Indians, goes through the sun initiation ritual, marries the chief's daughter, teaches the tribe British infantry tactics, and, in the end, his wife and adopted mother being dead, he splits for the white world.)

His girlfriend has that Ali McGraw look which probably is supposed to allow the audience to "identify" better with the Indians, but looks about as fitting as it did among the Jews of New Jersey (*Goodbye, Columbus*). Even a stab at righting the wrongs Westerns have done to language has similarly dismal result. The movie's makers, reacting to the common use of pidgin-Hollywood by Indian characters in normal Westerns, allow the Sioux in this movie to speak their own language. As all but two of the characters are Sioux, much of the movie is conducted in the Sioux language. If this were a French movie, there would naturally be subtitles; but as these are Sioux *au naturel,* and as here is already a conveniently English-speaking character, an alternate means is called upon. Another "prisoner" is created, an Indian who spent some time with the French and speaks broken English. At the behest of the English lord, he translates what is necessary to his and our understanding. In this way, the Indians, while retaining the dignity of their own language, are perhaps slightly less able to express themselves comprehensibly in this picture than in a normal Western. More important, just as if it were the normal wagon-train scenario, it forces us to see everything through white eyes.[11]

[11] For another recent example, see *Tell Them Willie Boy Is Here* (1970); and I feel certain (though I have yet to see it) that *Soldier Blue* (1970) will fall in the same general category.

As for the newness of "sympathetic" films—at least a couple of historical antecedents come to mind: first, *The General Died at Dawn* (1936) with Gary Cooper, and Akim Tamiroff as the warlord Yang (seems to have been a pretty popular name among warlords' mothers). This Clifford Odets script hangs heavy with the hand of the 30's Left. ("You ask me why I'm for oppressed people, because I have a background of oppression myself.") But despite its professed sympathy for the oppressed people of China, its protestations of Asian dignity and love for life, and its unbelievably murky politics, it is loaded with all the normal stuff: white-centeredness ("Mr. O'Hara, from the time you leave this room until you deliver the money, the fate of China is in your hands."); a Chinese super-evil villain; and a mass-suicide scene that only could have taken place among those for whom human life meant nothing at all (in the movie's climactic scene, General Yang—who is dying at dawn—has his troops line up in two facing lines several feet apart and shoot each other, to name just a few of the more salient points).

For an example from the earlier '60's, see John Ford's "bow" to the tribulations of the Indians, *Cheyenne Autumn* (1965). Exactly the same sort of process occurs, and a good book by Mari Sandoz, written from the viewpoint of the Cheyenne, is destroyed in the bargain. Even its historical ending is twisted to imply that Secretary of the Interior Schultz (Edward G. Robinson) allowed the remnants of the Cheyenne to return to their homeland—which he most definitely did not.

And as long as the eyes through which we see the world do not change, so long as the old frameworks for movies about the Third World are not thrown away, "intentions" go for little indeed. It is hard even to think of examples of films where sympathetic intentions are matched by deeds. Certainly one would have to venture beyond the bounds of the United States to find them—perhaps *The Battle of Algiers* (which, in reverse, does for the French colonizers what we were never willing to do for the Indians). Its view begins at least to accord with the brutal history of the Third World; to tell a little what it means, from the colonized point of view, to resist, to fight back, to rebel against your occupiers.

American moviemakers, however, are at heart still in love with an era when people could accept the six-year-old Shirley Temple telling Khoda Khan not to make war on the British because "the Queen wants to protect her people and make them rich." Their main substitution in later movies being to replace the Queen with (American) technology—machine guns to mow 'em down, and Band-Aids to patch 'em up. This mood is best captured by Gene Tierney in *Left Hand of God* when Humphrey Bogart says, "China's becoming a nightmare, Anne. . . . What are we really doing here? . . . We belong back in the States, marrying, raising a family." She replies, ". . . There's too much work to do here . . . the things we're doing here are what they need; whether medicine or grace. And we can give it to them. . . ." Of course, the historical joke of this being uttered in China's Sinkiang province in 1947, a time when the unmentioned Communist revolution is sweeping through the central provinces, passed the scriptwriters by. Yet, on the whole, just this distance between the film's "message" and Chinese reality about sums up the American approach to the Third World. In the end, no matter where the moviemakers may think their sympathy lies, their films are usually no more than embroideries on a hagiography of "pacification."

Within such a context, there is no possibility for presenting resistance, rebellion, or revolution by the intruded upon in a way that could be even comprehensible, no less sympathetic. Quite the opposite, the moviemakers are usually hell-bent on glorifying those Asians (or other Third Worlders) who allied with the Western invaders, not those who at some point resisted either the invasion or its consequences. However, there is an insoluble contradiction here. The method for judging nonwhites in these films is based on how dependent or independent they are of the white leads and the white world. To the degree to which they are dependent they are seen as closer to humanity. To the degree to which they are independent (i.e., resist), they are seen as less liable to humanization or outrightly inhuman and thus open to extermination. ("Mitchell, we must stamp this out immediately."—*Gunga Din.*) In other words, there is an inherent bias in these movies towards the glorification of those "natives" who have allied with us. Yet what makes the white hero so appealing is the audience's feeling that no matter how low he sinks, he retains some sense of human dignity. There is always that feeling (as Bogart and countless cowboy stars brought out so well) that despite appearances, *he is his own man.* Yet no movie Asians linked to the West can ever really be that.

Though they can bask in the light of humanity, they can never be much more than imitation humans. In only one nonwhite role is this possibility open— that is the role of villain (he who refuses white help and actively opposes him). Only the villain, already placed outside the pale (*sic*) of humanity, can be his own man.

The result is a knotty problem. If those close to the whites are invariably dependent, they cannot but be viewed in some way with contempt, no matter how the moviemakers go about trying to glorify them. On the other hand, if those most contemptible nonhumans, the villains, are the only Asians capable of "independence" in these films, they are also the only Asians who are the cinematic equivalents of the white leads. Thus, we cannot help but have a sneaking respect for those who oppose us and a sneaking contempt for those who side with us. (How similar this is to the attitudes of many American soldiers in Vietnam towards ARVN and towards the NLF forces.) No doubt this is at least partly responsible for the extremes American moviemakers have gone to in glorifying one and despoiling the other.

What Lewis and Clark's Indian guide Sacajawea was to American history high-school texts, Gunga Din was to Third World movies. He makes the classic sacrifice for the white world, and in death theoretically proves he is a "better man" than his British mentors. Yet how hollow this "triumph" is for the viewing audience. No one is fooled by the words. Doing his mimic marching shuffle, around the corner from the practicing British troops, what a pitiful imitation "human" he appears to be. And even his greatest hopes—to get one toe on the lowest rung of the white regimental ladder as company bugler—leave him second best to any white who comes along. On the other hand, the leader of the Kali worshippers (read: native resistance forces) is portrayed in a paroxysm of caricature ("Rise brothers and kill . . . kill for the love of Kali, kill for the love of killing, KILL, KILL, KILL!"). He is a mad murderer, a torturer, a loinclothed savage, a megalomaniac with bulging eyes. Yet he is the only Indian in the film who has the real ability to "love his country" like a white man. "I can die as readily for my country and my fate as you for yours," he says and voluntarily jumps into the snakepit, yelling "India farewell!"

This inability, despite pulling all the stops, to deny the enemy a certain dignity is not extraordinary. Even Mao Tse-tung, in the otherwise rabid *The Chairman,* proves in some grim sense, irrepressible. On the other hand, no matter how charmingly portrayed, our allies' dependency cannot be totally overcome. They are always, in a way, trained spies in the camp of their own people.

American movies about the Third World should not be given more credit than is their due. Despite the impression you might get in the theater, American moviemakers did not invent the world, nor even the version of world history they present in their films. However, they must be given full credit for developing a highly successful and satisfying cinematic form to encapsulate an existing ideological message. With this form, they have been able to relegate the great horrors of Western expansion into the rest of the world, and present-day American hegemony over great hunks of it, to another universe of pleasure and enjoyment. They have successfully tied extermination of nonwhite peoples to laughable relief, and white racial superiority to the natural order of things. They have destroyed any possibility for explaining the various ways in which nonwhite (not to speak of white) people could resist invasion, colonization, exploitation, and even mass slaughter.

Cowboy (-Third World) films are, in the end, a vast visual pacification program, ostensibly describing the rest of the world, but in fact aimed at the millions of people who for several generations have made up the American viewing audience. It's hardly a wonder that Vietnam did not sear the American consciousness. Why should it have? For years, Americans had been watching the whole scene on their screens: REV DEV, WHAM, endless My Lai's, body counts, killing of wounded enemy soldiers, aerial obliteration, etc. We had grown used to seeing it, and thrilling with pleasure while reaching for another handful of popcorn.

Such a "pacification" program is based on the inundation principle. It is not a matter of quality (probably there have been no good films on Asia since the 1930's), but quantity. So many cowboy-Third World movies have rolled factory-style off the production line that the most minute change of plot is hailed as a great innovation. In the end, all the visual "choices" available to a viewer just emphasize the way in which America is strikingly a one-channel country. In fact, it might not be too far wrong to say that while pacification may have failed in Vietnam, its pilot project here in America has generally succeeded; that we are a pacified population, living unknowingly in an occupied country.

Discussion Questions

1. Quickly jot down several forms of symbolic aggression discussed in this article.
2. What stereotypes of Indians and members of the Third World has the movie industry succeeded in perpetuating? How have these stereotypes affected governmental policy toward the Indians and the Third World?
3. Have television and other forms of mass media similarly contributed to the perpetuation of stereotypes? Have you seen an Indian, African, or Asian depicted in a normally daily routine?

GLEN GAVIGLIO

The Myths of the Mexican American

Another minority group yet to be assimilated in the United States is comprised of Americans of Mexican heritage. They have also become more conscious of their meager income and status, relative political impotence,

Reprinted from Glen Gaviglio, "The Myths of the Mexican American," with permission of Macmillan Publishing Co., Inc., from Society as It Is (pp. 420–427) by Glen Gaviglio. Copyright © 1971 by Macmillan Publishing Co., Inc.

and alienation from dominant-group culture. In the following article Glen Gaviglio outlines the major factors that have influenced the growing self-consciousness of Mexican Americans, and many of the myths that have thus far precluded their assimilation.

The Mexican Americans, or "Chicanos," have been referred to as the forgotten minority. They are supposedly a quiet, docile, passive, somnolent, and satisfied group of fatalistic near peasants. Therefore they have been erased from the conscience of most Americans. They have been invisible; they have been wiped from history, like the Indians. Yet Chicanos have not lost themselves, even though they have lived in a hostile environment for decades. Why have they been overlooked, ignored, and oppressed?

This brief essay is an attempt to synthesize some of the major sociohistoric factors that have influenced the development of *La Raza*. For purposes of analysis, this essay is arranged into four deeply ingrained myths of the Mexican American: (1) The Myth of the Border, (2) The Myth of the Docile Peasant, (3) The Myth of Ethnic and Racial Assimilation, and (4) The Myth of Mexican American Similarity.

Myths are important for societies; they influence every individual's definition of reality. People act in relation to the mythology of their society. Therefore myths are significant behavior inducing and shaping devices. (The social reality of the mind comes in all flavors of distortion.) The influence of some of these distortions is examined in each of the following myths.

The Myth of the Border

Historically, cries of "Spic," "Greaser," "Wetback," or "Taco Bender, go home" were very typical of the American Southwest. The cries are more subdued and sophisticated now, but invariably eruptions occur. For example, in 1969 in the Santa Clara Valley, just south of San Francisco, a venerable judge publicly excoriated a Chicano youth in court, saying that Hitler had a good thing going with the Jews and that a similar program should be undertaken with Mexicans. . . .

There is a political boundary separating Mexico and the United States, but the winds of change have modified that boundary immensely. In a very real sense that border does not exist. The border is totally artificial from a geographical perspective. It does not separate climatic or agricultural regions; in fact, it cuts across the natural topography of the area. The difference between Calexico and Mexicali, El Paso and Juarez, and Brownsville and Matamoros is economic and political, not geographical. The border does not really exist for the Chicano. It never has.

At one time the Southwest was part of Mexico. It was inhabited by a mixture of Spaniards and Indians; it was naturally an arid region that was sparsely settled. The region was the frontier or borderlands of Mexico, and it was never an integral part of that country. When the Spanish did come to settle this region, there actually were very few pure Spaniards in the expeditions. Most of the settlers who came north from Mexico were Mestizo and Indian. The Indians who were living in this area had already been strongly influenced by the Aztec civilization. On the eve of the Mexican–American War (1848), there were only about 82,000 Spanish-speaking people living in the Southwest, but they had been there for generations. (There were also an untabulated number of Indians and Mestizos in the area.) In California in 1848, there were 21,000 Spanish-speaking in a population of about 100,000. When California became a state (1850), the constitution was written in Spanish. This constitution, created in part by people of Spanish ancestry, established California as a bilingual state (and it remained bilingual until 1878). In southern California there were bilingual schools until the 1870's. In other words, California has gone from bilingual schools to denial to the Chicanos of the right to vote, because they cannot read the Constitution. (This has been recently changed by the California Supreme Court.)

When the United States wrested the Southwest from Mexico, many Spanish-speaking people automatically became residents of the United States. They did not immigrate from anywhere. Therefore, when an Anglo tells a Chicano to go home, he is less than amusing; he is grossly misinformed. The Chicano is more firmly rooted in the American past than an Anglo who may have just recently migrated from Europe.

The Treaty of Guadalupe Hidalgo (1848), which terminated the Mexican-American War, was supposed to protect and guarantee the rights of self-determination for the Spanish-speaking people in the newly acquired United States territory. In actuality the treaty did little to protect the rights of the Mexicans in his region. The Anglos immediately displayed a tremendous hostility and resentment toward these Hispanos. The creed of American racism became brutally apparent in the systematic oppression that followed. For example, in California the antagonism between Spanish-speaking and Yankee miners culminated with the Foreign Miners Tax Law of 1850, which effectively drove the Spanish-speaking from the gold fields. (Note the word *foreign*.) In 1851 the Federal Land Tenure Act was passed. This act made possible the systematic and gradual extraction of land from the hands of the Hispanos.

No Chicano is really an immigrant in America. When they "moved north," they felt that they were moving in an environment that was geographically, culturally, and historically familiar. I would even say that in a political sense the border has been a nebulous entity. There was no border patrol until 1924 and there was not even a quota on Mexican immigration until 1965. The reason the border did not exist in a political or economic manner for either the Anglo or Chicano was the need for cheap labor in the fields. As long as there was a ready supply of bodies toward the south, the indigenous labor force could not organize and demand higher wages. When the field workers did try to organize, their leaders were quickly "deported." The farm workers could not effectively unionize until the Bracero program was terminated in 1965. (The program allowed Mexican nationals to reside temporarily in the United States in order to harvest the crops.) The Delano movement still has not completely succeeded, because the border is still quite open. Migrant workers can enter both legally and illegally. "Green Card Holders" are now entering the United States to pick crops in times of emergency (meaning "during strikes"). In reality, the border has always been exactly what the United States has wanted it to be.

The Myth of the Docile Peasant

The Chicano has been stereotyped as a passive peasant. This is absurd on statistical grounds alone. Over 80 per cent of all Chicanos reside in urban areas and over 1 million Chicanos live in Los Angeles. The image of the Chicano is not really a static one. According to the stereotype, the Chicano can be either a fat and lazy peon, slumbering under a cactus and wearing his sombrero and poncho, or he can be a stinking, ferocious, foul-mouthed, greasy bandito. The stereotype of the Mexican American stems from two basic sources: (1) the popularized folk mythology of traditional American racism and (2) the distorted sociological image. We can expect the first; it bears no surprises, but the latter is more repulsive to us, because it comes from unbiased sociological sources.

There is nothing unique in saying that the society of America is racist, but when we confront the historical record of past American racial atrocities, the present looks as though peace and brotherhood abound (if you choose to ignore Vietnam). American literature, with but few exceptions, is filled with condescending racist drivel. One example from *The Oregon Trail* by Francis Parkman (Doubleday, 1948) will provide the proper flavor:

> Two or three squalid Mexicans, with their broad hats, and their vile faces overgrown with hair, were lounging about the bank of the river in front of (the gate of the Pueblo). They disappeared as they saw us approach [p. 260].
>
> A few squaws and Spanish women, and a few Mexicans, as mean and miserable as the place itself, were lazily sauntering about [p. 260].
>
> There was another room beyond, less sumptuously decorated, and here three or four Spanish girls, one of them very pretty, were baking cakes at a mud fireplace in the corner [p. 261].
>
> The human race in this part of the world is separated into three divisions, arranged in the order of their merits: white men, Indians, and Mexicans; to the latter of whom the honorable title of "whites" is by no means conceded [p. 263].

Usually the racism is not even this "subtle." Our history is replete with speeches of major political figures proclaiming a hypocritical and altruistic imperialism. We have always had an inclination to save the ignorant and backward colored masses of the world from themselves, witness this speech delivered by John C. Calhoun in the Senate on January 4, 1848 (after we had defeated Mexico in a war):

> We have never dreamt of incorporating into our Union any but the Caucasian race—the free white race. To incorporate Mexico, would be the very first instance of the kind, of incorporating an Indian race; for more than half of the Mexicans are Indians, and the other is composed chiefly of mixed tribes. I protest against such a union as that! Ours, sir is the government of a white race. The greatest misfortunes of Spanish America are to be traced to the fatal error of placing these colored races on an equality with the white race. That error destroyed the social arrangement which formed the basis of society. The Portuguese and ourselves have escaped—the Portuguese at least to some extent—and we are the only people on this continent which had made revolutions without being followed by anarchy. And yet it is professed, and talked about, to erect these Mexicans into a territorial government, and place them on an equality with the people of the United States. I protest utterly against such a project. . . .
>
> But . . . suppose all these difficulties removed; suppose their people attached to our Union, and desirous of incorporating with us, ought we to bring them in? Are they fit to be connected with us? Are they fit for self-government and for governing you? Are you, any of you, willing that your states should be governed by these twenty-odd Mexican states, with a population of about only one million of your blood, and two or three million of mixed blood better informed—all the rest pure Indians, a mixed blood equally ignorant and unfit for liberty, impure races, not as good as the Cherokees or Chocktaws?

Calhoun did not even believe in spreading the faith to the ignorant colored masses, because they were too inferior even to govern themselves and accept the gospel of Americanism.

The mythology of American racism has been updated and perfected since the heyday of blatant expansionism and imperialism. The myths may be a little more subtle but they are still extremely harmful. It can be effectively argued that the myths are even more destructive because of the pervasive influence in the mass media. The world is being turned into a McLuhanesque global village; therefore more people are influenced by the racist stereotypes portrayed in the mass media. At the moment one of the worst offenders is the advertising industry. One particularly offensive commercial was for Arrid deodorant. It shows a Mexican bandito spraying his underarm while a voice says, "If it works for him, it will work for you." Do Chicanos stink worse than blacks? Can you envision that same commercial with a sloppy, fat ghetto black wearing a dirty and torn T-shirt? Or is the black movement too powerful (or too violent) to allow that kind of defamation? There is a real battle in America to see who will be the new "niggers." The Chicanos or the Hippies?

These stereotypes are extremely important because people act upon these myths. Very insipid and disastrous self-fulfilling prophecies can be initiated by racial and cultural myths. If the dominant group treats the minority group as an inferior race or culture, the minority can become just that. In a political and economic sense racial oppression is very obvious, but it has more subtle manifestations. What happens in the school system when students are "tracked" or when the teacher has lower expectations for some students? What happens to the minds of minority group members? Can a people be taught to hate themselves? Can a minority group believe the myths the majority perpetrates? One of the most sickening aspects of race relations in America is that the preceding questions must be answered in a very negative manner.

Another form of stereotyping is of a more insidious variety because it is generated by the academic community and therefore carries with it scientific validity. In particular the work of Heller (*Mexican-American Youth*), Tuck (*Not with the Fist*), and Madsen (*Mexican-Americans of South Texas*) should be mentioned. The studies have some very major defects. The most obvious deficiency from a traditional sociological perspective is a methodological one, the authors over-generalize from a biased or partial sampling of Chicanos. These studies list "characteristics" or "attributes" of the typical Mexican American. Some of these characteristics seem like a sociological updating of racial mythology. Is being passive, accepting, and fatalistic much different from being lazy? Do all Chicanos display these traits? We cannot be sure of the limited regional sample of Chicanos in these studies. Another glaring omission in these studies is their completely historical nature. They speak of the Chicano as existing in the eternal present, as if his traditional culture were static and unchanging. The Chicano may not try to change his environment in the same manner as the robust and enterprising Anglo, for he has found that passive adjustment to his social milieu is necessary to his survival. This passiveness creates another blatantly false stereotype. Were those who rode with Villa and Zapata during the Mexican Revolution passively accepting their fate? Were the Chicanos who organized numerous strikes in the Southwest for the past seventy-five years accepting their fate? Are Reies Tijerina, Cesar Chavez, and Corky Gonsalez leaders of a passive and somnolent bunch of poncho-clad peasants?

The last significant error in these books is their tendency to equate and confuse ethnic and class characteristics. Many of the characteristics attributed to Mexican Americans in these studies are shared by all lower-class people. Cohen and Hodges, in a study done in California, found that lower-lower-class Chicanos, blacks, and Anglos all shared some basically similar characteristics: extended families, marked anti-intellectualism, *machismo* (a supermasculine, double-standard-type male), use of physical force, and a type of fatalism. Oscar Lewis has argued that throughout the world the lower classes generally share these traits. Lewis terms these characteristics a "culture of poverty"; he sees it as a functional adaptation to their oppressive social conditions. Therefore there is nothing unique in these traits that are supposedly typical of the Mexican American. Some statistical validity resides in the fact that a fairly large percentage of Chicanos live below the poverty level (16 per cent of the Anglos, 27 per cent of the blacks, and 37 per cent of the Chicanos). These figures may understate the degree of Chicano poverty. That 37 per cent basically represents United States citizens. According to the U.S. Department of Immigration, there are 1.5 million alien residents and 4.5 million illegal aliens below the poverty level.

The concept of the culture of poverty can also be interpreted in a very negative manner. It can be used to conclude that the cultural characteristics of the poor people themselves are responsible for their socioeconomic status. For example, take the noted fatalism of the lower classes. They feel that they have little control over the institutions and events that shape their lives. It is very possible that the pessimism, apathy, and fatalism of the lower classes is a valid adjustment to a historical social reality. The life chances of a minority group members have been severely and systematically restricted; these people have not had and still do not have very much control over the decisions that affect their lives. Is it really so hard to imagine accepting a religion, whether it is a folk Catholicism or a revivalist Protestantism, that promises an internal reward when the present and future look so bleak? When reality is unbearably ugly, fatalism may be the only answer among rotten alternatives.

It would be wise not to apply the concept of culture of poverty to minority groups unless its sociohistorical component is considered. Why is there a culture of poverty? How did it start? Why do so many different societies have subcultures of poverty with similar traits? The answer lies in an analysis of how people adjust to the conditions of poverty, racism, and oppression.

The Myth of Ethnic and Racial Assimilation

The huddled and hungry hordes of the world streamed to the shores of America, where golden opportunities awaited them. The saga of America is sometimes told as though it were a giant, bottomless cauldron where the oppressed masses of humanity mingled and produced an egalitarian and tolerant democratic society. This is the great myth of the melting pot. It is a romantic and nostalgic vision of the American past that does very little justice to reality. Assimilation in the American melting pot was meant for whites only. For example, Indians were almost exterminated like vermin, instead of being melted, and of course enough has been said recently of black Americans. The Chicano still forms an unassimilated and distinct cultural entity in America.

Glazer and Moynihan (*Beyond the Melting Pot,* 1963) argue that ethnic homogenization never completely took place in America. New York is a veritable hodge-podge of racial and ethnic groups that still function as political interest groups. Glazer and Moynihan succinctly conclude, "The point about the Melting Pot . . . is that it did not happen." Every act of racism and discrimination is a painful contradiction of the concept of the melting pot.

Why have the Chicanos not been assimilated into the American mainstream? The most obvious reason for this lack of assimilation is the dominant Anglo group itself; it has not been willing to let the Chicano assimilate. The Mexican American is in a caste position similar to that of the black man after emancipation. There are other factors that have contributed to the cultural distance between the Chicano and the Anglo. First, there is the fact that Mexico is adjacent to the United States. The homeland for many Chicanos is never far away. There is a continual cultural regeneration and reinforcement. Many Mexicans come to America "temporarily" and never psychologically divorce themselves from the values of Mexico. Then there is the continual immigration, both legal and illegal, from Mexico. There are also visits from relatives going in both directions. The communal and extended nature of the Chicano family further reinforces certain cultural values, like language. Three and four generations may live in the same household. This pattern can be contrasted with many white immigrant groups who left the homeland far behind in Europe, geographically if not psychologically.

Another reason why the Chicano has not been and may never be totally assimilated is that he does not want to be. Why accept the dominant culture? If Anglo youth rebellion is any indication of the viability of mainstream, middle-class American values, Chicanos may be correct in refusing to assimilate. In fact, many of the criticisms that young people level at America have been part of the Chicano cultural and historical tradition. Chicanos have never been "materialistic," or what the Anglo considers "property oriented." The land was usually for all to use or hold communally; their agricultural practices and use of the land were in harmony with nature. Chicanos have always displayed a sense of community, a tendency toward mutual aid, and a strong communal or extended family. They have always nurtured an emphasis on warm interpersonal relationships and a respect for people as individuals.

The Myth of Mexican American Similarity

As with most minority groups, the Mexican American has been stereotyped. The stereotype is usually one of a lower-lower-class Chicano, a rigid caricature which allows a minimum of diversity. The stereotype . . . has negative and racist connotations, and as a valid characterization of social reality, it is sadly lacking.

There are some statistical generalizations that can be made in relation to Chicanos. Many have parents or grandparents who migrated from Mexico, and as a consequence, many speak Spanish, Pocho (a combination of Spanish and English), or English with an accent. As a group, Chicanos tend to be Catholic (easily over 50 per cent). As a population they tend to be young (twenty years of age). The average yearly income for the Mexican American family is the lowest in the nation, except for the income of the reservation Indian. There are more Chicanos (60 to 70 per cent) living in poverty and more Chicanos with less education than blacks (less than eight years, on the average, for those over twenty-five). Chicanos as a group share certain cultural values, but within the broad contours just mentioned there is immense variety.

There are many physical differences in the Chicano population. Although Chicanos tend to be darker than the Anglo population, they range from swarthy to light skinned. All types of ethnic and racial groups have mingled in Mexico with the idigenous people, from black slaves to French immigrants. There are also Filipinos and Puerto Ricans who are culturally Chicano. There are rural and urban differences, generational conflicts, geographical differences, and class differences between Chicanos. Who is a Mexican American? How can you really stereotype the Chicano?

Here lies the strength and weakness of the Chicano. On one hand he is confronted in America with a severe "identity crisis." He is the true marginal man caught between cultures. Historically, he represents the uneasy compromise between the Hispano and the Indian who was delivered into a hostile Anglo world. Yet as a people, *La Raza* has developed a deeply ingrained humanism. The term *La Raza* does not simply mean the race or people, but the community or the family. *La Raza* stands in striking contrast to the cold and impersonal Anglo world.

Discussion Questions

1. Review the "four deeply ingrained myths of the Mexican American" this article discusses.
2. The nature of this article is a critique of one dominant—minority group relationship in the United States. Based on this critique, can you propose reforms that would bring about better relations acceptable to both dominant and minority groups?
3. Review the author's answer to this question: Why have Chicanos not assimilated and why may they never totally assimilate? Do you agree with Gaviglio's answer to this question? Discuss.

14 / Collective Behavior

"I dunno—hey, Moose! Why DO we have handlebars like this?"

It has been suggested throughout this book of readings that human behavior is generally orderly, organized, and somewhat rational. It must be recognized, however, that much of man's behavior is irrational, disorganized, and even bizarre. Crowds spontaneously releasing pent-up tension, lynchings, ecstatic religious revivals, fads of flagpole sitting, swallowing goldfish, teen-age games of "chicken," concern about barely discernible changes in the shades of lipstick and eye shadow, and the changing lengths of skirts all belong to the domain of collective behavior. *Collective behavior* may be defined as relatively spontaneous, unorganized, unplanned, and unpredictable behavior. It is behavior independent of cultural guidelines. The most dramatic examples oc-

cur when individuals are confronted with new situations in which they feel compelled to do *something*—anything— for which there are no guidelines. Young girls at a Beatle concert, for example, felt compelled to do more than simply applaud and shriek; they threw jelly beans and fainted!

There are basic kinds of collective groupings which cause behavior outside of established cultural patterns. Crowd behavior occurs when a temporary grouping of people engage in spontaneous and often uncontrolled interaction. It is illustrated by fans at a football game, or by a busload of passengers who have virtually no rules, leaders, traditions, or established patterns of interaction. Because of this lack of structure, individuals are more inclined to act upon suggestion, whether they scream encouragement to their team, loot property, or lynch a suspected criminal. The suggestion may have been given by an outspoken member of the crowd or by group consensus which develops as a kind of mutual reinforcement among the members of the crowd in their direct and indirect interactions. The *expressive crowd,* however, is not directed toward a specific goal. Cults and highly emotional religions where individuals express their joy and ecstacy through dancing, singing, and clapping are the most common form of expressive crowd. The *panic* also involves elements of crowd behavior. It is most likely to occur among individuals who perceive great danger with little hope of escape. Individuals on the upper floors of a burning building with only a small fire escape available may cause panic. A *mass* is a large number of people who react to a common stimulus but act individually without regard to one another. The "mass media" of television, radio, newspapers, and magazines convey advertising designed to persuade individuals to buy products in mass.

There is also a collectivity in modern democratic societies known as *the public.* The public is composed of people who display similar interest even though they have no face-to-face relationship. The public is not fixed or permanent. It emerges with an issue, divides itself in support or opposition to the issue, and dissolves when the issue fades. As members of the public debate the merits of a particular issue, a collective opinion called a *public opinion* is formed. The leadership elites of this society have long been concerned with public opinion—how to create and manipulate it through propaganda techniques for the achievement of political, economic, or other goals. They are also extremely interested in the measurements of the pollsters which have served as accurate indicators of public opinion.

Social movements are also considered a special form of collective behavior. They can be defined as collective enterprises that establish a new order of life. They can be distinguished from collective behavior, since they are more organized and persist over relatively long periods of time. They are collectivities that usually develop out of class, racial, political, and sexual struggles that require collectively organized action to remedy a perceived injustice.

Social movements have always existed in our society. For example, the Committees of Correspondence during the 1760s were the beginnings of the revolutionary movement. Its ideology was eloquently expressed by Thomas Jefferson in the Declaration of Independence. The civil rights movement in the 1960s transformed the ideals of the Constitution, which we venerate so deeply, into action through systematic lobbying in the U.S. Congress and courageous litigation in the U.S. judiciary. Perhaps the most widely known and most ardently debated social movement today is the women's liberation movement, which is concerned with the cultural, legal, and economic problems of male and female roles, guaranteed employment, fair wages, job discrimination, and child care. Although each of these social movements differs in its genesis and origin, they all have provided long-term shifts in our society.

JOHN HOUSEMAN

The Men from Mars

Spreading information by some form of communications network is one of the most significant processes underlying the development of collective behavior. In the article below, John Houseman gives a graphic account of the

Reprinted from John Houseman, "The Men from Mars." Copyright 1948 by Harper's Magazine. Reprinted from the December, 1948 issue by special permission.

panic and hysteria that resulted from a program designed for entertainment. The hysteria, it should be noted, was the result of a combination of factors, and not the broadcast alone.

On Sunday, October 30, at 8:00 P.M., E.S.T., in a studio littered with coffee cartons and sandwich paper, Orson swallowed a second container of pineapple juice, put on his earphones, raised his long white fingers and threw the cue for the Mercury theme—the Tchaikovsky Piano Concerto in B Flat Minor ♯ 1. After the music dipped, there were routine introductions—then the announcement that a dramatization of H. G. Wells' famous novel, *The War of the Worlds,* was about to be performed. Around 8:01 Orson began to speak, as follows:

WELLES

We know now that in the early years of the twentieth century this world was being watched closely by intelligences greater than man's and yet as mortal as his own. We know now that as human beings busied themselves about their various concerns they were scrutinized and studied, perhaps almost as narrowly as a man with a microscope might scrutinize the transient creatures that swarm and multiply in a drop of water. With infinite complacence people went to and fro over the earth about their little affairs, serene in the assurance of their dominion over this small spinning fragment of solar driftwood which by chance or design man has inherited out of the dark mystery of Time and Space. Yet across an immense ethereal gulf minds that are to our minds as ours are to the beasts in the jungle, intellects vast, cool, and unsympathetic regarded this earth with envious eyes and slowly and surely drew their plans against us. In the thirty-ninth year of the twentieth century came the great disillusionment.

It was near the end of October. Business was better. The war scare was over. More men were back at work. Sales were picking up. On this particular evening, October 30, the Crossley service estimated that thirty-two million people were listening in on their radios. . . .

Neatly, without perceptible transition, he was followed on the air by an anonymous announcer caught in a routine bulletin:

ANNOUNCER

. . . for the next twenty-four hours not much change in temperature. A slight atmospheric disturbance of undermined origin is reported over Nova Scotia, causing a low pressure area to move down rather rapidly over the northeastern states, bringing a forecast of rain, accompanied by winds of light gale force. Maximum temperature 66; minimum 48. This weather report comes to you from the Government Weather Bureau. . . . We now take you to Meridian Room in the Hotel Park Plaza in downtown New York, where you will be entertained by the music of Ramon Raquello and his orchestra.

At which cue, Bernard Herrmann led the massed men of the CBS house orchestra in a thunderous rendition of "La Cumparsita." The entire hoax might well have exploded there and then—but for the fact that hardly anyone was listening. They were being entertained by Charlie McCarthy—then at the height of his success.

The Crossley census, taken about a week before the broadcast, had given us 3.6 per cent of the listening audience to Edgar Bergen's 34.7 per cent. What the Crossley Institute (that hireling of the advertising agencies) deliberately ignored was the healthy American habit of dial-twisting. On that particular evening Edgar Bergen in the person of Charlie McCarthy temporarily left the air about 8:12 P.M., E.S.T., yielding place to a new and not very popular singer. At that point, and during the following minutes, a large number of listeners started twisting their dials in search of other entertainment. Many of them turned to us—and when they did, they stayed put! For by this time the mysterious meteorite had fallen at Grovers Mill in New Jersey, the Martians had begun to show their foul leathery heads above the ground, and the New Jersey State Police were racing to the spot. Within a few minutes people all over the United States were praying, crying, fleeing frantically to escape death from the Martians. Some remembered to rescue loved ones, others telephoned farewells or warnings, hurried to inform neighbors, sought information from newspapers or radio stations, summoned ambulances and police cars.

The reaction was strongest at points nearest the tragedy—Newark, New Jersey, in a single block, more than twenty families rushed out of their houses with wet handkerchiefs and towels over their faces. Some began moving household furniture. Police switchboards were flooded with calls inquiring, "Shall I close my windows?" "Have the police any extra gas masks?" Police found one family waiting in the yard with wet cloths on faces contorted with hysteria. As one woman reported later:

> I was terribly frightened. I wanted to pack and take my child in my arms, gather up my friend and get in the car and just go north as far as we could. But what I did was just sit by one window, praying, listening, and scared stiff, and my husband by the other sniffling and looking out to see if people were running. . . .

In New York hundreds of people on Riverside Drive left their homes ready for flight. Bus terminals were crowded. A woman calling up the Dixie Bus Terminal for information said impatiently, "Hurry please, the world is coming to an end and I have a lot to do."

In the parlor churches of Harlem evening service became "end of the world" prayer meetings. Many turned to God in that moment:

> I held a crucifix in my hand and prayed while looking out of my open window for falling meteors. . . . When the monsters were wading across the Hudson River and coming into New York, I wanted to run up on my roof to see what they looked like, but I couldn't leave my radio while it was telling me of their whereabouts.

Aunt Grace began to pray with Uncle Henry. Lily got sick to her stomach. I don't know what I did exactly but I know I prayed harder and more earnestly than ever before. Just as soon as we were convinced that this thing was real, how petty all things on this earth seemed; how soon we put our trust in God!

The panic moved upstate. One man called up the Mt. Vernon Police Headquarters to find out "where the forty policemen were killed." Another took time out to philosophize:

I thought the whole human race was going to be wiped out—that seemed more important than the fact that we were going to die. It seemed awful that everything that had been worked on for years was going to be lost forever.

In Rhode Island weeping and hysterical women swamped the switchboard of the Providence *Journal* for details of the massacre, and officials of the electric light company received a score of calls urging them to turn off all lights so that the city would be safe from the enemy. The Boston *Globe* received a call from one woman "who could see the fire." A man in Pittsburgh hurried home in the midst of the broadcast and found his wife in the bathroom, a bottle of poison in her hand, screaming, "I'd rather die this way than that." In Minneapolis a woman ran into church screaming, "New York destroyed. This is the end of the world. You might as well go home to die. I just heard it on the radio."

The Kansas City Bureau of the AP received inquiries about the "meteors" from Los Angeles; Salt Lake City; Beaumont, Texas; and St. Joseph, Missouri. In San Francisco the general impression of listeners seemed to be that an overwhelming force had invaded the United States from the air—was in process of destroying New York and threatening to move westward. "My God," roared an inquirer into a telephone, "where can I volunteer my services, we've got to stop this awful thing!"

As far south as Birmingham, Alabama, people gathered in churches and prayed. On the campus of a Southeastern college—

The girls in the sorority houses and dormitories huddled around their radios trembling and weeping in each other's arms. They separated themselves from their friends only to take their turn at the telephones to make long distance calls to their parents, saying goodbye for what they thought might be the last time. . . .

There are hundreds of such bits of testimony, gathered from coast to coast.

At least one book [1] and quite a pile of sociological literature has appeared on the subject of "The Invasion from Mars." Many theories have been put

[1] *The Invasion from Mars* by Hadley Cantril, Princeton University Press, from which many of the above quotations were taken.

forward to explain the "tidal wave" of panic that swept the nation. I know of two factors that largely contributed to the broadcast's extraordinarily violent effect. First, its historical timing. It came within thirty-five days of the Munich crisis. For weeks, the American people had been hanging on their radios, getting most of their news no longer from the press, but over the air. A new technique of "on-the-spot" reporting had been developed and eagerly accepted by an anxious and news-hungry world. The Mercury Theater on the Air by faithfully copying every detail of the new technique—including its imperfections—found an already enervated audience ready to accept its wildest fantasies. The second factor was the show's sheer technical brilliance. To this day it is impossible to sit in a room and hear the scratched, worn, off-the-air recording of the broadcast, without feeling in the back of your neck some slight draft left over from that great wind of terror that swept the nation. Even with the element of credibility totally removed it remains a surprisingly frightening show.

Radio drama was taken seriously in the thirties—before the Quiz and the Giveaway became the lords of the air. In the work of such directors as Reis, Corwin, Fickett, Welles, Robson, Spier, and Oboler there was an eager, excited drive to get the most out of this new, all too rapidly freezing medium. But what happened that Sunday, upon the twentieth floor of the CBS building was something quite special. Beginning around two, when the show started to take shape under Orson's hands, a strange fever seemed to invade the studio—part childish mischief, part professional zeal.

First to feel it were the actors. I remember Frank Readick (who played the part of Carl Phillips, the network's special reporter) going down to the record library and digging up the Morrison recording of the explosion of the Hindenburg at Lakehurst. This is a classic reportage—one of those wonderful, unpredictable accidents of eyewitness description. The broadcaster is casually describing a routine landing of the giant gasbag. Suddenly he sees something. A flash of flame! An instant later the whole thing explodes. It takes him time —a full second—to react at all. Then seconds more of sputtering ejaculations before he can make the adjustment between brain and tongue. He starts to describe the terrible things he sees—the writhing human figures twisting and squirming as they fall from the white burning wreckage. He stops, fumbles, vomits, then quickly continues. Readick played the record to himself, over and over. Then, recreating the emotion in his own terms, he described the Martian meteorite as he saw it lying inert and harmless in a field at Grovers Mill, lit up by the headlights of a hundred cars—the coppery cylinder suddenly opening, revealing the leathery tentacles and the terrible pale-eyed faces of the Martians within. As they begin to emerge he freezes, unable to translate his vision into words; he fumbles, retches—and then after a second continues.

A few moments later Carl Phillips lay dead, tumbling over the microphone in his fall—one of the first victims of the Martian Ray. There followed a moment of absolute silence—an eternity of waiting. Then, without warning, the network's emergency fill-in was heard—somewhere in a quiet studio, a piano, close on mike, playing "Clair de Lune," soft and sweet as honey, for many seconds, while the fate of the universe hung in the balance. Finally, it was interrupted by the manly reassuring voice of Brigadier General Montgomery Smith, Commander of the New Jersey State Militia, speaking from Trenton, and placing "the counties of Mercer and Middlesex as far west as Princeton and east to Jamesburg" under Martial Law! Tension—release—then renewed tension. For soon after that came an eyewitness account of the fatal battle of the Watchung Hills; and then, once again, that lone piano was heard—now a symbol of terror, shattering the dead air with its ominous tinkle. As it played, on and on, its effect became increasingly sinister—a thin band of suspense stretched almost beyond endurance.

That piano was the neatest trick of the show—a fine specimen of the theatrical "retard," boldly conceived and exploited to the full. It was one of the many devices with which Welles succeeded in compelling, not merely the attention, but also the belief of his invisible audience. "The War of the Worlds" was a magic act, one of the world's greatest, and Orson was just the man to bring it off.

For Welles is at heart a magician whose particular talent lies not so much in his creative imagination (which is considerable) as in his proven ability to stretch the familiar elements of theatrical effect far beyond their normal point of tension. For this reason his productions require more elaborate preparation and more perfect execution than most. At that—like all complicated magic tricks—they remain, till the last moment, in a state of precarious balance. When they come off, they give—by virtue of their unusually high intensity—an impression of great brilliance and power; when they fail—when something in their balance goes wrong or the original structure proves to have been unsound—they provoke, among their audience, a particularly violent reaction of unease and revulsion. Welles' flops are louder than other men's. The Mars broadcast was one of his unqualified successes.

Among the columnists and public figures who discussed the affair during the next few days (some praising us for the public service we had rendered, some condemning us as sinister scoundrels) the most general reaction was one of amazement at the "incredible stupidity" and "gullibility" of the American public, who had accepted as real, in this single broadcast, incidents which in actual fact would have taken days or even weeks to occur. "Nothing about the broadcast," wrote Dorothy Thompson with her usual aplomb, "was in the least credible." She was wrong. The first few minutes of our broadcast were, in point of fact, strictly realistic in time and perfectly credible, though somewhat boring, in content. Herein lay the great tensile strength of the show; it was the structural device that made the whole illusion possible. And it could have been carried off in no other medium than radio.

Our actual broadcasting time, from the first mention of the meteorites to the fall of New York City, was less than forty minutes. During that time men traveled long distances, large bodies of troops were mobilized, cabinet meetings were held, savage battles fought on land and in the air. And millions of people accepted it—emotionally if not logically.

There is nothing so very strange about that. Most of us do the same thing, to some degree, most days of our lives—every time we look at a movie or listen to a broadcast. Not even the realistic theater observes the literal unities; motion pictures and, particularly, radio (where neither place nor time exists save in the imagination of the listener) have no difficulty in getting their audiences to accept the telescoped reality of dramatic time. Our special hazard lay in the fact that we purported to be, not a play, but reality. In order to take advantage of the accepted convention, we had to slide swiftly and imperceptibly out of the "real" time of a news report into the "dramatic" time of a fictional broadcast. Once that was achieved—without losing the audience's attention or arousing their skepticism, if they could be sufficiently absorbed and bewitched not to notice the transition—then, we felt, there was no extreme of fantasy through which they would not follow us. We were keenly aware of our problem; we found what we believed was the key to its solution. And if, that night, the American public proved "gullible," it was because enormous pains and a great deal of thought had been spent to make it so.

In the script, "The War of the Worlds" started extremely slowly—dull meteorological and astronomical bulletins alternating with musical interludes. These were followed by a colorless scientific interview and still another stretch of dance music. These first few minutes of routine broadcasting "within the existing standards of judgment of the listener" were intended to lull (or maybe bore) the audience into a false security and to furnish a solid base of realistic time from which to accelerate later. Orson, in making over the show, extended this slow movement far beyond our original conception. "La Cumparsita," rendered by "Ramon Raquello, from the Meridian Room of the Hotel Park Plaza in downtown New York," had been thought of as running only a few seconds; "Bobby Millette playing 'Stardust' from the Hotel Martinet in Brooklyn," even less. At rehersal Orson stretched both these numbers to what seemed to us, in the control room, an almost unbearable length. We objected. The interview in the Princeton Observatory—the clock-work ticking monotonously overhead, the woolly-minded professor mumbling vague replies to the reporters' uninformed questions—this, too, he dragged out to a point of tedium. Over our protests, lines were restored that had been cut at earlier rehearsals. We cried there would not be a listener left. Welles stretched them out even longer.

He was right. His sense of tempo, that night, was infallible. When the flashed news of the cylinder's landing finally came—almost fifteen minutes after the beginning of a fairly dull show—he was able suddenly to spiral his action to a speed as wild and reckless as its base was solid. The appearance of the Martians; their first treacherous act; the death of Carl Phillips; the arrival of the militia; the battle of the Watchung Hills; the destruction of New Jersey —all these were telescoped into a space of twelve minutes without overstretching the listeners' emotional credulity. The broadcast, by then, had its own reality, the reality of emotionally felt time and space.

At the height of the crisis, around 8:31, the Secretary of the Interior came on the air with an exhortation to the American people. His words, as you read them now, ten years later, have a Voltairean ring. (They were admirably spoken—in a voice just faintly reminiscent of the President's—by a young man named Kenneth Delmar, who has since grown rich and famous as Senator Claghorn.)

THE SECRETARY

Citizens of the nation: I shall not try to cancel the gravity of the situation that confronts the country, nor the concern of your Government in protecting the lives and property of its people. However, I wish to impress upon you— private citizens and public officials, all of you—the urgent need of calm and resourceful action. Fortunately, this formidable enemy is still confined to a comparatively small area, and we may place our faith in the military forces to keep them there. In the meantime placing our trust in God, we must continue the performance of our duties, each and every one of us, so that we may confront this destructive adversary with a nation united, courageous, and consecrated to the preservation of human supremacy on this earth. I thank you.

Toward the end of this speech (*circa* 8:32 E.S.T.), Davidson Taylor, supervisor of the broadcast for the Columbia Broadcasting System, received a phone call in the control room, creased his lips, and hurriedly left the studio. By the time he returned, a few moments later—pale as death—clouds of heavy smoke were rising from Newark, New Jersey, and the Martians, tall as skyscrapers, were astride the Pulaski Highway preparatory to wading the Hudson River. To us in the studio the show seemed to be progressing splendidly—how splendidly Davidson Taylor had just learned outside. For several minutes now, a kind of madness had seemed to be sweeping the continent—somehow connected with our show. The CBS switchboards had been swamped into uselessness, but from outside sources vague rumors were coming in of deaths and suicides and panic injuries.

Taylor had requests to interrupt the show immediately with an explanatory station-announcement. By now the Martians were across the Hudson and gas was blanketing the city. The end was near. We were less than a minute from the Station Break. The organ was allowed to swirl out under the slackening fingers of its failing organist and Ray Collins, superb as the "last announcer," choked heroically to death on the roof of Broadcasting Building. The boats were all whistling for a while as the last of the refugees perished in New York Harbor. Finally, as they died away, an amateur shortwave operator was heard from heaven knows where, weakly reaching out for human companionship across the empty world:

2X2L Calling CQ
2X2L Calling CQ
2X2L Calling CQ
Isn't there anyone on the air?
Isn't there anyone?

Five seconds of absolute silence. Then, shattering the reality of World's End—the Announcer's voice was heard, suave and bright:

ANNOUNCER

You are listening to the CBS presentation of Orson Welles and the Mercury Theater on the Air in an original dramatization of *The War of the Worlds,* by H. G. Wells. The performance will continue after a brief intermission.

The second part of the show was extremely well written and most sensitively played—but nobody heard it. It recounted the adventures of a lone survivor, with interesting observations on the nature of human society; it described the eventual death of the Martian Invaders, slain—"after all man's defenses had failed by the humblest thing that God in his wisdom had put upon this earth"—by bacteriological action; it told of the rebuilding of a brave new world. After a stirring musical finale, Welles, in his own person, delivered a charming informal little speech about Halloween, which it happened to be.

I remember, during the playing of the final theme, the phone starting to ring in the control room and a shrill voice through the receiver announcing itself as belonging to the mayor of some Midwestern city, one of the big ones. He is screaming for Welles. Choking with fury, he reports mobs in the streets of his city, women and children huddled in the churches, violence and looting. If, as he now learns, the whole thing is nothing but a crummy joke—then he, personally, is coming up to New York to punch the author of it on the nose! Orson hangs up quickly. For we are off the air now and the studio door bursts open. The following hours are a nightmare. The building is suddenly full of people and dark blue uniforms. We are hurried out of the studio, downstairs, into a back office. Here we sit incommunicado while network employees are busily collecting, destroying, or locking up all scripts and records of the broadcast. Then the press is let loose upon us, ravening for horror. How many deaths have we heard of? (Implying they know of thousands.) What do we know of the fatal stampede in a Jersey hall? (Implying it is one of many.) What traffic deaths? (The ditches must be choked with corpses.) The suicides? (Haven't you heard about the one on Riverside Drive?) It is all quite vague in my memory and quite terrible.

Hours later, instead of arresting us, they let us out a back way. We scurry down to the theater like hunted animals to their hole. It is surprising to see life going on as usual in the midnight streets, cars stopping for traffic, people walking. At the Mercury the company is still stoically rehearsing—falling downstairs and singing the "Carmagnole." Welles goes up on stage, where photographers, lying in wait, catch him with his eyes raised up to heaven, his arms outstretched in an attitude of crucifixion. Thus he appeared in a tabloid that morning over the caption, "I Didn't Know What I Was Doing!" The *New York Times* quoted him as saying, "I don't think we will choose anything like this again."

We were on the front page for two days. Having had to bow to radio as a news source during the Munich crisis, the press was now only to eager to expose the perilous irresponsibilities of the new medium. Orson was their whipping boy. They quizzed and badgered him. Condemnatory editorials were delivered by our press-clipping bureau in bushel baskets. There was talk, for a while, of criminal action.

Then gradually, after about two weeks, the excitement subsided. By then it had been discovered that the casualties were not as numerous or as serious as had at first been supposed. One young woman had fallen and broken her arm running downstairs. Later the Federal Communications Commission held some hearings and passed some regulations. The Columbia Broadcasting System made a public apology. With that the official aspects of the incident were closed.

As to the Mercury—our new play, "Danton's Death," finally opened after five postponements. Not even our fantastic publicity was able to offset its generally unfavorable notices. On the other hand, that same week the Mercury Theater on the Air was signed up by Campbell Soups at a most lavish figure.

Of the suits that were brought against us—amounting to over three quarters of a million dollars for damages, injuries, miscarriages, and distresses of various kinds—none was substantiated or legally proved. We did settle one claim however, against the advice of our lawyers. It was the particularly affecting case of a man in Massachusetts, who wrote:

"I thought the best thing to do was to go away. So I took three dollars twenty-five cents out of my savings and bought a ticket. After I had gone sixty miles I knew it was a play. Now I don't have money left for the shoes that I was saving up for. Will you please have someone send me a pair of black shoes size 9B!"

We did.

Discussion Questions

1. Review the definition of panic given in the introduction to this chapter. Describe the ingredients of panic present in the reaction to "The War of the Worlds" broadcast.

2. Discuss some of the different panic-induced-reactions indicated in this article. Do you tend to agree with the "most general reaction [to the panic caused in many people] was one of amazement at the 'incredible stupidity' and 'gullibility' of the American public . . ."?

3. What are the keys to the "success" of "The War of the Worlds" as this article's author sees them? Do you find anything of sociological significance in Mr. Houseman's explanation of the broadcast's success? Discuss.

WILLIAM C. MARTIN

Friday Night in the Coliseum

Some of the most dramatic examples of collective behavior occur within a *crowd*. Crowds are common in ordinary life, and most adults have been a part of various kinds of crowds. Crowds can vary from a small number of street-corner gawkers to huge gatherings at spectator events such as a political rally or a football game. Crowds are characterized by *social contagion* where crowd members provide such an emotional buildup that the conventional system of norms and other features of organized social behavior become ineffective and inadequate. In the article below, William C. Martin describes the social contagion of the Houston Coliseum on wrestling night. As you read the article consider how the most successful wrestlers have contributed to the social contagion by reinforcing commonly held stereotypes.

"When I die, I want to be cremated, and I want my ashes scattered in the Coliseum on Friday night. It's in my will." Thus spoke a little old lady who hadn't missed a Friday night wrestling match for—well, she's not exactly sure, but "it's been a long time, son, a long time." On Friday night, fifty times a year, more than 6500 fans stream into the Coliseum in downtown Houston for promoter Paul Boesch's weekly offering of Crushers, Killers, Bruisers, and Butchers, Commies, Nazis, Japs, and A-rabs, Dukes, Lords, and Barons, Professors and Doctors, Cowboys and Indians, Spoilers and Sissies, Farmers and Lumberjacks, Bulls and Mad Dogs, Masked Men and Midgets, Nice Girls and Bitches, and at least one Clean-cut, Finely Muscled Young Man who never fights dirty until provoked beyond reason and who represents the Last, Best, Black, Brown, Red, or White Hope for Truth, Justice, and the American Way.

Though scoffed at by much of the public as a kind of gladiatorial theater in which showmanship counts for more than genuine athletic skill, professional wrestling enjoys steadily increasing success not only in Houston but in hundreds of tank towns and major cities all over America. This is not, of course, the first time around. Pro wrestling has been part of the American scene for more than a century and has enjoyed several periods of wide popularity. For most fans over thirty, however, it began sometime around 1949, with the arrival of television. Lou Thesz was world champion in those days, but the man who symbolized professional wrestling to most people was Gorgeous George, a consummate exhibitionist whose long golden ·curls,

Reprinted from William C. Martin, "Friday Night in the Coliseum." Originally published in *The Atlantic Monthly* (March 1972), 83–87. Copyright 1972 by William C. Martin and Geoff Winningham. This article was prepared in collaboration with Geoff Winningham.

brocade and satin robes, and outrageously effeminate manner drew huge crowds wherever he went, all hoping to see a local he-man give him the beating he so obviously deserved.

The Gorgeous One's success at the box office ushered in a new era of wrestler-showmen, each trying to appear more outrageous than the others. For many, villainy has provided the surest route to fame and fortune. The overwhelming majority of professional wrestling matches pit the Good, the Pure, and the True against the Bad, the Mean, and the Ugly, and a man with a flair for provoking anger and hatred has an assured future in the sport. Since shortly after World War II, the most dependable source of high displeasure has been the Foreign Menace, usually an unreconstructed Nazi or a wily Japanese who insults the memory of our boys in uniform with actions so contemptuous one cannot fail to be proud that our side won the war.

Houston's most recent Nazi was Baron von Raschke, a snarling Hun with an Iron Cross on his cape and red swastikas on his shoes, who acknowledged his prefight introductions with a sharply executed goose step. Raschke, however, managed to make one think of George Lincoln Rockwell more often than Hitler or Goebbels, and so never really achieved first-class menacehood. It must be disappointing to be a Nazi and not have people take you seriously.

Now, Japs, especially Big Japs, are a different story. For one thing, they all know karate and can break railroad ties with their bare hands. For another, they are sneaky. So when Toru Tanaka climbs into the ring in that red silk outfit with the dragon on the back, and bows to the crowd and smiles that unspeakably wicked smile, and then caps it off by throwing salt all over everything in a ceremony designed to win the favor of god knows how many of those pagan deities Japanese people worship, you just know that nice young man up there in the ring with him is in serious trouble.

Another major Foreign Menace is, of course, the Russian. Russian wrestlers are named Ivan, Boris, or Nikita, and although they have defected from Russia in quest of a few capitalist dollars, they still retain a lot of typically Communist characteristics, like boasting that Russians invented certain well-known wrestling techniques and predicting flatly that the World Champion's belt will one day hang from the Kremlin wall. Furthermore, they value nothing unless it serves their own selfish aims. After a twenty-year partnership with Lord Charles Montague, Boris Malenko states flatly, "I owe his lordship nothing. Remember one thing about us Russians. When we have no more use for anybody or anything, we let them go. Friendship means nothing to a Russian. When we get through with the Arabs and Castro, you will see what I mean. When we want something we don't care who we step on."

Wrestling fans are generally an egalitarian lot, at least among themselves, and they do not appreciate those who put on airs. So they are easily angered by another strain of crowd displeaser one might call Titled Snobs and Pointy-Headed Intellectuals. These villains, who love to call themselves "Professor" or "Doctor" or "Lord" Somebody-or-other, use the standard bag of tricks—pulling a man down by his hair, rubbing his eyes with objects secreted in trunks or shoes, stomping his face while he lies wounded and helpless—but their real specialty is treating the fans like ignorant yahoos. They walk and speak with disdain for common folk, and never miss a chance to belittle the crowd in sesquipedalian put-downs or to declare that their raucous and uncouth behavior calls for nothing less than a letter to the *Times,* to inform proper Englishmen of the deplorable state of manners in the Colonies.

A third prominent villain is the Big Mean Sonofabitch, Dick the Bruiser, Cowboy Bill Watts, Butcher Vachone, Killer Kowalski—these men do not need swastikas and monocles and big words to make you hate them. They have the bile of human meanness by the quart in every vein. If a guileless child hands a Sonofabitch a program to autograph, he will often brush it aside or tear it into pieces and throw it on the floor. It isn't that he has forgotten what it was like to be a child. As a child, he kicked crutches from under crippled newsboys and cheated on tests and smoked in the rest room. Now, at 260 pounds, he goes into the ring not just to win, but to injure and maim. Even before the match begins, he attacks his trusting opponent from behind, pounding his head into the turn-buckle, kicking him in the kidneys, stomping him in the groin, and generally seeking to put him at a disadvantage. These are bad people. None of us is really safe as long as they go unpunished.

Fortunately, these hellish legions do not hold sway unchallenged by the forces of Right. For every villain there is a hero who seeks to hold his own against what seem to be incredible odds. Heroes also fall into identifiable categories. Most of them are trim and handsome young men in their twenties or early thirties, the sort that little boys want to grow up to be, and men want to have as friends, and women want to have, also. Personable Bobby Shane wins hearts when he wrestles in his red, white, and blue muscle suit with the "USA" monogram; and when Tim Woods, dressed all in white, is introduced as a graduate of Michigan State University, older folk nod approvingly. They want their sons and grandsons to go to college, even though they didn't have a chance to go themselves, and it is reassuring to see living proof that not everybody who goes to college is out burning draft cards and blowing up banks.

Though quick to capitalize on the jingoist appeal of matches involving Menacing Foreigners, few promoters will risk a match that might divide the house along racial lines. So black and brown wrestlers usually appear in the role of Hero, behind whom virtually the entire crowd can unite. Browns— Mexicans, Mexican-Americans, and Puerto Ricans—are almost invariably handsome, lithe, and acrobatic. They fight "scientifically" and seldom resort to roughhouse tactics until they have endured so much that the legendary Latin temper can no longer be contained. If a black chooses to play the villain, he will soften the racial element; when Buster Lloyd, the Harlem Hangman, came into town, he belittled the skills of his opponents not because they were white, but because they were Texans and therefore little challenge for a man who learned to fight at the corner of Lenox Avenue and 125th Street. Several white grapplers might have been able to handle Buster, but the hero selected to take his measure and send him packing back to Harlem was Tiger Conway, a black Texan.

The purest of pure Americans, of course, and a people well acquainted with villainy, are Red Indians. Most wrestling circuits feature a Red Indian from time to time; in Houston, ex-Jets linebacker Chief Wahoo McDaniel is the top attraction and has wrestled in the Coliseum more than a hundred times in the last three years. Like Chief White Owl, Chief Suni War Cloud, and Chief Billy Two Rivers, Wahoo enters the ring in moccasin-style boots, warbonnet, and other Indian authentica. He can endure great pain and injustice without flinching or retaliating in kind, but when enraged, or sometimes just to get the old adrenaline going, he will zip into a furious war dance and level his opponent with a series of karate-like Tomahawk Chops to the chest or scalp, then force him into submission with the dreaded Choctaw Death Lock.

Although no Nazi fights clean and few Red Indians fight dirty, not all wrestlers can be characterized so unambiguously. The Masked Man, for example, is sinister-looking, and usually evil, with a name indicative of his intentions: The Destroyer, The Assassin, The Hangman, and Spoilers One, Two, and Three. But some masked men, like Mr. Wrestling and Mil Mascaras (who stars in Mexican movies as a masked crime-fighting wrestler), are great favorites, and Clawman has tried to dignify mask-wearing by having Mrs. Clawman and the Clawchildren sit at ringside in matching masks.

The majority of Houston's wrestling fans appear to be working-class folk. The white and Mexican-American men still wear crew cuts and well-oiled pompadours, and many black men and boys cut their hair close to the scalp. Family men, often with several children in tow, wear Perma-Prest slacks and plaid sport shirts with the T-shirt showing at the neck. Others, who stand around before the matches drinking Lone Star Beer and looking for friendly ladies, favor cowboy boots, fancy Levis, and Western shirts with the top two or three pearl buttons already unsnapped. Occasionally, a black dude in a purple jump suit and gold ruffled shirt shows up, but the brothers in non-descript trousers and short-sleeve knits far outnumber him. The women cling stubbornly to bouffant hairstyles, frequently in shades blonder or redder or blacker than hair usually gets, and at least 80 percent wear pants of some sort.

One basic reason these people come to the Coliseum is reflected in the motto displayed in Boesch's office: "Professional Wrestling: the sport that gives you your money's worth." Approximately half the Houston cards feature at least one championship bout or a battle for the right to meet the men's, women's, midgets', tag-team, or Brass Knucks champion of Texas, the United States, or the World. If fans grow jaded with championships, Boesch adds extra wrestlers to produce two-, three-, and four-man team matches, heavyweight-midget teams, man-woman teams, and Battles Royale, in which ten men try to throw each other over the top rope, the grand prize going to the last man left in the ring.

Grudge matches, of course, are the backbone of professional wrestling, and Boesch's skillful exploitation of grudges allows him to draw large crowds and to use wrestlers like Johnny Valentine and Wahoo McDaniel over and over again without having the fans grow weary of them. Men fight grudge matches for many reasons, all of which are elaborately developed in the printed programs and on television threat-and-insult sessions during intermissions.

They fight to uphold the honor of former associates, as when ex-gridders Ernie Ladd and Wahoo took on Valentine and Killer Karl Kox after the veteran wrestlers called them "big dumb football players" who did not have brains enough to engage in "the sport of the intelligentsia." They fight to avenge wrongs done to members of their family, as when Wild Bull Curry demanded to meet Valentine after the ruffian injured Wild Bull's popular son, Flying Freddy Curry, also known as Bull, Jr. And, in expression of a grudge more generic than personal, they fight to re-establish American supremacy over Foreign Menaces, as when Valentine turned hero-for-a-night by flying in from Asia to repay Toru Tanaka for the punishment the Dirty Jap had been handing out to the local heroes.

But not all grudge matches are fought for such lofty ideals. When Killer Karl Kox and Killer Kowalski wound up in Houston at the same time, they fought for the exclusive right to wear the nickname. In another long rivalry, marked by low but engaging comedy, Boris Malenko sought to humiliate Wahoo, who had kicked out several of the Russian's teeth a few weeks before, by challenging him to a match in which the loser's head would be shaved in the ring immediately afterward. Malenko lost, suffered the jeers of the fans for several weeks—"Hey, Baldy, why don't you go back to Russia?"—then challenged Wahoo to a rematch, the loser of which was to leave the state for a full year. The Russian, who had made himself doubly hateful by assuming the title of Professor, promised to punish Wahoo with his new steel dentures, and fans anguished over the possibility that their favorite Indian might bite the dust. Happily, Wahoo won the match, and Boris allegedly caught the first bus to Lake Charles, Louisiana.

To keep fans from tiring of a grudge series before it has yielded its full potential, promoters enhance the appeal of rematches by scheduling them under special rules and conditions that are something of a drawing card in themselves. The circumstances of previous matches often determine the conditions of the next. If one was decided by a questionable use of the ropes, the next might be fought with the ropes removed. If a cowardly villain frustrated a hero's attempt at vengeance by leaving the ring when the going got tough, he might find his way to safety blocked in the next match by a chain-link fence or a posse of eight or ten wrestlers stationed around the ring.

If Wahoo is involved, at least one match in the series will be an Indian Strap Match, in which the opponents are linked to each other by an eight-foot strap of rawhide. The strap can be used to beat, choke, and jerk, and the winner is the first man to drag his opponent around the ring twice. The Russian

Chain Match is based on the same principle, but an eight-foot length of heavy chain is considerably more dangerous than a strip of leather.

For guaranteed action, however, none of these can equal a Texas Death Match. In this surefire crowd-pleaser, usually arranged after several battles have failed to establish which of the two rivals is tougher, there are no time limits, no specified number of falls, no grounds for disqualification. A victor is declared when one of the wrestlers can no longer continue, usually because he lies unconscious somewhere in or around the ring. Fans seldom leave a Texas Death Match without feeling they got their money's worth.

For many regulars, Friday night at the Coliseum is the major social event of the week. All over the arena blacks, browns, and whites visit easily across ethnic lines, in perverse defiance of stereotypes about the blue-collar prejudices. A lot of people in the ringside section know each other, by sight if not by name. Mrs. Elizabeth Chappell, better known simply as "Mama," has been coming to the matches for more than twenty-five years. Between bouts, she walks around the ring, visiting with old friends and making new ones. When she beats on a fallen villain with a huge mallet she carries in a shopping bag, folks shout, "Attaway, Mama! Git him!" and agree that "things don't really start to pick up till Mama gets here." When a dapper young insurance salesman flies into a rage at a referee's decision, the fans nudge one another and grin about how "old Freddy really gets worked up, don't he?"

The importance of the opportunity to eat and drink and laugh and scream in the company of one's peers should not be underestimated, but at least two other basic drives manifest themselves quite clearly on Friday night: Sex and Aggression.

For women in a culture that provides its men with a disproportionate share of visual aids to sexual fantasy, the wrestling matches offer some redress. With little effort, an accomplished voyeuress can find considerable stimulation in the spectacle of husky gladiators of varied hues hugging, holding, and hurting one another while clad in nothing but boots and colored trunks that sometimes get pulled daringly low.

Male fans in search of similar titillation have fewer opportunities for fulfillment, since there are simply not enough girl wrestlers to enable promoters to book even one ladies' bout each week. But when they are scheduled, they make every effort not to disappoint. Whatever else may happen in a girls' match, certain maneuvers are inevitable. Hair will be pulled, first by the tough, dark-haired grapplerette in the gaudy-sparkly black suit, then by the sweeter looking blond youngster in the white outfit. Each girl will treat the other to a form of punishment known as the Keester Bump, in which the bumpee is bounced sharply on her behind, producing a pain that requires extensive patting and rubbing. And finally, one or both girls will manage somehow to roll over the referee virtually every time he lies down beside them to check their shoulders or start the three-count.

Some women fans seem to enjoy these antics as much as the men; throughout one contest, a laughing middle-aged woman kept elbowing her husband

and asking him, "How'd you like me to do that to you?" But others openly resent them, as did the young bride who said, "My husband is the only one I know that likes to watch the women. I really don't know why. This is a sport for men. Only thing I can figure is he's waiting for something to fall out."

Professional wrestling offers fans an almost unparalleled opportunity to indulge aggressive and violent impulses. A few appreciate the finer points of a takedown or a switch or a Fireman's Carry, but most would walk out on the NCAA wrestling finals or a collegiate match between Lehigh and Oklahoma. They want hitting and kicking and stomping and bleeding. Especially bleeding.

Virtually all bouts incite a high level of crowd noise, but the sight of fresh blood streaming from a westlers' forehead immediately raises the decibel level well into the danger zone. This is what they came to see. If both men bleed, what follows is nothing less than orgiastic frenzy. Mere main events and world championships and tag-team matches eventually run together to form murky puddles in the back region of the mind, but no one forgets the night he saw real blood. One woman recalled such a peak experience in tones that seemed almost religious: "One night, about six or seven years ago, Cowboy Ellis was sit against the post and got three gashes in his head. I grabbed him when he rolled out of the ring and got blood on my dress all the way from the neckline to the hem. I thought he would bleed to death in my arms. I never washed that dress. I've still got it at the house. I keep it in a drawer all by itself."

The lust for blood is not simply ghoulish, but a desire to witness the stigmata, the apparently irrefutable proof that what is seen is genuine. Wrestling fans freely acknowledge that much of the action is faked, that many punches are pulled, that the moisture that flies through the air after a blow is not sweat but spit, and that men blunt the full effect of stomping opponents by allowing the heel to hit the canvas before the ball of the foot slaps the conveniently outstretched arm. They not only acknowledge the illusion; they jeer when it is badly performed: "Aw my goodness! He can't even make it look good!" Still, they constantly try to convince themselves and each other that at least part of what they are seeing on a given night is real. When Thunderbolt Patterson throws Bobby Shane through the ropes onto the concrete, a woman shouts defiantly, "Was that real? Tell me that wasn't real!" And when Johnny Valentine and Ernie Ladd are both disqualified after a three-fall slugfest, a young man tells his buddy, "I think that was real. You know sometimes they do get mad. One time Killer Kowalski got so mad he tore old Yukon Eric's ear plumb off." But when blood flows, no one seeks or needs confirmation.

The effects on fans of viewing such violence are disputed. Some experiments with children and college students offer evidence that observing violent behavior either produces no change or raises the level of aggressive tendencies in the spectator. Other research, however, indicates that wrestling fans do experience a decrease in aggressive tendencies after viewing wrestling matches. Still, manipulating hatred and aggressive tendencies is not without its risks. Every wrestler has seen or heard about the time when some fan went berserk and clubbed or burned or cut or shot a villain who played his role too convincingly, and Tim Woods, it is said, has had only nine fingers since the night a challenger from the audience grabbed his hand, bit down extra hard, and spat the tenth out onto the mat. Then, too, the possibility always exists that in the highly charged atmosphere of the arena, a wrestler may lose control of himself and cause real damage to his opponent. If he were alive today, old Yukon Eric could tell you something about that.

At the Coliseum, as elsewhere, excitement, community, sex, and violence find their place in the context of a larger world view. One does not have to watch many matches or talk to many fans to sense that the action in the ring functions as a kind of quasi-religious ritual in which the hopes and fears of the gathered faithful are reflected in the symbolic struggle of Good and Evil. This ritual quality may help explain the indifference of fans to what happens at matches they do not see, either in person or on television. They may know that the same men they watch on Friday in Houston will wrestle on the other nights of the week, in some of the same combinations, in Fort Worth, Dallas, Austin, San Antonio, and Corpus Christi, but they do not care. It is not enough—it really isn't anything—that Wahoo defeat Tanaka in Fort Worth. For the event to have significance, for the ritual to work its power, it must occur on Friday Night in the Coliseum.

The Portrayal of Life that unfolds in the ring is no naïve melodrama in which virtue always triumphs and cheaters never win. Whatever else these folk know, they know that life is tough and filled with conflict, hostility, and frustration. For every man who presses toward the prize with pure heart and clean hands, a dozen Foreigners and so-called Intellectuals and Sonsofbitches seek to bring him down with treachery and brute force and outright meanness. And even if he overcomes these, there are other, basically decent men who seek to defeat him in open competition.

Nothing illustrates the frustration of the climb to the top more clearly than the Saga of Wahoo McDaniel. For three years, Wahoo has been a top challenger for the National Wrestling Alliance world championship owned by Dory Funk, Jr. A quiet and rather colorless man, who still wears his letter jacket from West Texas State rather than the theatrical garb favored by his rivals, Funk is rough but seldom really dirty, and he knows what he is doing in the ring. Folks may not particularly like him, but they have to respect him. He is no fluke champion, and they know that neither Wahoo nor anyone else can be Number One until he has defeated Dory Funk, Jr., fair and square.

They believe Wahoo can do just that. Wahoo believes it himself and on a dozen occasions has come within seconds of proving it, only to have what seemed certain victory snatched from his hands. Two of their matches ended in a draw. Wahoo lost a third when the referee missed an obvious pin. Funk was disqualified in their next meeting, but titles do not change hands on disqualifications. The champion then won a Texas Death Match by knocking Wahoo out cold with a steel folding chair, a legal but grossly unsportsmanlike tactic.

Two years after they first met, Wahoo and Dory are still at it. In their latest match, the third fall apparently ended with Wahoo the winner and new champion, but as he danced around the ring in triumph, the timekeeper informed the referee that Dory's feet had been over the bottom rope, thus nullifying the decision. The referee ordered the match to continue, but Wahoo missed the signal and Funk grabbed him from behind to gain a quick pin. Fans fumed and screamed, then filed out in silent despair. Long after most of them were gone, Freddy the insurance salesman maintained a noisy vigil at ringside, beating on the mat and shouting to nobody in particular, "People paid good money to come see this, and the damn referee is so stupid he has to ask the timekeeper what happened. There's got to be a rematch."

There will be, Freddy, there will be. And some day, if he actually is the best man, Wahoo will win. Life has its temporary setbacks and disappointments, to be sure, but we can be confident that over the long haul men eventually get what they truly deserve, genuine ability is always rewarded, and the scales of justice ultimately balance. For life is like that, too, isn't it? Isn't it?

Discussion Questions

1. Crowds respond readily and uncritically upon *suggestion*. What role do the promoters play in providing suggestions that cause social contagion?
2. The leadership of a crowd also affects the intensity and direction of the crowd. Would you classify "Mama" one of the leaders? Why?
3. Do you think the members of this crowd feel guilty about yelling ethnic obscenities to various fighters? Discuss.
4. Do you think you would be caught up in the social contagion if you went to the wrestling matches at the Houston Coliseum?

GEORGE F. GILDER

Suicide of the Sexes

There are obviously those who see a dramatically different result of women's liberation than the view provided by George F. Gilder. In the following article the author argues that there will be a very negative impact on our social structure if the women "win."

It is time to declare that sex is too important a subject to leave to the myopic crowd of happy hookers, Dr. Feelgoods, black panthers, white rats, answer men, evangelical lesbians, sensuous psychiatrists, retired baseball players, pornographers, dolphins, swinging priests, displaced revolutionaries, polymorphous perverts, and *Playboy* philosophers—all bouncing around on waterbeds and typewriters and television talk shows, making "freedom" ring in the cash registers of the revolution.

Nothing is free, least of all sex, which is bound to our deepest sources of energy, identity, and emotion. Sex can be cheapened, of course, but then, inevitably, it becomes extremely costly to the society as a whole. For sex is the life force—and cohesive impulse—of a people, and their very character will be deeply affected by how sexuality is managed, sublimated, expressed, denied, and propagated. When sex is devalued, propagandized, and deformed, as at present, the quality of our lives declines and our social fabric deteriorates.

Even the attitude toward sex and sexuality as concepts illustrates the problem. The words no longer evoke an image of a broad pageant of relations and differences between the sexes, embracing every aspect of our lives. Instead "sex" and "sexuality" are assumed to refer chiefly to copulation, as if our sexual lives were restricted to the male limits—as if the experiences of maternity were not paramount sexual events. In fact, however, our whole lives are sexual. Sexual energy animates most of our activities and connects every individual to a family and a community. Sexuality is best examined not in terms of sexology, physiology, or psychology, but as a study encompassing all the ulterior life of our society. . . .

The inflation and devaluation of sexual currency leads to a failure of marriage that subverts the entire society. The increasing incidence of divorce, desertion, illegitimacy, and venereal disease produces a chaotic biological arena. Anyone may be cut and slashed by the shards of broken families in the streets of our cities. When sex becomes a temporary release, to be prompted as well by one woman as by another, or by sex magazines; when sex becomes a kind of massage, which can be administered as well by a member of the same sex or by a machine for that matter—one's whole emotional existence is depleted. We can no longer fathom the depths of our biological beings, which are open only to loving sexual experience. Drugs and alcohol can substitute for erotic activity; and with a cheapened sexual currency, couples can no longer afford children emotionally. Babies come as mistakes, misconceived and misbegotten. They come back to get theirs later.

All these social problems are ultimately erotic. The frustration of the affluent young and their resort to drugs, the breakdown of the family among both the rich and poor, the rising rate of crime and violence—all the clichés of our social crisis spring from, or reflect and reinforce, a fundamental deformation of sexuality.

The chief perpetrators of these problems are men: Men commit over 90 per cent of major crimes of violence, 100 per cent of the rapes, 95 per cent of the burglaries. They comprise 94 per cent of our drunken drivers, 70 per cent of suicides, 91 per cent of offenders against family and children. More specifically, the chief perpetrators are *single* men. Single men comprise between 80 and 90 per cent of most of the categories of social pathology, and on the average they make less money than any other group in the society—yes, less than single women or married women. As any insurance actuary will tell you, single men are also less responsible about their bills, their driving, and other personal conduct. Together with the disintegration of the family, they constitute our leading social problem. For there has emerged no institution that can replace the family in turning children into civilized human beings or in retrieving the wreckage of our current disorder.

Yet what is our new leading social movement? It's Women's Liberation, with a whole array of nostrums designed to emancipate us. From what? From the very institution that is most indispensable to overcoming our present social crisis: the family. They want to make marriage more open, flexible, revokable, at a time when it is already opening up all over the country and spewing forth swarms of delinquents and neurotics, or swarms of middle-aged men and women looking for a sexual utopia that is advertised everywhere, delivered nowhere, but paid for through the nose (and other improbable erogenous zones). At a time when modernity is placing ever greater strains on the institutions of male socialization—our families, sports, men's organizations—the women's movement wants to weaken them further, make them optional, bisexual, androgynous. In most of the books the feminists speak of the need to "humanize" (emasculate?) men. . . .

Much of the recent debate over our sexual relations has focused on the question of power. Elizabeth Janeway maintains that in the past women exercised power but that "now it has evaporated." Kate Millett, on the other hand, believes that women have been oppressed throughout history. Many feminists see a gain in female power in recent years. Others regard the gains as illusory. Only Midge Dector perceives that the women's liberation campaign itself is a response to anxieties over the increasing power and freedom of women. In general, regardless of the assumptions about female power, men are said to dominate the society. . . .

[But] for most people, as Marx and others have observed, the one place they are least free, powerful, and individual is at work. Even the supposed titans of industry operate under severe marketplace constraints and psychological disciplines that cause them to labor some 70 hours a week. Few enjoy the kind of freedom that is fantasized by the movement of Herbert Marcuse. Leaving the great executives and entrepreneurs aside, most workers regard their jobs as bondage. When appraising the real power of the sexes, it is difficult to conceive of a measure less pertinent to the average man than the number of male Senators and millionaires. Most people enjoy their real gratifications not in the office or on the assembly line but in the domestic and sexual arenas, where female power is inevitably greatest.

The principal flaw of most of the literature of women's liberation is its incomprehension of the real power of women. Literally hundreds of tomes and pamphlets have been written on the need to establish "equality between the sexes." But since women are not presumed to have significant assets, the agenda always resembles an opening proposal in disarmament talks between the United States and the Soviet Union: Each side is willing to negotiate only about those "brutal weapons of aggression" in which the other side has the advantage. The feminist program thus usually consists of taking jobs and money away from men, while granting in return such uncoveted benefits as the right to cry.

It is on this issue of female power that Mrs. Janeway, the most sophisticated of the feminists, has a rare but disabling failure of perception. She sees that people behave as if women possessed important power. But it never occurs to her that women are actually powerful. Instead, in *Man's World, Woman's Place,* she asserts that female power is a "social myth." Then she labors for chapters to show that "social myths" are important enough to account for the pervasive male fear and respect of women.

It is a generous effort, since Mrs. Janeway could just as easily have dismissed these male fears as the typical sentiments, born of guilt, that most oppressors feel toward the oppressed. The usual feminist analogy is the slave owner's fearful attribution of great, mysterious sexual powers to the black male. But all these arguments or neurosis and myth fall before Occam's razor. The simplest explanation of male fear suffices: Women, in fact, possess enormous power over men. In a profound way, most women do not feel subordinated. For the conspicuous and calculable power of males is counterbalanced by a deep and inexorable power of women.

Sexual love, intercourse, marriage, conception of a child, childbearing, even breast-feeding are all critical experiences psychologically. They are times when our emotions are most intense, our lives most deeply changed, and society perpetuated in our own image. And they are all transactions of sexual differences.

The divisions are embodied in a number of roles. The central ones are mother and father, husband and wife. They form neat and apparently balanced paids. But appearances are deceptive. In the most elemental sexual terms, there is little balance at all. In most of those key sexual events, the male role is trivial, even easily dispensable. Although the man is needed in intercourse, artificial insemination has already been used in hundreds of thousands of cases. Otherwise, the man is altogether unnecessary. It is the woman who conceives, bears, and suckles the child. Those activities which are most deeply sexual and mostly female; they comprise the mother's role, defined organically by her body.

The nominally equivalent role of father is in fact a product of marriage and other cultural contrivances. There is no biological need for the father to be anywhere around when the baby is born and nurtured. In many societies the father has no special responsibility to support the specific children he sires. In some societies, paternity is not even acknowledged. The idea that the father is inherently equal to the mother within the family, or that he will necessarily be inclined to remain with it, is nonsense. In one way or another, the man must be made equal by society.

In discussing the erotic aspects of our lives, we must concern ourselves chiefly with women. Males are the sexual outsiders and inferiors. A far smaller portion of their bodies is directly erogenous. A far smaller portion of their lives is devoted to sexual activity. Their own distinctively sexual experience is limited to erection and ejaculation. Their rudimentary sexual drive leads only toward copulation. The male body offers no sexual fulfillment comparable to a woman's passage through months of pregnancy, to the tumult of childbirth, and on into the suckling of her baby. All are powerful and fulfilling sexual experiences completely foreclosed to men.

In very primitive societies, men have the compensation of physical strength. They can control women by force and are needed to protect them from other men. But this equalizer is relatively unimportant in a civilized society, where the use of force is largely restricted by law and custom. Here the men counterbalance female sexual superiority by playing a crucial role as provider and achiever. Money replaces muscle.

If women become equal in terms of money and achievement, there is only one way equality between the sexes can be maintained in a modern society. Women must be reduced to sexual parity. They must relinquish their sexual superiority, psychologically disconnect their wombs, and adopt the short-circuited copulatory sexuality of males. Women must renounce all the large procreative dimensions of their sexual impulse.

As anyone can attest who has associated much with "liberationist" women, this is what they try to do. They are as dogged in denying that they have a maternal instinct as they are resolute in their insistence that many men do. But despite the feminist protestations, the man remains inferior in procreation: He cannot bear children. Any special access to the child must be granted to him by the woman. She must acknowledge the man's paternity. And only the woman can acquire sexual affirmation from feeding the infant at her breast.

Neither the primacy of the biological realm, nor the immense psychological role of the woman in it, is well understood in our rationalist age. Man's predicament begins in his earliest years. A male child is born, grows, and finds his being in relation to his own body and to the bodies of his parents, chiefly his mother. His later happiness is founded in part on a physiological memory. Originating perhaps in the womb itself, it extends through all his infant groping into the world at large, which begins, of course, in his mother's arms. In trusting her he learns to trust himself, and trusting himself he learns to bear the slow dissolution of the primary tie. He moves away into a new world, into a sometimes frightening psychic space between his parents; and he must then attach his evolving identity to a man, his father. From almost the start, the boy's sexual identity is dependent on acts of exploration and initiative.

Throughout the lives of men we find echoes of this image, of a boy stranded in transition from his first tie to a woman—whom he discovers to be different, and subtly dangerous to him—toward identification with a man, who will always deny him the closeness his mother once provided. At an early age he is, in a sense, set at large. Before he can return to a woman, he must assert his manhood in action. The Zulu warrior has to kill a man, the Mandan youth had to endure torture, the Irish peasant had to build a house, the American man must find a job. This is the classic myth and the mundane reality of masculinity.

Female histories are different. A girl's sexuality normally unfolds in an unbroken line, from a stage of utter dependency and identification with her mother through stages of gradual autonomy. Always, the focus of female identification is clear and stable. . . .

Male sexual consciousness comes as an unprogrammed drive. Nothing about the male body dictates any specific pattern beyond a repetitive release of sexual tension. Men must define and defend the larger dimensions of their sexuality by external activity.

The male sexual repertory, moreover, is very limited. Men have only one sex organ and one sex act: erection and ejaculation. Everything else is guided by culture and imagination. Other male roles—other styles of masculine identity—must be learned or created. In large part, they are a cultural invention, necessary to civilized life but ultimately fragile.

A woman is not so exclusively dependent on copulation for sexual identity. For her, intercourse is only one of many sex acts or experiences. Her sexual nature is reaffirmed monthly in menstruation; her breasts and her womb further symbolize a sex role that extends, at least as a potentiality, through pregnancy, childbirth, lactation, suckling, and long-term nurture. Rather than a brief performance, female sexuality is a long, unfolding process. Even if a woman does not in fact bear a child, she is continually reminded that she can, that she is capable of performing the crucial act in the perpetuation of the species. She can perform the only act that gives sex an unquestionable meaning, an incarnate result.

Thus, regardless of any anxieties she may have in relation to her sexual role and how to perform it, she at least knows that she has a role of unquestionable importance to herself and the community. Whatever else she may do or be, she can be sure of her essential female nature. Women take their sexual identity for granted and assume that except for some cultural peculiarity, men also might enjoy such sexual assurance. Women are puzzled by male unease, by men's continual attempts to prove their manhood or ritualistically affirm it. . . .

Throughout the literature of feminism, in fact, there runs a puzzled complaint, "Why can't men *be* men, and just relax?" The reason is that, unlike femininity, relaxed masculinity is at bottom empty, a limp nullity. While the female body is full of internal potentiality, the male is internally barren (from the Old French *bar,* meaning man). Manhood at the most basic level can be validated and expressed only in action. For a man's body is full only of undefined energies. And all these energies need the guidance of culture. He is therefore deeply dependent on the structure of the society to define his role.

Nancy Chodorow ends her otherwise fine essay on "Being and Doing" by envisioning a world in which "male identity does not depend on men's proving themselves [by] doing." Like so many others in the movement, she wonders whether men can be "humanized." Chodorow laments that in our society men's "doing" is "a reaction to insecurity" rather than "a creative exercise of their humanity."

She is essentially right. The male sexual predicament, like the female, is not the sort of arrangement that might have been invented by social engineers. It has a tragic quality that is difficult to adapt to egalitarian formulas. But the essential need to perform is alterable only in sexual suicide. There is no short-cut to human fulfillment for men—just the short circuit of impotence. Men can be creatively human only when they are confidently male and overcoming their sexual insecurity by action. Nothing comes to them by waiting or "being." Even the degree of sexual confidence that most men *can* achieve in civilized society is dependent either on constant initiative or on culturally identifying and reserving certain roles and arenas as distinctively male. . . .

These differences in sexual experience, of course, account for the Victorian "double standard," whereby chastity was required for women but some promiscuity was acceptable for men. . . .

The chief difference is that, lacking the innate insecurity of males and possessing an unimpeachable sexual identity, women are not usually so reliant on intercourse. As Alfred Kinsey's colleague, Mary Jane Sherfey, observes in her liberationist book on female sexuality—and as the Masters and Johnson experiments show—women can both enjoy sexual relations more profoundly and durably and forgo them more easily than can men. In those ways they are superior. Whatever other problems a woman may have, her identity *as a woman* is not so much at stake in intercourse. She has other specifically female experiences and does not have to perform intercourse in the same sense as her partner; she can relax and virtually always please her man.

The man, on the other hand, has only one sex act and is exposed to con-spicuous failure in it. His erection is a mysterious endowment that he can never fully understand or control. If it goes, he often will not know exactly why, and there will be little he or his partner can do to retrieve it. His humilia-tion is inconsolable. Even if he succeeds in erection he still can fail to evoke orgasm—he can lose out to other men who can. And if he is impotent, it will subvert all the other aspects of his relationship and will undermine his entire personality. . . .

In general, therefore, the man is less secure than the woman because his sexuality is dependent on action, and he can act sexually only through a precarious process difficult to control. Fear of impotence is a paramount fact of male sexuality.

The women's literature, in its itch to disparage sexual differences, fails to comprehend these imperious facts of life, fails to understand that for men the desire for sex is not simply a quest for pleasure. It is an indispensable test of identity. And in itself it is always ultimately temporary and inadequate. Unless his maleness is confirmed by his culture, he must enact it repeatedly.

Thus there are times when sex may be psychologically obligatory for men.

Particularly in a society where clear and affirmative masculine activities are scarce, men may feel a compulsive desire to perform their one unquestionably male role. It is only when men are engaged in a relentless round of masculine activities in the company of males—Marine Corps training is one example—that their sense of manhood allows them to avoid sex without great strain.

Most young men are subject to nearly unremitting sexual drives, involving their very identities as males. Unless they have an enduring relationship with a woman—a relationship that affords them sexual confidence—men will accept almost any convenient sexual offer. This drive arises early in their lives, and if it is not appeased by women, it is slaked by masturbation and pornography. It is not a drive induced chiefly by culture. Rural boys, conditioned to avoid sexual stimuli, avidly seek pornography when they scarcely know what it is—and when it is outlawed. The existence of a semi-illegal, multi-billion-dollar pornography market, almost entirely male oriented, bespeaks the difference in sexual character between men and women. . . .

This view . . . [is] strongly confirmed by a cross cultural study of 190 different societies made by Clellan S. Ford and Frank A. Beach. Only in a very few, very primitive groups, do women equal males in promiscuity. Males almost everywhere show greater sexual aggressiveness, compulsiveness, and lack of selectivity. Over the whole range of human societies, men are overwhelmingly more prone to masturbation, homosexuality, voyeurism, gratuitous sexual aggression, and other shallow and indiscriminate erotic activity. In virtually every known society, sex is regarded either as a grant by the woman to the man, or as an object of male seizure. In most societies, the man has to pay for it with a gift or service. Although women are physiologically capable of greater orgasmic pleasure than men—and thus may avidly seek intercourse—they are also much better able to forgo sex without psychological strain. In the United States the much greater mental health of single women than single men may be explained in part by this female strength. But greater sexual control and discretion are displayed by women in virtually every society throughout history and anthropology. . . .

. . . In general, the sense of insecurity that impels the compulsive desire for promiscuity is a male phenomenon. In essence, the equivalent of nymphomania, a female aberration, is found in the healthiest of males.

This differing compulsiveness means that a woman's decision to pursue "illicit" sex ordinarily represents a more significant violation of love. It indicates a more deliberate repudiation of the values of ordered sexuality on which the social system depends. Thus, as a moral offense against the community, a woman's violation is more consequential than the man's temporary submission to his psychological and erotic demands. This is not to say that the woman is necessarily wrong in her decision; it is merely to say that one judges it differently. To uphold the double standard is merely to recognize the greater responsibility borne by women for the sexual prerequisites of civilized society. It is to acknowledge the much greater sexual power and responsibility inevitably exercised by women.

This difference also means that in most sexual encounters the woman has the superior position. The man is the petitioner; he bargains from the disadvantage. He can overcome his weakness only by aggressiveness. By controling the situation, he can gain the sense of security that enables him to perform. Like a tightrope walker, he must usually keep moving. He can compensate for his greater need by a great initiative. He can acquire the sense that he is preparing the woman and that he thus manages her readiness. In this way he escapes the extremely difficult challenge of performing on demand.

Aggressiveness on the part of the woman can jeopardize the whole process if it destroys the man's rhythm of control and enhances his insecurities. If conditions are right, he may succeed anyway. But the likelihood of impotence is increased. The key contingent variable in sex is the male erection, and it emerges from an internal psychochemistry of trust and confidence that is usually undermined by female activity. Germaine Greer's attempt to suggest that greater female aggressiveness will overcome male impotence reveals the complete failure to understand males that is omnipresent in her book. . . .

The crucial process of civilization is the subordination of male sexual impulses and psychology to long-term horizons of female biology. If one compares female overall sexual behavior now with women's life in primitive societies, the difference is relatively small. It is male behavior that must be changed to create a civilized order. Modern society relies increasingly on predictable, regular, long-term human activities, corresponding to the female sexual patterns. It has little latitude for the pattern of impulsiveness, aggressiveness, and immediacy, arising from male insecurity without women—and further enhanced by hormonal activity. This is the ultimate and growing source of female power in the modern world. Women domesticate and civilize male nature. They can destroy civilized male identity merely by giving up the role.

Female power, therefore, comes from what the woman can offer or withhold. She can grant to the man a sexual affirmation that he needs more than she does; she can offer him progeny otherwise permanently denied him; and she can give him a way of living happily and productively in a civilized society that is otherwise oppressive to male nature. In exchange modern man can give little beyond his external achievement and his reluctant faithfulness. It is on these terms of exchange that marriage—and male socialization—are based. . . .

. . . Male dominance in the marketplace, . . . is a social artifice maintained not for the dubious benefits it confers on men but for the indispensable benefits it offers the society: inducing men to support rather than disrupt the community. Conventional male power, in fact, might be considered more the ideological myth. It is designed to induce the majority of men to accept a bondage to the machine and the marketplace, to a large extent in the service of women and in the interests of civilization.

Any consideration of equality focusing on employment and income statistics, therefore, will miss the real sources of equilibrium between the sexes. These deeper female strengths and male weaknesses may be more important than any superficial male dominance because they control the ultimate motives and rewards of our existence. . . .

Women control not the economy of the marketplace but the economy of eros: the life force in our society and our lives. What happens in the inner realm of women finally shapes what happens on our social surfaces, determining the level of happiness, energy, creativity, and solidarity in the nation.

Discussion Questions

1. Review Mr. Gilder's discussion of the negative impact on our social structure if "the women win." Do you agree with Mr. Gilder? Why?

2. Would your answer to the above question change if it were asked with the following words in front of it?
   Individually . . .
   In terms of collective behavior . . .

15 / Population

"We moved out of the city so he wouldn't be exposed to all that crime, sex, and violence!"

Over the past decade the mass media has bombarded the American public with information and rhetoric on the subject of population growth. The United Nations estimates that world population increases by more than 5,600 people every hour. At current growth rates, each person alive will have about one square foot of living space in about 700 years. Paul Ehrlich argues that the present growth rate will have the same destructive effect as an atomic holocaust. He and others feel our only chance for survival is a "zero population growth." On the other hand, there are individuals who counter Paul Ehrlich and the other population "explosionists" by criticizing their approach and analysis as altogether too simplistic and inflammatory. Given the two opposing views on population growth and the implications these views hold for the future of mankind, students of demography must ask the question: What is the nature of "The Population Problem"?

Population growth is itself a complex phenomenon, neither analyzed nor controlled simply. Whether population growth poses a problem depends to some degree on an individual's perspective and expectations for the future. For many, the relatively low rate of population growth in the United States is a problem because it threatens the expected quality of life. While population growth in the United States has not yet threatened the food supply or flooded the labor market as it has in developing nations, it is seen as a major contributor to air and water pollution, urban decay, rising taxes, and is closely intertwined with the problem of race relations. Others argue that these social "ills" are simply a function of individual expectation, having no necessary connection to population growth. They consider the population crisis a spurious crisis, contrived by inept social scientists and various simplistic alarmists.

As students of social science it is important for us to inquire into the relationship between population growth and other elements of social life. Perhaps the science of demography can provide us with some insights. *Demography* is concerned with describing the population. It studies such matters as the changes over time in fertility and mortality. Demography's basic components are births, deaths, and migration. What particularly intrigues demographers are the social, cultural, economic, and political factors associated with increasing, decreasing, or stable birth rates, death rates, and migration.

Population growth occurs when birth rates exceed death rates. In 1798 Thomas Malthus, who is considered the first prophet of doom regarding uncontrolled population growth, argued that the very slow population growth of the world to that point in history had been the result of positive checks. *Positive checks* controlled population growth through natural forces such as disease, famine, and war. Malthus also discussed *preventative checks,* which included late marriages to prevent births, but felt they would be ineffective. He also concluded that positive checks would be inoperative in the future. These conclusions led him to assert that England's population would double in the next 25 years, and would arrive at the point of mass starvation in about 150 years. Obviously such dire predictions were never realized. Why not?

Beginning about 1650, England and the rest of the Western-industrializing nations experienced what has been called the *demographic transition.* Throughout the eighteenth and the nineteenth centuries death rates declined because of improvements in the areas of agriculture, public programs, personal hygiene, and medicine. Developments in these areas combined to improve the standard of living. Since the beginning of the twentieth century, however, the Western-industrialized nations have experienced a drop in their birth rates.

While population continues to grow, the rate is considerably slower. Demographers who support this explanation emphasize economic development, industrialization, and urbanization as the causes of both the initial decline of death rates and also the later decline of birth rates.

The developing nations are now experiencing the first stages of demographic transition. Low death rates and continuing high birth rates have produced dramatic increases in population. Given their limited space and resources, they cannot wait 200 years for the demographic transition to occur, precisely because their populations would double over the next 25 to 30 years and the prophetic declaration of doom uttered by Malthus in 1798, would be realized.

Since the large quantities of capital investment, technical skills, and leadership necessary to industrialize rapidly are not available to most of these developing nations, they have adopted a variety of alternate strategies to control population growth. These strategies include sterilizations, abortions, family planning, and birth control clinics. To this point these strategies have had little, if any, measurable success. Traditional values and beliefs undermine most such programs. Those who avail themselves of the programs are usually members of the emerging class in urban areas who probably would practice some form of private birth control even if the programs were unavailable. The traditional values and beliefs of most individuals in developing countries generally undermine the effectiveness of birth control programs. For example, the cultures of most of the developing nations view large families as proof of a man's virility and a woman's fertility.

The crucial question therefore becomes: How can the cultural values and beliefs be changed so that these people will want fewer children? Modernization will eventually lower the birth rate, but it will not necessarily produce zero population growth. Various programs stressing zero population growth depend on the support of the culture. But changing cultural attitudes and beliefs take time. Thus, for most of the world there is no strategy guaranteed to produce lower birth rates in the near future.

DAVID M. RORVIK

Paul Ehrlich: Ecology's Angry Lobbyist

What kind of problem is posed by the present rate of population growth in the United States and throughout the rest of the world? According to Paul Ehrlich, the problem is so great that it has him "running for his life." In his widely read book *The Population Bomb* he explains his fears about the population explosion. In the following article Dr. Ehrlich's major thoughts about over population and its effect on the environment are reviewed.

"I'm scared. I have a 14-year-old daughter whom I love very much. I know a lot of young people, and their world is being destroyed. My world is being destroyed. I'm 37, and I'd kind of like to live to be 67 in a reasonably pleasant world, not die in some kind of holocaust in the next decade."

Dr. Paul R. Ehrlich is running for his life. Lots of people are running after him. Magazines as diverse as *Ramparts, Playboy* and *McCall's* want his articles; television cameras are becoming a permanent fixture in his office at Stanford University, where the national networks and even the Voice of America seek his skull-splitting views on the state-of-the-environment ("going to hell, and Nixon is doing worse than nothing to stop it"); colleges are clamoring for his body ("I'm booked a year ahead on personal appearances and get around two dozen requests a day"); famous photographers want him to sit still for their cameras (Richard Avedon asked for a three-hour sitting, was offered ten minutes); Johnny Carson has featured him twice in six weeks.

And all the while, he keeps running—only faster, 18 hours a day, 80,000 miles a year, warning us that population has been increasing faster than the food supply since 1958, that 10 to 20 million people are already starving to death each year and that three-fourths of the world now goes to bed hungry each night, that the accumulation of DDT and similar poisons could bring the life-providing processes of photosynthesis to a halt and leave the oceans as dead as Lake Erie by 1979, that even Americans will probably be subjected to water rationing by 1974 and food rationing by the end of the decade, that hepatitis and epidemic dysentery rates could easily climb by 500 percent in this country between 1970 and 1974, on account of crowding and increasingly polluted water, that the prospects of worldwide plague and thermonuclear war grow more distinct each day as population pressures on a fragile environment and finite natural resources mount.

Paul Ehrlich an alarmist? "I certainly am," he says. "After all, I'm alarmed."

Reprinted from David M. Rorvik, "Paul Ehrlich: Ecology's Angry Lobbyist," *Look* (April 21, 1970), 42–44. Reprinted by permission of David M. Rorvik.

Professor of biology and former director of Graduate Studies for the Department of Biological Sciences at Stanford, author of 80 scientific papers and a number of books, including *The Population Bomb* (over 950,000 paperback copies in print), he strides to any platform and literally wraps his lanky 6'2" frame around the podium. He exhibits short hair but long sideburns ("I get away with a lot this way") and a wrinkled suit that hangs on him like camel skin. When he speaks, it is an urgent, nonstop, rapid-fire rumble.

It took one million years, he says, to double the world population from 2.5 million people to 5 million in 6000 B.C. Now we're pressing 4 *billion,* and the doubling time is only 37 years. If we kept on at this rate, Ehrlich says, we'd have 60 million billion people in another 900 years—"or about 100 persons for each square foot of the earth's surface." But surely we can ultimately move to some other planet? Forget it. Ehrlich marshals figures showing that even if Americans were willing to reduce their standard of living to 18 percent of its present level, they could still only export to the stars *one day's* increase in the population *each year*. And even if we did manage to get to the other planets, he says, "in a few thousand years, at the current growth rate, all the material in the visible universe would have been converted into people, and the sphere of people would be expanding outward at the speed of light!" Similarly, the notion that wars help check population is laid to rest with the disclosure that "all battle deaths suffered by Americans in all wars [more than 600,000] have been more than made up for by births in the last three days."

He flays the men he calls environmental villains, ecological Uncle Toms, "dum-dums and Yo-Yo's" of the Establishment:

Presidential Science Adviser Lee DuBridge—"His field, physics, is fading into the background; it deals with relatively simple systems and is no longer as relevant as it once was. Yet the politicians still think physics is the only real science and inevitably turn to physicists for advice. These are people who believe that scientists aren't supposed to take political, activist stances, hence not likely to give frank advice. The science adviser today should be a biologist or behavioral scientist, not a physicist."

The National Academy of Sciences—"Another part of the never-take-a-stand science establishment. It would be unable to give a unanmious decision if asked whether the sun will rise tomorrow."

The Atomic Energy Commission—"Its stand in regard to radiation levels is that if you can't prove they're going to kill you, they're all right. They're too busy promoting nuclear power to regulate it."

The Pope—"I have a great deal of compassion for serious Catholics who have been placed in a moral bind by the Pope's insistence on adherence to mindless policies against contraception. Why should anybody take sexual advice from the Pope? Thanks to the suppression of contraceptive devices, abortion is the commonest form of birth control in the world today, which is disgraceful. And abortion is most prevalent where the laws are most restrictive. In Italy, for example, the abortion rate is estimated to be nearly equal to the birthrate. Death is said to result in about four percent of these illegal Italian abortions; and in Santiago, Chile, bungled abortions are estimated to account for more than 40 per cent of all hospital admissions."

The so-called "Green Revolution," which some economists claim will increase the yield of the soil and thus save us all—"The Green Revolution, which puts emphasis on vast and dense plantings of single types of grain, creating monocultures, is going to turn brown. Among other things, without genetic variability in crops, you can't stay ahead of the bugs and the pests. They've got miracle rats to go along with their miracle rice now in the Philippines. Look at the Green Revolution created by the potato in Ireland a couple of centuries ago. The impoverished two million people there rapidly bred up to about eight million, and along came the potato blight. Two million people died of starvation and another two million managed to emigrate. If you consider that today there's no place to migrate to, the cost of giving a new food to two million people *without* population control could be the ultimate death of four million people! The economists never take these complexities into consideration."

Family planning—"Even if we prevented all *unwanted* children, the goal of family planning, we would still have a severe population problem. People *want* too many children. Family planning is a disaster because it is giving people a false sense of security. No one should have more than two children; anything beyond that is irresponsible, suicidal."

The Gross National Product—"Gross is the word for it. We've got to shift from what economist Kenneth Boulding calls our 'Cowboy Economy,' in which both production and consumption are regarded with great favor and which is, in his words, 'associated with reckless, exploitative . . . behavior,' to a Spaceman Economy, in which we recognize that there are no unlimited reservoirs, either for extraction or pollution, and in which consumption must be minimized."

The Department of Agriculture—"A subsidiary of the petrochemical industry that produces DDT and the other insecticides. The Department has no ecological knowhow whatever and is strongly in league with the very elements it ought to be regulating. Letting Agriculture control registration of pesticides is like letting the fox guard the henhouse."

The petrochemical industry—"Pesticides, in general, are *designed* to fail. The industry profits by this because when they do fail, their recommendation is to use *more* pesticides. The industry also cleverly recommends spraying on a regular schedule whether the bugs are there or not—a sort of 'preventive' approach that actually has the opposite effect. By spraying, as they recommend, late in the winter and then every two weeks in the season, you guarantee that the pests you are after will develop resistance. Beyond this, pesticides don't work because they almost always kill off far more of the predators that eat the plant pests than the pests themselves. The reason for this is simple: the pests, over a period of millions of years, have evolved means of handling poisons that the plants themselves produce as defenses. The pests are adept at this, but the predators aren't. And when the spray kills off the predators, the pest population explodes. The scientific approach to pest control is to enhance the plants' natural defenses, not introduce substances that dangerously upset the ecological balance."

President Nixon—"His State of the Union message makes it abundantly clear that he can be counted on to do practically nothing. He addressed himself to one tiny part of the problem—sewage disposal—and the $4 billion he allocated in Federal funds for use over the next five years is totally inadequate. To make matters worse, the type of sewage plants this money is going into are the type that foul up the water with phosphates and nitrates. And if we ever should get our own country on the right road with the right leaders, we're still going to have to work doubly hard to see to it that their counterparts in the Soviet Union, China and so on are also removed from power and put out on the happy farm where they belong."

Though Ehrlich denies that he's any sort of hero, he happily acknowledges the emergence of a new youth movement based on the population-pollution issue. He insists that it must become more than just a youth movement. "If anything is going to bring us all together, poor, rich, black, white, young, old, this has got to be it," he says. "Some of the black militants now are saying that population control is a white plot to commit genocide against the blacks. Unfortunately, some of the whites talking up population control *do* mean population control for the blacks, or the poor or the Indians. Like most racist plots, however, this one is incompetent—because if the blacks actually listened and had smaller families, it would mean more black power. Fathers would be more likely to stay with their families, the kids would get better educations, better nutrition and so on.

"But it's not for whites to tell the blacks what to do. Their birthrate is a little higher than ours, but they've been so stomped on that they haven't had a chance to do the looting and polluting of the environment that the whites have. Affluence and effluence go hand in hand. We Americans, comprising only six per cent of the world's people, consume 30 per cent of the world's available resources each year. So you can see that each American child puts far more strain on the world environment than each Asian child. We've got to put our own house in order before we start telling Asians and Africans what to do."

He also encourages the old to join in. "We ought to have swinging old people," he says. "The two groups of people most mistrusted are the very old and the very young. And they could form a great force for change, if they could come together and put pressure on the middle group that is responsible for much of the destruction of the environment."

Ehrlich argues that the young "share a disdain for material things, a fascination for nature and an interest in what might be called an ecological way of life. These attitudes are the antithesis of those of the Old Left, of

Socialism and Communism, which resemble Judeo-Christian attitudes in encouraging the exploitation of nature."

Ehrlich asks the young not to be misled by those who say the environment is a "safe" issue, that they are being co-opted, weaned away from the "real" issues of Vietnam, poverty, race and so on. "Your cause is a lost cause without population control," he says, "and race, war, poverty and environment are really part and parcel of the same big mess. The wars we're fighting in Vietnam and Laos, for example, are immensely destructive to the environment. We've defoliated an estimated 20 per cent of Vietnam, and much of the ecological destruction there is going to be permanent. Students have got to inform themselves on problems in their areas and then become teachers—fast. I think the Environmental Teach-In, April 22, is going to have tremendous impact. I hope that the participants will zero in on the politicians, make it clear we aren't going to settle for their lies and do-nothing attitudes. . . ."

"The movement is going to generate a lot of civil disobedience, similar to what we saw in the early days of civil rights: demonstrations, picketing, sit-ins. I think we will soon begin to see boycotting of the automobile industry, the big oil companies, the utilities and so on. Among other things, people are just going to stop paying their bills. One clue that we're making real progress will come when politicians start telling it like it is and to hell with the consequences."

Ehrlich's forthcoming book, *Population Resources and Environment,* sums it up: "Spaceship Earth is now filled to capacity or beyond, and running out of food. And yet people traveling first class are, without thinking, demolishing the ship's already overstrained life-support systems. . . . Thermonuclear bombs, poison gases, and super-germs are being manufactured and stockpiled. . . . [But] many of the passengers still view the chaos with cheerful optimism. . . ."

If neither party produces a presidential nominee in 1972 pledged to a crash program to save the environment, Ehrlich predicts a new party will offer such a man. An activist organization he helped start last year, Zero Population Growth, may provide the base. ZPG now has a membership of over 8,000 and it is doubling every two months. It wants legalized abortion, a maximum of two children a family, Government support of birth control, tax incentives for smaller families and candidates dedicated to environmental reform.

Ehrlich rules himself unsuited for public office. Rather than become more involved in public life after 1972, he may withdraw altogether. "When you reach a point where you realize further efforts will be futile, you may as well look after yourself and your friends and enjoy what little time you have left. That point for me is 1972."

In the meantime, though, he keeps running, burning up time he would much rather spend with his pretty wife Anne or his daughter Lisa, flying his own plane or carrying on research projects in evolution, finishing studies on the effects of crowding on humans, getting back to his field projects. "I'm no hair-shirt hero," he says again. "This is just a survival reaction. I'm running for my life. . . ."

Discussion Questions

1. Briefly review why Dr. Ehrlich is "running for his life." Do you agree with his fears? Discuss.
2. Summarize Dr. Ehrlich's list of "environmental villains, ecological Uncle Toms, 'dum-dums and Yo-Yo's' of the Establishment." Do you share his low regard for these individuals and groups? Discuss.

3. Dr. Ehrlich, a biologist, speaks negatively of the field of Physics in this article. He says: "The science adviser today should be a biologist or behavioral scientist, not a physicist." What leads him to this conclusion? Do you agree? Discuss.

―――――――――――――――――――

DONALD J. BOGUE

The End of the Population Explosion

During the past twenty years population "explosionists" such as Paul Ehrlich have terrorized themselves and others with the "scare rhetoric" of the hopelessness and inevitability of the population explosion. There are other scholars, however, who consider such doomsday prophecies as little more than inflamatory rhetoric based on tenuous assumptions and simplistic logic. Moreover, argue these other scholars, such rhetoric will in the long run hinder rather than help provide solutions to population and environmental problems. Contrary to the pessimism of the explosionists these scholars have observed some changes that bode well for the future of the world population growth rates. One such optimistic view is provided by Donald J. Bogue in the following article.

Recent developments in the worldwide movement to bring runaway birth rates under control are such that it now is possible to assert with considerable confidence that the prospects for success are excellent. In fact, it is quite reasonable to assume that *the world population crisis is a phenomenon of the 20th century, and will be largely if not entirely a matter of history when humanity moves into the 21st century.* No doubt there will still be problematic areas in the year 2000, but they will be confined to a few nations that were too prejudiced, too bureaucratic, or too disorganized to take action sooner, or will be confined to small regions within some nations where particular ethnic, economic, or religious groups will not yet have received adequate fertility control services and information. With the exception of such isolated remnants (which may be neutralized by other areas of growth-at-less-than-replacement), it is probable that by the year 2000 each of the major world regions will have a population growth rate that either is zero or is easily within the capacity of its expanding economy to support.

Reprinted from Donald J. Bogue, "The End of the Population Explosion," *The Public Interest,* Spring, 1967, pp. 11–20. Copyright © 1967 National Affairs, Inc.

The implications of these assertions for the feeding of the human race are obvious. Given the present capacity of the earth for food production, and the potential for additional food production if modern technology were more fully employed, mankind clearly has within its grasp the capacity to abolish hunger —within a matter of a decade or two. Furthermore, it is doubtful whether a total net food shortage for the entire earth will ever develop. If such a deficit does develop, it will be mild and only of short duration. The really critical problem will continue to be one of maldistribution of food among the world's regions.

These optimistic assertions are not intended to detract from the seriousness of the present population situation. Some years of acute crisis lie immediately ahead for India, China, the Philippines, Indonesia, Pakistan, Mexico, Brazil, Egypt, and other nations. Severe famines quite probably will develop within local areas of some of these nations unless emergency international measures are taken. My purpose here is to emphasize that the engineers and the agricultural technicians striving to increase the output of material goods in these nations are not working alone. Paralleling their activity is a very ambitious international fertility control program which is just starting to "pay off."

These remarks are certainly not intended to cause the participants in this international fertility control program to relax their efforts and be lulled into complacency. The successful outcome anticipated above is not one that will come automatically, but only as a result of a continued all-out "crash program" to make the widest and most intensive use of the medical, sociological and psychological knowledge now available, and of the practical experience that has recently emerged from experimental family planning programs. It also anticipates a continued flow of new research findings and enriched practical experience that is promptly fed back into programs of fertility reduction.

This view is at variance with the established view of many population experts. For more than a century, demographers have terrorized themselves, each other, and the public at large with the essential hopelessness and inevitability of the "population explosion." Their prophecies have all been dependent upon one premise: "If recent trends continue. . . ." It is an ancient statistical fallacy to perform extrapolations upon this premise when in fact the premise is invalid. It is my major point that *recent trends have not continued, nor will they be likely to do so.* Instead, there have been some new and recent developments that make it plausible to expect a much more rapid pace in fertility control. These developments are so new and so novel that *population trends before 1960 are largely irrelevant in predicting what will happen in the future.*

In times of social revolution, it often is fruitless to forecast the future on the basis of past experience. Instead, it is better to abandon time series analysis and study the phenomenon of change itself, seeking to understand it and to learn in which direction and how rapidly it is moving. If enough can be learned about the social movement that is bringing about the change, there is a hope that its eventual outcome can be roughly predicted. This procedure is followed here. The result is subjective and crude, but I believe it to be nearer the future course of demographic history than the official population projections now on record.

Limitations of space permit only a listing of major social developments which, in my view, justify the relatively optimistic prospect I have set forth.

1. Grass roots approval. All over the world, wherever surveys of the attitude of the public with respect to fertility have been taken, it has uniformly been found that a majority of couples with three living children wish to have no more. Of these, a very large proportion approve of family planning in principle and declare they would like to have more information about it. They also approve of nationwide health service that includes family planning. In other words, active objections among the masses on cultural, moral, or religious grounds are minor rather than major obstacles. This is true both in Asia and Latin America, and seems to be developing rapidly in Africa. Thus, at the "grass roots" level, the attitudinal and cultural conditions are highly favorable. Previously, it had been feared that traditionalism and religious attitudes would prove to be almost insuperable blocks to rapid fertility control. . . .

2. Aroused political leadership. . . . [I]n the nations with a population problem today the national political leadership openly accepts family planning as a moral and rational solution. Heads of state in India, Pakistan, Korea, China, Egypt, Chile, Turkey, and Colombia, for example, have made fertility control an integral part of the national plan for economic development. . . . The mass media are increasingly carrying official endorsements, public encouragements, and specific information.

3. Accelerated professional and research activity. Professional groups in the developing countries (as well as in the rest of the world) are rapidly losing whatever antipathy or prejudice against family planning they may have had. Everywhere, the medical profession is rapidly giving it a solid endorsement— even in nations where there have been problems of religious objection. Within religious groups where there formerly was a hard inflexible prohibition against the use of chemical or mechanical contraceptive appliances, there is now a great deal of difference of opinion. Gradually, the laity is reaching the belief that the control of natality is a matter for the individual conscience, or a medical matter to be discussed with a physician—but not with the priest. Physicians and priests alike tend to accept this interpretation without forthright challenge.

Universities, both in the United States and abroad, have undertaken large-scale and sustained research activities in the fields of family planning. Their activities cover the entire range of topics—medical, sociological, and psychological. Most of the nations with a national family planning program are sponsoring research into the problem. This includes not only projects to discover new and improved ways of promoting fertility control, but also the evaluation of present programs. . . .

Much of the credit for the development described above is due to the activities of not-for-profit organizations that have taken population control as a focus of their activities: the Ford Foundation, Rockefeller Foundation, Population Council, and International Planned Parenthood are the leaders. The Swedish Government, the Milbank Memorial Fund, the Planned Parenthood Association of America, and the Pathfinder Fund have also been highly important sponsors of these activities. These organizations have provided unprecedented financial and technical support.

4. The slackening of progress in death control. Immediately after World War II, the industrialized nations of the world realized that there was a series of public health and medical programs that could be accomplished quickly and cheaply to bring about a reduction in mortality. These have now been largely carried out—there have been campaigns against malaria, smallpox, cholera, yellow fever, and other diseases that can be brought under control with an injection, a semi-annual house spraying, etc. The results have been dramatic, and death rates have tumbled. However, further progress in death control will be slower, because the remaining problems are those for which a solution is more difficult or is as yet unknown. For example, the death rate in Latin America stands at about 14 per thousand now. Modern medicine could bring it, at best, only to about 8 per thousand—a fall of 6 points. But a very much greater investment must be made, and over a considerably longer span of time, to achieve these 6 points than was required to obtain the preceding six points. In Asia the death rate still stands at about 20, even after the advent of the "miracle drugs" and the mass-inoculation and mass-treatment programs. It may be expected to drift lower, but at a slower pace than before.

This slackening of death control has a most important implication—a decline in the birth rate would be more directly reflected in a decline in the rate of population growth. During the past two decades, even if birth rates were declining, death rates were declining still faster, so that the population growth rate increased. That trend now appears to be reaching the end of a cycle: the cycle appears to be on the verge of reversing itself.

5. A variety of sociological and psychological phenomena, previously unknown or underappreciated, are promoting the rapid adoption of family planning by the mass of the people. Here we can only list them, without explanation:

a. Privation is itself a powerful motivating force for fertility control.
b. Private communication about family planning is far greater than had been thought, and can easily be stimulated to attain flood proportions.
c. "Opinion leaders"—indigenous men and women who are knowledgeable about birth control and freely undertake to influence others to adopt it—

can be mass-produced cheaply and very rapidly by means of mass media and other action programs. . . .

d. It is becoming evident that fathers are very nearly equally as interested and responsible in controlling fertility as are wives. Programs aimed at couples, instead of at females, are highly effective.

e. We are discovering that illiterate rural populations will make use of the traditional methods of family planning—condom, suppositories, etc.—very nearly as readily as urban populations, after a brief period of information and trial. They will also adopt the newer methods as—or even more —readily.

6. Improved technology in contraception promotes massive adoption by uneducated people at a rapid pace. Oral contraceptives and the intrauterine devices have both proved to be highly acceptable after only short periods of instruction and familiarity. Even illiterate rural villagers make sustained use of these methods where they have been given unprejudiced trial. These developments are only half-a-decade old, but they already have had a profound impact upon fertility control programs and plans. . . .

. . . *Physiologists* insist that much superior methods are on the horizon—that soon there will be dramatic improvements, that costs will be cheaper, and that the need for "sustained motivation" to practice contraception will be greatly reduced. Millions of dollars are being poured into experimental research on this front each year. This activity is taking place both in the public and the private sector. The giants of the drug industry know that huge markets can be gained by improving upon present contraceptive technology—and that huge markets will be lost if a competitor discovers and markets a superior product. As a result, all of the leading motives that bring about frenzied activity for progress among scientists have been harnessed and are at work in behalf of improving contraceptive technology—prestige, economic gain, anxiety, compassion.

In order to illustrate the above points, let us take as an example the recent experience of Korea. In 1962, the Republic of Korea formally adopted family planning as one of its national policies. In 1965, a National Survey of Family Planning was conducted. Following are some points from that survey.

1. Eighty-nine per cent of the wives and 79 per cent of the husbands approved of family planning.
2. The rate of approval was only slightly lower in the rural than in the urban areas (88 per cent for rural women and 77 per cent for rural men).
3. Of the minority who disapproved, only 8 per cent mentioned religion or morals. Traditional resistance was as low in rural as in urban areas.
4. Inability to read was no barrier; 81 per cent of those unable to read nevertheless approved of family planning.
5. On the verbal level, the population declared itself willing to practice family planning if given services. Seventy-seven per cent of the urban

women and 71 per cent of the rural women made such a declaration. Among husbands, 71 per cent of the urban and 65 per cent of the rural made such a declaration.

6. Unwillingness to practice family planning was concentrated primarily among young couples who had not yet had the number of children they desired and older couples (past 40 years of age) who were approaching the end of their child-bearing. Couples in the years of prime importance for birth control, 25–40, were most positive in their attitudes. Moreover, the greater the number of living children, the greater the willingness to practice.

7. As a result of the national information program, 85 per cent of the urban and 83 per cent of the rural population had heard of family planning. Moreover, 67 per cent of the urban and 64 per cent of the rural population had knowledge of at least one contraceptive method. Even among the illiterate, 51 per cent knew of one method or more. Knowledge of the more reliable methods—oral pill, IUCD, condom—was only very slightly less widespread in rural than in urban areas.

8. At the time of the interview, 21 per cent of the urban and 14 per cent of the rural couples were practicing family planning. Even among the illiterate population, 10 per cent were currently practicing family planning. Although small, these percentages very obviously have sprung from a condition of near-zero within a span of three years. If only 2 per cent are added each year, within 35 years population growth would be near zero.

9. The methods used by rural families were equal to or superior to those of the urban population in terms of reliability:

| Method | Per cent of those using a method | |
	Rural	Urban
Condom	51.1	61.1
IUCD	18.4	27.0
Oral pill	8.5	3.5
Foam tablet	34.5	42.2

Note: Figures add to more than 100 because some couples employed more than one contraceptive.

10. In April of 1965 there were 2207 field workers in the national family planning service, stationed in the health centers or in local offices. This is only the first wave of a rapid build-up to a point where there will be one field worker for each 10,000 population. The medical and social science departments of Seoul National University are actively engaged in research, evaluation, and participation in the national program. A private organization, Planned Parenthood Federation of Korea, has a branch in each province and is providing service and information through its office.

Yonsel Medical College is conducting special experiments in rural areas, with assistance from the Population Council.

11. The progress of the national program in giving family planning services is most impressive. The progress that results when a well-designed family planning program is carried out in a population of low education is illustrated by the Sungdong Gu Action-Research Project on Family Planning, conducted by Seoul National University School of Public Health under the sponsorship of the Population Council. This program started in July, 1964. It included the use of mass media (TV, radio, newspaper, posters, pamphlets, leaflets), group meetings, and home visiting. During the first 15 months of the program, of a total of 44,900 eligible (married women in the ages 20–44), 9,809 visited the family planning station for family planning information. About 85 per cent of these visitors (19 per cent of all the eligible women) accepted a method of family planning. Acceptance was divided roughly equally between condoms and other traditional methods and the IUCD's. Within the period, a total of 5,722 insertions (13 per cent of the eligible women) were made. Even when allowance is made for the fact that the first year's experience would "skim off" the accumulated group of already-motivated people, the fact that one-fifth of the fertile population could be induced to adopt family planning within such short time is most impressive. . . .

The above brief notes on the progress of fertility control in Korea are not isolated instances. A recent report from the Pakistan Family Planning Programme suggests that more than one million families in that nation of 100 million (about 5 per cent of the eligible population) now are currently contracepted through this program alone. In India, more than a million insertions of IUCD's are being made annually—in addition, the use of other methods of contraception is rising. In Colombia in Latin America, the oral pills and the IUCD both are being accepted at phenomenal rates; it is estimated that more than 120,000 couples in this nation of 18 million persons are using the oral pills alone; this is roughly 3 per cent of the eligible population. In addition, large quantities of other methods are known to be used. In Santiago, Chile, the IUCD is so well known and widely used that it is a part of the medical service throughout the metropolitan area.

To summarize: wherever one looks in the underdeveloped segments of the world, one finds evidence of firmly established and flourishing family planning activity. By whatever crude estimates it is possible to make, it is quite clear that a sufficiently large share of the population already is making use of modern contraceptives to have a depressing effect upon the birth rate. Even conservative evaluation of the prospects suggests that *instead of a "population explosion" the world is on the threshold of a "contraception adoption explosion."* Because of lack of adequate vital statistics, the effects of this new "explosion" will not be readily measurable for a few years, but they will start to manifest themselves in the censuses of 1970 and will be most unmistakable in 1980.

Given the situation that has just been described, what can be said concerning the future population of the world? If we insist on extrapolating past trends, we are making the unrealistic assertion that conditions have remained and will continue to remain unchanged. If we predict a slow change of the type that was typical of Europe and Northern America before 1960, we are implicitly asserting that the current programs are having zero effect: this assertion is contrary to fact. The course taken here has been to try to comprehend the nature of the change that is taking place, and to predict its probable course and speed, so that its impact may be guessed. As crude and subjective as this procedure is, it appears to offer more valid predictions than conventional population projections. . . . [T]he following generalizations appear to be justified:

The trend of the worldwide movement toward fertility control has already reached a state where declines in death rates are being surpassed by declines in birthrates. Because progress in death control is slackening and progress in birth control is accelerating, the world has already entered a situation where the pace of population growth has begun to slacken. The exact time at which this "switch-over" took place cannot be known exactly, but we estimate it to have occurred about 1965 onward, therefore, the rate of world population growth may be expected to decline with each passing year. The rate of growth will slacken at such a pace that it will be zero or near zero at about the year 2000, so that population growth will not be regarded as a major social problem except in isolated and small "retarded" areas.

Discussion Questions

1. This author is not an explosionist. How is he different?
2. Do you tend to agree more with the explosionists or with Bogue's point of view? Discuss.

KINGSLEY DAVIS

Population Policy: Will Current Programs Succeed?

Although the previous article provided evidence to support an optimistic view of curbing world population growth, it is important to recognize that there are reputable scholars whose pessimistic views of population growth are equally well reasoned and convincingly argued. These scholars are not easily given to scare tactics designed to terrorize themselves, each other, or the public at large. In the following article, a highly respected U.S. sociol-

Reprinted from Kingsley Davis, "Population Policy: Will Current Programs Succeed?" *Science*, Vol. 158, pp. 730–739, Nov. 10, 1967. Copyright © 1967 American Association for the Advancement of Science.

ogist, Kingsley Davis, describes the dilemmas of population policies, which preclude optimism about future population growth rates.

Throughout history the growth of population has been identified with prosperity and strength. If today an increasing number of nations are seeking to curb rapid population growth by reducing their birth rates, they must be driven to do so by an urgent crisis. My purpose here is not to discuss the crisis itself but rather to assess the present and prospective measures used to meet it. . . . I . . . propose to review the nature and (as I see them) limitations of the present policies and to suggest lines of possible improvement.

The Nature of Current Policies

With more than 30 nations now trying or planning to reduce population growth and with numerous private and international organizations helping, the degree of unanimity as to the kind of measures needed is impressive. The consensus can be summed up in the phrase "family planning.". . .

As is well known, "family planning" is a euphemism for contraception. The family-planning approach to population limitation, therefore, concentrates on providing new and efficient contraceptives on a national basis through mass programs under public health auspices. . . .

Goals

Curiously, it is hard to find in the population-policy movement any explicit discussion of long-range goals. By implication the policies seem to promise a great deal. This is shown by the use of expressions like *population control* and *population planning*. . . . It it also shown by the characteristic style of reasoning. Expositions of current policy usually start off by lamenting the speed and the consequences of runaway population growth. This growth, it is then stated, must be curbed—by pursuing a vigorous family-planning program. That family planning can solve the problem of population growth seems to be taken as self-evident. . . .

When the terms *population control* and *population planning* are used, as they frequently are, as synonyms for current family-planning programs, they are misleading. Technically, they would mean deliberate influence over all attributes of a population, including its age-sex structure, geographical distribution, racial composition, genetic quality, and total size. No government attempts such full control. By tacit understanding, current population policies are concerned with only the *growth* and *size* of populations. These attributes, however, result from the death rate and migration as well as from the birth rate; their control would require deliberate influence over the factors giving rise to all three determinants. Actually, current policies labeled population control do not deal with mortality and migration, but deal only with the birth input. This is why another term, *fertility control,* is frequently used to describe current policies. But, as I show below, family planning (and hence current policy) does not undertake to influence most of the determinants of human reproduction. Thus the programs should not be referred to as population control or planning, because they do not attempt to influence the factors responsible for the attributes of human populations, taken generally; nor should they be called fertility control, because they do not try to affect most of the determinants of reproductive performance. . . .

The actual programs seem to be aiming simply to achieve a reduction in the birth rate. . . . The Pakistan plan adopted in 1966 aims to reduce the birth rate from 50 to 40 per thousand by 1970; the Indian plan aims to reduce the rate from 40 to 25 "as soon as possible"; and the Korean aim is to cut population growth from 2.9 to 1.2 per cent by 1980. A significant feature of such stated aims is the rapid population growth they would permit. Under conditions of modern mortality, a crude birth rate of 25 to 30 per thousand will represent such a multiplication of people as to make use of the term *population control* ironic. A rate of increase of 1.2 per cent per year would allow South Korea's already dense population to double in less than 60 years. . . .

. . . One suspects that the entire question of goals is instinctively left vague because thorough limitation of population growth would run counter to national and group aspirations. A consideration of hypothetical goals throws further light on the matter.

Industrialized nations as the model

Since current policies are confined to family planning, their maximum demographic effect would be to give the underdeveloped countries the same level of reproductive performance that the industrial nations now have. . . .

What does this goal mean in practice? Among the advanced nations there is considerable diversity in the level of fertility. At one extreme are countries such as New Zealand, with an average gross reproduction rate (GRR) of 1.91 during the period 1960–64; at the other extreme are countries such as Hungary, with a rate of 0.91 during the same period. To a considerable extent, however, such divergencies are matters of timing. The birth rates of most industrial nations have shown, since about 1940, a wavelike movement, with no secular trend. The average level of reproduction during this long period has been high enough to give these countries, with their low mortality, an extremely rapid population growth. If this level is maintained, their population will double in just over 50 years—a rate higher than that of world population growth at any time prior to 1950, at which time the growth in numbers of human beings was already considered fantastic. . . . Such facts indicate that the industrial nations provide neither a suitable demographic model for the nonindustrial peoples to follow nor the leadership to plan and organize population-control policies for them.

Zero population growth as a goal

Most discussions of the population crisis lead logically to zero population growth as the ultimate goal, because *any* growth rate, if continued, will eventually use up the earth. Yet hardly ever do arguments for population policy consider such a goal, and current policies do not dream of it. Why not? The answer is evidently that zero population growth is unacceptable to most nations and to most religious and ethnic communities. To argue for this goal would be to alienate possible support for action programs.

Goal peculiarities inherent to family planning

Turning to the actual measures taken, we see that the very use of family planning as the means for implementing population policy poses serious but unacknowledged limits on the intended reduction in fertility. The family-planning movement, clearly devoted to the improvement and dissemination of contraceptive devices, states again and again that its purpose is that of enabling couples to have the number of children they want. "The opportunity to decide the number and spacing of children is a basic human right," say the 12 heads of state in the United Nations declaration. . . .

Logically, it does not make sense to use *family* planning to provide *national* population control or planning. The "planning" in family planning is that of each separate couple. The only control they exercise is control over the size of *their* family. . . . There is no reason to expect that the millions of decisions about family size made by couples in their own interest will automatically control population for the benefit of society. . . .

Actually, the family-planning movement does not pursue even the limited goals it professes. It does not fully empower couples to have only the number of offspring they want because it either condemns or disregards certain tabooed but nevertheless effective means to this goal. One of its tenets is that "there shall be freedom of choice of method so that individuals can choose in accordance with the dictates of their consciences," but in practice this amounts to limiting the individual's choice, because the "conscience" dictating the method is usually not his but that of religious and governmental officials. Moreover, not every individual may choose: even the so-called recommended methods are ordinarily not offered to single women, or not all offered to women professing a given religious faith.

Thus, despite its emphasis on technology, current policy does not utilize all available means of contraception, much less all birth-control measures. . . . A greater limitation on means is the exclusive emphasis on contraception itself. Induced abortion, for example, is one of the surest means of controlling reproduction, and one that has been proved capable of reducing birth rates rapidly. . . . Yet this method is rejected in nearly all national and international population-control programs. . . .

The questions of sterilization and unnatural forms of sexual intercourse usually meet with similar silent treatment or disapproval, although nobody doubts the effectiveness of these measures in avoiding conception. . . .

On the side of goals, then, we see that a family-planning orientation limits the aims of current population policy. Despite reference to "population control" and "fertility control," which presumably means determination of demographic results by and for the nation as a whole, the movement gives control only to couples, and does this only if they use "respectable" contraceptives.

The Neglect of Motivation

By sanctifying the doctrine that each woman should have the number of children she wants, and by assuming that if she has only that number this will automatically curb population growth to the necessary degree, the leaders of current policies escape the necessity of asking why women desire so many children and how this desire can be influenced. Instead, they claim that satisfactory motivation is shown by the popular desire (shown by opinion surveys in all countries) to have the means of family limitations, and that therefore the problem is one of inventing and distributing the best possible contraceptive devices. Overlooked is the fact that a desire for availability of contraceptives is compatible with *high* fertility.

Given the best of means, there remain the questions of how many children couples want and of whether this is the requisite number from the standpoint of population size. That it is not is indicated by continued rapid population growth in industrial countries, and by the very surveys showing that people want contraception—for these show, too, that people also want numerous children.

The family planners do not ignore motivation. They are forever talking about "attitudes" and "needs." But they pose the issue in terms of the "acceptance" of birth control devices. At the most naive level, they assume that lack of acceptance is a function of the contraceptive device itself. This reduces the motive problem to a technological question. The task of population control then becomes simply the invention of a device that *will* be acceptable. The plastic IUD is acclaimed because, once in place, it does not depend on repeated *acceptance* by the woman, and thus it "solves" the problem of motivation.

But suppose a woman does not want to use *any* contraceptive until after she has had four children. This is the type of question that is seldom raised in the family-planning literature. In that literature, wanting a specific number of children is taken as complete motivation, for it implies a wish to control the size of one's family. The problem woman, from the standpoint of family planners, is the one who wants "as many as come," or "as many as God sends." Her attitude is construed as due to ignorance and "cultural values," and the policy deemed necessary to change it is "education." No compulsion can be used, because the movement is committed to free choice. . . . The effort is considered successful when the woman decides she wants only a certain number of children and uses an effective contraceptive.

In viewing negative attitudes toward birth control as due to ignorance, apathy, and outworn tradition, and "mass-communication" as the solution to the motivation problem, family planners tend to ignore the power and complexity of social life. If it were admitted that the creation and care of new human beings is socially motivated, like other forms of behavior, by being a part of the system of rewards and punishments that is built into human relationships, and thus is bound up with the individual's economic and personal interests, it would be apparent that the social structure and economy must be changed before a deliberate reduction in the birth rate can be achieved. As it is, reliance on family planning allows people to feel that "something is being done about the population problem" without the need for painful social changes.

Designation of population control as a medical or public health task leads to a similar evasion. This categorization assures popular support because it puts population policy in the hands of respected medical personnel, but by the same token it gives responsibility for leadership to people who think in terms of clinics and patients, of pills and IUD's, and who bring to the handling of economic and social phenomena a self-confident naiveté. The study of social organization is a technical field; an action program based on intuition is no more apt to succeed in the control of human beings than it is in the area of bacterial or viral control. Moreover, to alter a social system, by deliberate policy, so as to regulate births in accord with the demands of the collective welfare would require political power, and this is not likely to inhere in public health officials, nurses, midwives, and social workers. To entrust population policy to them is "to take action," but not dangerous "effective action.". . .

. . . By implying that the only need is the invention and distribution of effective contraceptive devices, they allay fears, on the part of religious and governmental officials, that fundamental changes in social organization are contemplated. Changes basic enough to affect motivation for having children would be changes in the structure of the family, in the position of women, and in the sexual mores. Far from proposing such radicalism, spokesmen for family planning frequently state their purpose as "protection" of the family— that is, closer observance of family norms. In addition, by concentrating on *new* and *scientific* contraceptives, the movement escapes taboos attached to old ones (the Pope will hardly authorize the condom, but may sanction the pill) and allows family planning to be regarded as a branch of medicine: overpopulation becomes a disease, to be treated by a pill or a coil.

We thus see that the inadequacy of current population policies with respect to motivation is inherent in their overwhelming family-planning character. Since family planning is by definition private planning, it eschews any societal control over motivation. . . . Unacquainted for the most part with technical economics, sociology, and demography, [family planners] tend honestly and instinctively to believe that something they vaguely call population control can be achieved by making better contraceptives available.

The Evidence of Ineffectiveness

If this characterization is accurate, we can conclude that current programs will not enable a government to control population size. In countries where couples have numerous offspring that they do not want, such programs may possibly accelerate a birth-rate decline that would occur anyway, but the conditions that cause births to be wanted or unwanted are beyond the control of family planning, hence beyond the control of any nation which relies on family planning alone as its population policy.

This conclusion is confirmed by demographic facts. . . . [T]he widespread use of family planning in industrial countries has not given their governments control over the birth rate. In backward countries today, taken as a whole, birth rates are rising, not falling; in those with population policies, there is no indication that the government is controlling the rate of reproduction. The main "successes" cited in the well-publicized policy literature are cases where a large number of contraceptives have been distributed or where the program has been accompanied by some decline in the birth rate. Popular enthusiasm for family planning is found mainly in the cities, or in advanced countries such as Japan and Taiwan, where the people would adopt contraception in any case, program or no program. It is difficult to prove that present population policies have ever speeded up a lowering of the birth rate (the least that could have been expected), [much] less that they have provided national "fertility control.". . .

Rising Birth Rates in Underdeveloped Countries

In ten Latin-American countries, between 1940 and 1959, the average birth rates (age-standardized), as estimated by our research office at the University of California, rose as follows 1940–44, 43.4 annual births per 1000 population; 1945–49, 44.6; 1950–54, 46.6; 1955–59, 47.7.

In another study made in our office . . . the recent trend was found to be upward in 27 underdeveloped countries, downward in six, and unchanged in one. Some of the rises have been substantial, and most have occurred where the birth rate was already extremely high. . . .

The Case of Taiwan

In discussions of population policy there is often confusion as to which cases are relevant. . . . [A] case of questionable relevance is that of Taiwan, because Taiwan is sufficiently developed to be placed in the urban-industrial class of nations. However, since Taiwan is offered as the main showpiece by the sponsors of current policies in underdeveloped areas, and since the data are excellent, it merits examination.

Taiwan is acclaimed as a showpiece because it has responded favorably to a highly organized program for distributing up-to-date contraceptives and has also had a rapidly dropping birth rate. Some observers have carelessly attributed the decline in the birth rate—from 50.0 in 1951 to 32.7 in 1965—to the family-planning campaign, but the campaign began only in 1963 and could have affected only the end of the trend. Rather, the decline represents a response to modernization similar to that made by all countries that have become industrialized. By 1950 over half of Taiwan's population was urban, and by 1964 nearly two-thirds were urban, with 29 per cent of the population living in cities of 100,000 or more. The pace of economic development has been extremely rapid. Between 1951 and 1963, per capita income increased by 4.05 per cent per year. Yet the island is closely packed, having 870 persons per square mile. . . . The combination of fast economic growth and rapid population increase in limited space has put parents of large families at a relative disadvantage and has created a brisk demand for abortions and contraceptives. Thus the favorable response to the current campaign to encourage use of the IUD is not a good example of what birth-control technology can do for a genuinely backward country. In fact, when the program was started, one reason for expecting receptivity was that the island was already on its way to modernization and family planning.

At most, the recent family-planning campaign—which reached significant proportions only in 1964 . . .—could have caused the increase observable after 1963 in the rate of decline. Between 1951 and 1963 the average drop in the birth rate per 1000 women (see Table 1) was 1.73 per cent per year; in the period 1964–66 it was 4.35 per cent. But one hesitates to assign all of the acceleration in decline since 1963 to the family-planning campaign. The rapid economic development has been precisely of a type likely to accelerate a drop in reproduction. The rise in manufacturing has been much greater than the rise in either agriculture or construction. The agricultural force has thus been squeezed, and migration to the cities has skyrocketed. Since housing has not kept pace, urban families have had to restrict reproduction in order to take advantage of career opportunities and avoid domestic inconvenience. Such conditions have historically tended to accelerate a decline in birth rate. . . .

The main evidence that *some* of this acceleration is due to the campaign comes from the fact that Taichung, the city in which the family-planning effort was first concentrated, showed subsequently a much faster drop in fertility

Table 1/Decline in Taiwan's Fertility Rate, 1951 Through 1966

Year	Registered births per 1000 women aged 15–49	Change in rate (per cent) *	Year	Registered births per 1000 women aged 15–49	Change in rate (per cent) *
1951	211		1959	184	−0.1
1952	198	−5.6	1960	180	−2.5
1953	194	−2.2	1961	177	−1.5
1954	193	−0.5	1962	174	−1.5
1955	197	+2.1	1963	170	−2.6
1956	196	−0.4	1964	162	−4.9
1957	182	−7.1	1965	152	−6.0
1958	185	+1.3	1966	149	−2.1

* The percentages were calculated on unrounded figures. Source of data through 1965, *Taiwan Demographic Fact Book* (1964, 1965); for 1966, *Monthly Bulletin of Population Registration Statistics of Taiwan* (1966, 1967).

than other cities. But the campaign has not reached throughout the island. By the end of 1966, only 260,745 women had been fitted with an IUD under auspices of the campaign, whereas the women of reproductive age on the island numbered 2.86 million. Most of the reduction in fertility has therefore been a matter of individual initiative. . . .

The important question, however, is not whether the present campaign is somewhat hastening the downward trend in the birth rate but whether, even if it is, it will provide population control for the nation. Actually, the campaign is not designed to provide such control and shows no signs of doing so. It takes for granted existing reproductive goals. Its aim is "to integrate, through education and information, the idea of family limitation *within the existing attitudes, values, and goals* of the people." Its target is *married* women who do not want any more children; it ignores girls not yet married, and women married and wanting more children.

With such an approach, what is the maximum impact possible? It is the difference between the number of children women have been having and the number they want to have. A study in 1957 found a median figure of 3.75 for the number of children wanted by women aged 15 to 29 in Taipei, Taiwan's largest city; the corresponding figure for women from a satellite town was 3.93; for women from a fishing village, 4.90; and for women from a farming village, 5.03. Over 60 per cent of the women in Taipei and over 90 per cent of those in the farming village wanted 4 or more children. In a sample of wives aged 25 to 29 in Taichung, a city of over 300,000, Freedman and his co-workers found the average number of children wanted was 4; only 9 per cent wanted less than 3, 20 per cent wanted 5 or more. If, therefore, Taiwanese women used contraceptives that were 100-per cent effective and had the number of children they desire, they would have about 4.5 each. The goal of the family-planning effort would be achieved. In the past the Taiwanese woman who married and lived through the reproductive period had, on the average, approximately 6.5 children; thus a figure of 4.5 would represent a substantial decline in fertility. Since mortality would continue to decline, the population growth rate would decline somewhat less than individual reproduction would. With 4.5 births per woman and a life expectancy of 70 years, the rate of natural increase would be close to 3 per cent per year.

In the future, Taiwanese views concerning reproduction will doubtless change, in response to social change and economic modernization. But how far will they change? A good indication is the number of children desired by couples in an already modernized country long oriented toward family planning. In the United States in 1966, an average of 3.4 children was considered ideal by white women aged 21 or over. This average number of births would give Taiwan, with only a slight decrease in mortality, a long-run rate of natural increase of 1.7 per cent per year and a doubling of population in 41 years.

Detailed data confirm the interpretation that Taiwanese women are in the process of shifting from a "peasant-agrarian" to an "industrial" level of reproduction. They are, in typical fashion, cutting off higher-order births at age 30 and beyond. Among young wives, fertility has risen, not fallen. In sum, the widely acclaimed family-planning program in Taiwan may, at most, have somewhat speeded the later phase of fertility decline which would have occurred anyway because of modernization. . . .

Is Family Planning the "First Step" in Population Control

To acknowledge that family planning does not achieve population control is not to impunge its value for other purposes. . . . My argument is therefore directed not against family-planning programs as such but against the assumption that they are an effective means of controlling population growth.

But what difference does it make? Why not go along for awhile with family planning as an initial approach to the problem of population control? The answer is that any policy on which millions of dollars are being spent should be designed to achieve the goal it purports to achieve. If it is only a first step, it should be so labeled, and its connection with the next step (and the nature of that next step) should be carefully examined. In the present case, since no "next step" seems ever to be mentioned, the question arises, Is reliance on family planning in fact a basis for dangerous postponement of effective steps? To continue to offer a remedy as a cure long after it has been shown merely to ameliorate the disease is either quackery or wishful thinking, and it thrives most where the need is greatest. . . .

Unfortunately, the issue is confused by a matter of semantics. "Family planning" and "fertility control" suggest that reproduction is being regulated according to some rational plan. And so it is, but only from the standpoint of the individual couple, not from that of the community. What is rational in the light of a couple's situation may be totally irrational from the standpoint of society's welfare.

The need for societal regulation of individual behavior is readily recognized in other spheres—those of explosives, dangerous drugs, public property, natural resources. But in the sphere of reproduction, complete individual initiative is generally favored even by those liberal intellectuals who, in other spheres, most favor economic and social planning. Social reformers who would not hesitate to force all owners of rental property to rent to anyone who can pay, or to force all workers in an industry to join a union, balk at any suggestion that couples be permitted to have only a certain number of offspring. Invariably they interpret societal control of reproduction as meaning direct police supervision of individual behavior. . . .

That the exclusive emphasis on family planning in current population policies is not a "first step" but an escape from the real issues is suggested by two facts. (1) No country has taken the "next step." . . . (2) Support and encouragement of research on population policy other than family planning is negligible. It is precisely this blocking of alternative thinking and experimentation that makes the emphasis on family planning a major obstacle to population control. . . .

New Directions in Population Policy

In thinking about other approaches, one can start with known facts. In the past, all surviving societies had institutional incentives for marriage, procreation, and child care which were powerful enough to keep the birth rate equal to or in excess of a high death rate. . . .

If excessive population growth is to be prevented, the obvious requirement is somehow to impose restraints on the family. However, because family roles are reinforced by society's system of rewards, punishments, sentiments, and norms, any proposal to demote the family is viewed as a threat by conservatives and liberals alike, and certainly by people with enough social responsibility to work for population control. One is charged with trying to "abolish" the family, but what is required is selective restructuring of the family in relation to the rest of society.

The lines of such restructuring are suggested by two existing limitations on fertility. (1) Nearly all societies succeed in drastically discouraging reproduction among unmarried women. (2) Advanced societies unintentionally reduce reproduction among married women when conditions worsen in such a way as to penalize childbearing more severely than it was penalized before. In both cases the causes are motivational and economic rather than technological.

It follows that population-control policy can de-emphasize the family in two ways: (1) by keeping present controls over illegitimate childbirth yet making the most of factors that lead people to postpone or avoid marriage, and (2) by instituting conditions that motivate those who do marry to keep their families small.

Postponement of marriage

Since the female reproductive span is short and generally more fecund in its first than in its second half, postponement of marriage to ages beyond 20 tends biologically to reduce births. Sociologically, it gives women time to get a better education, acquire interests unrelated to the family, and develop a cautious attitude toward pregnancy. Individuals who have not married by the time they are in their late twenties often do not marry at all. For these reasons, for the world as a whole, the average age at marriage for women is negatively associated with the birth rate: a rising age at marriage is a frequent cause of declining fertility during the middle phase of the demographic transition; and, in the late phase, the "baby boom" is usually associated with a return to younger marriages.

. . . In agrarian societies, postponement of marriage (when postponement occurs) is apparently caused by difficulties in meeting the economic prerequisites for matrimony, as stipulated by custom and opinion. In industrial societies it is caused by housing shortages, unemployment, the requirement for overseas military service, high costs of education, and inadequacy of consumer services. Since almost no research has been devoted to the subject, it is difficult to assess the relative weight of the factors that govern the age at marriage.

Encouraging limitation of births within marriage

As a means of encouraging the limitation of reproduction within marriage, as well as postponement of marriage, a greater rewarding of nonfamilial than of familial roles would probably help. A simple way of accomplishing this would be to allow economic advantages to accrue to the single as opposed to the married individual, and to the small as opposed to the large family. For instance, the government could pay people to permit themselves to be sterilized; all costs of abortion could be paid by the government; a substantial fee could be charged for a marriage license; a "child-tax" could be levied; and there could be a requirement that illegitimate pregnancies be aborted. Less sensationally, governments could simply reverse some existing policies that encourage childbearing. They could, for example, cease taxing single persons more than married ones; stop giving parents special tax exemptions; abandon income-tax policy that discriminates against couples when the wife works; reduce paid maternity leaves; reduce family allowances; stop awarding public housing on the basis of family size; stop granting fellowships and other educational aids (including special allowances for wives and children) to married students; cease outlawing abortions and sterilizations; and relax rules that allow use of harmless contraceptives only with medical permission. Some of these policy reversals would be beneficial in other than demographic respects and some would be harmful unless special precautions were taken. . . .

A closely related method of deemphasizing the family would be modification of the complementarity of the roles of men and women. Men are now able to participate in the wider world yet enjoy the satisfaction of having several children because the housework and childcare fall mainly on their wives. Women are impelled to seek this role by their idealized view of marriage and motherhood and by either the scarcity of alternative roles or the difficulty of combining them with family roles. To change this situation women could be required to work outside the home, or compelled by circumstances to do so. If, at the same time, women were paid as well as men and given equal educational and occupational opportunities, and if social life were organized around the place of work rather than around the home or neighborhood, many women would develop interests that would compete with family interests. . . .

In any deliberate effort to control the birth rate along these lines, a government has two powerful instruments—its command over economic planning and its authority (real or potential) over education. The first determines (as far as policy can) the economic conditions and circumstances affecting the lives of all citizens; the second provides the knowledge and attitudes necessary to implement the plans. The economic system largely determines who shall work, what can be bought, what rearing children will cost, how much individuals can spend. The schools define family roles and develop vocational and recreational interests; they could, if it were desired, redefine the sex roles, develop interests that transcend the home, and transmit realistic (as opposed to moralistic) knowledge concerning marriage, sexual behavior, and population problems. When the problem is viewed in this light, it is clear that the ministries of economics and education, not the ministry of health, should be the source of population policy.

The Dilemma of Population Policy

It should now be apparent why, despite strong anxiety over runaway population growth, the actual programs purporting to control it are limited to family planning and are therefore ineffective. (1) The goal of zero, or even slight, population growth is one that nations and groups find difficult to accept. (2) The measures that would be required to implement such a goal, though not so revolutionary as a Brave New World or a Communist Utopia, nevertheless tend to offend most people reared in existing societies. As a consequence, the goal of so-called population control is implicit and vague; the method is only family planning. . . .

The things that make family planning acceptable are the very things that make it ineffective for population control. By stressing the right of parents to have the number of children they want, it evades the basic question of population policy, which is how to give societies the number of children they need. By offering only the means for *couples* to control fertility, it neglects the means for societies to do so.

Because of the predominantly pro-family character of existing societies, individual interest ordinarily leads to the production of enough offspring to constitute rapid population growth under conditions of low mortality. Childless or single-child homes are considered indicative of personal failure, whereas having three to five living children gives a family a sense of continuity and substantiality.

. . . Hardships that seem particularly conducive to deliberate lowering of the birth rate are (in managed economies) scarcity of housing and other consumer goods despite full employment, and required high participation of women in the labor force, or (in freer economies) a great deal of unemployment and economic insecurity. When conditions are good, any nation tends to have a growing population.

It follows that, in countries where contraception is used, a realistic proposal for a government policy of lowering the birth rate reads like a catalogue of horrors: squeeze consumers through taxation and inflation; make housing very scarce by limiting construction; force wives and mothers to work outside the home to offset the inadequacy of male wages, yet provide few child-care facilities; encourage migration to the city by paying low wages in the country and providing few rural jobs; increase congestion in the cities by starving the transit system; increase personal insecurity by encouraging conditions that produce unemployment and by haphazard political arrests. No government will institute such hardships simply for the purpose of controlling population growth. Clearly, therefore, the task of contemporary population policy is to develop attractive substitutes for family interests, so as to avoid having to turn to hardship as a corrective.

Discussion Questions

1. How does the author answer the question of the title? Do you tend to agree? Discuss.

2. How does the author use "The Case of Taiwan" to back up his view? Discuss.

IRVING S. BENGELSDORF

Underdeveloped Lands Can Best Help Selves by Birth Control

Developing nations can employ a variety of strategies in combating their dramatic increases in population. In the following article Mr. Bengelsdorf

Reprinted from Irving S. Bengelsdorf, "Underdeveloped Lands Can Best Help Selves by Birth Control," *Los Angeles Times* (June 5, 1969), Section II, by permission of the author.

outlines some of those strategies. It is important to note the dilemmas involved in selecting a particular strategy. These are multifaceted dilemmas involving cultural, sociological, political, economic, religious, and other variables.

The year is 1970. You have been elected to serve a 10-year term as prime minister of Purizbad, a poverty stricken, underdeveloped nation. And you are faced with a dilemma.

Your economics minister tells you that if the country continues the way it is going, then by 1980 Purizbad's gross national product (GNP)—the total value of goods produced and services rendered—would be $2.5 billion. But, your minister of internal affairs tells you that if the country continues its present course, then by 1980 Purizbad's population would be 12.5 million people.

If you divide the 1980 GNP ($2.5 billion) by the 1980 population (12.5 million) the ratio, called the gross national product per capita (GNP/C), reveals that Purizbad's 1980 GNP/C would be $200. This is about the GNP/C of Ecuador or Senegal in 1969.

You would like to leave office in 1980 with the nation having a larger GNP/C than the $200 that would result if you decided to do nothing. But, what to do?

In arithmetic, a ratio such as GNP/C is called a fraction. The number above the line, the GNP, is the numerator, while the number below the line, the population, is the denominator. To increase the value of a fraction one either can increase the numerator—increasing the nation's GNP by building factories, irrigation canals, highways, harbors, dams, etc.—or decrease the denominator—decreasing the population growth by having a national birth control program.

Suppose you decide to increase the numerator—to increase the country's GNP. Starting in 1970, you spend an extra $2.5 million per year for the 10-year period to 1980 investing in factories, roads, etc. And suppose that the return on your investment is 10% per year—$250,000 on the $2.5 million invested annually. At the end of 10 years, therefore, you have added 10 times $250,000 or $2.5 million to the GNP. Since if you had done nothing, the GNP would have been $2.5 billion, then your 10-year investment program has increased the GNP by $2.5 million divided by $2.5 billion or 0.001 (0.1%).

But suppose you decide to decrease the denominator—to decrease the country's population growth. Starting in 1970, you spend an extra $2.5 million per year for the 10-year period to 1980 investing in contraception—both educational programs and materials. Assuming that it costs $5 per year to supply each user—man or woman—with contraceptive understanding and materials, you can provide contraceptive techniques for $2.5 million divided by $5 or 500,000 users per year for 10 years.

Suppose that without contraceptives each user would have been responsible for one-fourth of a live birth per year. Thus, contraception would prevent 500,000 times ¼ or 125,000 live births per year. So, because of contraception there would be 10 times 125,000 or 1.25 million fewer births by 1980 than if contraception were not practiced.

Since if you had done nothing the population would have been 12.5 million, then your 10-year expenditure for birth control would have cut the population by 1.25 million divided by 12.5 million or 0.1 (10%).

Thus, for the same investment of $2.5 million per year for 10 years, one could either increase the numerator of GNP/C by 0.1% or decrease the denominator by 10%. In other words, a 10-year birth control program in Purizbad could increase its 1980 GNP/C 100 times as much as a 10-year capital investment program in factories, dams, etc.

The above is a grossly oversimplified economic model of a nation. And it is a static model—it only looks at the situation in 1970 and 10 years later in 1980. Complex social interactions are neglected.

But real-life countries are not static but dynamic—as the years pass there are complex social interactions that change the conditions of the problem. So, writing in the May 16 issue of *Science,* Dr. Stephen Enke, manager of economic development programs at TEMPO, General Electric's Center for Advanced Studies, Santa Barbara, has considered a more elaborate dynamic model involving the numerous interactions of number of births, number of deaths, total population, capital, labor, savings, technology, GNP an GNP/C. And his conclusions essentially are the same.

For underdeveloped countries, money spent on national birth control programs is much more effective in increasing GNP/C than similar money spent in conventional capital investment.

Discussion Questions

1. Review the author's concluding statement. Do you tend to agree with it? Why?
2. Although the author of this article admits he has presented "a grossly oversimplified economic model of a nation" he goes on to offer evidence that reaches conclusions essentially the same. What is your reaction to this evidence? Discuss.

Drawing by Siggs. © Punch 1972.

"Know what I dread—driving home through all that traffic."

Although cities have existed in America for over 200 years, only recently have they housed the majority of Americans. The major cause of growth in both the number and size of America's cities has been the migration of rural people to the cities. With the influx of large numbers of people, the spatial patterns of the city changed along with the patterns of human life. The central core of the city, for example, has been abandoned by the wealthy to poor migrants, usually of ethnic origin. Sociologists refer to this transformation by the concept of urbanization. *Urbanization* refers to both *where* and *how* people choose to live. The basic characteristics of urban areas are large size, dense population, and heterogeneity of population.

Sociologists use the term *urban ecological processes* to refer to how American cities have grown and changed. Three of the most important processes are segregation, invasion, and succession. *Segregation* refers to the concen-

tration of individuals of similar race and culture in a particular area because of prejudice, discrimination, or poverty. The ghetto (traditionally a Jewish community, now largely black), Chinatown, and "Nob Hill" are examples of segregation on the basis of race, ethnicity, and economic status. *Invasion* refers to the penetration of a segregated area by an institutional function or population group different from the one already there. Residential areas may be invaded by business and commerce. People of a different race, ethnicity, or class may move into a residential area. When the invasion has become so successful that new types of institutions and population are established, sociologists say *succession* has taken place.

Urbanization is not simply a traditional city growing larger. It is a new and complex form which includes the trends of metropolitanization and suburbanization. *Metropolitanization* is the process whereby a number of cities expand toward and eventually merge with each other. A metropolitan area usually includes a "downtown" commercial and business district, an "inner-city" of slums and ghettoes, satellite towns and suburbs. Newspapers, television, radio, rapid transit, and freeways combine these diverse areas into one economic and social community.

Much has been written about the effect of urban life on personality development, especially life in the inner-city slums and ghettoes. In the past, writers and journalists have painted a pessimistic picture of urban life. Writing in the 1930s, for example, Louis Wirth depicted urban life as overstimulating, impersonal, fragmented, and alienating. The outlook of extreme indifference reflected in the behavior of so many city dwellers was seen by interpreters such as Wirth as a device used to insulate themselves from others. Robert E. Park also argued that cities disrupted primary relationships and cast individuals adrift on a sea of loneliness and isolation. More recently, sociologists have determined that primary groups such as the family are an important part of the social organization of slums, and that a generally oversimplified negativism by previous "experts" on urban life was not sustained by the evidence.

Suburbanization refers to the development of residential communities that are outside the corporate limits of a large central city, but which are culturally and economically dependent on the city. All suburbs are not "bedroom cities." Some suburbs are devoted to manufacturing and providing specialized services such as education and recrea-

tion. During the 1960s almost 15 million people moved to the suburbs. In fact, the expansion of the suburbs has been so great that suburbanites now comprise the largest sector of the population.

With the growth of suburban areas, social scientists, cartoonists, journalists, and others have depicted what they believe to be the suburban environment and the typical suburbanite. Writers most often portrayed the typical suburbanite as well-to-do, socially gregarious, politically conservative, and prejudiced against racial and ethnic minorities. While this "type" of individual may be found in suburban areas, sociologists do not consider him typical. Suburbs and suburban dwellers should not be stereotyped. Not all suburbanites are well-to-do or gregarious. Perhaps the only thing suburbanites have in common is the consideration of suburban areas as good places to live.

Much of the popular literature today views urbanization as the cause of the greatest domestic crisis facing America. Not only has urbanization made cities the location of the poor and the ethnic minorities, it has also become the major source of water and air pollution. Urban renewal is one commonly recommended antidote. The marginal success of urban renewal has led most theorists to argue that nothing short of a massive concerted effort by both government and private enterprise can solve the problems of education, unemployment, housing, and pollution in urban areas. Perhaps sociology can contribute to the solution by providing a clearer and more accurate picture of the urban process, and especially its sociocultural impact.

ALBERT N. VOTAW

The Hillbillies Invade Chicago

The ecological process of invasion occurs when new kinds of organizations or people enter an area. Residential areas may be invaded by industrial or commercial enterprises. People from a different social class, culture, or race may also move into an area. The movement of blacks into a traditionally all-white suburban area is a familiar example of invasion. In the article below, Albert Votaw describes what happened when the "hillbillies" invaded certain areas of Chicago. His description offers a cautionary note to those who would automatically link the sociological phenomenon of invasion to one particular racial minority.

The city's toughest integration problem has nothing to do with Negroes. . . . It involves a small army of white, Protestant, Early American migrants from the South—who are usually proud, poor, primitive, and fast with a knife.

A pathetic though bumptious minority of 70,000 newcomers among Chicago's motley population of four million is disturbing the city's peace these days—and incidentally proving to everybody who will listen that integration problems often have nothing to do with race, language, or creed. These are Chicago's share of the hundreds of thousands of Southern "hillbillies" who have been imported during and since World War II to offset labor shortages in the industrial centers of Ohio, Indiana, Michigan, and Illinois.

"In my opinion they are worse than the colored," said a police captain. "They are vicious and knife-happy. They are involved in 75 per cent of our arrests in this district."

"I can't say this publicly, but you'll never improve the neighborhood until you get rid of them," commented a municipal court judge.

"I've been in this business fifteen years," remarked the manager of a large apartment hotel, "but this is the first time I've had to carry a blackjack in the halls of my own building."

These farmers, miners, and mechanics from the mountains and meadows of the mid-South—with their fecund wives and numerous children—are, in a sense, the prototype of what the "superior" American should be, white Protestants of early American, Anglo-Saxon stock; but on the streets of Chicago they seem to be the American dream gone beserk. This may be the reason why their neighbors often find them more obnoxious than the Negroes or the earlier foreign immigrants whose obvious differences from the American stereotype made them easy to despise. Clannish, proud, disorderly, untamed to urban ways, these country cousins confound all notions of racial, religious, and cultural purity.

Hard times in the agricultural and mining counties of the South, combined with talk of high wages in the North, originally caused this push to the city. And the labor shortage is by no means over—though the Southern influx has leveled off somewhat. Industrial leaders in Chicago have estimated that a total of 300,000 new workers a year must be imported for the next five years. With European sources of immigrants almost cut off by restrictive quotas, these new workers must come mostly from the South (Negro and white) and from Puerto Rico, Mexico, and the Indian Reservations.

Whether the Southern rural whites—anti-social to the point of delinquency in the eyes of their neighbors—must remain a sore to the city and a plague to themselves depends both on their ability to learn and on the city's ability to treat them right. Unfortunately, they have an option not open to previous immigrants which keeps them from adapting to their new world. They can always pack up and go home—only an overnight drive away. Hence they remain transients in fact and in spirit.

Rebels for Good Cause

The Southerners bring along suspicion of the authorities—landlords, storekeepers, bosses, police, principals, and awesome church people. Often, in Chicago these authorities belong to groups whom the Southerners consider inferior—foreigners, Catholics, colored people—so the suspicion is reinforced by prejudice. But the most conspicuous reason why the Southerners look all wrong in the city setting is the domestic habits they bring from small backwoods communities.

Settling in deteriorating neighborhoods where they can stick with their own kind, they live as much as they can the way they lived back home. Often removing window screens, they sit half-dressed where it is cooler, and dispose of garbage the quickest way. Their own dress is casual and their children's worse. Their housekeeping is easy to the point of disorder, and they congregate in the evening on front porches and steps, where they find time for the sort of motionless relaxation that infuriates bustling city people.

Their children play freely anywhere, without supervision. Fences and hedges break down; lawns go back to dirt. On the crowded city streets, children are unsafe, and their parents seem oblivious. Even more, when it comes to sex training, their habits—with respect to such matters as incest and statutory rape—are clearly at variance with urban legal requirements, and parents fail to appreciate the interest authorities take in their sex life.

On the job they are said to lack ambition, but the picture is confused. Many workers are mechanically skilled though not highly competitive. Sometimes malnutrition and ill-health have left them weak. While relatively few enroll in on-the-job training, a good many attend television repair schools. Generally, where they are employed in offices (women mostly) or service work—where the irregular tempo suits the former miner or farmer—their work record is adequate. In theory they may be interested in accumulating a nestegg; in practice they are more likely to make do until they run out of money, and then go home for a spell.

Because of this constant commuting—a family funeral down South may empty an entire building in Chicago—Southerners are considered poor tenants. Even worse, some get wise to the practice of rent-skipping. One young man reportedly brought his wife home from the hospital with a new baby in the morning, and by lunchtime the whole family had disappeared bag, baggage, and a few of the apartment's furnishings to boot. Some know enough law to refuse to pay the rent, being sure of ninety days for the courts to act on the landlord's eviction request. If the landlord changes the lock to force out a tenant, an undercover guerrilla war may take place.

At school—perhaps the most intimate contact between immigrants and their city neighbors—Southern children are handicapped by coming from inferior rural classes. They are too old for their grades and too mature physically for their classmates. One principal tells of cotton-clad, sockless youngsters whimpering in zero weather at the school door, where they have been sent by working parents an hour before opening time. If the family goes home for the winter, the children are so much farther behind on their return that they must either be demoted or carried as a more or less passive and un-assimilated segment in the class. In some elementary schools which they attend, transfers outnumber regular pupils, and enrollment may vary as much as seventy-five a day among a total of one thousand.

Prone to disease—but fearful of authority—the Southern whites tend to avoid immunization officers, free dental care in the schools, polio inoculations. Sometimes fundamentalist religious beliefs complicate their fears. Positive TB tests have shown up in the Southern-infiltrated areas of Chicago in increasing numbers, and the 1956 polio epidemic was centered there too.

An added complication in the difficulties which keep the newcomers both separate and inferior in the eyes of city residents and authorities is their rock-hard clannishness. Settling together, keeping in touch with home by interminable telephoning and frequent trips, they isolate themselves by intent. One Chicago block, for example, is inhabited almost exclusively by transplanted Kentuckians; one elementary school district was flooded with fifty families from a West Virginia town where the mine closed. Their chief social diversion is to gather with friends, noisily, in the one institution they have orginated up North—the hillbilly tavern.

"Skid row dives, opium parlors, and assorted other dens of iniquity collectively are as safe as Sunday school picnics compared with the joints taken over by clans of fightin', feudin', Southern hillbillies and their shootin' cousins," said one ferocious exposé in the Chicago *Sunday Tribune*.

"The Southern hillbilly migrants," the story continued, "who have descended like a plague of locusts in the last few years, have the lowest standard of living and moral code (if any), the biggest capacity for liquor, and the most savage tactics when drunk, which is most of the time."

Many of the newcomers regard city churches as kin to the authorities they distrust. They either stop going to church or else frequent the store-front, "holiness" gospel centers conducted by itinerant preachers. Here they feel at home; the women are not embarrassed by the greater elegance of their neighbors; and they listen to the kind of old-time religion they are used to. Many modern ministers object to having to cater to their backwoods beliefs.

"I preached for years in a mountain church and school in Tennessee," one Chicago pastor, himself of Southern origin, said bitterly. "Those kids walked eight miles each way, but we weren't supposed to worry about that. We were supposed to teach them that Jesus would take care of all our worries by and by, and that was all. The South has had enough of that type of religion, and I'm not interested in preaching that way to them any more."

One possible avenue of religion for these migrants may be the regular Southern Baptist churches, now being formed in cities like Chicago. It is too soon to judge whether this missionary assault on the transplanted parishioners will tend to isolate them further, or to encourage their assimilation.

You Never Know How Much

If the Southerners are a nuisance to the city, the city is equally hard on them. The mountain folk, as one of their friends puts it, have been dodging revenue agents for hundreds of years, and there is no reason why their attitude should change overnight. Authority means trouble: police, court, jail; repossession of goods bought on time; snoopy social workers; the truant officer; the need to admit publicly—when asked to sign for their youngsters' library cards—that they don't know how to read or write.

One of their sorest complaints is against gouging landlords. An Alabama couple with eight children quartered in two and a half rooms, sharing a general bath, pay twenty dollars a week in rent plus a two dollar a week premium for each child. Total $160 per month.

"How can I keep this place clean?" asked one mother. "The landlord won't give us no garbage can, and the linoleum's so full of holes I can't sweep it."

What about moving to a better apartment?

"You find me a landlord going to rent to eight kids," was the bitter answer.

The police don't come fast enough when called and they won't run a bad man out of the neighborhood the way the string-tie, tobacco-chewing sheriffs down South would do.

"They's a law against them kids driving around so fast and burning rubber with them noisy mufflers. Why don't the cops grab them?"

But when it comes to taking away the TV set when the payment is overdue, the law comes all too fast. "How I wish you people would make it harder for us to buy things," one Tennessean complained. "Back home we have to get signatures and references, and it takes two or three days. Here you just walk in and order what you want, and you never know how much it costs until too late."

This man learned through bitter experience to limit his installment buying to two items—a television set and an automobile. He was luckier than many of his friends, who had their wages garnished and lost their jobs.

For many of the newcomers there is a terrible burden of loneliness. They are young, often newly married, and away from home for the first time. For the man there is at least work and the tavern. But for the woman, sometimes unable to leave the apartment for an entire winter, life in the big city may mean an aching homesickness. The patriarchal family disintegrates when jobs for women cut into the dominant role of the father, and the absence of chores leaves the children with idle time outside the home and away from parental influence.

A Disgrace to Their Race?

In the long run, the Southern whites will probably make their own compromise with city ways. But this is no answer for the very real problems of today, and city authorities have been reluctant to recognize that they require special attention. The first major approach was made in Cincinnati, the city first to receive Southern whites in any appreciable numbers. A 1954 workshop gathered together the Mayor's Friendly Relations Committee, various other city agencies, and several sociologists, including one from Berea College. This conference developed a program dealing chiefly with job discrimination. In Indianapolis and some industrial towns of Michigan, similar approaches have been made.

In Chicago the main problem is not employment, but housing. And this question, involving not just where men work forty hours a week but where women and children live and play twenty-four hours a day, is much more delicate and complex. The most comprehensive approach was initiated by a private community group concerned with housing, welfare, and planning in one of the areas of the city into which Southern whites had moved with the usual deleterious social effects. This group obtained a survey of the newcomers, the first and to date the only study of this group in Chicago; and called together a city-wide conference of church, school, administrative, and civic leaders to discuss the survey and to develop a program.

This program attempts to deal with the Southerner where he lives, where his insularity is most pronounced, and where the prejudices of the older groups are most violent. The proposal involves the following five points:

1. Development of Southern white leadership, to create social and fraternal organizations comparable to those created by other ethnic groups.
2. A pilot project to experiment with techniques for easing the Southerners' adjustment to the city and for relieving those problems associated with their arrival which are forcing more stable families out of adjacent areas. (The Welfare Council of Metropolitan Chicago is currently working up such a project.)
3. Organization of landlords and building managers to enforce higher standards of tenancy.
4. Increased attempts to deal with school transiency.
5. Continued development by existing youth and welfare agencies of specific services for this hard-to-reach group.

The focus of any program must be to prod the newcomers to help themselves. The women are the easiest to reach—sometimes through prenatal clinics for mothers; sometimes through their jobs. Although the men remain a hard core of resistance to change, hope lies in the fact that the Southern whites are not a solidly homogeneous group. The few who have come from cities are ripe for assimilation and critical of the rural folk, particularly of the mountaineers.

"If you think the hillbillies are making a mess of your schools, you should see what they did to ours down in Louisville," drawled one soft-spoken new arrival, an engineer. Chicago has a social club of Tennesseans—1,500 strong—not one of whose members comes from the hills.

This kind of rivalry within the group may provide a clue; for all—even the most clannish and stubborn—have potentially the ability to compete with city people on their own terms. The frequent comment, "They are a disgrace to their race," is an acknowledgment of this fact. For this Southern migrant—the white Protestant artisan or farmer—is the descendant of the yeoman of Jeffersonian democracy. No matter how anti-social he seems, he has every attribute for success according to the American dream—even in its narrowest form.

In a sense, this immigrant is hated because he proves our prejudices wrong. With all the ill will in the world, the worst detractors of the Southern white acknowledge that he has what it takes to make good. The question is, can he develop the desire to belong and to get ahead—before he packs up once and for all and goes home?

Discussion Questions

1. What is the irony in the following statement in reference to the transplanted Chicago "hillbillies"? "They are a disgrace to their race."
2. What reactions to the authority institutions of urban society are typical of these "hillbilly" invaders? What accounts for this kind of hostility?
3. How does this article demonstrate "that integration problems often have nothing to do with race, language, or creed"? Does this article lead you to the conclusion that the problems of "hillbilly" invasion and subsequent prejudice and discrimination against them are exactly the same as the problem of black invasion? Discuss.

A. M. ROSENTHAL

Study of the Sickness Called Apathy

Although the anonymity and isolation of personal life in the city have often been exaggerated, the urban environment has nevertheless wrought changes in interpersonal relations. Many theorists of urban life argue that the focus of interaction has moved away from the family and community to large-scale government and economic organizations. Urban residents have consequently become more formal and impersonal. Worst of all, the urban resident has lost sentiment of intimacy—of personally caring for his fellow man. In the article below, Rosenthal graphically describes what can happen when the focus of an individual's life is directed away from his fellow human beings.

It happens from time to time in New York that the life of the city is frozen by an instant of shock. In that instant the people of the city are seized by the paralyzing realization that they are one, that each man is in some way a mirror of every other man. They stare at each other—or, really, into themselves —and a look quite like a flush of embarrassment passes over the face of the city. Then the instant passes and the beat resumes and the people turn away and try to explain what they have seen, or try to deny it.

The last 35 minutes of the young life of Miss Catherine Genovese became such a shock in the life of the city. But at the time she died, stabbed again and again by a murderer in her quiet, dark but entirely respectable, street in Kew Gardens, New York hardly took note.

It was not until two weeks later that Catherine Genovese, known as Kitty, returned in death to cry the city awake. Even then it was not her life or her dying that froze the city, but the witnessing of her murder—the choking fact that 38 of her neighbors had seen her stabbed or heard her cries, and that not one of them, during that hideous half-hour, had lifted the telephone from the safety of his own apartment to call the police and try to save her life. When it was over and Miss Genovese was dead and the murderer gone, one man did call—not from his own apartment but from a neighbor's, and only after he had called a friend and asked her what to do.

The day that the story of the witnessing of the death of Miss Genovese appeared in this newspaper became that frozen instant." "Thirty-eight!" people said over and over. "Thirty-eight!"

It was as if the number itself had some special meaning, and in a way, of course, it did. One person or two or even three or four witnessing a murder passively would have been the unnoticed symptom of the disease in the city's body and again would have passed unnoticed. But 38—it was like a man with a running low fever suddenly beginning to cough blood; his friends could no longer ignore his illness, nor could he turn away from himself.

At first there was, briefly, the reaction of shared guilt. Even people who were sure that they certainly would have acted differently felt it somehow. "Dear God, what have we come to?" a woman said that day. "We," not "they."

For in that instant of shock, the mirror showed quite clearly what was wrong, that the face of mankind was spotted with the disease of apathy—all mankind. But this was too frightening a thought to live with and soon the beholders began to set boundaries for the illness, to search frantically for causes that were external and to look for the carrier.

There was a rash of metropolitan masochism. "What the devil do you expect in a town, a jungle, like this?" Sociologists and psychiatrists reached for the warm comfort of jargon—"alienation of the individual from the group," "megalopolitan societies," "the disaster syndrome."

People who came from small towns said it could never happen back home. New Yorkers, ashamed, agreed. Nobody seemed to stop to ask whether there were not perhaps various forms of apathy and that some that exist in villages and towns do not exist in great cities.

Guilt turned into masochism, and masochism, as it often does, became a sadistic search for a target. Quite soon, the target became the police.

There is no doubt whatsoever that the police in New York have failed, to put it politely, to instill a feeling of total confidence in the population. There are great areas in this city—fine parks as well as slums—where no person in his right mind would wander of an evening or an early morning. There is no central emergency point to receive calls for help. And a small river of letters from citizens to this newspaper testifies to the fact that patrols are often late in answering calls and that policemen on desk duty often give the bitter edge of their tongues to citizens calling for succor.

There is no doubt of these things. But to blame the police for apathy is a bit like blaming the sea wall for springing leaks. The police of this city are more efficient, more restrained and more responsive to public demands than any others the writer has encountered in a decade of traveling the world. Their faults are either mechanical or a reflection of a city where almost every act of police self-protection is assumed to be an act of police brutality, and where a night-club comedian can, as one did the other night, stand on a stage for an hour and a half and vilify the police as brutes, thieves, homosexuals, illiterates and "Gestapo agents" while the audience howls in laughter as it drinks Scotch from bootleg bottles hidden under the tables.

There are two tragedies in the story of Catherine Genovese. One is the fact that her life was taken from her, that she died in pain and horror at the age of 28. The other is that in dying she gave every human being—not just species New Yorker—an opportunity to examine some truths about the nature of apathy and that this has not been done.

Austin Street, where Catherine Genovese lived, is in a section of Queens known as Kew Gardens. There are two apartment buildings and the rest of the street consists of one-family homes—red-brick, stucco or wood-frame. There are Jews, Catholics and Protestants, a scattering of foreign accents, middle-class incomes.

On the night of March 13, about 3 A.M., Catherine Genovese was returning to her home. She worked late as manager of a bar in Hollis, another part of Queens. She parked her car (a red Fiat) and started to walk to her death.

Lurking near the parking lot was a man. Miss Genovese saw him in the shadows, turned and walked toward a police call box. The man pursued her, stabbed her. She screamed, "Oh my God, he stabbed me! Please help me! Please help me!"

Somebody threw open a window and a man called out: "Let that girl alone!" Other lights turned on, other windows were raised. The attacker got into a car and drove away. A bus passed.

The attacker drove back, got out, searched out Miss Genovese in the back of an apartment building where she had crawled for safety, stabbed her again, drove away again.

The first attack came at 3:15. The first call to the police came at 3:50. Police arrived within two minutes, they say. Miss Genovese was dead.

That night and the next morning the police combed the neighborhood looking for witnesses. They found them, 38.

Two weeks later, when this newspaper heard of the story, a reporter went knocking, door to door, asking why, why.

Through half-opened doors, they told him. Most of them were neither defiant nor terribly embarrassed nor particularly ashamed. The underlying attitude, or explanation, seemed to be fear of involvement—any kind of involvement.

"I didn't want my husband to get involved," a housewife said.

"We thought it was a lovers' quarrel," said another woman. "I went back to bed."

"I was tired," said a man.

"I don't know," said another man.

"I don't know," said still another.

"I don't know," said others.

On March 19, police arrested a 29-year-old business-machine operator named Winston Moseley and charged him with the murder of Catherine Genovese. He has confessed to killing two other women, for one of whose murders police say they have a confession from another man.

Not much is said or heard or thought in the city about Winston Moseley. In this drama, as far as the city is concerned, he appeared briefly, acted his piece, exited into the wings.

A week after the first story appeared, a reporter went back to Austin Street. Now the witnesses no longer wanted to talk. They were harried, annoyed; they thought they should keep their mouths shut. "I've done enough talking," one witness said. "Oh, it's you again," said a woman witness and slammed the door.

The neighbors of the witnesses are willing to talk. Their sympathy is for the silent witnesses and the embarrassment in which they now live.

Max Heilbrunn, who runs a coffee house on Austin Street, talked about all the newspaper publicity and said his neighbors felt they were being picked on. "It isn't a bad neighborhood," he said.

And this from Frank Facciola, the owner of the neighborhood barber shop: "I resent the way these newspapers and television people have hurt us. We have wonderful people here. What happened could have happened any place. There is no question in my mind that people here now would rush out to help anyone being attacked on the street."

Then he said: "The same thing [failure to call the police] happens in other sections every day. Why make such a fuss when it happens in Kew Gardens? We are trying to forget it happened here."

A Frenchwoman in the neighborhood said: "Let's forget the whole thing. It is a quiet neighborhood, good to live in. What happened, happened."

Each individual, obviously, approaches the story of Catherine Genovese, reacts to it and veers away from it against the background of his own life and experience, and his own fears and shortcomings and rationalizations.

It seems to this writer that what happened in the apartments and houses on Austin Street was a symptom of a terrible reality in the human condition—that only under certain situations and only in response to certain reflexes or certain beliefs will a man step out of his shell toward his brother.

To say this is not to excuse, but to try to understand and in so doing perhaps eventually to extend the reflexes and beliefs and situations to include more people. To ignore it is to perpetuate myths that lead nowhere. Of these the two most futile philosophy are that apathy is a response to official ineptitude ("The cops never come on time anyway"), or that apathy is a condition only of metropolitan life.

Certainly police procedures must be improved—although in the story of Miss Genovese all indications were that, once called into action, the police machine behaved perfectly.

As far as is known, not one witness has said that he remained silent because he had had any unpleasant experience with the police. It is a pointless point; there are men who will jump into a river to rescue a drowner; there are others who will tell themselves that a police launch will be cruising by or that, if it doesn't, it should.

Nobody can say why the 38 did not lift the phone while Miss Genovese was being attacked, since they cannot say themselves. It can be assumed, however, that their apathy was indeed of a big-city variety. It is almost a matter of psychological survival, if one is surrounded and pressed by millions of people, to prevent them from constantly impinging on you and the only way to do this is to ignore them as often as possible.

Indifference to one's neighbor and his troubles is a conditioned reflex of life in New York as it is in other big cities. In every major city in which I have lived—in Tokyo and Warsaw, Vienna and Bombay—I have seen, over and over again, people walk away from accident victims. I have walked away myself.

Out-of-towners, and sometimes New Yorkers themselves, like to think that there is something special about New York's metropolitan apathy. It is special in that there are more people here than any place else in the country—and therefore more people to turn away from each other.

For decades, New York turned away from the truth that is Harlem or Bedford-Stuyvesant in Brooklyn. Everybody knew that in the Negro ghettos, men, women and children lived in filth and degradation. But the city, as a city, turned away with the metropolitan brand of apathy. This, most simply, consists of drowning the person-to-person responsibility in a wave of impersonal social action.

Committees were organized, speeches made, budgets passed to "do something" about Harlem or Bedford-Stuyvesant—to do something about the communities. This dulled the reality, and still does, that the communities consist of individual people who ache and suffer in the loss of their individual prides. Housewives who contributed to the N.A.A.C.P. saw nothing wrong in going down to the daily shape-up of domestic workers in the Bronx and selecting a maid for the day after looking over the coffee to see which "girl" among the Negro matrons present looked huskiest.

Now there is an acute awareness of the problems of the Negroes in New York. But, again, it is an impersonal awareness, and more and more it is tinged with irritation at the thought that the integration movement will impinge on the daily personal life of the city.

Nor are Negroes in the city immune from apathy—toward one another or toward whites. They are apathetic toward one another's right to believe and act as they please; one man's concept of proper action is labeled with the group epithet "Uncle Tom." And, until the recent upsurge of the integration movement, there was less action taken within the Negro community to improve conditions in Harlem than there was in the all-white sections of the East Side. It has become fashionable to sneer at "white liberals"—fashionable even among Negroes who for years did nothing for brothers even of their own color.

In their own sense of being wronged, some Negroes of New York have become totally apathetic to the sensitivities of all other groups. In a night club in Harlem the other night, an aspiring Negro politician, a most decent man, talked on how the Jewish shopkeepers exploited the Negroes, how he wished Negroes could "save a dollar like the Jews," totally apathetic toward the fact that Jews at the table might be as hurt as he would be if they talked in clichés of the happy-go-lucky Stepin Fetchit Negro. When a Jew protested, the Negro was stunned—because he was convinced he hated anti-Semitism. He did, in the abstract.

Since the Genovese case, New Yorkers have sought explanations of their apathy toward individuals. Fear, some say—fear of involvement, fear of reprisal from goons, fear of becoming "mixed up" with the police. This, it seems to this writer, is simply rationalization.

The self-protective shells in which we live are determined not only by the difference between big cities and small. They are determined by economics and social class, by caste and by color, and by religion, and by politics.

If I were to see a beggar starving to death in rags on the streets of Paris or New York or London I would be moved to take some kind of action. But many times I have seen starving men lying like broken dolls in the streets of Calcutta or Madras and have done nothing.

I think I would have called the police to save Miss Genovese but I know that I did not save a beggar in Calcutta. Was my failing really so much smaller than that of the people who watched from their windows on Austin Street? And what was the apathy of the people of Austin Street compared, let's say, with the apathy of non-Nazi Germans toward Jews?

Geography is a factor of apathy. Indians reacted to Portuguese imprisoning Goans, but not to Russians killing Hungarians.

Color is a factor. Ghanaians reacted toward Frenchmen killing Algerians, not toward Congolese killing white missionaries.

Strangeness is a factor. Americans react to the extermination of Jews but not to the extermination of Watusis.

There are national as well as individual apathies, all inhibiting the ability to react. The "mind-your-own-business" attitude is despised among individuals, and clucked at by sociologists, but glorified as pragmatic national policy among nations.

Only in scattered moments, and then in halting embarrassment, does the United States, the most involved nation in the world, get down to hard cases about the nature of governments with which it deals, and how they treat their subject citizens. People who believe that a free government should react to oppression of people in the mass by other governments are regarded as fanatics or romantics by the same diplomats who would react in horror to the oppression of one single individual in Washington. Between apathy, regarded as a moral disease, and national policy, the line is often hard to find.

There are, it seems to me, only two logical ways to look at the story of the murder of Catherine Genovese. One is the way of the neighbor on Austin Street—"Let's forget the whole thing."

The other is to recognize that the bell tolls even on each man's individual island, to recognize that every man must fear the witness in himself who whispers to close the window.

Discussion Questions

1. Review the author's concluding statement about the "only two logical ways to look at the story of the murder of Catherine Genovese." Which way do you tend more to agree with and why?
2. This article attempts "to examine some truths about the nature of apathy." What are some of them that the author discusses? Does anything in these explanations indicate to you that apathy is more a symptom of urban society than of other types of society? Discuss.
3. Find a copy of John Donne's poem "No Man Is an Island." Do you find the thoughts expressed in it applicable to "The Kitty Genovese Story"? Discuss.

ARTHUR J. VIDICH and JOSEPH BENSMAN
Springdale's Image of Itself

The tendency to see the small-town environment as better than a big-city environment is deeply imbedded in American folklore. Residents of rural towns are especially prone to see their style of life as superior to that of the city dweller. In the following article, Vidich and Bensman describe some of the views small-town residents have of their community. "Springdale" is the fictitious name of a rural town of about 2,500 inhabitants in upstate New York. While the Springdalers spoke eloquently about the virtues of their rural lifestyle, researchers found that status distinctions prevailed. Like the city dwellers, Springdalers were given to ranking each other on the basis of income.

"Just Plain Folks"

When one becomes more intimately acquainted with the people of Springdale, and especially with the more verbal and more prominent inhabitants, one finds that they like to think of themselves as "just plain folks." The editor of the paper, in urging people to attend public meetings or in reporting a social event, says, "all folks with an interest" should attend or "the folks who came certainly had a good time." Almost any chairman of a public gathering addresses his audience as folks—"all right folks, the meeting will get underway"—and the interviewer in his work frequently encounters the same expression—"the folks in this community," "the townfolk," "the country folk," "good folks," and "bad folks." Depending on context, the term carries with it a number of quite different connotations.

First and foremost, the term serves to distinguish Springdalers from urban dwellers who are called "city people," an expression which by the tone in which it is used implies the less fortunate, those who are denied the wholesome virtues of rural life. City people are separated from nature and soil, from field and stream, and are caught up in the inexorable web of impersonality and loneliness, of which the public statement in Springdale is: "How can people stand to live in cities?" In an understandable and ultimate extension of this valuation one may occasionally hear references to the rural or country folk, in contrast to the villagers, the former being regarded by Springdalers as the "true folk."

The self-designation as "folk" includes everyone in the community; by its generality of reference it excludes neither the rich nor the poor, for everyone

Selections from "Springdale's Image of Itself," in Arthur J. Vidich and Joseph Bensman, *Small Town in Mass Society: Class, Power and Religion in a Rural Community* (revised edition © 1968 by Princeton University Press; Princeton Paperback, 1968), pp. 30–38. Reprinted by permission of Princeton University Press.

can share equally in the genuine qualities ascribed by the term. This is not to say that the community does not recognize scoundrels and wastrels in its own environment; quite the contrary, the scoundrel and allied types become all the more noticeable in the light of the dominant genuineness of rural life. It is rather to say that the standard of judgment by which character is assessed in Springdale includes no false or artificial values. To be one of the folks requires neither money, status, family background, learning, nor refined manners. It is, in short, a way of referring to the equalitarianism of rural life.

The term also includes a whole set of moral values: honesty, fair play, trustworthiness, good-neighborliness, helpfulness, sobriety, and clean-living. To the Springdaler it suggests a wholesome family life, a man whose spoken word is as good as a written contract, a community of religious-minded people, and a place where "everybody knows everybody" and "where you can say hello to anybody." The background image of urban society and city people gives force and meaning to the preferred rural way of life.

Rural Virtues and City Life

The sense of community-mindedness and identification has its roots in a belief in the inherent difference between Springdale and all other places, particularly the nearby towns and big cities. For the Springdaler surrounding towns all carry stigmata which are not found in Springdale: the county seat is the locus of vice and corruption, the Finnish settlement is "red," University Town is snobbish and aloof, and Industrial Town is inhuman, slummy and foreign. In the big city the individual is anonymously lost in a hostile and dog-eat-dog environment. Being in the community gives one a distant feeling of living in a protected and better place, so that in spite of occasional internal quarrels and the presence of some unwholesome characters one frequently hears it said that "there's no place I'd rather live . . . there isn't a better place to raise a family . . . this is the best little town in the whole country." In the face of the outer world, Springdalers "stick up for their town."

The best example of community identification occurs when newspapers of neighboring towns choose to publicize negative aspects of Springdale life: making banner headlines over the dismissal of a school principal, publishing the names of youthful criminal offenders who come from good families. In such instances, irrespective of issue or factional position, anyone with an interest in the community comes to its defense: "We may have our troubles, but it's nothing we can't handle by ourselves—and quicker and better if they'd leave us alone." A challenge to the image of Springdale as a preferred place cuts deep and helps to re-create the sense of community when it is temporarily lost.

It is interesting that the belief in the superiority of local ways of living actually conditions the way of life. Springdalers *make an effort to be friendly"* and *"go out of their way* to help newcomers." The newspaper always emphasizes the positive side of life; it never reports local arrests, shotgun weddings, mortgage foreclosures, lawsuits, bitter exchanges in public meetings, suicides or any other unpleasant happening. By this constant focus on warm and human qualities in all public situations, the public character of the community takes on those qualities and, hence, it has a tone which is distinctly different from city life.

Relationships with nearby towns, in spite of the occasional voicing of hostility, also have a sympathetic and friendly competitive aspect. No one in Springdale would gloat over another town's misfortunes, such as a serious fire or the loss of an industry. Athletic rivalries have long histories and although there is a vocabulary of names and yells for "enemies," these simply stimulate competitiveness and arouse emotions for the night of the contest. No one takes victory or defeat seriously for more than a day or two and only in a very rare instance is there a public incident when outsiders visit the town. "Nobody really wants trouble with other towns."

When one goes beyond neighboring communities, the Springdaler leaps from concrete images of people and places to a more generalized image of metropolitan life. His everyday experiences give him a feeling of remoteness from the major centers of industry, commerce and politics. His images are apt to be as stereotyped as those that city people hold concerning the country. Any composite of these images would certainly include the following:

1. Cities breed corruption and have grown so big and impersonal that they are not able to solve the problems they create.

2. Cities are an unwholesome environment for children and families, and have had an unhealthy effect on family morals.

3. Urban politicians and labor leaders are corrupt and represent anti-democratic forces in American life.

4. Washington is a place overridden with bureaucrats and the sharp deal, fast-buck operator, both of whom live like parasites off hard-working country folk.

5. Industrial workers are highly paid for doing little work. Their leaders foment trouble and work against the good of the country.

6. Cities are hotbeds of un-American sentiment, harbor the reds and are incapable of educating their youth to Christian values.

7. Big universities and city churches are centers of atheism and secularism and in spite of occasional exceptions have lost touch with the spiritual lesson taught by rural life.

8. Most of the problems of country life have their origin in the effects which urban life has on rural ways.

What is central, however, is the feeling of the Springdaler that these things do not basically affect him. While he realizes that machinery and factory products are essential to his standard of life and that taxation and agricultural policy are important, he feels that he is independent of other features of industrial and urban life, or, better, that he can choose and select only the best parts. The simple physical separation from the city and the open rural atmosphere make it possible to avoid the problems inherent in city life. Personal relations are face-to-face and social gatherings are intimate, churchgoing retains the quality of a family affair, the merchant is known as a person, and you can experience the "thrill of watching nature and the growth of your garden." Springdalers firmly believe in the virtues of rural living, strive to maintain them and defend them against anyone who would criticize them.

"Neighbors Are Friends"

Almost all of rural life receives its justification on the basis of the direct and personal and human feelings that guide people's relations with each other. No one, not even a stranger, is a stranger to the circumambience of the community. It is as if the people in a deeply felt communion bring themselves together for the purposes of mutual self-help and protection. To this end the community is organized for friendliness and neighborliness, so much so that the terms "friends" and "neighbors" almost stand as synonyms for "folk."

In its most typical form neighborliness occurs in time of personal and family crises—birth, death, illness, fire, catastrophe. On such occasions friends and neighbors mobilize to support those in distress: collections of money are taken, meals are prepared by others, cards of condolence are sent. A man whose house or barn has burned may unexpectedly find an organized "bee" aiding in reconstruction. Practically all organizations have "sunshine" committees whole sole purpose is to send greeting cards. These practices are so widespread and ultimately may include so many people that an individual, unable to acknowledge all this friendliness personally, will utilize the newspaper's "card of thanks" column to express his public appreciation.

Borrowing and "lending back and forth" is perhaps the most widespread act of neighborliness. Farmers say they like to feel that "in a pinch" there is always someone whom they can count upon for help—to borrow tools, get advice, ask for labor. In spite of the advent of mechanized and self-sufficient farming and consequently the reduction of the need for mutual aid, the high public value placed on mutual help is not diminished. Though a farmer may want to be independent and wish to avoid getting involved in other people's problems and, in fact, may privately resent lending his machinery, it is quite difficult for him to refuse to assist his neighbor if asked. Even where technological advance has made inroads on the need for the practice, to support the public creed remains a necessity.

For housewives in a community where "stores don't carry everything" domestic trading and borrowing is still a reality; they exchange children's clothing and *do* borrow salt and sugar. In Springdale they say "you never have to be without . . . if you need something bad enough you can always get it: of course, sometimes people overdo it and that makes it bad for everybody, but after a while you find out who they are." The process of selectively eliminating the bad practitioners makes it possible to keep the operation of the practice on a high plane.

Neighborliness has its institutional supports and so is given a firm foundation. Ministers and church groups make it a practice to visit the sick in hospitals and homes and to remember them with cards and letters, and all other organizations—the Legion, Masons, Community Club, book clubs—designate special committees to insure that remembrance is extended to the bereaved and ill. The Legion and Community Club "help our own" with baskets of food and clothing at Christmas time and organize fund drives to assist those who are "burned out." The ideology of neighborliness is reflected in and reinforced by the organized life of the community.

To a great extent these arrangements between friends and neighbors have a reciprocal character: a man who helps others may himself expect to be helped later on. In a way the whole system takes on the character of insurance. Of course some people are more conscious of their premium payments than others and keep a kind of mental bookkeeping on "what they owe and who owes them what," which is a perfectly permissible practice so long as one does not openly confront others with unbalanced accounts. In fact, the man who knows "exactly where he stands" with his friends and neighbors is better advised than the one who "forgets and can't keep track." The person who is unconsciously oblivious of what others do for him and distributes his own kindness and favor without thinking is apt to alienate both those whom he owes and doesn't owe. The etiquette for getting and giving in Springdale is an art that requires sensitive adjustments to the moods, needs and expectations of others. This ability to respond appropriately in given situations is the sign of the good neighbor. That this sensitivity is possessed by large numbers of people is attested to by the fact that friendliness and neighborliness contribute substantially to the community's dominant tone of personalness and warmth.

Of course, everyone does not participate equally or at the same level in being a good friend and neighbor. Deviations and exceptions are numerous. Neighborliness is often confined to geographical areas and to socially compatible groups. The wife of the lawyer is on neighborly terms with others like herself rather than with the wife of a carpenter. Farmers necessarily have less to do with people in the village and teachers are more apt to carry on friendly relations with each other. Those who are not willing to both give and take find themselves courteously eliminated from this aspect of local life. "People who are better off" simply by possessing sufficient resources do not find it necessary to call on friends and neighbors for help, though "everyone knows that if you went and asked them for something, they'd give it to you right away." Others have a more "independent turn of mind" and "will get by with what they have, no matter what, just to be free of mind"; the ideology of neighborliness is broad enough to include them "so long as they don't do anyone harm." The foreign elements, particularly the Poles, limit their everyday neighboring to their own group, but still by community definitions they are good neighbors because "you can always trust a Pole to deal square . . . if they owe you anything, they will always pay you back on time." Some folks are known as "just good people" who by choice "keep to themselves." By isolating themselves within the community they neither add nor detract from the neighborly quality of community life and so do not have an effect on the public character of the town.

The only group which does not fall within the purview of the conception of friend and neighbor is the 10 per cent of the population that live "in shacks in the hills." The people who live in shacks "can't be trusted"; "they steal you blind"; "if you're friendly to them, they'll take advantage of you"; "if you lend them something you'll never see it again"; "they're bad . . . no good people . . . live like animals." Hence by appropriately extending the social definition to give it a broader base than mutual aid, all groups in the community, except the shack people, fulfill the image of good friend and neighbor. The self-conception then reinforces itself, serves as a model for achievement and adds to the essential appearance of community warmth.

Good Folks and Bad Folks

"Of course, there are some people who just naturally have a dirty mouth. You'll find them anywhere you go and I'd be lying if I said we didn't have a few here." The "dirty mouth" is a person who not only fabricates malicious gossip about his enemies but also wantonly and carelessly spreads his fabrications. He commits the double *faux pas* of being deliberately malicious and of not observing the etiquette of interpersonal relations, and he is perhaps the most despised person in the community.

There are a whole range of personal qualities which are almost unanimously disapproved in Springdale. These are identified in the person

"who holds a grudge . . . who won't ever forget a wrong done to him."

"who can't get along with other people . . . who won't ever try to be friendly and sociable."

"who gives the town a bad name . . . always raising up a ruckus . . . always trying to stir up trouble."

"who tries to be something he isn't . . . the show-off . . . the braggart."
"who thinks he's better than everybody else . . . who thinks he's too good for the town . . . who thinks he's a cut above ordinary folks."

"who is bossy . . . thinks his ideas are always the best . . . tries to run everything . . . wants to be the center of attention all the time without working for it."

"who makes money by cheating people . . . who hasn't made his money honestly . . . you can't figure out where he got all that money."

"whom you can't trust . . . whose word is no good . . . who doesn't do what he says he was going to do . . . who doesn't carry through on anything."

In almost the exact reverse, the qualities of a good member of the community are found in the person who

"forgives and forgets . . . lets bygones be bygones . . . never dredges up the past . . . lets you know that he isn't going to hold it against you."

"is always doing something for the good of the town . . . gives willingly of his time and money . . . supports community projects . . . never shirks when there's work to be done."

"gets along with everybody . . . always has a good word . . . goes out of his way to do a good turn . . . never tries to hurt anybody . . . always has a smile for everybody."

"is just a natural person . . . even if you know he's better than you, he never lets you know it . . . never tries to impress anybody just because he has a little more money . . . acts like an ordinary person."

"always waits his turn . . . is modest . . . will work along with everybody else . . . isn't out of his own glory . . . takes a job and does it well without making a lot of noise."

"worked hard for what he's got . . . deserves every penny he has . . . doesn't come around to collect the first day of the month . . . you know he could be a lot richer."

"stands on his word . . . never has to have it in writing . . . does what he says . . . if he can't do it he says so and if he can he does it . . . always does it on time."

Springdalers affirm that on the whole most people in the community have these qualities. They are the qualities of "average folk" and "we like to think of ourselves as just a little above the average." "Average people can get things done because nobody has any high-blown ideas and they can all work together to make the community a better place to live."

Discussion Questions

1. Give a review statement of the Spring-daler's image of himself. How accurate do you think this self-image is?
2. Reread the section of this article on "Rural Virtues and City Life." Do you tend to see city life as being this "bad" and rural life as being this "good"? Discuss.
3. Review the "good" and "bad" personal qualities as described by Springdalers. What does this listing of personal qualities tell you about the differences between urban and rural patterns of living?

HERBERT J. GANS

The Future of the Suburbs

The 1970 U.S. census reported something many scholars had been asserting for years: that the suburbs had grown to a preeminent position and that more Americans lived in the suburbs (37.12 per cent) than lived in the cities (31.4 per cent). As a result, suburban communities officially became both the largest and the fastest-growing communities in the country. Given present growth rates, over the next twenty years more than half of all Americans will be living in the suburbs. But what does this change mean for the lives of those individuals who will live in the suburbs? Does it mean increased conformity, adultery, divorce, and alcoholism? What effect will it have on our social structure? Will the cities be inhabited only by blacks and other minorities, and the suburbs only by whites? Will our social system be more polarized and stratified? How will the political system respond to such changes? These and other questions are discussed by Herbert J. Gans in the following article.

In this unpredictable world, nothing can be predicted quite so easily as the continued proliferation of suburbia. Not only have American cities stopped growing for more than a generation, while the metropolitan areas of which they are a part were continuing to expand lustily, but there is incontrovertible evidence that another huge wave of suburban home building can be expected in the coming decade.

Between 1947 and about 1960, the country experienced the greatest baby boom ever, ending the slowdown in marriages and childbirths created first by the Depression and then by World War II. Today, the earliest arrivals of that baby boom are themselves old enough to marry, and many are now setting up housekeeping in urban or suburban apartments. In a few years, however, when their first child is two to three years old, and the second is about to appear, many young parents will decide to buy suburban homes.

Reprinted from "The White Exodus to Suburbia Steps Up," *The New York Times Magazine,* January 7, 1968. © 1968 by The New York Times Company. Reprinted by permission.

Only simple addition is necessary to see that by the mid-seventies, they will be fashioning another massive suburban building boom, provided of course that the country is affluent and not engaged in World War III.

The new suburbia may not look much different from the old; there will, however, be an increase in the class and racial polarization that has been developing between the suburbs and the cities for several generations now. The suburbs will be home for an ever larger proportion of working-class, middle-class and upper-class whites; the cities, for an ever-larger proportion of poor and nonwhite people. The continuation of this trend means that, by the seventies, a great number of cities will be 40 to 50 per cent nonwhite in population, with more and larger ghettos and greater municipal poverty on the one hand, and stronger suburban opposition to open housing and related policies to solve the city's problems on the other hand. The urban crisis will worsen, and although there is no shortage of rational solutions, nothing much will be done about the crisis unless white America permits a radical change of public policy and undergoes a miraculous change of attitude toward its cities and their populations.

Another wave of suburban building would develop even if there had been no post-World War II baby boom, for American cities have always grown at the edges, like trees, adding new rings of residential development every generation as the beneficiaries of affluence and young families sought more modern housing and "better" neighborhoods. At first, the new rings were added inside the city limits, but ever since the last half of the nineteenth century, they have more often sprung up in the suburbs. . . .

Moreover, studies of housing preferences indicate that the majority of Americans, including those now living in the city, want a suburban single family house once they have children, and want to remain in that house when their children have grown up. This urge for suburban life is not limited to the middle class or just to America; the poor would leave the city as well if they could afford to go, and so would many Europeans. . . .

Obviously, the popular antisuburban literature, which falsely accuses the suburbs of causing conformity, matriarchy, adultery, divorce, alcoholism, and other standard American pathologies, has not kept anyone from moving to the suburbs, and even the current predictions of land shortages, longer commuting, and urban congestion in the suburbs will not discourage the next generation of home buyers. Most, if not all, metropolitan areas still have plenty of rural land available for suburban housing. Moreover, with industry and offices now moving to the suburbs, new areas previously outside commuting range become ripe for residential development to house their employees. . . .

Of course, all this leads to increasing suburban congestion, but most suburbanites do not mind it. They do not leave the city for a rural existence, as the folklore has it; they want a half acre or more of land and all their favorite urban facilities within a short driving distance from the house. . . .

It goes without saying that almost all the new suburbanites—and the developments built for them—will be white and middle-income for, barring miracles in the housing industry and in Federal subsidies, the subdivisions of the seventies will be too expensive for any family earning less than about [$12,000]. Thus, even if suburbia were to be racially integrated, cost alone would exclude most nonwhites. Today, less than 5 per cent of New York State's suburban inhabitants are nonwhite, and many of them live in ghettos and slums in the small towns around which suburbia has developed.

Nevertheless, the minuscule proportion of nonwhite suburbanites will increase somewhat in the future, for, if the current affluence continues, it will benefit a small percentage of Negroes and Puerto Ricans. Some of them will be able to move into integrated suburban communities, but the majority will probably wind up in existing and new middle-class ghettos.

If urban employment is available, or if the ongoing industrialization of the South pushes more people off the land, poverty-stricken Negroes will continue to come to the cities, overcrowding and eventually enlarging the inner-city ghettos. Some of the better-off residents of these areas will move to "outer-city" ghettos, which can now be found in most American cities; for example, in Queens. And older suburbs like Yonkers and Mount Vernon will continue to lose some of the present residents and attract less affluent newcomers, as their housing, schools and other facilities age. As a result of this process, which affects suburbs as inevitably as city neighborhoods, some of their new inhabitants may be almost as poor as inner-city ghetto residents, so that more and more of the older suburbs will face problems of poverty and social pathology now thought to be distinctive to the city.

That further suburban growth is practically inevitable does not mean it is necessarily desirable, however. Many objections have been raised, some to suburbia itself, others to its consequences for the city. For example, ever since the rise of the postwar suburbs, critics have charged that suburban life is culturally and psychologically harmful for its residents, although many sociological studies, including my own, have shown that most suburbanites are happier and emotionally healthier than when they lived in the city. In addition, the critics have charged that suburbia desecrates valuable farm and recreation land, and that it results in "suburban" sprawl.

Suburbia undoubtedly reduced the supply of farm acreage, but America has long suffered from an oversupply of farmland, and I have never understood why allowing people to raise children where other people once raised potatoes or tomatoes desecrates the land. Usually, the criticism is directed to "ugly, mass-produced, look-alike little boxes," adding a class bias to the charges, as if people who can only afford mass-produced housing are not entitled to live where they please, or should stay in the city. . . .

The harmful effects of suburbia on the city are a more important criticism. One charge, made ever since the beginning of suburbanization in the nineteenth century, is that the suburbs rob the city of its tax-paying, civic-minded and culture-loving middle class. Actually, however, middle-class families are often a tax liability for the city; they demand and receive more services, particularly more schools, than their taxes pay for. Nor is there any evidence that they are more civic-minded than their non-middle-class neighbors; they may be more enthusiastic joiners of civic organizations, but these tend to defend middle-class interests and not necessarily the public interest. Moreover, many people who live in the suburbs still exert considerable political influence in the city because of their work or their property holdings and see to it that urban power structures still put middle-class interests first, as slum organizations, whose demands for more antipoverty funds or public housing are regularly turned down by city hall, can testify.

The alleged effect of the suburbs on urban culture is belied by the vast cultural revival in the city which occurred at the same time the suburban exodus was in full swing. Actually, most suburbanites rarely used the city's cultural facilities even when they lived in the city, and the minority which did, continues to do so, commuting in without difficulty. Indeed, I suspect that over half the ticket buyers for plays, art movies, concerts and museums, particularly outside New York, are—and have long been—suburbanites. Besides, there is no reason why cultural institutions cannot, like banks, build branches in the suburbs, as they are beginning to do now. Culture is no less culture by being outside the city.

A much more valid criticism of suburbanization is its effect on class and racial segregation, for the fact that the suburbs have effectively zoned out the poor and the nonwhites is resulting in an ever-increasing class and racial polarization of city and suburb. In one sense, however, the familiar data about the increasing polarization are slightly misleading. In years past, when urban census statistics showed Negroes and whites living side by side, they were actually quite polarized socially. On New York's Upper West Side, for example, the big apartment buildings are de facto segregated for whites, while the rotting brownstones between them are inhabited by Negroes and Puerto Ricans. These blocks are integrated statistically or geographically, but not socially, particularly if white parents send their children to private schools.

Nor is suburbanization the sole cause of class and racial polarization; it is itself an effect of trends that have gone on inside the city as well, and not only in America. When people become more affluent and can choose where they want to live, they choose to live with people like themselves. What has happened in the last generation or two is that the opportunity of home buyers to live among compatible neighbors, an opportunity previously available only to the rich, has been extended to people in the middle- and lower-middle-income brackets. This fact does not justify either class or racial segregation, but it does suggest that the polarization resulting from affluence would have occurred even without suburbanization.

Class and racial polarization are harmful because they restrict freedom of housing choice to many people, but also because of the financial consequences for the city. For one thing, affluent suburbia exploits the financially bankrupt city; even when payroll taxes are levied, suburbanites do not pay their fair share of the city's cost in providing them with places of work, shopping areas and cultural facilities and with streets and utilities, maintenance, garbage removal and police protection for these facilities.

More important, suburbanites live in vest-pocket principalities where they can, in effect, vote to keep out the poor and the nonwhites and even the not very affluent whites.

As a result, the cities are in a traumatic financial squeeze. Their ever more numerous low-income residents pay fewer taxes but need costly municipal services, yet cities are taking in less in property taxes all the time, particularly as the firms that employ suburbanites and the shops that cater to them also move to the suburbs. Consequently, city costs rise at the same time as city income declines. To compound the injustice state and Federal politicians from suburban areas often vote against antipoverty efforts and other Federal funding activities that would relieve the city's financial troubles, and they also vote to prevent residential integration.

These trends are not likely to change in the years to come. In fact, if the present white affluence continues, the economic gap between the urban have-nots and the suburban haves will only increase, resulting on the one hand in greater suburban opposition to integration and to solving the city's problems, and on the other hand to greater discontent and more ghetto rebellions in the city. This in turn could result in a new white exodus from the city, which, unlike the earlier exodus, will be based almost entirely on racial fear, making suburbanites out of the middle-aged and older middle-class families who are normally reluctant to change communities at this age and working-class whites who cannot really afford a suburban house. Many of them will, however, stay put and oppose all efforts toward desegregation, as indicated even now by their violent reaction to integration marches in Milwaukee and Chicago, and to scattered-site public housing schemes which would locate projects in middle-income areas in New York and elsewhere.

Ultimately, these trends could create a vicious spiral, with more ghetto protest leading to more white demands, urban and suburban, for repression, resulting in yet more intense ghetto protests, and culminating eventually in a massive exodus of urban whites. If this spiral were allowed to escalate, it might well hasten the coming of the predominantly Negro city.

Today, the predominantly Negro city is still far off in the future, and the all-Negro city is unlikely. Although Washington, D.C.'s population is about . . . [70] per cent Negro, and several other cities, including Newark, Gary and Richmond, hover around the 50 per cent mark, [in 1970, 13] of the 130 cities with over 100,000 population [were] 40 per cent or more Negro. . . . (New York's Negro population was [21] per cent in [1970], although in Manhattan, the proportion of Negroes was 27 per cent and of Negroes and Puerto Ricans, 39 per cent.)

Moreover, these statistics only count the nighttime residential population, but who lives in the city is, economically and politically, a less relevant statistic than who works there, and the daytime working population of most cities is today, and will long remain, heavily and even predominantly white.

Still, to a suburbanite who may someday have to work in a downtown surrounded by a black city, the future may seem threatening. A century ago, native-born WASPs must have felt similarly, when a majority of the urban population consisted of foreign-born Catholics and Jews, to whom they attributed the same pejorative racial characteristics now attributed to Negroes. The city and the WASPs survived, of course, as the immigrants were incorporated into the American economy, and suburban whites would also survive. . . .

Unfortunately, present governmental policies, local, state and Federal, are doing little to reverse the mounting class and racial polarization of city and suburb. Admittedly, the strong economic and cultural forces that send the middle classes into the suburbs and bring poor nonwhite people from the rural areas into the city in ever larger numbers are difficult to reverse even by the wisest government action.

Still, governmental policies have not been especially wise. The major efforts to slow down class and racial polarization have been these: legislation to achieve racial integration; programs to woo the white middle class back to the city; plans to establish unified metropolitan governments, encompassing both urban and suburban governmental units. All three have failed. None of the open housing and other integration laws now on the books have been enforced sufficiently to permit more than a handful of Negroes to live in the suburbs, and the more recent attempt to prevent the coming of the predominantly black city by enticing the white middle class back has not worked either.

The main technique used for this last purpose has been urban renewal, but there is no evidence—and, in fact, there have been no studies—to show that it has brought back a significant number of middle-class people. Most likely, it has only helped confirmed urbanites find better housing in the city. The attractions of suburbia are simply too persuasive for urban renewal or any other governmental program to succeed in bringing the middle class back to the city. . . .

Metropolitan government is, in theory, a good solution, for it would require the suburbs to contribute to solving the city's problems, but it has long been opposed by the suburbs for just this reason. They have felt that the improvements and economies in public services that could be obtained by organizing them on a metropolitan basis would be offset by what suburbanites saw as major disadvantages, principally the reduction of political autonomy and the loss of power to keep out the poor and the nonwhites.

The cities, which have in the past advocated metropolitan government, may become less enthusiastic as Negroes obtain greater political power. Since the metropolitan area is so predominantly white, urban Negroes would be outvoted every time in any kind of metropolitan government. Some metropolitanization may nevertheless be brought about by Federal planning requirements, for as Frances Piven and Richard Cloward point out in a recent New Republic article, several Federal grant programs, particularly for housing and community facilities, now require a metropolitan plan as a prerequisite for funding. Piven and Cloward suggest that these requirements could disfranchise the urban Negro, and it is of course always possible that a white urban-suburban coalition in favor of metropolitan government could be put together deliberately for precisely this purpose. Under such conditions, however, metropolitan government would only increase racial conflict and polarization.

What then, can be done to eliminate this polarization? One partial solution is to reduce the dependence of both urban and suburban governments on the property tax, which reduces city income as the population becomes poorer, and forces suburbs to exclude low-income residents because their housing does not bring in enough tax money. If urban and suburban governments could obtain more funds from other sources, including perhaps the Federal income tax, parts of the proceeds of which would be returned to them by Washington, urban property owners would bear a smaller burden in supporting the city and might be less opposed to higher spending. Suburbanites would also worry less about their tax rate, and might not feel so impelled to bar less affluent newcomers, or to object to paying their share of the cost of using city services.

Class polarization can be reduced by rent- or price-supplement programs which would enable less affluent urbanites to pay the price of suburban living and would reduce the building and financing costs of housing. But such measures would not persuade the suburbs to let in Negroes; ultimately, the only solution is still across-the-board residential integration.

The outlook for early and enforceable legislation toward this end, however, is dim. Although election results have shown time and again that Northern white majorities will not vote for segregation, they will not vote for integration either. I cannot imagine many political bodies, Federal or otherwise, passing or enforcing laws that would result in significant amounts of suburban integration; they would be punished summarily at the next election.

For example, proposals have often been made that state and Federal governments should withdraw all subsidies to suburban communities and builders practicing de facto segregation, thus depriving the former of at least half their school operating funds, and the latter of Federal Housing Authority (FHA) insurance on which their building plans depend. However desirable as such legislation is, the chance that it would be passed is almost nil. One can also argue that Washington should offer grants-in-aid to suburban governments which admit low-income residents, but these grants would often be turned down. Many suburban municipalities would rather starve their public services instead, and the voters would support them all the way.

The best hope now is for judicial action. The New Jersey Supreme Court ruled some years back that builders relying on FHA insurance had to sell to Negroes, and many suburban subdivisions in that state now have some Negro residents. The United States Supreme Court has just decided that it will rule on whether racial discrimination by large suburban developers is unconstitutional. If the answer turns out to be yes, the long, slow process of implementing the Court's decisions can at least begin.

In the meantime, solutions that need not be tested at the ballot box must be advanced. One possibility is new towns, built for integrated populations with Federal support, or even by the Federal Government alone, on land now vacant. Although hope springs eternal in American society that the problems of old towns can be avoided by starting from scratch, these problems seep easily across the borders of the new community. Even if rural governments can be persuaded to accept new towns in their bailiwicks and white residents could be attracted, such towns would be viable only if Federal grants and powers were used to obtain industries—and of a kind that would hire and train poorly skilled workers.

Greater emphasis should be placed on eliminating job discrimination in suburban work places, particularly in industries which are crying for workers, so that unions are less impelled to keep out nonwhite applicants. Mass transit systems should be built to enable city dwellers, black and white, to obtain suburban jobs without necessarily living in the suburbs.

Another and equally important solution is more school integration—for example, through urban-suburban educational parks that will build up integrated student enrollment by providing high-quality schooling to attract suburban whites, and through expansion of the bussing programs that send ghetto children into suburban schools. Although white suburban parents have strenuously opposed bussing their children into the city, several suburban communities have accepted Negro students who are bussed in from the ghetto; for example, in the Boston area and in Westchester County.

And while the Supreme Court is deliberating, it would be worthwhile to persuade frightened suburbanites that, as all the studies so far have indicated, open housing would not mean a massive invasion of slum dwellers, but only the gradual arrival of a relatively small number of Negroes, most of them as middle-class as the whitest suburbanite. A massive suburban invasion by slum dwellers of any color is sheer fantasy. Economic studies have shown the sad fact that only a tiny proportion of ghetto residents can even afford to live in the suburbs. Moreover, as long as Negro workers lack substantial job security, they need to live near the center of the urban transportation system so that they can travel to jobs all over the city.

In addition, there are probably many ghetto residents who do not even want suburban integration now; they want the same freedom of housing choice as whites but they do not want to be "dispersed" to the suburbs involuntarily. Unfortunately, no reliable studies exist to tell us where ghetto residents do want to live, but should they have freedom of choice, I suspect many would leave the slums for better housing and better neighborhoods outside the present ghetto. Not many would now choose predominantly white areas, however, at least not until living among whites is psychologically and socially less taxing, and until integration means more than just assimilation to white middle-class ways.

Because of the meager success of past integration efforts, many civil rights leaders have given up on integration and are now demanding the rebuilding of the ghetto. They argue persuasively that residential integration has so far and will in the future benefit only a small number of affluent Negroes, and that if the poverty-stricken ghetto residents are to be helped soon, that help must be located in the ghetto. The advocates of integration are strongly opposed. They demand that all future housing must be built outside the ghetto, for anything else would just perpetuate segregation. In recent months, the debate between the two positions has become bitter, each side claiming only its solution has merit.

Actually there is partial truth on both sides. The integrationists are correct about the long-term dangers of rebuilding the ghetto; the ghetto rebuilders (or separatists) are correct about the short-term failure of integration. But if there is little likelihood that the integrationists' demands will be carried out soon, their high idealism in effect sentences ghetto residents to remain in slum poverty.

Moreover, there is no need to choose between integration and rebuilding, for both policies can be carried out simultaneously. The struggle for integration must continue, but if the immediate prospects for success on a large scale are dim, the ghetto must be rebuilt in the meantime.

The primary aim of rebuilding, however, should not be to rehabilitate houses or clear slums, but to raise the standard of living of ghetto residents. The highest priority must be a massive antipoverty program which will, through the creation of jobs, more effective job-training schemes, the negative income tax, children's allowances and other measures, raise ghetto families to the middle-income level, using outside resources from government and private enterprise and inside participation in the planing and decision-making. Also needed are a concerted effort at quality compensatory education for children who cannot attend integrated schools; federally funded efforts to improve the quality of ghetto housing, as well as public services; some municipal decentralization to give ghetto residents the ability to plan their own communities and their own lives, and political power so that the ghetto can exert more influence in behalf of its demands.

If such programs could extend the middle-income standard of living to the ghetto in the years to come, residential integration might well be achieved in subsequent generations. Much of the white opposition to integration is based on stereotypes of Negro behavior—some true, some false—that stem from poverty rather than from color, and many of the fears about Negro neighbors reflect the traditional American belief that poor people will not live up to middle-class standards. Moreover, even lack of enthusiasm for integration among ghetto residents is a result of poverty; they feel, rightly or not, that they must solve their economic problems before they can even think about integration.

If ghetto poverty were eliminated, the white fears—and the Negro ones— would begin to disappear, as did the pejorative stereotypes which earlier

Americans held about the "inferior races"—a favorite nineteenth-century term for the European immigrants—until they achieved affluence. Because atittudes based on color differences are harder to overcome than those based on cultural differences, the disappearance of anti-Negro stereotypes will be slower than that of anti-immigrant stereotypes. Still, once color is no longer an index of poverty and lower-class status, it will cease to arouse white fears, so that open-housing laws can be enforced more easily and eventually may even be unnecessary. White suburbanites will not exclude Negroes to protect their status or their property values, and many, although not necessarily all, Negroes will choose to leave the ghetto.

Morally speaking, any solution that does not promise immediate integration is repugnant, but moral dicta will neither persuade suburbanites to admit low-income Negroes into their communities, nor entice urbane suburbanites to live near low-income Negroes in the city. Instead of seeking to increase their middle-income population by importing suburban whites, cities must instead make their poor residents middle-income. The practical solution, then, is to continue to press for residential integration, but also to eliminate ghetto poverty immediately, in order to achieve integration in the future, substituting government antipoverty programs for the private economy which once created the jobs and incomes that helped poorer groups escape the slums in past generations. Such a policy will not only reduce many of the problems of the city, which are ultimately caused by the poverty of its inhabitants, but it will assure the ultimate disappearance of the class and racial polarization of cities and suburbs. . . .

Discussion Questions

1. The author discusses the possibility of polarization between old-style metropolitan governments and emerging forms of urban-suburban governments. Why does he believe this polarization might occur? Do you agree? Discuss.

2. Compared to the past is "The Future of the Suburbs" optimistic or pessimistic? Discuss.

17 / Social and Cultural Change

Although the terms *social change* and *cultural change* are often used synonymously, basic distinctions do exist. Social change involves alterations in the social structure or social relations of society. It involves, for example, significant changes in population size or the expansion of a society's division of labor to include women. Social change also refers to such things as the decline in personal neighborliness and primary group relations as people move into the cities and become engulfed by bureaucratic and contractual relationships. Cultural change refers to the alteration or emergence of new traits that change the structure and function of morality and causes the emergence of new folkways and mores, new styles of hair, dress, music, dance, art, and so forth. It is important to recognize that most important changes include both social and cultural changes. As a result, sociologists employ the term *sociocultural change.*

Sociocultural change appears to be stimulated by such factors as whether or not the *physical environment* is conducive to change. Floods, droughts, and other natural disasters can disrupt life. Rivers and mountains have served as boundary lines and shaped political alliances. *Population growth* and *migration* have changed societies and cultures. Rapid growth during the eighteenth and nineteenth centuries, for example, rendered primogeniture impractical. Laws of primogeniture required that the family's entire property should pass on to the eldest son. This had the indirect effect of encouraging celibacy, as the younger sons had few options open to them other than life in the church or military service. *Ideologies* such as Marxism, democracy, and the Protestant ethic have also wrought profound changes in the societies where they have taken root. *Charismatic leadership* exhibited by such leaders as Ghandi, Nehru, Hitler, and Castro have also brought about significant changes. Charismatic leaders are considered by their followers to possess superhuman and supernatural powers. Consider, for example, the influence of Ghandi's leadership in bringing about the partition of India; Hitler's leadership and World War II; and Roosevelt's role in developing a special kind of United States welfare state.

Sociocultural changes occur through *discovery, invention,* and *diffusion.* As men discovered and invented quicker and safer methods of travel, for example, internal migration became more commonplace. Most sociocultural changes, however, occur through the process of diffusion. Diffusion refers to the spread of cultural traits from group to group, and from society to society. Americans sleep on beds built on a pattern originated in the East and modified in Europe. Americans sleep in pajamas, invented in India. Americans eat from plates made of a form of pottery invented in China. Americans smoke tobacco, a habit picked up from the Indians. Diffusion is also a two-way process. Japanese have become avid followers of country-western music. Other nations have adopted rock music and styles of dress exhibited in American-made movies.

Sociocultural change also has its costs. Innovations require a modification of the culture. Such modifications are usually associated with an increase in social problems. Social problems include deviant forms of behavior and perceived threats of the life and well-being of a society's members by disorienting and demoralizing them. A society in which a significant portion of its members feel demoralized tends to be apathetic and fatalistic. Such behavior is not only inconsistent with the values and beliefs of democracy, it also threatens the survival of the society. To prevent social problems and waste, social scientists and statesmen are increasingly emphasizing the necessity of *social planning.*

WILLIAM OPHULS

The Scarcity Society

The cultural values of our society have always supported change, with the belief that the future would always bring bigger and better things. It was simply taken for granted that we would have bigger homes, bigger swimming pools, together with all the other comforts of life, which included heating and air conditioning (Heaven forbid that anyone should experience discomfort!). All of this ongoing expansion was based on an abundant source of cheap energy. However, the Arab oil imbargo in 1974 changed everything. We have come to realize that we cannot continue blithely assuming that we can consume and waste energy as we have in the past. We must adjust ourselves—our entire life-styles—to the realities of scarcity. This change from an abundant to a scarce society holds implications for our democratic system of government.

Historians may see 1973 as a year dividing one age from another. The nature of the changes in store for us is symbolized by the Shah of Iran's announcement last December that the price of his country's oil would thence-forth be $11.87 per barrel, a rise of 100 per cent over the previous price. Other oil-producing countries quickly followed suit. The Shah accompanied his announcement with a blunt warning to the industrialized nations that the cheap and abundant energy "party" was over. From now on, the resource on which our whole civilization depends would be scarce, and the affluent world would have to live with the fact.

Our first attempts to do so have been rather pitiful. In Europe, the effect was to reduce once-proud nation-states to behavior that managed, as one observer put it, to combine the characteristics of an ostrich and a flock of hens. In America, which now lacks almost any observable leadership, the reaction to the statement was merely a general astonishment, followed by measures even more inappropriate than those adopted by the Europeans (except for Kissinger's efforts to promote international cooperation).

In one sense, Iran's move marked a dramatic geopolitical "return of the repressed," as the long-ignored Third World for the first time acted out its demand for a fair share of the planet's wealth. And the powerful new Organization of Petroleum Exporting Countries (OPEC) is only the first such group; resource cartels in copper, tin, bauxite, and other primary products may soon follow OPEC's example. But in another, more important sense, the Shah laid down a clear challenge to the most basic assumptions and procedures that have guided the industrialized democracies for at least 250 years. That challenge is the inevitable coming of scarcity to societies predicated on abundance. Its consequences, almost equally inevitable, will be the end of political democracy and a drastic restriction of personal liberty.

For the past three centuries, we have been living in an age of abnormal abundance. The bonanza of the New World and other founts of virgin resources, the dazzling achievements of science and technology, the availability of "free" ecological resources such as air and water to absorb the waste products of industrial activities, and other lesser factors allowed our ancestors to dream of endless material growth. Infinite abundance, men reasoned, would result in the elevation of the common man to economic nobility. And with poverty abolished, inequality, injustice, and fear—all those flowers of evil alleged to have their roots in scarcity—would wither away. Apart from William Blake and a few other disgruntled romantics, or the occasional pessimist like Thomas Malthus, the Enlightenment ideology of progress was shared by all in the West.[1] The works of John Locke and Adam Smith, the two men who gave bourgeois political economy its fundamental direction, are shot through with the assumption that there is always going to be more—more land in the colonies, more wealth to be dug from the ground, and so on. Virtually all the philosophies, values, and institutions typical of modern capitalist society—the legitimacy of self-interest, the primacy of the individual and his inalienable rights, economic laissez-faire, and democracy as we know

[1] Marxists tended to be more extreme optimists than non-Marxists, differing only on how the drive to Utopia was to be organized.

it—are the luxuriant fruit of an era of apparently endless abundance. They cannot continue to exist in their current form once we return to the more normal condition of scarcity.

Worse, the historic responses to scarcity have been conflict—wars fought to control resources, and oppression—great inequality of wealth and the political measures needed to maintain it. The link between scarcity and oppression is well understood by spokesmen for underprivileged groups and nations, who react violently to any suggested restraint in growth of output.

Our awakening from the pleasant dream of infinite progress and the abolition of scarcity will be extremely painful. Institutionally, scarcity demands that we sooner or later achieve a full-fledged "steady-state" or "spaceman" economy. Thereafter, we shall have to live off the annual income the earth receives from the sun, and this means a forced end to our kind of abnormal affluence and an abrupt return to frugality. This will require the strictest sort of economic and technological husbandry, as well as the strictest sort of political control.

The necessity for political control should be obvious from the use of the spaceship metaphor: political ships embarked on dangerous voyages need philosopher-king captains. However, another metaphor—the tragedy of the commons—comes even closer to depicting the essence of the ecopolitical dilemma. The tragedy of the commons has to do with the uncontrolled self-seeking in a limited environment that eventually results in competitive over-exploitation of a common resource, whether it is a commonly owned field on which any villager may graze his sheep, or the earth's atmosphere into which producers dump their effluents.

Francis Carney's powerful analysis of the Los Angeles smog problem indicates how deeply all our daily acts enmesh us in the tragic logic of the commons:

> *Every person who lives in this basin knows that for twenty-five years he has been living through a disaster. We have all watched it happen, have participated in it with full knowledge. . . . The smog is the result of ten million individual pursuits of private gratification. But there is absolutely nothing that any individual can do to stop its spread. . . . An individual act of renunciation is now nearly impossible, and, in any case, would be meaningless unless everyone else did the same thing. But he has no way of getting everyone else to do it.*

If this inexorable process is not controlled by prudent and, above all, timely political restraints on the behavior that causes it, then we must resign ourselves to ecological self-destruction. And the new political strictures that seem required to cope with the tragedy of the commons (as well as the imperatives of technology) are going to violate our most cherished ideals, for they will be neither democratic nor libertarian. At worst, the new era could be an anti-Utopia in which we are conditioned to behave according to the exigencies of ecological scarcity.

Ecological scarcity is a new concept, embracing more than the shortage of any particular resource. It has to do primarily with pollution limits, complex trade-offs between present and future needs, and a variety of other physical constraints, rather than with a simple Malthusian overpopulation. The case for the coming of ecological scarcity was most forcefully argued in the Club of Rome study *The Limits to Growth*. That study says, in essence, that man lives on a finite planet containing limited resources and that we appear to be approaching some of these major limits with great speed. To use ecological jargon, we are about to overtax the "carrying capacity" of the planet.

Critical reaction to this Jeremiad was predictably reassuring. Those wise in the ways of computers were largely content to assert that the Club of Rome people had fed the machines false or slanted information. "Garbage in, garbage out," they soothed. Other critics sought solace in less empirical directions, but everyone who recoiled from the book's apocalyptic vision took his stand on grounds of social or technological optimism. Justified or not, the optimism is worth examining to see where it leads us politically.

The social optimists, to put their case briefly, believe that various "negative feedback mechanisms" allegedly built into society will (if left alone) automatically check the trends toward ever more population, consumption, and pollution, and that this feedback will function smoothly and gradually so as to bring us up against the limits to growth, if any, with scarcely a bump. The market-price system is the feedback mechanism usually relied upon. Shortages of one resource—oil, for example—simply make it economical to substitute another in more abundant supply (coal or shale oil). A few of these critics of the limits-to-growth thesis believe that this process can go on indefinitely.

Technological optimism is founded on the belief that it makes little difference whether exponential growth is pushing us up against limits, for technology is simultaneously expanding the limits. To use the metaphor popularized during the debate, ecologists see us as fish in a pond where all life is rapidly being suffocated by a water lily that doubles in size every day (covering the whole pond in thirty days). The technological optimists do not deny that the lily grows very quickly, but they believe that the pond itself can be made to grow even faster. Technology made a liar out of Malthus, say the optimists, and the same fate awaits the neo-Malthusians. In sum, the optimists assert that we can never run out of resources, for economics and technology, like modern genii, will always keep finding new ones for us to exploit or will enable us to use the present supply with ever-greater efficiency.

The point most overlooked in this debate, however, is that politically it matters little who is right: the neo-Malthusians *or* either type of optimist. If the "doomsdayers" are right, then of course we crash into the ceiling of physical limits and relapse into a Hobbesian universe of the war of all against all, followed, as anarchy always has been, by dictatorship of one form or another. If, on the other hand, the optimists are right in supposing that we can adjust to ecological scarcity with economics and technology, this effort will have, as we say, "side effects." For the collision with physical limits can be forestalled only by moving toward some kind of steady-state economy— characterized by the most scrupulous husbanding of resources, by extreme vigilance against the ever-present possibility of disaster should breakdown occur, and, therefore, by tight control on human behavior. However we get there, "Spaceship Earth" will be an all-powerful Leviathan—perhaps benign, perhaps not.

A Bird in the Bush

The scarcity problem thus poses a classic dilemma. It may be possible to avoid crashing into the physical limits, but only by adopting radical and unpalatable measures that, paradoxically, are little different in their ultimate political and social implications from the future predicted by the doomsdayers.

Why this is so becomes clear enough when one realizes that the optimistic critics of the doomsdayers, whom I have artificially grouped into "social" and "technological" tendencies, finally have to rest their different cases on a theory of politics, that is, on assumptions about the adaptability of leaders, their constituencies, and the institutions that hold them together. Looked at closely, these assumptions also appear unrealistic.

Even on a technical level, for example, the market-price mechanism does not coexist easily with environmental imperatives. In a market system a bird in the hand is always worth two in the bush.[2] This means that resources critically needed in the future will be discounted—that is, assessed at a fraction of their future value—by today's economic decision-makers. Thus decisions that are economically "rational," like mine-the-soil farming and forestry, may be ecologically catastrophic. Moreover, charging industries—and, therefore, consumers—for pollution and other environmental harms that are caused by mining and manufacturing (the technical solution favored by most economists to bring market prices into line with ecological realities) is not politically palatable. It clearly requires political decisions that do not accord with current values or the present distribution of political power; and the same goes for other obvious and necessary measures, like energy conservation. No consumer wants to pay more for the same product simply because it is produced in a cleaner way; no developer wants to be confronted with an environmental impact statement that lets the world know his gain is the community's loss; no trucker is likely to agree with any energy-conservation program that cuts his income.

We all have a vested interest in continuing to abuse the environment as we have in the past. And even if we should find the political will to take these

[2] Of course, noneconomic factors may temporarily override market forces, as the current Arab oil boycott illustrates.

kinds of steps before we collide with the physical limits, then we will have adopted the essential features of a spaceman economy on a piecemeal basis —and will have simply exchanged one horn of the dilemma for the other.

Technological solutions are more roundabout, but the outcome—greater social control in a planned society—is equally certain. Even assuming that necessity always proves to be the mother of invention, the management burden thrown on our leaders and institutions by continued technological expansion of that famous fishpond will be enormous. Prevailing rates of growth require us to double our capital stock, our capacity to control pollution, our agricultural productivity, and so forth every fifteen to thirty years. Since we already start from a very high absolute level, the increment of required new construction and new invention will be staggering. For example, to accommodate world population growth, we must, in roughly the next thirty years, build houses, hospitals, ports, factories, bridges, and every other kind of facility in numbers that almost equal all the construction work done by the human race up to now.

The task in every area of our lives is essentially similar, so that the management problem extends across the board, item by item. Moreover, the complexity of the overall problem grows faster than any of the sectors that comprise it, requiring the work of innovation, construction, and environmental management to be orchestrated into a reasonably integrated, harmonious whole. Since delays, planning failures, and general incapacity to deal effectively with even our current level of problems are all too obvious today, the technological response further assumes that our ability to cope with large-scale complexity will improve substantially in the next few decades. Technology, in short, cannot be implemented in a political and social vacuum. The factor in least supply governs, and technological solutions cannot run ahead of our ability to plan, construct, fund, and man them.

Planning will be especially difficult. For one thing, time may be our scarcest resource. Problems now develop so rapidly that they must be foreseen well in advance. Otherwise, our "solutions" will be too little and too late. The automobile is a critical example. By the time we recognized the dangers, it was too late for anything but a mishmash of stopgap measures that may have provoked worse symptoms than they alleviated and that will not even enable us to meet health standards without painful additional measures like rationing. But at this point we are almost helpless to do better, for we have ignored the problem until it is too big to handle by any means that are politically, economically, and technically feasible. The energy crisis offers another example of the time factor. Even with an immediate laboratory demonstration of feasibility, nuclear fusion cannot possibly provide any substantial amount of power until well into the next century.

Another planning difficulty: the growing vulnerability of a highly technological society to accident and error. The main cause for concern is, of course, some of the especially dangerous technologies we have begun to employ. One accident involving a breeder reactor would be one too many:

the most minuscule dose of plutonium is deadly, and any we release now will be around to poison us for a quarter of a million years. Thus, while we know that counting on perfection in any human enterprise is folly, we seem headed for a society in which nothing less than perfect planning and control will do.

At the very least, it should be clear that ecological scarcity makes "muddling through" in a basically laissez-faire socioeconomic system no longer tolerable or even possible. In a crowded world where only the most exquisite care will prevent the collapse of the technological society on which we all depend, the grip of planning and social control will of necessity become more and more complete. Accidents, much less the random behavior of individuals, cannot be permitted; the expert pilots will run the ship in accordance with technological imperatives. Industrial man's Faustian bargain with technology therefore appears to lead inexorably to total domination by technique in a setting of clockwork institutions. C. S. Lewis once said that "what we call Man's power over Nature turns out to be a power exercised by some men over other men with Nature as its instrument," and it appears that the greater our technological power over nature, the more absolute the political power that must be yielded up to some men by others.

These developments will be especially painful for Americans because, from the beginning, we adopted the doctrines of Locke and Smith in their most libertarian form. Given the cornucopia of the frontier, an unpolluted environment, and a rapidly developing technology, American politics could afford to be a more or less amicable squabble over the division of the spoils, with the government stepping in only when the free-for-all pursuit of wealth got out of hand. In the new era of scarcity, laissez-faire and the inalienable right of the individual to get as much as he can are prescriptions for disaster. It follows that the political system inherited from our forefathers is moribund. We have come to the final act of the tragedy of the commons.

The answer to the tragedy is political. Historically, the use of the commons was closely regulated to prevent overgrazing, and we need similar controls— "mutual coercion, mutually agreed upon by the majority of the people affected," in the words of the biologist Garrett Hardin—to prevent the individual acts that are destroying the commons today. Ecological scarcity imposes certain political measures on us if we wish to survive. Whatever these measures may turn out to be—if we act soon, we may have a significant range of responses—it is evident that our political future will inevitably be much less libertarian and much more authoritarian, much less individualistic and much more communalistic than our present. The likely result of the reemergence of scarcity appears to be the resurrection in modern form of the preindustrial polity, in which the few govern the many and in which government is no longer of or by the people. Such forms of government may or may not be benevolent. At worst, they will be totalitarian, in every evil sense of that word we know now, and some ways undreamed of. At best, government seems likely to rest on engineered consent, as we are manipulated by

Platonic guardians in one or another version of Brave New World. The alternative will be the destruction, perhaps consciously, of "Spaceship Earth."

A Democracy of Restraint

There is, however, a way out of this depressing scenario. To use the language of ancient philosophers, it is the restoration of the civic virtue of a corrupt people. By their standards, by the standards of many of the men who founded our nation (and whose moral capital we have just about squandered), we are indeed a corrupt people. We understand liberty as a license for self-indulgence, so that we exploit our rights to the full while scanting our duties. We understand democracy as a political means of gratifying our desires rather than as a system of government that gives us the precious freedom to impose laws on ourselves—instead of having some remote sovereign impose them on us without our participation or consent. Moreover, the desires we express through our political system are primarily for material gain; the pursuit of happiness has been degraded into a mass quest for what wise men have always said would injure our souls. We have yet to learn the truth of Burke's political syllogism, which expresses the essential wisdom of political philosophy: man is a passionate being, and there must therefore be checks on will and appetite; if these checks are not self-imposed, they must be applied externally as fetters by a sovereign power. The way out of our difficulties, then, is through the abandonment of our political corruption.

The crisis of ecological scarcity poses basic value questions about man's place in nature and the meaning of human life. It is possible that we may learn from this challenge what Lao-tzu taught two-and-a-half millennia ago:

> Nature sustains itself through three precious principles, which one does well to embrace and follow.
> These are gentleness, frugality, and humility.

A very good life—in fact, an affluent life by historic standards—can be lived without the profligate use of resources that characterizes our civilization. A sophisticated and ecologically sound technology, using solar power and other renewable resources, could bring us a life of simple sufficiency that would yet allow the full expression of the human potential. Having chosen such a life, rather than having had it forced on us, we might find it had its own richness.

Such a choice may be impossible, however. The root of our problem lies deep. The real shortage with which we are afflicted is that of moral resources. Assuming that we wish to survive in dignity and not as ciphers in some ant-heap society, we are obliged to reassume our full moral responsibility. The earth is not just a banquet at which we are free to gorge. The ideal in Buddhism of compassion for all sentient beings, the concern for the harmony of man and nature so evident among American Indians, and the almost forgotten ideal of stewardship in Christianity point us in the direction of a true ethics of human survival—and it is toward such an ideal that the best among the young are groping. We must realize that there is no real scarcity in nature. It is our numbers and, above all, our wants that have outrun nature's bounty. We become rich precisely in proportion to the degree in which we eliminate violence, greed, and pride from our lives. As several thousands of years of history show, this is not something easily learned by humanity, and we seem no readier to choose the simple, virtuous life now than we have been in the past. Nevertheless, if we wish to avoid either a crash into the ecological ceiling or a tyrannical Leviathan, we must choose it. There is no other way to defeat the gathering forces of scarcity.

Discussion Questions

1. Do you agree with the author's assumption that the United States is going to say, "Farewell to the free lunch"? Discuss.

2. If the author is correct, and we become "The scarcity society," what are the major social changes the United States can expect?

U.S. NEWS & WORLD REPORT

The Ways "Singles" Are Changing U.S.

Social changes resulting from the growth of a group reflecting nontraditional family orientations are reviewed in this article. These "singles" are changing American values in very significant ways. Distinctions among singles as well as distinctions between them and groups reflecting more traditional life-styles are discussed in this article.

An emerging life style centered around the activities of unmarried men and women is adding a new dimension to American cities and towns.

Mainly evident in the nation's largest communities, the "singles phenomenon" is affecting housing, social contacts and recreation on a scale America has never seen before.

Behind these changes are living arrangements made by one or more unmarried adults whose residences, buying habits and personal concerns often are markedly different from those of traditional families.

According to new census reports, the number of Americans living alone or with unmarried roommates has risen more than 40 per cent over the last six

Reprinted from *U.S. News & World Report,* "The Ways 'Singles' Are Changing U.S.," *U.S. News & World Report* (Jan. 31, 1977). Copyright 1977 U.S. News & World Report, Inc.

years. That is seven times faster than the increase in married couples' setting up homes.

Singles, including those raising children, now make up 1 out of every 3 households in the U.S.

Some Results

Changes resulting from the trend are showing up in a variety of ways.

Already, potential slums are being revitalized by affluent singles seeking urban excitement and convenience.

Businesses are revising "family style" products to offer singles everything from more condominiums to single-serving soup cans.

Singles also are demanding—and often getting—an end to policies that favor families in tax payments, insurance plans, bank loans and air fares.

"What this means is that, for some time to come, all of us are going to be living in a world comprised to a far greater extent of people living alone and liking it," says Joseph Peritz, a pollster and market analyst in New York City. He observes: "This is a trend with enormous implications for business, Government and everyone else in our society."

One of the first cities affected by the changes was Chicago. There, according to Pierre de Vise, an urban-sciences professor at the University of Illinois, singles living in apartment complexes such as Carl Sandburg Village have helped to save the city's downtown from irreversible decay.

Before Sandburg was built with federal renewal money in 1963, its North Side neighborhood was a skid row that included rundown apartments, "greasy spoon" taverns and transient hotels frequented by prostitutes.

Today, the area is dominated by nine high-rise buildings surrounded by townhouses and renovated apartments. Nearly three quarters of the residents 18 years old and over are unmarried.

Land values have jumped from as little as $100 to as much as $3,500 a square foot in the last 20 years. Rents have more than doubled in a decade, too, reaching as high as $400 for a one-bedroom apartment. Those who cannot afford such leases often get roommates, contributing to an increase in unwed couples living together.

As a result of the new activity, more people are coming back to the neighborhood's churches and restaurants. At clubs catering primarily to singles, waiting lines are long and prices are high.

Typical of Chicago's singles is Carol Ignelzi, 29. She moved into a condominium in the downtown singles' area a year ago and started commuting to her home-town teaching job in the Indiana suburbs.

Now her routine includes attending college classes two nights a week and spending at least two more on the town with a date or girl friend.

Even though parking her car, for example, now costs $60 a month at home and $5 a visit at her favorite night club, Ignelzi declares: "I would never live single in the suburbs again. It's deadly boring, and people make you feel as though you should apologize for being single. Here, I feel alive."

On the Pacific

One of the most popular centers for singles on the West Coast is Marina del Rey in Los Angeles, where 9,500 apartment dwellers live on 400 acres of the Pacific waterfront. Single residents there outnumber married couples almost 2 to 1.

Because children are rare in this development, there are no schools or detached homes. Instead, residents live amidst office buildings, restaurants, bars and other small businesses. They also have the largest man-made harbor for pleasure boats in the world. Its 6,000 moorings are studded with sailboats, yachts and cruisers.

At the largest group of 16-story towers, called the Marina City Club, all but a handful of the 671 apartments are filled. Tenants pay monthly rents from $450 for a one-bedroom apartment to $2,500 for a four-bedroom penthouse.

Among the amenities are three private restaurants, a wine-tasting room, 341 private boat slips, swimming pools, courts for tennis, paddle tennis and handball, indoor golf, a European facial salon, and limousine, bodyguard and charter-jet services.

At Marina City Club, says one single resident, "you can get drunk and walk home. You are close to the airport if you want to fly somewhere."

Most local people say the development has brought cultural and economic vitality to what used to be a mosquito-infested marsh.

On the other hand, more and more singles are criticizing the way of life at places like Marina del Rey as rootless and superficial.

In many communities, "the age of the swinging-singles' apartment complex is over," says Houston developer Martin Fein. "Single people are looking for a more stable life style now."

One reason is that as today's large crop of singles grows older, Americans no longer regard bachelorhood as a brief fling before marriage. Joyce Rutledge, a single career woman in Houston, remarks: "When I hit 30, others began to take me as seriously as I took myself. I see this around me. Single people are more career-oriented and into their jobs than they used to be."

In many communities, singles have settled easily and quietly into traditional family neighborhoods.

Among those who did so is an Atlanta woman, Lil Friedlander, who became "very unhappy" two years ago with life in an affluent singles' community on the north side of Atlanta. Her reason: It was a homogeneous area with what she describes as too many "single women on the make." She says she "went to the grocery store for two years and only twice ran into somebody I knew."

Then the 29-year-old divorcée attended a block party given by a civic association promoting Atlanta's old midtown section, where 60 per cent of the residents are single.

Despite some initial worries about crime, Friedlander and her two sons moved into a duplex there because, she says, "they were warm, they invited me to parties, they helped me find a place right where I wanted to be and they thought it was great that I had small children."

Displeasure

In some areas, long-time residents, have been displeased by the advent of singles.

In New York City, unattached people are flooding new and restored apartments in the Yorkville section of Manhattan. In the process, soaring rents and crime are driving out many of the Irish and German families that police detective Joseph Spinelli calls "the social and cultural backbone of Yorkville."

Spinelli, a community-relations expert who has worked and lived in the area for more than 20 years, laments: "It used to be a family-oriented place. Now, it's much more commercial, and there's very little left for youth." He says that singles have no stake in the community.

Between 1970 and 1974, venereal-disease rates in this neighborhood jumped 71 per cent, four times the citywide increase. This could simply reflect more willingness to seek treatment here, health officials say.

Nevertheless, the figures coincide with nationwide increases in venereal disease since the singles boom and the "sexual revolution" began in the 1960s.

Complaints are also heard about call girls moving into the Yorkville area. Burglaries are increasing, too, because no one is at home in most singles' apartments during the day.

In San Francisco, where about half of the residents above the age of 17 are single, some citizens resent the changes that unattached people are bringing to the city.

Skyrocketing Prices

In the Noe Valley area, prices of some Victorian homes have jumped from $25,000 to $100,000 or more in five years as singles acquired renovated flats. New assessments reflecting these higher prices are forcing heavy increases in property taxes for the entire community.

With singles setting up crafts shops and restaurants, one quarter of the local businessmen have withdrawn from the Noe Valley Merchants Association to protest its new members.

Others, however, are enthusiastic. The head of the association, veteran shopkeeper Bob Sinclair, maintains: "This is the best thing that ever happened to us. This neighborhood was dying on the vine until the young people started coming in here with their money and their energy to help rebuild it."

The impact of the singles boom often is reckoned in cold cash. The reason is that most communities are eager for people who can pay their way without dumping more and more children onto welfare rolls or into costly and troubled schools.

At the national level, too, the singles phenomenon is having an impact in a variety of ways. One result is that families with children are showing up less often in advertising. Instead, a major wine company, for example, has built an entire ad campaign around the image of a mature bachelor or divorced man enjoying a casual style of living among a large group of friends.

Some demographers expect the nation to return to its traditional family orientation as soon as the big generation born in the 1950s and early 1960s settles down. But others, noting that divorce and anti-family attitudes are spreading to other segments of the population, expect an expansion of the singles trend.

Opinion-poll analyst Peritz says that young, unmarried people are carrying their attitudes with them as they grow older.

"In the process," he concludes, "they are transforming American values, especially among affluent and influential people who set the pace for the rest of the country."

Discussion Questions

1. In brief review form, list the ways singles are changing the United States.

2. In your opinion are these social changes beneficial? Discuss.

U.S. NEWS & WORLD REPORT

The Lure of Television—
Ways to Unplug Your Kids

Interview with Dr. Robert L. Stubblefield

This interview with a child psychiatrist indicates that television is a different kind of experience for today's children. Although it can be beneficial, it can also turn "many into passive receivers of canned experience." Dr. Stubblefield is concerned that the T.V.-saturated child may be deterred from being able to work out emotional problems through personal activity and play.

Q   Dr. Stubblefield, how can parents tell if their children are being emotionally harmed by viewing too much TV?

A   In younger children, you should look for such things as hyperactive behavior, loss of appetite, difficulty in sleeping, bad dreams, or refusal to play with children their own age.

These are the classic responses of children who are anxious—the same way they might feel if a member of the family became seriously ill or if mothering is done by a series of strange baby-sitters.

Q   Do symptoms change as children get older?

A   Yes. In early adolescence, heavy watchers are more likely to dwell in excessive fantasies, keeping themselves out of the new world of boy-girl relationships and social activities. They drift and become indecisive.

By the time they are supposed to leave high school, they may be unable to decide whether they want to take a job, go on to college or do anything at all.

Q   Is this a widespread problem?

A   It is being recognized by family doctors as a growing health problem, especially among children who watch television more than 25 hours a week, which is the national average. There also is some soft evidence that these children have more difficulty in school than those who don't watch as much TV.

Q   Is it all right to cut the child off from the set entirely?

A   Yes, particularly if it interederes with activities that are essential for his personal development, such as walking and talking at the age of 2 or 3.

In less-serious cases, however, it's usually enough to limit the child's viewing to a certain number of hours per week. Then as children get older, they can make more and more choices about what they want to watch within the time limit.

Q   How do you lay down this kind of rule?

A   Be firm—but accompany it with an explanation. Tell them the plain truth: that television is somehow interfering with their opportunities to learn more about themselves and about what other children are feeling and doing.

Remember that a child preoccupied with television is likely to be functioning at six to 18 months below his or her age level, so use simple words with no sign of vacillation.

Q   If a child wants to watch an "adult" show at 9 p.m., how can you get him to read, do homework without his resenting it?

A   The best way is for the parent to set the example. Children still model most of their behavior after their parents'—so you have to be prepared to turn the set off and pick up a book yourself.

And if the child co-operates, you should show your appreciation by bending the rules for certain special programs. If something worthwhile is on the air, children shouldn't have to disappear at 10:01.

If television is seriously interfering with homework, you should check with the child's teacher. Many teachers now have documents published by parents' organizations suggesting codes of television watching to be adopted in co-operation with the children and their parents. It isn't an attack on all TV but an attempt to improve children's viewing behavior.

Q Are there other devices that will help control viewing?

A One thing you need to cope with is pressure on a child to watch certain shows because all his friends are talking about it. What impresses me is that adolescents particularly will gang up on their parents and say, "Johnny's watching it and Jane is watching it, so why can't I?"

When that happens, I suggest parents find out from each other what they're actually permitting. Most parents want to lay down the same sort of rules, but if they don't check with each other, they'll get taken.

Q Why does TV have such a dramatic effect on children?

A It's a much different kind of experience than children were getting in the days before TV. Then most likely they were outside, involved in various kinds of games, and sharing; so they learned something about the rights and respect of others. Now too much watching turns many into passive receivers of canned experience. They never learn to work out emotional problems through personal activity and play.

Q What can parents do to cope with these troubles?

A First, you should get children involved at the earliest possible age in activities that will give them the curiosity and confidence they need to explore rewarding things that require effort. This means active pursuits. They can in-clude such things as painting, drawing, making music, playing games—both alone and with their parents. Doing chores together is a good antidote for tele-vision, too, even when children are really too young to be very helpful.

Children also need unstructured activities, like tinkering or exploring in the neighborhood, where they can learn to make their own discoveries and set their own rules.

Q Can television ever be beneficial for children?

A Yes, if parents help select the shows and take time to watch them with the child.

No matter whether it's a show about animals or a football game, there is much that children can learn about the world if parents ask questions, listen to remarks and help children learn to evaluate the things they see.

WHO WATCHES TV?

- 73 million households, or 97 per cent of all U.S. households, have television sets.
- Nearly 45 per cent of all homes have more than one set.
- 77 per cent of all home TV sets are color models.

Among the viewers—
- Adult women average 30 hours and 14 minutes a week before the television set.
- Children from ages 2 to 11 average 25 hours and 38 minutes.
- Adult men average 24 hours and 25 minutes a week.
- Teen-agers 12 through 17 average 22 hours and 36 minutes.

Source: A. C. Nielsen Company

Discussion Questions

1. What are the detrimental social changes caused by television to which Dr. Stubblefield alludes?

2. Despite these negative effects of television, Dr. Stubblefield says that television can be beneficial to children. How? Do you agree? Discuss.